Perfect your Italian

Sylvia Lymbery

The publisher has used its best endeavours to ensure that the URLs
for external websites referred to in this book are correct and active
at the time of going to press. However, the publisher and the
author have no responsibility for the websites and can make no
guarantee that a site will remain live or that the content will remain
relevant, decent or appropriate.

For UK order enquiries: please contact Bookpoint Ltd,
130 Milton Park, Abingdon, Oxon, OX14 4SB.
Telephone: +44 (0) 1235 827720. *Fax:* +44 (0) 1235 400454.
Lines are open 09.00–17.00, Monday to Saturday, with a 24-hour
message answering service. Details about our titles and how to
order are available at www.teachyourself.co.uk

For USA order enquiries: please contact McGraw-Hill Customer
Services, PO Box 545, Blacklick, OH 43004-0545, USA.
Telephone: 1-800-722-4726. *Fax:* 1-614-755-5645.

For Canada order enquiries: please contact McGraw-Hill
Ryerson Ltd, 300 Water St, Whitby, Ontario, L1N 9B6, Canada.
Telephone: 905 430 5000. *Fax:* 905 430 5020.

Long renowned as the authoritative source for self-guided
learning – with more than 50 million copies sold worldwide –
the *Teach Yourself* series includes over 500 titles in the fields of
languages, crafts, hobbies, business, computing and education.

British Library Cataloguing in Publication Data: a catalogue record
for this title is available from the British Library.

Library of Congress Catalog Card Number: on file.

First published in UK 1999 by Hodder Education, 338 Euston
Road, London, NW1 3BH.

First published in US 1999 by The McGraw-Hill Companies, Inc.

Previously published as Teach Yourself Italian Extra!

The *Teach Yourself* name is a registered trade mark of
Hodder Headline.

Copyright © 1999, 2004, 2010 Sylvia Lymbery.

Typeset by MPS Limited, A Macmillan Company.

Printed in Great Britain for Hodder Education, a division of
Hodder Headline, 338 Euston Road, London, NW1 3BH,
by Cox & Wyman Ltd, Reading, Berkshire.

Hodder Headline's policy is to use papers that are natural,
renewable and recyclable products and made from wood grown
in sustainable forests. The logging and manufacturing processes
are expected to conform to the environmental regulations of the
country of origin.

Impression number   10 9 8 7 6 5 4 3 2
Year   2014 2013 2012 2011 2010

Contents

Acknowledgements

I should like to thank Marina Bastianello, Emanuela Beltrami, Gabriella Bertone, Cinzia Buono, Silvia Lena, Paolo and Piera Ravarino, Annalisa Romizi, Mario and Nicola Rotondale, Renata Savio, Carlo Sigliano, Felicità Torrielli, Angioletta Viviani, three members of the Gruppo Mio and three members of the Moncalieri Branch of the Club Alpino Italiano for so kindly finding time to be interviewed, thus giving me the basis for this book. At the time of the interviews, it was not my intention to use the material verbatim, but it soon became clear that to do so would produce a more lively and stimulating book. I am therefore also grateful to those I have quoted for allowing me to do so and to attribute their words to them by name. Some people also helped in other ways, notably Cinzia Buono and Angioletta Viviani who made further recordings for me. I was unable to use more than a fraction of the material gathered but it has all proved valuable. I should also like to thank Sandra Silipo for reading the text as it was being written, acting as language adviser and writing a number of exercises; and Antonio Ravarino for drawing the two maps. Thanks also to everyone else who has helped me.

In addition I am grateful to: *La Stampa* for permission to reproduce various articles; *Repubblica* for permission to reproduce articles from their website; Ermete Realacci, National President of Legambiente, for permission to reproduce his article in *Legambiente Notizie*, October 1996; Giulio Einaudi Editore for permission to reproduce extracts from *Le piccole virtù* by Natalia Ginzburg, Copyright© 1962 Giulio Einaudi editore s.p.a., Torino; Zanichelli Editore, Bologna, for permission to quote definitions from *lo Zingarelli* 2010, *Vocabolario della lingua italiana di Nicola Zingarelli*; Little Brown and Company, London and New York, for permission to quote a sentence from *Long Walk to Freedom* by

Nelson Mandela; and Macmillan Children's Books for permission to reproduce *Jabberwocky* from Lewis Carroll's *Through the Looking-Glass: and what Alice found there* (London, 1948).

> Without language, one cannot talk to people and understand them, one cannot share their hopes and aspirations, grasp their history, appreciate their poetry or savour their songs.
>
> Nelson Mandela, *Long Walk to Freedom*
>
> (Little, Brown and Company, 1994)

Meet the author

Sylvia Lymbery learned Italian the hard way. No childhood in Italy, no Italian mother, no "unfair" advantage. Beginning at school, aged 16, she continued at university with Italian as a "second string" to a degree in French. So she understands what it is to learn a language from scratch. She realised as a student that a stay in Italy would help so she worked one summer as an "au pair" for an Italian family in the Veneto. Early in her post-university life she worked in the travel industry in Liguria before going into teaching. For many years she taught French with just one or two courses of Italian. Eventually she moved to a college where more Italian was needed and where she was also able to spend every summer with art and art history students in Tuscany. Then, once her family responsibility was at university, she went to live and work in Italy. This gave her the depth of knowledge of Italy and Italian to write books for students wanting to learn Italian. However she does also have a teaching qualification and an MA in Applied Linguistics. Throughout her teaching career she has found that every opportunity to learn more should be welcomed and exploited.

Only got a minute?

Italian is spoken by 60 million people in Italy and another 10 million Italians living abroad. It is the official language in Italy, San Marino, the Vatican City and one of the official languages in Switzerland and in Malta. It is the second language in Croatia, Istria and Slovenia.

Italian developed from Latin, the language of the Romans, and is related to French, Spanish, Portuguese, etc. Lots of English words are also from Latin (organisation, possible, moment, etc.), so some Italian words are easy to recognize.

Given your interest in Italian and your initial knowledge of the language, perhaps you can guess the meaning of some Italian sentences and phrases you'll meet in this course: **mi piacerebbe conoscere di più la Toscana** *I'd like to know Tuscany better;* **un uomo pragmatico, concreto, dotato di grande volontà** *a pragmatic man, down-to-earth, endowed with great* *willpower*; **mi si è presentata la possibilità di gestire questo centro** *the possibility was given to me to manage this centre;* **si trattò di un evento tragico** *it was a tragic event.*

Language, however, is much more than the study of vocabulary or grammar, so this course will provide you with ample opportunity to learn all aspects of it, always focusing on your needs as an intermediate speaker and on what you want to do and achieve through the medium of Italian. The aim is, above all, to help you interact with Italian-speaking people, not just socially but also in a number of situations where you may want to have closer contact with people and talk extensively on topics like: describing people, past events, the work you do, problems at work, how you combine career and family, personal experiences. These and a lot more are the topics you will be able to handle once you have completed this course.

5 Only got five minutes?

When you go beyond the elementary stage, Italian may appear to be a complex language but you soon discover that you can grasp the meaning of a whole article or a story you read by identifying the many Italian words that look like English words and have a similar meaning. The structure, too, is common to other languages spoken in the western world, and it follows patterns recognizable to the English-speaking reader.

Italian is a Romance language, that is a language developed from Latin, like French, Spanish, Portuguese, and a few others. Although English is a Germanic, not a Romance language, it was strongly influenced by Latin, both because of its French-speaking monarchs and aristocracy during the Middle Ages and because of the strong Latin influence during the Renaissance. So numerous English words borrowed from Latin give you a feel for similar Italian words.

See how much you can understand from these chunks of language you'll meet in the course. (English translations are provided at the end of this summary!) Talking about family life: **quando è scoppiata la guerra, papà è rientrato in Italia, logicamente si è portato la famiglia dietro.** Or talking about working in the world of fashion: **abbiamo avuto una crescita abbastanza limitata ... perché il campo della moda è così tanto cambiato in questi anni.** Or describing the activities of volunteers: **moltissimi giovani sono impegnati in attività sociali, di aiuto a persone anziane, persone handicappate, bambini.** It may be slightly difficult to get the full meaning when things are out of context, but even so you probably get the general gist. In the lessons you will get the full support you need from the author's comments and grammar explanations.

The course, with its interviews with real people, its newspaper articles and its short literary passages, is designed to expose you to a variety of contexts, to expand your vocabulary, to build on the basic structures you already know and thus to enable you to deal equally with the language spoken by adults and young people and with the more formal written language of journalism and literature.

You will be reading and hearing Italian as it is spoken today by the average person, not the language of soap operas or of the social networking sites, but common everyday speech which in Italy is still governed by sound grammar rules and by a richness of vocabulary, metaphors and imagery quite surprising in this all-flattening technological world.

When and where will you be using the Italian you learn in this course? You will use it in a variety of situations: in one-to-one exchanges in shops, restaurants, business environments, in more personal conversations with close family and friends, in discussions on general topics like education, work practices, voluntary organizations. Don't forget that Italian is spoken all over the western world, not only by 60 million people in Italy, but also by another 10 million living abroad. It is the official language in Italy, San Marino, the Vatican City and one of the official languages in Switzerland and Malta. It is the second language in Croatia, Istria and Slovenia. There are large Italian-speaking communities in Argentina, Brazil, the USA and Canada, as well as some in France, Germany, the U.K., Venezuela and Australia.

A good knowledge of Italian doesn't only help you with a tour of these countries but opens up the doors to the understanding of a rich cultural heritage, a world of art and architecture steeped in classical antiquity, a world of music which inspired great composers and singers, a world of many cultural elements which have influenced your own English-speaking civilization to this day. And if the present interests you more than the past, use the Italian you learn in these pages to understand the world of everyday fashion and high fashion, of modern design and the car industry, of films and musicals, of good food products and simple home-made dishes.

English translations of the Italian sentences quoted above:

quando è scoppiata la guerra ... *when the war broke out, dad came back to Italy, of course he brought the family along.*

abbiamo avuto una crescita abbastanza limitata ... *we had a fairly limited growth ... because the world of fashion has changed so much the last few years.*

moltissimi giovani sono impegnati in attività sociali ... *very many young people are engaged in social activities, helping the elderly, the disabled, children.*

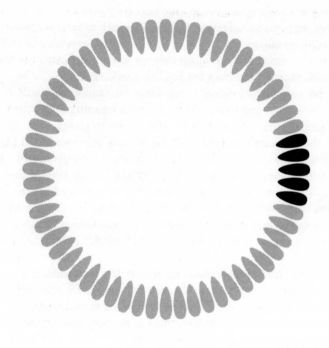

10 Only got ten minutes?

Is Italian an easy language to learn after the initial stages? Let us consider who may find it really easy. Italian is one of the Romance languages, which developed from the language spoken by common people in Roman times, as different from classical written Latin. Romance languages cover the main area of Western Europe. The most widely spoken today include, from west to east, Portuguese, Spanish, French, Italian, Romanian. So if you know any of these languages, you may find it easy to learn another one in the same family. English belongs to the Germanic, not the Romance family, but even for English speakers Italian can be easy because many English words share the same origin, either Latin or Greek, and usually have a similar meaning. Not only was English strongly affected by a Romance language, French, after the Norman conquest in 1066, but this influence lasted for centuries well into the Elizabethan era, where it compounded with the cultural input of classical historical and literary texts, either recently discovered or already known but now re-read in greater depth. Not surprisingly the great English writers of this period were inspired by the writings of antiquity and Queen Elizabeth I herself was said to be fluent in Italian, French, Latin and Greek.

You can test how close English can be to Italian by reading these short extracts from the course (English translations are provided at the end of this summary). **Era un esilio il nostro: la nostra città era lontana e lontani erano i libri, gli amici, le vicende varie e mutevoli di una vera esistenza.** (from *Le piccole virtù*, by Natalia Ginzburg); … **un sentimento comune, un voler bene all'Italia ed al suo patrimonio artistico, considerato a ragione patrimonio del mondo.** (from an article in *Legambiente Notizie*, 1996); **una marcia della pace attorno alle mura di Gerusalemme … è stata un'esperienza che praticamente ha cambiato la direzione della mia vita.** (from an interview with Silvia).

In this course you are going to read many texts and listen to many interviews with Italian native speakers and you'll be exposed to a variety of vocabulary, accents and structures. Why is that? Doesn't everybody speak the same Italian in Italy? They do and they don't. The influence of old regional dialects is still strong and it affects the way people speak standard Italian. Just as you can identify somebody's English speech as Cockney, US Deep South or Australian, so you can find that people from different regions in Italy have different 'accents'. Even after the unification of the country in 1861, and the transfer of the capital from Turin to Florence and then to Rome, there were still many different dialects, over and above one formal official language. One could say that only the influence of the media in the last fifty years has helped standardize common speech. Even now, you may find that you arrive in Milan and you understand what people say, then you move to Venice and it sounds somewhat different – there is a special sing-song sound to what you hear. Then you fly south and a whole world of new sounds explodes over you: consonants are soft and drawn, many are doubled and intensified, vowels are very open, many are dropped at the end of the word.

So what is 'Italian'? The saying goes that the best Italian is 'lingua toscana in bocca romana' (the language – the tongue – of Tuscany in the mouth of somebody from Rome). Tuscany, Florence in particular, is considered the cradle of Italian language and literature. You may be surprised to hear that the Italian spoken today is still the Italian forged by the Florentine poet Dante Alighieri in the 14th century. Dante lived about three hundred years earlier than Shakespeare and his impact on Italian language can only be compared to the one Shakespeare had on the English language. Dante was passionate about studying the origin of languages and about affirming the dignity of the 'volgare' (the language of the 'volgo' – the common people) vis-à-vis Latin (the language of the cultured élite). For this élite he wrote a treatise in Latin, *De Vulgari Eloquentia*, in which he proposed the adoption of an 'illustrious' Italian dialect as the main means of expression not only for common people, but also for literary production, and especially in the legal profession and at court where Latin and French were the dominant languages at the time. Putting his theory into practice, Dante wrote the *Divina Commedia* in a beautifully rich variety of Italian, based on the dialect spoken in Florence, and this language has been handed down through the centuries without much change. For this reason Dante has been called **il padre della lingua italiana** *the father of the Italian language.*

The defence of the Italian language was taken up in 1553 by the Accademia della Crusca, a society which fought to preserve the purity of the Florentine language as used by Dante and his contemporaries. Today the Academy is part of a European Federation which protects national languages.

A factor which contributed to the development of the Italian language in subsequent times was the long and protracted domination of foreign powers from the **Rinascimento** to the **Risorgimento**. The Spanish Hapsburgs occupied the greater part of Italy from the mid-1500s to the early 1700s and their language helped regularize Italian grammar. The Spanish Bourbons took over from them in the South and the Austrian Hapsburgs in the North until the unification of Italy in 1861. But for a brief period 1797–1814 Napoleon's influence was strong in Italy and helped develop a unifying system of education and government, reduce regional dialects and increase unity of language. Napoleon himself spoke Italian as his first language, since his mother was Italian and Italian was the language of Corsica before its annexation to France.

Another writer who felt passionately about the language and helped develop modern Italian was Alessandro Manzoni. In the years 1840–1842, after working at a number of revisions, he published the definitive version of *I Promessi Sposi* (The Betrothed), the first modern novel in the Italian language. Manzoni, born of an aristocratic family in Milan and fluent in the French language, felt his use of the Italian language in the first two versions of the novel (1821 and 1827) was affected by his Milanese upbringing and French influence, so he spent some time in Florence **a sciaquare i panni in Arno** *to rinse his clothes (i.e. his words) in the river Arno,* as stated in the Preface to the 1840 edition of the novel. Manzoni considered 'a cultured Florentine dialect' the purest form of Italian.

When Italy was unified (1861) only a very small percentage of the population spoke Italian. Most, from the King downwards, were more at ease speaking their local dialect. Italian, based on Manzoni's choice of educated Florentine/Tuscan, was taught in schools but it was only in the second half of the twentieth century that a common language became widely understood and spoken. An early factor was military service which brought men from all parts of Italy together with a need to communicate. In the 1950s and 1960s, came the flight from the land to work in towns and cities and many Italians moved from their home area to one where their home dialect did not meet their communication needs. The most important factor in developing some sort of standard Italian was the spread of radio and television. "Standard Italian" is no longer educated Tuscan but strongly influenced by Roman and Milanese, TV and radio being based in Rome and Milan. Nowadays it is rare to find someone who does not understand or speak a form of standard Italian although many, including highly educated people, still use dialect with friends and family.

Today an immense revolution is taking place under the influence of the media, of the internet, of the mobile phone and other technological innovations. The younger generation speak a language peppered with English words, borrowed from the world of technology, pop music, sport, computer games, soap operas, a language which is abridged, levelled out and shrunk to fit a hand-held screen. A far cry from Dante's and Manzoni's Italian!

In this course you will hear and read standard Italian which is understood wherever you go, but which also reflects personal nuances in vocabulary, inflection, structure. Since you are beyond the initial stage of Italian and have a solid grounding in its basic rules, you can now develop fluency, expand vocabulary and acquire an in-depth knowledge of more complex grammar structures. This course offers you the language as it is spoken by the average educated Italian (in its interviews with real people), the language as it is used by the media (in its newspaper articles), the language of good written prose (in its short literary passages).

You will be reading and hearing Italian as it is spoken today by the average person, not the language of soap operas or of social networking sites, but common everyday speech which in Italy is still governed by sound grammar rules and by a richness of vocabulary, metaphor and imagery quite surprising in this all-levelling technological world.

When and where will you be using the Italian you learn in this course? You will use it in a variety of situations: in personal conversations with close friends, in one-to-one exchanges in business environments, in discussions on general topics like education, work practices and voluntary organizations.

Don't forget that the countries where Italian is spoken are not only Italy, San Marino and the Vatican City, but also part of Switzerland, Malta, Croatia, Istria and Slovenia. Italian is understood in Corsica, on the Côte d'Azur, in Monaco, in Albania and in the ex-colonies of Libya, Eritrea, Somalia and Ethiopia. There are large Italian-speaking communities in Argentina, Brazil, the USA, Canada, Australia, as well as some in Venezuela, Uruguay and Chile. A number of Italian immigrants work and live in other European countries such as Germany, France and the UK.

According to the survey **Italiano 2000**, carried out under the direction of the authority on Italian language today, Tullio De Mauro of the 'La Sapienza' University in Rome, Italian is the fifth foreign language most frequently studied in the world. A European Union survey in 2006 found that it is the second language in Europe in terms of the number of speakers, after German, and the sixth most frequently spoken foreign language in the world (3%), after English (38%), French (14%), German (14%), Spanish (6%) and Russian (6%).

English translations of the Italian passages quoted above:

Era un esilio il nostro … *Ours was an exile: our city was far away and so were our books, friends, the various and changeable events of a real existence.*

un sentimento comune ... *a common feeling, a love for Italy and her artistic heritage, rightly considered a world heritage.*

una marcia della pace attorno alle mura di Gerusalemme ...
a march for peace around the walls of Jerusalem ... was an experience which practically changed the direction of my life.

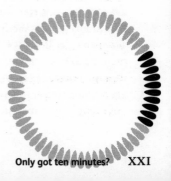

Introduction

Perfect your Italian is for you if you have learned some Italian and would like to widen and improve your knowledge of the language. If you are already following a course aiming to do that, you will find it offers valuable supplementary material. Teachers also will find much that they can exploit in the classroom in post-beginners classes.

Learning a language is best done by contact with the language. And you can always understand more than you can say. *Perfect your Italian* gives you rich experience of spoken Italian through interviews with Italians talking about the sort of topics people discuss everywhere. There is plenty of help with understanding what they say and the interviews have been recorded so that you can listen to them as often as you wish. In this way, you become really familiar with them, almost learning them by heart. This can be done while you are doing other things: washing up, waiting for a bus, travelling, so that you are using your precious time twice over. Gradually you will find you too can say the sort of things our speakers say. All the time, Italian will get easier!

Of course you also need to develop your understanding of the way the language works. To help you, we look at various aspects of the structure of Italian; this is followed by practice in using the language.

The conversations are organized into units around a single theme. The intention is that you should work through the text as you would any book. We have tried to make the style friendly and accessible, as if we were talking to you. To make the sections manageable, since you may not have long periods of time to devote to your Italian, each unit is subdivided into sessions which we hope are small enough for a single sitting. They vary in length as will your available time and the pace you work at. However, if you cannot manage to complete a 'session' in one go, don't worry. Go back to the beginning of that part when you next sit down to study and go through it again. Indeed you should consider going back over earlier units from time to time too. It will help you retain what you have learnt.

Perfect your Italian will give you other suggestions about the best way to go about learning a language. Different people learn in different ways and you need to try to find what works best for you. Language learning is not easy, for most people at least, so it is important not to be discouraged by the amount of time it seems to take. You will also probably find you have good patches and bad ones. Sometimes the language seems to flow, other days it just won't come. Don't worry! This is normal. But do try to persevere. And there is no doubt that regular sessions pay dividends. They need not be very long. Little and often is not a bad recipe. Three hours in six half-hour sessions during a week may well be more productive than one three-hour session. But you must do what fits in with your lifestyle.

At this point however we should like to stress just one thing: speaking a language is about saying what you want to say, about communication. You do not have to get it absolutely right to communicate. Mostly, your meaning will come over even if there are mistakes in what you say. Just think of all the non-native speakers of English you know who get by perfectly well speaking an English which you know is not what an English native speaker would use. So the most important rule of all is to try. Don't worry about making mistakes. If the listener understands, that is what matters. Many students of Italian report that when they try their Italian, native speakers are delighted. They are generally tolerant, patient and encouraging. So there's no need to worry! The worst you can do is make everyone laugh and that's no bad thing, anyway. Gradually, as you get more and more practice, you will get more and more right.

Good luck! **Buona fortuna! In bocca al lupo!**

1

....

I piaceri della vita

In this unit we shall
- *talk about what we like doing and things we like or dislike*
- *remind ourselves about Italian verbs: the infinitive*
- *say what we have to do*
- *revise the use of subject personal pronouns*
- *say what we should like to do: the conditional*
- *think about learning strategies*

_____

Session 1

Interview 1

We asked Angioletta Viviani, a teacher of English, to tell us what she enjoyed doing in her spare time; we also sought her advice on learning a foreign language (see Interview 2).

Read the interview which follows, listening to the recording at the same time if possible. If you need help understanding individual words, there is an Italian–English word list at the back of the book to help you. At the end of the passage, you will find comprehension questions which are designed to help you focus on the meaning of the passage.

Prof.ssa Angioletta Viviani is a high school teacher. She lives near Arezzo in a house with views over the Val di Chiana, a broad valley in southern Tuscany, between Arezzo and Siena.

Interviewer   Angioletta, cosa ti piace fare nel tuo tempo libero?

Angioletta   Nel mio tempo libero? Eh, direi la cosa che mi piace forse più di tutte è leggere. E leggo tanto in maniera molto disordinata nel senso che leggo tante cose di vario genere … e poi leggo molta narrativa contemporanea e se l'autore è un autore di lingua inglese lo devo leggere assolutamente in inglese. Mi rifiuto di comprare traduzioni e anzi devo dire che l'estate scorsa avevo comprato anche un romanzo in spagnolo, uno in francese perché volevo anche riprendere queste due lingue. E … poi mi piace camminare e … andare in giro, nei dintorni, mi piace.

Interviewer   In campagna?

Angioletta   In campagna, sì. Poi andare in bicicletta, sempre più o meno nella Val di Chiana. Poi mi piace cucinare … Soprattutto mi piace cucinare pasta e dolci. Se devo scegliere … La carne, non credo neanche di essere molto brava a cucinare la carne. Insomma non è una mia passione, infatti mi piace anche più mangiare i primi.

Interviewer   Sì?

Angioletta   Sì, sì, più della carne. E poi che mi piace fare? Eh, mi piace chiacchierare … Non so se è un pregio o un difetto comunque insomma … stare con amiche e parlare … Mi piace andare al cinema e …

Interviewer   Vai spesso?

Angioletta   Sì, andiamo con mio marito e con una coppia di amici che anche loro amano andare al cinema … più o meno l'inverno una volta alla settimana. Forse ogni dieci giorni, facendo la media. E poi mi piace andare in giro a visitare posti … nuovi … e pure rivedere vecchi posti dove sono stata. Mi piacerebbe conoscere di più la Toscana perché, sembra strano, ma ci sono ancora tanti piccoli paesi che non ho mai visto … e specialmente, per esempio, non so, nella parte nord della Toscana, Garfagnana, Lunigiana … Sono posti che non conosco.

Interviewer   Sei stata a Barga?

Angioletta	No.
Interviewer	È molto pittoresca.
Angioletta	Infatti. E poi che mi piace anche fare? Ah, mi piace leggere i giornali anche, leggere quotidiani; m'interessa proprio la politica e voglio essere sempre aggiornata, sapere le notizie. La prima cosa che faccio la mattina è accendere la radio o la televisione perché credo di essere anche un po' fanatica, cioè…. non posso resistere se non so che cosa è successo.

QUICK VOCAB

facendo la media on average (literally: making an average)
Garfagnana, Lunigiana areas in north-west Tuscany. Lunigiana also covers part of eastern Liguria.
Barga a small hill town in the Garfagnana, in the province of Lucca, well worth a visit.

Insight

Listen carefully to the soft sound of **c** or **ci** (as in *chair*) in pia**ce**, dol**ci**, spe**ci**almente, fa**cci**o. Listen to the hard sound **c** or **ch** (as in *cat*) in **c**omprare, **c**ampagna, **cu**cinare, ve**cchi**, an**ch**e. Spelling in Italian is very consistent and helps you identify the sound.

Practise also listening to the soft sound of **g** or **gi** (as in *jet*) in le**gg**ere, **gi**ro, **gi**ornali, Luni**gi**ana; and to the hard sound of **g** or **gh** (as in *get*) in le**gg**o, lin**gu**a, Bar**g**a.

Comprehension 1

These questions are designed to help you check you have understood the main points. Your answers should be in English.

1 What does Angioletta like doing most of all?
2 How does she organize her reading?
3 What sort of books in particular does she appear to enjoy?

4 What does she refuse to buy?

5 Why did she buy books in Spanish and French last summer?

6 Can you list two forms of physical exercise Angioletta says she enjoys?

7 Angioletta says she enjoys cooking, particularly preparing ... what?

8 What sort of food does she prefer eating and which does she enjoy less?

9 Angioletta is a very sociable person. How might you guess this from what she says?

10 What do she and her husband regularly enjoy, along with another couple, friends of theirs?

11 Angioletta lives in an area of Italy popular with tourists, Tuscany. She enjoys visiting places. What does she says she would like to do?

12 Finally, what does she need to start her day off properly?

Check your answers in the Key at the back of the book. This is important and you will also find the Key contains information to help you with possible difficulties.

Session 2

One of the aims of *Perfect your Italian* is to help you to a better understanding of the structure of Italian. Yes, the grammar. Some language learners go into a state approaching panic when they hear the word grammar but it is just another way of saying 'structure'. No language can work without structure; it would be just a jumble of sounds. To convey meaning, especially the subtleties human language is capable of, there has to be a structure. And when you study a foreign language, you need to develop an understanding of the structure so that you can make it work for you. If you are one of those who worry about grammar, your problem is probably that you are unfamiliar with the technical jargon used to talk about it. There is help for you at the back of the book in the section entitled **Grammar – the technical jargon explained**.

Saying you like doing something: piacere + infinitive

Angioletta said:

leggere	*reading*
camminare	*walking*
Mi piace andare in giro	*I like walking around the area*
andare in bicicletta	*cycling*
cucinare	*cooking*

and so on. What was the question the interviewer asked her at the beginning?

Che cosa ti piace fare?	*What do you like doing?*

The interviewer was an old friend of Angioletta's and therefore used the familiar form **ti piace**. The question using the formal form is:

Che cosa Le piace fare?	*What do you like doing?*

You will probably use the formal phrase more than the familiar one at first. The verb is the same in both cases, however; it is the pronoun (the word for *you*) which changes. What is going on? It helps if you understand precisely how the structure works. **Piace** is part of the verb **piacere** which means *to please, to be pleasing*. So the structure for expressing the idea *I like reading* is not the same as when you say **mi piace leggere**. You are in fact saying: *reading is pleasing to me*. Here is the whole picture:

Mi		**leggere**	*Reading*		*me*
Ti		**andare in bicicletta**	*Cycling*		*you (fam.)*
Le		**cucinare**	*Cooking*		*you (form.)*
Gli	**piace**	**stare con le amiche**	*Being with friends*	*is pleasing to*	*him*
Le		**parlare con le amiche**	*Talking to friends*		*her*
Ci		**chiacchierare**	*Chatting*		*us*
Vi		**andare al cinema**	*Going to the cinema*		*you (pl.)*
Gli		**camminare**	*Walking*		*them*

Note that **Le piace** can mean *You* (formal) *like* or *She likes.*
It usually becomes clear in context.

If you name the person who likes doing something you get:

A Giovanni piace cucinare.
Ai nostri amici piace andare
  al cinema.

John likes cooking.
Our friends like going to the
  cinema.

If you have already named them:

A lui piace cucinare, a loro
  piace andare al cinema, ma a
  me piace leggere in tranquillità.

He likes cooking, they like
  going to the cinema, but I like
  reading in peace and quiet.

Here you are using 'strong pronouns', which are needed after
a preposition.

Activity 1

Say you like doing the following things. To help you we have put
the Italian equivalents in a list, but not in the same order. So, using
your previous knowledge, guesswork, elimination and, if necessary,
a dictionary, pick the correct Italian verb from the list.

Example: *I like reading*   **Mi piace leggere.**

1 *dancing*	**guardare la televisione**
2 *going to the theatre*	**parlare italiano**
3 *travelling*	**ballare**
4 *surfing the Net*	**guidare la mia nuova macchina**
5 *gardening*	**andare a teatro**
6 *watching television*	**andare in discoteca**
7 *listening to classical music*	**viaggiare**
8 *going to the disco*	**lavorare in giardino**
9 *driving my new car*	**ascoltare la musica classica**
10 *speaking Italian*	**navigare su Internet**

Activity 2

Here are some things for you to say. Use the formal form **Lei** (**Le piace**) when speaking to the person you have just met and the familiar **tu** (**ti piace**) when speaking to your friend and her husband.

1 You are practising your Italian on a fellow-traveller in the aeroplane. How would you ask him: Do you like going to the cinema?
2 Ask him if he likes travelling by car.
3 You are having supper with an Italian friend. Ask her if she likes cooking.
4 Ask her what she likes cooking.
5 Ask her husband if he likes gardening.

Saying you like something

Have you checked your answers to Activities 1 and 2 in the Key at the back of the book? So far, we have looked at how you say you like *doing something*. You probably also know how to say you like *something*:

Mi piace la pizza.	*I like pizza.*
Mi piace il cinema.	*I like the cinema.*
Le piace il giardinaggio?	*Do you like gardening?*
Ti piace la carne?	*Do you like meat?*

Do you remember what happens when whatever is liked is plural? Think back to what **piace** actually means. You will realize, of course, it is singular, so that when what is liked is plural, you need to say:

Mi *piacciono* i libri di Antonio Tabucchi.	*Antonio Tabucchi's books are pleasing to me or I like Tabucchi's books.*
Ti *piacciono* di più i primi o i dolci?	*Do you prefer pasta dishes or puddings?*
Le *piacciono* i film italiani?	*Do you (formal) like Italian films?*

Saying you don't like something or doing something

Non mi piace la carne.	*I don't like meat.*
Non mi piacciono i gatti.	*I don't like cats.*
Non mi piace lavorare in giardino.	*I don't like gardening.*

There is another verb you can use to say what you like, perhaps with slightly more force. Angioletta uses it once, when talking about the friends they go to the cinema with. Can you find it?

una coppia di amici che anche loro amano andare al cinema	*a couple, friends, who also like going to the cinema*

Amare, *to love*, works as in English, i.e. as regards the structure of who likes what. **Amo la musica** = *I love music*. The difference in meaning between **mi piace** and **amo** is much the same as between *I like* and *I love*. And *to hate* is **odiare**.

Session 3

Verbs – infinitives
The infinitive is the part of the verb the dictionary gives you. The meaning will be given as *to read*, *to buy*, etc. But that is not always the most satisfactory translation. For instance, if you speak American English you probably say *I like to read*; if you speak British English you are likely to say *I like reading*. Either is fine, but remember that literal translations are not always right.

Activity 3

When Angioletta talked about what she likes doing, she used **mi piace** + the infinitive of the verb. Regular Italian verbs fall into three different types. Group 1 have an infinitive ending in **-are**; Group 2 have infinitives ending in **-ere** and Group 3 in **-ire**. (Sometimes the final **-e** of the infinitive, especially of **avere** and

essere, is dropped.) Look back to what Angioletta said and list all the infinitives she used, putting the infinitives into their respective groups. Make a group for any irregular verbs you find. Look up any words you do not know.

Example: Group 2: **rivedere**

Check your answer in the Key.

Saying you must/have to do something: dovere + infinitive

In Italian, the infinitive is used after **piacere**. It is also used after a number of other verbs. Angioletta uses a very common one, more than once. Can you pick it out?

devo leggere	*I must/have to read*
devo dire	*I must/have to say*
se devo scegliere	*if I must/have to choose*

Other verbs followed by the infinitive in this text include **volere** (**volevo riprendere** *I wanted to pick up … again*) and others which, in addition, require **di** before the infinitive (**mi rifiuto di comprare** *I refuse to buy*; **non credo di essere molto brava a** *I don't think I am very good at*). Note that **potere**, not in the text, also works like **dovere** and **volere** (e.g. **Posso aiutare?** *Can I help?*). Indeed, they make up a most useful trio. For the moment we will not investigate this point further. Let's get back to the infinitive itself.

Group 2 verbs – stress in the infinitive
You need to be aware which group a verb falls into in order to know how it will behave, i.e. what its form will be in its various parts. One small point: in the second group, some verbs are stressed on the ending **-ere** (**rivedere**), others (more) on the preceding syllable: **leggere, riprendere, scegliere, accendere, resistere.** Learners sometimes wonder about this. The way the stress falls has no relation to the way the verb works. And the only way to find out where the stress falls is to consult a dictionary – or check with an Italian.

The infinitive for polite instructions

The infinitive is often used for instructions, for instance on doors:

spingere *push* **tirare** *pull*

or other written instructions destined to be read by many people, e.g. cookery recipes:

Spuntare e tagliare a pezzetti le zucchine, lavarle, scolarle e gettarle in un tegame con cipolla tagliata sottilmente e olio.

Cut the ends off the courgettes and cut them into small pieces, wash and drain them and put them into a frying pan with finely chopped onion and oil.

Language learning tip

If you are unsure of a verb form, particularly for giving instructions, telling people to do something, use the infinitive. You may even find Italians do this to you with all verbs, thinking they are making themselves clearer – like the sort of pidgin some English speakers reserve for addressing non-English speakers. But you should gradually try to master the verb forms and this book will help you do so.

Subject personal pronouns – use

How often does Angioletta use the subject personal pronouns, **io, noi, loro** which are the ones we might expect when she is talking about herself, her husband and friends? Correct! She uses just one, once. Italians use subject personal pronouns for emphasis or contrast, that is when they are necessary to the meaning or add something. The rest of the time the verb alone is adequate. The ending is enough to indicate the subject in most contexts. Try to cut out inessential use of subject pronouns; this will give your Italian a more Italian flavour. Here is an activity which shows you the pronouns in action.

Reading

Read this extract from an essay by Natalia Ginzburg entitled 'Lui e io'. She is writing about her second husband (see p. 103) – and herself. At the end there are some activities for you.

Lui ama il teatro, la pittura, e la musica: soprattutto la musica. Io non capisco niente di musica, m'importa molto poco della pittura, e m'annoio a teatro. Amo e capisco una cosa sola al mondo, ed è la poesia.

Lui ama i musei, e io ci vado con sforzo, con uno spiacevole senso di dovere e fatica. Lui ama le biblioteche, e io le odio.

Lui ama i viaggi, le città straniere e sconosciute, i ristoranti. Io resterei sempre a casa, non mi muoverei mai.

Lo seguo, tuttavia, in molti viaggi. Lo seguo nei musei, nelle chiese, all'opera. Lo seguo anche ai concerti, e mi addormento.

Siccome conosce dei direttori d'orchestra, dei cantanti, gli piace andare, dopo lo spettacolo, a congratularsi con loro. Lo seguo per i lunghi corridoi, che portano ai camerini dei cantanti, lo ascolto parlare con persone vestite da cardinali e da re.

... A lui piacciono le tagliatelle, l'abbacchio, le ciliege, il vino rosso. A me piace il minestrone, il pancotto, la frittata, gli erbaggi.

'Lui e io' (written in 1962) in Natalia Ginzburg, *Le piccole virtù*, Einaudi 1962

senso di dovere dovere can be used as a noun, *duty.*
pancotto a simple soup containing bread
erbaggi vegetables, salads

Activity 4

1 Pick out the subject pronouns in the passage above.
2 What do you notice about Natalia Ginzburg's use of **amare** and
piacere?
3 Pretend to be her husband and say some of the things you like.
You probably think your wife also likes all your activities but you
know what she likes in the way of food. Say what she likes to eat.
You don't like these things; say so.

See the **Reference Grammar** for a table of the personal pronouns.

Activity 5

You've been asked by an Italian acquaintance about your leisure
time activities back home. Here is what you want to say. How
might you say it in Italian?

1 The children love swimming.
2 We like walking in the country round about.
3 My husband likes cooking and each of us (**ognuno**) prepares
part of the meal.
4 He prefers to cook meat.
5 I am good at puddings.
6 My husband likes reading. I prefer to play (**suonare**) the piano.
7 My daughter likes singing. She is very good.
8 We love visiting museums, going to the cinema and sometimes
concerts.
9 We don't like television.

Session 4

Saying what you would like to do

Reread what Angioletta says and pick out how she says she'd like to know Tuscany better:

Mi piacerebbe conoscere di più la Toscana …	*I'd like to know Tuscany better…*

She is using the form of the verb which is the equivalent of the English *would like*. Literally, *knowing Tuscany more would be pleasing to me*. Elsewhere she says:

Direi la cosa che mi piace forse più di tutte è leggere.	*I would say the thing I perhaps like most of all is reading.*

This is the 'I', first person singular, form. The tense is the conditional. The use of **direi** is common in spoken Italian where in English one might say: *I think* … Natalia Ginzburg also uses the conditional in the extract above to say what she would do, implying if it were not for her husband.

Io *resterei* sempre a casa. Non mi *muoverei* mai.	*I would always stay at home. I wouldn't ever move (go out).*

You will find you often want to say what you would do if … The first and third persons singular are probably the forms you will use most often, with the endings **-ei** (1st person) and **-ebbe** (3rd person).

Most verbs add these endings to the infinitive minus the final -e.

direi	*I would say*
mi piacerebbe	*I would like*
non mi muoverei	*I wouldn't move*
finirei	*I would finish*
capirei	*I would understand*

(Contd)

partirei	*I would leave*
conoscerebbe	*He/she would know/be acquainted with*
deciderebbe	*He/she would decide*

Group 1 verbs change the **a** of the infinitive to **e**.

comprerei	*I would buy*
cucinerei	*I would cook*
parlerei	*I would speak*
rifiuterebbe	*he would refuse*
mangerebbe	*he would eat*

Irregular verbs often have a bigger change to the root. You almost certainly know:

vorrei	*I'd like*

from **volere**. Others which also substitute double **rr** for **l** or **n** plus **r** are:

venire: verrei	*I would come*
rimanere: rimarrei	*I would stay, remain*

Other irregular verbs simply have a contracted form of the infinitive:

andare: andrei	*I would go*
avere: avrei	*I would have*
cadere: cadrei	*I would fall*
dovere: dovrei	*I would have to, I should, I ought to*
potere: potrei	*I would be able to, I could*
sapere: saprei	*I would know*
vedere: vedrei	*I would see*
vivere: vivrei	*I would live*

Essere is more irregular: **sarei** *I would be*

Note also:

fare: farei	*I would do/make*
dare: darei	*I would give*
stare: starei	*I would be/stay*

Activity 6

How would you say the following in Italian?

1 My partner (**compagno/a**) likes going to the gym (**la palestra**) in the evenings. I would prefer to stay at home. I'd read, or watch TV, or perhaps listen to a little music.

2 My partner would spend his/her holidays at home. He/she would go for walks in the surrounding area, play tennis and go to the cinema. I would prefer to go abroad. I like travelling. I would like to visit America. I would visit New York. I would see the Metropolitan Museum of Art, I would go to the Met and it would be interesting to visit the museum about immigration on Ellis Island. I am interested in Italian emigration to the USA.

Note: As well as **compagno/a** Italians also use the word **partner** (e.g. **il mio/la mia partner**).

Session 5

Getting your meaning across – communication

Language learning is about learning to communicate, to make yourself understood – and to understand the person speaking to you. Eventually, you will want to get things right, but when you are learning, it is more important to get the word out, even if incorrectly, than to be accurate. Accuracy will come gradually as you learn more. If in the heat of the moment, you use the infinitive of all verbs, or say *he reads* when you mean *I read*, because you are in a real-life situation, you will probably be understood. So don't worry too much about always getting it right. Try to learn the forms, but when you are trying to talk Italian, speak and forget about the mistakes. Think of all the foreign speakers of English you know who you understand even when they say things in a way which you never would and you know is not good English. They communicate – and that must be your primary aim.

Words – how to consolidate and extend your stock

To get your meaning over, what you need most of all is **words** (**vocabulary** is the technical word often used for a stock or list of words), lots of them, as many as you can muster. There are various aspects to this.

1 Learning the words you meet

This is one of the areas where you need to develop your own personal learning style. Were there any words you didn't know in what Angioletta said? What did you do about it? Assuming you looked them up, what did you then do? Many people find it helps to write new words down in a systematic way. Try dividing your page in half vertically and writing the Italian in one column and the English in the other. You can then cover up one half and test yourself on the other. Or you can make cards, initially perhaps one word per card, with Italian on one side and English on the other. You can also test yourself with these by putting the cards out on a table. And you can turn any card over when you can't remember the meaning. You can play a game: put a number of cards out, study them, and then cover them up and see how many you can remember. Try again a few days later and see if you have improved. And … even if you write the words down and then don't look at them again – in a busy life, these things can happen – just the act of writing the word down will help fix some of them. And they will be there for you to use when you go over the passage again – another important language-learning tool.

Another ploy is to group words: you might for instance group words connected with reading. From Angioletta you might take: **leggere, narrativa contemporanea, romanzo, giornale, quotidiano, traduzione, autore.**

You might follow this with some research of your own into words which in your mind relate to reading e.g. *reader* **lettore, lettrice;** *bookshop* **libreria;** *library* **biblioteca;** and you can probably guess the meaning of **storia; biografia; autobiografia; poesia; lettera; scrivere; scrittore, scrittrice; novella** – careful: you have had the word for *novel* in the interview with Angioletta – **novella** means *short story.* **Storia** means *history* as well as *story.*

A basic understanding of memory may be helpful: memory fades. Resign yourself to the fact that you will probably forget some words and have to re-learn them. But you can increase your chances of remembering if you have a follow-up learning session soon after the original one, say next day. Forgetting will not have set in to any great extent and re-learning slows down the forgetting process. If for some reason you are unable to work at your Italian for a long period, you will probably be upset at how much you have forgotten. Most speakers of foreign languages, even those who have achieved quite a high degree of fluency, find that a gap without using the language sets them back. So if you can work regularly it will help. But if you do have a gap and forget, don't despair. It will come back to you when you start working at it again.

Memory can also be helped by working out associations. Link the word in your mind with an image, another word, a context, something that will help you remember it. Many learners will find that becoming familiar with the Italian presented in a book like this is a possible way to extend their vocabulary, learning the words in a context. There is no need to learn by heart, but, over time, re-read, listen again and again to the recording, and you will get to know the material. Later you will find you can use the words in another context.

2 Understanding words you don't know, which you meet when you can't look them up or ask anyone.

You need to develop strategies for coping. In Activity 1, we suggested you use **guesswork** and **elimination**. Elimination won't work outside a limited context, like the list you had. Guesswork can however be refined:

a Is the word like any other Italian word you know? For instance, perhaps you didn't know **dintorni**. But you do know **intorno** = *around*. Maybe, looking at the context: **mi piace camminare e andare in giro, nei dintorni** ... you can guess that **dintorni** means *surroundings, surrounding area*.

b Is the word like an English word you know? For instance, **tempo libero**. Possibly you haven't met **libero**. But you do know *liberate* meaning *set free*. And of course, **libero** goes with **tempo**. Could the pair mean *free time, leisure*?

c Sometimes you may be thrown back on just guessing from the context. **Chiacchierare** doesn't look like any English or Italian word, you probably agree. But its context is: **mi piace chiacchierare ... Non so se è un pregio o un difetto comunque insomma ... stare con amiche e parlare.** What do friends do when they get together? *Talk* (**parlare**), or another word for that? Yes, *chat* (**chiacchierare**). Nicely onomatopaeic. But be a bit careful. Guessing can lead you horribly astray!

3 Increasing your vocabulary (stock of words) generally

Words are best learned in a context. It is unlikely to be profitable to learn lists of words, although if they are linked around a topic, it may work for you. Most people find words in use easier to grasp. This really means making efforts to 'meet' as much Italian language as possible. See the last part of this unit.

Activity 7

We are assuming you don't know the words in italic type taken from what Angioletta said in Session 1. How might you work out what they mean without using a dictionary?

1 **cose di vario** *genere*
2 *Mi rifiuto* **di comprare traduzioni**
3 **Non so se è un** *pregio* **o un** *difetto*
4 **una** *coppia* **di amici**
5 **visitare** *posti* **nuovi … rivedere vecchi** *posti*
6 **voglio sempre essere** *aggiornata*
7 **non posso resistere se non so che cosa** *è successo*

The spoken language

When we speak, the language we use is not the same as the written form. When we write, we have time to think and therefore we structure more carefully, correct, try to be concise, etc. In speech, we change direction in mid-sentence, we leave sentences unfinished and we include words that are not necessary, but which perhaps give us time to think or make it easier for the listener to follow. In English, you will be aware of the way some people use *sort of*, *I mean*, *anyway* and other expressions which when written down seem to be adding little to the meaning, but which we do not always even notice as we listen – or indeed when we use them ourselves. Angioletta uses some of the common equivalents in Italian, for instance:

direi, anzi, comunque, insomma, non so

Look back at how she uses these words.

Note also her use of **infatti**. It means *indeed, yes*. It is used to express agreement. The interviewer asked her whether she had been to Barga and she said she hadn't. When the interviewer followed up by saying how lovely Barga is, Angioletta felt that this provided support for what she had said about wanting to explore northern Tuscany which she doesn't know well. **Infatti** is very widely used in everyday Italian and it does not mean *in fact*. It is what is sometimes called a 'false friend', a word which sounds like an English word but which does not mean the same as the English word. You have met others in this unit, for instance: **libreria, novella**. We shall return to the question of 'false friends'.

Session 6

Interview 2

Imparare una lingua alla maniera di Angioletta Viviani

Angioletta was asked whether she, as a language teacher, had any advice to offer a student learning a foreign language. Here is what she said. Her answer showed, perhaps more than the interview at the beginning of the unit, some of the characteristics of the spoken language.

CD1, TR 2, 6:23

Angioletta Mah, io potrei dire quello che dico di solito ai miei studenti, che s'impara a scuola, ma s'impara anche tanto volendo … cercare l'occasione, no? per imparare. E io dico sempre, per esempio, guardate gli ingredienti dei biscotti quando fate colazione la mattina, per la lingua che volete imparare, per esempio, e lì sicuramente imparerete magari una o due parole nuove. Cercate le occasioni anche … se sentite … Io mi ricordo quando andavo all'università, viaggiando in treno da Arezzo a Pisa, se sentivo qualcuno che parlava l'inglese mi sedevo di sicuro vicino e tentavo di attaccare discorso per fare un po' di pratica. E poi ascoltare cose registrate, cercare di parlare a sé stessi ad alta voce nella lingua che si vuole imparare; io dico anche pensare dentro di sé ma aspettate l'occasione. Se siete in autobus e vedete un signore strano, pensate come lo descrivereste nella lingua che state studiando, no? E poi, che altro? Ecco: cercate di trovare delle cose, dei sistemi di memorizzazione che voi sapete funzionano per voi. Poi …È certo che per l'inglese è tutto più facile, voglio dire … non che l'inglese sia facile ma le occasioni sono moltissime. Trovi canzoni, trovi riviste, molto di più che non probabilmente, non so, per l'italiano oppure altre lingue. Però dev'essere un atteggiamento mentale, quello di volere imparare e effettivamente se faccio delle interviste ai ragazzi più bravi, scopro sempre che fanno tutte queste cose, soprattutto che parlano ad alta voce, si raccontano le cose quando sono soli e questo, secondo me, serve tantissimo perché si diventa più sciolti, più sicuri. Io facevo così e vedo che funziona.

QUICK VOCAB

volendo literally: *wanting to*. Frequently used to mean: *if you want to.*
gli ingredienti dei biscotti Angioletta is thinking of packets of biscuits which show the ingredients in several languages since they are sold in several countries. An equivalent for English people might be reading the labels on sauce bottles. Note also: many Italians breakfast on biscuits!
se sentite … A very obvious moment when Angioletta changes direction. She was clearly planning to say: If you hear someone speaking the language …
descrivereste *you* (plural) *would describe*. The **voi** form of the conditional.

Insight

The word **che** *which, who, that* can never be omitted in Italian: **la lingua che volete imparare** *the language (that) you want to learn*; **se sentivo qualcuno che parlava inglese** *if I heard somebody who spoke English*.

Activity 8

Reread Angioletta's advice and look for unfinished sentences using expressions of the same type as the English: *you know, well*, etc. Make a list of them and check your answer in the Key.

Comprehension 2

Make a list of the various suggestions Angioletta makes to students to help them learn a foreign language.

Further language learning suggestions

We would endorse everything that Angioletta said and add: **Reading** is also very valuable. It doesn't really matter what you read. If you can find newspapers or magazines, you may enjoy them. Following Italian politics is difficult for the uninitiated, but you can read about world events that you already know of. The *Cronaca* section which contains news of crime, accidents, etc. can be fascinating! Sometimes just going through the headlines concerning the latest natural disaster or world crisis provides plenty of new vocabulary. If there is a particular subject you are very keen on, try reading about it. Maybe you follow Italian football, for instance. You will find that your enthusiasm carries you along because you want so much to know.

Editions of Italian texts prepared by English-language publishers for students can be a good starting point for the more ambitious reader, since they often have notes and help with vocabulary. There are editions with parallel texts: the Italian on one page and on the facing page the translation. Natalia Ginzburg is a possible author to try since she writes in a style rather different to the flowery one once favoured by Italian writers. *Le voci della sera* might be an enjoyable starting point although the humour is rather black. Or another essay in *Le piccole virtù*: 'Elogio e compianto dell'Inghilterra' perhaps. This was written when Natalia came to London where her husband had become Director of the Italian Cultural Institute. She was suffering from writer's block at the time and the cultural shock was so great that she wrote *Le voci* *della sera* in a very short time. But be warned, in the essay she is expressing her homesickness.

The Internet: Try the sites mentioned in Unit 8 – newspapers, environmental groups, 'Slow Food' supporters ...

Music: It is true there is not much opportunity to hear Italian pop songs in the English-speaking world; if your taste lies in that direction, opera may offer you some practice – though the Italian may be a little old-fashioned.

Meeting Italians, hearing Italian: Seize every opportunity you can find for contact with the Italian language. In many towns an evening out at an Italian restaurant is a real possibility and if you are lucky some of the staff will speak Italian with you. Try Italian films, subtitled perhaps. You may be able to buy them on DVD or borrow them from your local library. See if there is an Italian circle near you. Many towns have an organization where people interested in Italy and Italians living locally meet for talks and social events. If you live within a reasonable distance of a capital city or any other very important city, contact the Italian Cultural Institute for their programme.

Coraggio e ... buona fortuna!

Activity 9

Talking to yourself

Before you leave this unit, re-read the texts in which people say what they like. Then think out how you would tell an Italian about what you *like* and *don't like*, what you *would like*, etc. During the next few days, come back to your thoughts, refine them, add to them. Then pretend to be someone you know and think out what they might say. Give yourself as much practice as you can on likes and dislikes. There is no entry in the Key for this activity since everyone will have a different answer.

Remember Angioletta's advice about talking to yourself and try it! It really does help. Throughout the book we shall suggest topics and you will doubtless have your own. It is an excellent use of time which might otherwise be quite wasted: time spent in traffic jams, in the bath, doing boring chores, waiting for a visitor to arrive. Just try saying out loud what you are doing, a kind of running commentary, it is all good practice.

Eccomi qui in questo ingorgo. Davanti a me c'è una Cinquecento gialla. Non riesco neanche a vedere il semaforo. Sono qui da cinque minuti ...

Here I am in this traffic jam. In front of me there is a yellow Cinquecento. I can't even see the traffic lights. I've been here for five minutes ...

If you are working with a friend or family member, or if you are learning in a group or class, you can of course also have real discussions.

TEST YOURSELF

1 My friends and I cannot agree on what to do together. Complete the text with these infinitives and add the correct pronoun for the verb **piacere**. Think carefully which person (or persons) likes what.

1 andare, 2 leggere, 3 passare, 4 camminare, 5 fare, 6 guardare

Serena ama gli sport pericolosi, specialmente quelli acquatici: (a) _____ piacerebbe molto (b) _____ windsurf o scuba diving. Michele e sua moglie preferiscono la musica: (c) _____ piace spesso (d) _____ ai concerti e all'opera. Io mi rifiuto di interessarmi di sport o di musica: (e) _____ piace (f) _____ romanzi, (g) _____ film alla tv e (h) _____ in campagna. Siamo tutti amici e (i) _____ piacerebbe (j) _____ un po' di tempo insieme, ma non riusciamo mai a metterci d'accordo su cosa fare.

2 In this unit you've found some Italian words which are slightly tricky for an English speaker. Choose the correct option in these sentences.

    a Vado in **biblioteca/libreria** a comprare una grammatica inglese.

    b Conosci **una novella/un romanzo** intitolato *Gone with the wind*?

    c Samantha legge molta **narrativa/finzione** contemporanea.

    d Mi sembrava inglese e **infatti/in realtà** ho scoperto che era nato a Londra.

    e È un sistema di memorizzazione che **lavora/funziona** per loro.

2

Mi presento

In this unit we shall
- *meet a number of different Italians*
- *examine how to talk about ourselves and others including descriptions of appearance and character*
- *review the present tense*
- *say how long we have been doing something*
- *revise vocabulary for talking about the family*
- *review the possessives:* my, your, his **etc.**

Session 1

Interview 1

Assuming you have the recording, listen to the interviews which follow. Try not to look at the text. If you do not have the recording, you will of course only be able to read the interviews.

First we meet three young people who belong to a group called **Il Gruppo Mio.** *(You will learn what this group does in another unit.)*

Antonella	Allora, io sono Antonella, ho 25 anni, sono studentessa all'università e studio scienze dell'educazione.
Riccardo	Io sono Riccardo, ho 31 anni e lavoro, faccio il rappresentante di farmaci e faccio parte del Gruppo Mio da parecchio tempo.

| Monica | Io mi chiamo Monica, ho 24 anni e mi sono laureata da poco in magistero delle scienze religiose, e … sono insegnante di religione … e niente. Sono nel Gruppo Mio dall'87. |

Insight

To say what your job is use **faccio** + the article: **Faccio il rappresentante** *I am a sales rep*. Or you can use **sono** + no article: **Sono insegnante** *I'm a teacher*.

Now a young man who manages a sports centre:

| Mario | Mi chiamo Mario Rotondale. Ho trent'anni, o quasi. Li compierò ad agosto di quest'anno, il 17 agosto. Sono nato a Torino. |

Insight

ad agosto *in August*: **d** is often added to the preposition **a** when the following word begins with the same vowel. **d** is also added to the conjunction **e** *and*: **ed era vero** *and it was true*. Adding **d** is not compulsory but it makes a better sound.

And now someone else with the same surname as Mario:

Interviewer	Si chiama?
Man	Nicola.
Interviewer	Nicola Rotondale?
Man	Sì. Figlio di Mario Rotondale.
Interviewer	Un altro Mario Rotondale?
Man	Quello lì era mio padre.

And two women:

| Silvia | Mi chiamo Silvia Lena. Abito a Bologna da circa vent'anni, però ho studiato a Milano. Sono laureata in lingue e letterature straniere. Ho insegnato nella scuola media per parecchi anni. |

(Contd)

Renata	Sono Renata Savio. Sono neuropsichiatra infantile come preparazione, come prima specializzazione, anzi naturalmente sono medico, sono laureata in medicina, sono specializzata in neuropsichiatria infantile, sono anche specializzata in igiene e medicina preventiva.

Insight

Many words in the field of medicine are similar in English and in Italian because of their common Latin or Greek root, but the pronunciation may be quite different: **neuropsichiatra** *neuropsychiatrist*, **specializzazione** *specialization*, **medicina** *medicine*, **igiene** *hygiene*.

QUICK VOCAB

io The three speakers from the **Gruppo Mio** use the personal pronoun **io** as they start to introduce themselves. This is because they are aware of representing a group but each is introducing him/herself rather than the group. In English speakers in the same circumstances would stress the word 'I' with their voice. None of the three uses the pronoun with subsequent verbs. Notice that the other speakers, who are being interviewed alone, do not do this. (See Unit 1.)

niente It usually means *nothing* but as used here by Monica it doesn't have much meaning at all. It is commonly used in this way in spoken Italian, when the speaker comes to the end of her/his thoughts. It would not be used in written Italian in this throwaway usage.

da parecchio tempo *for quite a long time*
per parecchi anni *for several years*

Comprehension 1

Read the questions, then listen to the speakers again and answer the questions.

1 What is the name of the person who
   a is still a student?
   b trained as a doctor?

c passes himself off as older (by a few months) than he actually is?

d sells pharmaceuticals?

e taught in middle schools for some years?

f lives in Bologna?

g teaches religion?

2 Two of the people mentioned are father and son. Can you work out which is the father, which the son?

Check your answers in the Key. Don't forget that the Key often contains useful explanations as well as straight answers.

Activity 1

To encourage you to listen to <u>how</u> people say things as well as <u>what</u> they say, listen to the interviews again and try to pick out:

1 two ways of saying: *my name is …*

2 two ways of saying: *I am a* + a job or profession.

3 how to say: *I have a degree in …*

4 the usual way of saying *how old you are.*

5 how to say *I was born in* + place …

6 how you say *you have been doing something for a certain amount of time*, with the implication you still are doing it.

7 how to say *you did something for a certain amount of time* but implying you no longer do it.

Check your answers in the Key.

Session 2

Saying how long you have done/been doing something

In Activity 1, question 6, the point is the way the speakers say this. What tense do they use? Compare the Italian and the English. Italian is simpler. You use the present tense of the verb and then **da** before the words saying how long.

Faccio parte del Gruppo Mio da parecchio tempo.	*I have been in the Gruppo Mio for some time.*
Abito a Bologna da circa vent'anni.	*I have lived in Bologna for about twenty years.*

Sometimes in English we would say: *I have been …ing*

Faccio questo lavoro da solo un mese.	*I've only been doing this job for one month.*
Mia sorella abita a Roma da un anno e mezzo.	*My sister has been living in Rome for a year and a half.*
Studio l'italiano da due anni.	*I have been studying Italian for two years.*

You can also indicate the time when you started doing whatever it is:

Sono qui da giovedì.	*I've been here since Thursday.*
Cerca alloggio da Natale.	*He/She has been looking for a place to live since Christmas.*

In Activity 1, question 7 draws attention to what you say when you did something for a while but no longer do it.

Ho insegnato nella scuola media per parecchi anni.	*I taught in middle schools for several years.*

In English too the tense is different. *I taught* not *I have taught* or *I have been teaching*.

Verbs – the present tense

Some learners may be at home with the present tense, others not very aware of how it works. It is not nearly as complicated as it might seem at first glance because verbs in the three groups differ only in certain parts. In Unit 1 we looked for infinitives and put them into groups. If you need to, remind yourself about them. Group 3 subdivides in the present tense with verbs of the type we have called 3b adding an extra syllable in some parts.

Question

What do you think the underlining in the text indicates? Study the table and try to decide before you look at the answer below.

Group 1	Group 2	Group 3a	Group 3b
<u>amare</u>	conoscere	<u>partire</u>	capire
amo	conosco	parto	capisco
ami	conosci	parti	capisci
<u>ama</u>	<u>conosce</u>	<u>parte</u>	capisce
amiamo	conosciamo	partiamo	capiamo
<u>amate</u>	<u>conoscete</u>	<u>partite</u>	<u>capite</u>
<u>amano</u>	conoscono	<u>partono</u>	capiscono

Answer

The underlining draws attention to parts of the verb where the ending is a characteristic one for that group, where the groups differ. However, look again. You must agree overall the differences are small. Each group has a characteristic vowel which we use to classify the infinitive: Group 1: **a**, Group 2: **e**, Group 3: **i**. This vowel appears in the infinitive and the second person plural for all Groups (indeed you may find it helpful to think of the latter as the infinitive, with the r changed to t); for Group 1 also in the third person singular and plural and for Group 2 also in the third person singular. Note that the third person plural of Group 2 and Group 3 verbs has the same ending. The same applies to their third person singular. Of course the Group 3b type of verb has an extra syllable but you will be familiar with that from common verbs such as **capire, capisco …**

A point to remember is that the ending indicates the subject. **Amo** = *I love*; **amiamo** = *we love*. The subject pronoun is usually omitted (see Unit 1). This means that in the long term, in order to speak Italian well, you need to learn to use the correct verb ending. But in the relatively early stages of speaking Italian, if you are not sure, just have a go. Gradually, as your confidence in communicating grows, you will find it easier and you can aim to become more correct.

Spelling and sound changes in the present tense

You may have learned that there are spelling changes in certain verbs. These are verbs where the letters **c** and **g** occur before the verb ending. Essentially, what happens is this:

a Group 1 verbs do not have a sound change and therefore have a spelling change.

b Group 2 verbs do the opposite: the sound changes so the spelling does not.

You have probably learned how Italian spelling reflects the sounds represented in English by the letters *k*, *g*, *ch*, *j*, and *sh*. We are sure you say: **ciao** (*ch*) and **chianti** (*k*) correctly. If you need to remind yourself, look at the section **The sounds of Italian**, at the back of the book.

Group 1 verbs

In the present tense, where the verb has the letters **c, sc, g,** before the **-are** infinitive ending, the spelling changes to reflect the fact that the sound stays the same in all persons of the present tense:

cercare	**cerco, cerchi, cerca, cerchiamo, cercate, cercano** (hard *k* sound throughout)
pagare	**pago, paghi, paga, paghiamo, pagate, pagano** (hard *g* sound throughout)

In addition, there is a minor point in the case of verbs where the **c, sc, g** in the spelling is followed in the infinitive by **-i-** (because the pronunciation is **ci** (*ch*), **sci** (*sh*), **gi** (*j*)). As with other Group 1 verbs, the sound does not change, but where **ci, gi, sci** + ending could result in there being two **i**s (e.g. with the ending (**tu**) **-i** or (**noi**) **-iamo**), then one **i** is dropped:

schiacciare	**schiaccio, schiacci, schiaccia, schiacciamo, schiacciate, schiacciano**
lasciare	**lascio, lasci, lascia, lasciamo, lasciate, lasciano**
mangiare	**mangio, mangi, mangia, mangiamo, mangiate, mangiano**

Just in case we have not made this clear, we will give a precise example using **cercare**: if we were to write **cerco, cerci** we would pronounce these [cherko, cherchi]. But that is not the correct sound, so the hard *k* in [cherki] needs to be indicated by the insertion of **h** after the **c**. (The square brackets indicate a use of letters to represent Italian pronunciation.)

Group 2 verbs

These do the opposite, i.e. the spelling does not change because the sound does.

vincere	**vinco, vinci, vince, vinciamo, vincete, vincono** (hard *k* in 1st person singular and 3rd person plural, soft *ch* in the others)
leggere	**leggo, leggi, legge, leggiamo, leggete, leggono** (hard *g* in 1st person singular and 3rd person plural, soft *j* in the others)
conoscere	**conosco, conosci, conosce, conosciamo, conoscete, conoscono** (hard *k* sound in 1st person singular and 3rd person plural, soft *sh* in the others)
scegliere	**scelgo, scegli, sceglie, scegliamo, scegliete, scelgono** (hard *g* sound in 1st person singular and 3rd person plural, the soft sound in the others – similar to *lli* in *million*)

Activity 2

Here and now, say the verbs above out loud to yourself once at least. If you think it will help you, always do this when learning a verb.

Session 3

Interview 2

We meet Gabriella and Piera who were asked to introduce themselves.

Gabriella	Mi chiamo Gabriella Bertone. Sono nata il 6 dicembre 1940 a Torino. Ho vissuto, potrei dire, un'infanzia meravigliosa in una famiglia molto semplice ma sempre allegra, questo mi ricordo. Mia madre era inglese, papà italiano. Mamma non ha mai bene imparato l'italiano per cui la prendevamo sempre in giro. Sono la terza figlia. Ho una sorella e un fratello maggiori. I miei genitori si sono sposati in Inghilterra ma hanno vissuto in Francia perché mio papà lavorava in Francia, infatti lì è nato mio fratello. Poi quando è scoppiata la guerra, papà è rientrato in Italia, e

Piera	logicamente si è portato la famiglia dietro, la mamma ... e per mamma sono stati tempi brutti, tempi duri. Dunque sono Piera Ravarino. Sono alta un metro e sessantotto e peso 63 chili e mezzo. Sono biondissima, ho gli occhi castani. Ho due figli, uno di 25 anni, l'altro di 30, ed ho anche un nipotino di un anno ... che vedo pochissimo e per questo mi dispiace tanto. Si chiama Thibaut e abita in Francia, in Bretagna, e vorrei tanto averlo più vicino e partecipare di più alla vita di questo bambino.

per cui *so, therefore* (literally: *on account of/for which*)
prendere in giro *to tease*
quando è scoppiata la Guerra *when the war broke out*. The subject (**la guerra**) coming after the verb shows it to be the important element in the phrase. Note also: **lì è nato mio fratello**.

QUICK VOCAB

....
Insight
il 6 dicembre *on 6th December*. When saying the date use the cardinal number, e.g. **sei** *six* (not *sixth*) preceded by **il** *the* (not by *on*). **Il** changes to **l'** in the case of **l'otto** *the 8th* and **l'undici** *the 11th*.
....

Comprehension 2

Listen more than once. As you listen, think about this: both are married women of about the same age and neither works.

1 What did you think they focussed on to define themselves?
2 Work out the family trees of Gabriella and Piera from what you hear.

Vocabulary for talking about the family

Both Gabriella and Piera talk about their families. Do you have the vocabulary you need to talk about your family? It is probably sensible to learn the words in pairs. If there is a word here you don't remember, look it up in the Glossary at the back of the book and write it down in your vocabulary notes.

bisnonno/bisnonna
nonno/nonna
padre/madre – genitori (sing: **genitore**)
marito/moglie
fratello/sorella
figlio/figlia
cognato/cognata
suocero/suocera
genero/nuora
cugino/cugina
zio/zia
nipote (m or f)

Note that nipote can mean either *nephew/niece* or *grandson/ granddaughter*. Often in the latter case, the diminutive **nipotino/a** is used. The context usually makes the relationship clear. Sometimes however the speaker clarifies by saying: '**nipote di zio**' or '**nipote di nonno**'. The article (**il nipote/la nipote**) or the possessive (**mio/mia**) normally indicate the sex.

Note the following:

papà	*daddy.* Affectionate, informal, also usually used when addressing one's father, e.g.: **Papà, c'è qualcuno al telefono per te.** Not to be confused with **il Papa** *the Pope.* The correct stress is important. The capital letter is usual in **Papa.**
babbo	*daddy.* Mainly in Tuscany but note: **Babbo Natale** *Father Christmas.*
mamma	*mummy.* As with **papà,** used when addressing one's mother and talking about her affectionately or informally.

Expressing possession

Below is a table of the possessive adjectives, the words for *my, your* etc. You will certainly have met some or all of these. Now you need to check you understand their correct use, so that you can aim to get it right.

Masc. Sing. noun	Fem. Sing. noun	Masc. Pl. noun	Fem. Pl. noun
il mio lavoro	la mia famiglia	i miei amici	le mie amiche
il tuo lavoro	la tua famiglia	i tuoi amici	le tue amiche
il suo lavoro	la sua famiglia	i suoi amici	le sue amiche
il nostro lavoro	la nostra famiglia	i nostri amici	le nostre amiche
il vostro lavoro	la vostra famiglia	i vostri amici	le vostre amiche
il loro lavoro	la loro famiglia	i loro amici	le loro amiche

Ti piace il tuo lavoro?	*Do you like your work/job?*
Il nostro itinerario comprende Siena e Orvieto.	*Our itinerary includes Siena and Orvieto.*

1 Don't forget that **suo, sua** etc. mean *his, her, your* (formal form). In other words you can't convey the gender of the possessor or owner as you can in English. This confuses Italians speaking English; listen to them. And you may remember the convention which uses the capital letter for the formal **Lei**, the possessives **Suo, Sua** etc. This helps reduce confusion in the written word.

Conosci Piero? Conosci anche sua madre?	*Do you know Piero? Do you know his mother as well?*
Conosci Anna? Conosci anche sua madre?	*Do you know Anna? Do you know her mother as well?*
Mi scusi, signor Rossi. Non conosco Sua madre, me la presenta, per piacere?	*Forgive me, Mr. Rossi. I don't know your mother, will you introduce her to me, please?*

2 Note the need for the definite article as well as the possessive adjective. There is an exception. Look for it in what Gabriella says. She talks about: **mia madre, mio papà, mio fratello**. The exception is singular words expressing family relationship. They have the possessive without the definite article – unless the noun is qualified (i.e. has an adjective describing it) or is a modified form (e.g. a diminutive etc.): **il mio giovane cugino, il mio fratellino, la mia mamma**. Note Gabriella makes (technically) a mistake by saying: **mio papà**. You would expect her to say: **il mio papà** as **papà** counts as a modified form. The way she says it is very common in the north. Similarly: **mia mamma, mio nonno** instead of **la mia mamma, il mio nonno**. In fact, you will meet either **il mio papà** or **mio papà**.

3 Loro always has the definite article: **il loro figlio**.

4 Un mio amico *a friend of mine*. **Questo mio amico** *this friend of mine*. After **questo, quello** and numerals, there is no definite article.

5 Il mio, il nostro, etc. are used as, in English, *mine, ours*, etc. that is to say, as the possessive pronoun.

'Piove e non ho un ombrello.'	*'It's raining and I don't have an umbrella.'*
'Prego, prendi il mio.'	*'Please take mine.'*
Abbiamo offerto un passaggio nella nostra macchina a Paolo e Marianna ma preferiscono venire con la loro.	*We offered Paolo and Marianna a lift in our car but they prefer to come in theirs.*

6 Note the following expressions:

i miei, i suoi, ecc.	are often used to mean *my family, his family, etc.*
la mamma	is very frequently used (i.e. without the possessive) to mean *my mother*. Similarly: **il papà, il babbo, il nonno, la nonna, lo zio, la zia**. For other family members, **mio cugino, mia sorella**, etc.
a casa mia, a casa tua ...	*at my house, at your house, at home ...*
dire la sua	*to have his/her say*
a ciascuno il suo	*to each his own*

Activity 3

Say in Italian:

1 *My friends.*
2 *Our family.*
3 *His book.*
4 *Her book.*
5 *Their brother.*
6 *Their brothers.*
7 *My friend.*
8 *His (female) friend*
9 *Her (female) friend.*
10 *Our mother.*

Activity 4

How would you say the following in Italian? If you don't know some of the words you need, try guessing, or even cheat and look at the Key. What is more important is that you should think out the various ways of expressing ideas such as saying what a person does, how old he/she is, how long they have been doing something etc.

1 My name is Jonathan. I am a teacher of foreign languages. I have been teaching for three years.
2 My sister's name is Olimpia. She is a doctor. She works in a hospital. She has worked in the hospital for 6 years.
3 George is 32 years old and works for a large company. They make accessories for the motor industry. George has worked for the company for 18 months.
4 My son is studying medicine. He is a student at the University of Southampton. He has been studying medicine for two years.
5 My brother is a psychiatrist. He works in Boston. He loves Boston. He was born in Cambridge, England, and now he lives in Cambridge, Massachusetts. He has lived in Cambridge for 8 years.
6 My wife is called Jane. She is a writer. Her mother is a famous actress. Her father is American. We have three children. Our eldest son is 8, our daughter is 6 and our second son is 4.
7 I've been learning Italian for nine months.
8 We understand Welsh. We lived in Wales for 24 years (in Wales: **nel Galles**). Now we live in London.
9 I've spoken French for twenty years.
10 I often read an Italian magazine which is called *Panorama*.

Session 4

Interview 3

In Session 3, Interview 2 Piera was asked to describe herself. Reread what she said. How did she describe herself? She didn't find it easy and gave very basic information: **Sono alta un metro e sessantotto e peso 63 chili e mezzo. Sono biondissima, ho gli occhi castani.** Note that Piera says: **Sono alta 1 m. 68.** *I am 1 m. 68 tall.* Spot the difference with English and imitate it!

Now listen to her husband.

CD1, TR 5, 15:33

Paolo	Allora, io mi chiamo Gianpaolo Ravarino. Sono nato a Torino nel gennaio del '45, appena finita la guerra. Sono una persona ... mi ritengo normalissimo, alto di statura, longilineo, abbastanza longilineo, sono ingegnere. Ho avuto problemi nella vita che tutti hanno avuto ... mi ritengo proprio perfettamente normale. Non sono un bell'uomo, sono una persona normale, come l'ho detto. Non ho niente di particolarmente sgraziato ma penso di non aver niente neanche di particolarmente aggraziato. Per quello che riguarda la testa, la testa è di una persona normale. Le capacità rientrano nell'ordinaria media delle persone. Non sono né deficiente né troppo intelligente. Forse sono un po' bonaccione ...

QV **bonaccione** *easy-going, good-natured*

> ## Insight
> Double negatives: when there is a negative word in the sentence (**niente, né ... né**) Italians make the verb negative too: **Non ho niente** *I have (not!) got nothing*, **Non sono né deficiente né troppo intelligente** *I am (not!) neither stupid nor too intelligent.*

Comprehension 3

1 What do you learn about Paolo's physical appearance?
2 About his character?
3 What do you think he means when he uses the word **testa**?

Activity 5

Describing yourself – and other people – is not easy. And it is not something you often need to do. At most, you sometimes need to give a few obvious characteristics so that someone can recognize you or a friend at the airport, for instance. So on paper pull together what you know how to say. Do you remember the names of the parts of the body, or other words relating to physique? Then look at the Key and compare your list with ours.

Language learning tip

This last activity probably sent you to your dictionary. As your knowledge increases, you should consider buying an Italian–Italian dictionary. It won't help when you do not know the Italian expression for an idea you want to put in words, of course. But if you use it when reading and working on texts you will find it will be a valuable tool. Thinking constantly from Italian to English and back again isn't always helpful. Nor are there always precise word-for-word equivalents between the two languages. And it can be instructive to see how the meaning is defined for Italians. In the Key for Activity 5 for instance, the differences between **snello** and **svelto** or **tarchiato** and **tozzo**, which are perhaps slight and subtle, become a little clearer. An Italian–Italian dictionary – a good one, fairly bulky, not a pocket one – will give you examples of how the word is used, what contexts it can be used in. And simply keeping your mind working in Italian helps. How much you enjoy the dictionary activity will depend upon how much you enjoy words, i.e. it's a question of taste.

(Contd)

For all the definitions in *Perfect your Italian*, we have used *Lo Zingarelli 2010, Vocabolario della lingua italiana di Nicola Zingarelli*, published by Zanichelli, Bologna, with their very kind permission. It is a hefty tome, and the publishers update it annually. It is also available on CD-ROM and on-line at www.zanichelli.it.

Activity 6

You are flying to Milan next week to meet an Italian business associate. His secretary is coming to meet you at the airport. Send him an email describing your appearance. Include height, hair colour etc. It need not be more than two or three sentences.

Activity 7

Practise your descriptive skills by thinking through a brief physical description of two or three people: relations, friends, colleagues, to help anyone needing to identify them.

Session 5

Interview 4

It is sometimes easier to sum up character, especially in other people. Listen to Gabriella describing her two grown-up daughters. Gianni, whom she mentions, is her husband.

CD1, TR 6, 17:03

| Gabriella | Ho avuto due figlie, Silvia e Barbara, molto vicine, infatti hanno solo due anni di differenza. Silvia assomiglia molto a Gianni, Barbara a mia mamma. È rossa di capelli e ha un carattere, diciamo, più inglese che italiano. È molto allegra. Silvia è molto posata, molto seria, molto ligia al dovere, quello che deve fare, lo fa. |

Mentre la Barbara, no. È più allegra, più spensierata, senza testa, molto disubbidiente. Adesso, Silvia è sposata e aspetta un bambino; mentre Barbara è andata a vivere per conto suo, ed è così felice e proprio contenta. Io ne ho fatto una grande malattia quando Barbara è andata via però adesso devo riconoscere che ha fatto bene. Sì, sì, ha fatto bene a lei e ha fatto bene a me. Il nostro rapporto è decisamente cambiato e lei è molto più vicina a noi adesso che è lontana e direi quasi che senz'altro capisce più tante cose lei che non Silvia. Alla quale abbiamo sempre attribuito doti insomma …

la Barbara In Tuscany and northern Italy, it is common to use the definite article before a female first name. It is also sometimes used before male first names.

Insight

Quello che, literally *that which*, corresponds to the English *what:* **Ti ho detto quello che pensavo** *I told you what I thought.*

Activity 8

Lots of useful words there for talking about people. Make a list. Where the word could have an opposite, do you know it? Compare your result with the one in the Key.

Activity 9

Think of some family members and work out character descriptions of them. How would you describe your own character?

Reading

Un manager senza compromessi

'Romiti ha una personalità e una professionalità sfaccettate e fuori dal comune ... L'elemento unificante della sua azione appare essere la sua fortissima volontà di vincere le battaglie che decide di affrontare e anche il vizio di volerle addirittura stravincere ... Non pare interessato, lui romano, all'arte tutta romana del compromesso e non si preoccupa troppo di piacere all'opinione pubblica.' (Mario Deaglio, in un articolo 'Un manager senza compromessi')

'Nei rapporti personali mi è parso meno feroce dell'immagine che se ne dà. Della sua durezza ho apprezzato l'esplicitezza, la chiarezza, la sincerità.' (Gianni Vattimo, filosofo)

'Un uomo pragmatico, concreto, dotato di una grande volontà. Una persona che non ha mai promesso a vanvera, che ha sempre realizzato.' (Enzo Ghigo, presidente della regione Piemonte)

'Ho un ricordo bellissimo. Appena arrivata nel '90 non avevo i soldi per pagare gli stipendi. Era il 250° anniversario del Teatro. Chiesi una sponsorizzazione alla Fiat. Romiti mi chiamò subito e mi disse che aveva firmato l'assegno di un miliardo. Era sensibile alla musica, ma anche al fatto che gli stipendi a chi lavora vanno pagati.' (Elda Tessore, ex-sovrintendente del Teatro Regio di Torino.)

'Lo descrivono come un burbero o un rude. Ma a tavola da noi con gli amici è sempre stato molto simpatico, aperto, semplice, colloquiale.' (Vittorio Urbani, titolare del ristorante preferito di Romiti)

(La Stampa, 22 giugno 1998)

In June 1998, Cesare Romiti left Fiat after nearly 25 years as Managing Director (**Amministratore Delegato**) and then, briefly, Chairman (**Presidente**). Such is the importance of Fiat in Italy that the event was given wide media coverage. Romiti had guided Fiat successfully through the effects of the oil crisis of the early 70s, the years of terrorism and a period of intense worker unrest. He used tough methods, notably with the trades unions, and won. He has a reputation for plain speaking and for determination to win battles. Although aged 75, he was leaving to take up an apppointment as Chairman of the publishing *group Rcs-Corriere della Sera*. Above, from *La Stampa*, are extracts from various people's descriptions of Romiti. It should be added *La Stampa* is published in Turin, Fiat is also based there, indeed Fiat stands for *Fabbrica Italiana Automobili Torino*. It is also the Latin for 'Let it be done/made'. Fiat also owns *La Stampa*! In 2003 Romiti created the influential Fondazione Italia Cina to promote business and cultural links between Italy and China, with offices in Milan, Beijing and Rome.

sfaccettato *multifaceted.* **Sfaccettato** is *faceted* – as a jewel is. It also has an idea of being cutting.

a vanvera *to no effect,* i.e. Romiti never made promises he did not intend to keep.

realizzare *to make real, to implement* (not: realize in the everyday English sense. Another false friend)

burbero *gruff, grumpy, crusty*

rude the English–Italian dictionary says *coarse.* The Italian dictionary explains that it is used to describe someone who is frank and determined, but not **grossolano** (*coarse*)! Note the value of an Italian monolingual dictionary!

Comprehension 4

1 What does Mario Deaglio consider the unifying element in the way Romiti behaves?

2 Romiti is from Rome. What Roman characteristic does he not possess? What is his attitude to public opinion?

3 How did Gianni Vattimo find Romiti in personal relationships?

4 From what Enzo Ghigo says, pick out the words which are the opposite of (a) **astratto**, (b) **teorico**.

5 What is the story which Elda Tessore, formerly in charge of the Turin Opera House (**Teatro Regio**), tells?

6 Vittorio Urbani whose restaurant Romiti patronized describes him as (a) **simpatico**, (b) **aperto**. What might be the opposites of these two words?

Interview 5

And finally, one more person introducing herself and clarifying ... well, what does she clarify? She is Emanuela and is married to an American called John. They live in an apartment. It is usual at the entrance to an apartment block to have a bell for each apartment and usually there is space for two names beside each bell.

CD1, TR 7, 19:11

Emanuela	Io mi chiamo Emanuela Beltrami e Beltrami è il mio cognome da nubile perché in Italia anche sposandosi, non si cambia cognome, si mantiene il cognome della famiglia. Questo vale per il lavoro, vale per la sanità, vale per tutto. Mentre è una cosa che ha lasciato un po' sorpresa la famiglia di John. Credevano non fossimo sposati quando hanno visto sopra il campanello della porta due cognomi diversi. Fa ridere quella cosa!

Insight
The article *the* is used a lot more in Italian than in English. It is always used when talking about things in general: **il lavoro** *work*, **la sanità** *health*, and in Activity 10: **la vita comincia a quarant'anni** *life begins at forty*.

Comprehension 5

1 What does Emanuela clarify?
2 What did John's family suspect when they saw the names over the bell at the entrance to the building where John and Emanuela live?

Activity 10

Talking to yourself

You remember we said that it has been shown that people who are good at learning a foreign language tend to talk to themselves in the foreign language they are learning. It really is good practice. Here are some possible topics.

1 Stereotipi nazionali: Gabriella considera che sua figlia Barbara, che è 'allegra, spensierata, senza testa, molto disubbidiente,' ha un carattere più inglese che italiano. Invece la figlia Silvia, che è 'molto posata, molto seria, molto ligia al dovere,' è più italiana. Cosa ne pensa Lei? Come vede Lei il carattere italiano, quello inglese, americano, ecc? Esiste il fenomeno di un carattere nazionale?

2 L'età pensionabile: al momento dell'articolo, Cesare Romiti, all'età di 75 anni, stava per cominciare un nuovo lavoro, come presidente di un importante gruppo editoriale. Secondo Lei, era troppo vecchio? In Italia, molte persone vanno in pensione il più presto possibile, qualche volta a 55 anni. Invece, altri, soprattutto in politica e nel mondo della finanza e degli affari, continuano ben oltre i 70 anni. Che cosa ne pensa? Ci dovrebbe essere un'età oltre la quale non è permesso continuare a lavorare? Quando, secondo Lei, si è troppo vecchi per lavorare? Lei ha progetti per la pensione? Come vede la prospettiva degli anni della pensione?

3 In inglese esiste un detto: la vita comincia a 40 anni. Quali sono secondo Lei gli anni più belli della vita?

TEST YOURSELF

1 How would you say the following in Italian?

(a) Last year I visited (*andare a trovare*) my friends Giulio and Anna in their village in Tuscany. (b) They've been living in this small village for ten years. (c) Giulio studied medicine in Florence and has been working as a pediatrician (*pediatra*) for quite a long time. (d) His wife, Anna, is a teacher of English in the local school where their two children also go. (e) The elder is Riccardo, a nine year old boy; he's tall with blond hair and brown eyes. (f) Renata is seven years old, so they are only two years apart. (g) Renata is a happy girl, she's very active and a bit naughty. (h) Her brother often teases her, but they are having a marvellous childhood in this place in the country. (i) Their parents like this life and this village very much. (j) I couldn't live in a small place far from the city, but I recognize that it is good for them.

2 Complete the sentences with an appropriate family name or possessive adjective. Put the article in front of the possessive if needed.
   a Il fratello di nostro padre è nostro _____.
   b Gianni ha una sorella sposata. Il _____ di sua sorella è _____ cognato.
   c Mio padre e mia _____ non vivono insieme. Come sai, _____ genitori sono separati.
   d Sabina, quando vai a trovare _____ nonni?
   e Erano preoccupati per _____ figlio più piccolo, sembrava che non fosse normale.

3

La mia storia

In this unit we shall
* *look at the Italian education system*
* *look at aspects of spoken Italian*
* *review ways of talking about past events*
* *do more guessing at meanings*

Session 1

Interview 1

We asked various people to tell us about their past, their story. First Marina Bastianello. Marina is **Amministratore Delegato**, *Managing Director, of Ristoranti Brek, a chain of self-service restaurants, and she has an office in Milan. She first knew the interviewer many years ago in England, in the school where she was a student. Listen to the interview on the recording, ideally without the text. If necessary go through it several times.*

Marina	Come sai, ho studiato, dapprima in Italia fino ai sedici anni, poi gli ultimi due anni del liceo ho fatto l'International Baccalaureate a Oxford, poi sono stata a Londra quattro anni, prima facendo la laurea in economia, poi un master, tutti e due alla London School of Economics, e poi sono tornata in Italia e qui

(Contd)

CD1, TR 8, 20:58

a Milano ho cominciato a lavorare per una società finanziaria dove sono stata, credo, un paio d'anni. Dopo sono andata ... mi sono trovata ad essere un po' forse impreparata al mercato italiano. Ero stata via parecchi anni, quindi mi trovavo un po' a disagio al mio ritorno. Quindi sono andata a fare un MBA, un Masters in Business Administration, alla Bocconi qua a Milano. E questo mi ha un po', diciamo, introdotto al mondo degli affari italiano. E quando sono uscita dalla Bocconi sono andata in una società della Fiat, una grossa impresa di costruzione, ho lavorato nella pianificazione strategica, anche lì per un anno e mezzo, due anni, e alla fine di questo iter sono arrivata in Brek, che è una società di ristorazione, quindi non c'entra assolutamente niente con quello che avevo fatto prima, però fa parte del gruppo di famiglia, è una società abbastanza piccola in un settore che mi diverte abbastanza perché mi piace mangiare, mi piace la cucina quindi la ristorazione è un settore, diciamo, più divertente dell'edilizia e quindi dall'89 circa lavoro qui.

un paio d'anni *a couple of years* (literally: *a pair*)

a disagio *uncomfortable, not at home* (opposite: **a mio/tuo/suo ecc. agio**)

la Bocconi l'**università Bocconi, Milano** – Founded by Ferdinando Bocconi, it is one of a small number of private universities in Italy; it specializes in economics, business administration, finance etc.

impresa *enterprise, undertaking, business* (cf. **imprenditore** *entrepreneur*)

pianificazione *planning* (**piano** *plan*. Don't forget your guessing strategies)

iter the Latin word for *a journey*. Normally used for journeys through procedure, e.g. **un iter legislativo, un iter burocratico.**

non c'entra niente con *it's nothing to do with*

fa parte del gruppo di famiglia Marina's family own a group which also includes the **PAM** supermarkets.

Interview 2

And now Mario Rotondale who runs **un circolo sportivo**, *a small leisure centre or club with tennis courts, a pitch for* **calcetto**, *five-a-side soccer, a gym* **una palestra** *and of course a bar for an after-match drink, with a terrace where you can also sit and watch others playing tennis.*

Mario	Ho fatto le scuole elementari e le medie inferiori a Poirino, in provincia di Torino. E poi sono passato a fare le scuole medie superiori a Chieri. Ho fatto ragioneria, dopodiché mi sono accorto di essere un pessimo ragioniere, di non ... che molto probabilmente non avrei mai potuto lavorare in una banca e allora ho proseguito facendo l'ISEF, l'Istituto Superiore di Educazione Fisica, qui a Torino. È un corso di tre anni, è un diploma di grado universitario, non è riconosciuto – unico paese in Europa – come laurea.

🎧 CD1, TR 9, 23:38

(Contd)

Interviewer	In che cosa consiste il corso?
Mario	28 esami più una tesi.
Interviewer	Quanti di questi esami erano pratici?
Mario	Contrariamente a quello che uno può pensare, una gran parte erano teorici. Spaziavano dalla medicina generale, la medicina dello sport, all'anatomia, alla fisiologia, alla endocrinologia, a tutte queste materie che … E una volta diplomato, ho – siccome qui in Italia non c'è possibilità alcuna di insegnare nella scuola, perché lo sbocco professionale principale è quello di insegnare nella scuola, nella scuola, di ogni ordine e grado …
Interviewer	Perché non c'è possibilità?
Mario	Non c'è possibilità perché c'è una situazione di cattedre sature da tanti anni, in poche parole non assumono e non fanno più concorsi e quindi mi sono lanciato nella … nelle attività private. Ho cominciato a lavorare in vari centri sportivi e poi mi si è presentata una … la possibilità di gestire questo centro. Mi sono, come si dice in italiano, mi sono tuffato, in gergo sportivo, e questo è successo nel novembre del '94 quando è iniziata questa gestione. Sotto questa gestione avevamo soltanto campi da tennis, e poi abbiamo aperto questa palestra. Abbiamo cominciato, o meglio ripreso, a fare attività giovanile, quindi sia per il tennis sia per altre cose. E adesso il futuro è questa piscina, quest'ampliamento con nuove, con probabilmente anche nuove palestre con possibilità di fare un discorso completo anche per quanto riguarda la palestra.

Comprehension 1 and 2

1 Marina's schooling was untypical. In what ways?

2 What was her reason for doing an MBA?

3 What link is there between the three areas of business she has worked in?

4 Why does she feel her present company is more fun than the construction company she worked for?

5 What made Mario decide to go to ISEF?

6 He appears to feel a little 'cheated' in respect of the status of his qualification. Why?

7 Why did he not take a job in a school?

8 How long has he been in his present job?

9 He mentions expansion of the facilities of the club. What sort of facilities will it have in the future?

Session 2

La scuola italiana

The overall scheme is:

(in brackets are the names they are often known by or have been known by in the past and the number of years the courses last).

Scuola dell'infanzia (scuola materna)

Scuola primaria (scuola elementare)
(5 anni)

Scuola secondaria di primo grado (Scuola media)
(3 anni)

Scuola secondaria di secondo grado (Scuola media superiore)
(5 anni)

Universita'
Istituti superiori statali (p.es ISEF)
Accademia Militare
Accademia di Belle Arti

Children may go to the **Scuola dell'infanzia** from the age of 2½ if their parents wish. They may enter the **Scuola primaria** at the age of 5½, again if their parents wish. Compulsory schooling (**la scuola dell'obbligo**) lasts 10 years, from the age of 6, so that the school leaving age is 16.

Scuola secondaria di secondo grado, high school: There is a variety of types, academic: **liceo classico, liceo linguistico, liceo scientifico**; or vocational: **istituto tecnico, istituto professionale**. There are a number of types of the last two.

There had been talk of reform of the Italian education system for many years and indeed some schemes were worked out but were not fully implemented or fell as governments fell. The final school leaving examination, **esame di stato**, once called **maturità**, after being "temporary" for some 30 years, was reformed in 1999 and in that year the school leaving age was raised from 14.

At the time of writing, a comprehensive series of changes, known as the Riforma Gelmini, after the Minister of Education in the Berlusconi government, is being phased in. These changes have been the subject of much discussion and protest; among the fears of the protesters is that the changes are being made largely to reduce the education budget and will be detrimental to the quality of the service. Their proponents would argue that they bring in much-needed simplification and will relate schools and programmes better to the world of work. Overall the main changes are:

Scuola primaria, (already operational) from a system of 3 teachers for two classes, so that there was specialist teaching for humanities, mathematics and English, with academic schooling extending into the afternoon, there is now a single class teacher for 18 hours. This effectively reduces the school day to mornings, although there

54

are activities in the afternoon with other teachers. English is taught from the first year.

Scuola secondaria di primo grado. As well as the **"esame di stato"**, the end of cycle test, children also do a test in Maths and Italian known as **INVALSI**. This is the name of the national testing service and the test, it makes possible comparisons of performance both geographically, between boys and girls, and Italian and non-italian speakers, etc. It is a test of the schools rather than individual children. This pre-dated the currrent reform.

Scuola secondaria di secondo grado o scuola secondaria superiore. The reform is scheduled to be phased in from September 2010. There will be a simplification in the number of types of school and a reduction in hours from 36 to 32 from September 2010. At the time of writing some details, particularly programmes, are not yet published.

It should be said that in all the high schools the programmes have historically offered students a very broad education and there is no reason to believe this will change.

Information can be found on the web site of the **Ministero della Pubblica Istruzione, dell'Università e della Ricerca:** www.pubblica.istruzione.it.

Mario went to an **istituto commerciale**, i.e. one of the **istituti professionali** mentioned above. There he learned the financial side of business and became a **ragioniere**. Other people you meet in the book who trained as **ragionieri** are Carlo and Emanuela.

Explaining the ISEF course, Mario said it consisted of **28 exami più una tesi**. Most university courses are not selective and a student with the **esame di stato** can enrol in the course of his choice. To get a degree the student has to take a number of modules and pass the end of module exam in each. The number of modules varies from course to course. Students also prepare a thesis. They usually start degree courses at the age of 19. The standard pattern is three years of a variety of courses plus two years of specialisation.

The drop-out rate is high. In recent years shorter courses (**laurea breve**) have been introduced. There is talk of further reform, but as yet there has been no change. Holders of full degrees in Italy are called **dottore**. As Mario said, however, his course, although equivalent to a degree course, did not confer a degree.

Mario refers to **cattedre sature** and **concorsi**. New teachers are recruited centrally at national level by competitive exam (**concorso**) to a **cattedra**, a permanent post in the school system. At the time Mario graduated, no new recruits were being taken on since falling pupil numbers meant there were too many teachers. Access to many jobs in the public sector is by competitive examination.

Spoken language, written language

Note how Marina says: **poi ... poi ... poi ...** She is talking off the cuff. Were she to write her life story she would avoid the repetition of **poi** (*then, next*) which in writing would be considered poor style. Other spoken language usages in what she says are: **quindi** (*so, then*), **diciamo** (*shall we say? let's say*), and the tendency to very long sentences of parallel clauses. Note the voice doesn't fall as it would if the speaker were intending to end the sentence. In writing, Marina would go for a more varied and perhaps more complex sentence structure.

Mario too was talking off the cuff. Note how his sentences change direction, as often happens in speech. As we think out what we are saying, our thoughts are just one jump ahead of our words and we realize things would be clearer, more effective if we restructured. As we listen to a speaker do this, we are scarcely aware of it. The same applies to Marina's repetitive clauses. The listener's mind follows the speaker's thought processes and focuses on the content rather than the structure of his/her sentences. It is only when the words are transcribed for us to read that we notice it.

Language learning tip

You can capitalize on this as you speak Italian. Your sentences do not, emphatically not, have to be well-formed, perfect sentences. You simply need to communicate.

Session 3

Talking about the events in our lives: 'il passato prossimo', the perfect tense

Activity 1

One of our aims in this unit is to talk about our life story. Both Marina and Mario were asked to talk about how they came to be in their current jobs. When you do this, you tend to spell out the stages of your education and career: *first I did this*, *then I went to X*, *after that I ...* You are talking about what you did, i.e. you use verbs. First for Marina and then for Mario, pick out the steps in their careers, just the verbs, what they <u>did</u>, what Marina calls her **iter**.

Example: **Marina: ho studiato, ho fatto (l'International Baccalaureate), ...**

Now that you have done that and checked your answers in the Key, you will have two lists of verbs, all in the tense used for completed actions in the past. You have probably met it and called it, perhaps, the *perfect* or in Italian **il passato prossimo**. It is a tense which we use often. Let's try and understand it.

The two parts of the perfect

The perfect is a compound tense, that is a tense composed of two parts:

a **an auxiliary verb**, i.e. a verb which helps form the tense, shedding its own meaning but not carrying the meaning of the main verb (e.g. in English: *have* as in *I have seen*)

b and **a past participle**. This comes from the verb with the main meaning and in English most of them end in *-ed* (*finished*, *received*, *wanted* etc). Some are irregular, such as *eaten*, *been*, *had*, *seen* – even English has its complications.

The regular past participle

Let's look first at the past participle. We come back to our three verb groups and they work as follows:

Group 1	Group 2	Group 3
cantare	ricevere	gestire
cantato	ricevuto	gestito

Activity 2

Probably you are familiar with this but for practice and to refresh your mind, make a few past participles. Give the English past participle too.

Example: **temere** *to fear*

past participle: **temuto** *feared*

1 andare	*to go*	
2 uscire	*to go out*	
3 tornare	*to return, go back, come back*	
4 lanciare	*to throw*	
5 sapere	*to know (fact, information)*	
6 conoscere	*to know (person, place – i.e. be acquainted with)*	
7 capire	*to understand*	
8 cadere	*to fall*	

Activity 3

What about the irregular verbs? They are mostly verbs in Group 2 (**-ere** type) with also some in Group 3 (**-ire** type). Can you pick out any irregular past participles in the list of verbs you made in Activity 1 from what Marina and Mario said? Check the answer in the Key.

Irregular past participles: Group 2 verbs

The translations are a guide only. They will not necessarily work in all contexts.

chiesto	**chiedere** to ask	**discusso**	**discutere** to discuss
rimasto	**rimanere** to remain	**messo**	**mettere** to put
risposto	**rispondere** to answer	**successo**	**succedere** to happen

scelto	**scegliere** to choose	**letto**	**leggere** to read
vinto	**vincere** to win	**rotto**	**rompere** to break

chiuso	**chiudere** to close	**scritto**	**scrivere** to write
preso	**prendere** to take	**nato**	**nascere** to be born
deciso	**decidere** to decide	**vissuto**	**vivere** to live

As you might expect, **essere** to be has an irregular past participle: **stato**.

You may notice we have grouped together verbs which work in a similar way. Some people find that helpful. It is important to realize that a verb made up of one of these verbs, preceded by a prefix, will also follow this model, e.g: **messo** (**mettere**) → **ammesso** (**ammettere** to admit); **preso** (**prendere**) → **sorpreso** (**sorprendere** to surprise). For a number of verbs in this group the form most commonly met is the past participle used as an adjective, e.g: **cotto** as in **prosciutto cotto**, **panna cotta**, from **cuocere**; **mosso** as in **mare mosso** rough sea, from **muovere**.

Verbs with more than one possible past participle

One or two verbs in this group have more than one possible past participle. The most common are: **perso/perduto** (**perdere** to lose) **visto/veduto** (**vedere** to see). It really doesn't matter which you use.

But don't despair! Many common verbs which are irregular in other ways have nice, regular past participles:

avuto	**avere** to have	**dovuto**	**dovere** to have to
potuto	**potere** to be able	**seduto**	**sedere** to sit
tenuto	**tenere** to hold	**voluto**	**volere** to want

And you have already seen **saputo** (**sapere** to know).

Verbs whose present-day infinitive is an abbreviated form

A small number of verbs can be classed as Group 2 because they have a present-day infinitive which is an abbreviated version of an earlier infinitive ending in -ere. They nearly all have irregular past participles:

fatto	**fare [facere]** to make, to do	**detto**	**dire [dicere]** to say
posto	**porre [ponere]** to place	**tradotto**	**tradurre [traducere]** to translate

The exception is **bevuto** (**bere [bevere]** to drink) which actually has the form of a regular Group 2 past participle.

Irregular past participles: Group 3 verbs

aperto	**aprire** to open
coperto	**coprire** to cover
sofferto	**soffrire** to suffer
morto	**morire** to die
venuto	**venire** to come

Language learning tip

As usual we would stress that when trying to get your meaning over, you should not worry too much about correctness. After all, small children using their own language often make things regular when they should be irregular, and we just laugh gently with them. But in the long run you will want to have the full picture and to aim at accuracy. As you listen to what Italians say, you will become familiar with these forms painlessly. Train yourself to listen – and then to imitate.

The auxiliary verb

But of course that is only half the story. We said the perfect had two parts: the past participle and another verb, called an auxiliary verb. You have probably learned or noticed that there are two possible auxiliary verbs. How do you know which to use?

Activity 4

Look back at the list you made for Activity 1. Pick out the two auxiliary verbs. Reorganize your list so that verbs using each are grouped together.

Verbs which use *essere*

Let's start with the verbs which use **essere**. Did you see any pattern?

1 You should have noticed that reflexive verbs make their **passato prossimo** with **essere: mi sono trovata, mi sono lanciato, mi sono tuffato, mi si è presentata.** The past participle agrees with the subject of the verb. So Marina says: **mi sono trovata** while Mario says **mi sono lanciato**.

2 Then you hear Marina using: **sono andata, sono tornata, sono uscita, sono arrivata** and Mario: **sono passato.** You will probably have already learned that verbs whose meaning relates to coming and going, moving from one place to another, make their **passato prossimo** with **essere.** Quite a large number of verbs make their perfect with **essere.** The essential point about them is that they are intransitive, which means they cannot have a direct object. This is for some language learners a difficult point to grasp. The verb **passare** can be transitive or intransitive. Compare:

Intransitive

L'errore è passato inosservato. *The mistake went unnoticed.*
Noi siamo passati per la strada *We went by the road but Mario*
   ma Marco è passato per i *went across the fields. So we*
   campi. Così non ci siamo visti. *didn't see each other.*

Transitive

Ho passato il mio ombrello a *I passed my umbrella to George/*
   Giorgio. *I let George have my umbrella.*
L'anno scorso abbiamo passato *Last year we spent the holidays in*
   le vacanze in montagna. *the mountains.*

In the last two sentences **passare** has an object (**il mio ombrello, le vacanze**). It is used transitively. In the first two sentences there is no direct object nor is one possible with this meaning. So in the first two sentences, **essere** is used as auxiliary.

Verbs using **essere** include verbs of movement from one place to another, as we have said: **andare, venire, entrare, uscire, arrivare, partire, scendere, salire, tornare, fuggire** and others with similar meanings.

Also verbs of not moving, of state, use **essere: stare, rimanere, restare, essere.**

And verbs expressing change of state: **arrossire, impallidire, dimagrire, ingrassare, nascere, morire, diventare, divenire, invecchiare, guarire, iniziare,** etc.

Anna è impallidita quando ha visto il professore.	*Anna turned pale when she saw the teacher.*
Quanto sei dimagrito!	*You've lost a lot of weight!*

Again, some of these verbs can also be used transitively: **Ho iniziato un sistema nuovo per** ... *I've started a new system for* ...

Verbs related to weather phenomena, e.g. **piovere**, also form their past with **essere**, although in everyday spoken Italian many people use **avere**.

Verbs which use *avere*

Transitive verbs use **avere**, whether the object is expressed or not; also many intransitive verbs, e.g. **parlare**:

Ho parlato con Gianna.	*I talked/have talked to Gianna.*

A good dictionary will indicate which auxiliary is used with a given verb. If in doubt, use **avere** and don't worry! Again, developing the habit of listening to Italians is important. Gradually, with experience, you will develop a sense of what is right, based on what you have heard.

The overall pattern

The overall pattern then can be presented thus:

capire	arrivare	accorgersi
ho capito	sono arrivato/a	mi sono accorto/a
hai capito	sei arrivato/a	ti sei accorto/a
ha capito	è arrivato/a	si è accorto/a
abbiamo capito	siamo arrivati/e	ci siamo accorti/e
avete capito	siete arrivati/e	vi siete accorti/e
hanno capito	sono arrivati/e	si sono accorti/e

The perfect infinitive

The perfect has an infinitive: **avere finito** *to have finished*, **essere arrivato** *to have arrived*. It is formed with **avere** or **essere** and the past participle. It is used after a preposition or after a verb which can be followed by an infinitive:

Dopo avere mangiato, sono usciti in giardino.
After eating (having eaten) they went out into the garden.

Non è ancora arrivato Paolo.
Paolo hasn't arrived yet.

Deve essere partito in ritardo.
He must have set off late.

We have devoted quite a lot of space to the **passato prossimo** because it is a tense we use frequently. We often want to tell people not only our life story but what we have just done. It occurs frequently in newspaper reports, especially the **cronaca** section. Here is a selection.

Session 4

Reading

Here are some short newpaper items. Read them carefully, more than once. Don't forget to exercise your skills at guessing meanings before looking words up. Then answer the questions at the end of the extracts.

1

Due esplosioni:
Lo Stromboli si risveglia. Allarme
sull'isola.

Ieri pomeriggio, intorno alle 17.30, due forti boati hanno
annunciato una piccola eruzione nella zona Sud del cratere
dello Stromboli, che ha provocato un incendio alla vegetazione
del costone. Le fiamme sono state prontamente domate
con l'intervento di un 'Canadair', mentre gli uomini della
Protezione Civile perlustravano la montagna con un elicottero
per soccorrere eventuali gitanti feriti e si tenevano in contatto
con gli abitanti della frazione di Ginostra, raggiungibile solo via
mare, isolata da due giorni per le cattive condizioni del mare.

(*La Stampa*, 24 agosto 1998)

QUICK VOCAB

Insight
Revise the use of the article **gli** for all masculine plural nouns
starting with a vowel (**gli uomini, gli abitanti**) or starting
with s + consonant or z (**gli studenti, gli zaini** *the rucksacks*).

Comprehension – Passage 1

1 Whereabouts on the mountain did the small eruption take place?
2 What was the consequence of the eruption?
3 What did the Canadair do?
4 Why did the Civil Protection squad search the mountain?
5 Ginostra already had other problems. What were they?

2

Con un coltello ha rapinato la Cariplo

Attimi di tensione e di panico l'altra mattina per una rapina avvenuta presso l'agenzia di Settimo Torinese della banca Cariplo …

L'assalto è avvenuto verso mezzogiorno e mezzo. Un bandito solitario, a viso scoperto, armato di un coltello a serramanico, ha fatto irruzione nell'istituto di credito.

… Il rapinatore ha subito varcato il bancone, e si è diretto deciso verso gli impiegati. Li ha minacciati con la tagliente lama e li ha quindi costretti a consegnargli quindici milioni.

Il colpo è stato messo a segno in pochi minuti, dall'esterno nessuno si è accorto di nulla. Il bandito è così riuscito poi a dileguarsi a piedi nel centro.

Scattato l'allarme, sul posto sono accorsi subito i carabinieri che hanno immediatamente istituito alcuni posti di blocco. Ma del rapinatore, però, nessuna traccia.

(*La Stampa*, 4 gennaio 1998)

Settimo Torinese a small town on the eastern outskirts of Turin
Cariplo the name of a bank (**Cassa di Risparmio della Lombardia**)
rapina *robbery* (c.f. **rapinare** *to rob*) Note past participle in title of piece.
quindici milioni *15 million lire = €7,700 approximately.* The article was written before the introduction of the Euro.
messo a segno *successfully completed;* **mettere a segno un colpo:** *to hit the target.*
dileguarsi *to vanish*

Comprehension – Passage 2

1 How many robbers took part in the attack?
2 How much was stolen?
3 Why do you think no one noticed the robber(s) during the getaway?
4 What did the carabinieri do?

3   **Incubo in ascensore**
Prigioniero per 10 giorni: allucinante avventura di un ex attore, custode del Club Med a Sestriere.

[Ha perso quindici chili ma si è salvato, i medici: 'Un miracolo']

Sestriere. L'hanno trovato ieri alle 13 i carabinieri. Vivo. Vivo dopo 10 giorni trascorsi chiuso dentro un ascensore guasto, senza né acqua né cibo. Armando Piazza, 64 anni, custode al Club Med, era entrato nella torre bianca dove ha sede il club, deserto d'estate, per ritirare alcuni fax. L'ascensore s'è bloccato a un metro e 70 dal primo piano e lui è rimasto là dentro fino a quando una barista ha dato l'allarme: 'Manca da troppo tempo, temo gli sia successo qualcosa'.

(*La Stampa*, 21 agosto 1998)

The above is the front page summary of a news item treated in greater depth inside the paper. Hence the rather 'telegraphic' style.

Insight

Many words ending in **-ista** indicate jobs, like **barista, elettricista, giornalista, musicista, pianista, violinista** etc. They can refer to a man or a woman, but the article changes: **una barista** *a barmaid*, **un barista** *a barman*. There are two separate plural forms: masculine **baristi** and feminine **bariste**.

Comprehension – Passage 3

1 Where had Armando Piazza spent 10 days?
2 Why had he gone into the building?
3 What made the barmaid call in the carabinieri?

4

Clandestino ritrova il papà dopo 15 anni
Da Tunisi a Torino

ROMA. È arrivato in Italia come clandestino dalla Tunisia per cercare
il padre, un tunisino con passaporto italiano che vive da oltre 15
anni a Torino. Ma le forze di polizia lo hanno sorpreso in Sicilia senza
permesso di soggiorno e, adesso, si trova nel centro di Ponte Galeria,
in attesa di sapere quale sarà il suo destino. Una storia degna del libro
'Cuore'. Tajeddine Abdel Karim, che ha appena compiuto 18 anni, ha
lasciato la madre per venire a trovare il padre. I militari e i volontari
della Cri, che gestiscono il centro di accoglienza di Ponte Galeria,
dopo lunghe ricerche sono riusciti a rintracciare, grazie anche alla
collaborazione con l'ufficio immigrazione della Questura, il padre, che
si è precipitato a Roma, con tutti i documenti necessari ad accertare
la paternità del ragazzo. Il consolato tunisino sta lavorando per far sì
che il ragazzo possa restare con il padre in Italia. [Ansa]

(*La Stampa*, 25 agosto 1998 – internet edition: www.lastampa.it)

centro di Ponte Galeria a reception centre for illegal immigrants,
near Rome
Cuore Title of a well-known sentimental novel by E. de Amicis,
published in 1886
Cri Croce Rossa Italiana *the Italian Red Cross*

QUICK VOCAB

Insight

The newspaper article starts with a verb **È arrivato (in Italia)**
and the subject of the verb appears quite a long way after:
un tunisino con passaporto italiano. This is a common
occurrence in Italian to give emphasis to the theme or topic,
in this case 'arriving in Italy'.

Comprehension – Passage 4

1 Who has been living in Turin for 15 years?
2 Why did the police take the young man into custody?
3 What did the father do when he heard his son was in Rome?
4 What did he bring with him?

....

Two aspects of Italy today are touched on in these passages: the risk of natural disaster and immigration. Italy is a high-risk country for natural disasters. Sadly there have been many in recent years. Much of the peninsula is potentially subject to earthquakes and there are areas of frequent volcanic activity. In addition a very high proportion of Italy is mountainous or hilly (one third mountain and one third hill, leaving only one third flat), leading to risks of landslide and flooding. This has been aggravated by the flight of the peasants from land which is difficult to farm so that the land is untended; by unwise building development; and lack of investment in geologists and appropriate personnel to manage prevention. Recent governments have appeared to take this more seriously than their predecessors but there is a long way to go and the basic nature of the land will mean the risk can never be eliminated.

Passage 4 relates to a fairly recent development. After the massive emigrations to the Americas in the late 19th and early 20th centuries and then the post-war flow of emigrants to other parts of Europe, Australia, and simply from one part of Italy to another (largely from South to North and from country to city), Italy is now learning to live with an unfamiliar phenomenon: immigration. This comes mainly from the former Communist countries of Eastern Europe and from North Africa. And much of the immigration is illegal. The long Italian coastline is difficult to patrol and in spite of unemployment, Italy seems to be a magnet, although undoubtedly many who land in southern Italy plan to move straight through to other parts of Europe. And as always in rich countries, there is work that the Italians prefer not to do. Reactions to immigration are mixed and there is no doubt that it is imposing strains on life, particularly in certain cities where racial tensions have led to disturbances.

It goes without saying that bank robberies are neither new nor specifically Italian. And being trapped in a lift is a common nightmare!

Session 5

Looking at the perfect in action

Let's return to the language of the passages in Session 4. How did that go? We hope you found you could get the meaning, even if you did not understand all the words. If you did, you can certainly get a lot from reading a newspaper. We will come back to the business of meaning shortly, but first let's look at the **passato prossimo** in the news items.

Activity 5

Read the news items again and pick out all the examples you can find of the **passato prossimo**.

More irregular past participles

You will have found irregular past participles not previously presented:

a costretti from **costringere** *to oblige, to compel*. This is often used when in English we might say *'I had to …'* meaning there was no other option for me. The base verb is of course **stringere**.

b rimasto from **rimanere** *to remain*. This is also common since it is used in expressions such as:

Ci sono rimasto male.	*I felt badly about it.*
È rimasto sorpreso dalla tua reazione.	*He was surprised by your reaction.*

There is a reference list of common irregular past participles in the
Reference grammar.

The passive form

You may have wondered about **Le fiamme sono state domate** in
Passage 1. This is a passive. *The flames were overcome.* You have the
passato prossimo of **essere** plus the past participle of **domare**. There
was a similar passive in another passage. Can you find it? (See Key.)

**Agreement of the past participle in verbs forming the 'passato
prossimo' with *avere*.**
You will also have noticed past participle agreements with **avere**.
We have not yet dealt with:

Li ha minacciati	*He threatened them*
li ha costretti	*he forced them*

Can you see what is happening in the examples which are from
Passage 2? The past participle agrees with the object of the verb,
the pronoun li, which refers to **gli impiegati della banca**. The
subject of the verb is *the robber*, who is singular. This is the usual
way for the past participle to behave with **avere**. It agrees with a
direct object pronoun placed before the verb. But it is not a point
you should worry about greatly until you are at quite an advanced
stage. The important point is the use of the **passato prossimo** to
recount the events in a story.

Activity 6

Now here are some things that have happened to you recently.
1 Yesterday you witnessed a road accident. A car didn't stop at
a red light and hit a car which was crossing on green. Tell your
Italian friend about it. Example: **Ieri ho visto un incidente stradale.
Una macchina ...**
2 You left your wallet on a table in the hotel bar last night. Tell
the receptionist and ask if by chance it was found.
3 You had a lovely walk yesterday with Paolo and Marco. You
took the path near the petrol station. You went up the hill and then

into the woods. You followed the path as far as Castiglione. Write a postcard to your mother telling her so.

4 You telephoned Anna last night. Her mother has broken her arm. She fell over in the street. Anna told you to give her greetings to Mario. Tell Mario.

Session 6

Dealing with vocabulary again

The newspaper items required some vocabulary guesswork from you. Here are some comments.

1 Words whose precise meaning is not crucial

There were words in the passages the meaning of which was not crucial to your overall understanding. You could read and understand the passage and knowing the precise meaning of those words would make very little difference. For instance, in Passage 2: **coltello a serra-manico** – does it matter what a **serra-manico** means? Isn't it enough to know the attacker had a knife? Similarly we are told **Il rapinatore ha subito varcato il bancone**. If you know all the other words, not knowing **varcato** really doesn't matter. As you develop your reading skills, you need not look up every word. So long as you are getting the gist, it is more enjoyable to carry on at a reasonable pace. Don't worry too much about the odd word here or there if you are following the story. Other words in these passages that this might apply to are: in Passage 1 **perlustravano**; in Passage 4 **Questura**.

2 Guessable words

There were some good guessing words in the passages, for example:

a words guessable from similar English words

Passage 5 contained several which were so easy, it may seem hardly worth mentioning them (the words in brackets are the English words which come to our mind, not necessarily the best translation or even a translation at all): **clandestino** (*clandestine*), **permesso di soggiorno** (*permit* or *permission to sojourn/stay*); **rintracciare** (*trace*) (cf. **traccia** in Passage 2); **collaborazione; ufficio immigrazione; accertare la paternità**. Or in Passage 1: **incendio** (*incendiary*).

b words guessable from Italian or a combination of Italian and English

In Passage 1 **gitanti** (Italian **gita turistica**); and **soccorre** (Italian **Pronto soccorso** *hospital emergency department* and English *succour*); in Passage 2 **viso scoperto** (English *visor* perhaps and Italian **coperto** *covered*: **scoperto**, *discovered, uncovered* (**s** prefix is often the equivalent of the English *un-*, *dis-*); in Passage 5 **ricerche** (Italian **cercare** and English *research*)

Sophisticated guessers may have been able to work out **costone** in Passage 1 from **costa** *rib* and the suffix **-one**, meaning *big*. It is a word with a dictionary entry (meaning *ridge*) but that is the way it is built up. There is a word built in a similar way in Passage 2. What is it? See key.

3 More false friends
Eventuale is a false friend (**eventuali gitanti** in Passage 1). We mentioned these in Unit 1. They are Italian words that look like English words but which do not have the same meaning. **Eventuale** means here *possible*, i.e. any tourists who might have happened to be on the volcano and have been injured. The adverb **eventualmente** is fairly common. It means *if this should be the case*. For instance you might be asked to give your name and (**eventualmente**) the name of your spouse. Meaning *if you have one*. Try to collect 'false friends' and get their use right. *Eventually* could be translated: **alla fine, finalmente**.

Activity 7

1 How would you tell Arturo's life story from the information below?

Example: **Mi chiamo Arturo Marullo, sono nato nel 1958 a Terni ...**

Nome: Arturo	Cognome: Marullo
Nato: il 6 febbraio 1958	Luogo di nascita: Terni (PG)*
Scuola elementare: Terni	
Scuola media inferiore: Terni	
Scuola media superiore: Liceo scientifico, Perugia	
Studi: Laurea in economia e commercio, Perugia, 1984	
Primo lavoro: Fratelli Alberti, commercianti in vino, Orvieto (3 anni)	
Secondo lavoro: Supermercati Gatti, Milano (7 anni)	
Lavoro attuale: Direttore di marketing, Pasta Bastoni, Milano	
*PG = the province of Perugia	

2 And now yours. Don't forget to say where you were born, where you went to school, and to tell us about any further studies and the various jobs you have held. Perhaps you might like to include the personal side: when you married (**mi sono sposato/a**), and who you married (**mi sono sposato/a con**), when your children were born etc. It's up to you! But make sure you do think it through.

Activity 8

Talking to yourself

1 Immagini di essere uno dei protagonisti di una o due delle storie in Session 4 e racconti quello che è successo dal Suo punto di vista. Per esempio, il bandito nel brano 2 (ho fatto irruzione ...) o uno degli impiegati della banca (Che paura oggi! A mezzogiorno e mezzo è entrato un bandito e ci ha minacciato con un coltello ...); o nel brano 4, Armando Piazza: Mi hanno trovato ...).

2 Racconti a Sé stesso la storia della vita di altre persone: amici, parenti, personaggi famosi. Il motivo per farlo è sforzarsi di parlare (e pensare) in italiano, cercare di usare la lingua. Non ha importanza di quali persone sceglie di parlare: l'importante è che siano interessanti per Lei.

3 Esiste nel Suo paese il fenomeno di una notevole immigrazione? Che cosa ne pensa Lei? Chi sono gli immigrati? Perché vengono? Ne conosce alcuni? Quali problemi incontrano? E quali sono i problemi creati dal loro arrivo? È mai stato residente all'estero anche Lei?

Quali sono i Suoi incubi ricorrenti? E i Suoi sogni?

TEST YOURSELF

1 *To be* or *to have* – that is the question. Test your feeling for the Italian **passato prossimo** by adding the correct auxiliary in the sentences.

  a Mel Gibson _____ nato a New York ed _____ andato a vivere a Sydney all'età di 12 anni.

  b L'attore _____ studiato alla scuola di arte drammatica di Sydney.

  c All'inizio _____ lavorato per il teatro, per la televisione e per il cinema.

  d Il suo nome _____ diventato famoso con il film d'azione *Mad Max* nel 1979.

  e Il suo maggior successo _____ stato il primo film della serie *Lethal Weapon*.

  f Ma l'attore _____ interpretato anche ruoli classici come quello di Amleto nel film di Zeffirelli del 1990.

  g Più tardi _____ diventato regista e _____ diretto film di grande successo come *Braveheart* per il quale _____ ricevuto l'Oscar.

  h Il suo maggior successo come regista _____ stato *The Passion of the Christ*.

  i Nel 1980 _____ sposato Robyn Denise Moore ed _____ avuto sette figli.

  j La coppia si _____ separata nel 2006 e _____ divorziato nel 2009.

2 Complete the sentences with the correct perfect tense of these verbs. Spot which verb must be used in the perfect infinitive.

laurearsi, lavorare, frequentare, essere, partire, aprire, conoscersi

  a Elisabetta _____ l'università a Milano e _____ in Economia e Commercio.

  b Nel passato tu e tua moglie _____ nel settore della ristorazione, ma perché non _____ un ristorante?

c Da quanto tempo _____ sposati Laura e Federico?

d Mara e suo marito _____ nel 1999.

e Non sono ancora arrivati? Potrebbero _____ in ritardo.

4

C'era una volta ...

In this unit we shall
- *meet various Italians reminiscing about the past*
- *use the preposition* da *to say*: something to eat, nothing to do, *etc.*
- *say how things used to be, describe what people were like and what they were doing at a time in the past: a review of the imperfect – form and use*
- *look at the pronoun* si *used impersonally*
- *meet the pluperfect*
- *meet the gerund, the past continuous and the present continuous*

Session 1

Interview 1

Angioletta talks about being a student and the early years of her marriage. She married before she had finished her degree.

Listen several times, preferably without looking at the text and then answer the questions which follow.

Angioletta	Ho studiato lingue a Pisa e stavo in un convento di suore che secondo i miei genitori era il posto giusto per una ragazza che stava fuori di casa … Si sentivano più sicuri. E poi, prima di finire l'università mi sono sposata … e siamo andati ad abitare a Firenze, dove lavorava mio marito.
Interviewer	Ti sei trasferita all'università di Firenze?
Angioletta	No, perché stavo finendo, non era conveniente e ho continuato ad andare a Pisa.
Interviewer	Raccontami la tua vita di giovane sposa a Firenze.
Angioletta	È stato un periodo un po' difficile perché io ero abituata a stare con molta gente. Mi sono trasferita alla periferia di Firenze dove ho trovato grandi difficoltà a entrare, a fare amicizia con le persone vicine. Avevo un'amica molto cara che era una compagna dell'università anche, quindi passavo molto tempo con lei.
Interviewer	Non lavoravi?
Angioletta	Non lavoravo. Avevo … facevo lezioni private. E studiavo. E soffrivo di solitudine, devo dire. Ho trovato molto difficile fare amicizia. Dicono che sia difficile per i toscani con i fiorentini e non avevo questa percezione, non l'avevo provata … E facevo molto da mangiare. Cucinavo tantissimo, a me piaceva sperimentare … e pulivo la casa, ero una padrona di casa molto attenta, lucidavo tutto, davo addirittura la cera alla cucina … (ride) che è una cosa molto …? Secondo me ora …
Interviewer	Quanto tempo siete rimasti a Firenze?
Angioletta	Due anni.
Interviewer	E Annalisa?
Angioletta	Annalisa è nata a Firenze. Due anni e mezzo veramente. Annalisa è nata a Firenze e poi noi ci siamo trasferiti quando lei aveva sei o sette mesi. Siamo venuti ad Arezzo.

non l'avevo provata Note the agreement of the past participle (see Unit 3). The pronoun **l'** stands for **la** and refers to **percezione** (f).

Insight

In this interview we hear a lot of reflexive verbs (see perfect tense in Unit 3): **mi sono sposata** *I got married*, **ti sei trasferita?** *did you move?* etc. Italians make a large use of reflexive verbs, in some case focusing on what people do for themselves: **comprarsi qualcosa** *buy (oneself) something*, **prendersi un caffè** *have a coffee (for oneself)* etc.

Comprehension 1

1 Where did Angioletta live in Pisa and why?
2 Why did she move to Florence when she married?
3 She could have transferred to the University of Florence but didn't. Why not?
4 What did Angioletta most miss living on the outskirts of Florence?
5 Why should she not have been surprised at how difficult it was to get to know people?
6 Who did she spend a lot of time with?
7 Did she have a job?
8 How did she console herself in her loneliness?
9 How long did she live in Florence?
10 Her daughter was born there. What did they do when Annalisa was six or seven months old?

Session 2

The use of prepositions da and di after certain adjectives and pronouns

The use of prepositions is possibly one of the most tricky areas when you are learning a foreign language. Of course, they often translate neatly on a one-to-one basis.

Da dove vieni?	*Where do you come from?*
Il negozio è aperto dalle otto	*The shop is open from*
all'una.	*eight to one.*

But there are also idiomatic usages, i.e. usages where there is not a straight translation. **Da** probably has more of these than other prepositions. You were reminded in Unit 2 of:

| **Studio italiano da due anni.** | *I've been studying Italian for two years.* |

Here is another idiomatic use of **da**. It is sensible to keep a section in your notes (just as you should have one for false friends) for these usages.

Certain indefinite adjectives and pronouns are followed by **da** plus an infinitive. (Indefinites are a group of adjectives and pronouns which, as their name implies, are generally imprecise about number.)

qualcosa		mangiare	something		eat
niente/nulla		bere	nothing		drink
molto	**DA**	fare	much/a lot	<u>TO</u>	do
tanto		dire	so much		say
troppo		vedere	too much		see

But note also:

qualcosa		bello	something	lovely
niente/nulla		nuovo	nothing	new
molto	**DI**	buono	much <u>that is</u>	good
tanto		importante	so much <u>that is</u>	important
troppo		sicuro	too much <u>that is</u>	certain

Can you spot where the difference lies? **DA** + verb; **DI** + adjective.

Tricky translations

Even as we translated from Italian to English in the previous section, we came up against the point that word-for-word translation does not always work, or produces a stilted result.

At the level of individual words, another point to look out for when learning any foreign language is that words are often not precise equivalents because no two countries are the same. They have different histories, different rates of development, different terrain, climate etc. And words which may perhaps have the same origin get used in different ways in different countries. This is an interesting point. Here are a couple of examples:

periferia: Italian cities do not really have suburbs. You are either *in the centre* (**in centro**), often **nel centro storico** meaning in the old, usually picturesque part; or **in periferia** on the *outskirts* but still within the city limits. Or else you go and live in another **comune** where you have a different local administration etc.

conveniente: *convenient* in English clearly has the same Latin origin as **conveniente** in Italian. However in Italian the word is often used colloquially to mean **vantaggioso dal punto di vista economico, adatto alle circostanze** – it seems to us that if you lived in the Florence area, it would be more convenient to be at university in Florence but Angioletta explained that she was so near the end of her course in Pisa it did not make sense to transfer. It was not convenient in the sense that she would have wasted time getting to know people and places and generally getting herself organized. Probably in English one would say: *advisable*.

Session 3

The imperfect tense

You will have noticed that, when talking about what they did, the stages in their career, our Italian speakers sometimes used another tense, not the perfect, **passato prossimo**. Much of what Angioletta says in Interview 1 is expressed in this other past tense which you may already know as the imperfect, **l'imperfetto**. Here are some examples from the part of the interview in which Angioletta is talking about the first year or two of her marriage:

Non **lavoravo**. **Avevo** … **facevo** lezioni private. **E studiavo**.

E **soffrivo** di solitudine, devo dire … E **facevo** molto da mangiare. **Cucinavo** tantissimo, a me **piaceva** sperimentare, … e **pulivo** la casa, **ero** una padrona di casa molto attenta, **lucidavo** tutto, **davo** addirittura la cera alla cucina.

Activity 1

A different tense must imply a different meaning. Try translating some sentences and phrases from Interview 1 given again below. The imperfect has been underlined to draw your attention to it. Can you work out why it is being used? Can you convey that in your translation?

Example: **Poi, prima di finire l'università, mi sono sposata … e siamo andati ad abitare a Firenze, dove <u>lavorava</u> mio marito.**

Then, before I had graduated from the university, I got married … and we went to live in Florence where my husband was working/worked/ used to work. (worked is a very acceptable translation, <u>was working</u> captures the meaning of the imperfect better in this case than used to work)

1 Mi sono trasferita alla periferia di Firenze dove ho trovato grandi difficoltà a entrare, a fare amicizia con le persone vicine. <u>Avevo</u> un'amica molto cara che <u>era</u> una compagna dell'università anche, quindi <u>passavo</u> molto tempo con lei.
2 <u>Facevo</u> molto da mangiare. <u>Cucinavo</u> tantissimo, a me piaceva sperimentare … e <u>pulivo</u> la casa, <u>ero</u> una padrona di casa molto attenta, <u>lucidavo</u> tutto, <u>davo</u> addirittura la cera alla cucina.

3 Annalisa è nata a Firenze e poi noi ci siamo trasferiti quando lei <u>aveva</u> sei o sette mesi.

Do you think you understood intuitively why a different tense was being used in that activity? As we show in our suggestions in the Key, English offers more than one possibility when it comes to translating. And here lies the key to understanding. The way the past is conveyed in English and Italian does not correspond exactly. Each language has its own system and it is not helpful to think from one language to the other – even though, as a language learner, you inevitably will to some extent.

Two past tenses in Italian

In Italian there are the two basic past tenses: the **passato prossimo** or *perfect* and the **imperfetto** or *imperfect*. The difference between them lies in *point of view*. Is the important aspect that the action was done once and completed? Or is that not what you are trying to convey? A clue lies in the names. The *imperfect* is not a bargain basement, 'only one tiny flaw' tense. The word comes from Latin and means incomplete. *Perfect* means completed. When what happened, happened once and is viewed as finished and done with, we use the *perfect*. The *imperfect* is used when the speaker is focussing on another aspect of the past event.

It may help to look at certain verbs where the force of the meaning is thrown into relief when translating as you really need different words in English, so different is the meaning. Compare:

Sapevo che Elena stava male.	*I knew Elena was ill. (**i.e. it was something I knew**)*
Ho saputo che Elena stava male.	*I learned/heard Elena was ill. (**i.e. knowing it was an event which happened at a precise moment and then it became part of my knowledge**)*

(Contd)

Conoscevo poche persone a Firenze.

I knew few people in Florence/ I didn't know many people in Florence.

Ho conosciuto mio marito a Firenze.

*I met my husband in Florence (**i.e. that was where I met him for the first time. It was an event which happened once – and changed my life! Well, no, perhaps it doesn't quite say that much!**)*

Gabriella, whom you can see here with her husband Gianni, told us (interview 3):

Ho conosciuto mio marito a una gita della parrocchia.

I met my husband at a parish outing.

Some learners find it useful to think of time as a line. The imperfect would fade in and out imperceptibly, while the perfect would be for specific chunks of time, points in time, with a clear beginning and end; the amounts of time can be longer or shorter, but the start and finish are clear.

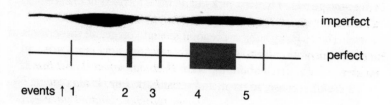

events ↑ 1   2   3   4   5

The uses of the imperfect

The imperfect is used in three main ways (all our examples here are taken from what Angioletta said above):

1 for repeated, habitual actions – finished, yes, but done many times:

non lavoravo; studiavo; facevo lezioni private; cucinavo tantissimo; pulivo la casa; lucidavo tutto

2 for describing what a person or a thing was like at a point in the past:

Ero una padrona di casa molto attenta.

3 when the verb is conveying things that happened but the start and finish of the action is not relevant, the action is seen as going on over an unspecified period, a background to other things:

dove lavorava mio marito; avevo un'amica molto cara; soffrivo di solitudine

With practice and familiarity, you will develop a feeling for it. In this unit you will get a good amount of practice.

Activity 2

This Activity is mostly for learners who have not met the imperfect before or who feel unsure of it. Forming the imperfect is easy. You can probably work it out for yourself from the examples you have already met. Try. First pick out all the imperfects in Interview 1. Then sort them into verb groups according to the characteristic vowel. Then sort by subject pronoun so that you get all those verbs in **-are** of which the subject is '**io**' together etc. See how much you can work out for yourself about the form of the imperfect on this basis. It is a useful exercise, so try it, and consult the Key before reading on.

Forming the imperfect

Each of the three verb groups keeps the characteristic vowel from its infinitive but otherwise the endings for all verbs are the same:

Group 1	Group 2	Group 3
passare	**avere**	**pulire**
passavo	avevo	pulivo
passavi	avevi	pulivi
passava	aveva	puliva
passavamo	avevamo	pulivamo
passavate	avevate	pulivate
passavano	avevano	pulivano

The verb **essere** is totally irregular: **ero, eri, era, eravamo, eravate, erano.**

Otherwise, very few verbs are irregular in the imperfect: they are the ones which have a contracted infinitive (see Unit 3, Session 3).

fare (facere)	facevo, facevi, faceva, facevamo, facevate, facevano
dire (dicere)	dicevo, dicevi, diceva, dicevamo, dicevate, dicevano
bere (bevere)	bevevo, bevevi, beveva, bevevamo, bevevate, bevevano
porre (ponere)	ponevo, ponevi, poneva, ponevamo, ponevate, ponevano
tradurre (traducere)	traducevo, traducevi, traduceva, traducevamo, traducevate, traducevano

Insight

For all three verb groups the **imperfetto** endings are: **vo, vi, va, vamo, vate, vano**, except for **essere**. But the vowel before these endings changes according to the verb group: **a** for **are** verbs, **e** for **ere** verbs, **i** for **ire** verbs.

This 'group' vowel is where the stress falls in all cases except for **noi** and **voi**: part-ivo, part-ivi, part-iva, part-ivamo, part-ivate, part-ivano.

As we said you need to become familiar with the imperfect in use, so to give you that practice, several reminders follow in the remainder of this Unit.

Session 4

Interview 2

Listen and answer the questions which follow. Try to listen without reading the text.

For many years Carlo worked for various Italian and foreign companies in Italy and abroad, in Brazil, Venezuela and Spain. Today he is Managing Director of Stock, a long established firm in Trieste. Here he is talking about his early days.

Carlo	Sono nato in un tipico ambiente astigiano di provincia, da genitori che erano figli di contadini e cercavano di emergere e hanno cominciato con una piccola attività commerciale con tante difficoltà, con tanta ristrettezza all'inizio. Era gente molto laboriosa che grazie alle prime economie ha permesso ai loro figli di fare i primi studi ad Asti. Si andava ad Asti in corriera, a circa quindici, venti chilometri, e si tornava la sera. Ed è in questo ambiente che evidentemente poi mi sono formato. D'estate si *(Contd)*

♦ CD1, TR 11, 34:48

> andava per nidi, si andava a pescare nei fiumi, si andava a
> pescare anguille. Ho imparato a nuotare nei ruscelli. Quelli
> erano praticamente i nostri svaghi. Si andava per tartufi,
> c'era sempre un vecchio che conosceva ...

QUICK VOCAB

astigiano *from the Asti area.* Asti (of **spumante** fame) is a town in
Piemonte to the southeast of Turin; it is the main town of the
province of Asti.

era gente molto laboriosa Gente is a feminine singular noun and is
accompanied by a singular verb (**era**).

si andava per tartufi *we went truffle hunting.* The area where
Carlo lived, is famous for its highly prized white truffles (**tuber
magnatum**).

Insight

Verb + preposition + infinitive: it is a good idea to memorize
which preposition goes after which verb, e.g. **cercare di** *to try
to,* **permettere di** *to allow to,* **andare a** *to go -ing,* **imparare** a
to learn to.

Comprehension 2

1 Carlo has had a successful career as a businessman. What did his
grandparents do?
2 What seems to have been his parents' ambition?
3 What did they do to further their ambitions and what does their
life seem to have been like?
4 Where did he go to school and what did that involve?
5 Carlo has fond memories of his childhood leisure activities.
What were they?

Impersonal si

Carlo says: **si andava ad Asti** ... *Si,* the pronoun, has many
functions. Here it is used impersonally (like English *one*). Carlo
means: **noi andavamo** ... He is including siblings and friends.

'Impersonal' is really a misnomer. **Si** refers to (an) unspecified person(s). We shall meet this again. Another use of impersonal **si** where in English we might use a passive:

Qui si parla italiano.   *Italian is spoken here.*

In English we also use <u>you</u>, meaning people in general:

Una piccola trattoria dove si   *A little restaurant where*
   mangia bene e si paga poco.   *you eat well and where*
                                                  the price is reasonable
                                                  (you pay little).

Something Italians are always trying to find. Aren't we all?

Activity 3

Pick out the verbs in what Carlo says (Interview 2). First make a list of the verbs in the perfect or **passato prossimo**. If you reflect on each, you will see that it refers to something which was done once and is finished. Then make a list of the imperfects which might be said to describe; those which convey habitual, repeated actions; and those which are describing the background.

We hope you found that useful. It takes time and practice to get the feel of the **imperfetto**. The **passato prossimo** is much more straighforward. Try to keep thinking about it as you listen and read. Here is some more practice.

Session 5

Interview 3

In Unit 1, Gabriella told us that her Italian father and English mother lived in France, that when war broke out her father had taken his family home to Italy and how difficult this was for her mother since, for Italy, Great Britain was an enemy country. Gabriella looks back at the war.

● CD1, TR 12, 36:54

Gabriella   Infatti, mio fratello che allora era molto piccolino non voleva più parlare con mia mamma perché diceva che era il nemico lei. E allora mio papà l'ha dovuto mettere in collegio, dalle suore, piccolino, perché temeva che dicesse cose … e … comunque tra una vicissitudine e l'altra … sono venuti fuori da questa guerra brutta per loro. Hanno perso la casa, han perso tutto, scappavano sempre; eravamo sfollati da tutte le parti e nessuno voleva darci da mangiare proprio perché mamma era inglese. E una volta mamma di notte si è alzata, è andata a mungere una pecora per darci del latte e le hanno sparato. Infatti questo pezzettino – non so come si possa dire – di pallottola ha sempre girato per casa, l'abbiamo sempre visto … Eravamo sfollati a Villafranca Piemonte, eravamo sfollati là. E io ricordo qualcosa vagamente. Non so se ricordo veramente o a furia di sentire raccontare … Però qualcosa ricordo di questa guerra.

QUICK VOCAB

in collegio *in a boarding school*. The school was run by nuns, **suore**.
han perso Gabriella abbreviates **hanno**: Speakers do sometimes abbreviate and/or slur words as they talk.
sfollati *evacuated*. They moved out of the city, which was a target for Allied bombing. Many families left the big cities.
a furia di sentire *by dint of hearing*

Insight
Sometimes words get shortened in Italian because they sound better in the flow of the sentence, e.g. **han perso tutto** *they lost everything*. Other examples: **man mano** *little by little*, **un gran bel libro** *a really good book*, **andar via** *to go away*, **far vedere** *to show*, **un po'** *a bit*.

Comprehension 3

1 Gabriella's brother was still very young and didn't understand. He used to say something which made her father fear the consequences. What did he say and what decision did their father take?

2 When they were evacuated, the fact that Gabriella's mother was English meant what for the family?

3 This drove her to do something unusual one night. What was it and what happened?

4 Does Gabriella have clear memories of the war? Why not?

Activity 4

As with Activity 3, examine the verbs in Interview 3 in the same way and make sure you understand the use of both the perfect and the imperfect.

Activity 5

As we said above, many Italians left the cities during the war. While they were living in the countryside they adapted to the new way of life and helped the local peasants in exchange for their hospitality. Here is a true story which happened to the Rossi family – yes, their name really was Rossi. Read the introduction and write the story using the verbs in brackets. Make appropriate use of the perfect and the imperfect.

Le tre bambine e le oche *The three children and the geese*

La casa della famiglia Rossi (padre, madre e tre figlie: Finetta, Cheche e Titti), a Torino, è stata bombardata e la famiglia Rossi ha perso tutto. Si sono rifugiati nel Monferrato, vicino ad Asti, in un piccolo paese di campagna, Quarto. A Quarto, vivevano ospiti in una fattoria. Le tre bambine andavano alla scuola elementare del paese la mattina, e il pomeriggio portavano a pascolare le oche del contadino.

Your story starts:

Era una bella giornata di primavera ...

Il sole (1 splendere). Le tre bambine (2 tornare) da scuola e (3 decidere) di portare le oche a pascolare al di là del fiume.

La riva al di là del fiume (4 essere) pericolosa. Spesso i partigiani (5 combattere) contro l'esercito tedesco. Le tre bambine (6 sapere) che non (7 dovere) andarci, ma (8 essere) curiose.

Mentre le oche (9 pascolare), le tre bambine (10 giocare) nel prato.

All'improvviso, le tre bambine (11 sentire) degli spari e (12 buttarsi) in un fosso con le oche.

Poco dopo, (13 arrivare) i partigiani e i tedeschi. Finetta e Titti (14 avere) paura e (15 volere) scappare; Cheche, invece, (16 dire): 'Voglio restare: non ho mai visto una battaglia vera!'

I partigiani (17 sparare) contro i tedeschi; i tedeschi (18 sparare) contro i partigiani. Le oche (19 essere) terrorizzate. Le bambine (20 prendere) in braccio le oche per tranquillizzarle.

Dopo qualche minuto, la sparatoria (21 finire) e gli uomini (22 andare) via. Tutto (23 essere) calmo di nuovo; le tre bambine e le oche (24 uscire) dal fosso: (25 essere) tutte salve. Le tre bambine (26 tornare) a casa e (27 decidere) che probabilmente non sarebbero mai più andate a pascolare le oche al di là del fiume ...

For the student who wants to pursue the topic of Italy during the Second World War, there is a considerable body of good writing on the subject. The incident which inspired the exercise brings to mind *La casa in collina* by Cesare Pavese.

Session 6

Interview 4

Here, as well as noting the imperfect/perfect relationship, think further about describing people. And of course listen as often as you need. Gabriella remembers her mother.

CD1, TR 13, 39:31

Gabriella	Mia mamma era una persona eccezionale, silenziosa, tranquilla, comunque non usciva mai, raramente, però sapeva tutto, leggeva tanto, sapeva tutti i film, ci raccontava tante cose, era una donna molto istruita ma purtroppo me ne sono accorta troppo tardi, di questo. Era la prima ad alzarsi e l'ultima ad andare a letto. Mamma è mancata che io avevo quarant'anni e posso dire d'averla vista in camicia da notte solo quegli ultimi giorni in ospedale. In tutta la mia vita non l'ho mai vista in camicia da notte. Se io mi dovevo alzare presto, io o i miei fratelli, per qualche motivo, lei si alzava un'ora prima di noi. E quando ci veniva a svegliare, prima di sentire la sua voce che ci chiamava, sentivo il profumo della saponetta. È l'ultima ad andare a letto. Sempre. Era molto rigida nelle sue idee che poi portava avanti senza ... cioè non è che lei pensasse: io devo fare così. No, no, no, era il suo modo di ... E si alzava presto al mattino per fare le cose che le piacevano: fumarsi una sigaretta, bere una tazza di caffè e fare le parole incrociate.
Interviewer	In italiano?
Gabriella	In italiano, e mio papà diceva sempre che era un'inglese sbagliata, che ... (ride) le piaceva anche molto bere il vino, l'apprezzava a tavola, ci preparava delle bellissime colazioni, tutti sempre a tavola, presenti, dovevamo essere a colazione, *(Contd)*

anche se non avevamo impegni, sempre, e vestiti. Mai in camicia da notte, mai in vestaglia. Cos'altro posso dire di mia mammina? Un'altra cosa curiosa di mia mamma è che verso le quattro e mezza del pomeriggio, lei si cambiava, si cambiava, e mi sono accorta quando mamma è mancata che in fondo lei non aveva niente, aveva poche cose: tre o quattro camicette, due magliette, però erano sempre in ordine, pulite, stirate, collettini ben lavati e stirati. Lei verso le quattro e mezza si ritirava, si lavava, si cambiava come se dovesse uscire e finiva lì la sua giornata perché aveva già organizzato la cena e allora parlava con noi, cantavamo, si suonava il piano, era una vita un po' particolare, infatti le mie compagne di scuola venivano volentieri a casa per vedere questa vita un po' strana che noi conducevamo, che io pensavo essere tipicamente inglese. Però quando poi sono andata in Inghilterra mi sono accorta che era una vita di mia mamma, non era una vita proprio inglese, era lei, così.

Mamma è mancata Mancare is the usual way of saying 'pass away, die' in Italian. Few people use **morire** referring to a recent death or the death of a loved one. Newspapers often report deaths using the verb **scomparire**: *È scomparso X …*

che io avevo quarant'anni che *when.* An idiomatic way of expressing the idea but one which is easily understood by the foreign learner.

per qualche motivo *for some reason.* Note that **qualche** must always be followed by a singular, whereas in English it is more usually followed by a plural. A useful way of remembering this is via a frequently used phrase such as **qualche volta** sometimes. **Volta** is patently singular.

fumarsi una sigaretta Making **fumare** reflexive underlines the enjoyment Gabriella's mother found in this quiet cigarette before the start of the day.

mammina The diminutive accentuates how very much Gabriella loved her mother. Notice Gabriella consistently uses the simple

possessive with no article with **mamma, papà, mammina**
  (see Unit 2)
come se dovesse uscire dovesse is an imperfect subjunctive
  (see Unit 8).
si suonava il piano Here is the impersonal **si** again, meaning *we*.

Insight

Italian can change the 'feeling' expressed by a noun or
an adjective by adding a suffix. In the last two interviews
Gabriella talks about her brother as **piccolino** *really young*,
questo pezzettino *this tiny bit*, **mammina** *my darling mum*.
The suffix **-ino** indicates that someone is much loved or
something is very small. See more of these in Unit 8.

Comprehension 4

1 Gabriella regrets that she didn't realize something about her
mother until it was too late. What was it?
2 What point do you think Gabriella is making by drawing
attention to the fact that she had not seen her mother in a
nightdress until her final illness in hospital?
3 What were her mother's little pleasures which she enjoyed before
the family got up?
4 What sort of behaviour does she seem to have demanded from
her children?
5 What habit of her mother's does Gabriella remember as being
curious – and, she thought, typically English?
6 What picture do you get of her mother?

Activity 6

Examine the text of Interview 4 for imperfects and perfects.

Session 7

Saying something had happened: the pluperfect

Activity 7

finiva lì la sua giornata perché aveva già organizzato la cena

Aveva ... organizzato she <u>had</u> ... organized. This is moving one stage back in time. It is called the pluperfect, **il trapassato**, and is formed ... Well how do you think it is formed, judging from this example? Check in the Key – there is a further question for you there.

Forming the pluperfect

Verbs which make the perfect with avere	Verbs which make the perfect with essere
avevo finito	ero uscito/a
avevi finito	eri uscito/a
aveva finito	era uscito/a
avevamo finito	eravamo usciti/e
avevate finito	eravata usciti/e
avevano finito	erano usciti/e

If you look back to Gabriella's account of her family during the war, you will notice she says:

Eravamo sfollati　　　*We had moved away*
a Villafranca ...　　　　*to Villafranca ...*

She uses the pluperfect. The verb **sfollare**, involving as it does movement, is conjugated with **essere**.

Activity 8

The story of the three little girls and the geese (Activity 5) can also be told using the pluperfect. It is a question of style. Try telling it again, leaving all the imperfects as they are and using the pluperfect for each perfect.

Further practice of the imperfect

Activity 9

Practise forming the imperfect, using Gabriella's description of her father. We have put nearly all the verbs which Gabriella used into the infinitive and we want you to find the correct form. ONE only was in the perfect. Which one was it and what would the form be? We have left other verbs, e.g. a subjunctive, unchanged. Think hard about the subject of numbers 7, 8 and 11; 9 has a different subject again and it is not **papà**.

Mio papà (1 essere) un gran buffone, gli (2 piacere) gli scherzi, (3 scherzare) sempre, (4 organizzare) riunioni in casa, parenti, feste, pranzi, gli (5 piacere) far da mangiare, era un gran cuoco … e ci (6 portare) sempre in giro … (7 avere) un giorno della settimana che era il nostro giorno, (8 uscire) con papà. Non (9 capire) mai se era il nostro giorno di libertà con papà o era il giorno di libertà di mia mamma …. Non (9 capire) mai. Papà (10 dedicarsi) alla spesa, (11 fare) sempre la spesa con papà perché mamma un po' per via della lingua o … oppure perché a papà (12 piacere). E questo (13 essere) molto strano perché parlo di quarant'anni fa quasi, anche di più per cui … allora gli uomini in Italia non (14 aiutare) in casa. Invece papà (15 fare) tutto in casa, tutto … perché gli (16 piacere), non perché volesse aiutare mamma, perché gli (17 piacere).

Activity 10

A little more practice. In the following sentences, choose for each verb which tense, perfect or imperfect, makes sense. Then put the verb given into that form.

1 Mentre io (tornare) a casa l'altra sera tardi, (vedere) un riccio (a hedgehog) che attraversava la strada.
2 Quando Gianni (abitare) qui vicino, noi lo (vedere) spesso. Ora lo vediamo raramente, ma l' (incontrare) giovedì. (Uscire) dalla banca.

3 Questa (essere) la casa dei nonni ma noi la (ristrutturare). Loro (avere) qui la sala da pranzo ma noi la (trasformare) in una grande cucina, come vedete.

4 I nonni (cucinare) su un forno a legna. Alla nonna (riuscire) a perfezione certi piatti cotti a fuoco lento.

Saying what was going on in the past: the past continuous

Look back to what Angioletta said at the beginning of Unit 4 about her move to Florence while she was still a student in Pisa. She was asked whether she transferred to the University of Florence and said:

No, perché stavo finendo ...   *No, because I was finishing ...*

She uses the imperfect of **stare** plus **finendo** to underline that she really was in the process of finishing at that time, there wasn't much left to do. You may or may not have met this type of imperfect. Just as in English you can say (indeed, have to say) *I was finishing* using a form which underlines that the action was going on at that time, so you can in Italian. You use the imperfect of **stare** plus what is called the **gerund**. The name may be unfamiliar but it is very easy to form. The root (the first part) is the same as for the imperfect and you add **-ando** for Group 1 verbs and **-endo** for all the rest.

Group 1	Group 2	Group 3
parlare → parlando	decidere → decidendo	partire → partendo

The verbs which are irregular in the imperfect (and you remember that is very few indeed) are also irregular in the gerund:

fare → facendo
dire → dicendo
bere → bevendo
porre → ponendo
tradurre → traducendo

And **essere** is NOT irregular!

essere → essendo

Activity 11

Try emphasizing that the actions in the following sentences were in progress at a time in the past.

Anna was preparing the supper.
Anna stava preparando la cena.

1 John was finishing a letter.
2 The train was coming into the station.
3 Father was reading the newspaper.
4 Mother was having a shower. (**fare la doccia**)

The tense lends itself to a murder mystery situation. The suspects are being interrogated by the police to discover what they were doing at the moment the murder was being committed and each has an alibi. X was doing this and Y was doing that ... Why not have some fun in your imagination and work out such a situation! Of course, the simple imperfect conveys the same idea, but **stare** + gerund emphasizes the action as ongoing at that point in time.

The present continuous

You can also use a form to say actions are ongoing in the present. If you haven't already met it, you might guess what it is. You use the present tense of **stare** and the gerund.

Sto studiando.   *I am studying.*
Stiamo cercando di risolvere   *We are trying to resolve*
  un problema.   *a problem.*

Session 8

Reading

This is an extract from another essay by Natalia Ginzburg written in Rome in the autumn of 1944. During the war her first husband, Leone Ginzburg, a former university teacher of Russian and a Jew, was sentenced to internal exile, **confino***, a punishment much used by the Fascist authorities for political dissidents. He was required to leave Turin and live in a small village in the mountainous Abruzzo region, at that time very much undeveloped and remote even though it is not far from Rome. His wife and three small children went too. For Natalia, used to big-city life, it was a different world.*

From 8 September 1943 to 25 April 1945 Italy was the theatre of a brutal civil war between the Fascists, who did not accept the armistice with the Allies, and the Partisans, who fought against fascism. In every town and village, communities were divided and executions and massacres were daily occurrences. Much literature has developed around the events of that period.

Quando la prima neve cominciava a cadere, una lenta tristezza s'impadroniva di noi. Era un esilio il nostro: la nostra città era lontana e lontani erano i libri, gli amici, le vicende varie e mutevoli di una vera esistenza. Accendevamo la nostra stufa verde, col lungo tubo che attraversava il soffitto: ci si riuniva tutti nella stanza dove c'era la stufa, e lì si cucinava e si mangiava, mio marito scriveva al grande tavolo ovale, i bambini cospargevano di giocattoli il pavimento. Sul soffitto della stanza era dipinta un'aquila: e io guardavo l'aquila e pensavo che quello era l'esilio. L'esilio era l'aquila, la stufa verde che ronzava, era la vasta e silenziosa campagna e l'immobile neve. Alle cinque suonavano le campane della chiesa di Santa Maria, e le donne andavano a benedizione, coi loro scialli neri e il viso rosso. Tutte le sere mio marito ed io facevamo una passeggiata: tutte le sere camminavamo a braccetto, immergendo i piedi nella neve. Le case che costeggiavano la strada erano abitate da gente cognita e amica: e tutti uscivano sulla porta e ci dicevano: 'Con una buona salute'.

Qualcuno a volte domandava: 'Ma quando ci ritornate alle case vostre?' Mio marito diceva: 'Quando sarà finita la guerra'. 'E quando finirà questa guerra? Te che sai tutto e sei un professore, quando finirà?' Mio marito lo chiamavano 'il professore' non sapendo pronunciare il suo nome, e venivano da lontano a consultarlo sulle cose più varie, sulla stagione migliore per togliersi i denti, sui sussidi che dava il municipio e sulle tasse e le imposte.

This short extract evokes the monotony and melancholy of Natalia's time of exile in a haunting, poetic style. The whole essay is not long and you may enjoy reading it. In the last paragraph you learn that Leone died in prison in Rome, not long after they left the village, a prisoner of the occupying Germans. The essay ends:

Allora io avevo fede in un avvenire facile e lieto, ricco di desideri appagati, di esperienze e di comuni imprese. Ma era quello il tempo migliore della mia vita e solo adesso che m'è sfuggito per sempre, solo adesso lo so.

'Inverno in Abruzzo' (written in 1944) in Natalia Ginzburg, *Le piccole virtù*, Einaudi 1962

s'impadroniva di noi Note the word **padrone** seems to be in this word. So 'the sadness became our ...'?

ci si riuniva ... si cucinava ... si mangiava This is the impersonal **si** we met earlier in the unit (Session 4). Note, however, that **riunirsi** is reflexive, which means if you use the impersonal **si** you have two identical pronouns together. Italian avoids this by changing the first **si** to **ci**.

gente cognita You may not know the meaning of **cognita** but you do know **conoscere** and the expression **incognito**. Can you guess? **cognita** is however very literary. More usual: **conosciuta**.

venivano a consultarlo It is difficult today to imagine the simple faith country people like these placed in someone who obviously knew a lot and probably didn't make any charge for the benefit of his advice. Since he knew a lot, he was expected to know everything. Similar experiences are described by Carlo Levi, another. Torinese also sent into internal exile, further south in the Basilicata, in his book *Cristo si è fermato a Eboli* (Christ Stopped at Eboli).

tasse ... imposte The latter are general taxes payable to the state such as income tax whereas the former are taxes on specific services or provisions and payable to specific agencies, for instance on cars, on school attendance (effectively *fees*), etc.

desideri appagati *wishes granted, fulfilled*

Comprehension 5

1 Natalia felt herself exiled from real life (**una vera esistenza**). What did she miss from the existence she had left behind?
2 How large a house do they seem to have had at their disposal?
3 Where did Natalia see an eagle and what did it come to symbolize for her?
4 What do you learn about the appearance of the women of the village?
5 What sort of advice did people come to seek from Leone Ginzburg?

Activity 12

Talking to yourself

Ora tocca a Lei! Now it's your turn. Think out how to talk (to yourself or someone else) about:

1 La Sua prima scuola. Com'era? Chi erano i Suoi amici? Che cosa Le piaceva fare? Che cosa detestava fare?
2 La vita della Sua famiglia quando era bambino/a. I Suoi genitori, fratelli, sorelle ... La casa dove vivevate. Le vacanze. Ricordi felici (o tristi, se vuole).

3 È abbastanza vecchio/a per ricordare la Seconda Guerra Mondiale? Che cosa si ricorda? Forse Lei ha avuto la sfortuna di vivere anche un'altra guerra. Ripensi alla Sua esperienza, e immagini di raccontarla a qualcuno, in italiano.

4 Cambiamenti nel corso della Sua vita. Com'era la Sua città (o il Suo paese) quando era bambino/a?

The more practice in reminiscing you can give yourself the better – remember the advice on language learning in Unit 1. But of course we don't know your life story. So you choose what to focus on and tell yourself what you used to do, what things and people were like ...

TEST YOURSELF

1 The villa of a famous sport star has been burgled. The cook is being interviewed by the police. Write their conversation in Italian. The cook is a male, the policeman addresses him in the **Lei** form.

Police   **a** Where were you yesterday at 5 in the afternoon?

Cook   **b** I was in kitchen.

Police   **c** What were you doing?

Cook   **d** I was cooking supper for the family.

Police   **e** Did you hear any noise (*dei rumori*)?

Cook   **f** No, I didn't. I was listening to the radio while I was making ravioli.

Police   **g** But somebody had come in through the window and had fired a shot (**colpo**).

Cook   **h** Sorry, sir, I didn't hear or notice anything strange. I thought the children were watching a western on TV.

Police   **i** Well, something strange happened in this house yesterday. The father was hurt and the money has disappeared.

Cook   **j** Are you accusing me, sir?

2 Complete these sentences with the prepositions **a**, **da** or **di**.

  a Non avevamo niente _____ fare ieri pomeriggio, perciò siamo andati _____ pescare.

  b C'è qualcosa _____ buono _____ mangiare oggi?

  c Era abituata _____ stare con molta gente. Non poteva fare niente _____ interessante in quel posto isolato.

  d Aveva tanto _____ raccontare dopo il suo viaggio a Londra. Ma non ha detto niente _____ specifico sul suo incontro con Joanna.

  e Raccontami qualcosa _____ bello. Che cosa c'era _____ vedere alla mostra dei fiori?

5

....

Al lavoro

In this unit we shall learn
- *how to talk about businesses and jobs*
- *how to express frequency and approximate amounts*
- *more prepositions:* fra/tra; in/a + place
- *relative pronouns:* che, quello che, cui, *etc.*
- *how to say* both ... and, either ... or, neither ... nor
- *the present subjunctive*
- *how to talk about repeated actions:* andare + gerund
- *how to say* 'having done this, I ...': past participles
- *the conditional perfect*
- *the use of* tu *and* Lei

Session 1

Interview 1

*Italian food is well known and widely enjoyed. Marina, whom we met in Unit 3, is Managing Director (**Amministratore Delegato**) of a chain of self-service restaurants, which aim to serve classic Italian food in pleasant surroundings. She was asked to describe the company.*

As usual, listen as often as you need and then answer the comprehension questions. If you can do so without looking at the text, you are giving yourself valuable practice at real-life situations.

Marina	Beh, la società è una società che gestisce questa piccola catena di ristoranti. Sono in tutto quindici ristoranti, apriremo il sedicesimo a Roma fra un paio di settimane. Poi ci sono un altro paio di locali un po' diversi, insomma diciamo che il core business, il filone principale è questi ristoranti self-service. Sono dei self-service un po' più di lusso del self-service classico, dove cioè cerchiamo di dare di più sia nella qualità del prodotto, di quello che prepariamo da mangiare, sia nell'allestimento, nell'arredo dei ristoranti. È una formula che funziona abbastanza bene anche se sono ristoranti molto grandi che hanno bisogno di investimenti piuttosto alti e hanno dei costi anche di gestione alti dunque funzionano solo se riescono a garantire un certo livello di attività. Che è abbastanza difficile da originare quindi si possono aprire solo in posti abbastanza particolari. Non è una formula che si presti a uno sviluppo a tappeto sul tipo McDonalds, ma a uno sviluppo un po' più lento.
Interviewer	Quanti ne avete aperti nei nove – dieci anni che ci lavori?
Marina	Una decina, circa uno all'anno, uno e mezzo all'anno che non è moltissimo. Nello stesso periodo McDonalds ne apre mille probabilmente, anche forse di più. Ma è una cosa diversa. È un po' il problema, diciamo, di questa formula che non riesce ad espandersi a dei ritmi molto veloci. Comunque, insomma, in complesso è una cosa che funziona quindi. Il primo ristorante è stato aperto a Trieste ma la sede del gruppo è in Veneto e diciamo che da lì, ci stiamo lentamente espandendo sul resto del territorio. Adesso abbiamo più o meno coperto il Nord Italia – beh, insomma siamo nelle principali città – e quindi ci stiamo un po' espandendo verso sud adesso.

Interviewer	La sede del gruppo è in Veneto?
Marina	Sì, vicino a Venezia. Io ho questo piccolo ufficio qui perché la mia famiglia, quella di mio marito, è qui a Milano, quindi è una base. Io sto qui anche se faccio poi abbastanza la pendolare, perché ogni settimana passo almeno un paio di giorni in sede.
Interviewer	Il tuo lavoro in che cosa consiste?
Marina	Sono amministratore delegato, quindi diciamo che mi occupo un po' di tutti gli aspetti di gestione della società da un punto di vista strategico se vogliamo, cioè non entro negli aspetti operativi, non li gestisco direttamente. Mi occupo abbastanza intensamente di tutto quello che è lo sviluppo, cioè la ricerca di nuove posizioni, contatti con controparti che ci offrono queste posizioni, la verifica se sono adatte o meno all'insediamento di nuovi ristoranti, lo studio … purtroppo per trovare una posizione che vada bene per un Brek, ne dobbiamo vedere cinquanta per cui è un'attività che porta via molto tempo, anche perché sono posti cosparsi per tutt'Italia qualche volta anche all'estero ci propongono delle cose, quindi devo viaggiare, girare.

sviluppo a tappeto Marina is coining a phrase here. The expression **bombardamento a tappeto** means *carpet bombing*, What Marina means is development leading to dense coverage.

Io ho questo piccolo ufficio qui Marina was interviewed in Milan.

la pendolare *commuter*. Don't forget your guessing skills. What does a pendulum (**pendolo**) do? It moves back and forth on the same path …

Sono amministratore delegato It is not usual to form a feminine for *managing director*.

adatte o meno *suitable or not* (lit: *suitable or less suitable*.) **Meno** means *less*.

Marina Bastianello
Amministratore Delegato

20122 Milano
Via dell' Unione, 3
Tel. e Fax (02) 867466

Brek Ristoranti s.p.a.
30038 Spinea (Ve)
Via delle Industrie, 8
Tel. (041) 5496111
Fax (041) 5496176

Brek

Comprehension 1

1 How many restaurants are there in the chain?

2 Is this all the company runs?

3 In what ways does the company consider it offers something special?

4 What is the problem which Marina seems to consider very important in ensuring that the company is profitable?

5 What kind of rate of expansion does Marina reckon the company is able to maintain?

6 Does she seem worried about the company?

7 There are two main reasons why Marina has to travel a lot. What are they?

8 One aspect of the company's business above all takes a lot of her time. What is it?

Session 2

Vocabulary for business

Often the words for talking about business are guessable, the English words having Latin origins and therefore being similar to the Italian, since Italian is close to its Latin parentage. Sometimes, however, you will find Italians use English words for standard concepts in the business world, which were usually first mooted in USA. There was an example in what Marina said.

Activity 1

Pick out words relating to business and commerce in the text of Interview 1. Using your knowledge and guessing skills, make a list with translations. Then consult the Key at the back of the book. It will help you with any you couldn't manage.

Activity 2

Here is a list of expressions related to the world of work (**Il mondo del lavoro**). They are divided into two groups, *nouns* (**nomi**) and *verbs* (**verbi**). For each noun, find the corresponding verb and for each verb the noun. You could use a dictionary if you get stuck.

Example: **nome:** una società → verbo corrispondente: associarsi
verbo: gestire → nome corrispondente: la gestione

Nomi: il prodotto – l'allestimento – il costo – il livello – lo sviluppo – l'amministratore – la ricerca – l'insediamento
Verbi: garantire – fondare – istituire – prestare – espandersi – investire – verificare – valutare

Activity 3

In Interview 1 Marina uses some of the points we have looked at in previous units.

1 Find an example of **stare +** gerund, the present continuous. In fact Marina uses the same expression twice.
2 Find examples of the preposition **da:** (a) used after an indefinite, as described in Unit 4 (**qualcosa da mangiare**);
(b) used after an adjective and followed by an infinitive.
3 Pick out at least three words or expressions which you think are characteristic of spoken language, words used by Marina as she hesitates, thinks, etc. For instance, when you first met Marina in Unit 3 we pointed out her use of **diciamo**.

Expressing frequency

Notice this idiomatic use of **a:**

uno all'anno (ristorante)	*one (restaurant) a year*
cinque riunioni alla settimana	*five meetings a week*
una volta al giorno	*once a day*

Activity 4

How then would you say in Italian:

1 once a week
2 three times a day
3 twice a month?

Activity 5

Here is part of a feature from a magazine:

Conducete una vita sana? Siete in forma? Scopritelo rispondendo a queste domande! *Do you lead a healthy life? Are you fit? Find out by answering these questions!*

Quante volte alla settimana (o al mese) ...

1 ... vai a lavorare a piedi?
2 ... fai sport?
3 ... vai a dormire prima di mezzanotte?
4 ... mangi verdura fresca?
5 ... mangi frutta fresca?
6 ... vai a passeggiare?

More prepositions: a special use of fra/tra
You probably know **fra/tra** meaning *between*:

fra amici	*between friends*
fra Pisa e Firenze	*between Pisa and Florence*
tra la vita e la morte	*between life and death,* i.e. *dying*
tra mezzogiorno e l'una	*between 12 o'clock and one*

Notice this use of **fra/tra**:

apriremo il sedicesimo a Roma *we shall open the sixteenth in*
 fra **un paio di settimane** *Rome in a couple of week's time*

With an expression referring to an amount of time, **fra/tra** means *in ... (amount of time) 's time*. **Fra** is interchangeable with **tra**. The choice of one rather than the other depends on which sounds best, i.e. to avoid repeating **f** or **t**.

fra tre giorni	*in three days' time*
fra un mese	*in a month's time*
fra poco	*in a short time, shortly*

Activity 6

It's the beginning of the new working year. Marina has a meeting with her colleagues to inform them about the new commitments and dates. Look at the notes she has written in her diary before the meeting and complete what she says at the meeting.

---

10 gennaio 2010

Ore 10.00 – riunione

Date da ricordare:

- apertura sedicesimo ristorante Brek a Roma, 25 gennaio '04

- apertura primo ristorante Brek all'estero (Germania, Monaco), gennaio 2011

- sopralluogo locali Brek di Monaco e conferma definitiva dell'accordo, prima settimana febbraio '10

- inizio lavori di ampliamento Brek Vicenza, settembre '10

- inizio lavori di ristrutturazione Brek Torino, Carlo Felice, giugno '10

Example: **Tra un paio di settimane**, il 25 gennaio, apriremo a Roma il nostro sedicesimo ristorante.

1 .... apriremo il nostro primo ristorante all'estero, a Monaco, in Germania.
2 .... faremo un sopralluogo per i locali del Brek di Monaco. Se va tutto come stabilito confermeremo definitivamente l'accordo.
3 Per quanto riguarda lavori su ristoranti già esistenti, quelli di ampliamento del Brek di Vicenza saranno iniziati .... Invece i lavori di ristrutturazione del Brek Torino, quello in Piazza Carlo Felice, inizieranno ....

More prepositions: a/in used with places

Don't forget that the way *a* and *in* work with places is different from the English *in/to*. In English whether you mean going to the place or being there affects your choice of preposition:

a Londra
    to London/in London

in Italia
    to Italy/in Italy

In Italian what is relevant is whether the place is a *village/town/city* or a larger area such as an Italian *region* or a *country*. Use **a** with the name of a village, town or city, **in** with a larger area:

Vado a Venezia.
    I'm going/I go to Venice.

Sono a Venezia.
    I'm in Venice.

Vado in Toscana e poi in Francia.
    I'm going to Tuscany and then to France.

Abito in Toscana. Mio fratello abita in Francia.
    I live in Tuscany. My brother lives in France.

Activity 7

You have just had a lovely holiday, a cruise up the Po in northern Italy. You visited various interesting towns in the three regions you went through: Milano, Cremona, Mantova in Lombardia; Parma and Ferrara in Emilia Romagna; and Verona, Padova and Venezia in Veneto. Write a postcard to some Italian friends telling them where you went, using the information from the tour brochure over the page and using **a** and **in** correctly.

Giorno 1	Arrivo all'aeroporto di Venezia. Notte a bordo della motonave Venezia.
Giorno 2	Visita guidata di Venezia: Basilica di S. Marco, Piazza S. Marco e il Palazzo Ducale, il Canal Grande, il Ponte di Rialto. In serata possibilità di andare in gondola.
Giorno 3	Partenza per Murano e Burano e poi Chioggia; gita facoltativa a Padova: Basilica di S. Antonio (bronzi di Donatello) e Cappella degli Scrovegni (affreschi di Giotto).
Giorno 4	Comincia il viaggio sul Po. Escursione: Ferrara: Palazzo dei Diamanti e Castello Estense.
Giorno 5	Continua il viaggio sul Po. Escursioni: Mantova: Palazzo Ducale e Palazzo Te; Verona: Arena – con teatro lirico in serata.
Giorno 6	Continua il viaggio. Escursione: Parma: Duomo e Battistero.
Giorno 7	Arrivo: Cremona. Piazza del Comune, Duomo.
Giorno 8	Viaggio in treno: Milano. Visita della città, shopping. Notte in albergo.
Giorno 9	Partenza.

Expressions of approximate amounts

un paio	*a pair*
una decina	*about ten*
una dozzina	*a dozen, about 12*
una quindicina	*about fifteen*
una ventina	*about twenty*

The suffix **-ina** can be added to any of these round numbers: 20, 30, 40, 50, 60, 70, 80, 90. It means 'about that number' and it is more common with those up to and including 50.

Siamo a una quarantina di chilometri da Firenze.	*We are about forty kilometres from Florence.*

Compare **quarantina** (*about forty*) with **quarantena** (*quarantine*), which was originally 40 days. At 'a hundred', the suffix for expressing approximation changes:

un centinaio   about a hundred
un migliaio   about a thousand

The plural is irregular and feminine:

Centinaia di vespe hanno invaso   *Hundreds of wasps invaded the*
** il giardino.**   *garden.*
Migliaia di tifosi stanno arrivando *Thousands of fans are arriving*
** per la partita.**   *for the match.*

The noun **un paio** works the same way. How would you say: *two pairs of shoes?* **due paia di scarpe.**

Activity 8

In your office there are a couple of terrible gossips. All day they ask each other about other colleagues. And if they don't know the information requested, they have a guess. Below are some of the questions. Answer them as they do, using one of the approximate quantity words just studied and the information given in brackets.

Example: Quanti anni pensi che abbia Carla? (40)
          Non lo so ... credo **una quarantina** ...
1 Quanti anni pensi che abbia Marco? (30)
2 Quanti anni pensi che abbia Paola? (50)

Example: Quanti soldi pensi che guadagni Carla al mese?
          (2 milioni)
          Non ne sono sicuro/a ... forse un paio di milioni ...
3 Quanti soldi pensi che guadagni Marco all'anno? (30 milioni)
4 Quanti soldi pensi che guadagni il nostro capo al mese (10 milioni)

Example: Quanti giorni di ferie ha preso Paola quest'anno? (10)
          Mah ... mi sembra **una decina.**

5 Quanti giorni di ferie ha preso Marco quest'anno? (2)
6 Quanti giorni di ferie ha preso Carla quest'anno? (15)

Example: Quante volte hai chiesto a Carla di non fumare
in ufficio? (100)
Almeno un centinaio!

7 Quante volte hai chiesto al tuo capo di darti un permesso per
uscire prima il mercoledì? (1000)
8 Quante volte hai chiesto a Marco di non lasciare la porta del suo
ufficio aperta quando è al telefono con le sue amanti? (100)

Session 3

Relative pronouns ('who', 'which', etc.)

There are a number of examples in what Marina said. Relative
pronouns are used to join two clauses or phrases so as to tell you
more about the first. They are straightforward in Italian once you
understand them.

Che

It can refer to people or things and be the subject or object of the
clause which follows it, so that it can mean *who*, *whom*, *which* or
that. In other words, it's much easier in Italian!

**Marina è una persona che ama
mangiare bene.** (refers to a person,
Marina, and is subject of **ama**)

*Marina is someone who loves
to eat well.*

**La società, che possiede ora quindici
ristoranti self-service, cresce a un
ritmo costante.** (refers to a thing
and is subject of **possiede**)

*The company, which owns
fifteen self-service restaurants
now, is growing at a steady
rate.*

**Marina, che conosco molto bene,
abita a Milano.** (refers to a person,
object of **conosco**)

*Marina, who(m) I know very
well, lives in Milan.*

La società che lei gestisce è ben conosciuta in Veneto. (refers to a thing, object of **gestisce**)

The company (which/that) she manages is well known in the Veneto.

Note: the relative pronoun can sometimes be omitted in English. **Che** must be present in Italian.

Activity 9

Match each person in the list on the left with the description of his or her profession (list on the right). Make a sentence, using the relative pronoun **che** to connect the two halves.

Example: Il direttore d'orchestra/dirigere l'orchestra
　　　　　Il direttore d'orchestra <u>è la persona che</u> dirige
　　　　　l'orchestra.

Il cantante lirico	**amministrare l'azienda**
Lo scrittore	**giocare in una squadra di calcio**
L'amministratore delegato	**controllare i biglietti sul treno**
Il cuoco	**curare i denti dei suoi pazienti**
Il controllore	**cantare le opere liriche**
Il calciatore	**cucinare i pasti in un ristorante**
Il dentista	**scrivere libri**

Cui

Cui is used instead of **che** after a preposition. Marina says (of the difficulty of selecting sites for the company's restaurants):

per trovare una posizione ... ne dobbiamo vedere cinquanta, per cui è un'attività che porta via molto tempo

to find a place ... we have to see fifty, so it is a task which takes a lot of time.

In this case, **cui** does not refer to a specific word, more to the whole problem. **Per cui,** is in fact often used to mean *therefore, on* *account of which.* **Cui** can however refer to specific words, denoting people or things:

E' una persona <u>con cui</u> non mi sento a mio agio.	*He/she is a person with whom I don't feel at ease.*
La casa <u>in cui</u> abita quell'amico è nuova.	*The house that friend lives in is new. (the house in which that friend lives …)*
dei self-service <u>in cui</u> cerchiamo di dare di più…	*self-service restaurants in which we try to give more …*

You can use **dove**, as Marina does, instead of **in cui**. If the preposition is **a** it can be omitted, although this is perhaps more usual in written than spoken Italian:

La signora cui ho parlato del Suo progetto era molto entusiasta.	*The lady I spoke to (to whom I spoke) about your plan was very enthusiastic.*

Activity 10

Marina, a busy woman, often gives her secretary detailed instructions to do what she will not have time to do herself. Read the instructions and transform them into a single sentence, using the relative pronoun **cui**, preceded by a preposition; in one case you can omit the preposition. Note: she uses **tu** to her secretary.

Example: Telefona all'Ingegner Rossi. Devo prendere un appuntamento **con lui** entro la fine della settimana.
Telefona all'Ingegner Rossi **con cui** devo prendere un appuntamento entro la fine della settimana.

1 Manda un fax alla Dottoressa Paolini. Devo sapere **da lei** se i lavori procedono regolarmente a Torino.
2 Telefona all'Avvocato Franceschi. Devo discutere **con lui** riguardo al nuovo contratto per il Brek di Monaco.
3 Scrivi una lettera di sollecito al Ragionier Barbato. Devo ricevere **da lui** i preventivi per i lavori al Brek di Vicenza entro la fine del mese.

4 Telefona all'Architetto Cappelli. Devo restituir**gli** i disegni e i progetti per il Brek di Roma con le correzioni al più presto.

Il cui, la cui, i cui, le cui

All these mean *whose* and the article should be that of the person or thing possessed:

Il mio amico Paolo, <u>il cui</u>
  padre è un noto scultore, mi ha
  invitato ad una mostra.
Il viaggiatore, <u>la cui</u> valigia è
  stata smarrita dalla compagnia
  aerea, era furibondo.

*My friend Paul, whose father is
  a well-known sculptor, invited
  me to an exhibition.*
*The traveller whose suitcase
  was mislaid by the airline was
  furious.*

Il quale, la quale, i quali, le quali

These can replace **che** or **cui** and are useful in particular to avoid ambiguity, since they show gender. Sometimes a speaker or writer will use them simply to avoid repetition of **che**.

La sorella del mio amico, <u>la quale</u>
  studia a New York, ci ha ospitati
  nel suo appartamento. (**la** shows it
  is the sister, not the friend, who is
  studying in New York.)

*My friend's sister, who is
  studying in New York, put us
  up in her apartment.*

Chi

What you need to remember, especially if you have studied French, is that **chi** is not commonly used as a relative pronoun. It is an interrogative pronoun, meaning *who?* As a relative pronoun it has very specific uses:

a Chi … chi … = *some … others …*

Chi ballava, chi cantava, chi
  stava a guardare …
Chi dice una cosa, chi un'altra.

*Some were dancing, some
  singing, others watching …*
Some say one thing, others another.

b To convey the idea *he who*, *she who*, *people who* as in sayings like:

Chi mai semina, mai raccoglie.
He who doesn't sow, doesn't reap. (You've got to put something in to get something out!)

Chi dorme non piglia pesci.
He who sleeps doesn't catch any fish. (Keep alert if you want results)

Also in ordinary speech:

Può venire chi vuole.
Anyone who wants to can come.

Activity 11

Here is a series of Italian proverbs and sayings. They have been split into two and the right-hand list is not in the correct order. Try matching them. Can you guess at the English equivalent?

Example: **Chi dorme non piglia pesci.**
He who sleeps doesn't catch any fish.

Chi dorme...	... la vince.
Chi tardi arriva ...	... raccoglie tempesta.
Chi va all'osto ...	... male alloggia.
Chi va piano ...	... l'aspetti.
Chi la fa ...	... non piglia pesci.
Chi va al mulino ...	... di spada perisce.
Chi semina vento ...	... s'infarina.
Chi la dura ...	... va sano e va lontano.
Chi di spada ferisce ...	... perde il posto.

Quello che, ciò che, quelli/quelle che

Quello che, ciò che both mean *what*, in the sense of *that which*. **Tutto quello che** means *everything that (all that which)*. The first two examples are from Marina's description of her work.

... nella qualità del prodotto, <u>quello che</u> prepariamo da mangiare.	... in the quality of the product, what we prepare to eat (the food we prepare).
Mi occupo di tutto quello che è lo sviluppo.	I deal with everything related to development (all that is related to ...)
Non capisco quello che dice.	I don't understand what he says.
Quello che mi preoccupa è la sua impetuosità.	What worries me is his/her impetuousness.

Quello che can also refer to a person (*the one who*). The plural is **quelli che, quelle che, tutti quelli che.**

Gianni è quello che indossa una maglia rossa.	Gianni is the one wearing a red sweater.
Tra i nostri clienti, quelli che non pagano puntualmente sono in genere i più benestanti.	Among our customers, those who (the people who ...) don't pay punctually are generally the most comfortably off.

Activity 12

Look at this photo. Say who's who, following the example.

Example: **Quello che indossa la giacca a quadri è mio fratello, Claudio.**

1 (Anna – sorella)
2 (la mamma)
3 (papà)
4 (Fausto – cugino)
5 (Antonio – il ragazzo di Anna)

Activity 13

Choose the correct relative pronoun from those explained above to complete the following sentences.

Example: Amo le donne interessanti, **quelle che** non trovi nelle sale da ballo.

1 Mah, io potrei dire .... dico di solito ai miei studenti.

2 Se sentivo qualcuno .... parlava inglese tentavo di attaccare discorso.

3 Mamma non ha mai imparato bene l'italiano per .... la prendevamo in giro.

4 Ho un nipotino .... vedo pochissimo.

5 Ho avuto i problemi nella vita .... tutti hanno avuto.

6 Silvia è molto seria, molto ligia al dovere, ... deve fare, lo fa.

7 Barbara capisce più tante cose lei che non Silvia. .... abbiamo sempre attribuito doti (di intuito).

8 Gli stipendi vanno pagati a .... lavora.

9 Non c'entra assolutamente niente con .... avevo fatto prima.

10 Contrariamente a .... si può pensare una gran parte (degli esami) erano teorici.

11 Armando Piazza, custode del Club Med, era entrato nella torre bianca .... ha sede il Club.

12 Tajeddine Abdel Karim, ... ha appena compiuto 18 anni, ha lasciato la madre per venire a trovare il padre.

sia ... sia ... *both ... and ...*
Marina says:

cerchiamo di dare di più **sia** nella qualità del prodotto, di quello che prepariamo da mangiare, **sia** nell'allestimento, nell'arredo dei ristoranti.

sia ... sia ... *both ... and ...*
You can also say: **e ... e ...**

Either ... or ... is **o ... o ...**
Neither ... nor ... is **né ... né ...**

This is another case of English and Italian working differently. In Italian you have the same word for both parts, in English, two different words. You can however use **che** as the second word if the first is **sia**.

Activity 14

Marina is constantly on the lookout for suitable places to open a new Brek. Imagine a meeting with the local council officers in a place which Marina considers suitable. Marina describes and promotes the hallmark characteristics of the restaurants in the Brek chain. Using the information given, construct sentences using **sia ... sia ...** correctly.

Example: **self-service/locali di altro tipo** (gestire)
> **Il nostro gruppo gestisce sia self-service sia locali di altro tipo.**

1 cibo di ottima qualità/ambiente elegante (garantire)
2 servizio veloce/salette da pranzo tranquille e silenziose (offrire)
3 costi di gestione alti/investimenti alti (avere)
4 nel Nord Italia/nel Centro-Sud (volere espandersi)

Activity 15

Re-read or listen again to what Marina said. Then close your book and try to summarize it in Italian using your own words. Here are some questions to guide you:

1 Qual è l'attività principale della società Brek?
2 Quanti ristoranti ci sono?
3 Che tipo di ristoranti sono?
4 Che cosa cercano di offrire?
5 Perché è importante garantire un certo livello di attività in un ristorante Brek?
6 In quale città è stato aperto il primo ristorante?
7 Perché Marina fa la pendolare tra Milano e la zona di Venezia?
8 Di che cosa si occupa soprattutto lei?
9 Perché porta via molto tempo la ricerca di posizioni adatte ad un ristorante Brek?

Session 4

Interview 2

The Italians were the first bankers. Emanuela, whom you met in Unit 2, is a branch manager in a small private bank (i.e. neither publicly owned nor quoted on the Milan Stock Exchange). We expected to find her rather pleased to have been made a manager.

Emanuela	Io lavoro in una banca, una banca privata, e attualmente dirigo una piccola agenzia. Molto piccola, siamo solo cinque elementi. Sono molto stanca, pagata poco e …
Interviewer	Dunque non sei molto contenta in questo momento?

◆ CD2, TR 1

Emanuela	No, non sono molto contenta perché non ho uno stipendio adeguato alla mia qualifica e quindi sto aspettando che loro decidano di cambiare il livello della mia posizione quindi di darmi lo stipendio giusto che è previsto per la legge. Sto aspettando da un anno.
Interviewer	Questo è perché sei una donna?
Emanuela	No, non è questo. Ci sono anche altri tre ragazzi che hanno lo stesso problema ... Sono maschi, sono l'unica, diciamo, l'unica ... be' ragazza, ormai non posso più dire ... visto che ho trentacinque anni mercoledì prossimo ... ma l'unica donna che nella nostra banca, a parte una signora molto più vecchia che ha una qualifica di alto livello .... gli altri che hanno la mia funzione sono tutti maschi. Anche loro purtroppo – sono tre ragazzi che hanno il mio stesso problema, fanno lo stesso tipo di lavoro, stesso tipo di impegno, lo stesso tipo di responsabilità, però lo stipendio non è quello previsto correttamente per la legge.
Interviewer	Ma sono molte le donne direttori di banca in Italia?
Emanuela	Qualcuna c'è. Io ne conosco diverse. Cassa di Risparmio, San Paolo, ne vedo diverse, ce ne sono abbastanza. Non credo (che)* sia una, ci sia una discriminazione ... Ammesso che si abbia il tempo e la voglia di dedicare di più dell'orario normale, previsto, per il lavoro. Però non credo ci siano problemi di ... forse più per i clienti ... magari vengono, trovano una donna giovane, è una cosa che non tutti apprezzano. Magari pensano sia necessario avere più il fisico del ruolo, no? Vecchiotto, capelli grigi, uomo. Questa è una cosa che disorienta un po' il cliente, trovo. Vengono, mi chiedono: 'Dov'è il direttore?' 'Mi dica!' 'No, volevo parlare con il direttore.' (ride) È un po'... però...

*Emanuela didn't say 'che'; it was added by the actress.

lo stipendio giusto previsto per la legge *the correct salary as laid down by law.* This may in fact be a trades union agreement (**un accordo sindacale**).

Cassa di Risparmio, San Paolo These are the names of banks.

Mi dica Lit. *Tell me!* The standard expression to indicate to a customer that a shop assistant, bank clerk etc. is ready to attend to his/her needs. The familiar (**tu**) form of this is: **dimmi!**

Insight

The pronoun **ne** *of it/of them* is used when talking about quantity. Emanuela talks about female bank managers and says **ne conosco diverse** *I know several (of them)*. She goes on to say: **ne vedo diverse** *I see several (of them)*, **ce ne sono abbastanza** *there are a fair number (of them)*. Note the position of **ne** <u>before</u> the verb, like all object pronouns. See a different use of **ne** in Activity 20 **Che cosa ne pensano i clienti?** *What do clients think about it?*

Comprehension 2

1 How many staff are there in the branch of the bank which Emanuela manages?

2 Emanuela is not happy. Why?

3 Is she the only woman manager in the small private bank she works for?

4 Does she feel there is sex discrimination (a) in the matter of her salary? (b) in the appointment of women bank managers generally?

5 What problem does she think a woman manager poses to the bank customers?

Session 5

False friends again

Add these to your collection:

attualmente *at the present time, at this moment, nowadays*
attualità *current events*
attuale *present, contemporary, current. (actual:* **reale, vero, effettivo;** *actually:* **di fatto, in verità, effettivamente, in effetti;** *actuality:* **realtà, verità, condizioni reali)**
stipendio *salary.* The Italian word doesn't have the limited use of *stipend* in English. But, once again, the link makes it guessable. Note: **salario** *wages,* i.e. the pay of manual workers.

Activity 16

Below is a summary of Emanuela's interview. Read it and think hard about its meaning. We want you to translate it into English and to think particularly about the translation of the words in bold type.

Tra il dire e il fare c'è di mezzo il mare
(Lit: *between saying and doing lies the ocean*)

1 Emanuela lavora in banca. Ha una posizione di una certa responsabilità, e si aspetterebbe di ricevere uno stipendio piuttosto alto. **In realtà** il suo stipendio è abbastanza basso.
2 Il motivo di questo stato di cose è che è stata solo recentemente promossa di livello, per cui **attualmente** non viene ancora pagata secondo quanto prescrive la legge. In futuro, però, verrà pagata di più.
3 Per quanto riguarda la sua credibilità, come donna, di fronte ai clienti uomini, Emanuela pensa che la condizione **attuale** delle donne lavoratrici in Italia sia migliore che nel passato, e non si ritiene discriminata.
4 Tuttavia, nonostante Emanuela sia ottimista a questo riguardo, la discriminazione sessuale sui posti di lavoro **in effetti** è un problema

vivo. Del resto, lei stessa dice che molti uomini che arrivano nella sua banca si stupiscono di trovare un direttore donna.

The present subjunctive

Earlier in this unit we met: **sia ... sia**, meaning *both ... and*. So what is meant when Emanuela says:

Non credo sia **una ... ci** sia **una discriminazione ...**

Sia here is clearly a verb: Emanuela in fact corrects herself to add **ci**. You might have expected, if you think about it, that she would use **c'è**. But she says: **non credo ci sia una discriminazione**. She uses the subjunctive. You can probably guess that the verb is **essere** and this is the present subjunctive. Why does she use it? What is this subjunctive which strikes fear into the heart of many a language learner? First let us say it should not do that! Like any part of the language, it needs to be studied, Italians need to be listened to and imitated, and gradually the learner will find it becomes a part of his/her Italian.

General remarks about the subjunctive

When analysing Italian verbs grammarians divide them into *moods*, **modi** in Italian. The subjunctive is a mood, as is the indicative (see **Grammar – the technical jargon explained**). As a general rule, the subjunctive is associated with subjectivity, point of view, not being categorical. The indicative is factual, the subjunctive deals with areas of doubt, possibility, uncertainty. The third mood, the conditional, deals with the hypothetical. The term mood as applied to the subjunctive may help you to remember it is related to feelings, uncertainties. The term *mode* might be more suitable, as it is perhaps more a question of *point of view*, the way the action is viewed. We should add that it is often said that the use of the subjunctive is diminishing. Maybe, but it is still widely used and not just by highly educated people. It still needs to be learned by the foreign student who aspires to a good command of Italian.

The subjunctive mood has four tenses: present, imperfect, perfect and pluperfect. It is not in itself a tense. For the moment we will stay with the present subjunctive, which is what Emanuela uses in the sentence we picked out. Emanuela says she doesn't think there is discrimination against women on the banks' part. She does not want to be categorical, it is her opinion. And the subjunctive brings that home.

The uses of the subjunctive

The most satisfactory way to approach the uses of the subjunctive is to consider them as you meet them, although we have put a reference list in the **Reference grammar** at the back of the book for you to consult when you need. For the moment we will draw your attention to the uses in the texts in *Perfect your Italian* as we meet them.

We must first be clear: the subjunctive is not normally used in main clauses. It is almost always used in a subordinate clause, that is a clause which doesn't stand by itself, but is introduced by something in the main part of the sentence. For instance in the sentence we have already looked at, the main clause is **Non credo**, and **credo** leads us into a subordinate clause. In almost all cases the subordinate clause starts with **che**. Emanuela happens to use two verbs (**credere, pensare**) which can be used without **che**, although other speakers use **che**; it's a matter of personal style. Let's look at more examples of the subjunctive in what Emanuela says, and a couple in what Marina says.

Emanuela:
<u>sto aspettando che loro decidano</u> di cambiare il livello della mia posizione.
I am waiting for them to make up their minds to change the level of my post.
<u>Ammesso che si abbia</u> il tempo e la voglia ...
Given that one has the time and the desire to ...
Però non <u>credo</u> ci <u>siano</u> problemi di ...
However, I don't believe there are problems of ...
Magari <u>pensano sia</u> necessario avere più il fisico del ruolo.
Perhaps they think it is necessary to have more the physical appearance for the role.

Marina:
Non è <u>una formula che si presti</u> a uno sviluppo a tappeto.
It's not a formula which lends itself to carpet development.

per trovare <u>una posizione che vada</u> bene per un Brek …
to find a location suitable for a Brek …

The subjunctive for opinions and beliefs

Of the examples we have, three involve verbs meaning thinking,
believing. When you say you think something is – or isn't – the
case or that you believe something is true or otherwise, you are
expressing an opinion, not offering the thought as fact. Doubt,
uncertainty, avoiding being categorical – all cases for the subjunctive.
So it will be associated with verbs such as **pensare, credere, dubitare**
(*to doubt*), **sperare** (*to hope*), **temere** (*to fear*), **avere paura** (*to fear, be
afraid*) etc. and expressions with similar meanings.

The subjunctive in clauses describing a type or category

per trovare <u>una posizione che vada</u> bene per un Brek.
to find a position suitable for a Brek.

Non è <u>una formula che si presti</u> a uno sviluppo a tappeto
It isn't a formula which lends itself to blanket development.

To go back to Marina's words, what sort of **posizione** is so
difficult to find? Not a healthy one, not a quiet one, but one
which is a good one for a Brek. The phrase **che vada bene per un
Brek** describes the location just in the same way as the adjectives
'*healthy*' or '*quiet*' might. This is why grammarians call this an
'adjectival phrase or clause'. It is describing a type of, rather than a
specific, location; '**una posizione**' rather than '**la posizione**'.

Grammarians call the word (**una posizione**) that the relative
pronoun (**che**) refers to 'the antecedent'.

antecedent   *relative pronoun*
posizione   che

When the antecedent does not refer to a specific person or thing,
they call it an 'indefinite antecedent'. Such expressions tend to occur
after verbs related to looking for, wanting, needing, etc. And they are
followed by a subjunctive. The second example from Marina is similar.

Look at two sentences and try to sense the difference:

Leggo un romanzo che stimola la curiosità.   *I'm reading a novel which stimulates curiosity.*

Cerco un romanzo che stimuli la curiosità.   *I'm looking for a novel which stimulates curiosity.*

(NB The translation here and below is word for word rather than the best possible.)

In the first sentence the words following **che** describe a specific novel and the quality it is known to have. In the second sentence the words after **che** describe the type of novel I am looking for. But I don't know whether or not there is one such available. Try two more:

Vado da uno psicologo che mi dà fiducia.   *I go to a psychologist whom I can trust.* (A fact. I am happy with my psychologist.)

Cerco uno psicologo che mi dia fiducia.   *I'm looking for a psychologist whom I can trust.* (This is the sort of psychologist I am hoping to find.)

And these. The first comes from the speech made by a new Prime Minister to Parliament when seeking its acceptance of the government he had just formed:

In una fase successiva è maturato l'accordo che consente oggi al Governo di presentarsi davanti alle Camere.   *In a subsequent phase the agreement which allows the Government to present itself to the (two) Chambers came into being.*

And here is what he might have said earlier, in the period in which he was canvassing support from various parties as he tried to form the government:

Ci vuole un accordo che consenta al Governo di presentarsi davanti alle Camere.   *We need an agreement which will allow the Government to present itself to the Chambers.*

In our experience the subjunctive in adjectival clauses is fairly common, but grammar books often leave it to last and skate over it when presenting the subjunctive, possibly because, as you will agree, it is not easy to explain!

Other cases

In our collection of examples we had two other types. For the moment we will just say that certain other categories of verb are followed by the subjunctive (e.g. **aspettare che**) and also that certain conjunctions are followed by the subjunctive (e.g. **ammesso che**).

Language learning tip

It is helpful to collect examples of the subjunctive. This is also true for other points you particularly want to remember. But it seems to us particularly useful with the subjunctive, which ultimately you will develop a feel for. Noting examples, thinking about them, going over them when you are revising, can help develop that feel. We recommend it.

Session 6

The form of the present subjunctive

All this is very well, you are probably saying, but how about the form of the subjunctive? Analyzing the use of the subjunctive may be tricky. Happily, forming it is not. Verbs divide into two types: (a) Group 1 verbs (-**are** type) (b) All other verbs.

	Group 1	Group 2	Group 3	Group 4
	parl**are**	decid**ere**	cap**ire**	part**ire**
io	parl**i**	decid**a**	capisc**a**	part**a**
tu	parl**i**	decid**a**	capisc**a**	part**a**
lui/lei	parl**i**	decid**a**	capisc**a**	part**a**
noi	parl**iamo**	decid**iamo**	cap**iamo**	part**iamo**
voi	parl**iate**	decid**iate**	cap**iate**	part**iate**
loro	parl**ino**	decid**ano**	capisc**ano**	part**ano**

As in the present indicative, the stress in the third person plural is on the same syllable as in the first person singular: **p<u>a</u>rlino, dec<u>i</u>dano, cap<u>i</u>scano, p<u>a</u>rtano**. Note also that verbs like **capire** have **-isc-** inserted where they would have it in the present indicative.

Activity 17

Study the tables and answer the following:

1 Why did we say verbs divide into two types in the present subjunctive? What is the characteristic of each type?
2 Which form is identical to the present indicative (the usual present you already know)?
3 Why do you think it is fairly common to use a subject pronoun with the singular forms of the present subjunctive?
4 Which forms have the same ending in both groups?

Irregular verbs

A number of verbs are irregular. Among the common ones are:

essere	avere	andare	dare	dire	fare	venire
sia	abbia	vada	dia	dica	faccia	venga
sia	abbia	vada	dia	dica	faccia	venga
sia	abbia	vada	dia	dica	faccia	venga
siamo	abbiamo	andiamo	diamo	diciamo	facciamo	veniamo
siate	abbiate	andiate	diate	diciate	facciate	veniate
s<u>i</u>ano	<u>a</u>bbiano	v<u>a</u>dano	d<u>i</u>ano	d<u>i</u>cano	f<u>a</u>cciano	v<u>e</u>ngano

(Underlining indicates stress.)

Notice the endings are the same for all irregular verbs and as we said are like Groups 2 and 3 verbs. This means if you are given the first person singular present subjunctive of an irregular verb, you should be able to work out the other persons. Try it (Activity 18).

It is also the case that for many irregular verbs the first person singular of the indicative has the same root as the subjunctive. Unfortunately it doesn't always work but it may be helpful to try this. For instance in the group above it is true for **andare, dire, fare** and **venire**.

Activity 18

Here are the infinitives of some irregular verbs and the first person singular, present subjunctive. Write out the complete form of the present subjunctive for each:

potere **possa**; sapere **sappia**; tenere **tenga**; volere **voglia**; uscire **esca**; dovere **debba**; produrre **produca**; piacere **piaccia**.

Note: verbs such as **uscire** and **dovere,** which have a vowel change in the present indicative, have a similar vowel change in the present subjunctive. Similarly verbs with soft **c, g, sc,** before any **i** in the endings of the present indicative (**tu, noi** endings) have the same sound change in the present subjunctive where the ending starts in **i**. **Piacere** is of course mostly used in the third persons, singular and plural, but the other forms exist and can be used: **Non credo che tu piaccia ai miei genitori.**

Activity 19

Study the following sentences and decide whether the verb should be indicative or subjunctive; then choose that form for the verb indicated.

1 Pensi che (essere) vero?
2 Sono certo che (essere) falso.
3 Marta è una persona che (dimostrare) sempre molta pazienza.
4 Ci vuole una persona che (avere) molta pazienza.
5 Non credo che il pranzo (essere) pronto.
6 So che il pranzo non (essere) pronto.
7 Credo che il direttore (avere) torto.

8 Il direttore è una persona che (dire) sempre quello che pensa.

9 La società ha bisogno di personale che (fare) il lavoro con entusiasmo e professionalità.

10 Mauro pensa che il direttore (volere) cambiare il sistema.

Activity 20

Che cosa ne pensano i clienti? *What do the customers think?*
On the one hand, Emanuela says there is no discrimination in her workplace. On the other hand, she tell us how some male customers are sometimes not entirely pleased to find the bank manager is a woman. Write down the thoughts of one male customer after he has met Emanuela, using the information given below and deciding whether to use the present subjunctive or the present indicative. You are practising using the subjunctive after certain verbs.

Example: **Penso/una donna (essere) in gamba come un uomo.**
Penso che una donna sia in gamba come un uomo.

1 Mi hanno detto/questa direttrice (avere) sufficiente preparazione ed esperienza.

2 Credo/le donne (essere) intelligenti e affidabili come gli uomini.

3 Però so anche/ad alti livelli le donne (non ricevere) rispetto e attenzione.

4 Ho paura/una donna (non avere) abbastanza autorità quando deve difendere gli interessi dei suoi clienti.

5 Spero/(non essere) vero, ma temo/un direttore donna (non garantire) i miei investimenti come un direttore uomo.

Activity 21

Complete the following sentences choosing whether to use the present subjunctive or the present indicative. You are practising using subjunctives to describe a type or category.

Examples: **Lavoro in una banca che (essere) è molto piccola.**
(Not a type – it's the one I work in)
**Sto cercando un posto di lavoro in una banca
che non (essere) sia troppo piccola.** (That is the
type of bank I want to work in).

1 Attualmente, ho uno stipendio che non (essere) ....
adeguato alle mie responsabilità.

2 Voglio uno stipendio che (essere) .... adeguato alle
mie responsabilità.

3 Molti clienti uomini vogliono un direttore che (sapere)
.... difendere i loro interessi ad alti livelli, e pensano
che una donna non sia adatta a questo compito.

4 Molte banche, tuttavia, hanno un direttore donna che (sapere)
.... svolgere il proprio lavoro professionalmente proprio
come un direttore uomo.

5 È necessario un nuovo contratto di lavoro che (garantire)
.... agli impiegati di banca lo stipendio adeguato al
loro livello.

6 Al momento, abbiamo un contratto che (non garantire)
.... agli impiegati uno stipendio adeguato.

Activity 22

You're chatting to a colleague and you discover that your ideas on
your working conditions differ. Answer each of his/her remarks
as shown in the example, using the correct form of the present
subjunctive.

Example: **Il Suo collega**   **La pausa pranzo è troppo corta!**
         Lei   **(essere abbastanza lunga) Non sono
                      d'accordo! <u>Penso che</u> la pausa pranzo
                      sia abbastanza lunga.**

1 Il Suo collega   **Nel nostro ufficio l'aria condizionata non
                    funziona: fa freddo in inverno e caldo in estate!**
         Lei   **(funzionare benissimo; fare caldo in inverno;
                    essere fresco in estate)**

2 Il Suo collega   Il nostro direttore non dà mai ascolto alle nostre richieste!

     Lei   (dare sempre ascolto; fare attenzione ai problemi di tutti)

Insight

The 3rd person of the verb **dare** is written with an accent, **dà** *gives*, to distinguish it from the preposition **da** *from*. The pronunciation is the same.

3 Il Suo collega   I colleghi più giovani non sanno fare il loro lavoro e vengono sempre a chiederci aiuto perché non hanno voglia di fare niente!

     Lei   (saper fare il loro lavoro; venire a chiedere aiuto per imparare)

4 Il Suo collega   Il personale che fa le pulizie deve lavorare di più: escono troppo presto la sera e arrivano troppo tardi la mattina!

     Lei   (non dovere lavorare di più; tenere gli uffici molto puliti; uscire all'ora prevista dal loro contratto di lavoro)

Session 7

Interview 3

Felicità Torrielli is an example of an entrepreneur, **un imprenditore,** *running a small business. Italy tends to produce energetic entrepreneurs and small businesses. Signora Torrielli created her own business 25 years ago and makes ready-to-wear garments for some well known designer labels, including Valentino and Ungaro. Here she answers a question about the aims of her firm.*

Signora Torrielli	Lo scopo, quando uno fa un'azienda, è quello di creare della produttività e quindi dei posti di lavoro. Io ho cominciato con un'unica dipendente, nel secondo mese siamo diventate due e nell'arco di dieci anni siamo diventati 20 e attualmente siamo al venticinquesimo anno e siamo 30.
Interviewer	Mi racconti come ha cominciato?
Signora Torrielli	Io volevo separarmi da mio marito, e non avevo nessun tipo di mestiere in mano, la cosa che mi piaceva di più fare era cucire i vestiti. Allora sono andata in una scuola di taglio e di cucito e ho detto alla direttrice che avrei seguito i suoi corsi ma non come le altre ragazze, perché io, che ero giovane, ma non ero più una ragazza, non volevo nessun tipo di diploma, avrei seguito i suoi corsi, ma a modo mio; cioè io entravo in una lezione, se lì insegnavano a tagliare una gonna, io appena avevo capito come si taglia una gonna, non avrei proseguito per settimane a fare gonne, sarei passata all'altra aula dove insegnavano a fare giacche o pantaloni, così, perché io volevo una infarinatura. Fatto questo tipo di scuola, ho assunto un maestro di taglio, ho comprato dei tessuti e ho cominciato a fare dei modelli. Poi ho fatto delle telefonate, ho detto alle mie amiche che io avevo aperto, allora si chiamava una sartoria, avevo aperto una sartoria e io ho cominciato.

Subito dopo però ho capito che questa cosa non mi piaceva come tipo di lavoro perché era troppo personale, non era una cosa che mi dava soddisfazione, a fare un vestito, ho capito che mi piaceva la produzione. Allora mi sono affittata un piccolissimo laboratorio, ho messo dentro due persone di cui una era una tagliatrice, c'è ancora, la prima persona c'è ancora, e ho cominciato a fare dei piccoli modelli che sono andata a vendere nei negozi e di lì ho cominciato. |

	Abbiamo avuto una crescita abbastanza limitata, se vogliamo, perché il campo della moda è così tanto cambiato in questi anni che la nicchia che noi c'eravamo riservata, che era quella di fare del pronto ad alto livello, è andata esaurendosi.
Interviewer	Come mai?
Signora	Perché le grandi firme, trovando difficoltà a vendere ai
Torrielli	loro prezzi alti, tutti quanti hanno fatto delle seconde linee, che si avvicinavano molto al nostro prodotto. Noi facevamo la nostra linea, che aveva praticamente i loro costi ma non poteva uscire ai loro costi perché non aveva il nome né il marchio. Quindi la nostra nicchia nel mercato è andata esaurendosi, perché fra comprare una giacca mia che costa 300.000 lire e comprarne una di Valentino che ne costa 420, beh, la gente, a questo punto, preferisce prendere quella firmata anziché quell'altra che ha forse il tessuto più bello, forse … Allora la nostra azienda si è cambiata e, anziché produrre una linea propria, è diventata un, come si chiama, un terzista e noi lavoriamo solo per le grandi firme che sono Valentino, Ungaro, Mila Schön, adesso.

lo scopo Another 'false friend' for your collection. It means *aim*.
posti di lavoro *jobs*
un/una dipendente *an employee*
nell'arco di dieci anni *over a period of ten years*
a modo mio *in my own way*
una infarinatura literally *a light dusting of flour* (**farina**). Signora Torrielli really wanted to be sure she had sufficient understanding of each process to be able to manage others doing it.
assunto irregular past participle of **assumere** (Unit 3 – Mario uses **assumere**)
nicchia *niche*
il pronto *ready-to-wear*; more usually Italians use the French expression **prêt-à-porter**.
marchio *brand-name*, or simply *name* in this context

le grandi firme big lit. *signatures* (**firmare** *to sign*, **una firma** *a signature*) but in this context, *designer labels*. Yet another 'false friend'.

tutti quanti *all of them, the lot of them*

300.000 lire ... 420 This interview was done before the introduction of the Euro in 2002.

Insight

Come mai? an informal way of saying *Why?* Its English equivalent could be *How come?*

Comprehension 3

1 How many years has Signora Torrielli been in business and how many people does she employ?

2 Why did she choose to set up this particular kind of business rather than one in another field?

3 What was untypical of her as a student in the dressmaking school she attended?

4 How did she launch her dressmaking business?

5 What did she very quickly realize?

6 Signora Torrielli started production of clothes (as opposed to dress-making) with two employees. What is she rather proud of?

7 Business hasn't been plain sailing for Signora Torrielli. In what way has her firm had to adapt to market conditions?

Session 8

Activity 23

Look at the interview with Signora Torrielli in Session 7.

1 Can you pick out any examples of the gerund, the form ending in **-ando** or **-endo**?

2 Can you find a past participle which seems not to have **avere/essere** with it?

3 Look also for any examples of the pluperfect (imperfect of **avere/essere** + past participle).
4 You should be able to find what looks like the conditional (see Unit 1) but with a past participle. Can you?

Gerund with andare

Firstly, when an object or reflexive pronoun is used with the gerund, it tacks on to the end, hence the **si** attached to **esaurendo** (**si è andata esaurendo** is also permissible). The use of **la nostra nicchia ... è andata esaurendosi** underlines that it was a gradual process: *our niche gradually disappeared.*

You remember **stare** + gerund to form the present continuous and the past continuous (Unit 4). You can also use **andare** with a gerund, to convey the idea of repeated action:

andare facendo, dicendo, scrivendo ...	*to be continually doing, saying, writing ...*

Activity 24

Every day Signora Torrielli has to face a series of problems. Here are some of the problems. Express each in a single sentence using **stare/andare** + gerund.

Example: **le tasse/aumentare**
   Le tasse <u>stanno aumentando</u>/Le tasse <u>vanno aumentando</u>.
   Taxes are going up.

1 Le stoffe/rincarare.
2 La concorrenza/crescere.
3 Il mercato/saturarsi.
4 Il campo della moda/cambiare.
5 La produzione/rallentare.
6 Le grandi firme/invadere il mercato del prêt-à-porter.
7 I guadagni/diminuire.
8 La situazione/peggiorare.

Past participles without an auxiliary verb

Fatto questo tipo di scuola ...

> *Having attended this type of school ...*

Finita la cena, la famiglia si è riunita attorno alla TV per la partita.

> *Having finished supper/supper being finished/when supper was finished, the family gathered round the TV for the match.*

The past participle is used as a neat way to join up the account of two past actions rather than say: I did this and then I did that. It is a stylistic device. Notice the participle behaves like an adjective, agreeing with the noun. (Those who know Latin will realize this derives from the ablative absolute.)

Notice also how Emanuela said:

Visto che ho trentacinque anni mercoledì prossimo ...

> *Seeing that I am thirty-five next Wednesday ...*

Ammesso che si abbia il tempo e la voglia ...

> *Given that one has the time and the desire to ....*

Here the past participle links with **che** and becomes a conjunction.

Activity 25

Read the following instructions for making a skirt. Change them using the past participle as in the example and then link with the next instruction.

Example: **Scegli una stoffa** che ti piaccia e che sia adatta al tipo di gonna che vuoi tagliare.
Una volta scelta la stoffa, prendi le tue misure.

1 Disegna il modello della gonna su carta, facendo attenzione a seguire le misure che hai preso. Una volta ...

2 Riporta il modello su stoffa, seguendo con più precisione possibile il disegno su carta. Una volta ...

3 Taglia la stoffa, lasciando almeno due centimetri di margine per le cuciture. Una volta …

4 Cuci la gonna a mano, usando il filo per imbastire: comincia dalla gonna vera e propria, per poi passare alla cintura e alla cerniera. Una volta …

5 Indossa la gonna per controllare che vada bene. Una volta …

6 Cuci la gonna a macchina. Una volta …

7 Stira la gonna.

Insight

All instructions in Activity 25 are given in the familiar form (**tu**) of the imperative. To give the instructions in the formal imperative simply swap the endings **i** and **a** (**scelga, disegni, riporti, tagli, cucia, indossi, stiri**).

Revision of the pluperfect

ho detto alle mie amiche che <u>avevo aperto</u> una sartoria.   *…I told my friends that I had opened a dressmaker's business.*

A straightforward use of the pluperfect, as you have seen in Unit 4 Session 7.

The conditional perfect in reported speech

This is another case where English and Italian differ. The use of the conditional with a past participle forms another tense, called the **conditional perfect**. Its name matters little. It is the use which matters: Signora Torrielli reported to us what she said to the principal of the dressmaking school she attended. When speaking she would have used the **future tense**, saying:

Seguirò i Suoi corsi … non proseguirò per settimane … passerò all'altra aula …
I shall follow your courses … I shan't continue for weeks … I shall move on to the next classroom …

We will meet **the future** in full in Unit 6, but note that when putting into reported speech words which were originally said in the future, Italians use the conditional perfect, whereas in English we use the conditional.

ho detto alla direttrice che <u>avrei seguito</u> i suoi corsi ... non <u>avrei proseguito</u> per settimane a fare gonne ... <u>sarei passata</u> all'altra aula ...

I told the principal I <u>would follow</u> her courses ... I <u>wouldn't continue</u> for weeks making skirts ... I <u>would move</u> on to the next classroom ...

Activity 26

Signora Torrielli often has meetings with a representative of Valentino, the fashion house, to agree about arrangements for production of the garments she makes for them. Read the following conversation and then imagine how Signora Torrielli reports it to her workforce so that they know what the firm's commitments and deadlines are. You will need to use the conditional perfect for the numbered verb phrases, as in the example.

Example: Line 5: Per quando **vorrete** il prodotto finito?
Ho chiesto alla rappresentante di Valentino per quando **avrebbero voluto** il prodotto finito.

Rappresentante	Questa è la collezione donna per il prossimo autunno-inverno: un modello per tailleur, una gonna sportiva, un vestito da sera, jeans, cappotto, camicette, ...
Torrielli	Sì... per quando vorrete il prodotto finito?
Rappresentante	Entro metà agosto? Poi bisognerà farlo arrivare ai distributori e poi i distributori ai negozianti ...
Torrielli	Beh, se è entro metà agosto ... allora ... avremo bisogno (1) della stoffa in maggio ... almeno per i capi eleganti, il tailleur e il vestito da sera, le camicette.

Rappresentante	Ai primi di maggio … va bene … e per gli altri capi forse un po' più tardi?
Torrielli	Sì, ma non troppo … dovremo cominciare (2) a lavorarla entro fine maggio, sicuramente. Se rispettiamo queste date, potremo garantire (3) un primo lotto di capi finiti … diciamo per fine luglio …
Rappresentante	Andrebbe benissimo.
Torrielli	… e poi saremo in grado (4) di consegnare il resto entro metà agosto, come dicevamo … Ma, senta, per le consegne ai distributori?
Rappresentante	Nessun problema … ci rivolgeremo (5) sempre allo stesso corriere. Dovrete risolvere (6) solo i problemi logistici, a quel punto.
Torrielli	Non c'è problema. Solo una cosa: sarà più pratico (7) dare direttamente il numero di telefono del magazzino, invece che quello del mio ufficio. Il responsabile per il magazzino si occuperà (8) di tutto.

Tu or Lei?

You may perhaps have noticed that our interviewees so far have mostly used **tu** to the interviewer, and vice versa. An exception was Signora Torrielli. She is also the only interviewee who has been referred to by her surname. This is simply because of the relationship of the interviewer with the various people. Mostly they are friends, in some cases old friends. They always use **tu** to each other. In the case of Mario Rotondale, it is more a case of usual practice. Mario runs a gym and tennis club and he very quickly finds himself saying to the members: **diamoci del tu**. In English, you would probably say: *my name is Mario, call me Mario* … and you would use first names to each other. He finds, with the many members he has and the friendly relationship which develops, particularly in the gym, that it is best to use **tu** with everyone, regardless of age or status. The interviewer's relationship with Signora Torrielli, however, has always been formal. They originally met at a dinner party and the interviewer has subsequently been a customer of Signora Torrielli's factory. Neither is young and they would have to meet socially much more for there to be a move to **tu**. Emanuela is an interesting case. Her husband and the interviewer were once colleagues. Colleagues almost always use **tu** to each other. But Emanuela has been brought up not to use **tu** a great deal, especially to people older than herself. There is therefore a situation where the interviewer uses **tu**, considering her a friend, but she does not reciprocate, aware of the age difference. This will also happen between adults and children: children have to be taught to use **Lei** because they don't always do so.

We were uncertain how to address you, dear learner, in the *Talking to yourself* suggestions. Had you been a class sitting before us, we would have used the collective **voi**. To each of you individually we would probably use **tu** (and first names). But in a book, we felt **tu** was too familiar; on the other hand **Lei** seems very formal. However since it is important for you to learn **Lei** so as not to give offence in casual encounters in Italy, we decided to use **Lei**.

This gives the impression that the whole situation is fraught. This is not really the case. When you do not know a person, you must use **Lei**. But in many relationships, when you are working or enjoying yourselves together, Italians are quick to say: **Diamoci del tu**. It is the Italian equivalent of using first names. They usually add: **è più facile**. For you as a student of Italian, that may not be the case, but try! And allowances will of course be made for you.

Remember that when you write **Lei**, formal *you*, and its related **La**, **Le**, **Suo/a** etc, there is a convention of using a capital letter. This is important in letters in particular since it is considered a mark of courtesy.

There has certainly been a shift in the way **tu** and **Lei** are used in the last twenty, thirty, forty years. The use of **Lei** is deferential, polite, distancing yourself out of courtesy, respect. **Tu** marks solidarity, closeness, friendship, affection. In the Fascist period **voi** was the compulsory mark of respect and the use of **Lei** was at one point forbidden as foreign – a mistaken view. **Voi** continued to be used for the formal *you* in rural areas for some time although it is unlikely you will hear it now, except perhaps in the south.

It may be of interest to know that Cesare Romiti (see Unit 2), who worked closely with Gianni Agnelli for some 25 years, for most of which Agnelli was President of Fiat and Romiti Managing Director, apparently always used **Lei** when addressing Agnelli. This is worthy of comment in the press, in other words Italians find it unusual.

Language learning tip

In one of the activities in this Unit we chose sentences from interviews or texts in previous units. Have you looked back at the earlier units recently? We strongly recommend you have a pattern of revision of earlier units, at least re-reading texts or listening again to the recording. We have purposely not simplified the Italian of the interviews and therefore, as the exercises made clear, points crop up before they are explained. Looking again helps to reinforce your understanding. Going over familiar texts also reinforces your memory of words and structures. If you haven't already tried it, why not give it a go? See if you can find any subjunctives!

Activity 27

Talking to yourself

Possible topics for your conversations in Italian with yourself – or if you are lucky, with the person or people studying with you – might be:

1 Descriva il Suo lavoro attuale e l'organizzazione (la ditta, la compagnia, l'ente …) per cui lavora.
2 Le piace l'abitudine di dare del tu? Trovi degli esempi di situazioni in cui si usa il 'tu' invece che il 'Lei' in un modo che è inappropriato. Per esempio, in ospedale un dottore potrebbe dare del tu a un paziente anziano che non aveva mai incontrato prima. Secondo Lei, ci sono situazioni in cui dare del tu rende la vita più facile o più difficile?

3 Il cibo italiano: le piace? Quali piatti preferisce? Perché? Mangia spesso nei ristoranti italiani? Come sono? Ne consiglierebbe alcuni?

4 Le piacciono i self-service? Quali sono i vantaggi e gli svantaggi dei self-service? Mangia mai da McDonald? Che cosa pensa della loro rapida diffusione? In Italia, sono spesso situati in posizioni di spicco, per esempio nelle piazze centrali di città famose. Certe persone pensano che rovinino la bellezza e lo stile della piazza: Lei, che cosa ne pensa?

5 Donne direttori di banca: ne conosce qualcuna? Che cosa pensa, in generale, delle donne con responsabilità manageriali? E delle donne in politica? Al momento, quasi nessuna donna, in Italia, ha ancora raggiunto posizioni di vero potere in politica. La sorprende? Pensa che sia più facile per le donne nel Suo paese raggiungere posizioni di potere in politica?

6 La moda italiana: Le piace? Che cosa pensa della moda italiana per uomo? Lei si veste secondo la moda o si lascia guidare da altre considerazioni nella scelta dei vestiti?

TEST YOURSELF

1 Join each pair of sentences with a relative pronoun referring to the word in bold.

   a La nostra è una piccola **società**. Gestisce alcuni negozi di abbigliamento in questa zona.

   b Il direttore ha chiamato in ufficio i **rappresentanti**. Gli ha detto di intensificare la campagna di vendita.

   c Lavoro in una **banca**. Ho una posizione di una certa responsabilità in questa banca.

   d Conoscevo un bravo **ragazzo**. Suo padre era un avvocato famoso.

   e Ricevo un piccolo **stipendio**. Lo stipendio non è adeguato alle mie responsabilità.

   f Abbiamo assunto tre nuovi **manager**. Le loro qualifiche sono eccezionali.

   g Si tratta di **problemi di gestione**. L'amministratore delegato si occupa di questi problemi.

   h Il principio delle pari opportunità è **la ragione principale**. Stanno discutendo un nuovo contratto di lavoro per questa ragione.

   i Erano tre **sorelle**. A loro piaceva vestirsi con abiti di grandi firme.

   j C'erano alcune **modelle**. Una di queste era altissima.

2 How would you say the following in Italian? Use the present subjunctive or the conditional perfect, as appropriate.

   a The manager thinks it is necessary to improve the quality of the food.

   b They say he has got a lot of experience.

   c I told her she would be successful (*avere successo*).

   d He's looking for a job that is paid well.

   e Everybody knew that taxes would go up.

Problemi di lavoro

In this unit we shall learn
- *about some of the problems Italians face in the workplace*
- *how to talk about what we intend to do in the future: the future tense*
- *how to say something is likely: a special use of the future*
- *how to say something must be done: the passive with* andare
- *another way of saying things are being done: the passive with* essere *and* venire

---

Session 1

Interview 1

You remember Emanuela was feeling tired and undervalued. We asked her about problems specific to work in an Italian bank.

◀ CD2, TR 3, 9:03

Emanuela	Sì, diciamo che … mah, ci sono problemi che adesso la concorrenza è diventata più agguerrita, arriveranno le banche europee, quindi sarà introdotto l'euro, quindi saranno anni un po' particolari per il sistema bancario italiano, anni in cui dovranno cambiare tantissime cose, e allora è richiesto uno sforzo grande, uno sforzo grande, una grossa attenzione, molto lavoro, questo credo in tutte le banche italiane. Tutte … dobbiamo veramente uscire dal medioevo. (*Ride*) Sì, è vero, abbiamo un sistema proprio arretrato e quindi dovremo lavorare molto.

We then asked Emanuela whether she derived any satisfaction from her work and she said (perhaps you can guess):

Emanuela (Ride) In questo momento vorrei una soddisfazione economica. Vorrei una soddisfazione economica perché è lo stupido parametro in … con cui misuriamo il nostro valore. Io sono apprezzata, lavoro tanto, quindi loro mi paghino … e questo perché vorrei comprare una bella casa, vorrei avere un futuro … più facile, no? per mia figlia, quindi vorrei più… più soldi.

sarà introdotto l'euro Emanuela was interviewed in the summer of 1998.

una soddisfazione economica We would add, though Emanuela might not agree, the employees of Italian banks have, in recent years, enjoyed favourable conditions in terms of hours and remuneration compared with bank staff in other EU countries.

uscire dal Medioevo *come out of the Middle Ages*. We would agree, from personal experience and as customers used to other banking systems, that Italian banks have rather out-of-date ways, although, as in many aspect of Italian life, things are gradually changing.

loro mi paghino *let them pay me*. An example of a subjunctive used in a main clause. It is in effect a third person imperative: the third person imperative is made using the present subjunctive.

Comprehension 1

1 Why does Emanuela think that in Italian banks there are difficult years ahead which will require much work and effort?

2 Why does she want what she calls 'economic satisfaction'?

QUICK VOCAB

Session 2

The form of the future

Emanuela looks ahead to the next few years and uses the future tense.

arriveranno le banche europee	*the European banks will come in*
sarà introdotto l'euro	*the euro will be introduced*
saranno anni un po' particolari	*they will be rather unusual years*
per il sistema bancario italiano	*for the Italian banking system*
anni in cui dovranno cambiare	*years in which so many things*
tantissime cose	*will have to change*

The future is formed on the same root as the conditional (Unit 1). Do you remember? For Groups 2 and 3 verbs, the base is the infinitive without the final **-e** and for Group 1 verbs the infinitive without the final **-e** and with the **a** of the ending changed to **e**.

arrivare	decidere	partire
arriverò	deciderò	partirò
arriverai	deciderai	partirai
arriverà	deciderà	partirà
arriveremo	decideremo	partiremo
arriverete	deciderete	partirete
arriveranno	decideranno	partiranno

The endings are the same for each group and for all verbs. Some verbs are irregular in that the first part, the root, is not formed as described above. These irregulars are exactly the same verbs as for the conditional, with the same irregularities.

1 essere: sarò, sarai, sarà, saremo, sarete, saranno
2 verbs whose infinitives contract:

  andare: andrò
  avere: avrò
  cadere: cadrò

dovere: dovrò
potere: potrò
sapere: saprò
vedere: vedrò
vivere: vivrò

3 verbs in which there is a contraction and a consonant change:
bere: berrò
tenere: terrò
venire: verrò
volere: vorrò
rimanere: rimarrò

4 As in the conditional, note also:
dire: dirò
fare: farò
stare: starò

It may be helpful at this stage for you to compare the future and
the conditional endings. We have not yet taken you through all
the persons of the conditional, only first and third person singular,
which you looked at in Unit 1. Here is the full picture.

Future		Conditional	
capirò	*I shall understand*	capirei	*I should understand*
capirai	*you will understand*	capiresti	*you would understand*
capirà	*he will understand*	capirebbe	*he would understand*
capiremo	*we shall understand*	capiremmo	*we should understand*
capirete	*you will understand*	capireste	*you would understand*
capiranno	*they will understand*	capirebbero	*they would understand*

Note: the third person plural of the conditional has the stress:
arriverebbero. The third person plural of the future is stressed on
the **a** of -**anno** (see The sounds of Italian).

Activity 1

Study the above table comparing the endings of the two tenses. Where in particular are you going to have to be very careful how you pronounce the two tenses to avoid saying the wrong one?

The uses of the future

1 It is used to express intended future actions, as Emanuela does. However, it is also common, as in English, to use the present to express what are in effect future plans:

La settimana prossima, vado in Francia per lavoro.	*Next week I am going to France for work reasons.*
Andiamo al cinema stasera. Vuoi venire anche tu?	*We are going to the cinema this evening. Do you want to come too?*

Note also, Italians use the present tense with **subito** to express something that they are about to do.

Vengo subito.	*I'll come immediately.*

2 A special case is the use of the future to express probability. This is different from English and like other such cases needs special attention.

A Dov'è papà?	*Where's dad?*
B Sarà in officina.	*He's probably in the workshop.*
A Portiamo delle mele dai nonni?	*Shall we take some apples to the grandparents?*
B Ne avranno già tante; i loro vicini gliene danno sempre.	*They're sure to have lots; their neighbours always give them some.*
A Che ore sono?	*What's the time?*
B Saranno le otto.	*It must be eight o'clock.*

The implication is that it is probable, likely, but can't be stated as fact.

Activity 2

Complete the following by putting the verbs in brackets into the correct person of the future tense. Then say what it all means.

Speaker A   Senz'altro, con un nuovo amministratore delegato, ci (1 essere) dei cambiamenti.

Speaker B   Sì. Sappiamo già che (2 modernizzare) il sistema di gestione. (3 Introdurre) per i vari direttori un sistema di traguardi da raggiungere. (4 Stabilire) con ogni direttore i suoi obiettivi e poi gli (5 lasciare) una grande libertà di decisione. Se il direttore (6 riuscire), (7 ricevere) un compenso a fine anno. Sennò...

Speaker A   Certo che questo (8 piacere) ad alcuni ma ad altri (9 mancare) la struttura attuale.

Activity 3

How would you put the following conversations in Italian?

1 **A**   Strange, there's a light on in Gianni's house. He went to the United States.
   B   He must have come back.
   A   I don't think so. It must be burglars.
2 **A**   Look, isn't that Pietro in that Mercedes at the traffic lights?
   B   Yes. Perhaps he has won the lottery.
   A   Or else it's his American uncle's car. He is in Italy at the moment.

Activity 4

Can you find any relative pronouns in what Emanuela says in Interview 1?

Session 3

Interview 2

Marina too was asked about problems at work.

CD2, TR 4, 11:20

Marina   Beh diciamo che ci sono soprattutto due ordini di problemi. Uno riguarda un po' l'Italia in generale, nel senso che lavorare in Italia è molto difficile perché ci sono moltissimi vincoli legislativi, burocrazie, permessi, leggi poco chiare che vanno sempre interpretate, quindi non si è mai sicuri di fare la cosa nel modo migliore e infatti, nel nostro settore in particolare, c'è la difficoltà anche di competere con degli operatori che sono in media molto piccoli, perché tipicamente il bar e la trattoria sono gestiti a livello familiare, che tendono a ignorare (*ride*) la buona gestione, quindi hanno dipendenti in nero, non pagano i contributi, non battono gli scontrini, non pagano le tasse, cioè è evidente che lì c'è una struttura di costi completamente diversa. È molto difficile per esempio assumere il personale perché il personale che lavora nel settore della ristorazione è abituato ad essere pagato in nero e essere pagato con delle cifre molto alte proprio perché sono in nero. Quindi è difficile attirare le persone e farle venire a lavorare da noi con dei salari decisamente più bassi però con i costi per l'azienda che sono molto alti perché bisogna aggiungere le tasse, i contributi, ecc. Questo sicuramente è un problema non tanto specifico nostro ma insomma un po' dell'Italia in generale.

E per me poi c'è forse un po' il problema di avere questa commistione tra il lavoro e la famiglia, cioè avere un intreccio di rapporti personali e professionali del lavoro che può essere un po' difficile da gestire, insomma, è un po' diverso avere a che fare con persone estranee, anonime o avere a che fare con i familiari. Delle volte questo facilita le cose, delle volte invece …

Interviewer	Perché questi ristoranti fanno parte …
Marina	Del gruppo di famiglia. Quindi ci sono sempre rapporti con mio padre, con i miei fratelli, con persone familiari o comunque persone diciamo con cui c'è un rapporto personale prima che professionale e questo appunto può essere qualche volta un po' difficile da gestire …
Interviewer	Mi puoi dare un esempio?
Marina	Mah, per esempio, mio padre quando tratta con me, è evidente che non tratta con me come la manager di un'azienda ma tratta con me come sua figlia, per cui mi tratta come figlia e quindi … (ride) quindi insomma è un rapporto diverso che … delle volte magari non c'è il rispetto che avrei se fossi un'estranea con cui c'è un rapporto di un altro livello.

nel senso che Another little phrase much used in spoken Italian (lit: *in the sense that*)

vincoli legislative *legal constraints*. **Vincoli** are *chains*, of a restricting type, *bonds, fetters*.

non si è mai sicuri *one is never sure*. With impersonal **si** any adjective is made masculine plural. If this seems odd, all we can say is that the reason lies in the history of Italian.

dipendenti in nero Employees who do not appear on the firm's books, who are paid in cash. No **contributi** *contributions for social security* are paid for them.

non battono gli scontrini Bars, restaurants and shops are required to give customers a **scontrino**, *fiscal receipt*.

avere a che fare con fratelli *to deal with, to have dealings with brothers* but includes *sisters* if there are any.

QUICK VOCAB

Insight

Learn to distinguish between **c'è** *there is* and **è** *it is*. Marina uses **c'è** frequently: **c'è la difficoltà** *there is the difficulty*, **c'è la struttura** *there is the structure*, **c'è il problema** *there is the problem*, **c'è un rapporto personale** *there is a personal*

(Contd)

relationtionship, **non c'è il rispetto** *there isn't the respect.* Marina also uses the impersonal constructions **è difficile** *it is difficult to*, **è un po' diverso** *it is slightly different to*, **è evidente che** *it is obvious that*.

Comprehension 2

1 Marina sees problems at work as being of two sorts. The first are, she says, specifically Italian. What, in broad outline, are they?
2 What does Marina say, in detail, about employment practices in the restaurant business in Italy? Why does Brek find it difficult to compete for staff?
3 The second category of problem which she experiences is peculiar to her situation. What is it?

Marina's remarks touch on several aspects of Italian life. First the questions of laws and permits. It seems Italy has a very large number of laws on its statute book compared to other Western European states. And the procedures for doing things are often complicated and full of pitfalls. The first Prodi government made a start on simplifying many procedures with the two Bassanini laws (**leggi Bassanini**), so called after the Minister who saw them through Parliament.

Lavoro nero, *black work*, has long been a feature of the Italian economy although a moment's reflection will confirm that it is not unknown in other countries. It seems that the costs to an employer of the social charges he has to pay on each employee are higher in Italy than in most countries of Western Europe and there is therefore a temptation to avoid them. This is particularly true in the case of small firms. An organization the size of the one Marina works for would not, of course, employ people this way. **Lavoro nero** would also include the plumber who charges you less if you pay cash and the employee who moonlights. The high costs of employing workers – and indeed the difficulty of getting rid of them should you need to – has also led to giving work to consultants, sometimes in cooperatives of young people, rather than employing them direct.

Italy has a general problem with tax evasion. One aspect of it is the service industries. When you buy something in a shop or eat a meal in a restaurant you should be given a **scontrino** or **ricevuta fiscale**. Technically you can be fined if you leave the premises without one. The trader who fails to give you a receipt possibly does not put the transaction through his books, cheating on VAT (**IVA – imposta sul valore aggiunto**) and other taxes. In the early 90s, in a drive to stamp out such tax evasion, there were some well publicized cases of customers being stopped and fined: children who had bought lollipops and not demanded **scontrini**, for instance. The fines on the traders are far heavier than on the customers. You can imagine the scandalized tone adopted by reporting journalists, which of course brought the clamp-down to public attention – presumably as was intended – and probably reduced avoidance. You may, therefore, as someone unused to picking up a till receipt when buying very inexpensive items, be surprised to find the shop assistant calling you back to take your receipt. We would not wish to give the impression that most Italians are dishonest. Our experience is rather the opposite. And dishonesty knows no frontiers.

The firm Marina works for is part of a family group. Family businesses are a well-documented feature of the Italian economic scene, as readers may be aware. Famous family firms include Benetton, Ferragamo, and, possibly infamous and certainly no longer owned by the family, Gucci.

Session 4

Unfinished sentences – more about the spoken language

You may notice that Marina doesn't finish the sentence:

Delle volte questo facilita le cose, delle volte invece ...   *Sometimes this makes things easier, at other times, on the other hand ...*

Nor does the interviewer finish the sentence which follows:

Perché questi ristoranti fanno parte ...?   *Because these restaurants are part of ...?*

In both cases the two speakers understand each other without having to spell everything out. This happens in the spoken language, any language. And the better two people know each other, the more this will occur. You may be able to turn this to good effect, saving yourself the trouble of finishing every sentence in Italian. This will tend to be in informal situations.

The passive with essere

The story of the passive in Italian is broader than in English and incorporates some useful shades of meaning. First, what do we mean by the passive? Verbs can be either active or passive. Here are some examples:

Active:

[Subject]	*[Verb]*		*[Object (direct)]*
Il Papa	ha ricevuto	oggi	il Presidente degli Stati Uniti.

The Pope today received the President of the United States.

[Subject]	*[Object (direct)]*	*[Verb]*
La moglie del Presidente	lo	accompagnava.

The President's wife accompanied him/was with him

Passive:

[Subject]	*[Verb]*		*[Agent]*
Il Presidente degli Stati Uniti	è stato ricevuto	oggi	dal Papa

The President of the United States was received by the Pope today.

[Subject]	*[Verb]*	*[Agent]*
Il Presidente	era accompagnato	dalla moglie.

The President was accompanied by his wife.

In the active, the subject of the verb does something to a direct object. In the passive the sentence is turned round and the object is made the grammatical subject, with the former subject becoming what is called the agent, in other words, something introduced by the word *by* (in Italian **da**). It sounds very convoluted but we all use the passive frequently:

[Subject]	*[Verb]*	*[Agent]*
Il libro	è stato comprato	da oltre un milione di lettori entusiasti.

The book has been bought by over a million enthusiastic readers.

[Subject]	*[Verb]*	
Il prodotto	sarà richiamato	dopo la scoperta dell'errore.

The product will be recalled after the discovery of the mistake.

The point of putting the idea this way round is to highlight the subject of the passive verb, in the examples above, **il libro** and **il prodotto**, rather than **oltre un milione di lettori entusiasti**. Indeed in the second sentence who was going to recall the product (the agent) is left unstated.

In English the passive is formed with *to be* and a past participle. In Italian, you can use **essere** and the past participle but another possibility with a special shade of meaning is illustrated below.

The passive with andare

Marina, talking about unclear laws, says:

leggi poco chiare che vanno   *laws which are not clear and*
  interpretate   *which have to be interpreted*

She uses **andare** not **essere**. The force of this is: **le leggi devono essere interpretate**. *The laws must/have to be interpreted.* Forming the passive with **andare** rather than **essere** conveys what *should be done*, obligation.

| **Lo spumante va servito fresco.** | *Fizzy wine must be/should be served cool/chilled.* |
| **Va ricordato che ...** | *It must be/should be remembered that ...* |

This latter type of phrase is very common in discussion or where you are arguing a point.

| **va sottolineato che ...** | *it should be emphasized (underlined) that ...* |
| **va detto che ...** | *it has to be said that ...* |

Activity 5

Can you find any passives in what Marina said in Interview 2? Reread her words and then check the Key.

Activity 6

Here are some statements in the active voice. Rephrase them in the passive, according to the example.

Example: Active: **La polizia ha arrestato un giovane tunisino che è arrivato in Italia come clandestino.**

Passive: **Un giovane tunisino che è arrivato in Italia come clandestino è stato arrestato (dalla polizia).**

1 Dei volontari hanno rintracciato il padre del giovane.
2 La banca ha risolto il problema di Emanuela.
3 Ha cambiato il livello del suo lavoro e aumentato il suo stipendio di conseguenza.
4 Un'eruzione dello Stromboli ha provocato un incendio nei boschi.
5 Le cattive condizioni del mare hanno isolato per due giorni la frazione Ginostra.

Activity 7

And now a little practice of the passive with **andare**. Continue the following exchanges on the lines of the example and say what the last sentence in each case means:

Example: **A È stato rintracciato il padre?**
B No, signore.
A Allora va rintracciato al più presto.
Then he must be found as soon as possible.

1 A **È stato isolato il malato?**
B **No, dottore.**
A **Allora …**

2 A **È stato liberato il prigioniero?**
B **No, signore.**
A **Allora …**

3 A **È stato firmato l'assegno?**
B **No, signora.**
C **Allora …**

4 A **È stato dato l'allarme?**
B **No, professore.**
A **Allora …**

The passive with chiedere, dare, dire, **etc.**

The last question in this activity however requires a cautionary note. There are a number of common verbs which we frequently use in the passive in English and which cannot be used in the passive in the same way in Italian. **Dare** is one of them. We are thinking of sentences like:

He was given a present.
They were asked to arrive early.
I was told he had arrived.

This is because the equivalent verbs in Italian work thus:

	Direct	*Indirect*
Verb	*Object*	*Object*
dare	un regalo	a qualcuno

		Indirect
	Verb	*Object*
chiedere/domandare	a qualcuno	di fare qualcosa

	Indirect	
Verb	*Object*	
dire	a qualcuno	di fare qualcosa.

In each case, **qualcuno** is an indirect object (the **a** is the clue). Italian doesn't allow an indirect object to become the subject of a passive. So what do you do? You have to find another way of expressing the idea, for instance, making the subject **loro** *they*, i.e. some vague, unspecified people.

I.O.	Verb	Direct Object
Gli	hanno dato	un regalo.

I.O.	Verb	
Gli	hanno chiesto	di arrivare in anticipo.

I.O.	Verb	
Mi	hanno detto	che era arrivato.

Activity 8

Can you find any relative pronouns in what Marina says in Interview 2?

Session 5

Interview 3

Our interviewer found Signora Torrielli weighed down by her problems and very much in need of the holiday which she would be taking in a few weeks. The problems are so numerous, we have divided the interview into two parts (see Session 7).

📶 CD2, TR 5, 14:06

Signora Torrielli Le problematiche di quest'azienda sono il fatto che non viene più pagata l'idea, non viene pagato più niente ma viene solo pagato il minuto/lavoro. Quindi a noi arriva la giacca, il rotolo di tessuto, il rotolo dei modelli, i fili e i bottoni e noi abbiamo 100 minuti per rendere questa cosa appesa ad un attaccapanni imbustata e pronta per la spedizione. Non ci vengono più riconosciute le nostre – volevo chiamarle bravure artigianali – perché si pretende da noi l'industria con incluso il risultato dell'artigiano, quindi siamo

	proprio in una profonda crisi … Non si può ottenere il massimo del prodotto con il minimo dei minuti. Da me vogliono il massimo della … non della produttività ma della qualità e non mi danno il tempo per farlo. E quindi l'azienda è in crisi per questa ragione. Per fare quel lavoro in 100 minuti non ci stiamo, noi andiamo non fuori mercato ma andiamo in perdita.
Interviewer	Dunque La trovo in un momento difficile.
Signora Torrielli	Certo. Anche perché non vedo quale possa essere la soluzione. Siccome tutti avranno sempre meno soldi, potranno sempre spendere meno, però saranno sempre più sollecitati dalla pubblicità, dai giornali, da tutti a volere quelle firme lì e quelle firme lì per poter vendere continueranno a discapito della qualità del tessuto, della qualità della confezione, così, a scendere nei prezzi e quindi la gente, sì, metterà un capo firmato ma non avrà più il valore di quella firma perché il capo non viene più fatto come dovrebbe essere fatto. Se si parla di prêt-à-porter. Se si parla di alta moda è un altro discorso, ma quello non facciamo, insomma, quindi …

le problematiche il complesso dei problemi. Sig.ra Torrielli has more than one problem!

imbustata *bagged*, i.e. in its plastic wrapping for transport

si pretende da noi l'industria con incluso il risultato dell'artigiano Another 'false friend' **pretendere** is more to do with having pretensions, laying claims, than with make-believe. Here: *they expect us to produce in an industrial way but wanting the finished product of a craftsman.*

non ci stiamo *we can't do it*

non fuori mercato *not out of business*

ma andiamo in perdita *but we are going to make a loss*

a discapito di *to the detriment of*

un capo firmato *a designer label garment*

è un altro discorso *it's another matter*

alta moda *haute couture*

QUICK VOCAB

Comprehension 3

1 Describe the process which is undergone when Signora Torrielli
produces a jacket for Valentino or another well-known firm. e.g.
who supplies what, who does what.
2 Signora Torrielli complains that the firms are expecting
something they do not any longer really pay for, or in Emanuela's
terms, recognize economically. What is it?
3 Why do the firms need to cut costs so fiercely?
4 What consequence does this have on the finished article, in the
case of ready-to-wear?
5 What area of fashion does Signora Torrielli say is not affected by
this constant lowering of quality, value?

Session 6

Activity 9

Can you find anything that looks like the passive in what Signora
Torrielli said in Interview 3? Check the Key to see if you were right.

The passive with venire

Il capo non viene più fatto come dovrebbe essere fatto.	*The garment is no longer made as it should be (made).*

Several times in this interview, Signora Torrielli uses a very
common form of the passive, made with **venire** (not **essere**) + the
past participle. You will find that this is much used by Italians, but

it can only be used in simple (one word) tenses. It is not used with compound tenses such as the perfect, where you need **essere**. Otherwise **essere** and **venire** are interchangeable, although possibly **venire** is used to suggest process, action, while **essere** is to do with state. For example, Signora Torrielli could have equally said:

Il capo non è più fatto come dovrebbe essere fatto.

Here is another example:

Il panettone viene mangiato a Natale. *Panettone is eaten at Christmas.*

(**Panettone** is a cross between a very light bread and cake, made of a yeast dough and containing candied peel.)

So there are three ways of forming the passive:

essere
venire } + past participle
andare

but the meaning when **andare** is used is distinctly different, as we saw in Activity 7.

Activity 10

Suggest how you might say:

1 Here's the coffee. It's hot. It should be drunk immediately.
2 The situation is difficult. It should be said that John is a stubborn person.
3 Usually in Italy meals are accompanied by wine.
4 The long working day is recognized in our remuneration.
5 Our work is valued.
6 The price must be increased.

Activity 11

In Interview 3 Signora Torrielli uses some of the forms we have just been working on.

1 Can you find examples of the future in what she says?
2 How about the present subjunctive?
3 She also uses the impersonal **si**. Can you find any examples?

Session 7

Interview 4

More aspects of Signora Torrielli's crisis. We should explain the interviewer had met Signora Torrielli for the first time the previous year.

◀ CD2, TR 6, 6:11

Interviewer	È molto cambiato dall'anno scorso?
Signora Torrielli	No, no, no. Assolutamente. È proprio una cosa che è in escalation da anni, questa, perché tutti trovano meno mercato, allora diminuiscono i prezzi, diminuiscono la qualità dei tessuti, diminuiscono la qualità della produzione, sempre però a discapito dell'ultimo che è quello che produce. Non a discapito della fotomodella, non a discapito del servizio fotografico, non a discapito di ... a discapito però dell'ultimo che mette insieme il capo, che è quello che non può difendersi. Che per lo meno si difende molto poco anche perché ci sono tutti i mercati emergenti che producono – non ancora bene – ma che produrranno nel giro di poco tempo bene. Dunque l'Italia, se non fa qualche cosa, perderà completamente tutta questa fascia di ... e le persone perderanno i posti perché non ci sarà più il mercato per fare questo tipo di lavoro. Tutti quelli che hanno potuto, proprio per tutte le grane sindacali, per tutti

	gli obblighi sindacali, per tutti gli obblighi di legge, per l'USSL e tutte quelle altre cose … tutti quelli che avevano la potenza, quindi quelli più grossi, sono andati, hanno trasferito le loro produzioni, all'estero, e il governo non ha fatto niente per tenerli in casa. Dalle scarpe alle borse, le confezioni, le maglierie, tutti. Noi facciamo ancora quest'élite di firme ma sicuramente quest'élite di firme, le loro linee più basse sono già state portate sicuramente fuori d'Italia a fare. Invece noi siamo a Torino, abbiamo la fortuna di essere a Torino … abbiamo certamente un mercato più favorevole perché siamo su Torino ma credo che a Torino nel giro di quest'anno abbiano già chiuso cinque o sei laboratori.
Interviewer	Mi è sembrato l'anno scorso, quando L'ho incontrata per la prima volta, che Lei era molto orgogliosa della Sua azienda …
Signora Torrielli	Sono orgogliosa ma non sono più gratificata, allora quando uno non viene più gratificato … quando si deve combattere contro … i minuti, proprio il minuto, che non può permettere a una ragazza di andare due volte a prendere l'acqua perché Lei, vedendo fare quello, sa che quella giacca non esce più in 100 minuti, esce in 102, e siccome tutte vanno due volte, non è più 102, ma 130 minuti. 130 minuti e noi ci abbiamo rimesso 30 minuti, 30 minuti vuole dire moltiplicato per 35 moltiplicati per 22 giorni di lavoro e noi alla fine andiamo a meno anziché a più. Difficilissimo già trovare ragazze che hanno voglia di fare questo lavoro. Forse hanno ragione loro perché è un lavoro di grande impegno, bisogna avere la testa tutto il giorno, non è una fabbrica dove uno schiaccia il bottone o … Con i contratti che i dipendenti ormai hanno, loro si attengono strettamente al contratto e non c'è più il rapporto interpersonale se non raramente, no, no, perché se loro decidono che non vogliono fermarsi un'ora di più perché quell'ora di

(Contd)

più – giustamente hanno fatto otto ore di lavoro – non si fermano e non gliene importa niente se andiamo in mora perché siamo in ritardo.

Quando ho iniziato non era così… Devono diminuire i prezzi e dove loro possono sicuramente stringere più facilmente è solo sull'ultimo gradino che è la produzione.

Domanda Ma non è la cosa più importante?

Signora Torrielli Certo ma non è che la gente capisca la differenza … Basta che ci sia il nome, per loro il marchio è la garanzia, quindi chi vede quello crede che sia già stato fatto tutto dentro quel marchio, invece dentro quel marchio è stato fatto tutto per risparmiare, per permettere gli utili a quel marchio.

in escalation Another English phrase in an Italian business context

nel giro di poco tempo *very soon* (**nel giro di 3 mesi** *within three months*)

grane sindacali *troubles caused by the unions* (**sindacati**)

USSL Unità Socio – Sanitaria Locale *the local Health Authority*

30 minuti … moltiplicato per 35 … The working week is 35 hours and there are 22 working days in a month … That would seem to be the calculation Signora Torrielli is doing. We confess to not quite understanding the 130 minutes – perhaps it is 2 minutes for each of 15 workers – but understand the overall problem.

non gliene importa niente *they couldn't care a jot.* (lit: *nothing of it matters to them*)

andare in mora Signora Torrielli's contracts will specify a delivery date and she probably *incurs a penalty for lateness*. **Mora** is a legal term for unjustified lateness in fulfilling an obligation, contract etc. but is often used to mean the penalty which that incurs.

chi vede quello *the person who sees that* (the name label) (this is the relative **chi**, see Unit 5)

gli utili *profits*

Insight

The threefold repetition of **diminuiscono** *they are lowering* and **non a discapito di** *not to the detriment of* at the beginning

of Signora Torrielli's reply express her frustration and her
mounting disillusionment.

Comprehension 4

1 Which elements in the chain which is involved in producing
designer label garments does Signora Torrielli say are exempt from
the economy measures? Which areas suffer from savings being made?
2 She fears competition from which quarter?
3 What does she say the most powerful firms are doing?
4 What has happened to five or six workshops similar to hers in
Turin this year?
5 What other problems does she consider Italian employers have to
contend with, which lead to their moving production away from Italy?
6 The interviewer found her to be very proud of her business last
year but thinks this might be no longer the case. What is Signora
Torrielli's comment?
7 Apart from the time problem, what staff problems does Signora
Torrielli mention?

Session 8

Activity 12

Look through Interview 4 for examples of some of the points we
have dealt with recently:

1 Relative pronouns
2 The subjunctive
3 The passive
4 The future

Reading

And finally, here's a happy worker. It's someone you've already met.

Il mio mestiere è quello di scrivere e io lo so bene e da molto tempo. Spero di non essere fraintesa: sul valore di quel che posso scrivere non so nulla. So che scrivere è il mio mestiere. Quando mi metto a scrivere, mi sento straordinariamente a mio agio e mi muovo in un elemento che mi par di conoscere straordinariamente bene; adopero degli strumenti che mi sono noti e familiari e li sento ben fermi nelle mie mani. Se faccio qualunque altra cosa, se studio una lingua straniera, se mi provo a imparare la storia o la geografia o la stenografia o se mi provo a parlare in pubblico o a lavorare a maglia o a viaggiare, soffro e mi chiedo di continuo come gli altri facciano queste stesse cose, mi pare sempre che ci debba essere un modo giusto di fare queste cose che è noto agli altri e sconosciuto a me. E mi pare d'essere sorda e cieca e ho come una nausea in fondo a me. Quando scrivo invece non penso mai che c'è forse un modo più giusto di cui si servono gli altri scrittori. Non me ne importa niente di come fanno gli altri scrittori. Intendiamoci, io posso scrivere soltanto delle storie. Se mi provo a scrivere un saggio di critica o un articolo per un giornale a comando, va abbastanza male. Quello che allora scrivo lo devo cercare faticosamente come fuori di me. Posso farlo un po' meglio che studiare una lingua straniera o parlare in pubblico, ma solo un po' meglio. E ho sempre l'impressione di truffare il prossimo con delle parole prese a prestito o rubacchiate qua e là. E soffro e mi sento in esilio. Invece quando scrivo delle storie sono come uno che è in patria, sulle strade che conosce dall'infanzia e fra le mura e gli alberi che sono suoi. Il mio mestiere è scrivere delle storie, cose inventate o cose che ricordo della mia vita ma comunque storie, cose dove non c'entra la cultura ma soltanto la memoria e la fantasia. Questo è il mio mestiere, e io lo farò fino alla morte. Sono molto contenta di questo mestiere e non lo cambierei per niente al mondo.

'Il mio mestiere' (written in 1949) in Natalia Ginzburg, *Le piccole virtù*, Einaudi 1962

QUICK VOCAB

mestiere *trade* (rather than *job*). Italian definition from Lo Zingarelli 2010: **esercizio di una attività lavorativa, spec. manuale, frutto di esperienza e pratica, a scopo di guadagno**. N. Ginzburg indeed refers to holding her tools nice and firmly in her hands.

frainteso *misunderstood*
qualunque altra cosa *any other thing whatsoever*

Insight

Sometimes a shorter form **quel che** is used instead of **quello che**.
Ginzburg writes **quel che posso scrivere** *what I may be writing*.

Comprehension 5

The questions are in Italian. Mostly a small change to the original
sentence will produce the answer. Your reply need not be a
complete sentence, just a natural answer.

1 Che cosa sa da molto tempo Natalia Ginzburg?
2 Su che cosa dice di non sapere nulla?
3 Come si sente quando scrive?
4 Che cosa adopera per fare il suo mestiere?
5 Che cosa succede se prova a studiare una lingua straniera o a parlare in pubblico, ecc?
6 Scrive di tutto, Natalia Ginzburg?
7 È più brava a scrivere articoli per un giornale o a parlare in pubblico?
8 Con quali immagini spiega le sensazioni che prova (a) quando scrive un articolo (b) quando scrive una storia?
9 Come sappiamo che le piace il suo mestiere?

Written style

Natalia Ginzburg's hallmark is a simple, direct style of writing.
Nevertheless you will probably realize that when Natalia Ginzburg
writes, the style is more literary than when one of our interviewees
speaks. A simple example in the first few lines is the abbreviation
of the present tense of **parere: par** instead of **pare**. This may
also be done in speech. And of course the sentences are carefully
structured, balanced, finished.

You may notice too that in this passage there are subjunctives
underlining her uncertainty about how various activities are best
carried out.

... mi chiedo ... come gli altri **facciano** queste stesse cose, mi pare
sempre che ci **debba** essere un modo giusto di fare queste stesse cose ...

Activity 14

Talking to yourself

1 In banca: tutti noi abbiamo qualche storia da raccontare: il
Bancomat che non funziona proprio quando non ne possiamo fare
a meno, il Bancomat ci ha 'mangiato' la carta, la banca non ha
pagato le nostre bollette da un anno o altri errori della banca ...
Racconti le Sue disavventure!

2 Imprese/attività a conduzione familiare: ne conosce qualcuna?
Quali sono i vantaggi? Quali gli svantaggi?

3 Lavorare con il marito, la moglie o con un altro familiare o
parente. Quali sono i pro? E quali i contro?

4 Il distacco generazionale e i rapporti tra genitori e figli. I Suoi
rapporti con gli anziani della famiglia o con la famiglia del Suo
coniuge/partner. Racconti le Sue esperienze.

5 Lavora troppo, Lei? Fa troppi straordinari? Il Suo datore di
lavoro riconosce il lavoro che fa? Come sono cambiate le Sue
condizioni di lavoro nel corso della Sua vita lavorativa? Ne parli!

6 Forse Lei è datore di lavoro: quali problemi ha con i Suoi
dipendenti? È facile o difficile trovare gli impiegati giusti, quelli
con le caratteristiche di cui ha bisogno per la Sua attività? I Suoi
dipendenti sono disposti ad essere flessibili quando ce n'è bisogno?

7 La Sua attività è minacciata dai concorrenti all'estero? Che cosa
può fare per difendersi? Che futuro vede per la Sua azienda?

8 Compra vestiti firmati Lei? Perché? Quali stilisti Le piacciono?
Secondo Lei, perché per molte persone la firma è così importante?

TEST YOURSELF

1 Cristina is daydreaming and perhaps making plans for the future. Complete her thoughts, hopes and ambitions with the future of the verbs in brackets.

La mia famiglia è inglese e vive a Londra, ma un giorno io
(a) _____ (partire) per un lunghissimo viaggio.
(b) _____ (andare) a insegnare l'inglese nell'America Latina.
(c) _____ (vedere) paesi che non ho mai visitato.
(d) _____ (conoscere) popoli diversi e diverse tradizioni.
(e) _____ (lavorare) in tante scuole con bambini e con adulti. Penso che i bambini (f) _____ (imparare) una lingua straniera facilmente e la (g) _____ (parlare) senza studiare la grammatica. Insieme, noi (h) _____ (fare) giochi divertenti,
(i) _____ (guardare) film in inglese e
(j) _____ (vivere) la vita quotidiana parlando inglese.

2 More transformation! Can you make these sentences passive? Use the auxiliary in brackets and the highlighted words as the subject of the passive sentence.

   (a) Questa organizzazione finanzia **i loro progetti** per il miglioramento dell'ambiente. (venire)
   (b) Hanno presentato **una petizione** al parlamento. (essere)
   (c) Uno sportivo famoso accenderà **la fiamma olimpica** durante la cerimonia d'apertura. (venire)
   (d) Bisogna servire **la pasta** al dente. (andare)
   (e) Non hanno firmato **l'assegno**. (essere)

7

La persona e il lavoro

In this unit we shall
- *look at the effect of work on the personal lives of some Italians*
- *look at the reality behind some Italian stereotypes: the Italian husband,* 'la mamma italiana'
- *look at the prepositions required after certain verbs, adjectives and nouns*
- *look further at the gerund and meet the present participle*
- *revise question words*
- *consider other uses of the subjunctive and ways to avoid it*
- *revise object pronouns and emphatic pronouns*

Session 1

Interview 1

For the women we interviewed, managing family, home and career is a big preoccupation. First Marina who is married and has two daughters, 8 and 6. She was asked how she managed to combine career and family.

Marina	Eh, ci si arrangia, insomma. Come tutte le donne, trovo in qualche modo delle soluzioni. Io ho avuto la fortuna di avere un marito che è molto bravo con le bambine, quindi quando sono via, il che succede abbastanza spesso, si occupa lui della gestione domestica in un certo senso. Non è molto contento di questo ma insomma lo fa. E poi ho una serie di aiuti quindi, ho una ragazza alla pari per le bambine, una signora che viene a fare le pulizie …
Interviewer	Dunque tuo marito forse non è tipico?
Marina	Mah, insomma anche gli uomini italiani si stanno evolvendo. Sì, credo che ormai, non tutti ma insomma … sicuramente rispetto a qualche anno fa sono molto cambiati, partecipano alla vita domestica. Mio marito comunque ha avuto un'educazione molto spartana, è sempre stato abituato ad arrangiarsi anche in casa, aveva i genitori separati, quindi è sempre stato allevato in modo molto … molto poco italiano, non c'è dubbio. Non c'era questa figura della mamma che pensa a tutto, che si occupa di tutto … Però ripeto, sì, penso che mio marito forse sia meglio da questo punto di vista, però io vedo che gli uomini, gli uomini giovani insomma … D'altra parte non c'è scelta, se la donna lavora credo non ci sia alternativa …

QUICK VOCAB

ci si arrangia arrangiarsi *to manage, to find a solution somehow, to get by somehow.* Note: **arrangiarsi** is a reflexive verb. Marina uses it with the impersonal **si** (*one*). Italian avoids **si si**: the first **si** is made into **ci**. Hence: **ci si arrangia**. We mentioned this in the note to the N. Ginzburg passage at the end of Unit 4.
il che *which,* referring to **quando sono via**
una ragazza alla pari *an au pair girl*
una signora che viene a fare le pulizie *a lady who comes to clean.* Often referred to as **una donna di servizio**, often simply

una donna. For instance you offer to help your hostess and she will say: **No, no, lo farà la donna**. See also **colf**, *home help* (formed from <u>col</u>laboratrice <u>f</u>amiliare).

rispetto a *compared with*

sono molto cambiati *they have changed a lot*. Note: **cambiare** when intransitive forms the **passato prossimo** with **essere**.

Insight

As we found in Unit 5, Marina uses a lot of extra words in her speech to mitigate her statements or to take time to think. How often does she use the word **insomma** in this interview? Why do you think she does that? Is she embarrassed about describing her husband as atypical of the Italian male?

Comprehension 1

1 Marina seems to have things very much under control. What makes one think it isn't as easy as all that?
2 Does Marina think Italian men help on the home front?
3 Why is her husband better prepared than many for having a wife with a successful career?
4 What notion of the typical Italian mother do you get from what Marina says?

Session 2

Verbs requiring prepositions before following infinitives

Notice how Marina says:

una signora che <u>viene a</u> fare le pulizie

Already in Unit 1 we met **dovere, potere, volere** and of course **piacere** (**mi piace, mi piacerebbe**) followed by the infinitive. We mentioned in passing that other verbs needed a preposition before a following infinitive. We drew attention to **mi rifiuto di comprare** and **non credo di essere molto brava**. **Rifiutarsi** and

credere both need **di** before an infinitive which follows them. Many verbs require **a**, for instance, **venire** (see above). We have provided a list in the **Reference grammar**. Sometimes expressions like this form up into a chain of prepositions:

Devo <u>cercare di</u> <u>ricordarmi di</u> fare la spesa prima della riunione.	*I must try to remember to do the shopping before the meeting.*
<u>Hai voglia di</u> <u>andare a</u> vedere un film?	*Do you want to go and see a film?*

Adjectives and nouns requiring prepositions before following infinitives

Similarly, certain adjectives and nouns require an **a** or a **di** when an infinitive is to follow. Marina says of her husband:

è sempre stato <u>abituato ad</u> arrangiarsi	*he's always been used to managing by himself*

She could have said:

non è <u>contento di</u> farlo ma insomma lo fa	*he's not pleased to do it but he does it*
è <u>capace di</u> cucinare	*he can cook/he is capable of cooking*

Verbs requiring a preposition before a following noun

The learner needs also to be aware that some verbs require a preposition before their object (usually a noun). Examples in what Marina says are:

... la mamma che <u>pensa a</u> tutto, che <u>si occupa di</u> tutto.	*... the mother who takes care of everything, who looks after everything*

You will notice that the two phrases are similar in meaning but different in structure, one using **a**, the other **di**. If there is to be a pronoun instead, the preposition will affect the choice of a pronoun. For example, if you are making plans for something and you offer to look after a certain aspect, you may say:

Ci penso io.   *I'll take care of it* (lit: *I'll think of it*).
                              (**ci** because it is **pensare a** …)
Me ne occupo io.   *I'll look after it.* (**ne** because it is
                              occuparsi di …)

You need to note particularly those verbs which work differently from their English equivalent. There is a list of some common ones in the **Reference grammar**. You need to be especially careful when trying to express the passive with verbs which take an indirect object in Italian (**a** + noun; or indirect object pronoun). It can't be done as you have seen in Unit 6, Session 4.

Direct Object	**Indirect Object**
The manager answered my letter.	**Il direttore ha risposto <u>alla mia lettera</u>.**
My letter was answered by the manager.	This cannot be translated directly. The letter is the direct object in English, but the indirect object in Italian.
Emanuela often asks John to do the shopping.	**Emanuela chiede spesso a John di fare la spesa.**
John is often asked by Emanuela to do the shopping.	No direct translation is possible.

There are also cases when a preposition is needed in English and not in Italian.

ascoltare qualcosa, qualcuno   *to listen to something, someone*
cercare qualcosa, qualcuno   *to look for something, someone*

Language learning tip

We would not advise attempting to learn lists of points, unless you are quite sure that that suits your style of learning. However, what we suggest strongly is that you try to be observant when listening to Italian, reading etc. and try to absorb the whole package rather than just the single word, e.g. **ascoltare qualcuno** ... rather than just **ascoltare**. It may also be helpful to make your own lists as you go along. Dictionaries usually tell you how a particular word functions.

Activity 1

Hai provato a ... ? *Have you tried ...?*

One of your friends has a husband who doesn't help in the home at all. She telephones you often to talk about the situation. This is one of your conversations. Complete it by filling in the gaps. Use the following expressions for her: **cominciare a; accorgersi di; continuare a; essere abituato a; rifiutarsi di; essere contenta di** and these for you: **provare a; fare finta di; essere stufa di.**

Example:

Amica	Non ne posso più! **Sono** veramente **stufa di** dovere fare sempre tutto io!
Lei	Secondo me dovresti **smettere di** lamentarti con me e **cominciare** a lamentarti con tuo marito ... !
Amica	Ci ho provato, sai?! Il risultato è che dice che gli dispiace, ma poi (1) .... comportarsi esattamente come prima!
Lei	E allora, senti, fai così: (2) .... fare finta di dimenticarti che ci sono dei lavori da fare ...
Amica	Non conosci mio marito! Lui proprio non (3) .... quello che c'è da fare in casa! Non li vede neanche, i lavori da fare!
Lei	Ma scusa, perché tu non glieli fai notare?
Amica	Quando glieli faccio notare, lui (4) .... farli, perché dice che lavora già abbastanza fuori casa,
	(Contd)

	e che non (5) .... fare i lavori domestici, dice che sono cose da donne!
Lei	Secondo me tu non sei abbastanza furba ... io ogni tanto (6) .... non stare bene ... che so ... di avere un gran mal di testa ...
Amica	E tu dici che lui ci crederebbe?! No, guarda ... io le bugie non le so dire ... e poi, scusa, non (7) .... ottenere il suo aiuto in questo modo ... vorrei che cambiasse per davvero ... forse un giorno (8) .... capire il mio punto di vista ...
Lei	Aspetta e spera! Da quello che mi dici di tuo marito, è il tipo che non cambierà mai! E per di più, io (9) .... dover ascoltare ogni giorno le tue lamentele!

Activity 2

Mr Rossi is very disorganized. He always has good intentions at the beginning of the week but he rarely manages to do what he has decided to do. Imagine what he says to himself on Friday evening when he looks back over what he intended to do but didn't.

Example: lunedì pomeriggio – avere intenzione di andare a trovare la zia Franca – non riuscire a trovare il tempo – mettermi ad aggiustare un rubinetto che perdeva

Lunedì pomeriggio <u>avevo intenzione di andare a trovare</u> la zia Franca, ma non <u>sono riuscito a trovare</u> il tempo perché all'ora di pranzo <u>mi sono messo ad aggiustare</u> un rubinetto che perdeva e quando ho finito il lavoro era troppo tardi per uscire!

On Monday afternoon I meant to go and see Aunt Franca but I didn't manage to find the time because at lunch-time I started to see to a leaking tap and when I had finished the job it was already too late to go out.

1 martedì mattina – avere intenzione di comperare un regalo per il
compleanno di mia figlia – non riuscire a trovarlo – dimenticarmi
di chiedere a mia moglie in che negozio lo vendevano
2 mercoledì sera – avere intenzione di andare allo stadio con
gli amici per vedere insieme la partita di calcio – non riuscire a
organizzare la serata – dimenticarsi di comperare i biglietti
3 giovedì mattina – avere intenzione di andare alla Posta per
pagare la bolletta del telefono – non riuscire a pagarla – accorgersi
troppo tardi di non avere abbastanza contanti nel portafoglio
4 venerdì pomeriggio – avere intenzione di prenotare le vacanze per
l'estate – non riuscire ad andare all'agenzia di viaggi – cominciare a
leggere un libro molto interessante e dimenticarsi di uscire

Session 3

Interview 2

*Emanuela has a daughter, Anna, aged 5, and as we have said,
her husband, John, is American. Not being so high on the career
ladder, she doesn't have the paid help Marina has, but her parents,
now retired, live close by and help to some extent. She was asked
whether in fact she saw herself as a career woman.*

Emanuela	In un senso mi piacerebbe, certe volte mi sembra una cosa che posso apprezzare. Altre volte quando magari al mattino mia figlia non vuole lasciarmi uscire, vuole andare a spasso, un periodo in cui ha bisogno di suo papà, di sua mamma, vorrei non lavorare. Sto pensando che perdo, lavorando, gli anni più belli della mia famiglia, quello è brutto. Spero che lo sforzo valga la pena, ecco non sia inutile …
Interviewer	Dunque veramente il problema di abbinare famiglia e lavoro per te …
Emanuela	È difficile, è difficile, sì, devo dire che dopo cinque anni sono proprio stanca, è difficile e, purtroppo, anche chiacchierando con altre amiche che hanno più o meno la mia età, hanno bambini piccoli, loro hanno lo stesso problema. Nel lavoro è richiesta molta competizione, molte ore, un grosso sforzo e comunque la famiglia ha delle esigenze che non possono essere disattese. E quindi è una cosa che pesa a tutte, ecco.
Interviewer	Hai un marito americano, lo conosco, so che in casa lui condivide …
Emanuela	Sì, lui è bravissimo, no, non voglio dire bravissimo, lui fa esattamente quello che io penso sia il dovere di ogni coniuge. Mio marito è molto apprezzato dalle mie amiche, mi dicono che sono molto fortunata, che è bravissimo, che è un tesoro, che è un papà magnifico. È vero, credo sia un bravissimo papà, è un marito che condivide assolutamente l'impegno della casa. Però anche gli altri mariti che hanno una moglie che lavora devono per forza aiutare, non c'è scelta, è un obbligo perché la giornata è veramente troppo pesante, quindi … C'è qualche scemo … Si può dire scemo?
Interviewer	Perché no?
Emanuela	C'è qualche scemo che non aiuta e questo è causa di problemi familiari seri. Perché sono situazioni che poi danneggiano l'armonia familiare.
Interviewer	Allora l'uomo italiano giovane veramente …

184

Emanuela	Sì, sì, io trovo che i nostri coetanei, se non altro, magari non si occupano specificamente della casa però comunque fanno la spesa, lasciano il bagno in ordine, guardano i bambini, li portano al parco, vanno a prenderli in piscina, non è proprio più concepibile, lavorando tutti e due, avere una sola persona che si occupa della casa e dei figli. Non è assolutamente possibile. Mio cognato non fa nulla in casa perché mia sorella non lavora, quindi l'impegno della famiglia è esclusivamente quasi di mia sorella. Però lei ha la grossa fortuna di non dover lavorare fuori casa quindi … Suo marito ha una giornata molto intensa, molto stressante, tutto il carico familiare è suo, di lei, ecco. Però quella è una cosa anche equa, potendo permettersi di mantenere la moglie a casa …
Interviewer	E anche a te, piacerebbe stare a casa?
Emanuela	Sì, sicuramente sì. È una scelta che scontenterebbe mia mamma che non ha lavorato fuori casa dopo il matrimonio e lei trova l'indipendenza economica assolutamente necessaria. Evidentemente, pur essendo lei l'amministratrice delle finanze familiari, il fatto di non poter essere lei una fonte di guadagno autonoma forse pensa abbia limitato le sue scelte. Io in questo momento baratterei l'indipendenza economica che ho con più tranquillità, con una vita più semplice.
Interviewer	Sì?
Emanuela	Sì. Invece di avere una vita costantemente impegnata, organizzare la giornata, cosa farò questa sera per cena, chi va a prendere mia figlia? chi la porta in piscina? cosa facciamo adesso che lei è in vacanza? Quindi una continua rincorsa all'organizzazione familiare, ecco. Sacrificando tante volte anche la bambina che invece avrebbe bisogno di avere più tempo con noi. Potrei rinunciare al lavoro tranquillamente oggi, oggi

(Contd)

in particolare … (*ride*) Oggi in particolare. Io starei qui volentieri una settimana senza vedere nessuno, senza lavarmi neanche la faccia proprio, niente make-up, niente tailleur, niente scarpe con tacco alto. Starei qui una settimana ad andare in bicicletta, fare dei pranzi semplici, qua è molto tranquillo, svegliarsi al mattino, andare a prendere i lamponi e non fare niente tutto il giorno. Mi piace tanto questo posto.

coniuge *spouse* i.e. *husband or wife*; Lo Zingarelli 2010: **ciascuna delle due persone unite in matrimonio (sia il marito che la moglie)**. Latinists will have found guessing easy. **Coniugato** means *married* and in official documents **già coniugato** is sometimes used rather than *divorziato*; also **libero/a di stato**.

si può dire …? *can you say* (lit: *can one say?*). **Si può** is neater than **è possibile** which learners sometimes use. Try to adopt it!

scemo *fool, silly person* (Lo Zingarelli 2010: **che manca di giudizio, di senno, di intelligenza**). Emanuela's hesitation in using the word would seem to be related to her personal judgment of what might be described as lazy, thoughtless or selfish husbands. Here she is saying that they haven't the sense to understand the consequences of their behaviour.

coetani A good one for guessing: **co + età**. *People of the same age as us.*

scontenterebbe Can you guess? **contento**, preceded by the **s** which makes it negative: *it would make (my mother) unhappy.*

Oggi in particolare … Io starei qui … questo posto The interview took place on a lovely Sunday late in June, in the attractive hills of the Alte Langhe (southern Piemonte) where Emanuela's ancestors used to farm and where her parents still have a rather dilapidated, very old house. The idea of being back in the noise of the city and going to work the next morning was obviously not appealing!

lamponi *raspberries*. Emanuela and her family have a kitchen garden at the farm, with some particularly prolific raspberry canes.

Comprehension 2

1 From what is said here, summarize Emanuela's attitude to being a career woman.

2 What is her big worry?

3 What does she find she has in common with friends of her own age?

4 Her friends think Emanuela is very lucky in her husband, but she takes back the word **bravissimo** which she initially uses to talk about his sharing of the household tasks. Why?

5 In talking about the husbands of working wives generally, she uses the same phrase as Marina. What is it?

6 What sort of tasks does she say young Italian husbands undertake?

7 Her life and her sister's are very different. What do you learn about her sister and her brother-in-law?

8 What seems to be the position of Emanuela's mother as regards working wives?

9 Emanuela is feeling particularly tired. What seems to plague her life?

10 What would Emanuela like to do for a week, rather than go back to the city and her job?

The general opinion, when you ask various people, not just our interviewees who each had rather special situations, seems to be that sharing of domestic duties between husband and wife is still unequal in many cases even though the wife is, like her husband, trying to make a career. Italian women attribute this in part to **la mamma italiana** who – and this is a generalization of course – tends to be indulgent towards her sons and do everything for them while requiring her daughters to help in the house.

Session 4

The gerund again

You may have noticed both Marina and Emanuela use **stare +** *gerund* for on-going actions:

Marina
anche gli uomini italiani si stanno evolvendo.	*Italian men too are evolving, making progress.*

Emanuela
Sto pensando che …	*I keep thinking that …*

In the second case, in English we probably wouldn't say *I am thinking*. What Emanuela means seems to be that the thought recurs to her quite often, it is on-going in that sense.

But Emanuela uses the *gerund*, the form ending in **-ando/-endo**, several times without the verb **stare**:

Sto pensando che perdo, <u>lavorando</u>, gli anni più belli …
I keep thinking that by working I am losing the best years …

anche <u>chiacchierando</u> con altre amiche …
also when chatting with other friends …

non è proprio concepibile, <u>lavorando</u> tutti e due, avere una sola persona che si occupa della casa e dei figli.
it's not really conceivable, with both working/since both are working, to have one single person who looks after the house and the children.

tutto il carico familiare è suo, di lei, ecco. Però quello è una cosa anche equa, <u>potendo</u> permettersi di mantenere la moglie a casa …
the whole burden of home and family falls on her. However that is also fair, since he can (afford to) maintain his wife at home …

pur <u>essendo</u> lei l'amministratrice delle finanze familiari ...
even though she is the administrator of the family finances ...

From the above examples you can see that there is a variety of ways in which the gerund can be translated. It is used when in English you might say:

on
by } + verb +*ing*
when
since + clause with verb

Note that the subject of the gerund should be the same as that of the main verb. Emanuela says: **Sto pensando che perdo, lavorando, gli anni più belli.** *She is thinking and she is working.* Note: clarity is lost when this is not the case, as in the last example but one.

Activity 3

In the sentences which follow, change the part in bold print to the gerund.

Example: **Dal momento che ha** un lavoro molto impegnativo, Emanuela non può passare molto tempo con sua figlia.
Avendo un lavoro molto impegnativo, Emanuela non può passare molto tempo con sua figlia.

1 Certe mattine Emanuela non vorrebbe andare a lavorare, **poiché sa** che sua figlia sentirà la sua mancanza.
2 La vita di Emanuela è al momento molto faticosa, **perché deve** abbinare famiglia e lavoro.
3 Dal momento che condivide tutti i lavori domestici con lei, il marito di Emanuela le è di grande aiuto.
4 Certi mariti non si rendono conto che, **se non aiutano** in casa, danneggiano l'armonia familiare e rendono la vita difficile a sé stessi prima ancora che alla moglie.

5 La maggior parte dei giovani mariti italiani è di sostegno alla moglie **perché lascia** il bagno in ordine, **fa** la spesa, **guarda** i bambini, **li porta** al parco, **li va** a prendere in piscina.
6 **Visto che non deve** lavorare fuori casa, mia sorella ha molto più tempo di me per badare alla casa e alla famiglia.

The adjectival form: the present participle

The gerund is a verbal form. The -*ing* ending in English can be adjectival and there is also an adjectival form in Italian ending in **-ante** (Group 1, -are verbs) and **-ente** (all other verbs). Its technical name is the present participle. This is a tricky area and we suggest you limit yourself to using present participles you have met, in similar contexts to those in which you met them.

un'esperienza sconvolgente   *a shattering experience*
(*Lo Zingarelli* 2010: sconvolgere: mettere in disordine, in agitazione, in scompiglio)

un fatto raccapricciante   *a horrifying fact*
(*Lo Zingarelli* 2010: raccapricciare: provare orrore, turbare profondamente)

Here the -*ing* word (**-ante/-ente** word in Italian) tells us more about the noun. The Italian has a plural form in **-i**: **scene commoventi** *moving scenes*.

As with other adjectives, this form can be used as a noun. Indeed some are also nouns: **un credente** *a believer*; **un principiante** *a beginner*.

Activity 4

Change the expression in bold print to the correct form of the present participle.

Example: Un risultato **che incoraggia**. Un risultato **incoraggiante**.

1 Una persona **che resiste** a grandi fatiche. = Una persona ...
2 Un rumore così forte da **assordare**. = Un rumore ...
3 Un oggetto **che pesa** molto. = Un oggetto ...
4 Un calciatore **che ha la funzione di attaccare**. = Un ...
5 Un vestito **che aderisce** al corpo. = Un vestito ...
6 Un film che non era bello come ti aspettavi e **che** ti **delude**. = Un film ...
7 Un criminale **che traffica** in armi. = Un ... d'armi.
8 Una persona **che presiede** un'associazione. = Un ...

The student may be perplexed occasionally to find a present participle which does not seem to obey the rules for its formation given above. This is because the Italian participle derives directly from the Latin participle, whereas the verb over the centuries has changed its form. One of the little fascinations of language study! Here are some examples:

Una persona **che prevede** i problemi e si organizza per tempo.
Una persona **previdente**. (i in participle, **e** in verb)

Un coltello affilato **che taglia** molto bene.
Un coltello **tagliente**. (**-are** verb but participle in **-ente**)

Una persona **che diffida** di tutto e di tutti.
Una persona **diffidente**. (**-are** verb but participle in **-ente**)

Question words – interrogative pronouns

Emanuela finds herself daily plagued by finding solutions to certain problems:

Cosa farò questa sera per cena? *What shall I do for supper tonight?*
Chi va a prendere mia figlia? *Who is going to fetch my daughter?*

This highlights the words used for asking questions, interrogative pronouns, the Italian equivalents of *who* and *what*. **Chi?** is *who?* and *whom?* i.e. subject or object.

Chi è?	*Who is it?* (subject)
Chi arriva?	*Who is arriving?* (subject)
Chi vedi?	*Who can you see?* (object)
Con chi parli?	*Who are you talking to?* (object)

Cosa? che cosa? or **che?** can all be *what?* Probably **cosa** is the most common in spoken, everyday Italian, while **che** belongs more to formal, even literary usage. All three can be subject or object:

Che cosa è?	*What is it?* (subject)
Cosa fai?	*What are you doing?* (object)
Con che cosa lo apri?	*What do you open it with?* (object)

There is a list of question words (interrogative) in the **Reference grammar**.

Questions which expect the answer *yes* or *no* need no question word and are made by using the question intonation in speech, or, in writing, by adding a question mark.

Ti piace il formaggio?	*Do you like cheese?*
Conosci Anna Pavese?	*Do you know Anna Pavese?*
Hai visto il nuovo film di Benigni?	*Have you seen Benigni's new film?*

Activity 5

A curious child, who asks questions all the time, is plaguing you. Here are the replies you give him. Work out what his questions were. Use the interrogative pronouns **chi** and **che cosa**. A clue: all the questions are about types of work or workers.

Examples: È la persona che ci consegna la posta ogni mattina.
Question: **Chi è il postino?**

Ci consegna la posta ogni mattina.
Question: **Che cosa fa il postino?**

1 Scrive gli .articoli sui giornali che leggiamo ogni giorno.
   Question:

2 È la persona che vende la frutta e la verdura.
   Question:

3 È la persona che aggiusta i rubinetti quando sono rotti.
   Question:

4 Suona il pianoforte.
   Question:

5 Dipinge quadri.
   Question:

Session 5

Personal pronouns: object, direct and indirect, and reflexive

These are usually covered in beginners' courses since you can't go far without them. There is a table in the **Reference grammar**, should you need it. Emanuela's interview however provides a useful springboard for reminding you about their place in relation to the verb. Study the following;

quando magari mia figlia non vuole lasciar_mi_ uscire
when perhaps my daughter doesn't want to let me leave

Hai un marito americano, <u>lo</u> conosco
You have an American husband, I know him

(i nostri coetanei) guardano i bambini, <u>li</u> portano al parco, vanno a prender<u>li</u> in piscina ...
(men of our age) look after the children, take them to the park, go and fetch them from the swimming pool

senza lavar<u>mi</u> neanche la faccia proprio
without even washing my face

Object pronouns, whether direct or indirect or indeed reflexive, usually precede the verb. However there are certain parts of the verb where they are attached to the end. Can you see some cases in the examples above? Yes, with the infinitive. This is also the case with the gerund:

Mio marito si occupa dei bambini, portandoli al parco, prendendoli da scuola, accompagnandoli dal medico.
My husband looks after the children, taking them to the park, picking them up from school, going with them to the doctor's.

Note that the stress does not change. Pronouns are also attached to the imperative:

dimmi	(**tu** form)	*tell me*
scusami	(**tu** form)	*forgive me, excuse me*
diamoci del tu	(**noi** form)	*let's use* **tu** *to each other*
ditelo con i fiori	(**voi** form)	*say it with flowers*

Note also that the formal, third person form of the command is really a subjunctive so this rule does not apply, hence:

mi scusi	*forgive me, excuse me*
mi dica	*tell me (see Unit 5, Session 4)*
s'accomodi	*please sit down*

Language learning tip

Learn some common examples, for instance: **mi dica, dimmi; mi scusi, scusami.** Use them as models.

Personal pronouns: subject, emphatic pronouns

Did you notice that both Marina and Emanuela used pronouns to stress and/or make clear who they are referring to?

quando sono via ... si occupa <u>lui</u> della gestione domestica
when I am away ... he takes care of the household management

Sì, <u>lui</u> è bravissimo, ... <u>lui</u> fa esattamente quello che io penso sia il dovere di ogni coniuge ...
Yes, he is very good, ... he does exactly what I think is every husband's duty

pur essendo <u>lei</u> l'amministratrice delle finanze familiari, il fatto di non poter essere <u>lei</u> una fonte di guadagno autonoma forse pensa abbia limitato le sue scelte.

even though she runs the family finances, perhaps she thinks that the fact of not being able, herself, to be an autonomous source of earning has limited her choices.

And in another place Emanuela puts in **di lei** to help clarify what would otherwise be ambiguous, although she still leaves the following sentence possibly unclear because the subject of the main verb, **è**, is not the same as that of the gerund, **potendo**. In the English translation the differentiation between the possessives, *his* and *her*, helps as does the avoidance of the gerund. When you feel the possessives are leading to a lack of clarity in Italian, you can put in: **di lui, di lei …**, as Emanuela does.

Suo marito ha una giornata molto intensa, molto stressante, tutto il carico familiare è <u>suo, di lei</u>, ecco. Però quella è una cosa anche equa, potendo permettersi di mantenere la moglie a casa.

Her husband has very intensive, stressful days, and all the burden of the family falls on her. However that is only fair, since he is able to afford to keep his wife at home.

Activity 6

Emanuela is very lucky: her husband shares equally with her the responsibility for their home and for the upbringing of their daughter. Here is an imaginary conversation between the two of them. Emanuela suddenly remembers something urgent to do and her husband immediately offers the solution. Write the husband's answers, using personal pronouns correctly as in the example.

Example: Emanuela **Domani bisogna pagare la bolletta del telefono!**
     The telephone bill has to be paid tomorrow.

     Suo marito **Non preoccuparti! <u>La</u> pago <u>io</u>!**
     Don't worry. I'll pay it.

1 Emanuela: Domani bisogna portare la bambina in piscina!

Suo marito:

2 Emanuela: Domani viene a cena mia mamma! Chi prepara la cena?

Suo marito:

3 Emanuela: Domani bisogna spedire quelle lettere!

Suo marito:

4 Emanuela: Domani dobbiamo andare a fare la spesa!

Suo marito:

Insight

Note the difference between **bisogna** *it is necessary* and **ha bisogno di** lit. *she has need of*, which Emanuela uses in Interview 2. **Bisogna** is a verb and is always followed by an infinitive. **Bisogno** is a noun and is always followed by **di** + noun or infinitive. It can be used with '**avere**' **ha bisogno di suo papà** *she needs her daddy*, or with '**essere**' **c'è bisogno di molto aiuto** *there is a need for a lot of help*.

Activity 7

In this exercise you practise using personal pronouns both before and after verbs. The text is based on what Marina says and the pronouns (subject, direct and indirect object and reflexive) have been omitted. Your job is to provide them! You may find it useful first to glance at the table of pronouns in the **Reference grammar**.

La famiglia di Marina *Marina's family*

A Marina è una donna in carriera, che deve trovare ogni giorno una soluzione per conciliare la sua vita di mamma e moglie con la sua vita lavorativa. Si ritiene fortunata, perché suo marito le è di grande aiuto quando ___ (1) è via per lavoro, si occupa delle bambine, ___ (2) va a prendere a scuola, ___ (3) aiuta a fare i compiti, organizza la giornata per ___ (4). Spesso viene aiutato

in questo da una ragazza alla pari, ma è ___ (5) che deve
telefonar___ (6), discutere con ___ (7) la giornata e gli orari
delle bambine, pagar___ (8).

> ## Insight
>
> You can say **le va a prendere a scuola** or **va prenderle a
> scuola**. This happens also with **potere, dovere, volere**:
> **lo posso fare or posso farlo** *I can do it*, **dobbiamo capirlo** or
> **lo dobbiamo capire** *we must understand it*, **volevo vederlo** or
> **lo volevo vedere** *I wanted to see it*.

B Marina e suo marito possono anche contare sull'aiuto di una
donna delle pulizie, però non ___ (1) conoscono molto bene,
quindi non si fidano di lasciare la pulizia della casa completamente
nelle sue mani. Quando Marina non è via per lavoro, si occupa ___
(2) di dar___ (3) istruzioni e di mostrar___(4) quali sono i lavori
più urgenti. Invece, quando Marina è fuori città, è il marito che
deve preoccuparsene: è ___ (5) che deve aspettar___ (6) la mattina
prima di uscire per andare al lavoro, è ___ (7) che deve scrivere
per ___ (8) la lista dei lavori più urgenti, è ___ (9) che deve
controllare che tutto sia stato fatto alla fine della giornata e che
deve pagar___ (10) alla fine della settimana.

C A quanto pare, il marito di Marina non è entusiasta di tutto
questo! ___ (1) adatta, perché sa di non avere scelta. Quando
Marina è via, ___ (2) sveglia più presto del solito la mattina, sveglia
le bambine, controlla che ___ (3) lavino, ___ (4) vestano, facciano
colazione e arrivino in orario a scuola. La sera, quando torna
dal lavoro, cucina per ___ (5) e per sé stesso e ___ (6) preoccupa
di controllare che la loro giornata sia andata bene. Ha imparato
a fare tutte queste cose perché non è mai stato viziato da sua
mamma, ma in fondo in fondo pensa che la sua vita sarebbe molto
più facile se avesse sposato una donna più tradizionale!

The subjunctive after sperare and other verbs

Emanuela refers to the difficulties of being a working mother and then says:

Spero che lo sforzo valga la pena, ecco, non sia inutile. *I hope the effort is worthwhile, that it is not pointless.*

The subjunctive underlines her doubts, which come through the whole interview. She works in order to provide a better life for her daughter, but finds it all very stressful and wonders whether the game is worth the candle.

After **sperare**, the subjunctive is not always used. This may be partly a personal choice, part of the speaker's style. To use a subjunctive after **sperare** may however be subconsciously underlining one's uncertainty. Apart from the present indicative, the future is sometimes used after **sperare**:

Spero che farà bel tempo domani. *I hope the weather will be good tomorrow.*

The subjunctive is used after other verbs which introduce an element of subjectivity. You have already met it after **credere**, **pensare**, in other words when opinions are involved. It is also required in clauses which follow verbs expressing other emotions such as wanting, regret, fear, doubt.

Voglio che dica la verità. *I want him to tell the truth.*
Teme che il risultato sia negativo. *He's afraid the result will be negative.*
Dubito che riesca a convincere sua moglie. *I doubt he will succeed in convincing his wife.*

Do you appreciate that the first verb is introducing the subject's point of view on the second? I want him to tell the truth – that is my wish, but may not be his, or his boss's, etc. You will also realize there is some cross-over in the emotions. For instance, **non credo che** may well be expressing doubt as well as opinion.

Avoiding the subjunctive

If the subject of both verbs is the same, there is no need for a subjunctive:

Voglio dire la verità.	*I want to tell the truth.*
Teme di essere noioso.	*He's afraid of being boring.*
Dubito di convincere mia moglie.	*I doubt I'll convince my wife.*

And when giving your opinion you can always say:

Secondo me, è un'impresa impossibile.	*In my opinion it's an impossible undertaking.*

Activity 8

Imagine you are an Italian woman and you are very sceptical about the possibility of a change in the position of women in Italy. You have read an article in the newspaper which says that Italian men in the younger generation are changing. You decide to write a letter to the editor to put your point of view which is that Italian men are not changing at all and you see the future for Italian women as very black! Explain your ideas using the following expressions, followed by the subjunctive: **penso/non penso che ...; credo/non credo che ...; temo che ...; dubito che ...; ho l'impressione che ...; spero che ...**

Example: **Non credo che** gli uomini italiani della nuova generazione <u>siano</u> <u>diversi</u> da quelli delle generazioni precedenti.
I don't believe the new generation of Italian men is different from preceding generations.

The choice of arguments and words is yours, so we cannot give a right answer but there is a letter written by an Italian for you in the Key.

Session 6

Interview 3

Signora Torrielli's two daughters now have children of their own and she is a grandmother. When she was younger, however, in addition to the difficulties of being a working mother, she had a sense of guilt, since she was a single mother. This was by choice, but didn't mean she was without regrets.

Interviewer	Lei tiene molto alla famiglia, vero?
Signora Torrielli	Sì. Io mi sono sposata, che ero molto giovane, ho avuto subito due figlie e dopo due anni mi sono separata. Il cruccio della mia vita è stato il fatto di riuscire a fare la mamma separata e mantenerle con un certo reddito per poter fare le cose cui ero abituata prima, e nonostante questo … tentare di mantenere il più vivo possibile il rapporto con le mie figlie. Adesso alla luce degli anni passati, le mie figlie hanno ormai 41 anni e 39 anni, mi sembra di esserci riuscita. Certo con molto sacrificio da parte mia e molti rimpianti adesso che forse valeva più la pena privilegiare meno le cose materiali, quindi dire: ahimè, se non ci possiamo permettere quella cosa lì, io lavoro due ore in meno al giorno, non ci permettiamo quella cosa lì, ma stiamo insieme … Però è un senno di poi, invece se non avevamo quella cosa lì, magari il nostro rapporto non sarebbe stato bello com'è stato, chissà?
Interviewer	Aveva aiuti?
Signora Torrielli	Sì, sì, ma io sto proprio parlando del rapporto personale che è quello che conta, non è chi gli dà la minestra, chi gli dà la pastasciutta. Quello che io intendevo è proprio il tempo mancato della quotidianità, del minuto col minuto … comunque

tutte le donne che lavorano questo problema ce l'hanno, in più io avevo la colpa di essere separata, sentivo questa colpa qui. Ma qui tutte hanno i bambini e i bambini stanno a casa e la mamma li porta dalla nonna, li porta all'asilo nido, insomma, non ha importanza, ma per nove ore al giorno chi lavora non vede i figli. Adesso poi che uno sia una buona mamma, paziente, per tutte le 24 ore o che invece per il suo carattere è meglio che faccia la mamma tre ore al giorno piuttosto che 21 ore, io penso di appartenere a quel gruppo, preferisco vederli nel momento in cui sono più disponibile piuttosto che vederli tutto il giorno poi magari essere nervosa come vediamo in certe mamme in giro ...

Lei tiene molto alla famiglia, vero? *The family means a lot to you, doesn't it?*

il cruccio Difficult to translate in one word. *Lo Zingarelli 2010:* **tormento, afflizione, dolore morale**; **seccatura, fastidio**. Perhaps Signora Torrielli just means *anxiety*.

ahimè *oh dear, alas.*

un senno di poi *Senno* is *wisdom, sense*, so can you guess? *Hindsight.*

chi gli dà la minestra, chi gli dà la pastasciutta. minestra is *soup*, usually with pasta or rice in it. But it can also mean *first course* (pasta course) of a meal. **pastasciutta is what we know as simply** *pasta*. But Signora Torrielli means the children's food in general. An interesting sidelight on the centrality of pasta in the Italian diet.

la colpa *guilt.* Don't forget separation was less common then. Indeed it would have been before divorce was possible in Italy, i.e. before 1970. But separated parents will possibly understand Signora Torrielli's feeling anyway.

qui tutte hanno bambini Signora Torrielli is at her workplace: she is referring to her employees.

vederli nel momento in cui sono disponibile Signora Torrielli is talking about 'quality time', time when the mother's attention is devoted entirely to the children.

Comprehension 3

1 Signora Torrielli says that as a mother separated from her husband she tried to do two things for her daughters, which were very difficult to combine. What were they? And does she think she achieved her aims?

2 What was the cost to her personally? What does she wonder?

3 Signora Torrielli had help with the children of course. But what does she think is important for a mother?

4 What does she say of the women who work in the factory?

5 What does she feel made her situation particularly difficult?

6 What sort of mother does she think she was?

Session 7

The subjunctive after impersonal expressions

Signora Torrielli says:

> per il suo carattere è meglio che <u>faccia</u> la mamma tre ore al giorno piuttosto che 21 ore

A number of impersonal expressions are usually followed by a subjunctive. A list of common ones is provided in the **Reference grammar**. An element of judgment, of subjectivity, is always present. (Subjunctive – subjectivity, point of view, do you remember? See Unit 5.) For instance, in the example above, one might ask: **meglio** *better* according to what criteria? These impersonal expressions relate to judgments about necessity, importance, advisability, possibility and similar concepts.

Reading

Read this extract from an article from *La Stampa*.

Studio dell'Istat: 'Colpa del marito'

La donna sposata lavora due ore in più al giorno

Sul posto di lavoro pubblico e privato resta la discriminazione contro le femmine

ROMA. È colpa dei mariti: sono loro, infatti, a procurare alle donne due ore di fatica in più ogni giorno. Come se non bastassero le 60 ore settimanali di lavoro, dentro e fuori le pareti domestiche, che vengono svolte da oltre la metà di loro. Più di un terzo, poi, supera anche le 70 ore a settimana.

Il vantaggio di non avere un partner per le donne occupate e con figli è emerso da uno studio presentato ieri, nella sede dell'Istat, dal ministero delle Pari Opportunità …

E i 'numeri' presentati dicono tanto. A scuola, per esempio, le donne riescono senz'altro di più degli uomini: su 1000 femmine con la licenza media, 160 arrivano alla laurea contro appena 107 maschi. Ma, poi, quando si tratta di trovare un lavoro, la musica cambia bruscamente: se nella categoria 'impiegati' sono più numerose dei colleghi maschi, nei luoghi dove si decide la presenza femminile è davvero ridotta.

Tra i dirigenti dei ministeri, le donne sono appena il 7,8 per cento, tra i primari ospedalieri il 6,9 per cento, tra i prefetti il 5,4 per cento. E, se nell'università raggiungono l'11,1 per cento dei professori ordinari, la carica di rettore si riduce ed è riservata appena al 3,1 per cento. Per non parlare delle istituzioni pubbliche: senza scomodare i 'record' stabiliti dalla Norvegia e dalla Svezia, dove la presenza femminile si aggira intorno al 40 per cento, ci sono più donne nei Parlamenti dell'Africa del Sud, del Portogallo e della Spagna che nel nostro.

Eppure qualcosa sta cambiando, anche se molto lentamente, è emerso dai dati elaborati dall'Istat. Le donne delle nuove generazioni – ha sottolineato il ministro Balbo – 'non sono più quelle delle campagne italiane di 50 anni fa'. Dal '93 al '98 sono aumentate le imprenditrici (da 54.000 a 83.000), le libere professioniste (da 125.000 a 200.000), le socie di cooperative (da 65.000 a 128.000), le donne quadro (da 240.000 a 324.000).

Il problema è che questa crescita procede disordinatamente, a macchia di leopardo, e perciò il tasso di disoccupazione femminile, ad esempio, oscilla in maniera vistosa tra Emilia Romagna (8,4 per cento) e Calabria (39 per cento) ...

(La Stampa, martedì 9 febbraio 1999)

QUICK VOCAB

Istat Istituto Centrale di Statistica
licenza media The *diploma* awarded to those who pass the final examinations at the end of middle school.
primari ospedalieri *hospital consultants*
prefetti *prefect,* senior civil servant who represents the government in a province
rettore *rector,* the senior academic who presides over a university. English equivalent: *Vice-Chancellor.*
donne quadro *women executives*
a macchia di leopardo *in an uneven way*

Activity 9

Imagine you are the Minister for Equal Opportunities and you are reporting on the Istat findings to your colleagues. However, there is to your mind some doubt about the statistics. Transform the following statements inserting **sembra che** and changing the verbs to reflect your doubts, as in the example:

Example: **Più di un terzo delle donne italiane supera le 70 ore di lavoro alla settimana.**
More than a third of Italian women work over 70 hours a week.
In base ai dati Istat, **sembra che** più di un terzo delle donne italiane **superi** le 70 ore di lavoro alla settimana.

1 A scuola le donne riescono più degli uomini.
In base ai dati Istat, sembra che ...
2 Su 1000 femmine con la licenza media, 160 arrivano alla laurea contro appena 107 maschi.
In base ai dati Istat, sembra che ...
3 La presenza femminile è davvero ridotta nei luoghi in cui si decide.
In base ai dati Istat, sembra che ...
4 Nell'università, le donne raggiungono l'11,1 per cento dei professori ordinari.
In base ai dati Istat, sembra che ...
5 Il tasso di disoccupazione femminile oscilla in maniera vistosa tra il nord e il sud.
In base ai dati Istat, sembra che ...

Ce l'hanno: **word order**

In the following sentence, Signora Torrielli illustrates together two usages which are common in spoken Italian:

Tutte le donne che lavorano questo problema ce l'hanno.   *All working women have this problem.*

One usage is to put the object before the verb and then in effect to repeat it by using a pronoun which stands for it. Here the object is **questo problema** and the l' refers to it. It is a way of stressing, emphasizing the object. If you look back through the texts in the book you will find other examples. You had no difficulty in understanding, and once you are in Italy, with ears pricked, listening hard to the way people speak, you will find yourself doing exactly the same thing, although in English you would not dream of saying: *All working women this problem they have it.*

Sometimes, particularly in speech, the object comes after the verb but is emphasized by a pronoun standing for it being inserted before the verb. There is an example in the extract from Natalia Ginzburg's account of winter in the village where her husband was exiled: the peasants say to them:

'Ma quando ci tornate alle case vostre?'

It is useful to remember that in Italian word order is more flexible than in English. Look out for this and gradually try to imitate what Italians say.

Ce l'hanno: a peculiarity of the verb avere

It is common practice, in spoken Italian, to use **ci** with the verb **avere**. This is particularly so when there is an object pronoun, but not only then.

Activity 10

You are setting off on an important business trip. You will be away for a week. You are rather apprehensive about the trip. In the taxi taking you to the airport you check mentally that you have everything you need with you.

Example: Il passaporto: Il passaporto, ce l'ho? Sì, ce l'ho!
            Passport: *Have I got my passport? Yes, I have.*

1 **Le chiavi di casa:** ....
2 **Gli appunti per il convegno:** ....
3 **L'indirizzo dell'albergo:** ....
4 **Il telefonino:** ....
5 **La patente:** ....
6 **Gli occhiali:** ....
7 **L'agendina:** ....
8 **Le pastiglie per il mal di testa:** ....

Session 8

Interview 4

We have looked a lot at the problems of working women.
We must redress the balance of the sexes a little! Carlo's career,
a very successful one, has presented rather different problems.
Indeed, Carlo has an approach to life which means problems
are simply a challenge. He is now Managing Director of an old
established firm in Trieste but, as he told you in Unit 4, he came
from humble origins in the countryside near Asti. His first job,
immediately after his military service, was selling office furniture at
shows. Here's how he describes his first moves up the career ladder.

Carlo Guadagnavo molto poco, però all'epoca, era una cosa
molto curiosa, c'era l'Ente Risi, che promuoveva il riso,
e facevo tutte le fiere con l'Ente Risi, per coincidenza, e
quindi mangiavo mattina, cena, a colazione, questi risi che
erano offerti a prezzi di promozione quindi, ero pagato
poco ma riuscivo a sbarcare il lunario. Dopo sei mesi, ho
mandato il mio cv alla Nestlé e sono entrato alla Nestlé
come amministrativo, usando il mio diploma. Ma non
mi piaceva, non ero capace, allora ho chiesto di passare
dalla parte commerciale e ho avuto fortuna perché mi
hanno mandato in Val d'Aosta a sostituire un ispettore
che c'era. Io ho sempre avuto veramente molta fortuna,
sono sempre andato o in mercati facili o a sostituire degli
incapaci o della gente che non erano granché lavoratori
ecc. Allora in Nestlé ho avuto molta fortuna perché
ho vinto vari premi come quello che aveva venduto le
maggiori quantità o ottenuto il maggior numero di nuovi
punti di vendita, e grazie a tutte queste piccole vittorie,
sono passato alla Cinzano come ispettore nella filiale di
Milano e poi direttore vendite. A 28 anni ero già dirigente,
una cosa importante a quell'epoca.

(Contd)

♠ CD2, TR 10, 30:21

He worked hard, improving his academic skills in evening classes.

E poi ho chiesto alla società di mandarmi all'estero perché capivo che era più facile fare carriera all'estero per la semplice ragione che c'era meno concorrenza. Mi avevano prospettato di andare in Inghilterra ed ero entusiasta. Pensavo: imparerò bene l'inglese, avrò la possibilità di confrontarmi con un mondo molto competitivo, molto professionale. E invece è saltata fuori un'opportunità in Brasile e io all'inizio non ero per niente interessato perché dicevo: vado in Brasile, mi sfrutteranno come un frutto e poi mi butteranno via. Invece ho imparato tantissimo in Sud America. Ho imparato a essere duro, a sporcarmi le mani, affrontare le responsabilità. In Brasile ho avuto anche dei buoni risultati grazie al fatto che era un mercato che stava sviluppandosi molto bene.

Poi ho lasciato la Cinzano, sono diventato direttore generale per la Moët et Chandon. La mia prima iniziativa imprenditoriale era aprire una fabbrica nel Rio Grande del Sud, una terra ricca di immigrati italiani e tedeschi e che produceva del vino buono ...

Poi la Cinzano mi ha richiamato e mi ha chiesto se non volevo fare il direttore generale su in Venezuela, una piccola società ... e ho avuto delle soddisfazioni enormi, ho tirato su una società che aveva 50 dipendenti a 180 a distanza di un anno circa, lanciando tre prodotti che erano dei pilastri che poi si esportavano ... poi sono diventato presidente nel Sud America.

Nel frattempo la famiglia, ho capito che si stava un po' troppo incentivando, perché lì fai la vita di club, golf club, con persone di servizio, ecc. E capivo che questo è bello se tu lo fai con umiltà, però se tu lo fai per troppo tempo, finisci che ti convinci che tu sei fra quei pochi privilegiati, che questa è la vita, e siccome né io, né Anne ci divertivamo a fare la vita dei ricchi, e specialmente temevamo un pochino per le implicazioni negative per i figli, ho deciso di fare ritorno in Europa.

In quel momento gli inglesi hanno comprato la Cinzano e mi
hanno promosso, mi hanno offerto la direzione generale della
Spagna e del Portogallo. Allora sono venuto in Spagna e anche
lì ho avuto fortuna perché ho sostituito ancora una volta
qualcuno pieno di arie ma poco lavoratore, poi erano anche
gli anni che si preparavano i mondiali, gli Olympic Games,
Madrid Capitale della Cultura, Siviglia Expo, quindi c'era tutto
boom, è andato tanto bene però non avevo più la possibilità
di fare l'imprenditore perché in una multinazionale tutto è già
stabilito, tu ricevi solamente, la campagna pubblicitaria è già
fatta, il prodotto c'è, e allora un headhunter mi ha cercato,
e mi è stata offerta una posizione che era quella di una
società a Trieste, la Stock, dove c'erano gli azionisti che erano
litigiosi e che volevano mettere la società praticamente nelle
mani non più della famiglia ma di qualcheduno che avesse
un'esperienza diversa … Così ho accettato.

*In fact, the family shareholders made Carlo's job impossible as they
were hopelessly divided on policy. After six months he handed them
his resignation. The shareholders' reaction was:*

'Se tu dici che non possiamo gestire quest'azienda, allora
l'unica prospettiva è quella di vendere.' In quel momento,
l'azienda è stata venduta ai tedeschi e i tedeschi in questo
momento sono i miei azionisti. Ho una esperienza molto
bella perché ho degli azionisti molto intelligenti che mi
hanno fatto delle proposte molto chiare: 'Il business è
tuo. Se funziona, bene. Se non funziona, una fucilata al
cuore e via.' E l'azienda nel frattempo stava andando
molto male ed è lì che è cominciata quella triste storia di
ristrutturazione che è cominciata esattamente al febbraio
dell'anno '97 e mi ha obbligato a fare dei tagli di ben
107 persone. Era la prima volta che io avevo un bilancio
negativo e che dovevo licenziare delle persone, tutte le
mie esperienze erano affari positivi, ero sempre in crescita
e in questo momento mi accingo a fare la seconda
ristrutturazione per garantire un ulteriore sviluppo della
nostra azienda.

le fiere *trade fairs, shows* (e.g. agricultural shows). But *a funfair* in Italian is **luna park**.

sbarcare il lunario *to make ends meet*

usando il mio diploma You may remember, Carlo is a **ragioniere**.

direttore generale *general manager*

iniziativa imprenditoriale Carlo had managed established businesses. Now his work was more that of an entrepreneur, starting a new activity from scratch, even if he had Moët behind him.

su in Venezuela *up in Venezuela.* Carlo was then in Brazil, so he sees a northward move as 'up'.

incentivando An unusual use of the verb. It is normally used in the context of business meaning: *motivate.* Of course, what he means is he and his wife feared the children were getting too used to the artificially high standard of living of an expatriate **direttore generale**.

Anne Carlo's (Scottish) wife.

pieno di arie Carlo means: all appearance rather than substance. **Darsi delle arie** *to give oneself airs.*

i mondiali *the World Cup* (1984 soccer – and Italy won!)

una fucilata al cuore *a bullet through your heart* (**fucilata**: *(gun)shot*)

Insight

Carlo spoke of his past career. List all the verbs in the past putting them into 5 categories: the perfect with **avere**, the perfect with **essere**, the passive form of the perfect, the imperfect and the few cases of pluperfect.

Comprehension 4

1 Carlo's first job was not well paid but he managed to get by. How?

2 Carlo reckons he has had a lot of luck in his career. What sort of luck?

3 He is proud of his early success. What does he say that reveals this?

4 Why did he not want to go to Brazil?

5 Why does he not regret going?

6 He enjoyed his job with Moët and the place he worked in. Why?

7 He also found his job in Venezuela satisfying. In what way?

8 What did he and his wife feel about their life style in South America?

9 Why did Carlo consider himself lucky when he came to work in Spain and Portugal?

10 Why does Carlo consider his German shareholders good to work for?

11 What experiences has he had with Stock which were new to him – and which he has not enjoyed?

12 What is your overall impression of Carlo?

Session 9

Carlo's interview was a long one, but the Italian was not very difficult. We thought you would enjoy a man's view. Now you should go over the various interviews and articles in this unit. You should find them easier. And we hope they will give you things to talk about to yourself – or others. Here are some suggestions.

Activity 11

Talking to yourself

1 Quanto conta la fortuna nella vita? Lei si considera fortunato/a? E quanto conta essere avventuroso, intraprendente? Quali altri fattori contribuiscono al successo nella vita, secondo Lei? Infatti, per Lei, che cosa è il successo nella vita?

2 Per una coppia che ha figli da educare, essere ricchi costituisce un problema nella Sua opinione? Quali sono le difficoltà? E per una famiglia povera, quali problemi esistono nell'educazione dei figli? Se Lei è di una generazione che ha educato figli qualche anno fa, secondo Lei, a parte le condizioni materiali personali, sarebbe più difficile oggi, nella società in cui ci troviamo ora?

3 La signora Torrielli ha sollevato la questione della qualità del tempo che la madre (e il padre, perché no?) passano con i figli. Secondo Lei, è meglio essere sempre con loro, ma magari squattrinati, stanchi, ecc. o avere un lavoro, migliori condizioni economiche – e dedicargli forse tre/quattro ore al giorno – tutte per loro?

4 Molti uomini vedono poco i loro figli, a causa delle ore lavorative che richiede la società. Nei paesi nordici, pare che ci siano leggi per combattere questo problema e infatti per dare ad ogni genitore la possibilità di partecipare pienamente all'educazione dei figli. È una buona idea, secondo Lei?

5 E la gestione della famiglia e della casa? Quale dovrebbe essere il contributo di ogni coniuge alla casa e alla famiglia?

You can probably think of plenty more topics arising from the interviews in this unit. Don't get into any arguments! But keep thinking in Italian!

TEST YOURSELF

1 How are you coping with the subjunctive? Choose the correct alternative in these sentences.

    a Mi sembra che **stia/sta** per piovere.

    b Dice che i pacchi **siano/sono** già arrivati.

    c Speriamo che il treno non **ha/abbia** un grosso ritardo.

    d Ho l'impressione che **è/sia** successo qualcosa di grave.

    e Lo so che non gli **piace/piaccia** la birra, ma non ho altro da offrirgli.

2 This short text describes the work of a charity helper in Africa. Complete it with the correct personal or reflexive pronouns.

Ebele inizia la sua giornata alle sei di mattina e non (a) _____ ferma fino alle otto di sera. Vengono da (b) _____ i bambini delle famiglie povere del villaggio e lei (c) _____ occupa di (d) lavar_____ (e) e vestir_____. Poi (f) _____ insegna a leggere e a scrivere. A mezzogiorno (g) _____ dà da mangiare e (h) _____ fa giocare. Quando deve andare al mercato in un paese lontano, il marito (i) _____ sostituisce e (j) _____ prepara la cena.

3 Transformation once more! Try to say these sentences using the gerund or the present participle as appropriate.

    a Ho incontrato Claudio **mentre andavo** in biblioteca.

    b Abbiamo ricevuto una notizia **che ci ha allarmato**.

    c **Se scegli** questo lavoro, avrai molte soddisfazioni.

    d **Dal momento che deve** mantenere i figli, si è messa a insegnare.

    e Sulla sua scrivania c'era il ritratto di un bambino **che sorrideva**.

8

··

Senza scopo di lucro

In this unit we shall
* *learn about voluntary work in Italy*
* *meet some people who give some of their spare time to helping others*
* *learn how to say what you would do if ...*
* *meet the imperfect subjunctive*
* *look at some suffixes to produce shades of meaning*
* *meet the subjunctive after certain conjunctions*
* *meet the past definite*

Session 1

Reading 1

The voluntary sector in Italy is flourishing. Here are some statistics:

Gli adulti italiani che si dedicano attualmente, o si sono dedicati in passato, ad attività di volontariato, sono quasi 9 milioni, il 18, 1 per cento della popolazione che ha superato i 15 anni.
È questo il risultato di un sondaggio svolto dalla Doxa nel giugno scorso ... Secondo il sondaggio, 3.900.000 persone, l'8 per cento di tutti gli adulti, sono i volontari 'certamente' attuali, in quanto hanno svolto qualche attività negli ultimi 12 mesi. Per il 57,8 per cento di loro si tratta di attività molto impegnative, perché svolte regolarmente, almeno una volta alla settimana. I tipi di attività più

frequentemente citati dagli intervistati sono i seguenti: ecologiche, ambientali, 16,9 per cento; parrocchiali in genere, 15,5 per cento; sportive, ricreative, 11,9 per cento. Seguono le citazioni dei destinatari di attività di assistenza: i malati (11,8 per cento), gli anziani (10,1 per cento), i disabili (9,6 per cento), i bambini (3,5 per cento). Non mancano le citazioni della raccolta di indumenti, medicinali, ecc. (5 per cento) e donazione di sangue (5 per cento).

From the website of *Repubblica* (**www.repubblica.it**),
'*Dall'ambiente alla parrocchia, sono 9 milioni i volontari.*'
15 settembre 1998.

The passage throws up a number of words which do not translate literally from Italian. We hope you haven't forgotten your false friend: **attuale**, **attualmente**.

il 18,1 per cento Note the definite article: **il 18 per cento**, **l'8 per cento**

superato i 15 anni Note the definite article.

Doxa From the Greek **doxa** = opinion. It is the Italian institute for opinion polls and market research, founded in 1946.

3.900.000 Note that the decimal place is indicated in Italy by a comma (**virgola**) and the thousands by a full-stop (**punto**), i.e. the opposite of the Anglo-Saxon practice.

si tratta di lit. *it is a question of*. Perhaps here it might translate: *this means*. Often in English it is appropriate to say: *it's about*.

impegnativo Un impegno is *a commitment, an engagement*, **impegnarsi** *to commit oneself*. Here **impegnativo** might be translated *demanding, exacting, requiring commitment*.

assistenza The main meanings of **assistere** are: 1 *to be present at* (a meeting, for instance); 2 *to look after* (a sick or injured person; or the interests of, say, a client). In other words, it has overtones not there in the English *assist*. Similarly, perhaps *assist*, with its Latin origins, has overtones in English not present in Italian. English words of Latin origin tend to be thought more formal, even learned: compare *assist* and *help*. **Assistenza**, the noun, relates solely to the second meaning of the verb (above). Here, as you can see from the context, it means *giving help* to the sick, the elderly, children, the handicapped. Simply *to help* is **aiutare**.

Insight

Plural nouns preceded by the definite article are used to indicate categories of people or things: **i malati** *sick people*, **gli anziani** *the elderly*, **i disabili** *the disabled*, **i bambini** *children*.

Reading 2

An earlier article gives slightly different statistics, gathered in a different way, with a different definition of **volontariato**, *but the basic message is the same:*

Gli italiani propensi all'altruismo? Sembrerebbe di sì. Sono infatti oltre cinque milioni le persone (per esattezza 5.397.000) che nel 1997 si sono impegnate in prima persona in attività di volontariato sociale e civile ...

Gli italiani, dunque, sono persone di cuore, capaci di prodigarsi gratuitamente per cinque ore e mezzo a settimana; se lo stesso tempo fosse regolarmente retribuito ci vorrebbero in un anno circa 750 mila lavoratori a tempo pieno. Di fatto il 12 per cento della popolazione adulta svolge attività di volontariato, un dato nella media con i paesi europei ...

From the website of *Repubblica*, 'Cinque ore alla settimana ecco l'Italia dei volontari.' 7 luglio 1998

in prima persona *personally*, i.e. actually working, not just giving money.
ci vorrebbero *would be needed*, conditional of **ci vuole**.

QV

Comprehension: Readings 1 and 2

1 Can you detect the reason for the differences in the figures given in the two articles?

2 What might be the implication behind the words: **sociale** and **civile** when applied to **volontariato**?

3 Is Italy exceptional in the numbers of people involved in voluntary work?

....

The voluntary sector is indeed lively in Italy today. Much of the work is done to high, even professional, standards. Serious training is often required of the volunteer. Some of the voluntary organizations are connected to the Catholic Church, catholicism being the traditional religion of Italy, but many are *secular* (**laico**). One often heard complaint is that volunteers do work that should be done by the state, filling the gaps in provision which arise from state inefficiency. We would add that there seems to be a great capacity in Italy for criticism of the Italian state and Italian institutions, linked to a conviction that things are better ordered in other countries. Which is not necessarily the case!

As an aside, however, it has to be said that Italy has suffered more than many advanced countries from poor government for much of the postwar period. This is not the place to examine the problem in any detail other than to say the blame lies partly in the fact that there was not, until very recently, what Italians call **alternanza**. In other words, the same group of political parties held power for a very long period, without the opposition ever coming to power. These parties governed in coalition governments which were often fragile and short-lived. When a government falls, so does the legislation it is trying to put through. What looked like political instability in fact led to too much stability. Reforms have not been made as in other countries. This has certainly contributed to the inefficiency of the state.

(Contd)

However, while Italians are sure every other country runs itself better than Italy, has a more efficient civil service, etc., when it comes to the fabric of everyday life – food, fashion, friendships and social life – in those areas Italians know Italy is best!

Mention is made in the first article of being a blood donor. It may be of interest to know the blood donor service is run by a voluntary organization: **AVIS (Associazione Volontari Italiani del Sangue)** which, according to its website (**www.avis.it**), supplies 70% of the country's requirements for blood.

Session 2

Introducing the imperfect subjunctive

In the second article we read:

se lo stesso tempo fosse regolarmente retribuito ci vorrebbero in un anno circa 750 mila lavoratori a tempo pieno.	*if the same amount of time had been paid for (in wages) in a year about 750,000 full time workers would be needed.*

Look at the verbs. As we said in the Notes at the end of the passage, **ci vorrebbero** is a conditional. What about the other? You have seen it before but not had your attention drawn to it. It is the imperfect subjunctive of **essere**. This type of sentence is one we often use. *If this were the case, then we should ...* Here are some more examples:

Cosa faresti se vincessi il primo premio alla lotteria?	*What would you do if you won the first prize in the lottery?*
Se avessi tempo, andrei più spesso al cinema.	*If I had time, I'd go to the cinema more often.*
Se i bambini fossero più grandi, andremmo all'estero in vacanza.	*If the children were older, we'd go abroad for our holiday.*

If you look back to Unit 7 you will see that Emanuela several times said what she *would like to do, would do* – but she did not spell out the other part of the condition: **se potessi permettermi di non lavorare,** *if I could afford not to work.*

The form of the imperfect subjunctive

This is very easy: you need to think back to the imperfect. Take the same root as for the imperfect. Any verb which had a special root for the imperfect will have that same special root again in the imperfect subjunctive, with three exceptions.

passare	avere	pulire	fare
passassi	avessi	pulissi	facessi
passassi	avessi	pulissi	facessi
passasse	avesse	pulisse	facesse
passassimo	avessimo	pulissimo	facessimo
passaste	aveste	puliste	faceste
passassero	avessero	pulissero	facessero

Note the stress in the first and third persons plural. The three exceptions are:

essere	dare	stare
fossi	dessi	stessi
fossi	dessi	stessi
fosse	desse	stesse
fossimo	dessimo	stessimo
foste	deste	steste
fossero	dessero	stessero

You can see the endings are always the same so, given the first person singular, you should be able to form all the parts.

Activity 1

Complete the sentences using the correct form of the imperfect subjuncive.

Example: Cosa faresti se (**vincere – tu**) .... il primo premio alla lotteria?

Cosa faresti se **vincessi** il primo premio alla lotteria? *What would you do if you won the first prize in the lottery?*

1 Cosa faresti se (**essere – tu**) .... il Presidente della Repubblica Italiana?

2 Signora Rossi, cosa farebbe se (**avere – Lei**) .... più tempo libero?

3 Ragazzi, che cosa fareste se vi (**dire – io**) .... che la settimana prossima la scuola sarà chiusa e sarete in vacanza?

4 Cosa faresti se un tuo amico ti (**chiedere – lui**) .... di occuparti del suo cane durante le vacanze estive?

5 Signor Rossi, cosa farebbe se (**scoprire – Lei**) .... che Sua moglie ha un amante?

6 Che cosa fareste se una persona vi (**passare – lei**) .... davanti in una coda?

7 Che cosa faresti se (**essere – tu**) .... in una coda al supermercato, (**avere – tu**) .... il carrello strapieno di acquisti, e (**scoprire – tu**) .... di avere dimenticato a casa il portafoglio?

8 Signor Bianchi, che cosa farebbe se (**essere – loro**) .... le tre di mattina e il vostro vicino di casa (**stare – lui**) .... ascoltando musica a tutto volume?

9 Che cosa faresti se il tuo datore di lavoro ti (**dare – lui**) .... una vacanza di tre mesi?

10 Che cosa faremmo se non (**avere – noi**) .... tutte le comodità che abbiamo al giorno d'oggi e (**dovere – noi**) .... vivere allo stesso modo in cui vivevano i nostri nonni?

Session 3

Interview 1

Silvia Lena, whom you were introduced to briefly in Unit 2, is not a trained volunteer worker but she has given much of her time to helping others, particularly the victims of conflict. So we asked her about some of her experiences.

● CD2, TR 11, 37:34

Silvia Non ho fatto volontariato sociale. In Italia il volontariato sociale è diffusissimo, moltissimi giovani sono impegnati in attività sociali, di aiuto a persone anziane, persone handicappate, bambini. Ecco, questa cosa io l'ho fatta solamente in un breve periodo all'università quando andavamo ad aiutare i vecchietti di ringhiera. Si chiamano così quei … quelle persone che vivono in delle case minime, chiamate così 'case minime', case povere fatte di una sola stanza, nella periferia di Milano. Eravamo universitari, e per caso abbiamo incontrato dei vecchietti che ci chiedevano aiuto per fare i loro documenti e abbiamo creato un gruppo di studenti disponibili a fare tutte le pratiche – mediche, negli uffici, accompagnare queste persone anziane a comprare gli occhiali, dall'oculista, dall'ortopedico … Per un breve periodo abbiamo fatto questa cosa, all'università, ma era più un divertimento, per stare insieme, infatti io ho conosciuto lì mio marito.

QUICK VOCAB

vecchietti di ringhiera case di ringhiera are a type of housing typical of the late 19th century, with several floors and balconies along each floor, with metal balustrades (**ringhiere**); the doors of the individual dwellings open on to these balconies. Sometimes originally they shared **servizi igienici** *lavatories*. A possible translation is *tenement*.

case minime *tiny houses*. **minimo: piccolissimo** is the irregular form of the superlative. See **Reference grammar**. They would be flats/apartments, not individual houses. **Casa** is often used in this way.

disponibili *available and willing*

fare tutte le pratiche *carry out bureaucratic procedures*. It refers to filling in forms and going through procedures, often necessitating visits to offices, so as to take advantage of medical and other services, pensions etc.

Insight

Note two adjectives followed by a preposition + noun or infinitive: **impegnati in** *engaged in*, **disponibili a** *willing to, available for*.

Comprehension: Interview 1

1 What sort of thing did Silvia and her fellow students do for the old people they helped?

2 What was the students' main motivation?

3 What does Silvia cite to support this?

Session 4

Suffixes in Italian

Silvia says:

il volontariato sociale è diffusissimo	*voluntary work is very widespread*
moltissimi giovani sono impegnati in attività sociali	*very many young people are committed to voluntary work*
aiutare i vecchietti	*to help old people*

You will be familiar with **-issimo** added to adjectives, meaning *very*. And you will know **-etto** being added to nouns to form a diminutive (cf. English *piglet*, *lambkin*). In Unit 3 we referred to **-one** which means *big*. There is quite a range of suffixes which can be added to nouns, changing their meaning slightly. The Italian word for these slight changes in meaning is **sfumature**. Good guessers will note that this contains the word **fumo**, *smoke*. The word is used, as is the verb **sfumare**, in relation to gradual, subtle, imprecise changes of colour, tone, etc. In Italian the suffixes are traditionally classified as:

diminutivi (which indicate size smaller than usual)
accrescitivi (which indicate greater size than usual)
vezzeggiativi (adds an idea of being lovable)
spregiativi (which indicates the person or thing is despised; it can also hint at irony)

However, some cross boundaries or vary in meaning according to the sense of the noun they are attached to or even the context. So they are not easy to use and you are advised at first just to note examples you hear and their meaning. Gradually you will feel able to use at least some of them. Probably one needs to have grown up in Italy to feel really at home using them. A good Italian dictionary will tell you which suffixes you can add to any given word. Some are also more common than others.

-etto, -ino, -ello, -cello, -icello, -erello

These are usually considered diminutives, but affection often comes in too. Gabriella referred to her **mammina** and there affection came into play. Also in **vecchietti**.

ragazzo, ragazzino	*boy, little boy*
casa, casetta	*house, small house*
sorella, sorellina	*sister, little sister*
gatto, gattino	*cat, kitten*
vento, venticello	*wind, little breeze*

-ino can also be added to adjectives and adverbs:

carino	*pretty, sweet, cute*
piano, pianino	*softly, very softly*
bene, benino	*well, quite well*

Note also: **pian pianino** meaning *little by little, step by step.*

-one

This indicates large size (**accrescitivo**) and has the peculiarity that when it is added to a feminine noun, the noun becomes masculine. However a feminine ending also exists, **-ona**.

una donna, un donnone	*a woman, a large woman*
gatto, gattone	*cat, large cat*
una cena, un cenone	*supper, the usually huge meal traditionally eaten late on New Year's Eve, to welcome in the New Year.*
uomo, omone	*man, large man*

This suffix can also be added to **bene**.

'Come sta?' 'Benone.'	*'How are you?' 'Very well indeed.'*

The suffixes **-otto, -ozzo** are usually listed as **accrescitivi**. They can also have diminutive force and/or express contempt, the idea of the object being a bit of a joke! **Ragazzotto** can, for instance, mean *a stocky young boy* (**accrescitivo** – in size) or *not yet a full boy* (17–18 years) *but not a child* (**diminutivo** – in years). Not easy for the foreign learner!

-accio, -astro, -onzolo, -ciattolo, -ucolo, -ipolo

These usually indicate unpleasantness, nastiness (**peggiorativi**).

parola, parolaccia	*word, swear word*
tempo, tempaccio	*weather, dreadful weather*

verme, vermiciattolo	*worm, nasty little worm*
professore,	*teacher, an ineffectual teacher (one*
professorucolo	*not worthy of respect)*
vino, vinaccio	*wine, poor quality wine*
uomo, omaccio, omaccione	*man, nasty man, great big nasty man*

-icino, -olino, -uccio, -uzzo

These indicate affection (**vezzeggiativi**).

porta, porticina	*door, tiny little door*
corpo, corpicino	*body, poor thin little body*
cane, cagnolino	*dog, puppy*
tesoro, tesoruccio	*darling, dear sweet darling*

Note also: 1. Many words formed with the use of suffixes have become words in their own right: e.g. **violino, violoncello**. 2. In addition there are also words which look as though they are formed with a suffix but this is in fact not the case, e.g. **mattone** *brick*; **padrone** *master, proprietor, boss*; **rubinetto** *tap*; **bottone** *button*.

Looking at the question of suffixes at another way, the word: **ragazzo** (*boy*) can be altered thus: **ragazzaccio** (*bad*); **ragazzetto** (*small*); **ragazzino** (*small*); **ragazzone** (*big*); **ragazzotto** (*big*); **ragazzuccio** (*small*); **ragazzuolo** (*small*). They have varying **'sfumature'**. The important thing, as we have said, is to be aware, and not to worry! Just use words and suffixes you hear Italians using.

Activity 2

You almost certainly know the story of **Treccedoro e i tre Orsi**, *Goldilocks and the Three Bears*. So we won't tell it to you, but here are some illustrations. Can you put labels to them in a way which fits the story?

Example:

a orsone
b orsa
c orsino

1

2

3

Activity 3

Study the following words and, using a dictionary, decide which are words modified by suffixes and which are not:

1 cassetto
2 tacchino
3 giornataccia
4 filetto

5 cagnolino
6 cappuccio
7 focaccia
8 casetta

Session 5

Interview 2

The motivation of 'stare insieme', *which perhaps reflects an aspect of the Italian character, the enjoyment of being with a group of friends, was also at the origin of the* **Gruppo Mio**. *You may remember we met three members of the group briefly in Unit 2: Antonella, Riccardo and Monica. Here, they tell us something about the group. They, again, are not volunteers of the sort referred to by Silvia in the phrase:* **volontariato sociale**.

This is a long extract from an even longer interview but you are becoming proficient now and we suggest you listen and try to pick out the main points, in particular: 1 how the group came into being 2 what its various activities are and 3 what motivates the speakers.

Interviewer	Che cosa vuol dire MIO e che cosa è il Gruppo?
Riccardo	La sigla MIO vuol dire Moriondo Insieme Ovunque. E' un gruppo che è nato da un incontro di alcuni amici. Hanno passato una giornata di ritiro riflettendo insieme ed hanno avuto un po' questa proposta e questa voglia di mettersi insieme e iniziare a lavorare per i poveri. Quindi lo scopo era di andare al di là, non trovarsi solo come amici per divertirsi o comunque per passare il tempo insieme ma fare anche qualcosa di utile, visto che c'erano queste opportunità e questa voglia dentro ognuno così di noi di creare qualcosa per gli altri, per chi ha bisogno, quindi per la realtà locale di Moriondo e anche per i più poveri. Quindi ovunque, insieme ovunque, insieme perché uniti in gruppo visto che l'unione di più forze dà frutti migliori, ovunque per tutti, quindi dove c'era maggior bisogno si è cercato di coinvolgere le nostre forze.
Interviewer	Ma lo stare insieme fa parte anche della motivazione del Gruppo, no?
Antonella	Sì, diciamo che il nostro gruppo è un gruppo un po' strano, no? Perché è un gruppo parrocchiale, perché si occupa della realtà della parrocchia, con tutte le attività di animazione ai più giovani, ai bambini, ai ragazzi, e tutte le attività che ci sono nella parrocchia, tipo animazione della messa ecc. È anche un gruppo missionario, e come gruppo missionario, facciamo parte dell'Operazione Mato Grosso, dalla quale poi siamo nati e ci occupiamo in particolar modo del Brasile e di un lebbrosario in Brasile. E poi siamo un gruppo di amici, infatti la caratteristica del nostro gruppo è che raggruppa un po' gente di tutte le età, no? Abbiamo i genitori, i neo-genitori, cioè ragazzi che hanno fondato 15 anni fa il Gruppo, che adesso hanno formato una loro famiglia ma abbiamo anche ragazzi giovani, 14, 15, 16 anni, no? E quello che ci raggruppa è questa voglia di stare insieme, no? Quest'amicizia che è nata fra di noi.
Interviewer	E vi incontrate, dunque, una volta alla settimana?

Monica	Noi c'incontriamo generalmente il lunedì sera. Noi abbiamo avuto la possibilità di avere come nostra sede la vecchia chiesa di Moriondo, che veniva utilizzata per la messa prima che venisse costruita l'attuale chiesa. Noi ci raduniamo lunedì sera appunto intorno alle nove così e, niente, programmiamo un pochino le attività che normalmente facciamo. Sosteniamo appunto questo lebbrosario in Campo Grande in Mato Grosso e poi al di là di quest'attività, che comunque ha portato alcuni nostri amici a stare giù per un po' di tempo, no? proprio per testimoniare in modo più concreto, no? questo voler aiutare il prossimo, abbiamo comunque anche attività che svolgiamo nell'ambito della parrocchia. Facciamo animazione liturgica alla messa la domenica …
	E poi ci occupiamo dei ragazzini per i quali, insomma, organizziamo nel periodo estivo l'Estate Ragazzi, per i bimbi più piccolini e poi anche perfino i ragazzi delle medie …
Interviewer	Che cos'è Estate Ragazzi?
Monica	Estate Ragazzi è un periodo di circa 15 giorni dove, utilizzando l'Oratorio, diamo la possibilità ai ragazzini tutti i pomeriggi di, insomma, di restare insieme. Organizziamo ogni anno generalmente un Estate Ragazzi a tema, nel senso che fissiamo magari un tema particolare da portare avanti durante tutto il periodo, per esempio quest'anno abbiamo scelto come tema il Circo e ai ragazzi appunto presenteremo delle attività, dei lavoretti manuali, dei giochi, ecc. sul tema del circo e verranno ogni giorno a trovarci in persona, qui da noi, i personaggi del circo, quindi verrà a trovarci un domatore di animali, verrà un giocoliere … Normalmente i ragazzi accorrono abbastanza volentieri, i genitori ce li portano, ce li mandano … hanno fiducia e così cerchiamo di dare il nostro contributo. Oltre a questo Estate Ragazzi, facciamo anche i Campi Scuola che sono periodi di

(Contd)

circa una settimana che facciamo fuori parrocchia,
e facciamo esattamente in Val Varaita, a Sampeyre,
dove appunto i ragazzini delle elementari, poi
successivamente, in un secondo turno, i ragazzi delle
medie e delle prime superiori, hanno la possibilità di
riflettere su dei temi stabiliti. Quest'anno abbiamo
proposto le Gemme di Hazan, un racconto, che è
un sussidio estivo che viene preparato dalla diocesi
e offerto alle parrocchie per poter proprio animare,
gestire sia i Campi Scuola o eventualmente l'Estate
Ragazzi qualora i Campi Scuola non venissero fatti
…È centrato sul tema dello Spirito Santo … E legato
a questo, si fanno attività, si fanno giochi, è un modo
per riuscire comunque ad aggregare questi ragazzi
… si cerca di trasmettere i valori che sono quelli che
abbiamo ricevuto a nostra volta dai più grandi.

E durante l'anno, Don Giacomo ci lascia l'Oratorio
per i ragazzini, la domenica pomeriggio dalle tre fino
intorno alle sei e mezza e quest'anno abbiamo tentato
anche una cosa un po' diversa, abbiamo utilizzato
l'Oratorio anche il sabato. Il sabato, dividendo in due
parti: c'era la possibilità di iscriversi ad una squadra di
pallavolo o di calcio, e poi la possibilità di fare attività
di laboratorio, attività manuali, si è insegnato a fare gli
aquiloni, a fare le magliette,

Antonella	la telecamera, abbiamo insegnato a riprendere, la fotografia,
Monica	Esatto … Un sacco di cose e poi la possibilità anche di far parte di queste squadrette di calcio e di pallavolo che sono nate così come una prova l'anno scorso … tra l'altro funziona abbastanza bene perché quest'anno le nostre ragazzine in pallavolo sono arrivate seconde al torneo della zona, invece i ragazzini l'anno scorso si sono beccati il primo posto.
Interviewer	Se non facevano questo, questi ragazzi …?
Riccardo	Innanzitutto l'Oratorio è stato per un lungo tempo chiuso, quindi è stata una conquista anche riaprire

	l'Oratorio, perché non c'era nessuno che lavorasse coi ragazzini, invece noi abbiamo cercato di riaprire l'Oratorio proprio per dare poi possibilità ai ragazzini di fare qualcosa d'utile per gli altri, quindi cominciare ad aggregarsi e non passare soltanto il tempo sulle panchine perché l'alternativa è quella, sui seggiolini della piazza coi motorini …
Interviewer	E come aiutate il lebbrosario in Brasile, a parte quelli di voi che sono andati a lavorare lì?
Antonella	Noi innanzitutto organizziamo delle attività, ad esempio la raccolta carta, ferro e stracci, che facciamo per il ricavato; organizziamo delle mostre artigianali, dei lavoretti in legno, in cuoio, in stoffa e li andiamo a vendere nelle scuole, cercando proprio di non mettere solo il banchetto e vendere, ma anche facciamo vedere delle diapositive, dei filmati, portando la testimonianza di persone che ci sono state, persone che vivono questa realtà… E poi c'è anche un discorso di farmaci, che vengono inviati, essendo un ospedale comunque ha bisogno, di medicinali …
Riccardo	Vorrei aggiungere che c'è un altro tipo di missionarietà vissuta molto più vicino, ad esempio, è stata forse una delle prime attività che abbiamo portato avanti e tuttora continuiamo a portare avanti ed è appunto andare a trovare delle nonnine alla Piccola Casa di Trofarello, che è un ospizio, molto piccolo quando abbiamo iniziato 15 anni fa, adesso si è ingrandito molto ma l'abbiamo sempre seguito, visto passare tutti i nonnini … L'attività nostra consiste nell'andare a trovarli il sabato pomeriggio e non fare nulla di particolare se non stare con loro, parlare con loro, cantare, far passare due ore di allegria a queste persone che spesso sono sole, tristi, quindi hanno proprio la necessità di avere qualcuno che vada a sorridere, a parlare con loro, che si metta a cantare con loro, quindi … Sappiamo a memoria tutto il repertorio delle canzoncine …
Antonella	un po' vecchie …

(Contd)

Riccardo	Poi distribuiamo tè, caffè, biscotti, è un momento di incontro ...
Antonella	Festeggiamo una volta al mese i loro compleanni, cioè festeggiamo tutti i compleanni del mese, facendoli soffiare delle candeline, portando delle torte ... Loro ci tengono a vederci ...
Interviewer	Dalle vostre facce vedo che prendete grande piacere ... c'è gioia ...
Antonella	Sì.

QUICK VOCAB

Moriondo Moriondo is a **frazione** of Moncalieri, a town of about 60,000 inhabitants just on the southern edge of Turin. Moriondo is on the fringe of Moncalieri, adjacent to Trofarello, the neighbouring **comune**, mentioned later.

una giornata di ritiro *a day spent in retreat*. The group is a church group.

andare al di là lit. *to go beyond*; perhaps *to go a bit further*

tipo animazione della messa *such as helping with mass*. This use of the word **tipo** is common in spoken Italian. More formal usage would say: **per esempio**.

la vecchia chiesa ... che veniva utilizzata Note the use of **venire** to form a passive: *was used*.

stare giù per un tempo *to stay down there for a while*. Down there: at the leper hospital in Brazil.

Estate Ragazzi: Campi Scuola Often organized by local authorities but also by churches in Italy, between the end of the school year and the start of the main summer holiday period. It is probably useful for working parents, but in these days of small families and urban living, children miss the mixing with others they get at school, are often not able to go out and play in the streets, etc.

Val Varaita In the Southern Alps, south-west of Turin. Sampeyre is at about 950 metres above sea level.

Oratorio This can mean a place for prayer. But it is also commonly used for the building most churches have available for use by children and young people in the afternoons. Italian schools usually finish their day around 13.30 hours. The idea originated with the Salesian Order, founded by Don Bosco.

tra l'altro Common in spoken Italian, adding little to meaning: *furthermore, moreover*.

li andiamo a vendere *we go and sell them.* You can also say: **andiamo a venderli.**

un sacco di cose *lots, loads of things.*

si sono beccati il primo posto *they won/walked off with first place.* The expression is however more vivid than the translation we give: **beccarsi** is related to **becco**, *the beak of a bird.*

facciamo vedere *we show.* The usual way of expressing the idea of showing.

hanno ... la necessità di avere qualcuno che vada a ... che si metta a cantare ... Note the subjunctives (**vada, con loro si metta**), following the indefinite antecedent.

Comprehension: Interview 2

These are the points we suggested you try to listen out for. Don't forget you can listen to the interview again and again, as often as you like.

1 How did the group come into being?
2 What are its various activities?
3 What motivates the speakers?

Session 6

Study of words and their use

The interviews throw up a number of interesting points to do with use of words:

a suffixes: notice the frequency of diminutives, often used affectionately: **i bimbi più piccolini, le nonnine, i nonnini, canzoncine, un pochino, lavoretti,** etc.

b some words which are difficult to translate although the meaning is clear: 1) **realtà** as in **la realtà locale**, and **la realtà della parrocchia. Realtà** means, of course, *reality*, but might perhaps be better translated here by *community*. Dictionaries define it as **il**

complesso dei fatti. 2) **animazione**: *bringing to life*, making events lively and meaningful by an organizational contribution. In the context of the summer camp etc. **animare** is really just *leading, organizing*.

c frutto, fruttificare: you will know **la frutta**, a collective noun, in the way *fruit* can be in English. *I must buy some fruit. We eat a lot of fruit*. A single fruit is **un frutto**, also used in the figurative sense. The plural is **frutti**. The verb **fruttificare** means *to bear fruit*.

d un discorso di farmaci: **discorso** is often used when in English we might use *matter, subject*. (See Unit 3, Interview 2, Notes.)

Activity 4

The spoken language

The three representatives of the Gruppo Mio were excited about being interviewed and full of enthusiasm for their group. Whether this affected the way they spoke, we can't judge, but it was very much **lingua parlata**, spoken language, with, in particular, words slipped in as props which contributed little to the meaning but perhaps helped them 'keep their balance', so to speak. Can you pick some of these out in the first speech of each of the three participants?

Insight
You may have found that the 'props' in the students' speeches were a bit annoying. Compare them to similar expressions used by young people in English, for example 'things', 'and stuff', 'like', 'you know' and other meaningless words.

The subjunctive after certain conjunctions

Monica says:

la vecchia chiesa di Moriondo, che veniva utilizzata per la messa <u>prima che venisse</u> costruita l'attuale chiesa.

the old church of Moriondo which was used for mass before the
present church was built.

**un racconto, che è un sussidio estivo che viene preparato dalla
diocesi e offerto alle parrocchie per poter proprio animare, gestire
sia i Campi Scuola o eventualmente l'Estate Ragazzi <u>qualora</u> i
Campi Scuola non <u>venissero</u> fatti.**
*a story, which is a summer (teaching) aid which is prepared by the
diocese and offered to parishes precisely to help lead, organize, either the
School Camps or Summer for Children if the School Camps are not held.*

You will notice the imperfect subjunctive. But why the subjunctive?
Because certain conjunctions require the verb in the clause
they introduce to be a subjunctive. See the list in the **Reference
grammar**. Note however **prima che** *before* needs the subjunctive
but **prima di** is followed by an infinitive. You can use **prima di** only
if the subject of both verbs is the same:

**Prima che arrivi Giorgio, cerchiamo di mettere in ordine il
soggiorno.**
Before George arrives, let's try to tidy the living room. (George is
arriving but we are doing the tidying.)

Prima di uscire, devo finire di scrivere questa lettera.
Before I go out, I must finish writing this letter. (I am both writing the
letter and going out.)

Prima di partire, telefona alla nonna.
Before you leave, phone grandma. (You are going out and the speaker
wants you to telephone grandma.)

The conjunctions requiring the subjunctive are always
subordinating conjunctions. A moment's reflection will confirm
that sentences with conjunctions are fairly complex. We tend to
keep to relatively simple structure when speaking. So this use of
the subjunctive is more common in written language and you will
normally be recognizing subjunctives after conjunctions rather than
having to produce them.

Activity 5

The following sentences are based on an **article 'Il volontariato non seduce più'** (*La Stampa*, 12 febbraio 1999), printed at the end of this unit. It is not necessary to have read the article to do this exercise. We found it interesting however and put it in for you, hoping you do too. Complete the sentences using the correct form of the subjunctive.

Example: Sebbene molti volontari (fare) **facciano** lavori faticosi e difficili, come scavare nel fango o assistere i malati, senza ricevere nessuna ricompensa, non si considerano degli eroi ma delle persone normali.

1 Sebbene i volontari (essere) .... sia uomini che donne, le donne volontarie sono in numero leggermente più alto degli uomini.

2 Nonostante il numero dei volontari che si impegnano attivamente all'interno delle associazioni (sembrare) .... essere in calo, le associazioni volontarie continuano a prosperare perché molti italiani versano loro dei soldi affinché (potere) .... proseguire la loro attività.

3 Benché il volontariato (avere) .... successo ovunque in Italia, la maggior parte delle organizzazioni opera nelle regioni settentrionali piuttosto che nelle regioni meridionali.

4 Sebbene (esistere) .... ancora molti gruppi volontari senza alcuno scopo di lucro, molti di loro si sono 'professionalizzati' e sono diventati cooperative sociali, che danno lavoro e reddito.

5 Benché la Chiesa Cattolica (giocare) .... un ruolo molto importante nella società italiana e all'interno del volontariato, in Italia esistono anche molti gruppi volontari aconfessionali.

6 Affinché le statistiche sul lavoro volontario in Italia (risultare) .... affidabili, bisogna escludere dal conteggio i semplici simpatizzanti, come per esempio i donatori di sangue.

The subjunctive after a negative antecedent

Riccardo says:

non c'era nessuno che   *there was no one working with the*
lavorasse coi ragazzini   *children*

This is similar to the use we saw in Unit 5, Session 5, with an indefinite antecedent. Here we have a negative antecedent, **nessuno**. The subjunctive would also be required after **niente**:

Non c'è niente che faccia più *There is nothing which frightens more*
paura che …   *than …*

Look for another example of **niente che** + subjunctive in the next Interview.

Session 7

Interview 3

Some of Silvia Lena's work has been with single individuals whose cause she has embraced. We asked her to tell us one particular story again. It involved helping a Kurdish refugee from Turkey who had been living in Switzerland with his wife and small daughter.

Silvia	Sì ma questa è stata un'esperienza molto particolare. Sono stata coinvolta con i curdi, ma questa è una cosa personale, cioè io non ho mai fatto niente che non passasse attraverso l'amicizia. Cioè tutte le cose che ho fatto, le ho fatte perché avevo degli amici che avevano bisogno di essere aiutati. La storia è così, molto sinteticamente: io conosco la causa dei curdi perché ho un'amica in Svizzera che ha fondato un'associazione Suisse-Kurdistan perché in Svizzera ci sono tantissimi immigrati curdi e lei, avendoli conosciuti nella loro vita sciagurata, nella loro disperazione, *(Contd)*

CD2, TR 13, 49:25

abitanti di cantine, perseguitati, accusati da turchi immigrati in Svizzera di cose non commesse, quest'amica si è dedicata alla loro causa e un giorno mi ha telefonato se potevo muovere l'amministrazione comunale di Bologna in aiuto di un curdo che era stato accusato di avere commesso un omicidio ed era stato poi assolto perché l'accusa veniva da un turco a lui ostile. La cosa è stata smascherata quindi lui doveva essere rilasciato dal carcere ma, in base alle leggi svizzere, messo su un aereo e inviato in Turchia dove lo aspettava una condanna a morte. Lui aveva una moglie bambina con una piccola di pochi mesi e quest'amica non si rassegnava a pensare che lui morisse e si è data da fare finché ha saputo che se c'era uno stato che avesse accolto questo curdo avrebbe potuto essere inviato e salvato. Io andai direttamente dal sindaco di Bologna che fu di una disponibilità meravigliosa. Mise a disposizione un'automobile con un autista e uno psicologo, perché pensava che questa persona sarebbe stata molto male, e prese contatto con il carcere svizzero dove lui si trovava, e lo ha mandato a prendere. Poi dovevo interessarmene io, perché il comune non poteva assumersi questa persona, quindi questo curdo è stato qua a casa mia; la moglie e la bambina lo hanno raggiunto, sono arrivate di notte, con un taxi svizzero … E io li ho ospitati in un istituto di suore che non avevano mai ospitato un uomo ma, commosse da questa storia, le suore sono diventate delle grandi sostenitrici del popolo curdo.

The tense is the pluperfect subjunctive and the usage is similar to the use in reported speech which we met in Unit 5. This is quite complex. But you understand, surely, without the explanation! And that is what matters.

un istituto di suore *a convent*

Insight

pensava che questa persona sarebbe stata molto male *he thought that this person would be very ill*: the conditional perfect (**sarebbe stata**) is used to express a future idea in reported speech after an imperfect (**pensava**) or another past tense, as you have studied in Unit 5.

Comprehension: Interview 3

1 Why did Silvia's Swiss friend found the Switzerland Kurdistan Association?

2 She telephoned Silvia seeking her help and that of the Bolognese city administration for a Kurdish man. What was he accused of?

3 Who was his accuser?

4 Injustice apart, why did Silvia's friend find it impossible to accept that the man should be returned to Turkey?

5 What did the mayor of Bologna do to help?

6 Once the man arrived, what did Silvia have to do?

7 Who gave the man and his wife shelter and what effect did his story have on them?

The end of the story

The stay in the convent for the Kurdish family was short term and Silvia was able to move them to a small hostel for immigrants that she had started together with a young priest in response to another need – another story. And how did the story of the Kurdish family end? Silvia wrote in response to the question:

Ora Imam vive con Aynur e quattro bambine in una banlieue (*suburb*) di Parigi, fa il giardiniere comunale, guadagna abbastanza, si sente ricco e felice. Lo andrò a trovare in ottobre con la mia amica svizzera Jacqueline che si occupava dei curdi.

And this in reply to a question about the mayor at the time:

Renzo Imbeni era il sindaco di Bologna. L'amministrazione comunista era allora molto aperta ai problemi internazionali. Imbeni ora è parlamentare europeo. Certamente è stata un'iniziativa esemplare ed eccezionale, ne parlò la stampa.

It should perhaps be added that Bologna had a Communist administration for some 50 years after the war. Bologna was indeed the Italian Communist Party's showpiece.

Session 8

Talking about the past: the past definite

When Silvia started to tell what she did on receiving her Swiss friend's call for help, she used some verbs you may not have met before:

Io <u>andai</u> direttamente dal sindaco di Bologna che <u>fu</u> di una disponibilità meravigliosa. <u>Mise</u> a disposizione un'automobile con un autista e uno psicologo.

I went straight to the mayor of Bologna who was marvellously willing to help. He made available a car with a chauffeur and a psychologist.

This single word past tense is known as the *past definite*, in Italian **passato remoto**. It is used when recounting events in the past, as is the perfect. The classic rule, based on Tuscan Italian, is that it is used for a past which is viewed as no longer having any link with the present, not necessarily very remote in time, but no longer having a relationship to today. But Tuscan Italian is no longer viewed as the model all must follow. Other regional varieties are equally acceptable. Notice that Silvia, who is not Tuscan, uses it in story-telling mode, as it were. She used it again in the message about the mayor of Bologna: **ne parlò la stampa** *the press reported it*.

The use varies from one part of Italy to another so that a hard and fast rule cannot be given. It is rarely used in speech in Northern Italy. In Central and even more so in Southern Italy you will hear it. And it is more widely used in writing. Writing necessarily distances events from us. But it does depend on the type of writing. It will be used particularly in academic writing, in novels written in 'classic' Italian. For instance, Natalia Ginzburg normally used it in her novels, but in *Caro Michele*, which consists largely of letters interspersed with some narrative, the narrative is in the **passato remoto**, and the letters in the **passato prossimo**.

As a student of Italian, at first you need only learn to recognize it. Indeed you might never need to use it yourself. You will find the meaning very guessable. The form is as follows:

firmare	vendere	partire
firmai	vendei (-etti)	partii
firmasti	vendesti	partisti
firmò	vendè (-ette)	partì
firmammo	vendemmo	partimmo
firmaste	vendeste	partiste
firmarono	venderono (-ettero)	partirono

The forms in brackets are alternative forms which exist for Group 2 verbs. You may meet them. The underlining indicates stress.

Many verbs in Group 2 are irregular in this tense. You met **mise** (**mettere**) and **prese** (**prendere**) above. However, they are irregular in the first and third person singular and in the third person plural only. In the second person singular and first and second person plural they are regular. Here are some examples:

avere	chiedere	decidere	leggere	prendere	scrivere
ebbi	chiesi	decisi	lessi	presi	scrissi
avesti	chiedesti	decidesti	leggesti	prendesti	scrivesti
ebbe	chiese	decise	lesse	prese	scrisse
avemmo	chiedemmo	decidemmo	leggemmo	prendemmo	scrivemmo
aveste	chiedeste	decideste	leggeste	prendeste	scriveste
ebbero	chiesero	decisero	lessero	presero	scrissero

If you are given the first person singular of the past definite of an irregular verb, you should, consulting this table, be able to work out the whole pattern, given that the second person singular will be regular. This is not true of **essere** which has the following forms: **fui, fosti, fu, fummo, foste, furono. Dare** and **stare** are also irregular in all persons. There is a list of common irregular past definites in the **Reference grammar**.

Activity 6

Look back to the story in Unit 4, Activity 5, about the three Rossi girls during the war. Imagine you are rewriting it for publication and decide the past historic would be a more suitable tense. Make the necessary changes.

Session 9

Reading 3

Gli 'Angeli del Fango'

A remarkable phenomenon in recent years has been the way people, particularly young people, have helped in the event of natural disasters, of which there have been many. The following article recalls, 30 years afterwards, the flooding of the city of Florence in 1966, an event which, in addition to loss of life and damage to buildings, caused widespread damage to art treasures. Note that it is recounted in the past definite.

L'Arno smise di tagliare in due la città e diventò Firenze. Tutto era fiume alle 7,26 del 4 novembre 1966. In quell'istante l'Arno aveva rotto gli argini e l'onda di piena (4.100 metri cubi al secondo) raggiunse, travolse e invase botteghe, case, musei e qualsiasi cosa incontrasse sul suo cammino. Si trattò di un evento tragico, frutto insieme delle precipitazioni eccezionali e soprattutto del dissesto idrogeologico che tuttora, in misura sempre maggiore, interessa l'intero bacino dell'Arno e non solo quello. Un evento che ferì gravemente un patrimonio d'arte e cultura di valore inestimabile e di appartenenza universale.

Eppure quell'alluvione fu contemporaneamente l'occasione di una straordinaria mobilitazione civile che coinvolse migliaia di giovani provenienti da ogni parte d'Europa: i cosiddetti 'Angeli del Fango', che per giorni prestarono la loro opera contribuendo a liberare dall'acqua, dalla mota e dalla nafta le strade del capoluogo toscano, le centinaia di migliaia di volumi della Biblioteca Nazionale, decine e decine di tele, i reperti del museo archeologico, i monumenti cittadini. Una identica molla spinse centinaia e centinaia di ragazze e ragazzi a raggiungere Firenze nei giorni successivi all'alluvione, ed a lavorare instancabilmente per ridare splendore alle opere ferite dalla melma: un sentimento comune, un voler bene all'Italia ed al suo patrimonio artistico, considerato a ragione patrimonio del mondo.

In questo numero di 'Legambiente Notizie' troverete un ampio servizio dedicato alla settimana di manifestazioni che la nostra associazione ha voluto dedicare – nel trentennale dell'alluvione di Firenze – agli 'Angeli del Fango': il loro impegno è un simbolo, un invito ad impegnarsi in prima persona che non va dimenticato. Così come non va dimenticata l'alluvione di Firenze e le tante, troppe, che l'hanno seguita, che hanno dimostrato come l'incuria, la cementificazione selvaggia e spesso abusiva del territorio, il conseguente dissesto idrogeologico rendano estremamente fragile il tesoro d'arte e natura che possediamo.

Ermete Realacci, Presidente Nazionale Legambiente,
Legambiente Notizie, 30 ottobre 1996

QUICK VOCAB

... **diventò Firenze** i.e. the Arno no longer flowed between its banks, but through the whole city. The Arno is the river which in normal circumstances flows through the centre of Florence.

qualsiasi cosa incontrasse imperfect subjunctive after an indefinite antecedent.

dalla mota e dalla nafta nafta is a word commonly used for the oil burned in central heating boilers, traces of which could be clearly seen on some buildings in Florence long after most signs of the flood had gone, at a height of up to two metres. It indicated the level the water reached. **Mota** is *mud*, as is **fango**: earth mixed with water to a paste.

... **del capoluogo toscano** Florence is the capital of the region of Tuscany. **Capo** *head*, *main*, **luogo** *place*; cf. **capostazione** *station master*, **capolavoro** *masterpiece*, **capolinea** *terminus* (of a bus route, for instance), etc.

melma is the word for the *mud* at the bottom of a river, or in a marsh, or indeed left by a flood when the water subsides.

che non va dimenticato *which should not be forgotten*. The passive with **andare** (see Unit 6, Session 4).

Insight

It is a good idea to make a note of the forms of the past definite when reading the description of a historical event, like the 1966 floods in Florence. Knowledge of the past definite will allow you to read many Italian novels and encyclopedia entries about historical events!

Comprehension: Reading 3

1 What did the 'Angeli del Fango' do?
2 The writer sees their commitment as constituting an invitation. To do what?

3 The writer seems to be pessimistic. Pick out the words which indicate this.

··

The mention of **dissesto idrogeologico** is not infrequent in discussions of environmental issues in Italy today. **Dissesto** is difficult to translate: *confusion, disorder, imbalance.* It is the opposite of **sesto:** *the normal position or state,* used in phrases like **sentirsi fuori sesto** *not to feel right;* **rimettersi in sesto** *to get back to normal.* The expression **dissesto idrogeologico** refers to the set of environmental problems which make flooding and landslides likely. First it must be remembered that much of Italy is mountainous or hilly, so that heavy precipitation leads inevitably to fast-flowing rivers and streams. Add to that centuries, not to say millennia, of deforestation; much more recently the flight from the land, land that is tough to farm and doesn't give as good a living as a factory job, usually in hilly areas which are then left in a state of neglect (**l'incuria**) – for instance drainage ditches become clogged up and the water flows elsewhere; then, lower down the rivers, building on land known to flood, and building, sometimes without permission, without making any – or adequate – provision for possible flood water (**la cementificazione selvaggia e spesso abusiva del territorio**). Thus land which was once like a natural sponge can no longer cope with heavy rainfall. As we said in Unit 3, Session 4, the problems are now being taken more seriously. Current law requires a geological report on any building site before permission to build is granted. And, in some areas at least, prevention is beginning to be considered.

On a historical note, it should be added that another great art city of Italy, Venice, also suffered exceptionally bad flooding in November 1966. But of course it is sadly no stranger to flooding. And the causes are perhaps more complex. The exceptionally heavy rain was common to both events.

··

Session 10

Here are your last pieces of practice in *Perfect your Italian*. Silvia talks about another project she has been involved with over the years. It is still not classic **volontariato sociale** but we hope you'll find it interesting. And an article in *La Stampa* questions whether the **volontariato** picture is perhaps changing. We hope these passages will show you what a lot of progress you have made since Unit 1.

Interview 4

● CD2, TR 14, 52:12

Silvia Mah è difficile parlare di volontariato veramente perché io ho solamente fatto delle … cioè m'interessava essere viva e partecipare, fare qualche tipo di intervento … fare qualche tipo di intervento in politica internazionale, delle donne. È molto ambizioso, questo termine, però è un po' così. Non ho fatto volontariato sociale.

Invece dopo anni di lavoro per la famiglia, anni in cui non ho fatto nulla di particolare per gli altri, quando sono venuta ad abitare a Bologna era molto vivo un centro di documentazione della donna. All'inizio ero un po' ostile su queste … Perché c'erano delle donne molto femministe e io non sentivo di condividere molto con loro. Poi, c'è stato un viaggio importantissimo nella mia vita, 1990, quando andai a Gerusalemme con loro in una marcia della pace attorno alle mura di Gerusalemme. Mi sembrava una cosa molto bella e infatti è stata un'esperienza che praticamente ha cambiato la direzione della mia vita. Perché era una marcia internazionale e io ho conosciuto tantissime donne e soprattutto ho conosciuto delle donne palestinesi e israeliane che manifestavano insieme con una metodologia particolare che è quella delle Donne in Nero, una forma di protesta silenziosa che ogni giorno nella piazza principale di Gerusalemme mettevano in pratica, cioè stando in piedi, vestite di nero in segno di lutto per le morti di palestinesi che ci sono state in questi anni … Questa manifestazione

(Contd)

Italy: physical geography.

è iniziata da delle donne israeliane molto aperte alla causa palestinese e a loro si sono associate delle donne palestinesi. Per anni hanno manifestato così coperte di insulti e di sputi. Noi ci siamo unite a loro e loro ci hanno chiesto di portare questa pratica in giro per il mondo E noi l'abbiamo fatto. Ero con altre quattordici donne di Bologna. Appena siamo tornate a Bologna abbiamo deciso di fare come loro. E poi abbiamo deciso un'altra cosa: di organizzare un campo di pace con ragazzini italiani, palestinesi e israeliani. Questa è una tradizione che è iniziata nel '91 e che è ancora in piedi con solamente un anno di interruzione nel momento più drammatico degli scontri fra gli israeliani e i palestinesi, ma anche quest'anno ci sarà un campo di pace, un'iniziativa molto bella nella quale mi sono impegnata con passione anche perché allora, all'inizio, erano coinvolti parecchi amici di Amnesty International di cui io sono sempre stata socia.

QV

un campo di pace The group had help again from the local authorities; for instance they made available premises at Cattolica, on the coast of Emilia Romagna, for the peace camp.
quest'anno The interview was given in July 1998.

Reading 4

Uno studio rivela: 'Si riducono i gruppi cattolici, ma le organizzazioni raccolgono maggiori risorse'

Il volontariato non seduce più
In calo chi si impegna per gli altri

Roma. Scavano nel fango, assistono i malati, spengono gli incendi, difendono il patrimonio artistico. C'è chi diventa un eroe, chi si fa fratello di chi assiste, chi trasforma quell'anelito ad aiutare gli altri in una professione. Ma il volontario è soprattutto una persona normale. È un adulto (il 31,5 % ha tra i 30 e i 45 anni, anche se uno su tre ha meno di 29 anni), può essere uomo o donna (con leggera prevalenza di quest'ultime, il 50,3%), ha una occupazione (il 45%) o comunque l'ha avuta (il 18,7% sono pensionati), ha un diploma di scuola superiore (4 su 10, mentre il 14,1% è laureato), si impegna in modo costante: fino a tre ore la settimana (36,4%), da 4 a 5 ore (18,2%), da 6 a 8 (25,6%) ma anche più di 8 ore (19,8%).

La fotografia del volontario-tipo, più nitida e meno enfatica che nel passato, viene dal secondo rapporto della Fivol – la Fondazione Italiana del Volontariato, una delle centrali più importanti del settore, nata dalla Banca di Roma, presentata ieri a Roma.

La prima indagine fu nel '93, questa si ferma al '97, ed è la più aggiornata. Che cos'è cambiato in quattro anni? La 'sorpresa' dello studio, curato dai ricercatori Fivol Renato Frisanco e Costanzo Ranci, arriva a pagina 40: 'Assistiamo ad una riduzione del lavoro volontario e ad un aumento delle risorse finanziarie utilizzate'. In pratica ci sono meno italiani disposti ad impegnarsi per gli altri, ma più persone che si mettono a posto la coscienza versando qualche soldo. Ecco le cifre: il 41% delle associazioni ha avuto dal '93 al '97 un calo del numero di volontari superiore al 20% (e il 29% è stabile), mentre una su due segnala un incremento delle entrate annue. Cambia anche la matrice ideologica: quelle aconfessionali (sono la maggioranza) crescono dal 67,5% al 61,2, mentre le cattoliche calano dal 40,4 al 36,3.

Nel '93 la Fivol aveva azzardato una stima di 3 milioni e 700 mila volontari. Nel rapporto presentato ieri questa cifra invece non si trova, ci si ferma a quota 400 mila, censiti. Perché? 'In quel dato – spiega Renato Frisanco – erano compresi i simpatizzanti, come i donatori di sangue o quanti partecipavano saltuariamente all'attività della loro associazione. Ora abbiamo individuato 12.909 gruppi, con gli effettivi aderenti.'

Ma quello che colpisce di più non è il calo della partecipazione – tocca soprattutto le associazioni più tradizionali come la San Vincenzo o i gruppi parrocchiali, bensì l'aumentato divario tra Nord e Sud. Oltre metà delle organizzazioni opera nelle regioni settentrionali, mentre nel Mezzogiorno è presente solo il 29% dei gruppi.

(Gigi Padovani, *La Stampa*, 12 febbraio 1999)

si mettono a posto la coscienza *they soothe their consciences*
(lit: they put their consciences straight)

crescono dal 67,5% al 61,2 There seems to be some mistake here;
probably the first figure should be 57.5 % but this was how it
appeared in the newspaper and we have been unable to get a
correction.

censiti counted carefully, as in a census

San Vincenzo A Roman Catholic organization which helps the poor,
in the footsteps of Saint Vincent de Paul.

Il divario tra Nord e Sud

This is an aspect of Italy today we have not touched on. It is
something for your future studies! Suffice it to say here that
whatever measure of economic well-being, often of social
well-being, you take, the North is ahead, often a long way
ahead, of the South. The North is often referred to as the
Centro-Nord, which means Tuscany and Umbria are being
included, even Rome. Tuscany and Umbria certainly belong
with the North in terms of economic prosperity.

Session 11

Talking to yourself

We hope this is a real habit by now. Unit 8 should have provided
plenty of subjects to think about. Here are some:

1 Lei fa un lavoro volontario di qualche tipo? In che cosa consiste?
Quanto L'impegna? Perché lo fa?

2 Forse non ha il tempo di svolgere lavoro volontario, ma sostiene
opere di carità, o associazioni volontarie, facendo donazioni e
offerte. Che tipo di associazione e attività aiuta? Perché? Di che
cosa si occupano?

3 Lei pensa che il lavoro volontario debba essere un complimento o un sostituto dello stato? Quanto dobbiamo aspettarci di diritto dallo stato in cambio del nostro voto e delle tasse che paghiamo?
4 Conflitti e guerre nel mondo: quali conosce? Di quali segue le vicende? Come sono iniziati? Che conseguenze hanno portato?
5 Disastri naturali: Lei è mai stato colpito da un disastro naturale? Saprebbe parlare di un disastro naturale che ha colpito il Suo Paese? o qualche altro paese?

....
Language learning tip

You will have noticed that this unit did not contain many exercises. What it did contain was lots of authentic Italian. As you become more proficient, that is the way to learn. So what you need to do now is get practice. We made some suggestions in Unit 1.

One very useful source of material is the Internet. A good search engine is **www.google.it**. You will gradually find the sites that interest you but the following may be a useful start. They also provide useful web links to other interesting sites.

www.corriere.it	
www.lastampa.it	three leading newspapers
www.repubblica.it	
www.internazionale.it	The web page of the magazine, where you will find articles on world news, mostly in Italian.
www.legambiente.eu	The web site of the environmental group, now a European site.
www.slowfood.it	The Slow Food movement started in Italy.
www.italmensa.it	another site for lovers of Italian food
www.istat.it	The Italian statistical institute with information about the voluntary sector and much else.

(Contd)

www.informagiovani-italia.com	For young people, with interesting links.
www.comune.roma.it	Comuni have web sites. This is Rome's. For Torino:
www.comune.torino.it	The pattern is the same. Try some.
www/rainews24.rai.it	The Italian state Radio and TV site has an online news service.
www.pianetabimbi.it	For children and their parents. Includes riddles, etc.
www.nonsolomamma.com	A journalists's blog about life with her children.
www.chetempochefa.rai.it	You can watch Italian TV on line. This is a popular chat show.
www.mediaset.it	The private TV network
www.striscialanotizia.mediaset.it	A popular Mediaset programme

You can also explore Italy this way. You will find some sites are in English or offer a choice of languages. The vocabulary for the web is English, e.g. **server, provider, link**, or derived from English, e.g. **cliccare**. Sites do to some extent come and go, so we apologize if something proves unavailable. Have fun surfing Italy.

Even better: go to Italy!

We hope you have enjoyed working through *Perfect your Italian*. We wish you much enjoyment as you learn more Italian – and many happy visits to Italy!

TEST YOURSELF

1 Match the two parts of the conditional sentences.

a Se lei andasse in Kenya,

b Se facessimo del volontariato,

c Se i ragazzi non sapessero cosa fare,

d Se il tempo fosse migliore,

e Se non capissi la loro lingua,

1 mi cercherei un inteprete.

2 potrebbero andare al centro ricreativo.

3 potrebbe partecipare a un safari fotografico.

4 aiuteremmo le popolazioni dei paesi poveri.

5 potresti andare in spiaggia.

2 Complete the sentences with the correct form of the present or the imperfect subjunctive.

a Volevo salutarlo prima che _____ (partire).

b Benché Chiara _____ (essere) molto socievole, non trovava mai un fidanzato.

c Non c'è nessuno che _____ (sapere) dove si è trasferita quella famiglia

d Vorrei qualcosa che mi _____ (fare) passare il mal di testa.

e Nel caso che gli ospiti _____ (arrivare) prima di me, puoi servire gli antipasti.

f Voleva andare in ufficio nonostante _____ (avere) l'influenza.

g La società cercava una persona che _____ (gestire) i rapporti con i clienti.

h Bisogna che tu _____ (prendersi) le tue responsabilità.

i Non c'era niente che _____ (potere) calmare la sua ansietà.

j È difficile che la comunità _____ (accettare) persone così diverse.

Grammar ...

The technical jargon explained

Many people find the study of a language off-putting because of references to adverbs, conjunctions, subordinate clauses, etc., terms which they are unfamiliar with. They speak and write their own language perfectly well without knowing the words for analyzing it. Why does learning a foreign language have to involve learning all these grammatical terms? Well, of course, it doesn't. However, if they are used, they enable us to make generalizations about patterns: instruction and learning can become more efficient. And, in fact, people subconsciously understand grammar; it is just the terminology that foxes them. You don't think you understand grammar? Well, look at this:

'Twas brillig, and the slithy toves
  Did gyre and gimble in the wabe:
All mimsy were the borogoves,
  And the mome raths outgrabe.

'Beware the Jabberwock, my son!
  The jaws that bite, the claws that catch!
Beware the Jubjub bird, and shun
  The frumious Bandersnatch!'

He took his vorpal sword in hand:
  Long time the manxome foe he sought –
So rested he by the Tumtum tree,
  And stood awhile in thought.

And, as in uffish thought he stood,
  The Jabberwock, with eyes of flame,
Came whiffling through the tulgey wood,
  And burbled as it came!

One, two! One, two! And through and through
  The vorpal blade went snicker-snack!
He left it dead, and with its head
  He went galumphing back.

'And hast thou slain the Jabberwock?
  Come to my arms, my beamish boy!
O frabjous day! Callooh! Callay!'
  He chortled in his joy.

JABBERWOCKY by Lewis Carroll

It's nonsense. And yet, we feel it's English. It conjures up images in our imagination, we can give it meaning even though among ourselves we might disagree about that meaning. We recognize it as acceptable as English. And yet many of the words are unknown to us and indeed to any dictionary we might consult.

Think about what happens in your mind when you read *Jabberwocky*. At least three things go on:

1 You use the words you understand as springboards for guessing what the ones you don't understand might mean. e.g. 'Twas is understandable as *it was*, and you know that in a sentence of the sort the poem starts with, *it was* usually introduces information about the weather, the conditions.

2 You give meaning to the nonsense words by comparing them to words which are similar in sound, e.g. *brillig* – *brilliant*, *bright*. You assume *brillig* is related to the quality of the light.

3 Most importantly, you can give a role, a function to the words in the sentences even when they are unknown to you, for instance, you know that the … *toves* can be completed by the addition of a word such as *little*, *ugly*, *blue*, *fascinating* and you accept *slithy* as a word of that type. You know that it would not work to insert a word like: *here*, *now*, *tomorrow*; nor would *have*, *sing*, *are*, *think* be suitable. You have an instinctive ability to attribute a role to words in sentences. You know that *little*, *ugly*, *blue*, *fascinating*, all have the same function, they describe the word that follows them: in *blue moon*, *blue* describes *moon* and *slithy* must describe *toves*.

So you see, you have a feeling for English grammar, you know what sort of word is needed in any given slot – even if the sentence is full of nonsense words. Really all you need to do is to learn the names of the technical words used for talking about language. For instance *little*, *ugly*, *blue*, *fascinating* are all examples of adjectives.

Definitions of grammatical terms can be tortuous and hedged around with provisos. Intuition is often a more effective way of understanding them. Of course, dictionaries contain definitions and this may help but we have tried to provide a way for you to understand the terms we use intuitively, taking our examples, as far as possible, from *Jabberwocky* and supplementing that with some ordinary, straightforward words.

The definitions which follow are arranged as far as possible logically. When we use another grammatical word in an explanation we have tried to deal with that next or soon afterwards.

Sentence Probably not a problem for you. A chunk starting with a capital letter and ending with a full stop, question mark or exclamation mark and containing a verb. (Carroll also makes use of the colon and technically that is not a sentence boundary. It ends a clause.) A sentence will have at least one **main clause** and may have **subordinate clauses**. Examples: *He chortled in his joy. The sun was setting behind the hill. Napoleon was finally defeated at the Battle of Waterloo.*

Main clause *And … The Jabberwock … came whiffling through the tulgey wood …* As its name suggests, the main frame of the sentence, which could stand alone. You can have parallel main clauses, as is the case here where the sentence continues: *and burbled as it came!*

Subordinate clause *as in uffish thought he stood* – effectively another sentence inserted into the main clause; it could not stand alone.

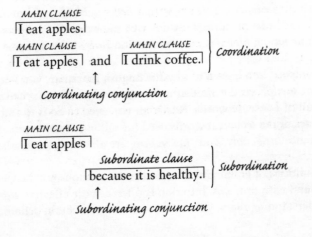

256

MAIN CLAUSE
┌─────────────┐
│ I eat apples │
└─────────────┘
  Subordinate clause   *Sub clause*   *Sub clause*
┌──────────────────────┐   ┌───────────────┐ ┌───────────┐
│ because it is healthy │ and │ the doctor says │ │ I should. │
└──────────────────────┘   └───────────────┘ └───────────┘
MAIN CLAUSE   MAIN CLAUSE
┌─────────────┐   ┌───────────────┐
│ I eat apples │   and │ I drink coffee │
└─────────────┘   └───────────────┘
  Subordinate clause   *Subordinate clause*
┌──────────────────────┐   ┌──────────────────┐
│ because it is healthy │   │ because I like it. │
└──────────────────────┘   └──────────────────┘

Phrase *the jaws that bite; by the Tumtum tree; with eyes of flame.* A group of words that together make a chunk of meaning. The difference between a phrase and a **clause** is that in a phrase there is no **verb**. (*that bite* is a subordinate clause).

Noun *The Jabberwock, toves, wabe, son, jaws ... thought.* (The word *thought* can of course also be used as a **verb**.) If it can have *the* or *a* in front of it, it is probably a noun, or being used as one: *the world, a hope, a grandfather.* A noun is a word used as the name of a person, place, quality, state or thing.

Adjective *brillig, slithy, mimsy, frumious, frabjous,* etc. from the poem. As we said above: *little, ugly, blue, fascinating* are adjectives. An adjective tells you more about a noun. The technical term for that is **qualify**. The adjective qualifies the noun. More examples: *long, futile, extraordinary, fictitious ...*

Verb *was, did gyre, (did) gimble, beware, catch, shun, took, rested,* etc. The heart of the sentence. A verb expresses action, being or occurrence. Note: *beware* is unusual in English in the way it works: you cannot say *I beware, he bewares.* You normally can with a verb: your innate grammatical sense tells you that it is possible to say *I gimble, he gimbles.* You also know: *I am, he is, I catch, he catches, I take, he takes,* etc. Other non-nonsense verbs are: *to try, to sneeze, to decide, to hope.*

Verbs have a variety of technical terms associated with them which it is helpful gradually to become familiar with:

Infinitive: this is the part of the verb you find in dictionaries: *to gimble*, *to be*, *to catch*, *to take*, etc.

Finite verb: the verb in use with a **subject**: *I gimble*, *I used to gimble*, *The slithy toves **will gimble** tomorrow.*

Non-finite: certain parts of the verb are non-finite: *to gimble*, *gimbling*, *gimbled* (see below). There is no **noun** or **pronoun**. In English, words like *gimbled*, the past participle, can also have another function: simple past tense. The Italian equivalent cannot.

Transitive, intransitive: finite verbs can be **transitive** or **intransitive**. A transitive verb can have a direct **object**: *He slew the Jabberwock. Mary had a little lamb.* Intransitive verbs cannot have a direct object. *I went to London. They despaired. The King reigned for 40 years. To go, to despair, to reign* are intransitive verbs.

Conjugate, conjugation: when you go through person by person, *I am, you are, he is*, you are conjugating the verb. In our text we have used this word in particular to say that in compound tenses some verbs use **avere** and others **essere**: they are *conjugated with* **avere** or **essere**. We have also called the different types of verb Group 1, Group 2, etc. These groups are often referred to as *first conjugation, second conjugation*, etc.

Root: this is used to refer to the unchanging part of the verb to which all the endings are added. It can also apply to other words (**nouns, adjectives**, etc.), especially when you are looking at how the word came into being and/or acquired its current meaning. The use is a simple analogy with plants, the root being the basis.

Tense: verbs have tenses: present, past, future.

Mood, mode: Italian categorizes **finite verbs** into four moods:

1 indicative: the form you will already be used to: present, past, future. It is for factual statements rather than the hypothetical (see conditional below) or actions viewed as being the wish, fear, belief etc. of the speaker (subjunctive – see below and units).

2 conditional: this is the equivalent of the English: *I would (do)*. You almost certainly know **vorrei** *I would/should like*. The conditional is subject to a condition: *if this were the case then B would ...*

3 subjunctive: this has almost disappeared from English but some people still use it in sentences like: *I wish it **were** true*. The subjunctive is not about fact, but rather uncertainty, wishes, etc. It is more fully explained in the text. Note: we tend to say that certain conditions **require** the subjunctive.

4 imperative: for telling people what to do, orders, instructions, advice: *Come to my arms ...*; *Beware the Jabberwock ...* and *shun the frumious Bandersnatch!*

It is also usual for Italian grammarians to talk about **non-finite moods** which are:

1 the infinitive (see above): *to be, to laugh, to hide, to surmise.*

2 the participles (see Units): *being, been; hiding, hidden; laughing, laughed; surmising, surmised.* You may perhaps see that some can act as adjectives.

3 the gerund (see Units): it ends in *-ing*, i.e. it has the same form as the present participle in English: *hiding, laughing, being, surmising.*

Pronoun *'Twas brillig* ('*T*' is really '*it*'); *He took his vorpal sword; He left it dead; And hast thou slain.* All these are **personal pronouns**; they stand for nouns which the writer does not want or need to repeat. *Jabberwocky* does not give much scope for illustrating other types of pronoun. In *The jaws that bite*, *that* is a **relative pronoun**: it relates what follows to the preceding noun. In fact it stands for the noun. The word the relative pronoun stands for is called the **antecedent**. So *jaws* is the **antecedent** of *that*.

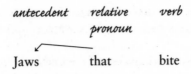

antecedent	relative pronoun	verb
Jaws	that	bite

This particular clause is an **adjectival clause** because it acts as an adjective. It tells you more about the *jaws* in just the same way as *huge* or *strong* would. There are other types of pronoun: **interrogative** (for asking questions): *who? which?*; **demonstrative** (for pointing out): *those*, etc.

Subject A **noun** or a **pronoun** showing who is doing the action of the **verb**: e.g. *I* or *the slithy toves*. It is subject of both the **verb** and the **clause**.

Object A **noun** or **pronoun** on which the action of the **verb** is performed. *He took his vorpal **sword** in hand; He left **it**; And hast thou slain the **Jabberwock**?* The words in bold print are the **direct object** of the verb. *Come to **my arms**:* in this case, *my arms* is the **indirect object**. The **preposition to** is a clue but English does not always need the preposition. (*He gave me chocolates:* He – subject, *gave* – verb, *me* – indirect object, *chocolates* – direct object. It is clumsy to analyze in words, but you might say *chocolates* underwent the action of the verb directly – they were given; *me* benefitted. Your intuition probably seizes the idea better.)

S. V.   D.O.   I.O.
|I|sent |a letter| |to my love.|

            Subject   Verb   Direct Object
    |The sudden thunderstorm| |ruined| |the concert.|

Adverb *Jabberwocky* doesn't contain a good example. But most adverbs are easy. In English they usually end in *-ly*: *silently, quickly, fearlessly, he slew the Jabberwock. She sings **well**, beautifully, loudly.* They are said to **modify** the **verb** they go with. They can also modify **adjectives**. *That coat looks **beautifully** warm. His work is **incredibly** interesting. I like my coffee **very** strong.* Less easy to identify are adverbs like: *And stood **awhile** in thought.*

Awhile is an adverb. *In thought* is an adverbial **phrase** (i.e. a phrase doing what an adverb does).

Preposition *in* the wabe; He took his ... sword *in* hand; *by* the Tumtum tree; The Jabberwock, **with** eyes of flame, came whiffling **through** the tulgey wood; Come **to** my arms. Other English prepositions include: *under, on, beside, at,* etc. and phrases such as: *next to, at the side of* etc. They mark the relationship between a **noun** or **pronoun** and another word.

Conjunction Just as a junction is where roads or railway lines meet and so connect, so a conjunction connects **words, phrases, clauses.** The most common are *and* and *but* called **coordinating conjunctions** because they simply join or relate two clauses or two words to each other. However in studying a language the ones you need to look out for are the **subordinating conjunctions** which introduce a subordinate clause. These are words like: *because, although, while, if, when,* and phrases like *in spite of the fact that.* They introduce a clause which is inserted into the main clause. See previous diagrams in this section which illustrate coordination and subordination.

Prefix This is simply a group of letters which can be put before the beginning of a word to make a new word. An example might in fact be *pre* which placed before *fix* forms another word. Others are: *dis-: appear, disappear; approve, disapprove; in-: appropriate, inappropriate; hospitable, inhospitable.*

Suffix This is similar except that the group of letters is placed at the end of the word: *pig, piglet.* Many adverbs are formed by adding the suffix *-ly* to an adjective: *slow, slowly.*

Interjections This is what you would call the exclamations *callooh! callay!* in Lewis Carroll's poem.

We hope the above was helpful – and that it doesn't ruin *Jabberwocky* for you for ever! It has a magic which we would be loath to destroy.

Reference grammar

This section contains lists for reference and help with certain points not covered in the text. For students who want to perfect their Italian grammar, a book devoted exclusively to Italian grammar is recommended. Particularly helpful are:

Derek Aust with Mike Zollo, **Azione Grammatica**, Hodder & Stoughton, new edition 2006. A full, clear and concise treatment of the main points of the grammar of Italian, with plenty of help for those not used to studying grammar and well thought-out exercises to practise the various points.

Denise De Rôme, consultant Paola Tite, **Soluzioni!: A Practical Guide to Italian Grammar**, Hodder Arnold, 2010. A clearly laid out and fairly full guide to Italian grammar for the learner wanting to know more; intended to be useful to beginners and accessible to readers unused to grammatical terminology, it will also be valuable for the more sophisticated and advanced student. Includes exercises.

Martin Maiden and Cecilia Robustelli, **A Reference Grammar of Modern Italian**, Arnold, 2000. A comprehensive work of reference but written with the intention of being accessible to learners of Italian of all levels of competence. Recommended for those who want to know all the details and for more advanced learners becoming aware of points not covered by course books.

Nicola Zingarelli, **Lo Zingarelli 2010 – Vocabolario della lingua italiana**, Zanichelli Editore, Bologna. Readers wanting to buy an Italian monolingual dictionary may like to consider the one used for our definitions. It is updated annually and is available with a CD-ROM and also on-line. See www.zanichelli.it.

Comparative and superlative of adjectives

interessante *interesting*	**più interessante** *more interesting*	**il più interessante** *the most interesting*	**interessantissimo** *very interesting*
allegro *happy*	**più allegro** *happier*	**il più allegro** *the happiest*	**allegrissimo** *very happy*

Common irregular forms are:

buono	*good*	**migliore** also **più buono**	*better*	**il migliore**	*the best*
cattivo	*bad*	**peggiore**	*worse*	**il peggiore**	*the worst*
piccolo	*small*	**minore** **più piccole**	*smaller*	**il minore**	*the smallest*
grande	*big*	**maggiore** **più grande**	*bigger*	**il maggiore**	*the biggest*
alto	*high*	**più alto, superiore**	*higher*	**il più alto**	*the highest*
basso	*low*	**più basso, inferiore**	*lower*	**il più basso**	*the lowest*

ottimo *very good*	
pessimo *very bad*	
minimo *very small* **il minimo** *the least*	
massimo *very big* **il massimo** *the utmost*	
altissimo *very high*	
bassissimo/ **infimo** *very low*	

Comparative and superlative of adverbs

lentamente *slowly*	**più lentamente** *more slowly*	**il più lentamente possibile** *as slowly as possible*	**molto lentamente, lentissimamente** *very slowly*

Note: **bene, meglio** *well, better* **male, peggio** *badly, worse*
molto, più *much, more* **poco, meno** *little, less*

Personal pronouns

Subject		Direct object (unstressed)		Indirect object (unstressed)		Reflexive		Strong (stressed)	
io	I	mi	me	mi	to me	mi	(to) myself	me	me
tu	you	ti	you	ti	to you	ti	(to) yourself	te	you
lui	he	lo	him	gli	to him	si	(to) himself	lui	him
lei	she	la	her	le	to her	si	(to) herself	lei	her
Lei*	you	La*	you	Le*	to you	Si*	(to) yourself	Lei*	you
noi	we	ci	us	ci	to us	ci	(to) ourselves	noi	us
voi	you	vi	you	vi	to you	vi	(to) yourselves	voi	you
loro	they	li (m.), le (f.)	them	gli	to them	si	(to) themselves	loro	them

*The formal *you*, singular. The usual plural is **voi**. Only in very formal speech/circumstances is **Loro** used as a plural formal *you*. Its form is as **loro** *they* given above.

Notes:

1 You may also meet the subject forms **egli, ella** (*he, she*), but usually in elegant, written style rather than in speech. Similarly **esso, essa** (*it*), **essi, esse** (*they*). Also in more elegant speech or writing, *to them* is **loro** and it follows the verb.

Informal speech: **Gli parla.** *He's talking to them.* Formal speech: **Parla loro.** *He's talking to them.*

2 Strong or stressed pronouns are used:
    a after a preposition: **Viene con me?** *Are you coming with me?*
    b for emphasis: **Cerca lui, non te.** *He's looking for him, not you.*

3 The direct and indirect object pronouns usually come before the verb but are added to the infinitive, the imperative (**tu** and **voi** forms), the past participle standing alone, and the gerund.

Combining pronouns

When both direct and indirect object pronouns are used, they are combined in this order:

1 the indirect pronouns **mi, ti, si, ci, vi** become **me, te, se, ce, ve** and are followed by **lo, la, li, le, ne**.

2 the indirect pronouns **gli, le** and the plural **gli**, all become **glie** and precede and are joined to **lo, la, li, le, ne**.

	lo	la	li	le	ne
mi	me lo	me la	me li	me le	me ne
ti	te lo	te la	te li	te le	te ne
gli	glielo	gliela	glieli	gliele	gliene
le	glielo	gliela	glieli	gliele	gliene
Le	Glielo	Gliela	Glieli	Gliele	Gliene
ci	ce lo	ce la	ce li	ce le	ce ne
vi	ve lo	ve la	ve li	ve le	ve ne
loro	glielo	gliela	glieli	gliele	gliene
si	se lo	se la	se li	se le	se ne

Tip

Rather than try to learn that as a rule, learn examples as you come across them:

Glielo dico.	*I'll say it to him/her/them* – or *you* (formal)
Me lo dai?	*Are you giving it to me?* (Often: *will you give it to me?*)
Non me ne parla.	*He/she doesn't talk to me about it.*

Negatives

Simple: **non** before verb. **Non abito qui.** *I don't live here.*
Strong negatives:

| non ... mica | non ... per niente |
| non ... affatto | non ... per nulla |

Non sono mica un suo amico.   *I'm definitely not a friend of his/hers.*

non ... nessuno	no one
non ... niente	} nothing
non ... nulla	
non ... ancora	not yet
non ... mai	never

non ... più	no longer, not any more
non ... neppure	} not even
non ... nemmeno	
non ... neanche	

Prepositions

Warning: The use of prepositions, particularly the commonest (**a**, **di**, **da**, **su**), is often tricky. Some meanings have been dealt with in the text. Further help is available in dictionaries or books such as *Azione Grammatica* (above). The list below is not exhaustive.

a	to, at	invece di	instead of
accanto a	next to	lontano da	far from
attraverso	across	lungo	along
circa	about	malgrado	in spite of
con	with	nonostante	in spite of
contro	against	per	for, through
da	from, by	presso	near
davanti a	in front of	prima di	before
dentro	inside	quanto a	as for, as regards
di	of, from	rispetto a	compared to
di fronte a	opposite	secondo	according to
dietro	behind	senza	without
eccetto	except	sopra	above
fino a	as far as, until	sotto	under
fra	between, within	su	on
in	to, in	tra	between, within
in fondo a	at the bottom of, at the end of	tramite	by means of
		tranne	except
in mezzo a	in the middle of	verso	towards
intorno a	around	vicino a	near

Interrogative pronouns and adjectives

che cosa? cosa? che?	what?
chi?	who? whom?
come?	how?

come mai?	how come? how (can it) possibly (be so)?
dove?	where?
perché?	why?
quando?	when?
quanto? quanti?	how much? how many?
quale?	which? which one?
quali?	which? which ones?

Cases where the subjunctive is required

1 After verbs expressing:

a *an opinion* or *casting doubt:* **pensare che, credere che,** (which, in the negative, both imply doubt), **dubitare che, non essere sicuro/certo che,** etc.

b *an order, a request, a wish that something be done or not done:* **comandare che, ordinare che, insistere che, desiderare che, volere che, proibire che, suggerire che, aspettarsi che,** etc.

c *necessity* – see list of impersonal expressions below.

d *fear, pleasure, and other emotions:* **avere paura che, temere che, essere contento/a che, essere felice che, essere triste che, stupirsi che, essere deluso che,** etc.

2 The subjunctive is also used after certain common impersonal expressions:

basta che	it is sufficient that
bisogna che	
è necessario che	it is necessary that
occorre che	
è importante che	it is important that
importa che	it matters that
è probabile che	it is likely that
è bene che	it's a good thing that
è meglio che	it's better that
è possibile che	
può darsi che	it's possible that
sembra che	
pare che	it seems that
è un peccato che	it is a pity that

3 The subjunctive is used after certain subordinating conjunctions. Common, or fairly common, are:

benché, sebbene, quantunque	*although*
perché, affinché, in modo che	*so that*
nonostante (che), malgrado (che)	*in spite of the fact that*
qualora, nel caso che, caso mai	*in the event that, in case*
purché, a condizione che	*provided that, on condition that*
a meno che	*unless*
prima che	*before*
finché non	*until*

Note: When **perché** means *because*, it does not require the subjunctive.

Imperative

Tu form
Group 1 (**are**) verbs end in **a**.
All other verbs (including all irregular verbs), end in **i** (the **tu** form of the present indicative.)

e.g. Group 1	**scusa, guarda, mangia**
e.g. All others	**senti, finisci, vieni**

Exceptions: verbs which do not use the **tu** form of the present indicative:

essere → sii	**sapere → sappi**
avere → abbi	**dire → di'**

Some common verbs have two possible forms, one abbreviated, the other regular:

andare → va'/vai	**dare → da'/dai**
stare → sta'/stai	**fare → fa'/fai**

Voi form (plural *you*)
Use the **voi** form of the present indicative:
scusate, guardate, decidete, finite, sentite, venite

Noi form (*Let's …*)
Use the **noi** form of the present indicative:
andiamo, mangiamo, decidiamo, finiamo

Lei form

This uses the present subjunctive:

-**are** verbs end in **i**: **scusi, guardi, mangi, s'accomodi**

All others end in **a**: **decida, senta, finisca, dica, venga**

Verbs which are irregular in the present subjunctive have that form in the imperative (**dica, venga**). Here are some other common ones:

essere → sia	fare → faccia
avere → abbia	sapere → sappia
andare → vada	stare → stia
dare → dia	

Note: Object (and reflexive) pronouns are attached to the end of the **tu** and **voi** forms, but precede the **Lei** form. This gives you:

tu form:	scusami	dimmi*	ascoltami	accomodati
voi form:	scusateci	diteci	ascoltateci	accomodatevi

BUT

Lei form:	mi scusi	mi dica	mi ascolti	s'accomodi

*When pronouns other than **gli** are attached to the abbreviated **tu** forms listed above, the first consonant of the pronoun is doubled: e.g. **dimmi**.

Tip

Use these or other commonly heard verbs as models to help you remember.

The negative imperative

It is formed by putting **non** in front of the positive imperative, except in the **tu** form, which uses **non** before the infinitive:

voi form:	non venite
Lei form:	non venga
BUT **tu** form:	non venire

Common irregular past participles and past definites

Since there is sometimes a link between the past participle and the past definite, it may be useful to have them listed together. Given the first and second persons singular of the past definite, it is possible to form the complete tense. Compounds of these verbs behave in the same way: e.g. **coinvolgere** behaves like **volgere**, **sorprendere** like **prendere**.

Infinitive meaning	Past participle	Past definite
essere to be	stato	fui, fosti, fu, fummo, foste, furono
avere to have	avuto	ebbi, avesti
assumere to take on (staff)	assunto	assunsi, assumesti
bere to drink	bevuto	bevvi, bevesti
chiedere to ask	chiesto	chiesi, chiedesti
chiudere to close	chiuso	chiusi, chiudesti
conoscere to know (person)	conosciuto	conobbi, conoscesti
correre to run	corso	corsi, corresti
dare to give	dato	diedi/detti, desti
decidere to decide	deciso	decisi, decidesti
dire to say	detto	dissi, dicesti
dirigere to direct	diretto	diressi, dirigesti
discutere to discuss	discusso	discussi, discutesti
escludere to exclude	escluso	esclusi, escludesti
fare to do, to make	fatto	feci, facesti
includere to include	incluso	inclusi, includesti
leggere to read	letto	lessi, leggesti
mettere to put	messo	misi, mettesti
nascere to be born	nato	nacqui, nascesti
perdere to lose	perso/perduto	persi/perdetti, perdesti
persuadere to persuade	persuaso	persuasi, persuadesti
prendere to take	preso	presi, prendesti
ridere to laugh	riso	risi, ridesti
rimanere to remain	rimasto	rimasi, rimanesti

Infinitive meaning	Past participle	Past definite
rispondere to answer	**risposto**	**risposi, rispondesti**
rompere to break	**rotto**	**ruppi, rompesti**
sapere to know (fact)	**saputo**	**seppi, sapesti**
scegliere to choose	**scelto**	**scelsi, scegliesti**
scendere to go down	**sceso**	**scesi, scendesti**
scrivere to write	**scritto**	**scrissi, scrivesti**
spegnere to extinguish	**spento**	**spensi, spegnesti**
stare to remain, stay	**stato**	**stetti, stesti**
stringere to grasp, squeeze	**stretto**	**strinsi, stringesti**
succedere to happen	**successo**	**successi, succedesti**
uccidere to kill	**ucciso**	**uccisi, uccidesti**
vedere to see	**visto, veduto**	**vidi, vedesti**
venire to come	**venuto**	**venni, venisti**
vincere to win	**vinto**	**vinsi, vincesti**
vivere to live	**vissuto**	**vissi, vivesti**
volere to want	**voluto**	**volli, volesti**
volgere to turn	**volto**	**volsi, volgesti**

Common verbs followed by the infinitive without a preposition

amare	to love	**interessare***	to be interesting
bastare*	to be enough	**lasciare**	to allow
bisognare*	to be necessary	**occorrere***	to be necessary
convenire*	to be advisable	**odiare**	to hate
desiderare	to desire, to want	**osare**	to dare
detestare	to detest	**piacere***	to be pleasing
dispiacere*	to be displeasing	**potere**	to be able
dovere	to have to	**preferire**	to prefer
fare	to make, to have done	**vedere**	to see
importare*	to matter	**volere**	to want

*Usually used impersonally.

Devo uscire.	*I have to go out.*
Fammi vedere la foto.	*Show me the photo.*
Faccio costruire una casa.	*I am having a house built.*
Lascia fare a me.	*Leave me to do it, let me do it.*

Mi piace andare al cinema.	*I like going to the cinema. (see treament of **piacere** in Unit 1)*		
Posso aiutare?	*Can I help?*		
Preferisco partire presto.	*I prefer to set off early.*		
Basta telefonare.	*All you need to do is telephone.*		
Bisogna telefonare.	*It is necessary to telephone (You/we need to telephone).*		
Conviene comprare qui.	*It is advisable to buy (it) here.*		

Common verbs requiring a, ad or di before an infinitive

Many speakers use **ad** before a verb beginning with a vowel, especially when the vowel is **a**, e.g. **aiutami ad alzare questo pianoforte** *help me lift this piano.*

Note: Verbs with similar meanings tend to work the same way, e.g. **chiedere** and **domandare**; **avere vergogna di** and **vergognarsi di**.

accettare di	*to accept to*	**convincere a**	*to persuade to*
aiutare a	*to help to*	**costringere a**	*to force to*
andare a	*to go to, to go and*	**credere di**	*to believe*
		decidere di	*to decide to*
avere intenzione di	*to intend to*	**dimenticare/ dimenticarsi di**	*to forget to*
avere paura di	*to be afraid of …ing*	**domandare (a qualcuno) di**	*to ask (someone) to*
avere ragione a	*to be right to*	**finire di**	*to finish …ing*
avere torto a	*to be wrong to*	**impedire (a qualcuno) di**	*to prevent (someone) from …ing*
avere vergogna di	*to be ashamed of …ing*		
avere voglia di	*to want to*	**insegnare a**	*to teach to*
cercare di	*to try to*	**mancare di**	*to fail to*
chiedere (a qualcuno) di	*to ask (someone) to*	**meritare di**	*to deserve to*
		mettersi a	*to start to, to start …ing*
cominciare a	*to begin to, to begin …ing*	**minacciare di**	*to threaten to*
consigliare (a qualcuno) di	*to advise (someone) to*	**non vedere l'ora di**	*to look forward to …ing*
parlare di	*to talk of …ing*	**scegliere di**	*to choose to*

permettere (a qualcuno) di	to permit/allow (someone) to	**scusarsi di**	to apologize for ...ing
pregare di	to beg/ask to	**servire a**	to be used for ...ing
promettere di	to promise to		
rendersi conto di	to realize	**smettere di**	to stop ...ing
		sopportare di	to stand/put up with/bear ...ing
ricordare/ ricordarsi di	to remember to		
		sperare di	to hope to
rifiutare di	to refuse to	**tentare di**	to try to
rinunciare a	to give up ...ing	**venire a**	to come to
riuscire a	to succeed in ...ing, to manage to	**vergognarsi di**	to be ashamed of ...ing
		vietare (a qualcuno) di	to forbid (someone) to
sapere di	to know		

Common verbs which take a direct object in one language and an indirect in the other

ascoltare qualcuno/qualcosa	to listen to someone/ something
assomigliare a qualcuno	to resemble someone
cercare qualcuno/qualcosa	to look for someone/something
chiedere qualcosa a qualcuno	to ask someone something
credere a qualcuno, qualcosa	to believe someone/something
but credere in qualcuno/qualcosa	to believe in someone/something
dare qualcosa a qualcuno	to give someone something
dire qualcosa a qualcuno	to tell someone something
entrare in un luogo	to enter a place
guardare qualcuno	to look at someone
occuparsi di qualcosa	to look after something
pensare a qualcuno	to think about someone
piacere a qualcuno	to please someone
rinunciare a qualcosa	to give something up, to go without something
rispondere a qualcuno/qualcosa (ad una domanda, al telefono)	to answer someone/something (a question, the telephone)
telefonare a qualcuno	to telephone/call someone
volere bene a qualcuno	to love someone, be fond of someone

Note also other differences between common verbs in the two languages. Collect others as you learn!

dipendere da	*to depend on*
leggere sul giornale che ...	*to read in the newpaper that ...*
parlare con qualcuno	*to talk to someone*
sognare qualcosa	*to dream about something*
sposarsi con qualcuno	*to marry someone*
vedere qualcosa alla tv	*to see something on TV*

The sounds of Italian

Notes on pronunciation

The purpose of this section is not to take you through all the sounds of Italian, but to help you with the problem areas which English speakers encounter. Italian is, for English speakers, fairly straightforward to pronounce. And the language has the bonus that it is, by and large, written phonetically. In other words, the spelling reflects the sound. There are however a few areas which can cause difficulty.

Double consonants
These must be pronounced differently from single ones, otherwise there is a risk of misunderstanding – or of sounding silly! You don't after all want people hearing the word *anus*, **ano**, when what you meant to say was *year*, **anno**! Try to linger on the two consonants, saying one and then the other before moving on. Of course, the preceding vowel is affected: it is shorter before a double consonant. Just practise saying:

babbo; cotto; cappa; mamma; ninna nanna; freddo; terra; ecco; cappuccino; stesso.

Pronunciation of r
The spelling reflects what is said, so try to pronounce each consonant including **r**. This is particularly difficult for speakers of certain varieties of English. By now, you surely know about the trap of saying **cane** (*dog*) when you mean **carne** (*meat*). The **r** is the difference between them. Always pronounce **r** if it is there in the spelling. And twice if there are two as in: **birra** (*beer*). If you have difficulty with a rolled r, you could try a guttural r. Some Italians do use this, it's called **erre moscia** (*soft r*). But you must say the **r**. If you practise hard, you will probably find you can learn to do a rolled r. We advise perseverance!

Stress

Stress in Italian words, as you probably know, generally falls on the syllable before the last, the penultimate syllable:

andi_a_mo; rom_a_no; ferrov_i_a; generalm_e_nte.

If it falls on the last syllable there is no problem because an accent (grave – i.e. backward leaning) is put on the vowel to show this:

città; più; possibilità; tivù; mercoledì.

The difficulty comes where the stress falls earlier in the word. And if you have not heard the word spoken, you have no means of knowing where to put the stress, except to guess 'penultimate', which in some cases will be wrong. We advise you to get into the habit when you write words down for learning purposes of marking stress in by some system of your own – we use underlining in this book. You can check stress in a dictionary if you are unsure. They will have some way of showing where the stress falls. There are also words where stress changes meaning, for example:

t_e_ndine (m.s.) *tendon* and **tend_i_ne** (f.pl.) *curtains*
princ_i_pi (pl. of **princ_i_pio**) *principles and* **pr_i_ncipi** (pl. of **pr_i_ncipe**) *princes*
s_u_bito *immediately* and **sub_i_to** *endured, suffered.*

You could argue that the context usually leads the mind to the correct meaning but in practice the wrong stress can obscure meaning. In fact it can create more problems in communicating than a bad Italian 'accent'. It may help to know there are certain groups of words which all work the same way i.e. the stress falls on the antepenultimate syllable:

a the adjectives ending in **-_a_bile, -_i_bile, -_e_vole,** or simply **-ile.** These often correspond to English words ending in *-ble.*

amabile *amiable, lovable;* **flessibile** *flexible;* **possibile** *possible;* **socievole** *sociable;* **umile** *humble;* **difficile** *difficult*

b nouns ending in -**agine**, -**aggine**, -**igine**, -**iggine**, -**udine** (which are all feminine)

immagine *image;* **testardaggine** *obstinacy;* **origine** *origin;* **vertigine** *giddiness, dizziness;* **fuliggine** *soot;* **abitudine** *habit*

Stress patterns in verbs

In the third person plural of the present, imperfect, past historic, present and imperfect subjunctive the stress is on the antepenultimate syllable, or occasionally the fourth syllable from the end. If you remember that the stress in the third person plural in any tense falls on the same syllable/vowel as in the first person singular of that tense it should help you get it right:

canto → cantano; cantavo → cantano; cantavo → cantavano;
      cantai → cantarono; canti → cantino; cantassi → cantassero;
telefono → telefonano (fourth syllable from the end – but on -le- as in the first person singular)

This applies to the other tenses where you get:

canterò → canteranno; canterei → canterebbero;
cantassi → cantassero

English/Italian spelling conflict

The fact that, for a limited number of sounds, the English spelling conventions conflict with those of Italian is an area of difficulty until the learner gets used to the Italian rules. This happens within the areas of the sounds *k, g, ch, j, sh, gl, gn* (English spelling). The rules of Italian apply consistently and just have to be learned. Imitating Italians speaking will help you. Try also fixing sounds in your mind by reference to words you know well. Try learning one word for each case.

gli	The letters **gli** represent a sound which is similar to the middle of the English word *million*.
	figlio; **Gigli** (the legendary tenor); **aglio** *garlic*; **foglia** *leaf*; **dirgli** *to tell him*
	In a few words **gli** is pronounced as in *glee*: **glicine** *wisteria*, **anglicano**, **glicemia**, **glicerina** and other chemistry words.
	In front of other vowels **gl** is pronounced as in *glue*: **gloria**, **gladiolo**, **glucosio**.
gn	These letters represent a sound similar to the middle of the word *onion*.
	ogni every; **Mascagni** (the composer); **giugno** *June*; **gnocchi**.
sc(i)	This is the Italian spelling convention for the sound spelt in English *sh*. The **i** is necessary before **a, o, u,** but not before **e**:
	sciarpa *scarf*; **sciopero** (stress on **o**) *strike*; **sciupare** to spoil; **scendere** *to go down*; **sci** *ski*
sc	+ **a, o, u** is pronounced as in English (*sk*):
	scala *staircase*; **scopo** *purpose*, aim; **scultore** *sculptor*.
	sch is the way to write the English sound *sk* before **e** or **i**: **scherzo** *joke*, **schifo** *disgust*.

English sounds **ch, j**

In Italian these are written:

before **e** or **i**	→ **c**	**cento**, **violoncello**, **San Francesco**, **Puccini**
	→ **g**	**gelato** *ice-cream*; **gente** *people*; **gita** *excursion*; **Gina**.
before **a, o, u**	→ **ci**	**ciao**, **Luciano**; **socio** *member*; **ciò** *that*; **ciuffo** *tuft of hair*
	→ **gi**	**giallo**, **Gianni**, **giorno**, **Giotto**, **giù**, **Giulia**, **Giuseppe** (often mis-spelt and mis-pronounced by English speakers).

English sounds **k, g**

In Italian these are written:

before **a, o, u** → **c** casa, Canada, cosa, Como, curioso, Cuneo (a town in Piemonte, stressed on **u**)

→ **g** galleria, Garda, gondola, gorgonzola, guardare, Guttuso (20th century painter), Guido, Gucci.

before **e** or **i** → **ch** orchestra (stressed on **e**, not on first syllable as in English); Cherubino, Michelangelo, chilo, Chianti

→ **gh** spaghetti, ghetto, ghiro *dormouse*; Lamborghini, Ghiberti, Ghirlandaio.

Key to exercises

Unit 1

Comprehension 1
1 Most of all she enjoys reading. 2 She feels she doesn't organize it.
3 Contemporary fiction. 4 Translations (of books written in English).
She likes to read in the original language. 5 Because she wanted to
brush up on those two languages. 6 She likes walking and cycling.
7 Pasta and puddings. 8 She most enjoys eating the pasta courses, more
than meat. (You will probably have learned that the pasta course is the
first course of an Italian meal, followed by the meat course and then
the pudding.) 9 She likes chatting, spending time with girlfriends and
talking. 10 Going to the cinema. She and her husband go with another
couple approximately once a week in the winter. Perhaps every ten
days, taking an average. 11 She would like to know Tuscany better
because, surprising as it may seem, there are lots of little villages she
hasn't yet seen, especially in the northern part. 12 She needs a 'fix'
of news. She always wants to be up-to-date with the latest news. She
turns on the radio or the television. She can't survive if she doesn't
know what has happened (in the wider world).

Activity 1
Mi piace … 1 ballare 2 andare a teatro 3 viaggiare 4 navigare su
Internet 5 lavorare in giardino 6 guardare la televisione 7 ascoltare
la musica classica 8 andare in discoteca 9 guidare la mia nuova
macchina 10 parlare italiano.

Activity 2
1 Le piace andare al cinema? 2 Le piace viaggiare in macchina?
3 Ti piace cucinare? 4 Che cosa ti piace cucinare? 5 Ti piace
lavorare in giardino?

Activity 3
Group 1: comprare camminare cucinare mangiare chiacchierare
parlare visitare

Group 2: leggere riprendere scegliere rivedere conoscere accendere resistere
Irregular: dire andare essere fare stare sapere

You will have noted that Angioletta didn't actually use any third group verbs. This was just chance.

Activity 4
1 Subject pronouns: **Lui ama il teatro ... Io non capisco niente di musica ... Lui ama i musei, e io ci vado con** sforzo. **... Lui ama le biblioteche, e io le odio. Lui ama i viaggi, ... Io resterei sempre a casa ...**

She uses the pronoun when she is contrasting their tastes which seem to be diametrically opposed. Once it is clear who she is referring to, in Paragraphs 4 and 5, she omits the pronoun. In the last paragraph of the extract: a lui piacciono ... A me piace ... These are underline *strong* pronouns used after the preposition a. In the case of **lui**, the form is the same as the subject pronoun.

2 She uses **piacere** when referring to food and **amare** for everthing else: the cultural pursuits, travel, etc. You may care to note that she seems to like simple country food. Her husband's tastes are perhaps more middle class.

3 A lei piace (mangiare) il minestrone, il pancotto, la frittata, gli erbaggi. A me non piacciono queste cose. Preferisco le tagliatelle, l'abbacchio, le ciliege, il vino rosso. The verb in the first sentence could equally be plural: A lei piacciono il minestrone, il pancotto, ecc. It would have to be plural if you had no single nouns in the list, just, perhaps, gli erbaggi.

Activity 5
1 I bambini amano/Ai bambini piace (molto) nuotare/il nuoto. 2 Ci piace camminare nei dintorni/nella campagna intorno. 3 A mio marito piace cucinare e ognuno prepara una parte del pasto. 4 Lui preferisce cucinare la carne. 5 Io sono brava a cucinare dolci. 6 A mio marito piace leggere. Io preferisco/A me piace di più suonare il pianoforte. 7 A mia figlia piace cantare. È molto brava. 8 Ci piace visitare i

musei, andare al cinema e qualche volta ai concerti. 9 Non ci piace la televisione.

Activity 6
1 Al mio compagno/Alla mia compagna piace andare in palestra la sera. Io preferirei rimanere/stare a casa. Leggerei, guarderei la TV o forse ascolterei un po' di musica. 2 Il mio compagno/La mia compagna passerebbe le vacanze/ferie a casa. Andrebbe in giro/farebbe delle passeggiate nei dintorni, giocherebbe a tennis e andrebbe al cinema. Io preferirei andare all'estero. Mi piace viaggiare/Amo i viaggi. Vorrei visitare l'America/gli Stati Uniti. Visiterei New York. Vedrei il Metropolitan, andrei al Met e sarebbe interessante visitare il museo dell'immigrazione a Ellis Island. M'interessa l'emigrazione italiana in America.

Activity 7
1 'Things of all kinds, sorts': a possible link is **genus**, pl. **genera**. It refers to kinds of plants, animals, etc. Or maybe literary *genre*, again, *type, kind*. 2 'I refuse, don't allow myself': surely, very like *refuse*. Using it reflexively stresses determination. 3 'A good point or a failing, a virtue or a weakness': **difetto** is easier to work out, *defect, fault*. The context indicates **pregio** is an opposite. 4 'A couple': surely the sound gives this one away. 5 'Places': here it is probably a case of guessing from the context. 'Visiting new … seeing old … again'. 6 'Up-to-date': **aggiornata** contains the word **giorno**, *day*. That should be the clue. 7 'What has happened': as a noun, **successo** is *success*, but here we have a past participle. Perhaps there is no obvious clue, and one is having to guess from the context. Why would someone who is really interested in politics switch on the radio or TV first thing in the morning? In Italy you will find **succedere** is very frequently used: **Cosa succede?** *What's happening?*

Activity 8
Expressions Angioletta uses which are common in speech and which seem to give thinking time are: **Mah; no?; E poi; Ecco; voglio dire; non so.**

Comprehension 2

You may not have picked out everything, depending on your way of interpreting what Angioletta said. 1 You can learn a lot (outside school) if you want. (In your case: outside the book) 2 Seek opportunities to learn. 3 Read the ingredients on biscuit packets to see if you can learn new words. Here Angioletta was effectively saying: every time you see something in the language you are trying to learn, make the most of it, see what you can learn from it. 4 When you hear the language being spoken, see if you can't get a little practice by initiating a conversation with the speaker. 5 Listen to recordings in the language. 6 Try to talk to yourself in the language. 7 Think in the language. Think out how you might describe someone you can see, for example, on a bus. 8 Try to find ways of remembering which work for you. 9 Adopt a determined mental approach, the approach of *wanting* to learn.

Test yourself

1 (a) le, (b) 5, (c) gli, (d) 1, (e) mi, (f) 2, (g) 6, (h) 4, (i) mi, (j) 3
2 (a) libreria, (b) romanzo, (c) narrativa, (d) infatti, (e) funziona

Unit 2

Comprehension 1

1 (a) Antonella. (b) Renata. (c) Mario Rotondale. He says he is 30, but then explains he will be 30, on 17th August, his birthday. (d) Riccardo. (e) Silvia. (f) Silvia again. (g) Monica. 2 Nicola and Mario Rotondale are father and son, respectively. The first Mario we heard is 30 and could not be the father of a man with an adult man's voice. Nicola refers to another Mario, his father.

Activity 1

1 (Io) sono or (io) mi chiamo. 2 (Io) sono or faccio il/la … 3 Sono laureato/a in … 4 (Io) ho (from avere, *to have*) + the number of years. 5 Sono nato/a a … 6 Faccio parte del Gruppo Mio da parecchi anni. Abito a Bologna da circa 20 anni. 7 Ho insegnato nelle scuole medie per parecchi anni.

Comprehension 2
1 Both focus largely on family, in Gabriella's case her parents and siblings, in Piera's case her sons and grandson. This is probably because of the importance of their families in their lives. Piera tries to describe her physical appearance but keeps to very obvious aspects: height, weight, hair colour, eye colour.

2 Gabriella: Italian father = English mother

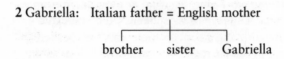

       brother   sister   Gabriella

She tells you about her parents and that her brother and sister are older than she. She also says her brother was born in France and that at the outbreak of war her parents left France and came to Italy. One can deduce therefore that the sister was born in Italy as well as Gabriella and therefore the brother is the oldest.

Piera: Piera = husband (*we assume*)

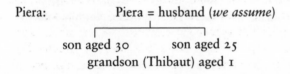

    son aged 30   son aged 25
      grandson (Thibaut) aged 1

We can't deduce which son is the father of Thibaut from what Piera says – you may say it is likely to be the older one. We know Thibaut lives in France, in Brittany.

Activity 3
1 I miei amici (if we know they are all female: le mie amiche).
2 La nostra famiglia. **3** Il suo libro. **4** Il suo libro. **5** Il loro fratello.
6 I loro fratelli. **7** Il mio amico/la mia amica – depending on gender. **8** La sua amica. **9** La sua amica. **10** Nostra madre.

Activity 4
1 Mi chiamo/Sono Jonathan. Sono insegnante/faccio l'insegnante di lingue straniere. Insegno da tre anni. **2** Mia sorella si chiama Olimpia. È medico. Lavora in un ospedale. Lavora nell'ospedale da

sei anni. **3** George ha trentadue anni e lavora per una grossa società. Fanno/fabbricano accessori per l'industria automobilistica. George lavora nella società da diciotto mesi. **4** Mio figlio studia medicina. È studente all'università di Southampton. Studia medicina da due anni. **5** Mio fratello è psichiatra. Lavora a Boston. Gli piace moltissimo Boston. È nato a Cambridge, in Inghilterra, e ora vive/abita a Cambridge, nel Massachusetts. Vive/abita a Cambridge da otto anni. **6** Mia moglie si chiama Jane. È scrittrice. Sua madre è un'attrice famosa. Suo padre è americano. Abbiamo tre figli. Il nostro figlio maggiore ha otto anni, nostra figlia ne ha sei e il nostro secondo figlio maschio ne ha quattro. **7** Studio italiano/imparo l'italiano da nove mesi. **8** Capiamo il gallese. Abbiamo abitato per ventiquattro anni nel Galles. Ora/adesso abitiamo a Londra. **9** Parlo francese da vent'anni. **10** Leggo spesso una rivista italiana che si chiama **Panorama**.

Comprehension 3

1 He is tall (**alto**) and **longilineo**, which means that he is long-limbed with a relatively slight torso. He doesn't consider himself handsome: **non sono un bell' uomo**. But at the same time he doesn't think he is in any way unpleasant-looking: **sgraziato** means lacking in grace and could apply to appearance, way of moving, or even manners. **Aggraziato** is its opposite. **2** As for his character, he says perhaps defensively that he is 'very normal' and easy-going, **bonaccione**. **3** He appears to be referring to intelligence, to what is in the **testa**. This is gathered from the two sentences which follow.

Activity 5

Definitions from *Lo Zingarelli* Italian dictionary. The full entry gives examples of usage too. We have made quite a wide range of suggestions, many of which we would not expect you to know but which you may want to adopt.

Statura e corporatura (*height and build*):
alto, grande *tall*
basso (di statura), piccolo *short*
grande can be *tall, large*
grasso *fat*, referring to excessive fat (Zingarelli: '**Che presenta abbondante sviluppo del tessuto** (*tissue*) **adiposo**')

grosso usually *fat, large* (Zingarelli: 'Che supera la misura ordinaria per massa, per volume')

longilineo *long-limbed*

magro *thin*

robusto *sturdy, strong*

snello *slim, agile, active, quick* (Zingarelli: '1. Agile, svelto, leggero, nei movimenti; 2. Che ha forma slanciata, sottile ed elegante. contr. tarchiato, tozzo')

svelto *slender, lively, quick-witted* (Zingarelli gives four meanings: 1. Che si muove, agisce … con prontezza …; 2. Lesto, sollecito … 3. Sottile e slanciato, agile … 4. Sveglio, vivace …) So **svelto** can refer to quickness of mind; it is also associated with quickness of movement, whereas **snello** is more usually used to describe slimness, i.e. size, shape. But as you can see, the meanings overlap

tarchiato *thickset* (Zingarelli: 'Di persona dalla corporatura robusta e massiccia') So it indicates a person with a sturdy or bulky frame. Zingarelli gives an opposite: **slanciato**.

tozzo *stocky* (Zingarelli: 'Di cosa o persona eccessivamente grossa rispetto all'altezza') Is our translation a good one? It is standard in translating dictionaries.

TESTA E FACCIA (*head and face*):

capelli neri/bruni/biondi/rossi/castani

occhi bruni/azzuri/castani; bocca carnosa (*fleshy*)/piena (*full*)/ sottile (*thin*, the opposite of *full*)

naso curvo/aquilino/greco/all'insù or nasino alla francese (*turned up*); camuso (*flat*)/a patata (*big and shapeless, like a potato!* You may also be amused to learn **ficcanaso**: someone who pokes their nose into other people's business, *nosy*)

sopracciglia (*eyebrows*) folte (*bushy*)/ben disegnate/disordinate/ sottili

una mascella quadrata *a square jaw*

un mento pronunciato *a prominent chin* opposite: un mento sfuggente a receding chin; doppio mento *double chin;*

orecchie a sventola *ears that stick out*

guance scavate *hollow cheeks*

zigomi pronunciati *prominent cheekbones.*

Activity 8

assomigliare a; rossa di capelli; avere un carattere … inglese;
allegro opp: triste; posato opp: impulsivo; serio opp: leggero; ligio
al dovere; spensierato opp: serio, prudente, sollecito, premuroso,
riflessivo; disubbidiente opp: ubbidiente; felice opp: infelice, triste;
contento opp: scontento; avere doti.

Comprehension 4

1 His strong will to win any battle he decides to take on. And to
win hands down – Deaglio considers this latter a vice (**un vizio**).
2 The art of compromise. He is not worried about what people
think of him. 3 Less fierce than he is painted. 4 (a) **concreto**,
(b) **pragmatico** 5 She had only just started the job and she had
no money to pay the wages. It was the 250th anniversary of
the opera house. She asked for sponsorship from Fiat. Romiti
telephoned her immediately and said he had signed a cheque for
one thousand million lire. Her explanation was that, yes, he cared
about music, but he also cared that workers should get their wages.
6 (a) **antipatico**, (b) **chiuso**.

Comprehension 5

1 She clarifies the custom – and law – concerning a married woman's
surname. Italian women, for official purposes, do not change
surname when they marry. Socially, however, many do use their
husband's surname. 2 They thought Emanuela and John were not
married, since Emanuela was still using her maiden name.

Test yourself

1 (a) L'anno scorso sono andato a trovare i miei amici Giulio e
Anna nel loro paese in Toscana. (b) Abitano in questo paesino da
dieci anni. (c) Giulio ha studiato medicina a Firenze e lavora come
pediatra da parecchio tempo. (d) Sua moglie, Anna, è insegnante/
fa l'insegnante d'inglese nella scuola locale dove vanno anche i loro
due bambini. (e) Il più grande/il maggiore è Riccardo, un ragazzino
di nove anni; è alto, con i capelli biondi e gli occhi castani. (f)
Renata ha sette anni, quindi hanno solo due anni di differenza.
(g) Renata è una bambina contenta, molto attiva e un po'
disubbidiente/birichina. (h) Suo fratello la prende spesso in giro,

ma hanno un'infanzia meravigliosa in questo posto di campagna.
(i) Ai loro genitori piacciono moltissimo questa vita e questo paese.
(j) Io non potrei vivere in un posto piccolo lontano dalla città, ma riconosco che per loro va bene.

2 (a) zio, (b) marito, suo, (c) madre, i miei, (d) i tuoi, (e) il loro

Unit 3

Comprehension 1 and 2
1 She went to England for the last two years of high school, did an International Baccalaureate (rather than the **maturità**) and she then took her degree and Master's – presumably an MSc. – at the London School of Economics, University of London. 2 Because she felt poorly prepared for working in an Italian business environment, having been away from Italy for so long. 3 There is no link except insofar as that management of all businesses has things in common no matter what the end product. 4 Because it owns restaurants and since she likes eating and cooking, she finds it more fun than construction, building. 5 He had trained in bookkeeping, accountancy but he felt he would be very bad at it and was unsuited to working in a bank. He doesn't add that he loves sport but that must have been a factor. 6 Because in any other European country students doing courses similar to the one he completed get degrees. 7 At the time he graduated recruitment of teachers was at a standstill. No jobs were being made available. 8 He has been there since November 1994. 9 A swimming pool and probably new gyms.

Activity 1
Marina: ho studiato, ho fatto, sono stata, sono tornata, ho cominciato, sono stata, sono andata, mi sono trovata, sono andata, mi ha ... introdotto, sono uscita, sono andata, ho lavorato, sono arrivata.

Mario: ho fatto, sono passato, ho fatto, mi sono accorto, ho proseguito, mi sono lanciato, ho cominciato, mi si è presentata, mi sono tuffato, è successo, è iniziata, abbiamo aperto, abbiamo cominciato, (abbiamo) ripreso.

Activity 2

1 andato *gone*; 2 uscito *gone out*; 3 tornato *returned*; 4 lanciato *thrown*; 5 saputo *known*; 6 conosciuto* *known*; 7 capito *understood*; 8 caduto *fallen*

*Note an *i* is needed after the *sc* to indicate you use a s̲h̲ sound, not a hard k̲. As in the present, verbs in the second group usually keep the sound throughout.

Activity 3

Marina: fatto (fare); stata (stare – note this could be the past participle of **essere** too); introdotto (introdurre)

Mario: fatto (fare); accorto (accorgersi – a reflexive verb); successo (succedere); aperto (aprire); ripreso (riprendere)

Activity 4

The two auxiliary verbs are **avere** and **essere**. Using **avere: Marina:** ho studiato, ho fatto, ho cominciato, mi ha introdotto, ho lavorato, **Mario:** ho fatto (twice), ho proseguito, ho cominciato, abbiamo aperto, abbiamo cominciato, abbiamo ripreso.

Using **essere: Marina:** sono stata (twice), sono tornata, sono andata (three times), mi sono trovata, sono uscita, sono arrivata. **Mario:** sono passato, mi sono accorto, mi sono lanciato, mi si è presentata, mi sono tuffato, è successo, è iniziata.

Comprehension – Passage 1

1 In the southern part (zone) of the crater. 2 A fire broke out in the vegetation on the ridge (nearby presumably). 3 It put out the fire. 4 In case they needed to help possible injured tourists. 5 The village, which can be reached only by sea, had been cut off for two days by bad sea conditions.

Passage 2

1 One. 2 15 million lire. 3 Possibly because the man had not covered his face. Had he been wearing a mask he would have been more noticeable! 4 They set up road blocks. But to no avail.

Passage 3
1 In a lift which stalled 1m.70 from the first floor in the Club
Med tower at Sestriere. The tower is not used in summer. 2 To
collect faxes, presumably from an office in it. He is the caretaker.
3 She felt that he had been missing for too long, she was afraid
something had happened to him.

Passage 4
1 The father of the young Tunisian who was arrested in Sicily.
2 Because he had entered Italy clandestinely – and illegally, since
he had no permit to stay. 3 He rushed to Rome. 4 The documents
needed to prove the young man was his son.

Activity 5
Passage 1: due boati hanno annunciato; che ha provocato;
Le fiamme sono state domate ...

Passage 2: l'assalto è avvenuto; un bandito ha fatto irruzione;
il rapinatore ha varcato; (il rapinatore) si è diretto; Li ha minacciati;
li ha costretti; il colpo è stato messo a segno; nessuno si è accorto;
il bandito è riuscito; (i carabinieri) sono accorsi; hanno istituito.

Passage 3: L'hanno trovato; l'ascensore s'è bloccato; lui è rimasto;
una barista ha dato.

Passage 4: È arrivato; le forze di polizia lo hanno sorpreso;
T.A. Karim, che ha appena compiuto; ha lasciato; i militari ...
sono riusciti; il padre che si è precipitato.

The passive form: The other passive was: il colpo è **stato messo** a
segno (Passage 2).

Activity 6
(*Possible answers*) 1 (Oh, Maria, sai che cosa?) Ieri ho visto
(sono stato/a testimone di) un incidente stradale (automobilistico).
Una macchina non si è fermata al semaforo rosso ed è finita dentro
un'altra che traversava con il verde. 2 Mi scusi, signorina. Ieri

sera ho lasciato il mio portafoglio nel bar dell'albergo. È stato ritrovato, per caso? 3 Cara Mamma, ieri ho fatto una passeggiata bellissima con Paolo e Marco. Abbiamo preso il sentiero vicino alla stazione di servizio. Siamo saliti per la collina (abbiamo salito la collina) e siamo entrati nei boschi. Abbiamo seguito il sentiero fino a Castiglione. 4 Mario, ho telefonato a Anna ieri sera. Sua madre si è rotta il braccio. È caduta per strada. Anna mi ha chiesto di salutarti.

Guessable words
Il bancone is the word ending in **-one**. It is the word for the kind of counter used in banks and other offices where the staff are separated from the public. It is based on the word **banco** which is also the basis for the word **banca**. Note: some banks are actually called **banco**, e.g. Banco di Napoli, Banco di Santo Spirito. The word **bancone** is in fact more usually used for *counter* in shops and bars. In a bank, more commonly one talks of **gli sportelli**.

Activity 7
(*Possible answer*) Mi chiamo Arturo Marullo. (Many Italians would say: Marullo, Arturo, putting the family name first.) Sono nato il 6 febbraio 1958. Sono nato a Terni in provincia di Perugia. Ho fatto le scuole elementari e medie a Terni e poi sono andato a fare le scuole medie superiori a Perugia. Ho fatto il liceo scientifico di Perugia. Poi ho fatto l'università, sempre a Perugia. Mi sono laureato in economia e commercio nel 1984. Poi sono andato a lavorare per dei commercianti in vino, i Fratelli Alberti, a Orvieto. Sono stato lì tre anni. Quindi mi sono trasferito a Milano e ho lavorato 7 anni per i Supermercati Gatti. E poi sono entrato nella ditta Pasta Bastoni, come direttore di marketing.

Test yourself

1 (a) è, è, (b) ha, (c) ha, (d) è, (e) è, (f) ha, (g) è, ha, ha, (h) è, (i) ha, ha, (j) è, ha
2 (a) ha frequentato, si è laureata, (b) avete lavorato, avete aperto, (c) sono, (d) si sono conosciuti, (e) essere partiti

Unit 4

Comprehension 1

1 In a convent, because her parents thought that was the right place for a girl living away from home. 2 Because her husband worked there. 3 Because she had nearly finished and it wasn't advisable. 4 She missed people. She was used to living with others and she was alone. 5 Because they say in Tuscany that it is difficult to be accepted by the Florentines. 6 Her one close friend, who was a fellow-student. 7 No. She gave private lessons and she studied. 8 By cooking – you remember it is one of her favourite activities – and by cleaning the house, polishing everything. 9 Two, two and a half years. 10 They moved to Arezzo, which happened to be near Angioletta's parents, family and friends, so, although the interview doesn't say so, the unhappy period was over.

Activity 1

1 I moved to the outskirts of Florence where I found great difficulties getting to know/making friends with the neighbours. I had a very good friend who was also at university with me and so I spent/used to spend a lot of time with her. (Apart from the suggestion *I used to spend*, it is difficult to convey in English the underlying sense of the imperfect as used here.) 2 I made/used to make/would make lots to eat. I used to cook a lot (meaning possibly *frequently*, possibly *large quantities of food*, probably both), I liked experimenting ... and I used to clean the house, I was a very careful housewife, I polished/used to polish everything, I even waxed/used to wax the kitchen floor. (Note: this would have been of ceramic tiles which do not need polish!) 3 Annalisa was born in Florence and then we moved when she was six or seven months old.

Activity 2

You should have been able to group the verbs thus:
Group 1: **io** stavo, passavo, lavoravo, studiavo, cucinavo, lucidavo, davo; **tu** lavoravi; **lui/lei** stava, lavorava; **loro** si sentivano.
Group 2: **io** avevo, facevo; piaceva.
Group 3: **io** soffrivo, pulivo.
And you will have found: **ero** and **era**. You will have quickly spotted that each of the three types of verbs has its characteristic

vowel throughout the imperfect and, that apart, the endings for all verbs are the same.

You found the 1st, 2nd and 3rd person singular and the 3rd person plural in the text. You may well have felt confident enough to deduce the following:

Group 2: (tu) avevi, facevi; (lui/lei) aveva, faceva; (loro) avevano, facevano. Group 3: (tu) soffrivi; pulivi; (lui/lei) soffriva, puliva; (loro) soffrivano, pulivano.

More than that by yourself you can't really do. For ease of reference the form is given in the text. (Note: in the above answer we treated **dare** and **stare** as regular verbs since they behave regularly in the imperfect.) For **fare**, see text.

Comprehension 2

1 They were peasant farmers (**contadini**). 2 They wanted to do better than their parents, get out of their agricultural background (**emergere**). 3 They set up a small business, probably a shop. It was a great struggle and things were very tight (financially) but they were hard workers. 4 He went to school in Asti. It meant travelling 15–20 km daily by bus. 5 He (and his friends) went birdnesting, they fished in the rivers for eels, he learned to swim in streams, he went collecting truffles.

Activity 3

Passato prossimo: Sono nato; hanno cominciato; hanno permesso; mi sono formato; ho imparato. If you reflect, you will realize all these are 'one-off' events; and they are (long) finished.
Imperfetto: *describing*: erano figli di contadini; era gente; Quelli erano praticamente; *habitual, repeated actions*: Si andava ad Asti; si tornava la sera; si andava per nidi; si andava a pescare (*twice*); Si andava per tartufi; *background*: cercavano di emergere; c'era sempre un vecchio che conosceva.

You can argue about the way the imperfects are classified, but the point of view, the aspect of the action which the speaker has in mind, is different from that in the **passato prossimo** verbs, which definitely view actions as past and completed.

Comprehension 3 1 He used to say his mother was the enemy. His father decided to send him away to school. 2 That people wouldn't give them food. 3 She went to milk a ewe to get milk for her children and she was fired at. 4 No, she was very young (born at the end of 1940, Unit 2, Interview 2).

Activity 4
Passato prossimo: mio papà l'ha dovuto (meaning not just *he had to*, but viewing the necessity as a finished action – he had to do it once – and did it); sono venuti fuori; Hanno perso, han perso (Gabriella uses **perso**; **perduto** is also possible); si è alzata; è andata; hanno sparato (notice this series of verbs is preceded by **una volta** – Gabriella's mother did this once); ha sempre girato; abbiamo sempre visto (here you might almost have expected an imperfect, seeing **sempre** and knowing it meant the action was repeated. But those times are over, Gabriella is seeing the actions as finished).

Imperfetto: *describing*: era (molto piccolino); era il nemico; mamma era; *habitual, repeated actions*: diceva; scappavano; (perhaps) eravamo sfollati; voleva darci da mangiare; *background*: mio fratello … non voleva, temeva.

Other verbs: ricordo (present); dicesse (imperfect subjunctive – we'll come to that later); possa (present subjunctive – we'll come to that later too).

Activity 5
1 splendeva; 2 sono tornate; 3 hanno deciso; 4 era; 5 combattevano; 6 sapevano; 7 dovevano; 8 erano; 9 pascolavano; 10 giocavano; 11 hanno sentito; 12 si sono buttate; 13 sono arrivati; 14 avevano; 15 volevano; 16 ha detto; 17 sparavano; 18 sparavano; 19 erano; 20 hanno preso; 21 è finita; 22 sono andati; 23 era; 24 sono uscite; 25 erano; 26 sono tornate; 27 hanno deciso

Here is a part translation to help you grasp the meaning: *It was a lovely spring day. The sun was shining. The three little girls came home from school and decided to take the geese to graze on the other side of the river. The other bank of the river was dangerous.*

Often the partisans used to fight the German army there. The three little girls knew that they ought not to go there but they were curious about it. While the geese were grazing the three girls played in the meadow. Suddenly the three girls heard gunshots. They threw themselves into a ditch with the geese. Shortly afterwards the partisans arrived.

Comprehension 4

1 How well educated her mother was. (Note: **istruito** *educated*; **educato** *well-behaved*; **maleducato** *rude*. **Educazione** refers to *behaviour, upbringing.* Note also **il Ministero dell'Istruzione, dell'Università e della Ricerca.**) **2** What high standards her mother adhered to in her personal life, dress, habits etc. **3** She liked to have a cigarette and a coffee and do crosswords. **4** Very much the same as her own: they had all to be dressed and come to breakfast together even if they had no reason to be up and about. No lying in bed! **5** Once she had organized the supper, at about 4.30 p.m., she used to wash and change as though getting ready to go out. **6** She appears to have been a person with high standards, devoted to her family, always finding time to attend to their needs and to be with them.

Activity 6

In this interview there are very few perfects: **Mi sono accorta quando mamma è mancata** *I realized when mother passed away* – both events, completed. **Quando poi sono andata in Inghilterra mi sono accorta.** Another completed event: Gabriella went to England and there she realized … Otherwise the imperfect is used, since every verb is expressing either a repeated action, or describing or filling in background. Except in a case dealt with next: the pluperfect.

Activity 7

You are right to say that the **trapassato** is formed using the imperfect of **avere** (**avevo, avevi, aveva, avevamo, avevate, avevano**) and the past participle of the verb, on the same lines as the perfect. It expresses one stage back in time, rather as in English *he had finished*. Question: If this is the case, what do you think might happen in the pluperfect to verbs which use **essere** to form the perfect? Answer: They use the imperfect of **essere** (**ero, eri, era, eravamo, eravate, erano**) plus the past participle.

Activity 8

You need not change any of the verbs which were in the imperfect in Activity 5. So that leaves: 2 erano tornate; 3 avevano deciso; 11 avevano sentito; 12 si erano buttate; 13 erano arrivati; 16 aveva detto; 20 avevano preso; 21 era finita; 22 erano andati; 24 erano uscite; 26 erano tornate; 27 avevano deciso

Here is a partial translation to help you understand the way we have changed the text. *It was a lovely spring day. The sun was shining. The three little girls had come home from school and had decided to take the geese to graze on the other side of the river. … Suddenly the three girls had heard gunshots. They had thrown themselves into a ditch with the geese. Shortly afterwards the partisans had arrived.*

Activity 9

1 era; 2 piacevano (remember how **piacere** works); 3 scherzava; 4 organizzava; 5 piaceva; 6 portava; 7 avevamo (subject: **noi**); 8 uscivamo; 9 ho mai capito (yes, that is the perfect – it was understanding that Gabriella has never achieved. If you like, an event which has not happened! However, if you suggested a future (capirò), that is also acceptable); 10 si dedicava; 11 facevamo; 12 piaceva; 13 era; 14 aiutavano; 15 faceva; 16 piaceva; 17 piaceva.

Activity 10

1 tornavo; ho visto/veduto. 2 abitava; vedevamo; l'abbiamo incontrato. Usciva. 3 era; l'abbiamo ristrutturata; avevano; l'abbiamo trasformata. 4 cucinavano; riuscivano (subject: piatti)

Activity 11

1 John stava finendo una lettera. 2 Il treno stava entrando nella stazione. 3 Papà stava leggendo il giornale. 4 Mamma stava facendo la doccia.

Comprehension 5

1 She obviously missed the city she had left behind; and all it offered, particularly books, friends, and the many and varied happenings of city life. **2** The house seems to have been small. The housing stock of a small village in the Abruzzo is likely to have been limited. But it may have been that only one room was heated and this is why they all crowded into it. **3** The eagle was painted on the ceiling of the main room and for her it came to symbolize her exile. **4** The women wore black shawls and had red faces. The black was typical of villages since mourning was taken seriously and lasted some time. The red faces occurred presumably because of the cold. **5** They consulted him about the best time to have teeth extracted, about subsidies available from the local authority and about various taxes. In other words about anything they did not understand.

Test yourself

1

Poliziotto	(a) Dov'era Lei ieri alle cinque del pomeriggio?
Cuoco	(b) Ero in cucina.
Poliziotto	(c) Che cosa faceva/stava facendo?
Cuoco	(d) Cucinavo/Stavo cucinando la cena per la famiglia.
Poliziotto	(e) Ha sentito dei rumori?
Cuoco	(f) No. Ascoltavo/Stavo ascoltando la radio mentre facevo/stavo facendo i ravioli.
Poliziotto	(g) Ma qualcuno era entrato dalla finestra e aveva sparato un colpo.
Cuoco	(h) Mi dispiace, signore, non ho sentito o notato niente di strano. Pensavo che i bambini guardavano un film western alla TV.
Poliziotto	(i) Be', qualcosa di strano è successo in questa casa ieri. Il padre è stato ferito e i soldi sono scomparsi.
Cuoco	(j) Mi sta accusando, signore?

2 (a) da, a, (b) di, da, (c) a, di, (d) da, di, (e) di, da

Unit 5

Comprehension 1

1 There are 15 at present and a 16th is about to be opened in Rome. 2 Marina mentions that there are two other establishments of a different sort but she doesn't say what they are and doesn't consider them part of the core business. 3 The self-service restaurants it runs are a little more luxurious than self-service restaurants usually are, in the surroundings they offer as well as the quality of the food. 4 The costs of setting up one of the restaurants are very high, as are the running costs and therefore they need to be sited so as to have what she calls 'a certain level' of business. In other words they need to generate a high turnover. 5 So far she has opened one or one and a half a year and that seems to her about right. 6 No, she feels the formula works quite well. 7 One is that the head office of the company is near Venice and she lives in Milan. She has a small office in Milan but needs to spend at least a couple of days each week in the head office. And secondly, she spends a lot of time going to see possible sites for new restaurants, scattered throughout Italy and occasionally abroad. 8 Looking at possible sites for new restaurants.

Activity 1

You will probably have found the vocabulary very guessable. Did you list the following, or most of them? (The English expression Marina used is *core business*.)

una società	*company*
gestire (*NB like*: capire)	*manage*
una catena	*a chain* (literal or figurative)
un locale	*premises*
il filone principale	*the core business* (filone: lit. *(coarse) thread*)
il prodotto	*the product*
allestimento	*the fitting out* (This word refers to the preparation for a performance, a party, a meal. It can be used for the fitting out of a ship.)

arredo	*furnishings*
formula	*a formula*
funzionare	*to work* (in the sense of *to function*)
un investimento	*an investment*
un costo	*a cost*
gestione (f) (*cf.* gestire)	*management*
garantire (*also like*: capire)	*to guarantee*
livello	*level*
attività	*activity, business*
originare	*to generate*
prestarsi	*to lend itself*
sviluppo	*development*
espandersi	*to expand*
sede (f) (linked to: sedere – to sit)	*head office*
amministratore delegato	*managing director*
strategico (*cf.* strategia (n)	*strategic*
aspetto	*aspect*
operativo	*related to the day-to-day running*
ricerca	here *search;* can mean *research*
controparte (f)	*counterpart*
verifica (cf. verificare)	*check, inspection (verification)*
insediamento (*cf.* sede)	*siting*

You may have picked out fewer or more words, depending really on where you see the world of business beginning and ending! But you must agree that, with a little thought, many of these words are guessable. Can you see also the value of making links between, say, nouns and verbs (**gestione, gestire**) and a word and its root (**in<u>sed</u>iamento** from **sede**; la **Santa Sede** is, incidentally, the *Holy See*). When guessing meanings, a very literal approach helps. For instance, you remember that **-one** is a suffix indicating that something or someone is large. **Un filo** is a thread, **un filone** might be the main strand.

Activity 2
Nouns: the corresponding verbs are: produrre (pp prodotto); allestire; costare; livellare; sviluppare; amministrare; ricercare; insediare.

Verbs: the corresponding nouns are: garanzia; fondazione (f); istituzione (f); prestito; espansione (f); investimento; verifica; valutazione (f).

(Note that most nouns ending in **-ione** are feminine. Note also that the importance of this exercise was less in getting it right than in thinking about the connections between words, so that your stock becomes ever larger.)

Activity 3
1 Ci stiamo espandendo. *We are expanding*, underlining that it is a process happening even now! **2a** quello che prepariamo **da** mangiare (*what we prepare to eat, the food we prepare*); **2b** un certo livello di attività che è difficile **da** originare (*a certain level of business which is difficult to generate*). 3 Beh, insomma, cioè, comunque, quindi.

Activity 4
1 una volta alla settimana; 2 tre volte al giorno; 3 due volte al mese.

Activity 5
We don't know what your answers were, but here are some recommendations: Bisognerebbe camminare almeno trenta minuti al giorno, per esempio andare o tornare dal lavoro a piedi. Bisognerebbe praticare uno sport almeno una volta alla settimana. Bisognerebbe andare a dormire prima di mezzanotte tutti i giorni lavorativi, quindi almeno cinque volte alla settimana. Bisognerebbe mangiare frutta e/o verdura fresca almeno tre volte al giorno. Bisognerebbe fare una lunga e rilassante passeggiata una volta alla settimana.

Activity 6
1 Tra un anno (dodici mesi); 2 Tra un mese (tre/quattro settimane); 3 tra nove mesi; tra solo cinque/sei mesi (note: **Fra** is also correct)

Activity 7
You are free to write the postcard as you like, picking the places and sights that interest you most. The important point is that you

use: **in** Veneto, Lombardia and Emilia Romagna; and **a** Venezia, Verona, Padova, Parma, Ferrara, Cremona, Milano, Mantova and any other town you mention. Use **a** also for the islands of Murano and Burano – they are small. If you were to go to a large island you would say: **in Sicilia, in Sardegna.** Here is a possible text:
Cari Anna e Andrea, Sono appena tornata da un viaggio bellissimo. Sono andata a Venezia in aereo e lì ho raggiunto una motonave che poi ci ha portati a fare una crociera lungo il Po. In Veneto, a Venezia, Padova e Verona abbiamo potuto fare visite guidate, molto interessanti. A Verona abbiamo anche visto l'Aida di Verdi all'Arena – magnifica! Poi abbiamo raggiunto la Lombardia dove siamo andati a vedere Mantova. Dopo, abbiamo potuto visitare Parma in Emilia Romagna e la crociera è finita a Cremona in Lombardia, da dove siamo andati in treno a Milano – poi ritorno a casa. Tanti cari saluti.

Activity 8
1 Non lo so … credo una trentina. 2 Non lo so … credo una cinquantina. 3 Non ne sono sicuro/a … forse una trentina di milioni. 4 Non ne sono sicuro/a … forse una decina di milioni. 5 Mah … mi sembra un paio. 6 Mah … mi sembra una quindicina. 7 Almeno un migliaio. 8 Almeno un centinaio. (Note: an Italian might also say 7 **mille**; 8 **cento**. It is not unusual to use both **cento** and **mille** when in English we might say: *hundreds, thousands.* The context will make it clear.)

Activity 9
Il cantante lirico è la persona che canta le opere liriche.
Lo scrittore è la persona che scrive libri. L'amministratore delegato è la persona che amministra l'azienda. Il cuoco è la persona che cucina i pasti in un ristorante. Il controllore è la persona che controlla i biglietti sul treno. Il calciatore è la persona che gioca in una squadra di calcio. Il dentista è la persona che cura i denti dei suoi pazienti.

Activity 10
1 Manda un fax alla dottoressa Paolini **da cui** devo sapere se i lavori procedono regolarmente a Torino. 2 Telefona all'Avvocato Franceschi con cui devo discutere riguardo al nuovo contratto per

il Brek di Monaco. 3 Scrivi una lettera di sollecito al Ragionier Barbato **da cui** devo ricevere i preventivi per i lavori al Brek di Vicenza entro la fine del mese. 4 Telefona all'Architetto Cappelli **cui/a cui** devo restituire i disegni e i progetti per il Brek di Roma con le correzioni al più presto.

Activity 11

Chi tardi arriva male alloggia. (Lit. *the person who arrives late gets the worst place, worst bed.* Obviously going back to days when late arrival in a town might mean there was nowhere left to sleep. It is often used to chide any lateness.)

Chi va all'osto perde il posto. (The Italians asked did not know what **osto** meant although they knew and used the saying. Children use it meaning: *If you give up your place, you can't expect to have it back when you come back.* It derives from **hostis**, the Latin word for *enemy.* So the idea is: *if you go and fraternize with the enemy, you can't expect a warm welcome on your return!*)

Chi va piano va sano e va lontano. (*The person who proceeds slowly, travels safely and goes a long way.* If you do things slowly and calmly, you'll get a lot done and done well.)

Chi la fa l'aspetti. (*Those who do harm to others should expect others to harm them.*)

Chi va al mulino s'infarina. (*You can't go to the mill without getting flour on you.* In other words, you can't undertake certain activities without them leaving their trace – often meaning a moral or character trace.)

Chi semina vento raccoglie tempesta. (*If you sow wind, you reap storms.* In other words, if you create negative situations, you'll get the consequences.) Chi la dura la vince. (*The person who keeps to his plans and pursues them with determination succeeds.*)

Chi di spada ferisce di spada perisce. (*The person who injures with a sword, will die by the sword.* If you hurt others, you can expect them to do the same to you. The meaning is really the same as: Chi la fa l'aspetti.)

Activity 12

1 Quella che indossa una minigonna è mia sorella, Anna. 2 Quella che indossa un vestito a fiori è la mamma (è Mamma). 3 Quello

che fuma la pipa è Papà. **4** Quello che porta gli occhiali è mio
cugino, Fausto. **5** Quello con i capelli lunghi è Antonio, il ragazzo
di Anna.

Activity 13

1 quello che; **2** che; **3** cui; **4** che; **5** che; **6** quello che (ciò che);
7 Alla quale (A cui); **8** chi; **9** quello che (ciò che); **10** quello che
(ciò che); **11** dove (in cui); **12** che.

Activity 14

1 Il nostro gruppo garantisce sia cibo di ottima qualità sia un
ambiente elegante. **2** offre sia servizio veloce sia salette da pranzo
tranquille e silenziose. **3** ha sia costi di gestione alti sia investimenti
alti. **4** vuole espandersi sia nel Nord Italia sia nel Centro-Sud.

Activity 15

1 La società gestisce dei ristoranti/una (piccola) catena di ristoranti.
2 Ci sono 15 ristoranti. **3** Sono dei ristoranti self-service. **4** Cercano
di offrire di più di un self-service classico. Cercano di offrire un
ambiente un po' più di lusso, curato, e un menù un po' migliore.
5 I ristoranti hanno dei costi piuttosto alti sia di investimenti sia di
gestione. Dunque, funzionano solo se garantiscono un certo livello
di attività. **6** Il primo ristorante è stato aperto a Trieste. **7** Marina
abita a Milano, perché suo marito è lì, ma la sede del Brek è nel
Veneto. Lei ha un piccolo ufficio a Milano, ma deve andare in sede
ogni settimana. **8** Si occupa soprattutto della gestione strategica
della società, dello sviluppo. **9** Perché deve andare a studiare ogni
possibilità ma è difficile trovare un posto adatto, che garantisca il
livello di attività necessaria.

A possible summary might be: Marina è amministratore delegato
di una società che si chiama Ristoranti Brek. La società gestisce
una catena di ristoranti self-service, un po' più di lusso del
self-service classico sia nell'arredo sia in quello che offrono da
mangiare. I costi di investimento e di gestione sono piuttosto alti
per cui ogni ristorante deve garantire un certo livello di attività. Il
primo ristorante è stato aperto a Trieste ma la sede del gruppo è
vicino a Venezia. Marina abita con il marito a Milano dove ha un

piccolo ufficio ma fa la pendolare tra Milano e il Veneto dove ogni settimana deve andare in sede. Si occupa soprattutto della gestione strategica e passa molto tempo a visitare posizioni possibili per nuovi ristoranti Brek.

Comprehension 2

1 Five including her. 2 Because she is not being paid the salary which should go with her job. 3 No, there is another but she is much older and has a high level qualification (which, by implication, it seems Emanuela does not have). 4 No, in both cases. (a) She says there are three other young people, all men, in her situation, doing the job of bank manager and not paid the correct salary. (b) She doesn't feel the banks discriminate provided the women in question are prepared to give the commitment required, which seems to be hours beyond the normal working day. 5 They expect a bank manager to be old, grey-haired and male.

Activity 16

1 Emanuela works in a bank. She has a position of some responsibility and she would expect to receive a fairly high salary. In fact her salary is rather low. 2 The reason for this state of things is that she has only recently been promoted to this level and so at the moment she is not yet paid as the law provides. In the future, however, she will be paid more. 3 As regards her credibility, as a woman, with male customers, Emanuela thinks that the current position of working women in Italy is better than in the past and she doesn't feel she has been the object of discrimination.
4 Nevertheless, in spite of the fact that Emanuela is optimistic on this count, sex discrimination in the work place is actually a live issue. Moreover, she herself says that many men who come into her bank are amazed to find a woman manager. (You will notice from the above that translation can be tricky! We have tried not to distort the English and yet render the flavour of the Italian.)

Activity 17

1 Group 1 verbs have an -i- in the ending of the 1st, 2nd, 3rd person singular and the 3rd person plural, all the other verbs have -a-. Irregular verbs also have -a, as you will see. 2 The **noi** form.

This is true of all verbs. 3 Because the forms for 1st, 2nd and 3rd person singular are identical and therefore the pronoun is often needed to avoid ambiguity. 4 **Noi** and **voi**.

Activity 18
potere: possa, possa, possa, possiamo, possiate, possano
sapere: sappia, sappia, sappia, sappiamo, sappiate, sappiano
tenere: tenga, tenga, tenga, teniamo, teniate, tengano
volere: voglia, voglia, voglia, vogliamo, vogliate, vogliano
uscire: esca, esca, esca, usciamo, usciate, escano
dovere: debba, debba, debba, dobbiamo, dobbiate, debbano
produrre: produca, produca, produca, produciamo, produciate, producano
piacere: piaccia, piaccia, piaccia, piacciamo, piacciate, piacciano

Activity 19
1 sia; 2 è (it is a fact); 3 dimostra (we are referring to Marta specifically, not to a type of person in general); 4 abbia (here we are describing the type of person who is needed); 5 sia; 6 è; 7 abbia; 8 dice; 9 faccia (you might possibly feel it should be plural because the idea is plural – facciano); 10 voglia.

Activity 20
1 Mi hanno detto che questa direttrice ha (indicative: **dire che** does not imply doubt) ... 2 Credo che le donne siano ... 3 Però so anche che ad alti livelli le donne non ricevono ... 4 Ho paura che una donna non abbia abbastanza ...; 5 Spero che non sia vero ma temo che un direttore donna non garantisca ...

Activity 21
1 è; 2 sia; 3 sappia; 4 sa; 5 garantisca; 6 garantisce.

Activity 22
1 Non sono d'accordo! Penso che funzioni benissimo, che faccia caldo in inverno e che sia fresco in estate. 2 Non sono d'accordo! Penso che dia sempre ascolto alle nostre richieste. Penso che faccia attenzione ai problemi di tutti. 3 Non sono d'accordo! Penso che loro sappiano fare il loro lavoro. Penso che vengano a chiedere

aiuto per imparare. 4 Non sono d'accordo! Non penso che debbano lavorare di più. Penso che tengano gli uffici molto puliti e che escano all'ora prevista dal loro contratto di lavoro.

Comprehension 3

1 25 years; 30 people. 2 She had no training at all in anything but what she enjoyed most was sewing, making clothes. 3 Firstly although she was still young she was no longer a girl, in other words, she was older that the usual students; secondly she didn't want any diplomas, she wanted to understand the techniques, rather than practise doing each until she was expert at it. She wanted an understanding of the whole process rather than a high level of skill in performing any one technique. 4 She made some model clothes and then telephoned round all her friends to say she was in business. 5 She found dressmaking for individual customers too personal, she didn't like it and wanted to produce in quantity. 6 That her first two employees are still with her, in her twenty-fifth year. 7 She had planned to make high quality ready-to-wear but has found it impossible to compete with the famous name designer labels, even though her garments were less expensive, better quality fabric, etc. People want the name, the designer label.

Activity 23

1 La nostra nicchia è andata **esaurendosi**; 2 **Fatto** questo tipo di scuola; 3 ho detto alla mie amiche che io **avevo aperto** ... una sartoria; 4 ho detto alla direttrice che **avrei** seguito i suoi corsi ... non **avrei** proseguito per settimane a fare gonne, **sarei** passata all'altra aula.

Activity 24

1 Le stoffe stanno/vanno rincarando. 2 La concorrenza sta/va crescendo. 3 Il mercato (si) sta/va saturando/saturandosi. 4 Il campo della moda sta/va cambiando. 5 La produzione sta/va rallentando. 6 Le grandi firme stanno/vanno invadendo il mercato del prêt-à-porter. 7 I guadagni stanno/vanno diminuendo. 8 La situazione sta/va peggiorando. (Note: You can use either **stare** or **andare**. **Stare** indicates that the action is going on. **Andare** underlines that it is a gradual process. In English you might use the continuous tense + **gradually** or **continually**.)

Activity 25

1 Una volta prese le misure, disegna il modello della gonna su carta. 2 Una volta disegnato il modello, riporta il modello/riportalo su stoffa. 3 Una volta riportato il modello su stoffa, taglia la stoffa. 4 Una volta tagliata la stoffa, cuci la gonna a mano. 5 Una volta cucita/imbastita la gonna a mano, indossala per controllare che vada bene. 6 Una volta controllata, cuci la gonna a macchina. 7 Una volta cucita a macchina stirala.

Activity 26

Ho chiesto al rappresentante per quando **avrebbero voluto** il prodotto finito. Io gli ho fatto notare che in quel caso noi **avremmo avuto bisogno 1** della stoffa in maggio, che **avremmo dovuto cominciare 2** a lavorarla entro fine maggio. Gli ho detto che rispettando queste date, **avremmo potuto garantire 3** un primo lotto di capi finiti per fine luglio e che **saremmo stati in grado 4** di consegnare il resto entro metà agosto. Per le consegne il rappresentante ha detto che **si sarebbero rivolti 5** sempre allo stesso corriere, così noi **avremmo dovuto risolvere 6** solo i problemi logistici. Gli ho spiegato che **sarebbe stato 7** più pratico dare al corriere il numero di telefono del magazzino così il responsabile del magazzino **si sarebbe occupato 8** di tutto.

Test yourself

1 (a) La nostra è una piccola società che gestisce alcuni negozi di abbigliamento in questa zona. (b) Il direttore ha chiamato in ufficio i rappresentanti a cui ha detto di intensificare la campagna di vendita. (c) Lavoro in una banca in cui ho una posizione di una certa responsabilità. (d) Conoscevo un bravo ragazzo il cui padre era un avvocato famoso. (e) Ricevo un piccolo stipendio che non è adeguato alle mie responsabilità. (f) Abbiamo assunto tre nuovi manager le cui qualifiche sono eccezionali. (g) Si tratta di problemi di gestione di cui si occupa l'amministratore delegato. (h) Il principio delle pari opportunità è la ragione principale per cui stanno discutendo un nuovo contratto di lavoro. (i) Erano tre sorelle a cui piaceva vestirsi con abiti di grandi firme. (j) C'erano alcune modelle di cui una era altissima.

2 (a) Il manager pensa che sia necessario migliorare la qualità del cibo. (b) Dicono che abbia molta esperienza. (c) Le ho detto che

avrebbe avuto successo. (d) Cerca un lavoro che sia pagato bene/
ben pagato. (e) Tutti sapevano che le tasse sarebbero aumentate.

Unit 6

Comprehension 1
1 Because competition is becoming fiercer as European banks
start operating in Italy; the introduction of the Euro means many
changes; and Italian banks will have to modernize their practices.
All this will mean hard work for the staff. **2** Because she works
hard, she knows she is appreciated and salary is the way value is
measured for an employee. Professionally, she wants the salary due
to her level. Personally, she wants it to provide her daughter with
an easier future (easier, she means, than her own life), with a lovely
house etc.

Activity 1
In the first person plural form, where the only difference between
the two tenses is that the future has one **m** and the conditional a
double **m**:

Future: capiremo *we shall understand*; saremo *we shall be*;
potremo *we shall be able to*.

Conditional: capiremmo *we should understand*; saremmo *we
should be*; potremmo *we should be able to*.

Activity 2
1 saranno; **2** modernizzerà; **3** Introdurrà; **4** Stabilirà;
5 lascerà; **6** riuscirà; **7** riceverà; **8** piacerà; **9** mancherà.

Note that with **lasciare** the -i- after **sc** is no longer necessary to
indicate the soft sound in **lascerò**, etc. Similarly, in **mancare**
the **h** after the **c** is necessary to indicate the hard **c** in **mancherò** etc.
This applies to all verbs of this sort in Group 1 when forming the
future.

A Of course, with a new managing director, there will be changes.

B Yes. We already know he will modernize the management system. He will introduce a system of targets to achieve. He will set his targets with each director and then he will leave him a wide freedom for decision-making. If the director is successful, he will get a bonus at the end of the year. If not ...

A Of course this will please some but others will miss the present structure.

Activity 3
1 A Strano, c'è una luce da Gianni. (Lui) è andato negli Stati Uniti.
B Sarà tornato. **A** Non penso. Saranno dei ladri. **2 A** Guarda.
Non è Pietro in quella Mercedes al semaforo? **B** Sì. Avrà vinto la lotteria. **A** Oppure sarà la macchina dello zio americano. È in Italia in questo momento.

Activity 4
You should have found: **1** anni in **cui** dovranno cambiare tantissime cose. **2** lo stupido parametro con **cui** misuriamo il nostro valore.

Comprehension 2
1 There are two, possibly related, areas. One is the legal situation, with numerous, often unclear, regulations, requirements for permits etc. The other is employment practices in the restaurant business which make it difficult for Brek to compete for staff and which add to the high costs of running the company. **2** According to Marina, most operators in the restaurant and bar business are small family enterprises and their management practices are not good: they pay staff cash in hand, thus avoiding the considerable costs due to the Italian state in taxes and social security payments, they fail to issue receipts, thus avoiding VAT and other taxes. They also tend to pay high wages, probably to tempt staff to accept the illegal deal. Brek finds it difficult to compete since they are doing things legally and, because of the costs involved, they cannot pay the same wage level. **3** The business is a family one and Marina sometimes finds it difficult to be working with family members with whom she has a relationship which is not primarily professional.

Activity 5

We hope you picked out 'tipicamente il bar e la trattoria sono gestiti a livello familiare; il personale che lavora nel settore è **abituato*** ad **essere pagato** in nero e **essere pagato** con delle cifre molto alte ...' *You may think this is just the verb **essere** + adjective; this is an acceptable analysis. Past participles are used as adjectives. We included it because the passive analysis is also possible.

Activity 6

1 Il padre del giovane è stato rintracciato da volontari. **2** Il problema di Emanuela è stato risolto dalla banca. **3** Il livello del suo lavoro è stato cambiato e il suo stipendio è stato aumentato di conseguenza. **4** Un incendio nei boschi è stato provocato da un'eruzione dello Stromboli. **5** La frazione Ginostra è stata isolata per due giorni dalle cattive condizioni del mare.

Do you think you understand the passive better? You are likely to choose the passive when the person or thing mentioned first in the above sentences (i.e. the subject) is what you want to emphasize. You would choose the active, as in the original sentences, if you consider the subject of those (the agent above) is the important item. For instance in number 1, it will depend on whether you consider it important that someone has managed to find the young man's father; or alternatively that the father was found by volunteers rather than by professionals. You will have recognized some of the items as being related to the reading passages in Unit 3, Session 4. If you read all five again, you will find they contain a number of passives – which we are sure did not bother you at the time!

Activity 7

1 Allora va isolato al più presto. *Then he must* be *isolated as soon as possible.* **2** Allora va liberato al più presto. *Then he must be freed as soon as possible.* **3** Allora va firmato al più presto. *Then it must be signed as soon as possible.* **4** Allora va dato al più presto. *Then it must be given as soon as possible.*

Activity 8

There are several examples of che as a relative pronoun: leggi poco chiare che vanno … interpretate; operatori che sono … molto piccoli; il bar e la trattoria …. che tendono a ignorare …; il personale che lavora …; i costi per l'azienda che sono molto alti …; un intreccio di rapporti personali e professionali del lavoro che può essere …; il rispetto che avrei se fossi … Towards the end of the interview you should have found: persone … con cui c'è un rapporto personale; un'estranea con cui c'è un rapporto … You can see in this interview that che is singular or plural, it can refer to people, objects or concepts and also that not every che is a relative pronoun: for instance, nel senso che; è evidente che … .

Comprehension 3

1 The fashion house delivers to her the jacket – possibly a sample garment – the roll of fabric, the roll of paper patterns, the threads and the buttons. Her workers have 100 minutes to transform this into a jacket, on a coat-hanger, wrapped and ready for despatch. This would seem to imply that the price her firm is paid for their work allows 100 minutes of labour input, no more. 2 The craftsman's skill. They want her to perform like a factory (l'industria) but they still expect high craftsmanship in the finished product (il risultato dell'artigiano). 3 The customers have less money to spend but they want the designer clothes which are constantly promoted in advertising, newspaper articles etc. So the firms bring their prices down, to the detriment of the quality of the fabric and of the tailoring (confezione). 4 The customers get their designer label garments but they no longer have the value that the designer label once had, since the garments are no longer made as they ought to be. 5 High fashion, haute couture: l'alta moda. Presumably those who can afford to buy at this price scarcely need to look at the price ticket!

Activity 9

You will find two passives with essere: saranno sollecitati; come dovrebbe essere fatto as *it ought to be made*. In the second case Signora Torrielli could have said andrebbe fatto, but it probably doesn't express sufficiently strongly the contrast she wants to make.

You will also find a number of passives made not with **essere**, nor indeed **andare**, but with **venire**: non viene più pagata l'idea, non viene pagato più niente, ma viene solo pagato il minuto/lavoro *the idea is no longer paid for, nothing is paid for any more, but the only thing that is paid for is the 'working minute'*; **non ci vengono più riconosciute le nostre ... bravure** *our exceptional skills are no longer recognized*; **il capo non viene più fatto** the *garment is no longer made*. Turn back to Unit 6 for an explanation.

Activity 10
1 Ecco il caffè. È caldo. Va bevuto subito. 2 La situazione è difficile. Va detto che John è una persona testarda. 3 Di solito in Italia i pasti sono/vengono accompagnati dal vino. 4 La lunga giornata lavorativa è/viene riconosciuta nella nostra remunerazione. 5 Il nostro lavoro è stimato. 6 Il prezzo va aumentato.

Activity 11
1 Future: tutti **avranno** sempre meno soldi, **potranno** sempre spendere meno, però **saranno** sempre più **sollecitati** (a passive in the future); quelle firme ... **continueranno** a discapito della qualità; la gente, sì, **metterà** un capo firmato ma non **avrà** più il valore ... 2 Present subjunctive: non vedo quale **possa** essere la soluzione. 3 Impersonal si: **si pretende** da noi l'industria; Non **si può**; Se **si parla** di (twice).

Comprehension 4
1 Most levels really, although she specifically mentions the girls who model the clothes and the photographic services which produce the publicity photos. But she says the only place savings can really be made is in the production of the garment itself and in the quality of the fabric. 2 From 'emerging markets' (third-world countries or countries of the former Soviet bloc) which she says don't at the moment produce good work, but very soon will. 3 Moving their production abroad. 4 They have closed, gone out

of business. 5 Problems with the trades unions, legal requirements, and the USSL. These would include contracts, health and safety at work legislation, the level of social security payments employers have to make (cf. Marina) and possibly other constraints. 6 She is indeed proud of the business she has created but she no longer derives satisfaction from the work. The word **gratificata** implies the satisfaction bringing peace of mind, professional satisfaction. She is not happy that she is not able to produce the quality of work she considers her hallmark within the constraints she now works with. 7 She has difficulty finding staff. The job demands concentration and she implies women may prefer to work in a situation where they just press buttons and don't have to think. She also feels that there is no longer the relationship between employer and employee which there used to be. Working hours are strictly adhered to whereas years ago, we understand, staff would be willing to do a little extra if they were behind on a contract.

Activity 12
1 Relative pronouns: ... una cosa <u>che</u> è in escalation; dell'ultimo che è <u>quello che</u> produce; a discapito dell'ultimo che mette insieme il capo; <u>che</u> è <u>quello che</u> non può difendersi; i mercati emergenti che producono ... ma <u>che</u> produrranno ...; <u>Tutti quelli che</u> hanno potuto; <u>tutti quelli che</u> avevano la potenza; Difficilissimo ... trovare ragazze <u>che</u> hanno voglia di fare questo lavoro; non è una fabbrica <u>dove</u> uno schiaccia il bottone; i contratti <u>che</u> i dipendenti ormai hanno; è solo sull'ultimo gradino <u>che</u> è la produzione; quindi <u>chi</u> vede quello crede ...
2 Subjunctive: **credo che a Torino nel giro di quest'anno già <u>abbiano chiuso</u> cinque o sei laboratori** (this is a perfect subjunctive: five or six factories have closed. The reason for the subjunctive rather than the indicative is **credo che**. Signora Torriellli is not sure, she does not want to be categorical); **non è che la gente <u>capisca</u> la differenza** (the subjunctive here is required by the negative impersonal expression, again casting doubt); **chi vede quello crede che <u>sia</u> già stato fatto tutto dentro quel marchio** (in fact, this is passive, and a perfect subjunctive again. *Those who see this believe that everything has been made inside that company* – i.e. the company whose label is on the garment). Note the contrast with

what follows: **è stato fatto tutto** – here Signora Torrielli is giving as fact that everything has been done (to save money for the profits of the company) not saying it is someone's belief – note it is another passive. Did you perhaps wonder why there was no subjunctive in the sentence **Difficilissimo già trovare ragazze che hanno voglia di fare questo lavoro?** You might say: this is a 'type' of girl, shouldn't it be subjunctive? Possibly another speaker would have used the subjunctive. An example of the dying subjunctive almost certainly.

3 Passive: we have already pointed out two passives in Activity 9. A third: le loro linee più basse <u>sono</u> già <u>state portate</u> ... fuori d'Italia a fare.

4 Future: i mercati emergenti ... che <u>produrranno</u>; <u>perderà</u>; le persone <u>perderanno</u> i posti perché non ci <u>sarà</u> più il mercato.

Comprehension 5

1 (Sa) che il suo mestiere è quello di scrivere. 2 (Dice di non sapere nulla) sul valore di quello che può scrivere/di quello che scrive.
3 (Si sente) straordinariamente a suo agio. 4 Degli strumenti che le sono noti e familiari. 5 Soffre e si chiede di continuo come gli altri facciano queste cose. 6 Dice che può scrivere soltanto delle storie.
7 A scrivere articoli per un giornale, ma solo un po'. Fa fatica a farlo.
8 (a) si sente in esilio. (b) si sente come uno che è in patria. 9 Dice che farà questo mestiere fino alla morte, che è molto contenta di questo mestiere e che non lo cambierebbe per niente al mondo.

Test yourself

1 a partirò, b Andrò, c Vedrò, d Conoscerò, e Lavorerò,
f impareranno, g parleranno, h faremo, i guarderemo, j vivremo

2 (a) I loro progetti per il miglioramento dell'ambiente vengono finanziati da questa organizzazione. (b) Una petizione è stata presentata al parlamento. (c) La fiamma olimpica verrà accesa da uno sportivo famoso durante la cerimonia d'apertura. (d) La pasta va servita al dente. (e) L'assegno non è stato firmato.

Unit 7

Comprehension 1
1 Firstly, Marina's choice of the verb **arrangiarsi**, with its implications of the solutions not being ideal, but the best one can do in the circumstances. Then the fact that although her husband is good at running the household, he's not pleased to have to do it. 2 Yes. She thinks they are making progress, changing – and in the last resort, as she says at the end, they simply have to get involved in the domestic arrangements if their wife is working, '**non c'è scelta**'. As you probably thought when we mentioned stereotypes, many men of earlier generations did nothing in the house, indeed would have thought it demeaning. 3 His parents were separated so that he had quite a tough upbringing and had to look after himself at home more than is usual. He didn't have a mother to do everything for him. 4 The stereotype Italian **mamma** thinks for her children, takes care of everything for them, particularly perhaps for her sons.

Activity 1
(1) continua a; (2) prova a; (3) si accorge di; (4) si rifiuta di; (5) è abituato a; (6) farei finta di; (7) sarei contenta di; (8) comincerà a; (9) sono stufa di.

Activity 2
1 Martedì mattina avevo intenzione di comperare un regalo per il compleanno di mia figlia ma non sono riuscito a trovarlo. Ho dimenticato (avevo dimenticato) di chiedere a mia moglie in che negozio lo vendevano. 2 Mercoledì sera avevo intenzione di andare allo stadio con gli amici per vedere insieme la partita di calcio ma non sono riuscito a organizzare la serata. Mi sono dimenticato di comperare i biglietti. 3 Giovedì mattina avevo intenzione di andare alla Posta per pagare la bolletta del telefono ma non sono riuscito a pagarla. Mi sono accorto troppo tardi di non avere abbastanza contanti nel portafoglio. 4 Venerdì pomeriggio avevo intenzione di prenotare le vacanze per l'estate ma non sono riuscito ad andare all'agenzia di viaggi.

Ho cominciato a leggere un libro molto interessante e mi sono dimenticato di uscire.

Comprehension 2

1 She is ambivalent about it. Sometimes she thinks she would enjoy it, but often she wishes she didn't work. This happens particularly when her daughter seems to be needing her a lot.
2 That by working she is missing the best years of her family life. She means, really, of her daughter. 3 They all find it difficult to combine work and family. Work makes big demands on them and yet their families too have needs they cannot ignore. 4 Because while recognizing that he shares all the household tasks, she feels this is only right, it is the duty of any married person. 5 **Non c'è scelta**. *There is no choice.* In other words: they have to share in the household tasks. 6 They do the shopping, they leave the bathroom tidy, they look after the children, take them to the park, fetch them from swimming (lessons), etc. 7 Her sister does not work outside the home and therefore takes on all aspects of running the house and family. Her brother-in-law does nothing at all at home. But he works very hard – and clearly earns enough to have the luxury of a wife who doesn't work. 8 She herself never worked outside the home but she seems to feel regret. She certainly considers economic independence very important. 9 It seems to be one long round of trying to organize the household (meals for instance) and her daughter's activities. The reference to **la piscina** is a reminder that Italian children tend to have all sorts of lessons and activities outside school. Most schools operate in the mornings only and the afternoons can therefore be devoted to these activities. 10 She would like to 'go back to nature'. Not see anyone, not even wash, certainly not put on make-up, smart suit, high-heeled shoes ... She would go cycling, eat simply and just do nothing all day long!

Activity 3

1 Certe mattine Emanuela non vorrebbe andare a lavorare, <u>sapendo che</u> sua figlia sentirà la sua mancanza. 2 La vita di Emanuela è al momento molto faticosa, <u>dovendo</u> abbinare famiglia e lavoro. 3 <u>Condividendo</u> tutti i lavori domestici con lei, il marito di Emanuela le è di grande aiuto. 4 Certi mariti non si rendono

conto che <u>non aiutando</u> in casa danneggiano l'armonia familiare
e rendono la vita difficile a sé stessi prima ancora che alla moglie.
5 La maggior parte dei giovani mariti italiani è di sostegno alla
moglie <u>lasciando</u> il bagno in ordine, <u>facendo</u> la spesa, <u>guardando</u>
i bambini, <u>portandoli</u> al parco, <u>andando</u> a prenderli in piscina. *or*
andandoli a prendere in piscina. 6 <u>Non dovendo</u> lavorare fuori
casa, mia sorella ha molto più tempo di me per badare alla casa e
alla famiglia.

Activity 4

1 resistente 2 assordante 3 pesante 4 attaccante 5 aderente
6 deludente 7 trafficante 8 presidente.

Activity 5

1 Che cosa fa il giornalista? 2 Chi è il fruttivendolo? 3 Chi è
l'idraulico? 4 Che cosa fa il pianista? 5 Che cosa fa un pittore?

Activity 6

1 Non preoccuparti. La porto io. 2 Non preoccuparti. La preparo
io. 3 Non preoccuparti. (Te) le spedisco io. 4 Non preoccuparti.
Ci vado io. (La faccio io).

Activity 7

(Note: a hyphen indicates the pronoun is attached to the preceding
word) A (1) lei (2) le (3) le (4) loro (5) lui (6) -le (7) lei
(8) -la B (1) la (2) lei (3) -le (4) -le (5) lui (6) -la (7) lui (8) lei (9) lui
(10) -la. C (1) Si (2) si (3) si (4) si (5) loro (6) si

Activity 8

Here is a possible letter. Gentile Direttore, Ho letto recentemente
un articolo pubblicato sul Suo quotidiano, in cui si diceva che
gli uomini italiani della nuova generazione non sono più come i
loro padri e i loro nonni, e che le giovani mogli italiane hanno di
fronte a loro un futuro molto più roseo di quello che potevano
aspettarsi le loro madri (e le loro nonne). Fosse vero! Sono una
donna di quarant'anni, sposata da dodici e con figli adolescenti.
Ho scelto di rinunciare alla mia carriera per occuparmi della
famiglia, e per evitare di lavorare otto ore fuori casa e altrettante

in casa tutti i giorni della settimana … Io **non penso** che gli uomini italiani **stiano** cambiando, anzi. **Credo che** i giovani uomini italiani **crescano** ancora più viziati e coccolati di una volta, perché spesso sono figli unigeniti. **Ho l'impressione che** i loro genitori (e in particolare le madri) non li **educhino** per nulla all'indipendenza e all'autosufficienza, e che anzi li **proteggano** e li **aiutino** in maniera quasi ridicola. **Dubito che** le madri dei giovani uomini italiani **abbiano insegnato** loro a stirare, a lavare i piatti, a cucinare e a passare l'aspirapolvere. E sono sicura che quelli più 'avventurosi' che hanno scelto di lasciare la famiglia e di andare a vivere da soli … sono sicura che il sabato e la domenica portano alla mamma la biancheria sporca perché gli **faccia** il bucato! Non credo che gli uomini italiani **siano cambiati**, né che cambieranno mai!

Comprehension 3

1 She tried to guarantee a certain level of income so as to be able to do the things they were used to and at the same time keep alive and well her relationship with her daughters. She thinks, looking back, that she did succeed. 2 She herself made many sacrifices; and she regrets now that perhaps she should have forgone certain material things in favour of an hour or two more with her daughters. But she wonders whether, if they had forgone certain possessions, their relationship would have been as beautiful as it has been. She doesn't know. 3 She thinks the important thing is not necessarily feeding the children, catering to their physical needs, but the time spent with them. But she thinks being with your children all the time is not necessarily best. What is important is to be completely available to respond to their needs for a certain amount of time each day, and this may only be for three hours. Not all mothers can be with their children 24 hours a day and remain patient, available … 4 They have the same problems as she had. For nine hours a day they don't see their children. 5 Being separated from the children's father. She felt guilty about this. 6 She thinks she was the sort who was a better mother for being with her children less, but available to them fully at certain times. She doesn't think she would have been able to be patient etc. had she been at home all the time.

Activity 9

1 le donne riescano più degli uomini. 2 su 1000 femmine con la licenza media, 160 arrivino alla laurea contro appena 107 maschi. 3 la presenza femminile sia davvero ridotta nei luoghi in cui si decide. 4 nell'università le donne raggiungano l'11,1 per cento dei professori ordinari. 5 il tasso di disoccupazione femminile oscilli ... .

Activity 10

1 Le chiavi di casa, ce le ho? Sì, ce le ho. 2 Gli appunti per il convegno, ce li ho? Sì, ce li ho. 3 L'indirizzo dell'albergo, ce l'ho? Sì, ce l'ho. 4 Il telefonino, ce l'ho? Sì, ce l'ho. 5 La patente, ce l'ho? Sì, ce l'ho. 6 Gli occhiali, ce li ho? Sì, ce li ho. 7 L'agendina, ce l'ho? Sì, ce l'ho. 8 Le pastiglie per il mal di testa, ce le ho? Sì, ce le ho.

Comprehension 4

1 At the fairs where he worked there was an organization promoting rice. He was able to get a good supply of rice at promotional prices and by eating rice at all meals, he was able to make ends meet. 2 He sees himself as having been lucky in two ways: he has always worked in easy markets and he has always succeeded people who were either incompetent or not very hardworking, a bit lazy. 3 He was a manager by the age of 28 and he points out that in those days this was important, quite something! 4 He thought the firm would exploit him for what they could get from him and then jettison him. 5 Because he learned an enormous amount: to be tough, to do demeaning jobs when necessary, to face up to responsibility. **Sporcarsi le mani** means *to do things beneath one's status*. 6 It was his first experience as an entrepreneur – we learn later that he enjoys that, when he implies that he got less enjoyment from his work when Cinzano was bought out by a multinational. And he obviously enjoyed being in an area where there were many Italian and German immigrants, and where good wine was produced; perhaps the vineyards were planted by the immigrants. 7 He was running a company and was able to expand it at quite a remarkable rate: from 50 employees to 180 in about a year, with three new products which he also exported. 8 They didn't particularly enjoy the 'rich man's' lifestyle.

And they obviously worried about their children coming to take it for granted. **9** Because he took over from someone who was all show, not a reliable worker; and also because it was a time when he could easily expand his company's market, with a number of events in Spain drawing visitors from over the world. (Cinzano produces and sells alcoholic drinks. Its fame rests on vermouth: wine with a high alcohol content, infused with herbs. A speciality of Piemonte, Carlo's home region.) **10** Because they have given him very clear instructions; and probably too because these instructions leave all the responsibility in his hands. If he succeeds, fine; if he fails, he is out! **11** Stock is the first company he has worked for which was not prospering. By the time the present owners took over, it was in serious difficulties and his first task for them was to restructure, which meant reducing the labour force. The restructuring was not covered in the interview but we know that he is proud of the way he did it, in collaboration with the unions, trying to make sure that each worker made redundant was in a position to go forward in his/her life. This was helped by a generous financial allowance from the German shareholders to make that possible. He was at the time of the interview embarking on more restructuring, but this time by deals with multinationals to share products and markets – if we understood correctly; it was not entirely clear! **12** Our impression during the interview was of a man who enjoys his work; who is very competitive – or at least certainly was as a young man; who is modest about his successes, saying they came easily; who knows how to seize opportunities; who tends to turn everything positively, an optimist who gets the most out of situations; who enjoys a challenge – for instance he is clearly pleased to be given a free hand to try to turn his company round. He gives the impression of being at peace with himself, a confident man, in charge of his life. He is also a 'family man'. His family means a lot to him, witness his decision to leave a very comfortable position rather than allow his children to be spoilt by having life too easy.

Test yourself
1 (a) stia, (b) sono, (c) abbia, (d) sia, (e) piace
2 (a) si, (b) lei, (c) si, (d) lavarli, (e) vestirl, (f) gli, (g) gli, (h) li, (i) la, (j) le **3** (a) Ho incontrato Claudio andando in biblioteca.

(b) Abbiamo ricevuto una notizia allarmante. (c) Scegliendo questo lavoro, avrai molte soddisfazioni. (d) Dovendo mantenere i figli, si è messa a insegnare. (e) Sulla sua scrivania c'era il ritratto di un bambino sorridente.

Unit 8

Comprehension: Readings 1 and 2 1 It seems to lie in the fact that the first article counted not only Italians currently active in voluntary work but also those who had done such work in the past. This gave a figure of nearly 9 million, 18.1% of the population over the age of 15. The second figure in the first article is of those who had done some sort of voluntary work in the previous 12 months, presumably up to June 1998. This gave a figure of 3,900,000 people. In the second article on the other hand, the figure was for 1997. And the second paragraph implies that those who were counted were those who had given at least 5½ hours of their time a week. The figure given was 5,397,000. **2 Sociale** would probably mean helping the less fortunate; **civile** is more likely to be environmental work or help in natural disasters. They would inevitably overlap. **3** It would seem not. The second article concludes by saying the statistic falls within the European average: **un dato nella media con i paesi europei.**

Activity 1
1 fossi 2 avesse 3 dicessi 4 chiedesse 5 scoprisse 6 passasse 7 fossi, avessi, scoprissi 8 fossero, stesse 9 desse 10 avessimo, dovessimo

Comprehension: Interview 1 1 They helped the old people with various bureaucratic procedures, went with them to the optician to buy glasses, the orthopaedic doctor, etc. **2** They did it largely for fun, to be together. **3** She met her husband in this group.

Activity 2
1 a. sediona b. sedia c. sediolina 2 a. ciotolona b. ciotola c. ciotolina or ciotoletta 3 a. lettone b. letto c. lettino. It is usual to use **-ona,** rather than **-one,** with the feminine words above. We said the whole business was difficult for non-Italians. Don't worry! You'll be understood.

Activity 3

(a) **Not modified by suffixes** (some of these, e.g. **cassetto**, probably originated as a modified word but are not viewed as such nowadays): 1 *drawer* (the diminutive is **cassettino** *small drawer*) 2 *turkey*, the large edible bird (the diminutive of **tacco** heel is **tacchetto**). 4 fillet, as in fillet steak, a fillet of sole. 6 hood, as worn by some monks, for instance. Sometimes barmen call a cappuccino **cappuccio**, possibly making the assumption **cappuccino** is a diminutive of **cappuccio**, whereas it is more likely the name comes from the colour of the milky coffee which is the same as that of the habits of Capuchin monks. 7 a type of bread. (b) **Modified by suffixes**: 3 *really dreadful day* (**giornata** + **-accia**.) 5 *puppy, dear little dog* (**cane** + **-olino**) 8 *a little house* (**casa** + **etta**).

Comprehension: Interview 2 1 The Gruppo Mio was formed when some friends spent a retreat day together and decided not just to meet as a group of friends but to do something for others, for those in need, both in the locality where they live and beyond, wherever help was most needed. **2** They do a number of things: (a) they are part of a missionary group and help support the work of a leprosy hospital in Brazil. They do this in two ways: largely by raising funds and collecting medicines to send; the funds are raised by collecting waste paper, metal and rags; by selling handicraft work and talking to schools about the work; by holding charity events (the interview was conducted in a room off the new, main church in Moriondo, while in the background were the sounds of a spirited rehearsal in the church of a musical, *Joseph and his Amazing Technicoloured Dreamcoat*, to be performed to raise funds); and also some members of the group have gone out to Brazil to help personally in the work of the hospital. (b) they help in strictly church activities such as providing music at mass; (c) they run the Sunday School and more recently have also started a Saturday club for local children; (d) they run a two week summer activity programme for local children; (e) they run a summer camp for local children in the mountains; (f) they visit an old people's home on Saturday afternoons and spend time with the old people, trying to cheer up those who are sad and lonely. **3** Their motivation lies partly in their religious faith, but they also enjoy the friendship of the group – perhaps that was the first motivator. They also seem aware of the way they have been helped by the group, the enjoyment and fulfilment it has given them and they want the younger generations to share this too.

Activity 4
Riccardo: the use of **questo** when really the definite article would do; **hanno avuto <u>un po'</u> questa proposta ...; questa voglia dentro ognuno <u>così</u> di noi ...**; perhaps the use of **quindi**; certainly his repetitions or rephrasing of the same or a similar idea. There is much 'redundancy' in what he says, a feature of spoken language, saying more than is strictly necessary, which actually helps the listener get the general gist without too much effort. Antonella: **diciamo che il nostro gruppo è un gruppo un po' strano, <u>no</u>?** The **no?** at the end of a phrase is frequent in certain people's speech. There is much redundancy in what Antonella says, too. Monica: **Noi ci raduniamo lunedì sera <u>appunto</u> intorno alle nove <u>così e, niente</u>, programmiamo <u>un pochino</u> l'attività ...**: **così e, niente,** has really no meaning (we have already drawn attention to this frequent use of **niente** in speech); **appunto** and **un pochino** add little to the meaning and are all part of the redundancy. Monica also adds **no?** to phrases.

Activity 5
1 siano; 2 sembri; possano; 3 abbia; 4 esistano; 5 giochi; 6 risultino.

Comprehension: Interview 3
1 Because she was moved by the desperate conditions of the lives of Kurdish refugees in Switzerland. 2 Murder. 3 A Turk, another immigrant. We assume readers will be aware of the relations between the Turks and the Kurds in Turkey and also know that the death sentence (question 4) may well have been imposed for actions which elsewhere would not be considered worthy of punishment, let alone such punishment. 4 He was under sentence of death in Turkey. Moreover he had a young wife and a baby daughter. 5 He made contact with the Swiss jail where the man was being held, provided a chauffeur and a car to go and collect

him, and a psychologist to go to help cope with any problems
the man might be facing as a result of what he had been through.
6 She had to look after the man since the city of Bologna could
not take on that responsibility. 7 A convent, where the nuns had
never before had a man as a guest. As a result, the nuns started to
support the cause of the Kurds.

Activity 6
You should have changed all the perfects to the past definite. The
imperfects should have remained unchanged. Both the perfect
and the past definite are for events. The imperfect does its jobs (see
Unit 4) alongside both. 1 splendeva; 2 tornarono; 3 decisero; 4 era;
5 combattevano; 6 sapevano; 7 dovevano; 8 erano; 9 pascolavano;
10 giocavano; 11 sentirono; 12 si buttarono; 13 arrivarono;
14 avevano; 15 volevano; 16 disse; 17 sparavano; 18 sparavano;
19 erano; 20 presero; 21 finì; 22 andarono; 23 era; 24 uscirono;
25 erano; 26 tornarono; 27 decisero.

Comprehension: Reading 3
1 They freed from water, mud and oil the streets, the books in
the National Library, paintings, the objects on display in the
Archaeological Museum, the monuments of the city. Once the
immediate emergency was past, they worked on the restoration
of the works of art damaged by the mud. 2 To commit oneself
personally to voluntary work, particularly, one imagines, to
work for the environment. 3 In the first paragraph he refers
to the **dissesto idrogeologico che tuttora, in misura sempre
maggiore, interessa l'intero bacino dell'Arno e non solo quello.**
*The hydrogeological mess which even now still threatens the Arno
basin and not only that*! He sees flooding almost as a fact of life,
although he implies it need not be so if only more were done to
prevent it. At the end of the passage he says a number of things
(neglect, uncontrolled building) make the art and natural treasures
of Italy very fragile: (this flood and the many which have followed
it) **hanno dimostrato come l'incuria, la cementificazione selvaggia e
spesso abusiva del territorio, il conseguente dissesto idrogeologico
rendano estremamente fragile il tesoro d'arte e natura che
possediamo.**

Test yourself
1 (a) 3, (b) 4, (c) 2, (d) 5, (e) 1
2 (a) partisse, (b) fosse, (c) sappia, (d) facesse, (e) arrivino,
(f) avesse, (g) gestisse, (h) ti prenda, (i) potesse, (j) accetti

Italian–English glossary

This glossary is selective. The meaning given is the one relevant to the texts in this book. Words easily guessable (e.g. **descrizione**) are not included nor are words which are almost certain to be known from basic courses. Gender is indicated for nouns not ending in -o or -a; the feminine of adjectives is given where is it different from the masculine. Where a verb has an irregular past participle, it is given.

Abbreviations: n = noun; v = verb, adj = adjective, adv = adverb, m = masculine, f = feminine, s = singular, pl = plural. (These are indicated only to avoid ambiguity.) A vowel underlined indicates that the syllable is stressed, either because the stress is irregular or because the student might be unsure about stress (e.g. in nouns ending in **-io**).

abbacchio   *roast lamb*
a mio agio   *at (my) ease*
abbastanza   *fairly*
abbinare   *to combine*
abusivo/a   *illegal*
accendere (acceso)   *to turn on (appliance); to light (fire)*
accingersi a (accinto)   *to get ready to*
accogliere (accolto)   *to receive, to welcome*
accorgersi (accorto)   *to realize*
accorrere (accorso)   *to run to help*
aconfessionale   *not linked to a church*
acquisti (m.pl)   *purchases*
adatto/a   *suitable*

addirittura   *downright, frankly*
addormentarsi   *to fall asleep*
adeguato/a   *right, fitting*
adoperare   *to use*
affari (m.pl)   (s: **affare**) *business*
affidabile   *to be trusted*
affinché   *so that*
affittare   *to rent*
affrontare   *face up to*
aggiornato/a   *brought up to date*
aggirarsi   *to be approximately*
aggiungere (aggiunto)   *to add*
aggraziato/a   *graceful*
aggregarsi   *to get together*
agguerrito/a   *ready for war*
ahimè!   *alas!*
aiuto   *help*

al di là di beyond, on the other side of

allegria happiness

allegro/a happy

allestimento preparation

alloggio lodging

alluvione (f) flood

almeno at least

alto/a tall, high

altro/a other

alzarsi to get up

ambiente environment

(nell') ambito di in the confines/compass of

amicizia friendship

ampliamento enlargement, expansion

andare in giro to go around and about

anelito strong desire

anguilla eel

annoiarsi to be bored

anzi indeed, on the contrary, or rather

anzi che, anziché rather than

anziano/a (n or adj) elderly person; elderly

appartenenza ownership

appartenere a to belong to

appena scarcely, only just

appendere (appeso) to hang

appunto precisely

aprire (aperto) to open

aquila eagle

argine (m) bank (of river)

arrangiarsi to get by, to manage

arredo furnishing

arretrato/a backward

arrossire to turn red, to blush

artigianale belonging to/ produced by a craftsman

ascensore lift, elevator

ascoltare to listen to

asilo nido day nursery

aspettare to wait for

aspettarsi to expect

aspirapolvere (m) vacuum cleaner, hoover

assegno cheque

assolvere (assolto) to find not guilty

assomigliare a to resemble, to take after

assumere (assunto) to take on, to appoint (staff)

attaccapanni (m) coat-hanger

attaccare discorso to strike up a conversation

atteggiamento attitude

attenersi a to abide by

attirare to attract

aula classroom

autista chauffeur, driver

avvenire (m) future

avvicinare to come close to

azienda company, firm

azionista (m or f) shareholder

bacino basin (of river)

ballare to dance

banchetto stall

barattare to barter, to exchange, to trade

battere uno scontrino to key a sum into the till to generate the receipt

benché *although*

benedizione (f) *benediction (a church service)*

biblioteca *library*

bisnonno/a *great grandfather/ mother*

bolletta *bill (for utilities, items consumed before payment)*

bonaccione *easy-going, goodnatured*

bottega *workshop (of craftsman)*

(a) braccetto *arm in arm*

braccio *arm*

bravura *skill, ability*

bruscamente *suddenly*

brutto/a *ugly, nasty*

buffone *joker, jester*

bugia; dire bugie *lie, fib; to lie*

buttare *to throw*

buttarsi *to throw oneself*

calcio *football, soccer*

calo (in) *declining*

camerino *dressing room (theatre)*

camicetta *blouse*

camicia da notte *nightdress*

camminare *to walk*

campagna *country (as opposed to town), countryside*

campana *bell (of church, for instance)*

campanello *doorbell*

campo *field*

cantante (m or f) *singer*

cantina *cellar*

canzone (f) *song*

capo *boss, person in charge; also: item of clothing, garment*

Capodanno *New Year*

capoluogo *main town, capital*

cappotto *overcoat*

carica *office*

carne (f) *meat*

carrello *supermarket trolley*

carta *paper*

castani (m.pl form) *chestnut (of hair); hazel (of eyes)*

catena *chain*

cattiveria *nastiness*

cattivo/a *bad, naughty*

cena *supper*

cera *wax, wax polish*

cercare *to seek, to look for, to try*

cerniera *zip fastener*

chiacchierare *to chat, chatter*

chiarezza *clarity*

chiedere (chiesto) *to ask*

chiesa *church*

chiudere (chiuso) *to close*

ciascuno/a *each, each one*

cibo *food*

cieco/a *blind*

cifra *figure*

ciliegia *cherry*

cintura *belt*

circa *about*

circo *circus*

clima (m) *climate*

coda *queue*

coetaneo/a *of the same age*

cognato/a *brother/sister-in-law*

cognome (m) *surname*

coinvolgere (coinvolto) *to involve*

colazione (f) *breakfast*

collettino *little collar*

colpa *fault, blame*
commettere (commesso) *to commit*
commistione (f) *(unusual) mixture*
commuovere (commosso) *to move (emotionally)*
comodità *'mod. cons.', convenience*
compagno/a (n) *partner*
comperare, comprare *to buy*
compiere gli anni *to have a birthday*
compleanno *birthday*
comportarsi *to behave*
comprare *to buy*
comprendere *to comprise, to take in*
comunque *however*
concorrenza *competition*
condividere (condiviso) *to share*
condurre (condotto) *to lead*
confezione (f) *tailoring, dressmaking*
confine (m) *frontier*
coniglio *rabbit*
coniuge (m or f) *spouse (husband or wife)*
conoscere *to know, to be acquainted with (person or place)*
consegnare *to hand over, to deliver*
contadino *peasant farmer*
contanti (m.pl) *cash*
controllare *to check*
convegno *conference*

coprire (coperto) *to cover*
correre (corso) *to run, to race*
corriera *country bus, mail bus*
corriere *carrier (of goods)*
cosa *thing*
così *so, thus*
cosiddetto/a *so-called*
cospargere (cosparso) *to sprinkle, to strew*
costeggiare *to be alongside*
costruire (costruito) *to build, to construct*
crescere *to grow*
crescita *growth*
cucinare *to cook*
cucito *sewing*
cuciture (f.pl) *stitches, seams*
cuoco *cook*
cuoio *leather*
cuore (m) *heart*

danneggiare *to damage, to cause harm to*
dappertutto *everywhere*
datore (m) **di lavoro** *employer*
decidere (deciso) *to decide*
deficiente *stupid*
degno/a *worthy*
dente (m) *tooth*
dentro *inside*
destinatario *addressee, recipient*
diapositiva *colour slide*
difetto *defect*
diffuso/a *widespread*
dimagrire *to lose weight*
dimenticarsi *to forget*
diminuire *to decrease*
(i) dintorni *the surrounding area*

dipendente (m or f) *employee*
dipingere (dipinto) *to paint*
direttore generale *general manager*
dirigere (diretto) *to direct, to manage, to be in charge of*
(a) disagio *not at ease, uncomfortable*
disatteso/a *not heeded*
discapito *detriment*
discutere (discusso) *to discuss*
disegnare *to draw*
disegno *drawing*
disponibile *available*
ditta *firm*
divario *variation, discrepancy, difference*
divenire (divenuto) *to become*
diventare *to become*
diverso/a *different*
dolce (m) *pudding, sweet*
domare *to control*
domatore (m) *tamer*
dote (f) *gift, natural quality*
dovere (n.m) *duty*
dovere (v) *to have to*

economie (f.pl) *savings*
edilizia *building trade/industry*
ente (f.) *organisation, bureau (usually public)*
entrarci; non c'entra *to come into it, to be relevant; it is nothing to do with ...*
entro; entro sabato *by (with expression of time); by Saturday*
equo/a *fair, equitable*
esempio *example*
esercito *army*

esigenza *demand, necessity, need*
esilio *exile*
esplicitezza *explicitness*
estate (f) *summer*
(all') estero *abroad*
estivo/a *summer, summery*
estraneo/a *outsider, who does not belong*
età (f) *age*

fabbrica *factory*
facile *easy*
facoltativo/a *optional*
fango *mud*
fantasia *imagination*
fare finta di *to pretend to*
fare parte di *to belong to, to be a member of*
farmaci *pharmaceuticals*
fatica *effort*
faticare *to have difficulty, to work hard to*
faticoso/a *needing a lot of effort, tiring*
fattoria *farm*
felice *happy*
ferie (f.pl) *paid holidays*
ferire *to wound*
ferito/a *wounded, hurt*
ferro *iron*
festa *party*
festeggiare *to celebrate*
fianchi (m.pl) *hips*
fiera *trade fair, market, show*
filiale (f) *branch (of business)*
fiore (m) *flower*
fiume (m) *river*
fonte (f) *source*

forse   *perhaps*
fosso   *ditch*
fotomodella   *the model (photographed wearing the designer's clothes)*
frainteso/a   *misunderstood, misinterpreted*
francese   *French*
(nel) frattempo   *(in the) meanwhile*
fresco/a   *cool*
frittata   *omelette*
funzionare   *to work*
fuori   *outside*

gamba: in gamba   *competent*
gatto   *cat*
gemma   *gem, jewel*
genere (m)   *kind, sort*
(in) genere   *generally*
genero/nuora   *son/daughter-in-law*
genitore   *father or mother*
gente (f.s)   *people*
gergo   *jargon*
gestione (f)   *management*
gestire   *to manage*
giardinaggio   *gardening*
giardino   *garden*
ginocchio   *knee*
giocare   *to play*
giocattolo   *toy*
giocoliere (m)   *juggler*
giornale (m)   *newspaper*
giovane   *young*
(nel) giro di poco tempo   *in a short time*
gonna   *skirt*
gradino   *step, rung (of ladder)*

grana   *irritation, problem*
(non) granché   *not very*
guadagnare   *to earn*
guadagni (m.pl)   *earnings*
guardare   *to look (at)*
guarire   *to get better (from an illness)*
guasto/a   *out of order, broken*
guerra   *war*
guidare   *to drive*

idraulico   *plumber*
igiene (f)   *hygiene, public health*
imbastire   *to tack*
imbustare   *to put into a (plastic) bag/into an envelope*
impallidire   *to turn pale*
imparare   *to learn*
impegno   *commitment, engagement*
impiegato/a   *office worker, employee*
impresa   *enterprise*
(all') improvviso   *suddenly*
in attesa di   *waiting to/for*
in fondo a   *in the depths of, at the bottom of*
incentivare   *to stimulate*
incubo   *nightmare*
incuria   *carelessness, indifference*
indossare   *to wear, to put on (clothing)*
indumento   *garment, clothing*
infatti   *indeed*
ingrandire   *to enlarge*
ingrassare   *to get fat, to put on weight*
iniziare   *to begin*
inizio   *beginning*

innanzitutto *first of all*

insediamento *establishment, setting up*

insegnante (m or f) *teacher*

insegnare *to teach*

insieme, insiemea *together, together with*

insomma *in short, in conclusion*

instancabilmente *tirelessly*

intendere (inteso) *to understand*

intreccio *interlacing*

introdurre (introdotto) *to introduce*

inutile *useless, pointless*

invecchiare *to grow old, to age*

invece *on the other hand, instead*

inverno *winter*

istituire *to set up*

istruito/a *educated*

laboratorio *workshop*

lamentarsi *to complain*

lasciare *to leave, to let*

latte (m) *milk*

lebbrosario *a leper hospital*

legare *to tie, to tie up*

legge (f) *law*

leggere *to read*

leggero/a *flighty*

legno *wood*

lento/a *slow*

letto *bed*

lettore (m), **lettrice** (f) *reader*

libero/a *free*

libreria *bookshop*

libro *book*

licenziare *to dismiss, to sack, to fire*

ligio/a *loyal, true*

lingua *language*

lirico/a; teatro lirico *opera; opera house*

litigioso/a *quarrelsome*

locale (m) *premises*

lucidare *to polish*

luna *moon*

lutto *mourning*

macchia *spot*

macchina *car*

magari *maybe, perhaps*

magazzino *warehouse*

magistero *teaching*

maglia: lavorare a maglia *to knit*

maglieria *knitware factory*

maglietta *lightweight sweater, jumper*

mai *never*

mal di schiena *backache*

mal di testa *headache*

malattia *illness*

mancare *to be missing, to pass away*

marito *husband*

materia *(school) subject*

media (n) *average*

medio/a; scuola media *average; middle school*

medioevo *Middle Ages*

meno *less, minus*

meridionale *southern*

messa *mass*

mestiere *skill*

metà (n.f); **metà agosto** half; mid August, half way through August

mettere (messo) to put

mettersi a to begin to

mezzo half

migliorare to get better

modelli patterns

modo; a modo mio; modo giusto mode, way; (in) my way; right way

moglie (f) wife

molla spring, trigger

molto (adv) very, a lot

molto/a/i/e much, a lot of

mondo world

morire (morto) to die

morte (f) death

mostra exhibition

motivo reason

motorino motor scooter

mungere (munto) to milk (animal)

muoversi (mosso) to move

mura (f.pl) walls (outer, defensive walls)

museo art gallery, museum

mutevole changeable

nascere (nato) to be born

nascita birth

neanche not even

negozio shop

nemico enemy

neve (f) snow

nido nest

niente nothing

nonno/a grandfather/mother

nonostante in spite of the fact that

noto/a known, well-known

nubile unmarried woman

nulla nothing

nuotare to swim

obbligo obligation

oca goose

occasione (f) opportunity

occuparsi di to take care of, to look after

odiare to hate

ogni each, every

oltre beyond, more than

onda di piena wave of flood water

opera work

oppure or

ordine (m) order

orgoglioso/a proud

ormai now

ospitare to give hospitality to

ospite (m or f) guest

ospizio old people's home

ottenere to obtain

ovunque everywhere, anywhere

paese (m) village; country, nation

pagare to pay

palestra gym

pallottola bullet

panchina bench

pantaloni (m.pl) trousers

parametro parameter

parecchio/a quite a lot

parecchi/ie several

parente (m or f) *relation*
parere (parso) *to seem*
parete (f) *wall (of house)*
parola *word*
parole incrociate *crossword puzzle*
parrocchia *parish*
partigiano/a *partisan*
partire *to depart, to leave*
partita *match (e.g. soccer match)*
pascolare *to graze*
passaggio *a lift (in a car)*
passeggiata *walk*
pasto *meal*
patria *homeland, fatherland, mother country*
pausa pranzo *lunch break*
pavimento *floor*
pecora *sheep*
peggiorare *to get worse*
pendolare (m or f) *commuter*
per via di *on account of*
perché + indicative *because; why*
perché + subjunctive *so that*
perciò *therefore*
perdere (perduto or **perso)** *to lose; (of tap) to leak*
perfino *even*
perlustrare *to search (a place)*
permesso di soggiorno *residence permit*
permettere (permesso) *to allow*
però *however*
perseguitare *to persecute*
pesare *to weigh*
pescare *to fish*
pesce (m) *fish*

piacere (n.m) *pleasure*
piacere (v) *to be pleasing*
piacevole *pleasant*
pigliare *to catch, to take*
pilastro *pillar, core product*
piovere *to rain, to be raining*
pittura *painting*
più *more, plus*
piuttosto *rather, fairly*
politica *politics; policy*
porre (posto) *to place*
portafoglio (m) *wallet*
posato/a *poised, sedate*
posto *place*
posto di lavoro *job;* also: *workplace*
potenza *power, capacity*
potere (n.m) *power*
potere (v) *to be able to*
pranzo *dinner, main meal*
pratica – fare pratica *to practise*
precipitarsi *to rush*
preferire *to prefer*
pregio *a good point, quality*
premio *prize*
prendere (preso) *to take*
prendere in giro *to tease*
presentare *to introduce*
presso *at the premises of*
prestare *to lend*
prestarsi *to lend itself*
presto *early*
pretendere (preteso) *to expect, to demand*
prevedere (previsto) *to foresee, to make provision for*
preventivo *estimate*
prima che *before*

(il) primo *the first course of an Italian meal is the pasta/risotto course; meat comes in the second course*

problematiche (f.pl) *range of problems*

prodigarsi *to devote oneself to*

prodotto *product*

promuovere (promosso) *to promote*

pronto/a *ready*

propenso/a a *inclined to/towards*

proporre (proposto) *to propose*

proprio (adv) *really*

proseguire *to continue*

prova *trial*

provare *to try*

pulire *to clean*

pulizia *cleaning*

purtroppo *unfortunately*

(a) quadri *checked*

qualcheduno, qualcuno *someone*

qualcosa *something*

qualora *if, in case*

qualsiasi *any, no matter which*

qualunque *any, any whatever*

quasi *almost*

quotidiano/a *daily*

raccolta *collection*

raccontare *to tell (a story)*

radunarsi *to meet, to get together*

(a) ragione *rightly*

(avere) ragione *to be right*

ragioniere *book-keeper, accountant*

rallentare *to slow down*

rapporto *relationship*

rassegnarsi *to resign oneself*

reddito *income*

registrato/a *recorded*

reperto *object in a collection*

resistere *to hold out, to endure*

restare *to remain*

restituire *to hand back*

retribuire *to remunerate, to recompense*

ricavato *proceeds*

riconoscere *to recognize*

ricordarsi *to remember*

ridere (riso) *to laugh*

rientrare *to be within*

rifiutare *to refuse*

rimanere (rimasto) *to remain*

rimetterci (rimesso) *to lose*

rimpianto *regret*

rincarare *to get expensive*

rincorsa *run-up*

rintracciare *trace*

riprendere (ripreso) *to take up again*

risparmiare *to save*

rispetto a *compared with*

rispondere (risposto) *to answer*

ristrettezza *poverty*

ristrutturare *to modernize, to rebuild*

ristrutturazione (f) *re-building*

ritenere *to consider, to maintain*

ritenersi *to consider oneself*

ritmo *rhythm*

riunione (f) *meeting*

riuscire a   to succeed in, to manage to

riva   bank (of river)

rivista   magazine

romanico/a   romanesque

romanzo   novel

rompere (rotto)   to break

ronzare   to hum

rotolo   roll

rovinare   to ruin

rubacchiare   to pilfer

rubinetto   tap

ruscello   stream

sacerdote (m)   priest

saggio   essay

sala da ballo   dance hall

salvaguardare   to safeguard

sangue (m)   blood

sanità   health, (colloquially) health service

sapere   to know (a fact)

saponetta   bar of soap

sbagliare   to make a mistake

sbocco   outlet, opening

scappare   to run away

scattare   to go off (of an alarm)

scavare   to dig out, to excavate

scegliere (scelto)   to choose

scelta   choice

scemo/a   silly, stupid, half-witted

scherzare   to make jokes

scherzo   joke

schiacciare   to press, to squash

sciagurato/a   wretched

sciolto/a   fluent

scomodare   to make uncomfortable

sconosciuto/a   unknown

scontentare   to make unhappy

scontrino   receipt

scontro   clash

scopo   aim, purpose

senza scopo di lucro   not for profit, charitable

scoppiare   to explode; (war) to break out

scoprire (scoperto)   to uncover, to discover

scorso/a   last (i.e. one just finished)

scrittore (m), **scrittrice** (f)   writer

scrivere (scritto)   to write

sebbene   although

secondo   according to

sede (f)   head office

sedere, sedersi   to sit

seggio, seggiolino   seat, little seat

seguire   to follow

selvaggio/a   uncivilized, ferocious

seminare   to sow (seed)

sentire   to hear, to feel

senz'altro   without a doubt, of course

servire   to be helpful, to be useful

settentrionale   northern

settimana   week

sforzo   effort

sfruttare   to exploit

sgraziato/a   ungainly

siccome   since, for the reason that

sicuramente   undoubtedly, certainly

sicuro/a; di sicuro *sure, confident; definitely, certainly*

sigla *acronym*

sindacale *related to trades unions*

sinteticamente *in outline, briefly*

sistema (m) *system*

smarrire *to lose, to mislay*

smascherare *to unmask*

smettere (smesso) *to stop, to cease*

soccorrere (soccorso) *to help, particularly the sick and wounded*

società *company*

soddisfazione (f) *satisfaction*

soffiare *to blow out*

soffitto *ceiling*

soffrire (sofferto) *to suffer*

sogno *dream*

soldi (m.pl) *money*

solito/a; di solito *usual; usually*

(lettera di) sollecito *letter urging prompt action*

solo (adv) *only*

solo/a *alone*

sondaggio *survey*

sopralluogo *on-site meeting*

soprattutto *above all*

sopravvivere (sopravvissuto) *to survive*

sordo/a *deaf*

sorridere (sorriso) *to smile*

sostenitore (m), **sostenitrice** (f) *supporter*

spagnolo/a *Spanish*

sparare *to shoot*

sparatoria *burst of gunfire*

sparo *gunshot*

spasso; andare a spasso *enjoyment, pleasurable activity; to go for a walk*

spaziare *to range*

spedizione (f) *despatch*

spensierato/a *carefree, thoughtless*

sperimentare *to experiment*

spesso *often*

spettacolo *show*

spiacevole *unpleasant*

spingere (spinto) *to push*

splendere *to shine*

sporcare *to dirty*

sposarsi *to get married*

sposo/a *bridegroom/bride*

sputo *spit*

squadra *team*

squattrinato/a *penniless*

stabilire *to establish*

stampa *press*

stanco/a *tired*

stenografia *shorthand*

stentare a *to find it hard to*

stesso/a *same*

stipendio *wage, salary*

stirare *to iron*

stoffa *fabric*

stracci *rags*

straniero/a *foreign*

strapieno/a *very full*

stravincere (stravinto) *more than win* (**stra:** *suffix meaning extra, over*)

stringere (stretto) *to squeeze*

stufa *stove*

stufo/a *fed up*

stupido/a   *stupid*

succedere (successo)   *to happen*

suocero/a   *father/mother-in-law*

suonare   *to play (musical instrument)*

superare   *to overcome, to get over, to exceed*

sussidio   *subsidy; teaching aid*

svago   *amusement, recreation*

svantaggio   *disadvantage*

sviluppo   *development*

svolgere (svolto)   *to carry out*

tacco   *heel*

tagliare   *to cut*

taglio   *cutting, cut*

tailleur   *(ladies') suit*

tanto   *so much*

tappeto   *carpet*

tardi   *late*

tartufo   *truffle*

tasso   *rate*

tedesco/a   *German*

tela   *canvas*

tema (m)   *theme*

temere   *to fear*

tempo   *time; weather*

tenere   *to hold*

tentare   *to attempt, to try*

tesoro   *treasure; darling*

tessuto   *material, fabric*

testimoniare   *to bear witness*

tifoso   *fan (e.g. soccer fan)*

tirare su   *to pull up*

titolare (m or f)   *owner*

togliere (tolto)   *to take out*

tornare   *to go back, to return*

torneo   *tournament*

torta   *cake*

tra l'altro   *by the by*

tradurre (tradotto)   *to translate*

traduzione (f)   *translation*

tramonto   *sunset*

trascorrere (trascorso)   *to spend (time)*

trasferirsi   *to move (house)*

trattare con   *to deal with, to negotiate with*

trattarsi di   *to be a question of*

travolgere (travolto)   *to sweep away, to overwhelm*

troppo (adv)   *too*

troppo/a   *too much*

trovare   *to find*

truffare   *to cheat, swindle*

tuffarsi   *to dive in*

turno   *session, sitting*

tuttavia   *nevertheless, all the same, however*

tuttora   *still now*

uscire   *to go out, to come out*

utile (adj)   *useful*

utile (m)   *profit*

utilizzare   *to use*

valere (valso/valuto)   *to be worth, to be valid for, to apply to*

valere la pena   *to be worth it*

valigia   *suitcase*

vecchiotto/a   *aging*

veloce   *fast*

verifica   *check, inspection*

vespa   *wasp*

vestaglia   *dressing gown*

vestito   *dress; (men's) suit*

vestito/a da *dressed as*
viaggiare *to travel*
vicenda *happening, event*
vicino *near*
vincere (vinto) *to win*
vincolo *chain, fetter*
viso *face*
vistoso/a *showy, very visible*
vita *waist; life*

vivere (vissuto) *to live*
voce (f)**; ad alta voce** *voice; out loud*
volere *to want*
volere bene a *to be fond of, to love*
volontà *will*
volta *time, occasion*

zio, zia *uncle, aunt*

Index

References are to page numbers. See also the following sections: **Grammar – The technical jargon explained** and the **Reference grammar**, both at the end of the book.

....

Credits

NEW WRITING VIEWPOINTS
Series Editor: Graeme Harper

Power and Identity in the Creative Writing Classroom
The Authority Project

Edited by
Anna Leahy

MULTILINGUAL MATTERS LTD
Clevedon • Buffalo • Toronto

Library of Congress Cataloging in Publication Data
Power and Identity in the Creative Writing Classroom: The Authority Project
Edited by Anna Leahy.
New Writing Viewpoints: 1
Includes bibliographical references.
1. English language–Rhetoric–Study and teaching. 2. Creative writing (Higher
education) I. Leahy, Anna. II. Series.
PE1404.P618 2005
808'.042'0711–dc22   2005016342

British Library Cataloguing in Publication Data
A catalogue entry for this book is available from the British Library.

ISBN 1-85359-847-X / EAN 978--1-85359-847-0 (hbk)
ISBN 1-85359-846-1 / EAN 978-185359-846-3 (pbk)

Multilingual Matters Ltd
UK: Frankfurt Lodge, Clevedon Hall, Victoria Road, Clevedon BS21 7HH.
USA: UTP, 2250 Military Road, Tonawanda, NY 14150, USA.
Canada: UTP, 5201 Dufferin Street, North York, Ontario M3H 5T8, Canada.

Typeset by Gilbert Composing Services Ltd.
Printed and bound in Great Britain by MPG Books Ltd.

Contents

Acknowledgments

On behalf of all the contributors to this collection, I thank Anna Roderick of Multilingual Matters and Heather Beck of Manchester Metropolitan University, both of whom supported and helped us focus our work. Many others also offered us words of encouragement as we shared our research and ideas at conferences and in conversations.

I acknowledge North Central College, which provided me with a Junior Faculty Enhancement Grant that allowed the time and energy for revision of *The Authority Project*. The college also recognized my research and writing with the Dissinger Award for Faculty Scholarship. Several individual colleagues there, both within and beyond the English Department, have encouraged my professional development, particularly at those times when I felt overwhelmed by other obligations.

A partial fellowship from the Vermont Studio Center supported time for this project at an early stage and for other, creative writing projects.

I thank my mother, sister, and aunt for their encouragement over the past several years. Thanks also to my father, who wanted to be a writer himself but who did not live to see my first publication. Finally, thanks to Douglas Dechow, my most vociferous supporter and most insightful reader, with whom I'm lucky to collaborate on a number of endeavors.

Foreword

ANNA LEAHY

With hundreds of undergraduate and graduate creative writing programs in existence and with numerous other colleges and universities offering at least creative writing coursework, many of us, though we may have been hired because we write, are paid *to teach*. Articulating a coherent creative writing pedagogy – as we have done here in *Power and Identity in The Creative Writing Classroom: The Authority Project* – is now important for several reasons: to establish creative writing as a distinct and valuable field in English studies more than a decade after Joseph Moxley's (1989) edited collection, *Creative Writing in America*, laid groundwork; to rethink prevalent assumptions about workshops and other common practices in order to both understand and revise them; to document and share a unified but adaptable approach for those entering and continuing to teach in the field; and to demystify teaching and separate it from writing in ways that ultimately benefit both student learning and faculty satisfaction.

Authority is an often little-discussed concept central both to pedagogy in general and to the writing process. Our project does not embrace authoritarianism, the simplistic sense of authority as the teacher's power to give orders to young creative writing students; authority is not simple, centralized dissemination in the classroom. Instead, our work as a whole offers and plays with various ways to configure authority: as the expertise of the teacher or of the students, as an agency or action for accomplishing things, as a set of mutually beneficial or agreed-upon guidelines for fostering success, as a set of evaluation criteria, as seemingly inherent forces in writing and teaching, and even as authorship itself. Authority, for the contributors to *The Authority Project*, involves exploring who has permission to do what, who has which rights in the creative and academic processes, how ideas and individuals are privileged, who has control in the creative writing classroom, and how all these are in flux. The goal we have achieved in *The Authority Project* is to configure an adaptable pedagogy in which authority guides us as teachers in encouraging student learning.

Over the last several decades, creative writing teachers have built edifices for our pedagogy so that instructors might move around among them with little guidance to find their own ways. *The Authority Project* articulates, questions, and makes adaptations to the pedagogical paths that have emerged on our landscape. This collection asserts that by becoming conscious of authority – in various forms – as the guiding pedagogical principle, we can understand the theoretical underpinnings of the field and also make positive decisions about our classrooms. Authority, as a guiding principle in our teaching, makes central the human, the cultural, and the textual elements of our pedagogy – or andragogy, as tenets of adult learning are called in Europe – and encourages college-level teachers to participate most thoughtfully and productively in their professional lives so that students, too, flourish.

The Authority Project grew out of a panel for the Associated Writing Programs Conference (now called the Association of Writers and Writing Programs), where seven of this book's authors shared basic ideas about how they teach creative writing and why some ways of thinking about teaching and of designing courses and assignments are working or not working. An overriding concern with how authority functions in workshop-style classrooms – those in which students share and respond to each other's writing – was evident even in our early discussions. Our initial group grew to include the 17 writer-teachers represented here as The Authority Project, which asserts that authority-conscious pedagogy can and should shape our field in general and should guide our individual decisions about how we define ourselves and how we teach the subject in today's classrooms.

Wallace Stegner (2002), in *On Teaching and Writing Fiction*, points out that, while Europe developed literary centers where young writers apprenticed themselves to master-writers in cafés and pubs, the United States, because of its geographical expanse, has developed colleges and universities as gathering places for writing talent to be encouraged. Which college or university deserves credit for putting into place the first academic creative writing course or program and, thereby, initiating this phenomenon is up for debate, particularly when considered on both sides of the Atlantic. According to the web site of the Iowa Writers' Workshop, that program was established in 1936, 14 years after the institution deemed creative work acceptable as a graduate thesis. Other programs and scholars suggest creative writing emerged in U.S. academe even earlier. D.G. Myers, for instance, notes that Henry Wadsworth Longfellow accepted a professorship in 1829, though he quit as soon as his writing could support him (p. xvii), and that 'creative writing was first taught under its own name in the 1920s' (p. 101). Certainly, by the end of the 1940s the underpinnings of numerous creative writing programs were established in the United States, and opportunities such as the Bread Loaf Writers' Conference were founded by the likes of Robert Frost, publisher John Farrar, and others. In the 1960s, M.F.A. – Master of Fine Arts – programs appeared in such varied places as the University of Alaska, Bowling Green State University, the University of British Columbia, and the University of Oregon, according to Moxley's (1989) appendices in *Creative Writing in America*. Then, in 1967, 15 writers, including R.V. Cassill, from 13 programs established the Associated Writing Programs, thereby defining the field and profession as distinct from other English studies and arguing that living practitioners of literature could enhance English studies in the academy. Since 1975, the number of the association's member programs has quadrupled; the number of terminal degree programs (Ph.D. and M.F.A.) increased from 20 to 140, the number of intermediate (M.A.) programs is growing, and the number of undergraduate programs is now impressive at more than 350, according to the Association of Writers and Writing Programs' web site.

As the number of undergraduate and graduate course offerings expanded dramatically, graduate creative writing programs began, in large part unintentionally or uncritically, to produce not only writers but also teachers for these new creative writing courses and programs. But the field, long focused on cultivating writers, has not yet caught up with this role of producing college-level teachers. In fact, only recently have researchers, namely Moxley in 1989 and Myers in his 1996 *The Elephants Teach: Creative Writing Since 1880*, documented the rise of creative writing as an academic discipline. Myers recognizes that the field's 'plan [...] was not always adequate to the task. And too sometimes the nature of the task was not fully grasped [...]' (p. 167). In the wake of these texts and the continued growth of creative writing programs, writer-teachers such as David Radavich and Shirley Geok-lin Lim have pointed to the field's lack of attention to its place and roles in academia. Geok-lin Lim (2003), in an article in *Pedagogy*, calls this lack '[t]he absence of reflective and theoretical substance, of research in the history and pedagogy of this "complementary" field' (p. 163). Both Radavich and Geok-lin Lim, in broad strokes, argue that it's time to face our new roles, to rethink our relationships with other disciplines, and to thoughtfully document and revise what we do as creative writing teachers in colleges and universities.

Even now, the Iowa Writers' Workshop asserts that writing is unteachable and that the program attracts the most talented young writers and, therefore, produces very successful graduates. While this tack works very well for the Iowa Writers' Workshop, it is ill adapted for the expanding field as a whole. With few exceptions, creative writers have not studied, documented, and analyzed their teaching. The danger for the larger field, then, is the presumption that writers can learn to be good teachers merely through their participation in workshops *as students*.

Those graduate programs in the United States that do train their teaching assistants most often do so in composition; graduate students become steeped in rhetorical approaches to teaching and in how to instruct first-year college students in research and academic writing. So, the teaching of writing is often not defined specifically for the creative writing workshop. Instead, the preparation of future creative writing professors is heavily influenced by compositionists like Patricia Bizell, Kenneth Bruffee, Peter Elbow, and Donald Murray whose approaches to pedagogical components can be adapted – often uncritically or even unconsciously – to suit the new professor's new goals, texts, and students in the creative writing classroom. Kelly Ritter's (2001) study, 'Professional writers/writing professionals: revamping teacher training in creative writing Ph.D. programs,' documents well the influence composition theory and teacher training in composition has had on creative writing. While pragmatic in terms of preparing graduate students to teach first-year, required courses in general education during graduate school and while such compositionists have borrowed creative writing approaches in significant ways, this approach to pedagogy leaves creative writing instructors and professors ill prepared to teach in their specialization and in need of continuing guidance. Save for a few exceptions, such as Moxley's edition of essays and somewhat more recently *Colors of a Different Horse* edited by Wendy Bishop and Hans Ostrum in 1994, the field has defined creative writing pedagogy neither consistently nor thoroughly. It's as if creative writing professors can best learn through osmosis, individual trial and error, and reinvention of wheels without yet knowing very much about the vehicle from the driver's seat.

So, college-level, creative writing teachers learn largely without field-specific teaching mentors, pedagogy guidebooks, or shared bodies of knowledge about what it means to lead a creative writing course.

Importantly, graduate programs, such as the one at Indiana University, have begun to develop coursework or orientation programs to prepare their students specifically in the theory and practice of teaching creative writing, but texts and models for those efforts are few. Susan Hubbard, former Vice President of the Association of Writers and Writing Programs and one of this collection's contributors, for instance, teaches a course at the University of Central Florida that introduces graduate students to pedagogical issues and practicalities of the creative writing classroom and has used *The Authority Project* as part of that course even before its publication. In general, though, the field's pedagogy has been sparsely articulated in writing and too largely based on hallway conversations or uncritical assumptions. While compositionists over the past several decades have mapped out classical, current-traditional, expressivist, social constructionist, and radical theoretical territories and have charted practical applications of these theories for course and assignment design, creative writers have largely failed to document the theoretical underpinnings of the workshop-style classroom; the assumed relationship between the writing process and the written poem, story, essay, or play; and the crucial roles of authority in the field; and the practical matters of how we do and can teach our subject with these roles in mind.

Here, as *The Authority Project*, 17 essays document philosophies, concerns, and approaches of new and experienced writer-teachers who are in the continual process of figuring out their roles in the classroom, who are developing styles that best suit themselves and their students, and who face issues particular to the workshop-style classroom. Each contributing author keeps in mind both the real-world classroom as well as the reasoning behind its dynamics as he or she explores the authority-conscious pedagogy that this collection defines. We, like Dorothea Brande in 1934, see both problems and possibilities in the way creative writing is taught and premise our project, in part, on one akin to Brande's assertion in *Becoming a Writer*: 'there is no field where one who is in earnest about learning to do good work can make such enormous strides in so short a time' (p. 27). The strides that our students make are encouraged by each of the four aspects – each of the four sections – of *The Authority Project*, where authority is employed as a useful, adaptable, guiding principle for creative writing classrooms.

The first and most theoretical section, 'Understanding the Larger Influences,' addresses cultural, institutional, and individual influences that shape the creative writing classroom. By seeing authority as the central pedagogical issue, we analyze assumptions about what creative writing is, how an author is defined, and how the larger culture influences the writer, the writing process, and the classroom. This section begins with Nancy Kuhl's and Anna Leahy's explorations of crucial influences in order that we make more theoretically informed and authority-conscious choices about our pedagogical approaches; Kuhl addresses concepts of and assumptions about therapeutic writing and popular representations of writers, whereas Leahy addresses concepts of the writing and teaching processes and their relationships to caring. Brent Royster's 'Inspiration, Creativity, and Crisis: The Romantic Myth of the Writer Meets the Contemporary Classroom' takes on the question of why creative writers do and can teach a supposedly unteachable subject; he asserts that a play, a poem, an essay, or a story is not necessarily solely the product of an individual author but of a complex social and historical interaction. Evie Yoder Miller defines the commonalities and distinctions of two pedagogical fields – creative writing and composition – and considers the relationship of the two kinds of writing when constructing a workshop; Miller's essay is particularly helpful for those of us trained in graduate school to teach composition and to those who continue to teach both creative writing and composition. Finally, this section concludes with a thoughtful analysis by Carl Vandermeulen of what happens when the best of widely accepted ideas about seemingly decentered classrooms, individual expression, and collaborative communities goes terribly awry. This opening section, then, maps the field, examines the cultural influences that individuals bring to the classroom, and defines and challenges prevalent concepts about who and what holds authority in the creative writing workshop.

The second and most narrative section, 'The Teacher's Place, Voice, and Style,' proceeds to define several ways of thinking of oneself as a teacher – as an authority – in the classroom. Mary Cantrell's essay offers a lively discussion of what we too often hesitate to document about ourselves as teachers of creative writing: our role as evaluator. Audrey Petty, in 'Who's the Teacher?: From Student to Mentor,' explores the transition most of us go through as we move from graduate student to professor, a transition that she, in hindsight, recognizes was guided at first by the unquestioned methods of those who had taught her and also by her perceptions of students' assumptions about her age, gender, and race. Rachel Hall uses her experience with motherhood – as a reality and as a metaphor – to critically examine the teacher–student relationship in a workshop setting, particularly as that relationship is shaped by the teacher's and students' assumptions about authority, physicality, and emotionality. Katharine Haake's 'Dismantling Authority: Teaching What We Do Not Know' asks that we both risk and re-energize our own authority by teaching what seems to be beyond our present knowledge, just as we ask our students to move beyond what they can already do comfortably. This second section, as a whole, examines and orients the authority of the instructor.

The final two sections move to practical applications for authority-conscious pedagogy. The section on 'Course Design' provides four different ways to structure creative writing courses by using authority as the underlying principle. Wendy Bishop, perhaps the leading expert in the field of creative writing pedagogy, outlines a course based on four components that can structure the roles of the teacher and the students: evaluation-free risk-taking, contract grading, radical revision, and the portfolio as the culmination of a process within a writing-intensive zone. Suzanne Greenberg provides a discussion of a subject that we must face as teachers with institutional authority: how evaluation and grading shape a course and the creative process. Other essays by Susan Hubbard and Argie Manolis offer course designs based on gender studies and service-learning workshops and that reconfigure the relationships among texts, teachers, students, and communities. In offering an analysis of both prevalent practices and alternative course structures, this third section rethinks and moves beyond the seemingly typical, seemingly self-evident workshop by using authority as a central orientation for overall course planning.

'In the Classroom' offers four authority-conscious methods for creating positive classroom experiences for students and teachers. Cathy Day, in 'Where Do You Want Me To Sit?: Defining Authority through Metaphor,' outlines in detail a first-week activity that brings a discussion of authority, the individual, and the workshop to the forefront by asking students to articulate their assumptions about how class dynamics might operate. Mary Swander challenges the coach-type workshop leader that lingers in our classrooms and in our students' minds and offers in its place step-by-step, process-oriented assignments and critical encouragement. Other essays by Amy Sage Webb and Sandy Feinstein delineate the uses of mythology and of published models in assignment sequences that offer students common reference points and encourage experimentation. While each contribution to this section draws from specific classroom experiences, the approaches and assignments can be adapted to fit various genres and course levels.

Each essay in *Power and Identity in the Creative Writing Classroom: The Authority Project* complements the others, with an afterword by Graeme

Harper and Stephanie Vanderslice, to form a wide view of how authority, the individual, and community do and should work together in workshop-based creative writing classrooms. These authority-conscious theories and practices form an organizing principle or agenda that can be used on the whole or selectively by instructors in college-level creative writing classrooms. Readers will not agree with every essay, nor, perhaps, with every idea within a given essay. Instead, the variety of voices and experiences makes for a comprehensive reference where little has existed for those of us who want to understand ourselves better as writer-teachers, who want to continue growing in our work, and who envision creative writing pedagogy as a distinct field. This collection describes and revises many of the well-established structures of the field and, importantly, cements a distinct system of paths among those that continue to emerge as our field develops. *Power and Identity in the Creative Writing Classroom: The Authority Project* unravels and re-maps creative writing pedagogy for the 21st century so that concepts of authority can shape both our theoretical approaches and also the meanings and applications of our approaches in our day-to-day decisions as college teachers.

References

The Association of Writers and Writing Programs (2004) 10 April 2004 <http:// www.awpwriter.org>.

Brande, D. (1981/1934) *Becoming a Writer.* New York: Tarcher/Penguin.

Geok-lin Lim, S. (2003) The strangeness of creative writing: An institutional query. *Pedagogy* 3 (2), 151–69.

Moxley, J. (1989) *Creative Writing in America: Theory and Pedagogy.* Urbana, IL: National Council of Teachers of English.

Myers, D.G. (1996) *The Elephants Teach: Creative Writing Since 1880.* Englewood Cliffs, NJ: Prentice-Hall.

Ritter, K. (2001) Professional writers/writing professionals: Revamping teacher training in creative writing Ph.D. programs. *College English* 64 (2), 205–27.

Stegner, W. (2002) *On Teaching and Writing Fiction.* New York: Penguin.

Writers' Workshop: The University of Iowa (1997) University of Iowa. 20 December 2003 <http://www.uiowa.edu/~iww/>.

Part 1

Understanding the Larger Influences

Chapter 1
Personal Therapeutic Writing vs. Literary Writing

NANCY KUHL

Lately, I can't help but notice the relationship between writing and psychotherapy in American popular culture – it's everywhere. Take, for instance, *Moulin Rouge*, a recent film musical that is a wacky post-modern version of the back stage musicals of the 1930s, a la Busby Berkely and Ruby Keeler. The film opens with Christian, a young writer played by Ewan McGregor, weeping over his typewriter. He is about to write the story of his true love, a dancer named Satine (played by Nicole Kidman), whose untimely death has left him utterly grief stricken. The story unfolds as Christian writes of their meeting and falling in love, of the obstacles they faced together, and ultimately of Satine's death. When the film returns to this frame at its close, Christian's grief has been transformed into a bittersweetness. The film implies that, for Christian, writing his story has been a kind of solitary talking cure. He has gotten his grief off his chest, and now he can begin to move on with his life.

Another example of this popular connection between writing and psychotherapy is HBO's thirty-something-single-girl-sex-comedy *Sex in the City*. Carrie, the main character, played by Sarah Jessica Parker, writes a newspaper column about the sexual trials and tribulations of Manhattan party girls. The column, which is used to structure each episode around a particular topic or question ('Are all men freaks?' Carrie asks in one episode), provides a way for Carrie to sort out her boyfriend troubles, examine her life's goals and choices, and evaluate her feelings about various sexual-political issues. Carrie's column (and the show) is a kind of diary – a place where Carrie can work through difficult times and personal problems.

The idea that writing is primarily a means of self-expression, as opposed to a craft or a creative discipline, has been widely held by members of my classes and, for a variety of reasons, it has created challenges for me as a teacher. Not the least of these challenges has been to my authority in the classroom, as both a teacher and a writer.

3

Because I promote writing as a matter of craft and skill with language and because I challenge the idea that writing is primarily a means of exploring one's psyche, I find myself in conflict with popular images and with the vast marketplace of goods that support that very idea.

As a young woman teaching writing in academic and non-academic environments, I've faced various challenges to my authority. I've had students suggest that, because I am younger than they are, I am not qualified to teach them. I've even had a student physically intimidate me. Those challenges to my authority were difficult to address, but I always felt that I could prove myself and refuse to be intimidated simply by doing a good job teaching the course. The challenges to my authority that I've faced as a result of the popular relationship between writing and self-discovery have been significantly more difficult to overcome. The marketing of this idea has been so convincing, and the commodification of the artistic process so undermines the reality of that process, that I sometimes have found it nearly impossible to have meaningful classroom interactions with students heavily invested in the popular mythologies dealing with writing and creativity.

I do not disagree or take issue with the idea that writing can help one work through difficult personal problems, or even with the idea that good literary writing can rise out of exploratory personal writing. Articles with titles like 'Expressive Writing and Coping with Job Loss,' 'Prison Poetry: A Medium for Growth and Change,' 'Postmodernism, Spirituality, and the Creative Writing Process: Implications for Social Work Practice,' and 'Establishing a Creative Writing Program as an Adjunct to Vocational Therapy in a Community Setting' indicate that writing can indeed have a positive therapeutic effect for the writer. There is even a periodical entitled *The Journal of Poetry Therapy*, devoted to the discussion of a therapeutic writing method. Clearly, writing is a great way for many to deal with difficulties in their lives and gain helpful insight into their emotions and experiences.

Private journal and diary writing, however, differs dramatically from literary writing. While I am glad that many find comfort and insight through the writing process, solace and self-discovery cannot be the goals of a productive literary creative writing workshop, which has become the dominant classroom teaching practice for creative writing in the United States. Generally, private writing is an end in itself. In other words, if consolation is one's goal, and the process of writing produces a feeling of consolation, the written product is somewhat beside the point; its quality as literature, at least, is really not at issue.

By contrast, the work of a literary writing workshop – where participants share work with the group, then listen silently as group members discuss the merits and weaknesses of the piece, and then revise the written product – even one that pays close attention to process, takes as its goal the production of literary writing. Therefore, the class must concentrate not primarily on the writer's feelings, but on craft, style, narrative conventions, and other elements of writing for an audience. The public writing produced in workshops *can* begin where private writing leaves off, but often work that begins in a private journal must be heavily revised or even wholly transformed before an audience can participate in it as public, literary writing.

In general, the workshop method emphasizes the role of revision in good writing largely by assuming that participants are still actively working on the pieces they present to the group. A workshop assumes that writers will consider, and perhaps incorporate, criticism and comments from their peers as they write, rewrite, work, and rework a piece; otherwise, what would be the point of hearing the feedback? Though, to first-time workshop students, it often seems that listening to criticism is the hardest part of a workshop, those who are serious about writing learn that revising is the really hard and invigorating part. Stepping back into a piece one has already spent a great deal of time on, cutting lines or paragraphs or even pages, restructuring major portions of a piece – these are often the most difficult parts of the writing process. So, the role of revision is one of the central differences between the private and public writing processes.

If students in my classes have been reluctant to recognize the differences between private and public writing, it is hardly their fault. In recent years, a tremendous commercialization of the act of writing and of the writing process has occurred. Many media forums, bookstores, and publishers have promoted writing as a means of psychological cure in various ways.

The Oprah Winfrey Show has been particularly successful in marketing this idea. Writing, as it figures in the world of *Oprah*, consists mainly of private journal writing exercises such as gratitude journals, which were made popular by the book *Simple Abundance*, in which viewers are encouraged to note five things each day for which they are grateful. On the show's website, viewers can create their own personal journals to explore their day-to-day experiences. In the online journal of the 'Your Spirit' section of the web page, Oprah notes, 'Keeping a journal will absolutely change your life in ways you've never imagined.' Even *Oprah's Book Club* invites readers/viewers to write to the show telling about their personal experiences with the book at hand. Moreover, selected books are primarily discussed and valued not as literary art, but as tools by which the reader might pursue self-discovery.

Discussions of journaling as a path to healing often include a pitch for one of a number of guidebooks to help one journal more effectively. Popular images of writing as a kind of therapy are well supported in book stores by these diary and journal writing guide books and by blank writing journals that encourage writing as a means of soul searching through the inclusion of writing prompts and inspirational quotes (one can easily imagine a blank book with a still image from *Moulin Rouge* or a photo of Oprah or the stars of *Sex in the City* on the cover).

A veritable industry has been built around one self-help writing guide, *The Artist's Way* by Julia Cameron (1992). *The Artist's Way*, Cameron states in the book's introduction, 'is, in essence, a spiritual path, initiated and practiced through creativity' (p. xi). The book outlines a process by which artists might '[create] pathways in [their] consciousness[es] through which creative forces can operate' (p. xiii). Each of the 12 chapters is devoted to another step in the process; if you are reminded of 12-step programs, there is a reason: Cameron, a recovering alcoholic, refers to *The Artist's Way* as a 'do-it-yourself recovery' (p. xvi). This creative process has become so popular that Cameron has published a variety of spin-off books and journals, including *The Artist's Way Morning Pages Journal, The Artist's Way at Work, The Vein of Gold, The Artist's Way Date Book, Reflections on the Artist's Way, Inspirations: Meditations from the Artist's Way, The Right to Write,* and *The Artist's Way Creativity Kit.*

The popularity of this kind of guide can be understood to mean that many people feel compelled to write and are in search of some kind of permission to do so. The pages of *The Artist's Way* are rich with quotations intended to offer permission: 'Saying no can be the ultimate self-care,' Claudia Black (p. 164); 'In the middle of difficulty lies opportunity,' Albert Einstein (p. 165). Additionally, the popularity of such books lends further support to the psychological benefits of writing. Many of the exercises suggested in the 'Tasks' sections of each chapter are, in fact, about self-improvement more than they are about writing. One task during Week 2 reads, 'List ten changes you'd like to make for yourself, from the significant to the small … (get new sheets, go to China, paint my kitchen, dump my bitch friend Alice)' (p. 58); tasks for Week 10 include 'Make a quick list of things you love, happiness touchstones for you. River rocks worn smooth, willow trees, cornflowers…' (p. 175).

My own teaching employs some methods that are at least theoretically similar to these: I am a teacher who starts each class by reading and discussing published works I hope will help my students grant themselves permission to take risks in their writing, and I often use writing exercises to help students explore stories, characters, and the writing process. But *The Artist's Way* and other writing-as-self-exploration tools fail to mention many steps in the writing process that might help to propel personal writing into public writing. Revision, for example, does not appear as a step in the Artist's Way process nor even as a term in its index. By contrast, poet Richard Hugo's *The Triggering Town* (1979), an older, less commercial, and more academic book about writing, one that guides those interested in producing literary writing for an audience, includes a chapter entitled 'Nuts and Bolts' that is almost entirely dedicated to practical tips for revising one's work. Hugo's warning that one should 'never want to say anything so strongly that you give up the option of finding something better' (p. 38) clearly has little in common with Cameron's view of the writing process.

The Artist's Way and similar books blur the differences and distinctions between personal or private writing and writing which is intended for an audience. Students who uncritically absorb the popularized lesson that the goals of creativity and writing are insight and self-expression are often ill equipped to deal with the constructive criticism at the center of workshops. These students expect a writing workshop to mimic the kinds of discussions they've viewed on *The Oprah Winfrey Show*, where everyone's contribution is equally praised.

As a workshop instructor in both academic and nontraditional educational environments, I have tried to embrace my students' enthusiasms about writing in whatever form they show themselves. The idea that writing is therapy, however, is so counter to a productive workshop that I have taken issue with it often and early in my classes. When I've confronted and disputed this idea, though, I've been faced with challenges to my authority as a writer and as a teacher that, on occasion, have brought the class to a stand-still.

In workshops that I've taught in a nontraditional setting, there has often been a class period that goes something like this: a student reads a short piece of private writing to the class, and I point out some good things about the piece, talk about how it might be revised to be made more accessible to an audience and how it might evolve into something other than a personal diary entry. 'Good writing,' I say, 'is about language and craft. It is not merely about self expression.' Inevitably, the students look at me, some in disbelief. 'If this is rude, then I'm sorry,' a student once said, 'but you're wrong about that.' Others nodded in agreement. In academic workshops, these student attitudes are often suggested less overtly but underlie many comments.

The discussion that follows this sort of classroom exchange, while in some ways productive, is often extremely difficult. I talk about the expectations of an audience, and the ways in which writers address or complicate those expectations. I quote William Stafford (1978: 12): 'A writer is a person who enters into sustained relations with the language for experiment and experience not available in any other way'. I quote Richard Hugo (1979: 6): 'The words should not serve the subject. The subject should serve the words'. I talk about ways we evaluate good writing and remind students that the writer's experience writing a piece doesn't necessarily have direct relationship to the reader's experience reading or judging it as literature. I quote Hugo (1979: 10) again: 'Get off the subject and write the poem'. 'Does it matter,' I ask, 'if the writer worked through his feelings about a personal matter?' I answer my own question quickly, 'No. What matters is how well the writer crafted her sentences, how she's created her characters, and how I, as a reader, am able to participate in the piece.'

Some students seem amazed that I, the writing teacher, could be so ignorant about writing. Students in both academic and community settings often voice their disagreement:

'The reader can get what ever he or she wants from a piece of writing.'

'If the writer has grown by writing something, the reader will know it.'

'When someone tells about his emotions, the reader can see himself in the writing.'

'Honesty about your feelings is the most important thing in writing.'

'If you aren't writing about your true emotions, what's the point?'

Occasionally, such conversations become somewhat combative, as students argue that writing is primarily about the experience of the writer, that self-expression is an important goal of any kind of creativity.

During one class, very near the end of the class meeting, one student interrupted me as I was talking about my own love of language and how that that is a driving force in my own writing. 'What?' he said loudly, 'You don't express yourself in your writing?' I was left feeling certain that his final rhetorical question had been a significant blow to my authority in the classroom.

A great many beginning and sometime writers buy into the popular connection between writing and self-discovery. At a college or university, however, one can and should use various pedagogical paths to meet such ideas. I assign readings by writers who discuss the issues in question, I send students to the library to examine literary magazines to see what kinds of writing are being published, and I invite local and faculty writers to class to discuss their writing processes and their reasons for writing. All of this lends support to my claims about literary writing as a separate activity from private writing.

The nature of my community school classes – those taught in non-academic environments – didn't allow for these measures and, therefore, led me to value what might seem like burdensome or stifling faculty obligations or options. Though I suggested readings, and even handed out copies of essays and stories I thought might be particularly useful, students rarely read anything in preparation for class. In addition, I was prohibited from requiring students to buy any books for the class, and though I often mentioned must-read titles in class, I saw little evidence that students sought these books. Because of the informal, grade-free nature of the class, I had few tools with which to motivate students to do much outside of class. The pedagogical tools readily available for and often demanded of creative writing courses in traditional, academic settings – including attendance policies, participation guide-lines, required assignments, and grading criteria – should never be undervalued.

Academic writing workshops, of course, have their own problems. It can seem, for instance, difficult to apply grades to the creative work of undergraduates trying writing for the first time, especially because they bring to class the assumption that writing is primarily self-expression. It can be difficult, too, to convince such students of the values of reading widely and revising heavily. Nevertheless, the more formal setting of the academic classroom, in spite of its problems, enables teachers to command a certain authority. The academic class, with its necessary evaluation, grades, and course credits, provides instructors with the basic tools of authority. Though students in each setting may enter the class with the same ideas about writing, the instructors are differently equipped to address these assumptions, and the instructor in the academic setting is apt to be more successful. In both cases, individual students who are seriously interested in improving their writing skills show themselves. Yet, even the instructor in the academic setting has difficulty convincing students that writing for an audience differs significantly from writing in a private journal.

If all students were like-minded and interested primarily in writing as a means of personal problem solving, we could modify course goals accordingly. Even my community courses, however, were billed in the school's literature as advanced creative writing workshops, and each section had several members who were accomplished writers looking for a serious literary writing community, constructive criticism about their work, and tools for improving their writing skills. The goals of these kinds of students often come to be in conflict with the goals of class members who pursue writing in hopes of sorting out personal feelings and gaining spiritual insight.

The primary obstacle to many workshop goals is that many students have been sold an idea about writing that can prevent them from developing and improving the skills necessary to successfully write for an audience. The idea of writing one's way to recovery from all kinds of problems has been successfully marketed and merchandised and consumed by students everywhere. Creative writing, as promoted by bookstores, publishers, and the talk-show/self-help industry, has been commercialized in such a way that it has been transformed into a new kind of creativity. This new creative mode is uncritical, self-absorbed, and ultimately unproductive in that it so values process that it renders the final product nearly valueless. Thus, those who embrace this creativity praise all creative efforts and products equally.

That is the real irony of this new marketplace creativity. At first glance, one might see this idea of creativity as one that serves to make art and writing accessible to many. It would be easy to argue that this kind of artistic mode rescues creativity from a sort of elitism and makes it more egalitarian; once available only to those privileged with education, economic security, and leisure time, the *Oprah/Artist's Way* notion of creativity makes it available to anyone with a pencil and the inclination to express herself. Upon closer look, however, this connection between creativity and psychotherapy is relativist and deeply marketplace oriented, making adherents in college and in communities better consumers, not better writers.

If we hold with a model that ties art to personal well-being, we must accept the relativist notion that any creative work can be judged only with criteria specific to its making: if the writer learned something about her relationship with her father, then her story is a success; if the writer is comforted, the poem is a winning accomplishment. While I certainly don't feel there is one set of criteria by which writing ought to be judged, I also don't believe that there are infinite sets of criteria appropriate to that purpose. Relativism renders any classroom authority meaningless and may even eliminate the need for an instructor by eliminating all fixed criteria for judgment.

The role of the teacher in any classroom has been hotly debated for years, especially in college writing classes where popular pedagogical ideas, such as Peter Elbow's 'Teacherless Writing Class,' encourage instructors to surrender the trappings of traditional teacherly authority and act as a member of the class's 'writing community' (p. 76). Though I am extremely uncomfortable with a teacher-centered classroom in an educational model that asserts complete authority of the instructor as the keeper of knowledge and as the evaluator of quality, the total surrender of instructor authority that results from a relativist approach in the college classroom is at least as problematic.

If we allow writing classes to devolve into writing therapy groups where we give up all criteria for evaluating writing in exchange for equal praise and encouragement for all, we do damage to writing and to those students who aspire to write something other than private journals. Such classes are destined to be about writers, not about writing. Though I, as an instructor, may be uncomfortable acting as an arbiter of value and quality in students' writing, this role is an essential one for any teacher to play, even a teacher who resists the traditional classroom authority structure in other ways.

As long as the popular connection between writing and self-discovery remains profitable, instructors of creative writing workshops will increasingly face challenges to their authority and to the value of any writing process that incorporates criticism, revision, and audience expectations. Even if *Sex in the City* shows Carrie revising and rewriting her column as she works with an editor who cuts out sentences and whole paragraphs, even if writing actually looks like work and not like a clever pastime with which an introspective single girl might fill hours in a swank coffee shop, workshop instructors will undoubtedly have to continue to develop pedagogical approaches that employ authority as a positive force that redirects students' attention beyond the self to language, writers' choices, and the written text.

References

Cameron, J. (1992) *The Artist's Way: A Spiritual Path the Higher Creativity*. New York: Jeremy P. Tarcher/Perigee.
Damianakis, T. (2001) Postmodernism, spirituality, and the creative writing process: Implications for social work practice. *Families in Society: The Journal of Contemporary Human Services* 82 (1), 23.
Hugo, R. (1979) *The Triggering Town: Lectures and Essays on Poetry and Writing*. New York: Norton.

Meunier, A. (1999) Establishing a creative writing program as an adjunct to vocational therapy in a community setting. *Journal of Poetry Therapy* 12 (3), 161–8.

Moulin Rouge (2001) Dir. Baz Luhrmann. With Nicole Kidman and Ewan McGregor. Twentieth Century Fox.

Oprah.com: Online Journal. Retrieved August 8, 2001 from the World Wide Web: http://journals.oprah.com/journal. *The Oprah Winfrey Show*. Chicago, IL: Harpo Inc. Prod. Oprah Winfrey.

Rothman, J.C. and Walker, R. (1997) Prison Poetry: A medium of growth and change. *Journal of Poetry Therapy* 10 (3), 149–58.

Sex in the City. Prod. HBO. Michael Patrick King. With Sarah Jessica Parker.

Spera, S.P. *et al.* (1994) Expressive writing and coping with lob loss. *Academy of Management Journal* 37 (3), 722–34.

Stafford, W. (1978) *Writing the Australian Crawl: Views on the Writer's Vocation.* Ann Arbor: University of Michigan Press.

Chapter 2
Who Cares – and How: The Value and Cost of Nurturing

ANNA LEAHY

I agree with writer-teachers like Robin Hemley and bell hooks whole-heartedly when they assert that pedagogy depends, in part, on nurturing. Hemley (2000: 53; my italics) writes, 'The best teachers I've had have always been the most generous, the ones who were able to forget their own egos and *care* about their students, who take *time* with their students and their stories'. Likewise, hooks (1998: 231; my italics) in *Teaching to Transgress*, writes, 'To teach in a manner that respects and *cares for* the souls of our students is essential if we are to provide the necessary conditions where learning can most deeply and *intimately* begin'. However, I question what they mean by *care*. How do students perceive nurturing in conjunction with authority, whether it be in classroom discussions, in challenges to myths of what a writer is and does, in overt guidance in conferences, in grading policies, or in course evaluations? Might students' expectations for caring be especially high in creative writing, and expectations for freedom, praise, forgiveness, and high grades be high, too? If so, authority embodied by or granted to a teacher might be low. By extension, when the teacher exhibits authority, students might perceive her as uncaring, impersonal, and even inhibiting creativity, rather than as knowledgeable or helpful.

Though a graduate workshop – the typical graduate classroom community of writers in the United States – full of what Hemley's student called 'uninformed peers' may be ideal, I find that particularly the undergraduate workshop, in which students gather to share and respond to each other's work, does not necessarily suggest, as Hemley interprets his student's comment, 'that the students and teacher are all after the same thing while acknowledging that the teacher has more experience, and techniques and insights worth imparting' (p. 52). Kathaerine Haake (1994: 80) rightly notes that workshops run under all sorts of false, even damaging, assumptions, including 'that such workshops will be composed of homogenous groups of talented students with strong vocational commitments to writing' (p. 13). If the teacher has more experience, techniques, and insights and is in the position to impart, then students are not really her peers even though the workshop style fosters a sense of equality among all participants.

So, when I contradict that workshop model or the power the students feel within it, I meet with resistance. When I assign a journal dictionary as a way for students to track their own thinking and approaches in terms of particular aspects or concepts of creative writing (i.e. character, line, etc.), some students tell me, either face-to-face or in course evaluations, that critical writing distracts them from creativity itself. When I ask students to write in traditional form, some moan about how unnatural, and therefore uncreative, it is and about how it prohibits them from saying what they want to say. Many students seem to believe that they know what's best for themselves because they already know how to write and be creative. When I challenge their assumptions and authority, is this evidence of nurturing or of lack of caring?

I resist the role of teacher as mere stamp of approval; I offer praise, criticism, and guidance, sometimes in class discussion but more often in written comments or in one-on-one tutorial conferences. As Hemley rightly notes, praise makes students want to write more. However, focused criticism and guidance can make the student want to write better. Many creative writing students want a conversational, uncritical environment in which they can feel good about what they can already do, an environment they do not necessarily expect from other classes.

Certainly, I am often confirmed for asserting authority. I talk about analysis as learning to read and articulate selfishly as a writer, as a way to become a better critic of one's own work, and as placing individual creative pieces in a larger context. I talk about traditional form as a way to write lines one wouldn't think to write otherwise, as a way to focus intensely on diction, and as a way to learn how sound contributes to meaning. I steer away from discussion of feeling and into discussion of language; I discourage comments such as 'I can relate to that' and 'This is good because readers can read it any way they want to' and encourage comments about the problems of cliché and the value of ambiguity as meaning two things at once rather than nothing at all. Most importantly, I treat everyone's work as unfinished, always; I try to have an ongoing dialogue with individual students and try to convince students that a piece deserving of critical comments is a deserving piece. These attitudes and approaches are especially important in the introductory courses I teach, where students are learning to learn in a new way. When students in my advanced creative writing courses have skipped the prerequisite for whatever reasons, they flounder not only with clichés and overtelling but with their role in workshop discussion and revision to an even greater extent. In other words, the classroom is structured around the concept that the learning process, particularly for creative writers, involves moving beyond what one already knows and can do. To be uncomfortable, as a writer, is not a bad thing. Those students who take it all in, even occasionally with reservations, most often admit that they learn a lot, that empowerment is about confidence, motivation, and challenging oneself.

Yet, the process of taking it all in can be an exhausting struggle for everyone involved. Issues of authority are at the heart of the struggle. Creative writing itself is deemed feminine in relation to literary studies or literary theory and based on notions of creativity as a right-brain, intuitive, spontaneous, emotional process. Myths about writers include that we are quirky, impassioned, disorganized, even unreliable and eccentric folks who teach because we can't earn a living writing. The field of creative writing, creative writers themselves, and the workshop classroom are marked as feminine, regardless of the gender of the instructor.

A recent study of best and worst teachers, indicated by education students, divided traits into two categories: personal and instructional. The first group of personal characteristics of good teachers was dominated by traditionally feminine traits: caring and compassion, listening and understanding, respect for everyone, patience, the ability to make students feel special, and smiling and friendliness (Black & Howard-Jones, 2000). Good instructional characteristics included many valuable approaches: using group activities, making learning fun, strong classroom management and organization, providing guidelines, knowing and loving the subject, and flexibility (p. 4). My own institutional evaluations often indicate organization, knowledge, and enthusiasm as my teaching strengths. In this study, however, 'approximately 60% of all best teacher descriptors involved personal characteristics[,]' and most of the comments fell into the first group, dominated by feminine characteristics (p. 5). Caring is, by far, the most important characteristic for a good teacher to have, according to this study and according to another, done in 1997 by the National Board of Professional Teaching Standards. One would think that feminine behaviors – regardless of the instructor's gender – contribute positively to a teacher's effectiveness and that the creative writing classroom, with its discussion basis, flexibility of texts and topics, and small class size, is an especially good venue for these best-teacher characteristics.

Advice on these personal characteristics abounds. *A Handbook for College Teaching* spends fewer than two pages on 'professional competency' and follows with more than six pages on 'personal competency.' The latter section begins, 'An individual's personal characteristics determine the way that person is perceived by others. Physical characteristics are obvious, but there is very little relationship between an instructor's height, weight, color, or sex and instructional effectiveness' (p. 7). While this news is great to hear, for it allows me to believe, briefly, that those biological and cultural attributes over which I have the least control do not affect my teaching, this outlook contradicts itself. As I near the age of 40, student evaluation comments on my attire have lessened, but I'm not convinced that my gendered appearance has no bearing on student perceptions of my pedagogical approaches. The longest sub-sections of the handbook concentrate on interpersonal skills, consideration for students, and friendliness. Even praise receives its own, separate sub-section. The sub-section on friendliness begins by reminding, 'The instructor who meets both students and associates with a smile and a word of greeting finds it easier to work with them' (p. 11). This friendliness is posed as the opposite of 'being tough' and of bullying students (p. 11), as if there is no middle ground and a smile alone conveys 'patience, tact, and self-control' (p. 11). One student expressed on the institutional evaluation that I did not consider his individual needs and his life's demands because I didn't accommodate his excessive absences, though I accommodated them enough that he didn't fail the course based on the attendance policy. To be a good teacher, I must 'consider the feelings of others' (p. 10) and use compliments to 'spur people to increased productivity and satisfaction' (p. 11), as if productivity and satisfaction are nearly interchangeable and generated best by comments from someone in authority. Certainly, friendliness and understanding are positive attributes.

The mounting advice, however, presumes a pre-existing authority that takes masculine socialization (i.e. logical thinking, assertiveness, etc.) as the norm and poses feminine socialization (i.e. attention to relationships, orientation to process, etc.) as what must be cultivated. This presumption isn't valid in the workshop classroom, and we should have moved beyond these assumptions with recent emphases on writing as process and on collaborative learning. Why not presume that a teacher's authority is in flux and that interpersonal connection is a given, particularly for creative writing courses which rely heavily on sharing work, peer response, and even dismantling the lecture podium in favor of the decentered circle of chairs?

The creative writing classroom, especially one founded on the workshop model, fosters even higher expectations for nurturing because it supposes more interpersonal interaction and individualized attention. In a conference with one student, I faced the following question in response to suggestions for improving her essay: 'Why don't you like me?' In an article about student evaluations, gender bias, and teaching styles across disciplines, Susan A. Basow (1998) asserts that the female professor is marked by her gender and must satisfy dual roles of woman and professor, whereas the roles of man and professor are unified. Does creative writing feminize *professor*? Creative writing, after all, may seem less organized and hierarchical than other disciplines. I may have an agenda for talking about enjambment and metaphor, whereas students may think we're just talking. Kristi Andersen and Elizabeth D. Miller (1997: 217), in an overview of the interactions between gender and student evaluations, agree with Basow: 'If these are the [adversarial and authoritative] techniques that students associate with (the more numerous) male professors, women may not be perceived as "legitimate" professors and academics if they choose, for example, to use more participatory or cooperative teaching methods'. By asking young poets about their own writing habits and processes, does a creative writing teacher of either gender imply to students that creative writing is less legitimate because it doesn't merit the lecture podium? Are teachers like me in the feminized workshop then viewed as illegitimate or unprofessional by students and colleagues?

Very importantly, according to Basow, professors of either sex are perceived less favorably when they break gender stereotypes. Andersen and Miller (1997: 217) conclude the same: 'When confronted with women faculty, students expect a more nurturing role, but then judge that behavior as less professorial. On the other hand, if a woman is more assertive, students may perceive her as too masculine'. So, while female creative writing teachers might be judged as less professorial, male teachers in a workshop might be seen as unusually feminine. The smaller and more advanced the class, the better perceived I am as a teacher according to student evaluations. I see little coincidence that students in smaller classes tend to be friendlier, more supportive, and more consistently better prepared because they understand they have significant responsibility. Nor do I see much coincidence that students in advanced writing courses feel familiarity with me. Perhaps, I have less need to be either assertive or nurturing in these courses.

This study also finds: 'Women tended to focus more on the student as the locus of learning; men, on themselves. Although both sexes claimed to use an interactive style, women did so more extensively, taking more pains to involve students and to receive more input from students' (Andersen & Miller, 1997: 218). *Interactive* undoubtedly means different things to different teachers in different workshops. Certainly, though, *interactive* means something more extensive in a creative writing course than in many other courses. Perhaps, too, teacher characteristics mean something different when one starts with different presumptions. We may too easily think, 'I don't have any authority – it's a workshop.' I find, though, that even in a workshop circle, students tend to raise their hands or seek organization of the conversation from me and that students often address comments to me, especially in the first half of the term or when they express concern over interrupting each other. When I am silent, students notice; when a female student is silent, it seems to go unnoticed. Only I have the authority to encourage students to talk with each other rather than only to me. Creative writing presumes interaction in ways other fields do not because of the workshop model, which redefines rather than dismantles authority.

On a related note, Basow (1998: 146), in her cross-disciplinary research, argues 'warmth and relationships with students appear to be more important for female professors than male professors'. Creative writing, as a feminized study and with feminine class dynamics, emphasizes this warmth. Andersen and Miller (1997: 218) cite a study that confirms Basow's findings:

> Women received positive evaluations the more they interacted with students by acknowledging their contributions, responding to their requests, and 'personalizing' instruction by revealing their own experiences and bringing students' experiences into the classroom. Women were judged less likable if they did not interact extensively with students, instead choosing simply to present material. Men's competence ratings and likability ratings, on the other hand, were higher when they adhered to stereotypical masculine styles in their classrooms, using a 'teacher as expert' style: presenting material, admonishing, and interrupting students.

I would add that warmth and relationships with students appear more important for both male and female creative writing professors and that praise is perceived as very warm. Our teaching behaviors create contradictions, including, perhaps, lack of nurturing or lack of competence.

Regardless of the instructor's gender many writing students expect an A and understand a B, grades are taken personally within the highly interpersonal class, and grades lower than B are perceived as lack of an instructor's warmth, support, and understanding. Students in my recent workshop brought up resentment for instructors who seem to dole a single A per class; when I brought up that they all could earn As in the poetry course because work is judged individually according to criteria on the syllabus and assignment sheets, they indicated that criteria may be designed to prevent an excess of high grades. Basow (1998: 146) also claims, 'if students expect to receive a low grade, they tend to evaluate their female professor lower than they would a male professor from whom they expected to receive that same grade'. She goes on to assert that males are perceived positively when they use authority to maintain classroom control, whereas females are perceived positively when they disperse authority with a give-and-take discussion and student-focused activity (p. 150). How might I – or any workshop instructor – relinquish authority to the workshop and know that authority will be there when I need it, when it can be most useful for learning? Because the workshop model undercuts status and encourages so-called feminine behavior from the teacher, we can struggle, consciously or unconsciously, when our authority emerges, whether it be in directing discussion, correcting students' misconceptions, assigning particular tasks, criticizing a piece of writing, or assigning a grade.

Certainly, most teachers negotiate these issues. I balance workshopping with other activities, such as discussions of readings, group work, and writing exercises. I focus criticism around potential for revision, so that negative comments help students move beyond their limits. Very recently, for instance, I wrote a response to a student's poem that called the last two lines 'fantastic' but suggested that the preceding section should live up to and lead to those last two in much stronger ways; in other words, in seeing the great lines of the poem, I, as an informed reader, recognize the potential of other sections, potential that students sometimes don't believe their work has. I also carefully rationalize assignments and design tasks to push students beyond what they can already do adequately. I use the portfolio method to defer much of the grading so that students feel more comfortable taking risks and envision the process rather than the end.

I rely, in fact, on written documents, organized plans, and things I've done and said before, even when the class meetings seem spontaneously generated and meandering. Many women 'prefer the written to the spoken voice, because in this form they can project authority and influence without engaging in confrontations that raise confusing issues of appropriate response' (Aisenberg & Harrington,

1988: 74). Logically, writers of either gender might prefer the written to the spoken voice. These documents I create may be an attempt to offer the students an authoritative and separate voice about evaluation of the creative work to which they are personally tied and to assert authority quietly. However, this multi-vocal approach has its drawbacks for male and female instructors alike. How does my in-class conversation and occasional joking collide with a checklist rubric for a response essay on a published poem? As Jeffrey Wolcowitz (1982: 14–15) points out:

> Students will generalize from their observations of the instructor's behavior and will accept these generalizations as the implicit contract between themselves and the instructor, upon which they can rely in planning their classroom behavior. The explicit contract is quickly set aside, however, when the implicit contract that is reinforced at each class meeting sets a different standard.

As the daughter of two attorneys, I'm irked that students glean an implicit contract and choose to honor it *instead of* the written documents I so carefully prepare. And, yet, I know it to be true.

Hard work is required to adhere to all the explicit and implicit contracts in the workshop format, particularly because workshops can seem unstructured and friendly. James Wilkinson (1982: 7) discusses two particular dangers of discussion-based courses: 'The greatest risk they run is lack of structure' and students can perceive the class meetings as 'talk fests' in which they feel warmly supported but in which 'no generalization truly withstands scrutiny'. As the teacher, my frustration comes because my workshop sessions are very organized, and we accomplish specific goals. I realize, too, what Kenneth Eble (1983: 9) points out: 'Students know teachers by patterns of utterance, pet expressions, speech rhythms, and words of emphasis and organization. Eloquence is an acquired skill; distrustful as our time is of eloquence, the well-spoken person still commands both attention and respect'. So, I strive for speech that is conversational and also eloquent, that is friendly and also organized, that is tied to texts and concepts. I have learned, through comments on past institutional evaluations, that even eloquent sarcasm is not welcomed by students, and I've heard the same conclusion from fellow female faculty. Moreover, regardless of how free-flowing the workshop sessions might seem, I do not lose sight of the structured contracts, and I, perhaps mistakenly, expect the same from my students.

Another area in which I, perhaps, am not in sync with my students is in the need to be liked. As a student myself, I wasn't friends with my writing professors nor did I want them to like me as a person, but I did want them to take me seriously as a young writer. Frankly, I don't want to know personally about students' heartbreaks, their family tragedies, or their enlightening experiences at raves, though these subjects emerge in their writing as well as in conversation. Conversely, though advice abounds about sharing personal experiences to define oneself as human, I choose very carefully the personal information I reveal. While I don't consider myself unfriendly, I don't socialize with students outside of an academic context, and I don't encourage conversations that stray far from their writing, their college experience, or their future plans. Yet, I worry because 'A laboratory study in which students read descriptions of teaching situations of which half included out-of-class socializing with students found no difference between nonsocial and social males, but female instructors who were unfriendly outside of class received lower ratings' (Anderson & Miller, 1997: 217). Do creative writing students expect socializing outside of class, even perceive workshopping as socializing? I, perhaps again mistakenly, expect students to cultivate a situation in which they like me for what I encourage them to do in their writing.

In my search to construct that situation, Basow has numerous suggestions, some of which I've tried. She suggests talking about one's qualifications the first day, but I'm unsettled by selling myself with my credentials. The workshop model makes self-promotion anomalous or vain; after all, I don't want my students to write like me, a common criticism of workshop methods, so students needn't rush out in search of my poems in literary journals to make sure I'm what they want. Basow also suggests dressing professionally. In *The Aims of College Teaching*, Eble directly discusses how dress can help a professor cultivate presence. While he asserts that appearance should not be an overriding concern nor fodder for student course evaluations, he does argue, 'At all times, my appearance had to have some fit with what I was, if only to free me from being ill at ease, self-conscious, lacking in presence. [...] I can, and do, bring myself to the classroom with some sense of fit between my inner and outer selves that in an important way defines my presence' (1983: 7). Representing one's inner self with one's outer self might offer a way to bring the explicit and implicit contracts of a course more closely together, though I don't want nurturing determined by dashing attire. A former student ran into me recently and said, 'Oh, you look so cute today,' as if I had never looked cute before and as if my appearance was a great improvement – as if, in fact, she *liked me* more in my dashing winter garb. What's worse is that I then made a comment about her hair, though I also asked if she were still writing.

Basow has other suggestions as well. She encourages the use of one's title rather than first name, and, surprisingly, students at one institution where I taught did use 'Dr.' or 'Professor' until they gleaned clear instructions that it was appropriate to do otherwise. Using one's title instead of one's first name might backfire with some students in creative writing classes because its formality directly undercuts warmth. At my current institution, my students seem to avoid the issue as much as possible. One student adopted *Dr. L*, which is a version of what my coworkers at the Gap during graduate school called me, Dr. Anna. But that student graduated before she could pass along the professional-personal nickname so that it sticks.

Other suggestions that could offset the feminized workshop model include designing supplemental evaluation forms and reviewing course goals and accomplishments regularly. Standard evaluation forms are traditionally poor at addressing the successes of workshop-based classrooms. For instance, many evaluations ask students to rate the organization of the course or professor but fail to ask directly about aspects most relevant to creative writing courses. I design supplemental evaluations that ask about particularly useful tasks, students' sense of exactly what they learned about being writers and about the writing process, and students' roles in helping each other learn. Students should be encouraged to put into words, and therefore realize, what's going well and what they are accomplishing that is particular to course goals.

Evaluations do usually ask students to rate instructor accessibility. Creative writing students expect a high level of interpersonal interaction, and, for me, individual and small-group conferences accomplish more than many other activities. In conferences, I feel particularly adept at being a writing teacher, at being assertive and directive while encouraging an individualized exchange. Some students have begun to end the conference with *thank you*. Here, in the nontraditional academic setting, in the so-called feminine realm of interpersonal communication, I feel at ease with my authority and understand the value of asserting it. Students, too, seem to appreciate the *ah-hah* moments of conferences in which I create an opportunity for them to learn something specific and important about their own writing and even about themselves.

Yet, I'm disturbed to think that the authority of the workshop leader fits most seamlessly in the most traditionally feminine situations, in situations not always valued by the academy, and in especially time-consuming activities. Andersen and Miller (1977: 217) confirm my suspicions about accessibility too: 'Because women are assumed to be supportive listeners, they often have more advisory roles, without recognition from students. Because creative writing is feminized, students say they do get more time from women faculty, they do not report women as more accessible than their male counterparts'. Writing teachers of both genders probably don't get enough credit in this area. Successes in conferencing and in addressing difficulties through dialogue lead me to value accessibility. On the other hand, my parents did not allow me to take typing in high school because they feared I might be asked to do secretarial work instead of leadership tasks; be careful when your strengths lead you into devalued and exhausting roles.

Most importantly, though, the advice and research disheartens me because it implies I – as a writing teacher – must live up to a higher standard of, or at least put greater thought into, both feminine and masculine teaching behaviors than many colleagues. If I take Robert Mangan's (1990: 2) advice to 'Be an ego ideal,' for instance, I must display my character always in my teaching because 'since teaching is fundamentally a personal activity, our personality has a direct – and sometimes crucial – influence on the outcome.' But what if that personality contradicts expectations? More importantly, what happened to teaching as a fundamentally professional activity? Mangan goes on to suggest that I 'Be human – in class and outside. Inspire trust in students. Encourage them to express their ideas and opinions and feelings freely' (p. 2). That's good advice, and he does begin his advice with 'Be the expert' and 'Be the authority' (p. 1). However, I find all these identities do not always fit easily together in the workshop.

In other words, I feel pressure to both assert and undermine my authority and wonder whether my constant – sometimes conscious, often unconscious or unintended – negotiations of authority benefit my students. Do I use words like *rapport, enthusiasm*, and *availability* because they are integral to my pedagogy or because they appear on institutional evaluation forms? As Hemley (2000: 51) notes, 'anger, as we know, is a great motivator, sometimes better than the limp whip of praise. Good teachers are not the same necessarily as teachers who make their students feel good'. For various reasons – professional, pedagogical, and personal – I don't want a bunch of angry writers in my classrooms. Neither do I want to slip into the role of counselor. Instead, I strive for authority that both is a motivator and makes students feel good, that nurtures – feeds, brings up, trains, supports through stages of growth – creativity and writing skills in my students. As hooks (1998: 235; my italics) puts it, 'Within professional circles, individuals often complain bitterly that students want classes to be "encounter groups." While it is utterly unreasonable for students to expect classrooms to be therapy sessions, it is appropriate for them to hope that the knowledge *received* in these settings will enrich and enhance them'. Pedagogy should work to impart knowledge or wisdom that enriches students, and the authority-conscious creative writing classroom seems the ideal place for students to become enriched. I continually work, then, to contextualize caring within professionalism, to define nurturing as authority.

The key, it seems, is to allow one's authority to become an integral part of one's pedagogical approach. The teacher's authority is a benefit both to myself and to my students. I hope that my students, too, recognize the benefits, and I have the sense that many, especially those who care as students, do. My authority need not be a tool of institutional indoctrination or oppression, though if it is, then it is also a model for moving beyond indoctrination through one's own writing. Neither need my authority be discarded in favor of indulgence mistaken for caring. Instead, authority must remain part of my professional life in order that I can nurture my students as creative writers and foster the learning process that I myself value. Authority, therefore, is essential to caring, is the means by which I am able to care for my students as students.

References

Aisenberg, N. and Harrington, M. (1988) *Women of Academe: Outsiders in the Sacred Grove*. Amherst, MA: University of Massachusetts Press.

Andersen, K. and Miller, E. (1997) Gender and student evaluations of teaching. *PS: Political Science*. June, 216–18.

Basow, S.A. (1998) Student evaluations: The role of gender bias and teaching styles. In L.H. Collins, J.C. Chrisler, and K. Quina (eds) *Career Strategies for Women in Academe: Arming Athena*. Thousand Oaks, CA: Sage.

Black, R.S. and Howard-Jones, A. (2000) Reflections on best and worst teachers: An experiential perspective of teaching. *Journal of Research and Development in Education* 34 (1), 1–13.

Eble, K. (1983) *The Aims of College Teaching*. San Francisco, CA: Jossey-Bass Publishers.

Haake, K. (1984) Teaching creative writing if the shoe fits. In W. Bishop and H. Ostrom (eds) *Colors of a Different Horse: Rethinking Creative Writing Pedagogy and Theory*. Urbana, IL: National Council of Teachers of English.

Hemley, R. (2000) Teaching our uncertainties. *The Writer's Chronicle* 32 (4), 50–3.

hooks, b. (1998) Engaged pedagogy. In J. Zlotnik Schmidt (ed.) *Teaching to Transgress: Education As the Practice of Freedom. Women/Writing/Teaching*. Albany, NY: State University of New York Press.

Mangan, R. (1990) *147 Practical Tips for Teaching Professors*. Madison, WI: Atwood Publishing.

Miller, W.R. and Miller, M.F. (1997) *Handbook for College Teaching*. Sautee-Nacoochee, GA: PineCrest Publications.

Wilkinson, J. (1982) Varieties of teaching. In M. Morganroth Gullette (ed.) *The Art and Craft of Teaching*. Cambridge, MA: Harvard-Danforth Center for Teaching and Learning.

Wolcowitz, J. (1982) The first day of class. In M. Morganoth Gullette (ed.) *The Art and Craft of Teaching*. Cambridge, MA: Harvard-Danforth Center for Teaching and Learning.

Chapter 3

Inspiration, Creativity, and Crisis: The Romantic Myth of the Writer Meets the Contemporary Classroom

BRENT ROYSTER

Thumb through any issue of the Association of Writers and Writing Programs' *The Writer's Chronicle*, and you'll discover the salient concerns of many professional writers. Alongside commentary on writing programs, interviews, and personal narratives about craft and technique, readers also discover competition deadlines, conference announcements, and advertisements for academic writing programs. On the one hand, there exists an emphasis upon the writer as professional, as artist; on the other hand, there's guidance and encouragement for the writer as student. The first narrative concerns *being*, while the second describes *becoming*. The tension between these two concepts, as well as the daily demands of the writer's discipline, underscores the split within teaching creative writing in an academic setting and begs the recurrent questions implicit in professional discussions: does *real* creative writing depend upon natural talent? Can creative writing be taught?

Any writing involves a substantial investment of both time and intellectual engagement. If only the very talented compose poetry, fiction, or creative nonfiction of merit, the very task of writing regularly – and of teaching creative writing – seems a waste of time for the insecure or uncertain novice. In light of a highly competitive publication market, the unlikeliness of being recognized for one's contributions, and the great personal anxiety of peer criticism in workshop classrooms, one wonders why, or rather, how creative writing persists as a flourishing vocation.

One possible answer highlights the mythical presence poets have maintained for centuries. Specifically, the Romantic portrayal of the writer wholly disassociated from society invests the craft of writing with particular gift and purpose. Definitions of the Romantic writer are punctuated by such loaded terms as *creativity*, *genius*, and *imagination*. Even in literature courses, anecdotes of extra-worldly creative prowess

26

permeate the history of literature. Consider two examples. Coleridge claimed *Kubla Kahn* came 'all at once during an opium-induced dream.' The poem, however, was discovered in earlier, cruder drafts, proving that the poem changed over time, rather than being produced whole from the mind of genius (Weisberg, 1986: 115). Similarly, Jack Kerouac is said to have written *On the Road* in a matter of weeks, furiously typed on paper ingeniously taped together to form one long scroll. Though a modicum of truth may exist concerning the early drafts' form and immediacy, the novel went through a series of revisions and editions before its eventual publication.

Unfortunately, these Romantic representations of inspiration are perpetuated by creative writing trade journals and workshops, and such dramatic narratives illustrate the real crisis still plaguing creative writers: the need to be individual, gifted, prolific. In other words, some writers hope to be talented before being taught, before developing discipline, even before *becoming* writers. Essays in *The Writer's Chronicle*, *The Poet's Market*, and *Poets and Writers* focus upon issues of ownership and competition in the monolithic publishing industry. We witness the talent-oriented machinery at work as other young writers are instantly legitimated with book deals, awards, and talk-show appearances. For students, the writer's life must seem a schizophrenic tragicomedy of glitz on the book tour and loneliness in the garret, a life of euphoria and madness. The real work of writing, however, remains hidden from view. This split reveals an inherent conflict of interest found also in the creative writing classroom.

While we focus upon making poems-as-products in a system of gains and losses, we lose sight of what should be the real goal of workshops, or student communities of writers who share and critique each other's work: our aim is to foster more dedicated writers. Compositionists will recognize this conflict from the process-not-product debate begun in the late seventies, a debate which still affects contemporary writing pedagogy. Rhetoricians such as Linda Brodkey and Karen Burke Lefevre have insisted that we view composition as a socially constituted act in which writers are mediated by numerous identities. Over the last decade, composition and creative writing studies have often traded modes, and some creative writing teachers have applied recent process pedagogy in the workshop environment. Don Bogen's (1984) 'Beyond the Workshop,' for example, offers alternative pedagogical options for a workshop format. Bogen's claim is that workshops have come to rely upon ritualized standards and values for writing, and alternatives for students' voices have not been fully explored. Traditional creative writing workshops generally caution students against speaking about their process in favor of listening to peer criticism. A process-oriented workshop, however, assumes that writing is not a one-way performance, but rather a reciprocal engagement with audiences and selves; in other words, the process itself is a text. The written artifact, the life of the artist, and the culture play active roles in shaping artistry.

Other studies focus less upon the practices of creative writers and more upon the creative process itself. Specifically, Diane Marsh and Judith Vollmer (1991) study the personal narratives of artists to examine how process is internalized and communicated by individuals. By examining responses of artists, the authors repeal the 'relatively narrow conceptions of the creative process' (p. 106) and offer theoretical inquiry into the cognitive processes of creators in the midst of their work. Since creative acts are defined as multidimensional and fluid, Marsh and Vollmer's study demonstrates how any single recognition of the creative process may be limiting and presents a broad, 'comprehensive conception of the creative process' in order to take into account the varying influences and behaviors of working artists (p. 106). Applying this thinking to the workshop means that facilitators must resist the Romantic representation of the autonomous author, while also maintaining an awareness of the crisis between subjective agency and a dynamic creative process.

Considering some recent research into creativity, students might engage a revised notion of inspiration as a psychological nexus of recognition, in which cultural influences, as well as those of the craft's history, come into play during – or rather, preceding – composition. This understanding contradicts assertions that the poet is filled with the breath of God and that the creative work is, thereby, a product fully formed, unpremeditated, unconsciously formed by the writer who – until now – acts as the catalyst. With this revised definition of inspiration, Mihaly Csikszentmihalyi's (1999) 'Implications of a systems perspective for the study of Creativity' offers a persuasive model of how creativity takes place. His model, coupled with recent criticism of the creative writing workshop, can allow teachers to redefine methods used to teach such an unteachable discipline. If we accept that the writer is both social and individual, we then can look to applications that highlight the dynamic involvement each writer has already begun before taking up the pen. In so doing, we may revise staid assumptions about the craft, notions we have already accepted, by and large, and which we continue to bequeath the burgeoning writers in our creative writing groups.

Writers everywhere struggle against seeming pretentious when claiming the lofty role of the writer. The hidden assumption in dubbing oneself a writer holds that if we can define writing, especially good writing, then we can also perform it. Australian author Kevin Brophy (1998: 187) notes this very real reluctance to call oneself a writer: 'I am a creative writer. I do it, but I cannot easily talk about it or analyze it. More accurately, perhaps, I think I do it – though I might have borrowed some vain emperor's non-existent new clothes – and who can I trust to tell me if I have?'. Since the writing process is in a perpetual state of flux, authors continually question their own performance of the craft – and others, too, question their legitimacy. With this crisis in mind, one might argue that a writer is a person in the process of *becoming* a writer.

To assuredly point to the writerly self and stake a claim in that esoteric territory seems to imply a moment of stasis never reached. Retellings of inspiration likewise limit our full recognition of the creative process and its attendant influences. Timothy Clark notes that authors often narrate an unrealistic scene of the inspired, or creative, moment. Writing and speaking about writing becomes a sort of sleight-of-hand trick, in which the author performs without showing the functions and underpinnings of that performance. Clark (1997: 1) recognizes the illusion taking place and cites an early confession by Edgar Allen Poe: 'Most writers – poets in especial – prefer having it understood that they compose by a species of fine frenzy – an ecstatic intuition – and would positively shudder at letting the public take a peep behind the scenes [...]'. Clark insists that the subjectivity of the writer is a site of inevitable conflict, and his theory of inspiration relies upon a 'crisis of subjectivity at odds with any humanist mythology of psychic power' (p. 11). For the student writer, the workshop is the most immediate influence, and the forum often can be a psychologically grueling experience. On the one hand, when the class widely accepts the writing and its writer, the praise generated can indenture the writer to a life of solitude and dedication. On the other hand, seemingly immediate rejection and correction can be devastating.

As a result of the increasing drive for creative writing and writers to be legitimated in an expansive industry, critics question the growth of creative writing in the academy. D.G. Myers (1996), for instance, delineates the creative writing program's illustrious, dynamic history but notes the inevitable concern with teachability. Joseph Moxley's (1989) collection bemoans the split between creative production and other modes of literary study. Greg Kuzma (1986), too, argues that writing programs confine writers, which leads to the inevitable decline in academic and artistic standards. Some critics, however, defend the traditional antagonism between creative writers and the rest of the English department. Proponents of the current workshop format argue that the workshop serves to weed out untalented, unmotivated students. What's more, some see the workshop as a way of tempering writers to criticism, while also providing lessons in audience expectation. Of central concern in this ongoing discussion is that this publication-oriented role of the workshop is at cross purposes with the real goals of workshop pedagogy. In short, the workshop focuses too much upon the products of the writer, whereas too little is done to nurture the process of the writer.

This diversity is reflected in how writers view their own process, and it also illustrates the way writers critique the existing teaching of creative writing. In the September 1999 issue of *English Journal*, Michael Lloyd Gray argues that the workshop method, currently practiced in many MFA programs, is 'faulty and needs modification' because the system focuses primarily upon the failures and inadequacies of individual students. By his account, workshop participants too often assume that since the material being submitted has been authored by fellow students, the workshop's role 'becomes a quest to ferret out the flaws.' For this reason, workshops are unhelpful and even destructive. Gray concludes that one way to address the workshop's inadequacy is to shift the focus from 'how' writers write to 'why' writers write. It seems clear that many writers romanticize their daily practice by leaving out the struggle involved in writing: the regular stints at the keyboard, the hours spent tinkering with one word after the next, the downright torture of the creative writing workshop. Or, these attributes are exaggerated, so that the task of being a writer is one of never ending struggle and pain. Both versions of the story leave all sorts of details out of the picture. Both versions also tend to emphasize the writer as an isolated genius, a producer of art, a literary machine who serves as a conduit for divine inspiration – the source of artistry.

Claims of inspiration discount the vast milieu of cultural influence that defines creative work. Compositionist Derek Owens refutes the idyllic and misleading notion of the universal *I* and asserts that the persona is a construct of selves both complex and infinitely untranslatable. He points out that style is an accommodation to comfortable and familiar norms, and the variety of styles present at any historical moment is testament to the fluid and complicated methods by which individuals represent themselves to an audience. These representations, or manifestations of rhetorical styles, can be 'envision[ed] as relative fictions or "masks" which writers present as one of many possible identities.' In short, all writing is performance. Moreover, 'To write (or paint or perform or compose) is to fashion not so much our identities but bridges that connect various facets of our experience within an incomprehensibly dense and unmapped personal landscape' (Owens, 1993: 165). Owens' assertion is key to the contemporary creative writing workshop, where students analyze dominant representations of style in order to offer alternate representations.

The crisis of subjective agency is certainly central to the stance writers take concerning both the production and consumption of creative writing. Brophy (1998) mediates the dilemma between writer and audience or between, in Csikszentmihalyi's terms, the *individual* and the *domain*. Noting the conflict within what the writer must see as the central purpose of the craft, the daily practice, as it were, Brophy (1998: 99) states, 'it is useful to come to some understanding of how tricky is the writer's part of the bargain struck between writer and reader. Perhaps too by spending some time writing creatively we can be moved towards greater awareness of what we are as readers'. In essence, this crisis of subjective agency melds writer with audience, makes the two seem less distinguishable, and reveals the integral parts they share. Brophy notes that when workshop participants insist upon being – or becoming – creative, their experience of self is inevitably limited. By contrast, Brophy calls for a workshop environment that does not depend upon formalized and rigid construction of authorial selves, but rather for an environment that separates creativity and authorship. Such a workshop offers freedom that the Romantic-driven workshop obscures by its own individual-centered rhetoric. 'It is possible to experience a model of writing which helps expose the illusions attached to the myth of the author as an original and individual source for texts' (p. 47). Definitions of *inspiration, creativity*, and *genius* assume that the individual is the sole agent in the production of remarkable work, and it is our job as writers to reconfigure these terms.

I'm not arguing that brilliant creations do not exist. After attempting to critically unmask great works of science and art as mere cultural constructs, essayist Benjamin Taylor (1995: 2) deduces, 'what was "higher" turned out not to be a cover for something else; what was "higher" turned out to be higher'. His assertion, then, is that while we can certainly see that social, cultural, and economic forces bear influence upon the creative act, the act itself contains no less measure of genius. In fact, he continues, the current concept is one grand delusion which humankind would suffer to dismantle: 'Genius, the Romantic idea of man transcending himself, is what we cannot not believe in' (p. 2). In the same vein, Timothy Lensmire and Lisa Satanovsky (1998) explore the impact of Romanticism upon contemporary writing workshops. The Romantic mythos, they argue, is attractive to new writing students, who face a creative process that is difficult to describe and investigate; the Romantic view of the artist as an autonomous agent, performing unconsciously, relieves artists of certain burdens. Recognizing the conflict between Romantic individualism and postmodern decentering, though, Lensmire and Satanovsky still rely upon terms such as *freedom*, which reiterates the Romantic notion and which is, for the most part, a lie to students itching to effectively express. So, it's not necessary to refute the concept of creativity, but we should assume that our definition of creativity must be expanded to include the vast matrix of influence which determines any creative act.

Csikszentmihalyi's model, simply put, refutes the idea that solely the individual generates a creative work. On the contrary, though his dynamic model of creativity still illustrates the individual's role in the creative process, equal agency is distributed among the social and cultural systems influencing that individual. Csikszentmihalyi's model names three interrelated loci of activity functioning all at once in the creative process, and these points of contact are what he terms 'dynamic links of circular causality' (1999: 329). According to his theory, 'each of the three main systems – person, field, and domain – affects the others and is affected by others in turn. One might say the three systems represent three "moments" in the same creative process' (p. 329). What's more, Csikszentmihalyi articulates time's significant role in determining the creativity of any act or artifact. Although some consider particular literary values to be common sense, a systems view of creativity illustrates how the passage of time and the evolution of taste affect the creative process.

Here's a recent example of the system at work: A few years ago, I assigned a collection to my creative writing workshop that I felt was an example of remarkable work. That collection, Campbell McGrath's (1996) *Spring Comes to Chicago*, is a delightful exploration delivered from the perspective of a blocked writer, sitting at his computer, near his window, reading *People* magazine, and thinking about the snow falling outside and the diabolical squirrels chattering nearby. What feels at first like a joy ride through oblivion turns out to be an accurate indictment of culture, money, the monumental task of excavating snow from one's sidewalk, and, of course, the egg rolls at Ho Wah Garden.

I requested that my students read the book because 'The Bob Hope Poem' blends poetic genres, from haiku to Whitmanesque catalogues, in sharp, precise, and elegant language. Moreover, I felt that the work represented some powerful ideas, and, for this reason, I suggested that my students keep track of McGrath's destined greatness. Several months later, I discovered that McGrath received a MacArthur genius grant – $380,000 over the course of the five years and one of the most prestigious awards for creative persons. While I must admit I felt redeemed, having aptly judged McGrath's work, I also winced at the economic strata that McGrath himself had called into question in *Spring Comes to Chicago*. The disparity between the haves and have-nots in the American literary scene is indeed almost as stark as the larger economic system in which such generous patronage is made possible.

It is, indeed, difficult to reconcile the fortune of a few gifted individuals with the squalor, isolation, and even suffering of countless other talented folks, but Csikszentsimalyi's model does offer an explanation for the way these influences function. Essentially, a caucus of esteemed individuals (the field) decides that McGrath (the individual) exhibits attributes of genius, his oeuvre is selected and instantly legitimated as a valid poetic achievement, and then his clout and the final editorial stamp of approval is transmitted to a larger collective readership (the domain). Given the element of time, this readership influences and is influenced by a set of working writers and is continually altered by past writers whose work is finally validated by the field. What we also see by this example is that fields vary, according to criteria for determining creativity and genius. Kenneth Hope (1993: 117) asserts that the MacArthur fellowship program's 'conception of creativity...is closely linked with the human attributes of curiosity: the love of exploration and discovery, a passion for making things, for seeing things anew, for tackling intractable problems, and the quest for growth, mastery, quality, and beauty'. The system works because there is social agreement upon the relative greatness of each selected (or refuted) work and, in this case, a defined set of criteria for assessing potential genuises. Though one may assume that great work exists and should be revered, the key issue, however, is how we view the creative process that spawned the great work.

This rethinking of the creative process does not discount the creative works that continue to be produced and discovered. In fact, some Romantic views of genius still work within the constraints of the dynamic model. For instance, when Benjamin Taylor (1995) asserts that the Romantic ideal of genius is 'something we cannot not believe in,' his main concern is that we do injustice to the keen faculties of individuals if we neglect to view excellence for what it's worth. Taylor relies upon an antiquated model of genius which gives sole possession of creative ability to the individual, but the model of the creative person to which he refers is not at odds with a dynamic view of creativity. He quotes from Diderot's 18th-century encyclopedia entry to describe the creative individual 'whose ranging soul occupies itself with all that is in nature, receiving from her no idea that is not roused by [a] distinctive play of emotion' (Taylor, 1995: 13). A striking resemblance exists between this definition and the MacArthur Foundation criteria. Yet, neither definition suggests that the individual is not acted upon by a host of significant influences. Rather, the individual and a host of other influences together define the creative process.

We see the process taking place at every level, but certain behaviors of particular individuals seem especially keen, and usually these are behaviors claimed to have been performed unconsciously: stories composed in an afternoon; poems that transfix the mind in wonder; portraiture leaping from the paintbrush, stunningly alive and with depth of feeling. Though the individual claims to have been inspired, these moments of heightened intensity illustrate a psychic state in which all three fields interact simultaneously. Consider the inspired moment when a poem leaps from the writer's imagination. Rather than claiming that this inspiration came from somewhere beyond the writer, it seems more apt to suggest that the mind of the artist has reached an opportune moment in which rhythms, sounds, and connotations seem to arise unbidden from memory. And yet, understanding that all these poetic constructs rise from memory, then memory and the knowledge within the individual are bound by a particular field, a particular domain, and a particular time period.

The workshop, then, is a hybrid classroom. The *work* of the class is the daily practice of writing, and the shared process of that practice. The *shop*, on the other hand, represents the daily critique that validates (or invalidates) the writer's work. The individual, the field, and the domain are evident. Each workshop participant is, of course, an individual charged with altering the transmitted codes from the domain; this newly organized information is then transmitted to the field – fellow workshop participants, including the workshop facilitator; the attributes of the new information are assessed, suggestions for alteration provided, and, in some cases, work may be immediately legitimated or devalued. If we view all three influences as equally affective in the system, the workshop can thereby foster the creative process and alternatives for investigating this process.

What, then, is at stake if a dynamic model is never implemented in the creative writing classroom? If creative writing workshops are growing in popularity, why is a revised notion of creativity and a restructuring of the workshop necessary? Simply put, a product-centered pedagogy stifles growth. Such a system places too much emphasis upon subjective agency, too much emphasis upon particular, validated modes of writing, while devaluing other valid, though unfashionable, styles and voices. Equally important is an awareness of those students whose abilities are driven by an intense need to know or, rather, to explore. Writer and teacher Stephen Minot (1976) cautions instructors not to proselytize by projecting specific values about creativity and what should be considered good. Rather, he suggests that teachers 'draw on a full range' of tastes and address particular student motives for coming to the creative writing classroom (p. 392). Many students delight in tinkering with language or are fascinated by the writerly mystique, some value current trends in writing and theory, and still others wish to explore writing as an extension of political aims. In other words, if we place too much emphasis upon individual poems or stories submitted to workshop, we may neglect to consider the real reasons students enroll in workshops and the variety of benefits they might gain. To this end, Minot (1976: 394) suggests that teachers read these motives and address them through course design: 'When we fail [to consider students' motives,] we begin to reward those whose approach to writing mirrors our own and unconsciously punish the rest'.

Minot's compassionate, sensitive, and proactive approach to teaching creative writing points us to yet another difficulty facing creative writing teachers: assessment. As teachers, those of us who draw upon process pedagogy to inform our grading practices are especially challenged in conversations about outcomes and objectives. It seems only fitting to bring this conversation into the classroom. As teachers, we already ask our students to consider audience, and we oftentimes compose assignment sheets that offer a situation to ground student writing. Oftentimes, these assignment sheets will include guides; for instance, there's the ever-present 'college-educated readership' some folks include in order to suggest that students choose the appropriate 'tone.' In this case, 'tone' implies a particular attitude and intensity of language directed toward the reader. Usually, noting that the readership is both enlightened and relatively stuffy, students will take on a bland sort of non-writing. In essence, there are conventions for the creative writing classroom – many of them unstated – which students are expected to abide by. It is our complex role, then, to see that students abide by certain conventions, while at the same time thinking beyond them. Geoffrey Chase (1988: 13) suggests that we examine these conventions, decode what our classroom practices signify in the larger cultural construct, the university. '[B]efore we ask students to engage in certain sets of conventions, we need to know how these conventions operate on the larger, theoretical level, and the implications of those conventions for our student'.

Wendy Bishop (1997) addresses one student motivation in a brief article entitled 'Poetry as a therapeutic process: realigning art and the unconscious.' She describes a classroom that encourages students' exploration and personal statement but that also recognizes the academic and aesthetic motivations that demand students resist Romantic and altogether disingenuous representation. She suggests that a confessional mode might allow students to develop authentic voices; such an authentic voice involves the reader in the writer's felt personal experience and offers the author an avenue for therapeutic healing. Most importantly, Bishop (1997: 262) calls for fresh ways of talking about writing that enliven the workshop environment: since 'poetry is the stuff of the self', the workshop should offer an environment where authors exist without presumption, without undue influence because motives for writing are varied and dynamic. The workshop environment, while not a therapy session, should foster continual writerly process and growth, rather than expect and reward finished products.

One effective way to affirm this growth process is to underscore the assumption that all writing is culturally mediated and that ideas are shared, even in their most inspired forms. In a brief study of creativity, Fern Tavalin (1995) articulates several key assumptions for the workshop that examines the constructedness of a writer's position. First, writers and their works are never fully formed, especially not in draft form – and talking through drafts offers an avenue for student writers to recognize the impression their work provides for a diverse, live audience. Additionally, one's knowledge and performance of any craft is cumulative and infinite; since writing is a continual process, young writers may avoid stylization and stagnation of craft and may look to innovative ways of constructing new work (Tavalin, 1995: 140).

One major criticism of the workshop atmosphere is that it is often passionless and uncreative and, therefore, engenders disengaged, even mechanical writing. A way to revitalize the art is to give back to the creative writing student what is most desired: an individual perspective. While the assumptions here figure the writer as constructed by a larger cultural context, the individual is a necessary component of the *becoming* matrix. Moreover, creative writing teachers can promise a great deal of rigorous, active writing and thinking; we can also point toward a wellspring of energy for writing and thinking about our perspectives and offer ways we might engage and resist various constructions. The creative writing workshop can facilitate the formation of self and voice – not by deterministic frames for authenticity and not by Romantic illusions of the writer's life, but by multimodal, multivocal exploration of text and craft.

References

Bishop, W. (1997) Poetry as a therapeutic process: Realigning art and the unconscious. *Teaching Lives* (pp. 252–63). Logan: Utah State University Press.

Bogen, D. (1984) Beyond the workshop: Suggestions for a process oriented creative writing course. *Journal of Advanced Composition* V, 149–61.

Brophy, K. (1998) *Creativity: Psychoanalysis, Surrealism, and Creative Writing*. Victoria, Australia: Melbourne University Press.

Chase, G. (1988) Accommodation, resistance, and the politics of student writing. *College Composition and Communication* 39, 13–22.

Clark, T. (1997) *The Theory of Inspiration: Composition as a Crisis of Subjectivity in Romantic and Post-Romantic Writing*. Manchester University Press.

Csikszentmihalyi, M. (1999) Implications of a systems perspective for the study of creativity. In R.J. Sternberg (ed.) *Handbook of Creativity*. Cambridge: Cambridge University Press.

Gray, M.L. (1999) Method and madness in the creative writing workshop. *English Journal* 89 (1), 17–19.

Hope, K. (1993) Giving it away at the MacArthur Fellows Program. In J. Brockman (ed.) *Creativity*. New York: Simon & Schuster.

Lefevre, K.B. (1987) Invention as social act. *Invention as a Social Act* (pp. 33–47) Carbondale: Southern Illinois University Press.

Lensmire, T. and Satanovsky, L. (1998) Defense of the Romantic poet? Writing workshops and voice. *Theory into Practice* 37, 280–8.

Kuzma, G. (1986) The catastrophe of creative writing. *Poetry* CXLVIII, 342–54.

McGrath, C. (1996) *Spring Comes to Chicago*. New York: Ecco.

Marsh, D. and Vollmer, J. (1991) The polyphonic creative process: Experiences of artists and writers. *Journal of Creative Behavior* 25, 106–15.

Minot, S. (1976) Creative writing: Start with the student's motive. *College Composition and Communication* 27, 392–4.

Moxley, J.M. (ed.) (1989) *Creative Writing in America* (pp. 159–75). Urbana: National Council of Teachers of English.

Myers, D.G. (1996) *The Elephants Teach: Creative Writing Since 1880.* Englewood Cliffs, NJ: Prentice-Hall.

Owens, D. (1993) Composing as the voicing of multiple fictions. In A. Ruggles Gere (ed.) *Into the Field* (pp. 159–75). New York: Modern Language Association of America.

Tavalin, F. (1995) Context and creativity: Listening to voices, allowing a pause. *Journal of Creative Behavior* 29, 133–42.

Taylor, B. (1995) *Into the Open: Reflections on Genius and Modernity.* New York: New York University Press.

Weisberg, R.W. (1986) *Creativity: Genius and Other Myths.* New York: W.H. Freeman.

Chapter 4

Reinventing Writing Classrooms: The Combination of Creating and Composing

EVIE YODER MILLER

The authority of blending reading, thinking, and writing skills into a useful whole serves the common goals and strategies of composition (general college writing) and creative writing classrooms in which literature – reading established texts – are models for students to consider in making choices about their own writing styles. This pedagogical position relates to Edward O. Wilson's view that the 'ongoing fragmentation of knowledge and resulting chaos in philosophy are not reflections of the real world but artifacts of scholarship' (Wilson, 1998: 8). While he refers to gaps among large disciplines such as the natural sciences, social sciences, and humanities, the same principle for consilience applies within the main areas of English study. People in college and university English departments function more efficiently and encourage more positive growth to students' lives when we see our areas of specialization as complementary, rather than competitive. Creative writing is, in fact, integral to everything we do in all our classrooms. Moreover, issues of authority in teaching creative writing can be managed by integrating creative writing, composition, and literature.

The nature of writing and the goals for teachers and students are foundational to the writing assignments that we develop as creative writing teachers. I expect to see playfulness *and* reasoning at work: I create writing assignments that require both imagination and skill in shaping ideas. Either emphasis in writing requires mastery of conventions: a thesis for composition assignments, appropriate use of point of view for fiction writing. Both analytical and imaginative writing require development of ideas and appropriate use of mechanics. Students must think of writing as a process with either type of writing, not simply an end-product. My goal – and I hope theirs – is to generate ideas, focus intent, and put everything together in a pleasing way.

Issues of authority may be most responsible for our failures to cooperate and to complement. Those who have authority in an English department may not want to recognize others who seek it, as if their own esteem may be reduced if they surrender any portion. Those who don't have authority may feel that they must fight and scrap for every bit of respect. This adversarial relationship damages everyone by promoting hostility among faculty and by suggesting for students a narrow vision of what the study of English means.

The pressure to carve individual turf starts early. From positioning ourselves for the most interesting composition courses – most often first-year, general education courses that prepare students for college writing across the curriculum – as graduate teaching assistants, to drafting a dissertation proposal with an unusual perspective, to marketing ourselves as candidates in tight job markets, we are encouraged to develop and emphasize our own distinctiveness, often at the expense of other equally-talented grad students. Once hired, we may become rancorous with our colleagues over how many English courses are offered in our specialty area, over the ratio of required courses for literature and writing emphasis majors. We may fight each other for the brightest students and for enough students to fill our upper-level courses so they're actually offered. We quarrel for what little prestige remains. Contributing factors come from forces outside English departments also. As universities increasingly become diminished by a reliance on business principles and that ever-present bottom line, English departments carry less weight because they don't produce graduates who immediately command large salaries. Increasingly, we fall into the category of being viewed by others as service departments, supporting other educational programs in the university. Creative writing faculty may work to create a niche or name for themselves in the institution.

Chris Green, in an article in *College English*, notes that 'the relationship of creative writing programs with the rest of an English department is often a point of contention and difficulty' (Green, 2001: 156). Creative writing is often considered less intellectual, more instinctual, and thus given a place on the fringe of English studies. Historically, both creative writing and composition have been assigned positions below literature and criticism. Perhaps because neither wants to be the 'lowliest,' composition and creative writing have fought to distinguish themselves as different types of writing, thus discouraging the transfer of skills from one to the other. Contrary to prevalent thought, composition is not the so-called *other* to creative writing, nor vice versa. We can design

English courses to lessen these tensions and increase collegiality. Rather than fighting to be different, both so-called camps can learn from the other.

While composition is often more informational and seemingly academic in its purpose, and while creative writing is often more imaginative, the two kinds of writing are more similar than different. Both composition and creative writing involve creating and composing. Both are grounded in some degree of reality, and both involve some use of the imagination. Both kinds of writing include the subjectivity of the writer. As David Smith says, '"creative" when applied solely to fiction, drama, or poetry is largely a misnomer ... all writing that has interest, value, passion, durability, and vision is necessarily creative' (quoted in Moxley, 1989: 26). Yet, to further complicate the labels that are intended to define types of writing, we've added creative nonfiction as a genre based on reality but that is perceived as more creative than other reality-based writing.

I don't mean to disparage all distinctions; these terms are useful to some degree. Wendy Bishop (1997: 228) asserts that our categories of genre are useful 'to maintain order within our communities.' I think I've failed in some way when my student labels her first short story 'Essay #1' and when another student refers to his personal essay as 'a little story.' What I'm arguing against is the effort to valorize in direct or subtle ways one type of writing over another. Students often perceive composition to be required writing, while creative writing is voluntary – an elective course – and, therefore, fun. Teachers may see first-year composition courses as drudgery, while creative writing courses are prized because of the opportunity to relate to smart students who thrive on the unorthodox. As writing teachers, though, we can model authority through collegial cooperation. We can help our students see the overlap between composition and imaginative writing, see that both are important, energizing work.

While creative writing has sometimes struggled for legitimacy within English departments, imaginative writing is not only for those inclined toward the artistic. Seeing the world metaphorically can improve any writing and can be a goal for students in all writing courses. Wilson (1998: 218) refers to metaphors as 'the building blocks of creative thought. They connect and synergistically strengthen different spheres of memory'. For example, a principle from physics – every action has an equal and opposite reaction – may strengthen a point about the sequence of historical events. Not only do metaphors connect ideas across disciplines and subjects, they also enhance different types of writing. Hans Ostrom (1994: xxi) puts it this way: 'It may well be that (so-called) imaginative writing has a greater role to play in (so-called) basic and first-year writing; one old assumption is that students had to master skills before they produced literary art, but increasingly it seems as if the connections among skills, mastery, creativity, and so forth are more complicated and less linear than we have assumed'. Ostrom's point argues for the integration, rather than the separation, of analytical and creative writing. Both are part of a basic literacy that college students need.

Psychoanalytic theory also reminds us that writing is not simply about the product. In the same issue of *College English* that carries Green's article, Judith Harris (2001: 183) writes, 'There is a need to broaden the *concept* of the writing act so that it will include not only the writing product but also the human being who is endeavoring to write'. We need to consider the most common goals of an undergraduate student when we plan teaching strategies. Students often write out of a desire for self-expression. While this motive is important, it may not be inclusive enough. David Radavich (1999: 111) states this point well when he says, 'any creative writing course worth its enrollment needs to teach reading, critical thinking, and awareness of historical context, as well as the particulars of form and evocative expression'. As teachers, we can push students beyond the obvious reasons to write, beyond what they can see easily. Few of our students will reap wealth from their creative endeavors, but many can benefit from instruction that presents discussions of form and content. Rather than viewing creative writing for undergraduates as an end in itself, it can be taught in the context of writing that has both beautiful *and* useful functions.

Whether students create characters bent on murder in an imagined world or argue vigorously for the elimination of the death penalty in our all-too-real world, they try to make sense of themselves and their world. 'Writing venues of all kinds can help students to assume more responsibility for themselves and for their world' (Harris, 2001: 185). As teachers, we often help students see their own contradictory impulses as they show up on paper. Without playing therapist or counselor, I can ask questions about what I see emerging in a student's thinking. I can show the student the slipperiness of language; I can illustrate where language both reveals and conceals, how words allow us to shape – or misshape – our ideas. I don't need to criticize or validate the emerging voice of the writer, so much as I need to keep on asking for more, asking any writing student to continue thinking and searching for the most precise words, the most apt metaphor, to accurately express ideas and communicate emotion.

Sometimes I wonder whether my teaching methods come from composition pedagogy or fiction-writing theory. Then I wonder why the question of origin matters. Like most creative writers in university settings, I was trained as a teaching assistant to teach composition and as a student to teach creative writing. I've taken bits and pieces and blended them in the courses I teach. Sometimes my theory leads to practical application; sometimes my practice informs my theoretical stances. Through borrowing and pasting together theory and practice, I ultimately ask students to identify what it is they want to say. I push them to consider the creative and compositional options of writing their ideas effectively and memorably. They might reconsider their diction and syntax; they might insert short narratives or rhetorical questions in the middle of explaining a persuasive stance; they might revise a poem by removing all pronouns.

What's of primary importance is that students learn to be confident in their own writing, that they hear the authority of their own experiences and voices. When they can find for themselves the appropriate words and shape to fit the rhetorical situation, then they will have demonstrated the most important authority of the teacher: the ability to pass on knowledge. Writing classrooms are for students' advancement, not for teachers' egos. I'm not creating younger versions of myself but helping students experience a broader range of writing possibilities.

Hence, my authority – what I have of it in the larger institution – teeters as I say, 'Try this.' I teach both composition and creative writing at a regional campus of a large university in the Midwest of USA. As is common for many newly hired creative writers, I teach more first-year students than any other group. Less frequently, I teach creative writing, fiction writing, or advanced composition. In any writing course, though, I require that students practice, analyze, and revise. All writing assignments, if effective, involve personal belief and passion. All result in mixtures of success and failure. For successful work in their ongoing academic experience, students need practice writing clear sentences and presenting ideas in logical, comprehensible ways. They need to be able to explain clearly the knowledge they're discovering. I might require a comparison/contrast essay about two stories, discussing the stories in terms of sibling conflict or their shared theme of rebellion as a necessary component of maturation. This kind of assignment encourages clear organization and the ability to understand one story in light of another. For beginning creative writing students, an analytical assignment might also include an oral presentation and a short, accompanying essay about one of the formal features at work in an essay, story, or poem (its circular structure or its repeated images of physical labor). My teaching goal is for students to explain an element of how a poem works, while acknowledging that there are always parts of a poem's effectiveness that go beyond articulation.

Sometimes in an attempt to prepare students for college work, our middle schools and high schools have squelched this imaginative voice in favor of the more stereotypically scholarly writing. The converse also happens; some students' past writing experiences fail to demand rigorous, critical writing in favor of emotive expression: 'But this poem is what I feel, and besides, my boyfriend likes it.' An imaginative perspective on the world, commonly found in children, can also be put to good use in academic work, making the student's writing more interesting, playful, and personal. In these cases, the student wants to convey knowledge less directly. Here I often face conflicts with students' expectations because I take students with varied writing backgrounds and nudge them in directions where they may be uncomfortable.

A related tension occurs when I have difficulty convincing students that there is authority in using first person; they may question my authority to require using *I* for an assignment because their high school English teachers never let them use *I*. Following these kinds of definitive rules of composition earned them grades that led to college, after all. I try to explain that authority rests in both voices, that different rhetorical situations require students to make different choices, depending on their goals. Some students want a simpler approach; they want to know which method is right. When I say, 'It depends,' they question me, as if the lack of a definitive answer signals incompetence. My right-brained pleasure in ambiguity sometimes frustrates my left-brained students. Without resorting to a sometime-you'll-understand attitude, I want students to come to the knowledge that both voices, both critical and creative approaches, can be useful in various writing contexts, depending on the purposes and audiences.

Another overlap in different types of writing is that all require some revision. While some of my creative writing students thrive at composing a piece on the strength of the inspiration that comes between two and four a.m. of the day a draft is due, I insist that they look again, perhaps a week or month later. Frequently, the student sees the gaps and unnecessary repetitions after some time has passed – along with the passing, glazed eyes of that wonderful burst of inspiration.

I maintain that the bursting instinct and the looking again are both invaluable. Students may question my authority with comments such as, 'why do I need to experiment with third person?' or 'but there were six of us at the cemetery; that's the way it really happened.' I hold to my view that learning includes trying out various stances and methods before fully informed choices can be made. I credit my training in composition for this view that good writing is a process that's often recursive.

Creating effective writing pedagogy also involves the literature that we read and discuss. In my current teaching situation, we read fiction during the first semester and then turn to poetry and drama during the second semester. I use texts in class that model an authority for students' own writing. I'm not comfortable with students saying that all stories or essays are equally good or bad, that value depends simply on what the individual likes. As teachers, we help students develop critical perspectives so that they can see for themselves why a given poem demands more of a reader, shows more control, or communicates more obliquely. Granted, these are elitist notions about art. But even the stance that writers can *improve* their skills suggests that value judgments are a necessary part of education. Teaching involves setting and communicating basic standards about the quality expected in students' work.

I'm not advocating that we need to read the so-called masters so that we can slavishly imitate them, but neither do I object to an imitation writing assignment. Marie Ponsot and Rosemary Deen (1982: 67) raise an important concern about students writing from models on the page: 'what is intended as a writing class becomes a series of exercises in literary analysis'. I agree that it's important tomov beyond analyzing. Yet analysis *is* an important part of the process of storing literature in the mind, internalizing it so the student can spill out an idea in a fresh way. I move again between left and right hemispheres. I don't present anthologized writers and their texts as if these models are the only way to write effectively. Rather, these poems and stories show us, in remarkable ways, our shared human experience. I ask students to try to create similar effects. For example, I've asked students to write an interior monologue that's a stream of advice, such as is heard in Jamaica Kincaid's 'Girl.' I've asked students to practice character development by describing objects of importance to their characters or by detailing the clothing worn, as seen in Tim O'Brien's 'The Things They Carried.' I underscore the essential point: details are convincing evidence, whether researching a stem cell controversy or developing resonance in a poem.

Another way to use literature as a positive authority in the classroom is to read a story such as Amy Tan's 'Two Kinds.' To follow-up on classroom discussion, students can write a story *or* a personal essay – show *or* tell, to use classic extremes – in which they have a conflict with an authority figure over how an object like Tan's piano should be viewed. Or students can write their own poem that imitates the rhythm of an accessible poem such as Langston Hughes' 'I, Too, Sing America' or Lucille Clifton's 'Homage to My Hips.' Or I ask them to write a narrative like Abe Akira's 'Peaches' in which they tell a story from their childhood and, in the process, question their memory (show *and* tell), thus recognizing how their views of the incident have changed as adults. These assignments require subtle variations of traditional genre differences and illustrate the overlap and blurring of genres that frequently occurs today. Another assignment requires the student to write a story that's almost entirely dialogue between two characters, much like what occurs in Ernest Hemingway's 'Hills Like White Elephants.' In all of these varieties of form and content, we discuss the conventions of the writing, the specific contexts of the stories, and the ways the conventions are being manipulated or played with by the authors. We talk about the complexity of language: that words say things (content) and do things (function). Assignments like this enhance learning about both writing and literature. All of this – analyzing and then creating and composing – explores how literature can be made.

I call these *creative* writing exercises, but I use variations in all of my courses. They require that the students understand original stories, poems, or essays before they try to write their own. Students are asked to avoid a detached, intellectual, written analysis of a text. Instead, they engage with the literary tradition through a more spontaneous, imaginative response at the level of writing a poem, personal essay, or story. Research has shown that the ability to create a story or poem reveals an advanced form of knowledge about literature. Jennifer Bailey reports on the efforts of British scholars to investigate the relationship between studying and analyzing a text – the Western classic literary tradition – and producing a new text. Traditionally, reading classic texts involves analysis through writing about these texts in an academic setting. Now, the question is whether attempting to reproduce the techniques of the original text can also be viewed as an exercise of academic knowledge (Bailey, 1997: 66). Based on my own classroom research, my answer is *yes*. When I ask my students to write creatively, they demonstrate knowledge about how writing works. I ask them to write new literature.

Creative writing belongs in a central position in English studies. It draws on literature, or models, and on the basic principles of composition – and supports both as well. Student writings-in-progress also offer important models for students. These less polished essays, stories, or poems written by peers can be catalysts for learning about writing. Not only can students see flaws in their peers' writing more easily than they can see the gaps in their own writing or thinking, they can also be inspired to stretch themselves and achieve the quality of writing that they see coming from their peers who are their equals. Creative writing has led the way in showing the advantages of workshop pedagogy. But small group critiques of thesis statements, peer reviews of first drafts, oral readings of revised drafts, and brainstorming about 'what's left out?' are also practical methods of peer exchange that work to advantage in the composition classroom. To divide the fields of English studies – in the department or in the classroom – is to deny the most productive pedagogy.

The creativity I advocate – 'a general fluency in writing based upon experiential learning' (Bailey, 1997: 68) – isn't separated from analysis. Rather, it's part of the process of learning, of moving from the text, to analysis, to creation. Moreover, authority exists at every step: reading the established text; analyzing the text; then rebuilding through the creation of a new text, based on what has been learned through reading and critical thinking. This learning process integrates the standard components of an English department: literature and criticism, composition, and creative writing. The student learns about the body of literature, learns to analyze through writing, and learns to create again through the imagination. By using all the strategies available, students and teachers increase their chances of understanding, enjoying, and creating literature.

All of this discussion of composition and creativity returns us to the nature of writing itself. Whatever goals we as teachers may claim, undergraduate students often view writing as an experience of self-exploration. This task may involve investigating the nature of human responsibility in order to identify when governmental or societal demands erode personal freedoms, or it may involve a satiric look at consumption practices in the 21st century, in order to point a wicked finger at human inclinations to excessive hoarding. Writing may also precipitate a needed break from parental oppression for a student who transfers personal feelings onto an imagined character. The specific form that the writing takes, while central to conveying the writer's ideas, may not be as important for college students as is the necessity that the writing, in fact, takes place, that the forum exists on paper for exploration of the young adult self in a complex world.

Rather than segregating writing courses according to the writing product, Harris (2001: 180) advocates that 'Writing courses should ideally work together in a more integrative and comprehensive process of developing ideas about the self (or the subject) and the social world that are always in dialectical formation'. This emphasis returns our focus in writing courses to the needs of the student (integrated learning about the self), rather than to the convenience of the teacher (organized strategies of delineating knowledge). From this perspective, we can create writing pedagogy that integrates the strengths of literature, composition, and creative writing. With our breadth of understanding about literature and composition, creative writing teachers can be a unifying, authoritative force in English departments and classrooms.

References

Bailey, J. (1997) Creative writing in higher education: Towards a redefinition of reading and writing. *Higher Education Review* 29 (3), 65–9.

Bishop, W. (1994) W. Bishop and H. Ostrom (eds) *Colors of a Different Horse: Rethinking Creative Writing Theory and Pedagogy*. Urbana, IL: NCTE.

Bishop, W. (1997) *Teaching Lives: Essays and Stories*. Logan, UT: Utah State Unversity Press.

Green, C. (2001) Materializing the sublime reader: Cultural studies, reader response, and community service in the creative writing workshop. *College English* 64 (2), 153–74.

Griffin, G.B. (2001) *Calling: Essays on Teaching in the Mother Tongue*. Pasadena: Trilogy.

Harris, J. (2001) Re-writing the subject: Psychoanalytic approaches to creative writing and composition pedagogy. *College English* 64 (2) 175–204.

Moxley, J.M. (1988) Tearing down the walls: Engaging the imagination. In J.M. Moxley (ed.) *Creative Writing in America: Theory and Pedagogy* (pp. 25–45). Urbana, IL: NCTE.

Ostrom, H. (1994) Introduction: Of radishes and shadows, theory and pedagogy. In W. Bishop and H. Ostrom (eds) *Colors of a Different Horse: Rethinking Creative Writing Theory and Pedagogy* (pp. xi–xxiii). Urbana: NCTE.

Ponsot, M. and Deen, R. (1982) *Beat Not the Poor Desk*. Montclair, NJ: Boynton/Cook.

Radavich, D. (1999) Creative writing in the academy. *Profession 1999* (pp. 106–12). New York: Modern Language Association.

Wilson, E.O. (1998) *Consilience: The Unity of Knowledge*. New York: Knopf, 1998.

Chapter 5

The Double Bind and Stumbling Blocks: A Case Study as an Argument for Authority-conscious Pedagogy

CARL VANDERMEULEN

Because I also brought a background in composition to the teaching of creative writing, I share Wendy Bishop's interest in 'investigating the personal, therapeutic, and affective aspects' of teaching writing (Bishop, 1997: 143). I find it easy to agree with her that learning to write involves a change in the *person*, in the way the person sees, thinks, feels, reads, even in the person's identity, not just in how she or he writes and revises. The following teacher-research, which examines a poetry writing class that went awry, supports Bishop's position that in such a writing process, students' high expectations for the teacher give us a great deal of authority – more than we find comfortable. The creative writing teacher's roles include model writer, listener and responder to students whose work may lie close to the person of the writer, as well as guide and encourager for their journey of becoming as artists. This is already a tricky combination. Add that students know that their admired model and trusted guide remains an institutional authority who will rank them by means of a grade – and it's a wonder that creative writing classes work as well as they do. What has been termed a pedagogical 'meltdown' (see Tassoni & Thelin, 2000) may even be more likely (and more traumatic) for those of us who have imported our pedagogy from composition because we *think* we've solved the problem of authority. Despite my investment in what can be called a therapeutic writing process, I find that problems arise not only from having more authority than we suppose but also from unacknowledged and therefore unexamined conflicts within and between our different kinds of authority. A case study of one class becomes here an argument for authority-conscious pedagogy.

Composition Theory and the Authority of the Teacher

Much of the recent history of composition theory can be understood as a deliberate limiting of the teacher's authority in order to create a

49

safe space in which students can develop their own authority as *authors*. One resulting practice I follow is delaying the grading until students have had time to revise their best work and collect it in a portfolio. Another is asking students to include with drafts a writer's memo in which they discuss where the piece came from, where they think it is going, and what guidance from me will help. A third is responding in the role of intended reader while limiting the advice associated with teacherly authority.

I also limit my authority by discouraging individual competition and instead authorizing and training students to collaborate in the process of enabling other students to develop as writers. Consequently, I've rejected as too divisive the whole-class critique session common in art and creative writing courses. Most student response to writing occurs instead in established smaller groups whose members learn to trust each other. And especially for early drafts, I ask responders to avoid offering any judgment of the piece as a whole. Instead of taking the role of critic, responders occupy the role of the intended reader, so I teach them to use Peter Elbow's (1981) modes of *descriptive* response: pointing to particulars of detail or style that catch their attention, summarizing, saying what is 'almost said' in the piece, and saying what, for them, is the center of gravity. Elbow's idea is that responders should read *with* the writer at first, saving reading *against* for final drafts.

By such practices, I thought I had achieved what Richard Boyd calls a 'peaceable classroom':

> With the emergence of the student-centered classroom and the influence of expressivist rhetoricians like Peter Elbow and Donald Murray, it was to be expected that the old narratives of instructor and students locked in a struggle of wills would be replaced by a new version of a far more peaceable classroom where teachers might act more as collaborators than as adversaries. (Boyd, 1999: 590)

But *because* I thought I had created a safe workshop – a classroom environment in which students were relatively comfortable sharing their own writing with their peers and responding to each other's drafts – I underestimated both the weight of my authority in the eyes of my students as well as the threat posed by classmates as competitors, not just collaborators.

Thrusting Ourselves into what Terrifies

I know that students new to writing poetry lack confidence and that they tend to focus this anxiety on grades. To deflect this concern, my syllabus argues, 'Compared to the pleasure of feeling a poem sing or sizzle or sigh, a good grade is a paltry gratification.' However, grade-consciousness ran deep, especially among the 13 female (of 15) students. But because I knew and admired most of the students, I expected confidence and didn't take very seriously the level of anxiety expressed in students' opening letters to me, such as in this one from Naomi:

> There is a fear when you share something intimate with others that they won't like or understand your work. I have a hard time showing others my work. I am also a horrible reader of poems. I could practice and never become good. I have to admit I am horrified and intimidated by our class. There is much diversity and many brilliant minds that I don't feel I can honestly contest with. Though I love poetry I am dreading the next class.

Because I knew Naomi well, I assumed she felt free to express herself to me in a way that seemed hyperbolic, so I reassured her and assumed that engaging in the process would push fears aside.

Brina expressed similar fears but also a determination to break through fear. 'I've learned that the best way to become comfortable with something that terrifies you is to thrust yourself into it without reservation and let it carry you.' I responded that I couldn't have expressed better what I wanted the course to help writers do. Yet when I found those words later, they seemed ironic, because instead of finding the confidence that we had hoped for, we were carried into crosscurrents we didn't expect and that I couldn't make sense of at the time.

At first, class sessions seemed to go well, but after three or four weeks, discussion was still tentative. I guessed that the problem was worry about their competition. Still, some routine questions should have generated better responses if students were reading the textbook. I mentioned this concern to Joonna Trapp, a colleague who was sitting in on the class. She said she suspected that students weren't doing enough with the text. I had told them to be steadily faithful, so I gave a quiz. I give no exams and few quizzes because I know that they can conflict with a collaborative pedagogy, but I reasoned that students shouldn't be upset if I assured them that the grades wouldn't count much.

The result bore out my suspicion. A few did well, but several who were used to getting A's and B's earned D's or F's – grades that must have confirmed their fears. The next graded assignment was a short paper for which students were to discuss the impact of a single revision to a draft of a poem. Several papers dealt instead with multiple revisions. I blamed carelessness in following guidelines, but now I think that worry about making a good impression led them to try too hard, do too much. As a result several students had *two* low grades.

To encourage them, I reminded the class that they were welcome to schedule a conference with me as they revised poems for the mid-semester portfolio. As an example of a kind of response they could ask me to do, I mentioned what Elbow calls a 'movie of the reader's mind' – a detailed running account of thoughts, reactions, and attempts to make sense while reading. After class, I decided I should demonstrate such a response, and since my colleague, Joonna, had asked for response to a poem draft, we agreed to use it for the demonstration.

In class, I read Joonna's poem aloud, pausing to say what I was noticing, what I was connecting, what expectations I was forming. Joonna listened and made notes. When I finished, I talked about how the first part of the poem raised expectations for me that didn't seem to be met in the last part, so that the poem seemed to be going in two directions. I thought I had offered no judgment of the poem as a whole. But when I looked at the class to see if they had questions, what I saw left me dumbfounded: the same expression of shock on more than half the faces. I couldn't imagine what they thought they had heard.

Joonna's observation email written after class that day confirmed my impression that I had offered useful reader-response. Then, she expressed the same bewilderment I had felt:

> What confuses me is why, then, did the following happen? I stopped and talked to two of the better students in the class. [...] They both said that they felt their poems were actually regressing. Before I could say anything else, they expressed their concern over my poem 'being torn to shreds' before the class. I was flabbergasted.

Later Joonna called to say that other members of the class had also stopped at her office to say how bad they felt when I 'ripped her poem apart.'

One student, Katie, came to my office to say she didn't feel she was making any progress. She said that my comments seemed mostly critical, so she didn't know if she was doing anything well. She added that class discussion was similarly discouraging because I seemed to reject any interpretation of a poem other than my own. A day or two later, Naomi stopped in and added that students thought I was expecting them to write poems like my own. I had no idea why a group of students I liked and had looked forward to teaching had formed impressions of me so contrary to those expressed by previous poetry classes. I was, after all, practicing all the supposedly proper pedagogical approaches.

Scapegoating

I guessed that a cause of students' bizarre reaction in class was anxiety over the approaching portfolio, and that's what I told them in the next class – that a state of panic had caused them to *think* they heard something that really hadn't happened. I added that portfolio grades had been high in previous classes and that drafts I had seen indicated that they would be high again. They *seemed* reassured, and midterm grades should have eased concerns. Yet class discussion remained tentative. Why had what worked for previous classes turned sour for what should have been my best class? What blinded them to the encouragement that I was sure I had included in my responses to their writing?

One form my frustration took was wondering if one of the students was saying things that poisoned students' regard for me or for the course. This dynamic can emerge in workshops, which have become the well-accepted pedagogical approach in creative writing in the United States, so I started suspecting Amanda. She seemed self-assured and her work had been excellent, yet in class she assumed an air of superior silence. Girard offers the valuable insight that the scapegoating that occurs in such baffling and threatening conditions is an *unconscious* process. Its participants are blinded by their own good intentions. When things go wrong in a relationship, those involved point to their own good intentions as proof that *others* must be at fault. Those others, equally well-intentioned, then feel falsely accused and betrayed, so they counter with their own accusations. Unless this cycle is broken, as Girard explains, it builds toward a violent conclusion.

While looking back at the course, I came to understand that the dramatic turn in many students' perception of me was mostly my doing and that the students who – unknowingly – contributed most to the problem were students I knew well and held in high regard. Three of them – Naomi, Brina, and Beth – had been or were my advisees. I knew that my commitment to them raised the stakes for me, but it wasn't until I pondered this passage from Lad Tobin that I realized that our prior relationship must also have raised the stakes for these students – and made them more likely to view me as an authority figure:

[F]rom a student's perspective a writing teacher is an authority figure, even – or especially – in process classrooms. In fact, the teacher in composition classes in which students are asked to write about their personal feelings and to meet in one-to-one conferences actually holds more authority, because the stakes are higher. (Tobin, 1993: 20)

I had thought of my relationship with these students more in terms of *service* than of *authority*, but if an authority is one whose judgment of you and your work matters, then our prior relationship, along with the personal nature of their writing, made me an authority in their eyes.

Double Binds

Complicating the problem was the fact that the person who had been these students' adviser and encourager became, in this class, a professor with high expectations who seemed oblivious to their worries that they might fall short. One of them, Naomi, in a later interview with Joonna described how my duality confused her: 'I knew Carl beforehand. I get along with Carl out of class really well. But it is hard for me to connect with him in class. Carl is very much concerned with your academics. He always wants to push you a little harder.' In my mind, I'm the same person who recruited her to the college with the promise that she could get a good edcuation there, now trying to keep that promise in my role as teacher. But if I *listen* to Naomi, I hear real confusion about who I am.

My reading of Girard led me to realize that I had placed students who knew me best in a double bind – a 'contradictory double imperative' (Girard, 1977: 146). Double binds are common. They are the seemingly unresolvable situations in which it feels impossible to do the right thing, because we receive contradictory messages about what is expected of us. An example was the quiz that turned me from collaborator into homework cop. And Naomi's comment reminds me that, although I claim to want a safe classroom, I also want one dangerous enough to spur creativity. Beth, another advisee, explained in an interview with Joonna that every class she had taken with me was harder than she expected and that what was hardest was wanting praise but getting criticism. Joonna asked her whether my responses to her writing seemed harsh. Beth said, 'Every time! I felt torn apart.' But she added, 'I'm not sure it was ever his fault. I wanted praise and didn't get it. I wanted encouragement. I didn't want "You can and should do better."' I thought she knew that I admired her and her work, so I did focus on ways she could make it better. Consequently, while I thought that she saw me as a teacher who was willing to help, she saw me as an authority she could do nothing to satisfy.

All collaborative teachers place their students in a serious double bind when they downplay authority in favor of the roles of coach, collaborator, and friend but nevertheless assign grades, that ultimate expression of institutional authority. Of this double bind, I was aware. I explain to students that I want to be a writing coach first, and only shift to the required role of judge of portfolios of poetry at midterm and at the end of the course. But students' need to do good work, coupled with teachers' high expectations for that work, make them see us as much more of an authority figure than we might imagine in the workshop model.

Blocked Expression

When someone we've counted on suddenly seems like a different person, we don't just say, 'Hmmm, must be he's a contradictory being like the rest of us.' We say, 'He's not at all who I thought he was.' It makes sense that one consequence of the double bind, according to Girard, is 'loss of faith in the capacity of language' (Girard, 1978: 292). How do we address someone when we can't decide who he is?

Blocked language was most obvious in Beth and Brina's prose. For the final paper, students were to choose a poet, identify aspects of technique or approach, and employ some of them in their own imitative poem. The paper called for careful description, but Brina and Beth seemed to believe that it demanded profound interpretation. Girard helps us to recognize a paradox that operates in such a case: 'Desire has its own logic, and it is a logic of gambling. Once past a certain level of bad luck, the luckless player does not give up; as the odds get worse, he plays for higher stakes' (Girard, 1978: 298). Beth insisted months later that this paper was one of the toughest she had ever written, so she tried harder. She brought a draft to a conference with me, then wrote another that was equally difficult to follow. I tried harder too, writing an extensive response to suggest how she might simplify. Yet the paper she submitted became even muddier. In some paragraphs, what seemed to be the topic sentence was repeated, as though her thoughts were stuck in a loop. 'As a writer Sandburg must continually keep his reader in mind. If they cannot understand his work through the tools he has chosen to convey meaning, then he has failed as a writer. Reader-writer relationship is imperative, without it, no work can hold meaning. Text has meaning only when it is read and understood. Sandburg places himself in the shoes of his readers to better ensure his own clarity and sense of seeing or understanding'. If read like a poem, Beth's paragraphs sound like a mantra, every sentence about getting in touch with one's reader – something Beth knew was 'imperative' but felt was impossible because she imagined me as a reader who insisted on her best while expecting something worse.

I knew Beth could write well – and I found confirmation in her accompanying writer's memo about her imitation of Carl Sandburg. There, instead of trying to impress, she simply says what she noticed as one writer trying to imitate another. Then, she explained these points in a readable style and in paragraphs that moved forward instead of looping back. Still, how does a workshop instructor grade a paper when one wonders if its faults arose partly from the instructor's own attempts to help? I did grade her partly on the clearer expression in the writer's memo. I should have leaned farther in that direction, and one reason I did not is that I was caught in a double bind between empathetic understanding and academic standards.

Brina's sentences and paragraphs had similar problems that I could account for in no more precise way than that she seemed to be trying too hard. When writing final comments, only a few minutes remained before the class period in which I wanted to return the papers, so I just described the problems I found and wrote at the end that I knew that she was a better writer than the paper showed. Frustration over her paper lowered my expectations for the poem. In her imitation of Robert Frost, I noticed that his first line, 'I have been one acquainted with the night,' became in hers, 'I have been one acquainted with the *light*.' I had cautioned students not to imitate too closely so I quickly wrote that she had used 'a form suitable for a dark poem in a poem about light, and that form won't let the light through.' I noticed that in other ways she had caught the sound and form, so I gave it – or it earned – a B.

I realized that some phenomenon I did not understand was preventing good students from doing their best work. I should have called Brina to talk about it; instead, I wondered why she didn't come to talk to me. I never guessed the reason was anger until, at the end of her final portfolio, I came to her Frost imitation, accompanied by this writer's memo:

I'm quite sure it is obvious to a learned person like you that I mimicked Frost's 'Acquainted with the Night.'

In your feedback, you suggested I scrap the format and try to write about a similar 'Frost' subject. My group and I disagree with your statement that this format is only suitable for a dark poem. Did you make that statement because you had 'Acquainted with the Night' stuck in your mind, and therefore could only see this format accompanying darkness? This may not be the best poem ever written, it's probably not even worthy of being called a Frost-copycat, but that was a baseless reason to tell me it is worthless. I'm sure you can think of better reasons for ripping my heart-work to pieces.

The reason I consciously chose to do it this specific way, was because I struggle with format and rhyming schemes and I was deliberately challenging myself to attempt the things I think I cannot do. I spent hours with the format and rhyming scheme trying to say something worthwhile. I don't care how you choose to evaluate this poem, the true values lie in the lessons learned. Maybe it wasn't worth your time, but it's what I have to offer you.

I couldn't believe I deserved such accusation. To assure myself that I didn't, I immediately re-read my earlier response to her poem – and saw that I had misread the poem. It was not about light but about *wanting* light. The poem ends, 'It is for this reason alone that I write. / I have been one acquainted with the light.' The poem is about having a glimpse of something hopeful, and about having writing as a means to apprehend what we have glimpsed.

I tried to call, but had to leave a message. Then she sent an email explaining that she had wanted to 'say exactly what I felt like saying after receiving your response to both my paper and to my poem' and apologizing for the writer's memo as 'a little harsh, emotionally based, and probably uncalled for.' It seemed to me that she was saying, 'You're my advisor and teacher, but now I find myself feeling very angry toward you, and you need to figure out what's going on.' It was the moment most responsible for my beginning this case study.

Brina's insistence several months later that I never offered her enough encouragement made me realize that this had become true late in the course but also had been true earlier. Looking back, I noticed that, at the end of my response to her first poem draft, I had written, 'It's good to have you in class. I've been looking forward to seeing you in such a place.' Finding this, I thought, 'Wasn't *that* encouragement?' But now I wonder if what Brina heard me saying was, 'I've invested a lot in you; you'd better be really impressive.'

Model Becomes Ogre

Because we who teach creative expression rely partly on another kind of authority, namely the example of our own artistic practice and our own lives as artist, those students in our classes who want most to become artists are likely to identify with us and idealize us. Instead of making *desire* primary for our development, as Freud does, Girard sees *imitation* as primary. People *form* powerful desires by identifying with a model and taking clues from the model about what is desirable. They do this because they admire the *being* of the model – he or she seems to have a fullness or plenitude that they lack. They think that this plenitude is accounted for by what they suppose the model *has*, so they want that object too (Girard, 1977: 146).

Most imitation of a model is mutually gratifying – up to a point. Problems occur when imitation arouses desire for something that is in short supply (such as opportunities to be published) or is somehow reserved to the model. Then the model can become an *obstacle*, apparently *preventing* the subject from achieving the desired object. Perceiving resistance where invitation was expected, the subject begins to act differently toward the model, and the model, sensing suspicion in a once-trusted subject, becomes more distant, confirming to the subject that the model's determination to keep the object for himself. This peculiar fix, which Girard calls 'mimetic rivalry,' forms apart from conscious awareness.

> The model considers himself too far above the disciple, the disciple considers himself too far below the model, for either of them even fleetingly to entertain the notion that their desires are identical – in short, that they might indeed be rivals. (Girard, 1977: 146–7)

Although I did not imagine it at the time, I now believe that I was caught up in mimetic rivalry, at least with Beth and Brina. According to Girard, it is not through words, 'but by the example of his own desire that the model conveys to the subject the supreme desirability of the object' (1977: 146). Like my best teachers, I teach partly through the example of my own desire. Sometimes I recite poems, and I sometimes distribute my own poems. Beth, Brina, and others did perceive me early on as a model who could help them become poets – and they later perceived me as a person who would 'tear apart' others' poems perhaps to keep them from comparing favorably with my own.

Caught in such a predicament, the subject re-imagines the model as the kind of cruel god who would lead someone to want something and then capriciously pull it away. Paradoxically, instead of renouncing the model, the subject becomes more fascinated, imagining the model as a godlike being who despises them, just as an inner voice tells them they deserve to be despised, while at the same time desiring to be similarly godlike and invincible. As Girard (1978: 296) explains, the object comes to seem even more desirable: 'Since the model obstinately bars access to it, the possession of this object must make all the difference between the self-sufficiency of the model and the imitator's lack of sufficiency, the model's fullness of being and the imitator's nothingness'. In short, the model comes to deserve the label stumbling block – a model who becomes a 'special form of temptation, causing attraction to the extent that it is an obstacle and forming an obstacle to the extent that it can attract' (1978: 416).

If the rivalry continues, the subject responds in one of two ways. The first is with anger focused upon the model/rival, which Brina illustrates when she adopts an authoritative tone to ridicule my failure to understand her work. The other response Beth illustrates: she turns against *herself* the accusations she imagined coming from me. First listen to Girard (1978: 296):

> Even if he holds himself to be persecuted, the subject will necessarily ask himself if the model has not got perfectly good reasons for denying him the object. An increasingly weighty part of himself will carry on imitating the model and, by virtue of this fact, will take the model's side, secretly justifying the hostile treatment he believes he is undergoing at the hands of the model and interpreting it as a special condemnation that he probably deserves.

Now listen to Beth: 'It killed me. In a good way,' she explained, 'I love Carl, I wanted him to think I can write, I wanted to please. Then I hated Carl. I was frustrated with myself, with being a poor writer. Then, I realized I wasn't willing to be critical of my own work.' But the blocked writing in her paper shows that she had become too critical, turning upon herself not only her habitual self-criticism but also the harsh critic she perceived me to be.

Collaboration as Mimetic Contagion

Beth, Brina, and a few others were probably caught up in the kind of mimetic rivalry with me that I have described. The means by which others in class formed a distorted picture of me is probably just good collaboration. Beth told Joonna that in her peer response group 'The comments were all negative.' She said that they included expressions of 'frustration with Carl, with his criticism. Some felt that he just talked and didn't listen.' Naomi reported much the same in her group, and yet she valued the peer response, calling it 'encouraging.' That's a mark of a good group; but when people feel disheartened, one form that encouragement takes is 'It's not your fault.' Such words of comfort are only a sigh away from naming the person whose fault it must then be. Girard gives collaborators the insightful label, 'partners in reciprocal imitation' (1978: 21). Under extreme conditions, the result can be what he calls 'mimetic contagion' – a more descriptive term than panic for the process by which much of the class came to see me as the kind of teacher who would 'rip apart' a colleague's poetry, perhaps to keep it from competing with my own.

Understanding the Risks

A motif in students' responses to the course is the phrase *torn apart*, which I now read symptomatically: we all were caught in something that was ripping us apart. It was Brina's angry memo that brought me to that realization. Later, I learned that identification with the victim is what Girard credits as the way out of scapegoating and violence (Brooke, 2000: 171). In Beth's words, Brina's message 'killed me, in a good way.'

I spent several months reexamining the course and viewing it from different perspectives before I could admit that the pedagogy I imagined as providing a safe but challenging space for becoming a writer could turn into a threatening space where expression was blocked instead of encouraged. The students named here do believe the story I've told. And I think that if experienced teachers of creative writing were to revisit such seeming anomalies as talkative classes that went silent, bitter remarks scattered in course evaluations, soured relationships with leading students, and other evidence of resistance, these teachers would be able to account for some of them with the help of the lenses of authority, mimetic rivalry, or mimetic contagion.

We should investigate where and how things can go wrong in the relationships that enable students to become writers and artists in order to become more capable of preventing or addressing the problems to which our pedagogy is vulnerable. For instance, to prevent mimetic contagion, I caution writers not to use group time for either venting or for anguishing about their supposed weaknesses. I am also more alert to signs that a group has gotten off track.

In addition, I work harder to avoid misunderstanding. Joonna says that in written responses to drafts, I perform the emotion of the reader who wants what the poem promises and who is bothered by what still impedes that promise. Such eagerness for excellence can lead to an impatient tone, especially with a promising but still flawed poem. I now explain *why* I respond the way I do and suggest how students should read and use my comments so that they are less likely to misread them. Kathleen Yancey's idea of a 'talk back' offers an effective strategy for preventing misreading. Students are asked to say or write what they heard the teacher saying in his response (Yancey, 1998: 37). Some misunderstandings clear up when they go back to read the comments more carefully. If any persist, the teacher has a new opportunity to clarify.

Another of Yancey's suggestions helps students take advice and criticism less personally. She suggests asking the writer to include with a draft an argument that it fails miserably, followed by an argument that it succeeds admirably (p. 32). Supporting either argument requires writers to view the work not as personal expression but as a performance whose readers evaluate it by discoverable criteria. Having distanced the work from their person, writers are more likely to view the instructor's response as help with assessing the performance instead of as judgment of them as a person. In addition, since making these arguments requires integrating the perspectives of the text with their own thinking and writing, this strategy is a better one than quizzes for encouraging thoughtful engagement with the text.

I now pay closer attention to students' expressions of anxiety, and I'm more aware of the writers who have difficulty distancing their writing from their person. I pay more attention to relationships too. If a student I already know well takes my class, I may tell him or her not to worry about having to impress me. And I trust students more and seek out their impression of how the course is working.

Certain risks come with any territory, but part of being an authority is knowing our territory. If we are the kind of authority known as *teacher* and if our territory is the writing workshop, we must not avoid Bishop's call for 'investigating the personal, therapeutic, and affective aspects' of teaching creative writing. We must continue to develop and improve authority-conscious pedagogy.

Note

1. Students mentioned gave permission to use their writing and requested that their names be used. Brina was one of two students who

joined me to present work at a panel of the Southwest/Texas Popular Culture Association.

References

Bishop, W. (1997) Writing is/and therapy. *Teaching Lives: Essays and Stories* (pp. 143–56). Logan, UT: Utah State University Press.

Boyd, R. (1999) Reading student resistance: The case of the missing other. *JAC* 19 (4), 589–605.

Brooke, R. (2000) René Girard and the dynamics of imitation, scapegoating, and renunciative identification: A response to Richard Boyd. *JAC* 20 (1), 167–75.

Elbow, P. (1981) *Writing with Power: Techniques for Mastering the Writing Process.* New York: Oxford University Press.

Girard, R. (1977) *Violence and the Sacred* P. Gregory (trans.). Baltimore: Johns Hopkins University Press.

Girard, R. (1978) *Things Hidden Since the Foundation of the World* S. Bann and M. Metteer (trans.). Stanford, CA: Stanford University Press.

Tassoni, J.P. and Thelin, W.H. (2000) *Blundering for a Change: Errors and Expectations in Critical Pedagogy.* Portsmouth, NH: Boynton/Cook Heinemann.

Tobin, L. (1993) *Writing Relationships: What Really Happens in the Composition Class.* Portsmouth, NH: Boynton/Cook Heinemann.

Yancey, K.B. (1998) *Reflection in the Writing Classroom.* Logan, UT: Utah State University Press.

Part 2

The Teacher's Place, Voice, and Style

Chapter 6
Teaching and Evaluation: Why Bother?

MARY CANTRELL

What is wrong with those of us who teach creative writing? Unlike professors in any other discipline, we seem eager to relinquish our authority in the classroom. We don't lecture or use the podium. We arrange our desks (if we even meet in a classroom) in a circle and tell our students they can call us by our first names. Some of us even participate in in-class writing assignments and share our works-in-progress with students during workshop. Evaluation and grading is especially agonizing for us; many of us, in fact, would prefer we eliminate grades altogether or establish a pass/fail policy for creative writing classes.

Yet few of us truly want a classroom in which we do not embrace, to some extent, roles of authority. If we wanted an authority-free classroom, we would begin by eliminating prerequisites: creative writing classes would be open to anyone who wants to write about any subject in any form. Once enrolled, students would determine for themselves how much they would like to write during the semester and, at the end of the semester, would determine their own grades. Instead of imposing our own limited aesthetic criteria, we professors would listen as students offered to one another praise and criticism based on uninformed personal taste. Comments such as 'I couldn't relate to this story so I don't like it' and 'My favorite thing about this poem is that you can interpret it any way you want' would be perfectly acceptable. Writers could take as much time as they'd like to share the background inspiration for their poems or stories or to defend aspects that readers found confusing or problematic. We would not require students to complete readings from expensive textbooks, nor would they have to waste precious writing time reading and analyzing contemporary writing by published authors whose works might confuse or bother some of them. The professor's job would be simply to discuss ways that students can publish and, at the end of the semester, to ensure that they receive college credit.

While some people may teach this way – in addition to eliminating problems associated with exerting authority, such an outlook allows the teacher more time for her own writing – most creative writing professors do not completely relinquish authority. The fact that students receive three hours of college credit (and move toward a degree with that credit) compels us to establish authority in the classroom. If a professor completely relinquishes authority, if the class becomes primarily a writers' therapy group designed to encourage writing by providing a nodding audience, if students are not held accountable for having learned or produced anything, if no guidance is offered, then why offer college credit for creative writing courses?

Moreover, our own sense of integrity dictates that we set some parameters and that students acknowledge our authority to some extent. We do, after all, hold degrees that reflect, if not expertise, at least experience. We may not mind when our students challenge us by questioning our publication record, resisting our criticism, or ignoring our instruction, but even when challenged, most of us continue to promote the skills and concepts we think important.

So what's the problem? Why are we conflicted about our own authority in the classroom? The discomfort we feel regarding our authority, as well as the problems students often have with the creative writing professor's authority, come from several assumptions we have about creative writing and our role as evaluator in the academy, assumptions we should examine and consider carefully not just for our own benefit but also to ensure that creative writing programs continue to thrive within colleges, universities, and community colleges.

Assumption #1: Creative Writing Teachers and Classes Should Challenge Existing Power Structure

David Radavich, in his article 'Creative writing in the academy,' writes that 'relations between writing programs and the academy have not always been smooth' (1999: 107). Because creative writing programs began to establish themselves 'in the wake of the Beat Generation and various civil rights movements, writers often disdained working too closely with traditional scholars and academicians' (p. 107). Radavich reminds us that the 'first wave' of creative writers in the academy had a political agenda that sought to include formerly marginalized groups. 'Such writers frequently and vociferously attacked established hierarchies,' he explains, including academic institutions, which were seen as part of those hierarchies (p. 108).

Today, the rebel's stance remains popular, and our proud tradition of attacking or at least questioning established hierarchies contributes to our resistance to the trappings of academia, especially grading. Yet, teachers exist as part of the hierarchy – one might even argue it sustains us – so we must balance our responsibility to the institution, which prescribes a degree of authority in the classroom, with our commitment to questioning authority. We may feel hypocritical – question authority, but not mine – or simply reluctant to impose specific standards on students, for fear that we might disenfranchise a certain perspective or operate on the limited aesthetics of the dominant culture or of the culture to which we belong, dominant or not.

Surely, though, one can maintain a set of standards and embrace conventions of higher education without being hypocritical and without being disrespectful or unaware of difference among our students. Unless a college degree represents nothing more than a capacity to conform to a narrow set of expectations, the goals of a creative writing class and those of the college or university offering the class need not conflict. Radavich (1999: 112), in fact, argues that 'if creative writing is to have meaning in the academy of the future, it needs to partake of those very qualities and purposes best representative of true scholarship – namely, broad, informed, intensive reading, thinking and writing and a commitment to social betterment of a troubled world'.

In the simplest of all worlds, students would enter our classes ready to partake without much guidance; they would achieve their goals without needing feedback, a planned series of assignments, or the threat of a grade looming. In my experience, though, students are only partially motivated and, like most of us, react not with long-term goals in mind but in response to immediate demands. They are more likely to succeed at any endeavor if they are provided structure, feedback, and evaluation. Can't the experience in a creative writing classroom incorporate both structure and a healthy skepticism?

Assumption #2: Creative Writing Teachers Aren't Really English Teachers

Once, during a long, long Greyhound trip, I sat next to an elderly woman who talked non-stop for the first hour and a half of the journey. Finally, she paused a moment to ask me where I was going. I told her I was a graduate student in English on my way home for the December holiday. She was horrified. 'You must think my speech is just terrible,' she said. 'All the grammar mistakes I've been making ...'

Wayne C. Booth (2000: 494–5) tells a similar story in his essay 'Boring from within: The art of the freshman essay' and concludes that, when meeting someone who teaches English, people usually confess their hatred for past English classes or apologize for their ineptness with the English language. The English-teacher stereotype of a fastidious old woman, tapping a pointer at diagrammed sentences on a blackboard, comes to mind for many people when they hear 'English teacher.' It is an unappealing image to most everyone, but especially to many of us who teach creative writing. We much prefer the Robin Williams version from *Dead Poets' Society*. Carpe Diem! Rip the pages from the boring text and go live life! Damned be those who would damper our passions with The Rules.

In their article, 'Creativity research and classroom practice,' Linda Sarbo and Joseph M. Moxley (1994: 142) explore research on creative thinking and conclude that '[f]amiliarity with creativity research increases our sensitivity to the negative effects of external evaluation' and argue that 'our role [as creative writing professors] is that of skillful midwife rather than critic/judge'. They believe that creativity can be developed in students by making the classroom 'a safe place for experimentation and self-expression, a place where unconventional solutions are sought and rewarded' (p. 143).

Absolutely. Creative thinkers in *any* discipline are going to be better learners and are going to produce better work than non-creative thinkers, but in a creative writing class especially, professors develop a pedagogy that promotes creativity and imagination. Similarly, the creative writing professors whom I know encourage students to be empathetic thinkers, capable of seeing the world from a multiplicity of perspectives. John Gardner (1983: 115) believes that writing teachers should help students avoid what he calls the 'faults of the soul,' problems related to character. For example, 'frigidity,' one of the faults, results from a student's inability to empathize and to understand the complexities of human nature (p. 118). Gardner insists that it is the writing professor's duty to help 'bring about a change in the writer's basic character' (p. 115). In other words, writing professors are supposed to help writers become better human beings.

As writers ourselves, we recognize that creativity, imagination, and empathy are qualities crucial to writing good literature. Nonetheless, we are not comfortable teaching or assessing students' creativity, imagination, and ability to empathize; we do not like to make judgments about a student's character. Perhaps, then, we should not evaluate these qualities. In his article 'The workshop's evolution and the writer's life,'

Tom Grimes writes, 'Imagination cannot be taught. Habits of art and virtues of mind can be encouraged, no more' (1999: 26). However, as Grimes argues, 'until craft is mastered, imagination is a useless, largely inapplicable abstraction. Mastering craft gives the writer access to the fullness of his or her imagination because it gives the writer the ability to deploy and apply it' (pp. 26–7). We *can* teach and evaluate an understanding of craft, and, at least at the undergraduate level, students should be held accountable for understanding it.

Some creative writing professors have argued that it is dangerous to introduce students to elements of craft before they discover what they want to say in their stories or poems. We can, of course, over-emphasize craft. Because it is easier to teach rules, to ask students to articulate definitions, to grade exams that measure only knowledge, not application, we may sometimes neglect the more important and less easily quantified aspects of writing, elements of craft that develop through rigorous practice and depth of character. The accusation that writing classes produce the dreaded workshop story is another cliché among writers. When teaching undergraduates, though, we can ensure that our students are empowered with an understanding of the mechanics of writing and that they are able to explain basic concepts. Do they understand omniscient points of view? Can they define allegory? Can they recognize a sonnet?

If asking students to understand some basic rules, techniques, or concepts related to writing diminishes their capacity to write creatively, perhaps their talent was rather fragile in the first place. Which leads to the third assumption.

Assumption #3: Talent is Fragile; Teachers Must Nurture it at All Times

Most of my creative writing professors – male and female – were nurturing, encouraging, accessible. Had I been subjected to less nurturing teachers, perhaps I would have lost confidence. Obviously, the abuse of authority in a creative writing classroom can damage a writer's talent. We have all heard stories about the egocentric, dismissive professor whose dominion over the workshop intimidates good writers and extinguishes creative impulses. But at the other end of the spectrum is neglect: we should neither abuse *nor* neglect our authority. In my experience, the tendency to eschew the responsibility of being the authority in the class – the tendency to neglect—is the far more common problem. As Susan M. Brookhart (1988: 3) argues, our role as advocates for the students 'provides much of the internal satisfaction and intrinsic motivation that teachers claim as the primary reason they teach'. In other words, we are much more comfortable being the cheerleader, the midwife, the coach, or whatever than we are being the authority, the master-writer, the critic, or the judge, and our comfort results primarily from an understanding that writing is difficult and that writers are easily discouraged, frustrated, depressed.

Our ability to sympathize and empathize with students may sometimes make it difficult to instruct and, especially, to grade. Brookhart, in fact, explains that teachers often inflate grades because

> teachers do not like to give low grades, feel bad when they do, and dislike grading in general. Reasons given include concern for students' developing self-image as learners, fear that a 'why bother' attitude may follow low grades, and worry that students may give up or even drop out of school as a result of academic failure. (Brookhart, 1988: 3)

Can we assess without damaging self-esteem, guide students without discouraging them, challenge them without frightening them? It isn't easy, but I think it can be done.

None of my nurturing teachers or professors offered unconditional praise. On the contrary, they offered honest and considered opinions regarding what did not work in my stories and poems. Everyone dreads hearing that a character is shallow, that a poem is sentimental, but if students develop the critical vocabulary with which to discuss poetry and fiction, if they understand that consistent perfection is not a requirement for becoming a writer, surely they will be better writers than they would be if they receive nothing but adulation and ingratiating responses to flawed or mediocre work.

Assumption #4: Teachers Cannot Evaluate Creative Writing Objectively (or Very Well)

'The results of memorization and rote learning are easy to evaluate,' writes Christopher M. Jedrey (1982). When the 'desiderate are clarity of expression and originality of thought,' however, grading isn't easy (p. 103). Jedrey is referring to essay grading, but the same holds true for short stories, poems, and memoir. Because creative writing professors must grade writing, we worry about imposing our own narrow ideas and tastes on a student's work. What if I'm too conventional to appreciate the student who doesn't want to use conjunctions and pronouns in his experimental work? Why should I require the 87-year-old retired architect in my poetry class to understand assonance when he simply wants to write rhyming poetry for his grandchildren? I don't like science fiction, so how can I judge a student's attempt at writing it?

In a creative writing class, students enter with enormously different writing abilities and with very different goals, all of which make establishing criteria for grading difficult. Nonetheless, unless we are awarding grades and credit for effort and/or a desire to write well, both of which are difficult to assess accurately, we are all burdened with the task of putting aside our personal preferences, establishing criteria and determining how well a student meets those criteria. We should also feel some obligation to articulate those criteria and to read each student's work carefully enough to determine how well it meets those criteria. Finally, we must be self-aware and confident enough in our level of expertise to apply the criteria.

We do not, however, have to give students bad grades on their poems and short stories. Instead, we can ask students to supply other evidence of learning, evidence that is both easier to assess and easier for the students to have assessed. We can, for example, quiz students to determine how well they can articulate the concepts we have discussed. Granted, quizzes measure only knowledge, not application, but doesn't knowing certain terms and concepts help students understand what they might be doing?

We can also ask students to produce more traditional essays analyzing and evaluating collections of stories and poems, literary magazines, or their classmates' works-in-progress. To write an effective analysis, students need to read carefully and recognize specific devices or strategies that a writer uses. They also need to support their opinions, follow the conventions of standard grammar, and present their ideas clearly and coherently. These are skills most people expect students in higher education to learn and practice, whether they major in creative writing or biology – and these thinking and writing skills may benefit students' own stories and poems.

We can also grade students based on revision. I tell my students that revision does not always produce a better story, but revisions they submit to me at the end of the semester should show an attempt to address concerns or questions raised during the workshop. In other words, I read their revised work to see if they are able to do something they did not appear able to do when they submitted the piece to the workshop. Finally, being objective when grading student writing may be more difficult than being objective when grading a math exam or a history paper, but anyone who grades is guilty of some degree of subjectivity. When students are being evaluated on how well they apply concepts as opposed to how well they can articulate concepts, evaluation is difficult, no matter what the discipline. Each poem or story we write requires us to relearn and apply the fundamentals of writing all over again, and knowing what we need to do doesn't mean we *can* do it. These truths help us understand why grading is difficult.

They also explain why the grade earned may not merely reflect whether I think a particular poem or story is very good. For the serious writers, my extensive comments on their work rather than the grade will help them understand my evaluation of the work. And regardless of the grades they earn on stories and poems, students who earn high grades for the course are students whose understanding of fiction or poetry is more complex and informed than it was before the class. Final grades, therefore, reflect progress rather than effort, an ability to master certain objectives rather than to write great literature. Perhaps grades can also reinforce the idea that great writing results from knowledge of craft, discipline and perseverance, and continual practice, not innate ability or deeply felt passions.

Is it too much, then, to ask our students to demonstrate that they have learned something significant in our class, and can't we do this with some conviction? We do know more about writing than most of our students, and while that doesn't always make us better writers or the best judges of their work, it does make it possible for us to establish a useful degree of authority.

Assumption #5: Teaching is What Failed Writers Do

There is, of course, the old cliché: those who can't write, teach. The truth is, though, those who can write often do teach poorly because they do not want to spend time studying pedagogy, reading student work, conducting lengthy workshops. Hans Ostrom (1994: xii) writes that 'seeing themselves as writers first and teachers second,' most creative writing professors do not study critical theory or pedagogy. Sometimes, professors do not even study their students' work. When I was at Iowa State University, Jane Smiley made no qualms about the fact that she sometimes read my story 10 minutes before we met to discuss it. Smiley was a brilliant reader and teacher, regardless of how little time she spent reading my work. But her time then (she was on leave) was devoted – fortunately for all of us – working on *A Thousand Acres,* which was published the year after I graduated.

It isn't that good writers make better teachers or that only mediocre or bad writers teach; the trouble is, both good teaching and good writing take time, and we have to make decisions about how to invest that time. Instead of being honest about their reluctance to spend time teaching, though, some people seem to want to justify it by claiming that writing can't really be taught, that grading can damage a student's self-esteem, or that we're too subjective when it comes to grading. Ostrom suggests, too, that some creative writing professors cling to the Romantic view of the writer as 'isolated author whose spirit breathes life into an organic art form, and when native talent or "genius" meets solitude, good artistic things happen' (1994: xv). Writers who promote this viewpoint, they argue, have no need for pedagogy or theory, for they see writers as needing no teaching, no guidance (p. xv). The view is convenient for those who want to justify their lack of involvement in and evaluation of their students' learning.

We continue to demand that colleges and universities recognize the differences between teaching writing classes and teaching classes like history, classes that do not require professors to read and evaluate student writing, but until universities reduce the workload for writing faculty, the workshop in which the professor is merely equal participant and not the authority remains tremendously appealing.

Instead, we should admit that our interest in teaching *does* diminish our commitment to writing and that the two will come into conflict. Perhaps, teaching even diminishes our ability to write well, to think creatively, to produce original work. Certainly it takes time, time that could be spent writing.

Assumption #6: Grades Are Meaningless

At the beginning of every semester, I ask my composition students to define what individual grades mean. Every semester, at least half of the class responds that A means a student tried hard, while B represents a pretty diligent effort, and C means the student didn't really try. The assumption students have is that grades reflect effort, not evidence of ability or of progress. To help them think about grades differently, I talk about my own valiant effort in math classes, where the highest grade I ever earned was a B– in a course referred to as 'Math for Tree Stumps' or 'Math for Poets.' I also assure them that it is unlikely that anyone will ever take their composition grade into account when making decisions related to employment. Grades are intended to communicate a student's performance to other instructors, to other schools, and to the student. As Jedrey (1982: 104) explains, 'The grade conveys a relatively unambiguous message about a student's progress in a universally understood system of academic notation.'

Grades *should* be unambiguous and universally understood, but I'm aware that, even in an academic setting and especially in creative writing classes, they rarely are. The most commonly given grade at both Tulsa Community College and at Yale University is an A, which could mean that most students at these institutions are brilliant or that they tried hard or that professors have decided to quit resisting the forces that contribute to grade inflation. In any case, the student who earns numerous As in her classes may or may not be a true scholar.

Bad grades, on the other hand, do not indicate whether a student will succeed in future endeavors, nor do they seem to prevent students from achieving the goals they have set. Sometimes, bad grades are actually an indication of true genius. Sometimes, I'm forced to recognize that my pedagogy caters mostly to the mediocre student, the one who has neither the resources nor the self-discipline to develop an appreciation for the elements of craft without the structure of a course. While my approach may help some students become better writers, those who are already quite talented sometimes choose not to complete certain assignments or participate in workshop discussions. As a result, they may earn lower grades than some students who earnestly and diligently complete assignments and participate in class discussions. And how frustrating is that? I end up feeling as if my composition students are partially correct: grades have to do with effort and a capacity to conform to the professor's specific expectations; grades have nothing to do with talent or ability or the poem or story itself.

Nonetheless, we must give grades, and we know that students feel they mean something. Jedry (1982: 103) writes, 'As students, most of us felt that a grade was in some sense an evaluation of our personal worth, not just our work.' He speculates that such feelings result from the fact that grades in a college environment appear authoritative and precise, and while evaluation occurs in other life experiences, 'outside college seldom is [evaluation] done so frequently or so explicitly'. So, while we understand that grades have a definite impact on writing students, we also know they have little meaning in terms of a student's talent or potential. Why grade at all, then? Why not give only A's and hope that, by doing so, we encourage the good writers and give the less talented writers confidence with which to continue developing their skills?

Grades may seem sometimes counterproductive to what we want to do in our classroom, but until grades are no longer assumed to be an 'unambiguous message about a student's progress,' we are stuck with them and should attempt to make them mean something useful. A grade merely indicates a student's ability to meet certain criteria, and as long as we make those criteria clear to students, as long as students understand the limited message that a grade conveys, we could feel comfortable about grading.

Conclusion

One of my colleagues in another department has adopted a new teaching strategy: he lectures on Mondays, then does not show up for class at all on Wednesdays and Fridays. Students are to use this time to read, review lecture notes, and to take a comprehension quiz, which is graded with a scantron in the writing lab. My colleague remains in his office in case students have questions about the reading. Most days, he's off campus by noon. Does anyone complain about this pedagogical approach? Certainly not the students. Some administrators were unhappy at first, but enrollment in his classes remains high and students are happy. Of course, some colleagues complained, but at least one other instructor has decided to teach this way, too.

So why don't I just relax, stop worrying about my authority and students' learning? I'd have more time for my own writing; more students would enroll in my easy-A, fun-filled creative writing classes; and revenues from high enrollment would please administrators. Since I teach at a community college, I could even justify this approach, since part of our mission is, after all, to provide greater access to higher education and to serve the needs of the community.

Our mission also states, however, that we will offer 'educational opportunities' to a variety of students 'in a supportive learning environment conducive to the development of the student's potential.' Some of my students will transfer to four-year programs, some perhaps will attend MFA programs. Aren't I, then, responsible for creating a learning environment, for trying to encourage students' potential, for ensuring that students can pursue a variety of opportunities?

Establishing authority takes time and effort. It requires that we develop criteria with which to judge work, clarify those criteria for students, and read their writing carefully so that we can apply those criteria fairly. Finally, we must evaluate students' progress toward learning certain elements of craft: we *must* make a judgment, and that judgment should mean something. Many of our assumptions work against embracing this role; yet to neglect it is to jeopardize the field's position in higher education. Even as more and more students enroll in creative writing programs and as colleges and universities – even community colleges – establish creative writing programs, the suspicion that creative writing professors are less academic, less rigorous, and that creative writing can't *really* be taught and therefore doesn't *really* belong in an academic setting lingers. We can address this suspicion by over-exerting our authority and dismissing anyone who questions it, by relinquishing our authority and creating the type of classroom I described in the opening, or, as I do, by struggling each semester to figure out just what we're doing, why we're doing it, and why it matters.

References

Booth, W.C. (2000) Boring from within: The art of the freshman essay. In L. H. Peterson, J.C. Brereton and J.E. Hartman (eds) *The Norton Reader* (pp. 494–504). New York: Norton.

Brookhart, S. (1988) Why 'Grade inflation' is not a problem with a 'Just say no' solution. *Phi Kappa Phi Journal* 78 (2), 3–5.

Gardner, J. (1983) *The Art of Fiction: Notes On Craft for Young Writers.* New York: Random-Vintage.

Grimes, T. (1999) The workshop's evolution and the writer's life. *The Writer's Chronicle* 32 (1), 19–30.

Jedrey, C.M. (1982) Grading and evaluation. In M. Morganroth Gullette (ed.) *The Art and Craft of Teaching* (pp. 103–115). Cambridge: Harvard-Danforth Center for Teaching and Learning.

Ostrom, H. (1994) Introduction. In W. Bishop and H. Ostrom (eds) *Colors of a Different Horse: Rethinking Creative Writing Theory and Pedagogy.* Urbana: National Council of Teachers of English.

Radavich, D. (1999) Creative writing in the academy. *Profession*, 106–12.

Sarbo, L. and Moxley, J.M. (1994) Creativity research and classroom practice. In W. Bishop and H. Ostrom (eds) *Colors of a Different Horse: Rethinking Creative Writing Theory and Pedagogy* (pp. 133–45). Urbana: National Council of Teachers of English.

Tulsa Community College (2002) 'Mission Statement.' 31 July. <http://www.Tulsacc.ok.us/catalogpages1-85.pdf>.

Chapter 7

Who's the Teacher?: From Student to Mentor

AUDREY PETTY

> We can only retell and live by the stories we have read and heard.
> We live our lives through texts. They may be read, or chanted, or
> experienced electronically, or come to us, like the murmurings of
> our mothers, telling us what conventions demand. (Heilbrun, 1988:
> 37)

Like many creative writing professors, I began teaching college writers
when I was a graduate student. The University of Massachusetts at
Amherst and its writing program, with theorists like Peter Elbow and
Anne Herrington as professor-administrators, privileged a process-
oriented approach to composition. Students were encouraged to
freewrite as they began drafts in class; they worked through at least
three drafts for every essay assigned, allowing ample time for peer and
teacher feedback; and final drafts were accompanied by process notes
in which students reflected upon their progress from draft to draft. The
program's method facilitated a student's own observations of herself in
process. From the start, teaching was an exhilarating process for me as
I witnessed my students gaining a deeper sense of ownership of and
connection to their writing over the course of a semester.

There, in a graduate composition pedagogy class at U-Mass, I
found the language and theory for my most deeply held beliefs
about productive teaching and learning. Paulo Freire's critique of
the 'banking system of education' – with teacher as depositor and
student as depository – was particularly compelling, as that very
system had been reproduced in the majority of the high school classes
I'd attended. (And I struggled, or sometimes refused to struggle, to
make the grade in many of those circumstances.) Fortunately, as
a college student, I experienced a different classroom, one in which
student experiences and insights were significantly brought into
dialogue. To me, the creative writing courses at Knox College seemed
most revolutionary in that sense. There, I felt authorized to read closely
and respond critically to published and student work. My writing

classes were integral to the college education that transformed me into a self-assured thinker.

I returned to my undergraduate alma mater six years ago to begin my college teaching career. The transition from being student to being faculty was, to put it mildly, a challenging one. While I enjoyed teaching composition and literature that first year at Knox College, I felt inept and awkward in my creative writing class. The roots of the problem lay in my desperate attempts to impersonate my most influential undergraduate teacher, whose colleague I had become.

In more ways than one, my mentor/colleague's positive influence had led me to my career. A graduate of Princeton University who went on to earn his M.F.A. from the Iowa Writers' Workshop, he had inspired me with his intelligence and compassion. At 19 years old, I'd never met anyone who read so widely or cared so intensely about the lives on a page. As a mentor, my colleague had inspired me by taking me seriously when I wrote my first story; he inspired me by demanding that I take myself seriously as well. His classroom was a space in which I felt the freedom to pursue questions about how an act of terrible violence leaves it traces on an elementary school playground or why the love of a parent cannot go far enough to save his teenage son. My mentor's classroom was a space in which the stakes felt intoxicatingly high. Writing was serious business.

By the time I returned to Knox as a new hire, my treasured professor, who had been teaching there for nearly 30 years, continued to ignite young writers across the campus. Had my first college teaching job been elsewhere, I'm certain that I still would have filed through memories of my mentor/colleague's classes to provide a standard for teaching fiction writing. Returning to my alma mater only intensified the desire that many new creative writing professors have to replicate those classes that made a difference to us as writers and to fit the teaching model that had been important to me as a student.

Imitation was the first creative strategy I reached for when I began writing poems at eight years old. (William Wordsworth and Gwendolyn Brooks were my first role models.) And imitation is an approach I have come to assign to my beginning writing students. Without fail, the pastiche exercise they perform (e.g. 'rewrite "Hills Like White Elephants" from the slant of John Updike's colorful and conflicted narrator in "A&P"') serves as a revelatory experience. The exercise demands that students read with meticulousness in order to discern 'the writer's signature' (Bailey, 2000). The exercise also sensitizes them to their own writing tendencies and makes plain the truth that creating a story means entering a series of choices.

I did my best, then, to imitate my mentor/colleague when I taught my first fiction workshop. I'd ask leading questions and wait for a discussion to unfold. Occasionally, I'd enter the conversation to ask another question or to point out a pattern that I had discovered in the work we were studying. My class wasn't awful, but it was sorely lacking. While we managed to address basic issues of technique and theme in student work, our conversations seemed flat and perfunctory; our dialogue did not connect from one class to the next. We had no momentum.

Within the first weeks of workshop, I painfully realized that I could not inhabit the same space my mentor/colleague did as a teacher. He taught as a storyteller. I couldn't. I couldn't tell long and colorful anecdotes about my personal experiences or share my own deep musings about the nature of sex and love and death even though my professor had modeled that very well, and had made me thoughtful and adult as his audience. I also couldn't keep my workshops running as long as he did. While we both started our classes at 7 p.m. on Wednesdays, mine ran until about 10:30 p.m. His ran – as they did when I was his student – until midnight or later. I couldn't meet with students for workshops at the local bar. I tried it twice and battled with the noise of the cash register, with the hard and clunky patio furniture, with the friendly waitress checking in regularly. My mentor taught as a confidante – the conference space being fluid, eternal, and open to disclosure of all sorts from students – and I couldn't be this kind of confidante.

My efforts to emulate my mentor/colleague confused my students, along with whom I had been asked for identification as proof of legal drinking age during our first meeting at the Cherry Street Brewing Company. And my instincts told me that this confidante approach might cause students to view me as someone less than professional and serious. I didn't know how to make such interaction meaningful to my teaching – and frankly, I wasn't sure I wanted to. As that first term progressed, I began to accept that that way of teaching wasn't me, all the while appreciating that my mentor/colleague's authority, was in part, rooted in a powerful intimacy forged between himself and his students. I began grasping the fact that my mentor/colleague's experience as well as his race and gender were crucial to his approach and to the reception he received.

By trying to imitate my mentor/colleague, I came up against the reality of my own body. After all, I had returned to Knox as myself:

a young, petite, baby-faced, mild-mannered, African-American woman. When I walked in my classroom and sat down that first day, I could tell that nearly all the students were still waiting for the teacher to arrive. My teaching experience had been different in graduate school, where, as a T.A., I had instructed composition classes taught almost exclusively by graduate students; furthermore, the University of Massachusetts' population was significantly more racially diverse than Knox's. My age and race had not set me apart as dramatically as they did at Knox, where I taught in the shadow of my mentor/colleague, a white man 20 years my senior.

At Knox, my authority was far from automatic. As is the case for many new creative writing faculty, my authority was dubious, up for grabs. As this reality set in, so did a spine-chilling panic. While I felt an ethical and intellectual obligation to decenter the class, I also began to fear that process. This ambivalence manifested itself daily. Taking a cue from former workshops, I had my workshops sit in a circle. I'd assign process notes to accompany student drafts. 'And yes,' I'd tell my students enthusiastically, 'you *can* and you *should* use personal pronouns in your readers' response papers.' On the other hand, I felt the incredible urge to purchase power suits and high-heeled shoes in which to teach. I even considered investing in expensive makeup in hopes of making myself look more mature. And I almost forbade students from calling me by my first name, in contrast to the tradition set by generations of creative writing professors at Knox and elsewhere. If any of the workshoppers had dared to ask me why we were reading *The Best American* short story anthology for our textbook, I'd have to respond: 'because I said so.' The real reason, of course, was because that's what my mentor/colleague had assigned to my classmates and me way back when. While I admired my mentor/colleague and firmly believed in encouraging my students' interaction and independence, I was also looking for my own structure and my own set of boundaries. How could I make myself appear a capable writing teacher? Could I convincingly perform authority?

In their dialogue, 'Building a teaching community,' bell hooks and Ron Scapp discuss the ways in which the teacher's gendered and racialized body may inform students' assumptions about that teacher's authority. Scapp asserts: 'as a white university teacher in his thirties, I'm profoundly aware of my presence in the classroom [...] given the history of the male body, and of the male teacher. I need to be sensitive and critical of my presence in the history that has led me there' (hooks, 1994: 135). hooks, an African-American woman, affirms

Scapp's observations about the teacher body's as a historicized one, and describes early teaching experiences that resonate with my own. She recounts her nervous reluctance, as young professor, to literally step away from her desk. 'I remember thinking, "This really is about power"' (hooks, 1994: 138). hooks insists that such a reckoning is fundamental to her commitment to a liberatory pedagogy, a 'practice of freedom':

> Once we start talking in the classroom about the body and how we live in our bodies, we're automatically challenging the way power has orchestrated itself in that particular institution. The person who is the most powerful has the privilege of denying their body. (hooks, 1994: 136–7)

A new faculty member, especially one who is young, African-American, and female, does not have this power and privilege. Neither I nor my students, however, could deny my physical self.

Ultimately, the impact of a lifetime of positive and negative classroom experiences inoculated me from giving in to my authoritarian impulses. I didn't resort to buying a single power suit, but I had to become a much more definite and defining presence in the classroom. And this presence had to be projected by who I was and what I valued. As much as I wanted my students to take ownership of our workshops, I needed to stake my own claims by claiming authority in ways that felt meaningful and sound. Gradually, I began to identify myself as a set of texts to offer to the class. I shared my questions about distinctions and links between genres by bringing in poetry, flash fiction, songs, and plays for us to unravel. I gave students time – something I desperately craved as a writer – to freewrite in class. I introduced them to stories I loved. And things improved.

When my first 10-week term of teaching had ended, I was humbler and wiser, and raring to teach workshop again. In addition to initiating broader conversations about fiction, I chose new textbooks and revised my syllabus, my assignments, and my basis for student evaluation. My syllabus has continued to change over the years. The assignments I've added allow for a more sustained, dynamic consideration of the craft of fiction. While I had encouraged students to use research as a tool in crafting work in my first two fiction classes, I now include narratives like Michael Ondaatje's (1996) *Coming Through Slaughter* as a text for close study. Through its unconventional use of point of view and artifact, *Coming Through Slaughter* addresses (or some might say that it inhabits) the life of the obscure, long-deceased Storyville musician,

Buddy Bolden. Additionally, I now assign each student a collection of short stories to read and present to the class. I ask that they enter these assignments with one very basic question in mind: what can I learn from this text as a writer? This question allows us to engage in vital discussions about craft, and I trust that it makes the students more reflective about the choices they make as they write. My developing pedagogy is now not a loose, uncritical adaptation of those who taught me; instead, my more aware, authority-conscious pedagogy is conveyed and supported through secondary texts.

Of course, such refinements in my teaching plan did not ensure a completely harmonious relationship with all of my fiction students. It was in the area of conferencing that I experienced the most significant, prolonged anxiety about the differences between my mentor/colleague and myself. My mentor/colleague scheduled one-on-one meetings to discuss poems, stories, or essays with students nearly twice as much as I did – or rather, I had chosen to conference with students half as much as he did. I felt considerable pressure from students to match his schedule. On several occasions early on in a given term, students would approach me to ask why I didn't plan to conference as often as they expected; some verged on requesting that I revise my syllabus. Evidently, they had come to understand, through experience or simply through grapevine anecdote, a specific equation: fiction class = x number of conferences. As a beginning teacher in a very small school that placed a premium on student evaluations, I, at first, had difficulty fielding these students' concerns with tact or clarity or self-confidence, but I relied on my graduate school experience as a composition instructor to sustain my resolve.

At heart, I believe that the conference can be a space in which students 'learn to read their own drafts with increasing effectiveness' (Murray, 1985: 148). I'm convinced that this learning is accomplished more by the content of conferences than by their frequency. My first creative writing conferences as a professor were horribly regrettable. Unable to clearly recall how my mentor/colleague conducted his conferences, I tended to leave it up to each student to provide an engine for discussion. It's not that I didn't read and reread their stories or have opinions about them – I simply didn't trust myself to set an agenda for the direction of our conversations and wanted to empower students, as mentor/colleague and others had, by encouraging students to set agendas.

The students' agendas were quite varied. Some came to conference to cultivate friendship; some wanted to explain their stories to me; others were raring to talk turkey: how to get published, how to find an agent;

and then, there were those few who had nothing at all to say. Fortunately, this conference free-fall didn't last too long. My composition-instructor reflexes kicked in and saved me. The key was to focus on the work and the process. As Donald Murray (1985) asserts in *A Writer Teaches Writing*, the 'conference will not be fully understood if it is seen just as a dialogue between teacher and student or writer and a writer. The text itself plays an important role, usually an equal role, sometimes a dominant role in the conference. What occurs is really a trialogue between student, teacher, and text' (Murray, 1985: 150). Conference time allows me to get to know each student's vision for his or her work, and it allows me to ask questions and provide a cogent critique for the student to consider. Most of all, the conference becomes about my relationship to the student's writing and the student's relationship to the writing.

As was the case when I taught writing in graduate school, conferences have become a crucial location for me to assess a student's process. Questions of authority and how it is forged, deflected, and/or re-negotiated are particularly fraught in the creative writing classroom, where teachers encourage an artistic process and, in most cases, must assess its results with an end-of-term grade. My aim as I grade is to view the final portfolio as manifestation of a process instead of as a freestanding project. Conferencing allows me to more closely observe how a student moves through drafts and to give considerable weight to how a student progresses as she re-thinks and refines her work. Conferences, then, served a key role in my own re-thinking and refining of an authority-conscious pedagogy that worked in my courses.

All in all, I felt mighty divided during my first years of college teaching, and I'm convinced that other writer-teachers share similar experiences related to the demands of the job. Even as I was reconsidering the specifics of the example set by my mentor/colleague, I was still adhering to a basic principle of being ever-accessible, devoting nearly all of my energies to serving the needs of others. Young, untenured, African-American, and female in an overwhelmingly white institution, I wore many hats at once. In addition to teaching, conferencing, and researching for classes and independent studies, I, like many creative writing professors, was a busy committee member and advisor. Less official, but equally important were my duties of advising and supporting students of color on campus. I had re-entered Knox with a strong vision of its strengths and needs and with a powerful sense of indebtedness for everything it had provided me. Without a doubt, I gained a great deal of satisfaction from the wide set of responsibilities

I assumed and from the contributions to the institution and the concept of education that mattered in my own development. But inevitably, my teaching self was at odds with my writing self.

What is more difficult than honing my syllabus, conferencing with students, or creating dialogue during workshop is going to my desk regularly and working on a piece of my own. I now believe that this role is crucial to my effectiveness as teacher. The Associated Writing Programs agrees: 'AWP reminds institutions that a teaching writer needs large amounts of time to do his or her own work. [...] As with other arts, the writing teacher will be effective as a teacher only insofar as he or she is active and engaged as a writer [...]' (AWP, 2003: 5). Just as conferencing with a student requires that we both focus on the text, being a creative writing professor demands, for me, that I remain immersed in my own writing and share that experience as a teacher. My great part in trust-building and instruction comes through modeling for my students – showing them my passion about a piece of writing; demonstrating how to read a story, an essay, or a poem with care; and working at being a writer myself: authorizing myself through regular work at the craft.

I'm now finishing my second year of teaching at the University of Illinois at Urbana-Champaign. Leaving my alma mater for the second time made for a bittersweet graduation. Fortunately, I stayed at Knox long enough to make some peace with my mentor/colleague's legend *and* advance in establishing my own agenda as a writing teacher; long enough to build rich relationships with students and witness their growth over time, even beyond their tenures at Knox; long enough to miss the place now. Knox offered me a safe and unsettling first home as a professor. I am grateful for the whole of it.

Although I've clearly left Knox, the contours of my new academic residence – a Big Ten, research-I university – are still materializing around me. There is much to discover. The English department faculty here is almost ten times the size of the department at Knox, the library is immense, and the campus sprawls for a good mile or two. I must admit, I haven't minded being rather clueless about what's where, who's who, and what's what at the U of I because my time in the classroom now offers the reassuringly familiar. Teaching – with a lower course load – bestows me with stimulating, intimate engagement in this new community. In addition, as the University of Illinois is in woeful need of more faculty of color, I am committed to assuming the same kinds of unofficial mentoring/community-building duties that I'd assumed elsewhere. I also welcome the institutional demands of becoming a more widely published, active writer and scholar. My future here relies upon maintaining the balance to which I already aspire, a balance I've come to slowly.

Much work remains to be done outside of the classroom when it comes to inhabiting and asserting my authority within it. In addition to creating texts through the practice of writing, it is vital that I continually seek existing ones to examine, to contest, and/or to live by. In *Colors of a Different Horse: Rethinking Creative Writing Theory and Pedagogy*, Patrick Bizzaro argues that teachers 'must spend less time telling our students what they should do when they write and more time showing them who they can be' (Bishop & Ostrom, 1994: 234). Like Murray (1985), Bizzaro envisions an evolving teacher-student relationship, one aimed toward empowering the student to rightfully claim authority as a writer and reader. The teacher, by modeling the use of a range of literary-critical methods of reading, equips the student with various lenses to critique and/or create their own writing and critique that of their fellow students.

Equally important are benefits that such engagement with literary *and* composition theory can provide to the teacher. Wendy Bishop observes that such 'cross-fertilization' allows for the integration of teacher and writer identities. 'If we write with our students in class, write about our classes, read theory and writers with an eye to developing the students in class the student in ourselves, we develop an ecologically sound system for our writing lives' (Bishop and Ostrom, 1994: 291). My professional, artistic, and pedagogical growth has relied upon a fundamental shift in the way I understand my own roles, authorities, and interests. To categorize them in binary terms – student and teacher; encourager of students and grader of students; reader of literature and reader of theory; writer and critic; and teacher and writer – needlessly sets them in opposition. bell hooks and Ron Scapp remind me that this, too, can be the case for the teacher who attempts to separate body and mind. Finally, these selves have begun to integrate within me so that I am now confident – as are my students – that the teacher has arrived and is still at work, arriving.

References

The AWP Director's Handbook (2003) Fairfax, VA: Associated Writing Programs.

Bailey, T. (ed.) (2000) *On Writing Short Stories*. New York: Oxford University Press.

Bishop, W. and Ostrom, H. (eds) (1994) *Colors of a Different Horse: Rethinking Creative Writing Theory and Pedagogy*. Urbana: National Council of Teachers of English.

Heilbrun, C. (1988) *Writing a Woman's Life*. New York: Ballantine.

hooks, bell (1994) *Teaching to Transgress: Education as the Practice of Freedom.*
New York: Routledge.
Murray, D. (1985) *A Writer Teaches Writing.* Boston: Houghton Mifflin.
Ondaatje, M. (1996) *Coming Through Slaughter* (1st international edn). New
York: Vintage International.

Chapter 8
The Pregnant Muse: Assumptions, Authority, and Accessibility

RACHEL HALL

> It was as Mother that woman was fearsome: it is in maternity that she
> must be transfigured and enslaved.
>
> (Simone de Beauvoir, *The Second Sex*)

After several years as a creative writing professor, I'd become relatively comfortable with my pedagogical approaches and my teacherly identity. Then my identity and my authority shifted. Because becoming a mother affected student response to me both in the classroom and outside, both during office hours and in more casual interactions, I am now aware of the way any instructor's physicality influences students' perceptions of creative writing teachers and classes. While all teachers interact as physical beings, my experiences as a teacher who is also a mother provide an examination of some of the assumptions students bring to and form within creative writing courses.

Even now, when it is generally believed that these seemingly non-pedagogical issues have been resolved, difficulties of all kinds face mothers in the academy: negotiating maternity leave; finding and securing quality child care; balancing the demands of teaching, writing, and community and campus service with parenting. The biggest challenge, however, was one I hadn't anticipated, one that emerged in conjunction with my motherhood but is undoubtedly at work even when not highlighted by such an identity shift: how to maintain my authority. Becoming a mother is an empowering creative act, but instead of inspiring respect, I was often dismissed, treated with a mixture of boredom and condescension. When a friend mentioned that television sitcoms suffer a drop in ratings after an infant is introduced into the story line, I had a moment of recognition. My ratings were dropping. As surprised as I was to discover the impact of motherhood on my teaching, I have been even more so by its impact on my writing life.

* * *

It is a dreary afternoon in western New York. In this beginning fiction writing class, the students are turning in their first assignment. We have to distribute them quickly in order to get to the discussion of two published stories. As I do every semester, I have given the class explicit directions about coming prepared, with the appropriate number of copies, already stapled and labeled. Only about half the class is prepared. The rest are madly collating on their desks' lima-bean-shaped tops. At eight months pregnant, I can no longer wedge myself into these desks. To join the circle, I have to ask a student to bring me the armchair from behind the lectern. Papers slip off the students' desk tops, sail through the air, and land on the scuffed wood floor. Someone asks if I have a stapler on me.

I'm tired from carrying around an extra 25 pounds, from waking every couple hours at night to pee. 'No, I don't have a stapler,' I say, measuredly. 'I thought I asked you guys to come prepared.'

I catch the eyes of one student, a young man whose writing and comments in class show promise. I intend to encourage him to take more writing classes. But his eyes startle me; they are steely, contemptuous. I imagine he is thinking 'Pregnant bitch,' 'Cow,' 'What's the big deal?' Behind me, the heater grinds loudly. One thing is clear: I am no longer who I think I am. My new girth, the loose smock and stretch pants, are speaking for me, telling students who I am, what I am, and in this role I am supposed to be patient and nurturing, uncritical, and unconditionally loving.

I'm aware of something else, too, another transgression: I have brought my body – my clumsy, swollen, female body – into the classroom, called attention to the fact that I am a woman in a place where man is still the model of authority. Of course, all professors have bodies, but some bodies can be overlooked in a way that others cannot. It isn't so long ago, really, that pregnant public school teachers were not allowed to teach after their fifth month, when many would still barely show. My students are not aware of such strictures, nor are they fully aware of their own conflicted feelings about their mothers. Does my pregnancy conjure up images of their mothers pregnant with younger siblings? Do they expect a sense of desertion they may have felt when their mothers were at the hospital, returning days later with a new baby? Do they desire creative writing teachers to be especially parental, and do I now validate that desire? A former colleague said that when she told students they needed to clean up their grammar, it was as if she had told them to clean up their rooms – a look of shame and anger and rebellion burned across their eyes. In *Of Woman Born*, Adrienne Rich (1976: 11) writes, because young humans remain dependent upon nurture for a much longer period than other mammals, and because of the division of labor long established in human groups, where women not only bear and suckle but are assigned almost total responsibility for children, most of us know both love and disappointment, power and tenderness, in the person of a woman.

Whatever my students think, it is clear that somehow I bring their mothers into the classroom, whoever she might be – kind, generous, demanding, withholding, distracted, devoted.

The intense discomfort of this ambivalence is surely brought into focus by a creative writing class that asks students to dig deep, to write from experience. Probably, a pregnant professor is noted with some consternation in any classroom, but I suspect it is heightened in the creative writing classroom by two things: (1) the general perception of creative writing as something without objective criteria, something suspiciously emotional and therefore female within the otherwise rational, male academy; and (2) the decentralized authority of the workshop model. In other words, my own experience has given me insight about my authority as a creative writing teacher of which I'd been previously unaware, though surely issues of authority exist for all of us.

Much later, when I tell a writer friend about my experience that dreary day, she tells me about Gordon Lish, the year *Esquire* dubbed him Captain Fiction, pointing to a pregnant woman in a workshop and saying that she couldn't be a serious writer of fiction. Writers, he said, put nothing before their work. My students don't articulate the sentiment that mothers can't be writers, but it is the unconscious assumption out of which many of them work. For them, writers dress in black, smoke pipes, drink bourbon straight from bottle, and die by their own hand or of syphilis. Mothers, on the other hand, are boring but dependable. Mothers are the ones holding up the line in the grocery store with their coupons. They are the ones demanding that dishes get put in the dishwasher, that feet get wiped. Mothers especially don't fit the cool stereotype, but many other creative writing teachers don't either.

By the time I was pregnant, I'd been teaching full-time for five years and was accustomed to some students' belief that writing couldn't be taught. They wouldn't put it that way; instead, they'd resist criticism and write subversive comments on peer's work: 'This is perfect!' or 'I wouldn't change a thing!' Years ago, I'd developed ways of handling this: emphasizing revision; requiring readings from texts which explained the elements, craft, and technique of fiction or poetry; assigning exercises before asking students to attempt full-length stories; and discussing published work in a way that reminded students that choices (first-person or third-person? past tense or present?) were made in its creation. More recently, I have devoted time on the first day of class to a discussion of my assumptions about students' presence in a creative writing classroom. It tells me, I say, that they believe writing is something that can be taught, that there are standards by which we can distinguish a good poem or story from a less successful one, and that they are interested in having an audience and communicating with that audience through their writing. By being explicit, I assert creative writing's legitimacy as a serious subject and prevent – I hope – some student resistance. Not infrequently, students who look annoyed during this discussion will drop the class, though sometimes they stick around and make me miserable for the whole semester, poisoning other students with their resistance to criticism.

While occasional students think that whim and personal preference guide my comments and grades, I seemed mostly successful until that February afternoon. That day, it was revealed to me the double-whammy to authority a woman teacher of writing faces: creative writing's place in the academy is still suspect, as is the woman writer-professor. My pregnant body overtly marked me *woman*, though of course I had been a woman for my entire teaching career. That day, I had become a certain kind of woman, and this kind was meant to be at home. Alicia Ostriker (1983: 126) puts it best: 'that women should have babies instead of books is the considered opinion of the Western civilization. That women should have books instead of babies is just a variation on that theme'.

Without a doubt, the double-whammy can be a time-consuming frustration and annoyance. In class and conferences, pains must be taken to make each student feel appreciated. In anticipation of it, one's response to student work must be both stern and yielding. I cannot, for instance, say, as my beginning poetry-writing teacher said to me, 'this is a waste of your time and mine,' though this sort of approach still exists. I just heard a story in which a young male professor told a graduate student to abandon her story about a mother and daughter set in suburbia. 'It's been done before,' he said. I can't imagine saying such a thing to a student, nor do I agree with the professor. What hasn't been done before? Over the years, I've read at least a dozen stories by male students in which the protagonist shoots his first deer, but not once have I said the subject was tired. The professor's maleness allows him the authority to make such proclamations, just as it did for my male professor nearly 20 years ago. It's not that I want to dismiss student work. My strategy is decidedly, consciously more nurturing, but whereas students balk at my gentle criticism, the male professor's summation of a story or poem as worthless is accepted.

Once in a creative non-fiction workshop I was teaching, a student raised his hand to say that the class wasn't thinking about the writer's intentions; we were too quick to criticize, he said. Later, discussing the goals of the workshop with the same class, I asked, 'what other class has the burden of making you feel good about yourself? Chemistry? British Literature?' Thankfully, we were able to laugh, but at the time of the outburst, it was very tense. Balancing the rigor that is required to be taken seriously with the compassion required of the mother – or the nurturing creative writing teacher – is tricky at best. And I had to use class time – already at a premium with a class of 25 – to reexamine assumptions about creative writing as a discipline.

I know my students are anxious about my dual roles as professor and mother because their concerns show up in class evaluations. Questions like 'How responsive was the instructor?' and 'Was the instructor sensitive and patient?' are loaded. Even the administration at my school is aware of the way gender affects student expectations, and students are now required to indicate their gender on the forms as well as other information such as year in school and major. But these questions are particularly loaded for the mother-professor, given cultural expectations for mothers to praise and admire without reservation, to be constantly available and responsive, and to love every minute of it.

While I maintain more than the required number of office hours, my student evaluations starting with the semester I was pregnant showed low marks in this area. One student put it directly: 'I wish Rachel had more office hours, but I understand babies are more important.' After my daughter was nine months old and I returned to teaching half-time, I needed to express breast milk a couple times a day. I never used office hours for this activity, but I did use my office. I would shut the door and assemble the pump, which came – thankfully! – in a black leather briefcase. Still, during this time, students regularly knocked on my door. I might call out that I was busy or I would stay silent, hoping they couldn't hear the whir of the breast pump through the hollow wooden door, but it was clear to me from the disgruntled sounds and comments that my closed door was an affront. How could I, a mother, turn them away? How can any caring creative writing teacher not welcome them openly always?

Where I teach, faculty accessibility to students is expected and emphasized; it is considered carefully in decisions about tenure and promotion. College guidelines and requirements aside, I knew that my writing had benefited from conferences and discussions with my mentors, both in college and graduate school, and I wanted to do this for my students. But the very assumptions about mothers which refused me authority, also made me readily accessible to students. I was the June Cleaver of professors, always available to chat about writing or boyfriends or roommate problems, while my male colleague sat alone in his office, his feet on his desk, listening to Billie Holiday. I was being sucked dry, a metaphor which motherhood gave new resonance. And eventually, I came to see that this wasn't necessarily good for my students either. One student, a talented writer of densely layered, complex essays about her struggles with eating disorders, started coming by my office to show me each new paragraph, every alteration. She had grown so dependent on me for feedback, praise, and validation that she surrendered her own authority. Part of what I want to teach students like this one is that they have authority too.

It's worth remembering that *author* and *authority* have the same root. *Author* descends from a Latin word for *originator*, and *authority* draws from that idea of an original, trustworthy, or powerful source. Authority can refer both to control or influence and to witnessing or expertise. *Authority*, then, stems from the practice, patience, and informed strength that I demonstrate myself as a writer-teacher and that I foster in my students.

On the other hand, I don't think this student could have written this essay were it not for my maternal presence in the classroom. She was able to tell her story of obsession and self-denial in part because of the safe, compassionate space I work hard to create. The goal for authority-conscious pedagogy, then, becomes to find a way to sustain this safe space where student writers can grow, but also to set some boundaries so they don't become too dependent.

If student evaluations are a good indication of the level of student anxiety, student writing is a gold mine. Perhaps my students always wrote about mothers and I didn't notice it until I was a mother myself. But the deluge of mother stories and essays that came my way in the months after my maternity leave were thick with assumptions and judgment. In one story, a mother gives up her floral dresses for dark suits. In the beginning, she loves her work for the identity it gives her; she isn't 'Mommy' or 'hon' on the job, but 'Elizabeth.' Things turn, though, when she has an affair while on a business trip. The final scene shows the young mother – repentant – snuggled in bed with her husband and young daughter, 'happy to just be Mommy again.' She has decided to quit her job. The story had all kinds of structural problems, not to mention issues of character motivation. These aspects were what I focused on, asking questions about Elizabeth's motivation and asking the author to allow her more complexity – a love for her daughter and a desire to make her way in the world without punishing her. Mostly, though, the student readers liked the ending. It was challenging to talk about this story, as I was very conscious of my status as a working mother. My authority felt compromised as if I were responding to the story in a defensive manner even though my comments and suggestions were primarily technical. This story and other student work has led me to ponder how the teacher's identity may unintentionally influence even the subject matter of the students' writing and how students may use their stories and poems to please or rebel against whomever – whatever authority – they perceive us to be.

Another student that same semester wrote an essay in which she compared working mothers to pet-owners who pay someone else to walk their dogs: 'The way I see it, if you can't walk the dog yourself, don't have a pet. It's the same with parents and children.' She then went on to write about her mother's devotion to her children, 'not because she had to, but because she wanted to.' This time, I tried to get the class – an upper-level nonfiction class – thinking about the difficulty of knowing another person, particularly a parent. I'd been trying all semester to talk about ambivalence with this class, trying to get them to see that their best writing was coming out of this place. Ambivalence has come to mean, in this anti-intellectual time, wishy-washy or indecisive, so it was difficult to reorient students to understand that ambivalence is the result of strong opposing desires. The student ended up abandoning this piece, understanding a little, I think, the assumptions she was making.

Neither of these students was antagonistic. Both of them, in fact, repeatedly signed up for my classes; they were simply reacting to deep-seeded societal beliefs. My presence in the classroom made them question their mothers' actions and choices and forced them to think about choices they would need to make if they decided to become mothers. Their stories and essays were ways of working out these perplexing issues, and I've come to see the value in these attempts. An authority-conscious pedagogy makes space for this kind of learning and recognizes the role of the teacher-writer, the student-writer, and the written work in the process.

In *Of Woman Born*, Rich (1976: 61–2) writes,

women have been both mothers and daughters but have written little on the subject: the vast majority of literary and visual images of motherhood come to us filtered through the collective or individual male consciousness. As soon as a woman knows that a child is growing in her body, she falls under the power of theories, ideals, archetypes, descriptions of her new existence, almost none of which have come from other women (though other women may transmit them) and all of which floated invisibly about her since she first perceived herself to be female and therefore potentially a mother.

The result is what she calls 'The Great Silence.'

Twenty years later, Jane Smiley (1993) makes a similar comment in her essay 'Can Mothers Think?' Writing about literature, she asks, 'Where were the mothers? Why didn't they speak up? Can mothers actually think and speak?' Novelist Anne Enright (2001: 28) asks the same question in her journal excerpted in *Harper's*: 'Can a mother not hold a pen? Or is it the fact that we are all children when we write?' The absence of mother's voices in our literature, these mother/writers assert, is detrimental for the individual mother and the culture. In becoming a mother, I have also become a writing teacher more aware of the various stereotypes, silences, and assumptions that come to my classroom with my students and the texts.

* * *

When my daughter was just six weeks old, I needed to go to my office to turn in independent-study grades. I had to time the 40-minute commute around evolving nursing times. This trip was the first time I would be on campus as a mother. I was self-conscious, unsure of the rules (though aware that there were indeed rules). I both wanted and feared the attention and fuss. The drive went well, and this instilled confidence. As I entered the department, I ran into a former student, a fiction writer whom I appreciated for his honest, subtle language and his intuitive sense of plot.

'Hey, Chris,' I said.

'Hey,' he said, slowing to look into the baby carrier. 'How are you?'

'Good, but exhausted.'

'So this is your little bundle of joy,' he said.

I checked his face, expecting his ironic grin. *Bundle of joy?*

I couldn't allow my daughter, who was already a personality with particular gestures and squeals, to be turned into a cliché, anymore than I could stomach the implication that motherhood was wholly joyful. 'This is the hardest thing I've ever done,' I told Chris, perhaps a bit too fiercely.

I knew vaguely that I was up against more than Chris here, but I pushed on. I told him how consuming motherhood was, how filled with worry and fear and chaos and the unknown, before I noticed he was nodding politely, his eyes glazed over.

While that interaction with Chris wasn't successful and in fact silenced me for awhile, I've come to see this kind of conversation as part of my work – both in my writing and in my interactions with students. Isn't it the job of the writer-teacher to expose cliché and stereotype? In her book *The Mask of Motherhood*, Susan Maushart writes about the conspiracy of silence surrounding mothering stories. By talking about myths and writing mothering stories, I work against 'The Great Silence' and help future generations understand the difficulty of the task. Smiley (1993: 8) writes that the lack of mothers' voices is damaging for potential mothers because they

> have no variety in their models of mothering, and no model for articulating what it means to be a mother. Thus it is more likely that these girls will internalize those externally formulated projections of motherhood they find in their culture and discover, to their disappointment and frustration, that their 'performance' as mothers is almost inevitably wanting.

Rewriting motherhood is challenging, I admit, because people don't always want to hear the truth, maybe particularly from women, as Francine Prose (1998: 62) comments in her essay 'Scent of a woman's ink'. It is much nicer to believe that motherhood is wholly gratifying and blissful. Even intelligent adults are reluctant to imagine that their mothers didn't love every minute of motherhood. It is scary to confront maternal ambivalence because mother's love has been held out as a panacea for all society's ills: violence, drugs, teen pregnancy. What will protect us now? And of course, the listener can always decide it's just me – not all mothers – who find motherhood so demanding.

Like Young Goodman Brown, students are still mostly caught in what William Perry calls dualism or binary thinking (Hays, 1995: 154). Which is it, they demand – good or bad? challenging or blissful? Nothing taught me ambivalence like motherhood. Never before have I felt so intensely conflicting desires: I want to be with my child as

I write, and when I am with her, I wish to write. As I struggle with my ambivalence, I like to think of F. Scott Fitzgerald's definition of a genius as someone who can hold two opposing ideas at the same time. Certainly, good writing comes from studying our ambivalence. One can't write complex fictional characters without understanding ambivalence, nor can one write compellingly about death, illness, aging, love, and loss without first confronting his or her own ambivalence.

After talking endlessly, it seemed, about ambivalence in that nonfiction class, we celebrated the end of the year with a picnic and all donned pink *A*s for ambivalence. We were marked writers by our willingness to reside in our ambivalence, to go there and stay, resisting all cultural pressure to decide pro or con.

Motherhood, like adolescence, in part for the way that both experiences threw me into my body, was for me a crisis of identity: Who was I? What did I know? What did I want to do with my life? How would I make my place in the world? Out of this upheaval, came a new sense of purpose and ambition. I wanted to write and to reach people with my stories, partly to show my daughter what a woman could do and partly because I felt connected to world in a new way and wanted to contribute in the way I knew best. I began writing more seriously than I ever had, and my work grew richer and more complex, as did my teaching. Having a child made this commitment to my work harder, but it also made it possible.

*   *   *

As part of my newly aware pedagogical approaches and to ensure that I wrote during the school year, I told my advanced fiction workshop that I would do the writing exercises with them. When they turned theirs in, I did too, and my pieces were workshopped when time permitted. In addition to making myself write, this sharing of my writing was valuable in establishing both the rigor of creative writing and my authority as a writer. By modeling my process, I made students aware of the many choices an author makes in crafting a piece of fiction. Even my advanced students need to be reminded that fiction is a made thing and that there are strategies and techniques one can learn and employ. Most importantly, they saw me as a writer in a very concrete way. After the class moved from exercises to complete stories, I didn't feel comfortable using class time to workshop an entire story of mine, but I did give a reading as part of the English department series and invited my fiction-writing students to attend.

Having been reminded of my body, brought home to it, even if unwillingly, I see the danger in trying to forget that we – all of us – have bodies or pretend that we are all brain. Flannery O'Connor (1969: 67), whose chronic illness no doubt was a constant reminder of the body, writes that we know the world through our bodies, through our eyes, nose, mouth, ears, fingers, and that these are the ultimate tools of the fiction writer. Robert Pinsky (1998: 8), too, points out, 'The medium of poetry is a human body: the column of air inside the chest, shaped into signifying sounds in the larynx and mouth. In this sense, poetry is just as physical or bodily an art as dancing'. I tell my students that the creative writing classroom may be one of the few places within the academy where they are allowed to have a body, where, in fact, it is required.

All teachers, of course, should consider how their physical selves affect their pedagogical approaches and how those physical and pedagogical selves are perceived by students. I have come to realize that the one thing a professor of creative writing can count on is that her or his authority in the classroom will always be in flux as she ages, bears children (or not), goes gray (or not), gains weight or works out, dresses fashionably or frumpily. I have spent a lot of time wondering how we writers–teachers can prepare for this. Perhaps, the only thing we can do is know that fluctuation is coming and understand where it is coming from. Just as a child goes through stages, throws tantrums, has nightmares, or demands *why why why?*, this too will pass. And in the meantime, we must keep writing.

References

Enright, A. (2001) My milk. *Harper's Magazine* May, 26–9.
Hays, J. (1995) Intellectual parenting and a developmental feminist pedagogy of writing. In L. Wetherbee Phelps and J. Emig (eds) *Feminine Principles and Women's Experience in American Composition and Rhetoric* (pp. 153–91). Pittsburgh: University of Pittsburgh Press.
O'Connor, F. (1969) The nature and aim of fiction. *Mysteries and Manners* (pp. 63–86). New York: Noonday Press.
Ostriker, A.S. (1983) A wild surmise: Motherhood and poetry. *Writing Like a Woman*. Ann Arbor: University of Michigan Press.
Pinsky, R. (1998) *The Sounds of Poetry*. New York: Farrar, Strauss & Giroux.
Prose, F. (1998) Scent of a woman's ink. *Harper's Magazine* June, 61–70.
Rich, A. (1997) *Of Woman Born: Motherhood As Experience and Institution*. New York: Norton.
Smiley, J. (1993) Can mothers think? In K. Brown (ed.) *The True Subject: Writers on Life and Craft* (pp. 3–15). Saint Paul: Graywolf.

Chapter 9

Dismantling Authority: Teaching What We Do Not Know

KATHARINE HAAKE

Some years ago, I participated in an early pedagogy panel at the Associated Writing Programs Conference in Philadelphia titled, in part, 'Claiming Our Own Authority: Feminism and Creative Writing Teaching.' It was 1989, and I had arrived, a new mother and teacher with plenty of anxiety about both. These days, babies, even children of all ages, are common enough at academic conferences, but Joey was AWP's first: before the night was out he was welcomed by the keynote speaker, Grace Paley, who scooped him up, kissed him, and announced in a loud voice – so everyone could hear – that she couldn't stand a reading without a baby.

Those were hopeful times in general. The creative writing world, stalled for so long in its own origins, seemed on the cusp of radical change. AWP was sponsoring panels on pedagogy, feminism, and gay and lesbian voices. Joseph Moxley's book, *Creative Writing in America*, was rumored to inaugurate a whole new NCTE series on creative writing. And yes, we were excited – or I was – for it seemed imminent that the discipline itself was opening up and out and that the inequities which had worked for so long to silence so many among us were largely unintended and about to be corrected. Like the boy in the 'Emperor's New Clothes,' we were convinced that if we just said out loud what seemed obvious to us – who got to speak, for example, and who did not – discourse would be suddenly open and free. And this, we believed, would make us not just better teachers, but also better writers. We believed that creative writing was about to come of age.

In 1989, I suppose I could be said to have been emerging from a lifetime of silence during which, unable, ever, to measure up against the way I thought I was supposed to speak/write/be, I simply didn't. At the time, it felt good to claim my own authority, and there was, for me, a kind of language-based euphoria just in learning how to say that things were the way they were, not for any natural reason but because of the general parsimoniousness which governed the getting and keeping of power. For a long time I worked to share this new sense of entitlement to speech itself with students, whose unbridled voices, too, were powerful and thrilling: one small-group performance in a theory class ended with the whole class chanting, 'No more silence.'

Then some more years passed. An earthquake came. My school fell down. And in the unstable world we had entered, I heard the very cadence of my own voice changing, assuming the certain authority of the already-known, and, over time, I began to recognize repetition as an organizing principle in my own classroom, to hear myself tell the same stories, say the same things – to teach, as it were, what I already knew. In the history of my life as a writer, I once came to a place where I knew exactly how to write what I knew how to write, and I hovered there a while near the end of writing. Now I found myself approaching yet another point where teaching might have ended too but for an accident of fate and maybe grace.

Now I wonder: is this what the others have always felt, that they know what they know. Is *knowing* the very condition by which authority – and its correlative, power – distributed within and among disciplines and discourse in such a way that things hold together firmly in the first place?

My proposition is simple, but I do not offer it without some trepidation. One possible role for authority in the creative writing classroom is to dismantle itself. For if we believe that alternative models for teaching should redistribute power in such a way that students may come into authentic writing of their own, we must probably begin by allowing that at least some of the time it is not the content, but the structure of how we teach that makes this possible. But authority, when linked to mastery and like a bad psychic habit, is terribly seductive. One possible way of testing ourselves to see if we mean what we say is simply to teach what we do not know.

When I was in college and graduate school, I carried an idea of authority inside me like a curse, believing that the process of an education was a simple one in which a particular body of knowledge was exchanged in a precise, orderly transfer from the professor, who possessed it, to the student, who was expected to absorb it. But this was before I met Professor Tillie Shaw. One of just two women professors I had in college, Shaw was an enigma and challenge – a small, braless woman with a mop of white hair and a destabilizing pedagogical practice of never asking questions she already knew the answer to. Shaw's classes were full of awkward silences and acutely nervous laughter, but as she pawed at her hair and groped to articulate concepts she didn't know and couldn't name, it was as if the very synapses of my own brain were somehow coming alive, and I carried the idea of the small, laughing woman around in my head for many years without fully understanding why the image was so powerful. If writing begins in the very moment of its own coming into being, what cannot ever be known before it becomes what it already is, my guess is that teaching does too.

When I first started teaching, I often taught a senior-level core course for creative writing majors called Theory of Fiction, the very subject I had most struggled with on my Ph.D. exams. Now convinced that I was soon to be discovered as a fraud, I wrote out long lectures beforehand and read them out loud to my class in a tedious imitation of the men who once had been my teachers. My class was like a well-constructed box, and students, accustomed to boxes, were happy enough. But another thing that writing and teaching share in common is that one of the worst things we can do is to proceed in it the way we think we are supposed to, Soon, I found myself as bored as my students, and I suspect that I was coming close to the end of teaching.

So I did what I'd done whenever I was failing at writing, and one day in the middle of a vexed semester with stronger than usual student resistance, I threw out my lecture notes, syllabus, and everything I thought I knew, and started all over again, as if for the very first time. I have never worked harder, nor been more afraid in class, but from that moment on, I was learning that the letting go of thinking meaning works the same way in the classroom as it does on the page. This is something we can model for our students, and when we do, though (or perhaps because) there is always risk, the classroom may become an authentic site of co-discovery and learning.

But there's a catch.

As a young teacher, I used to say that my goal was to disorient students sufficiently so as to force them into a new space for writing; but as the late Wendy Bishop cautioned at the time, there are, of course, productive and non-productive states of disorientation. Now, I was preparing to step into this same space with my students.

Shaw was an expert of the first degree, and brilliant to boot, who could work as she did – without a net – because of the profound reach of her curiosity, intellect, and knowledge, as well as the endearing quirkiness of her humility. My own way of proceeding is clumsier, but if there is any one thing I've learned is that what I don't know can't hurt me. Thus, I have also learned that if I am to maintain a proper skepticism about authority in my own classroom, I can rely on a simple trick that always seems to work: invent and teach classes about which I know nothing at all.

And it's not that I don't love the old model of the workshop, just the same way that I love all finely made things – pots, beds, fabric. It's enduring and endearing. Had it been a better fit for me, I'd have found a way to be there, and stayed.

Instead, over the past few years I've taught several topics-based writing seminars – classes with full reading lists and critical dimensions organized around a theme or body of knowledge in which students produce their own creative writing in response to the conversation of the texts and class. I develop these courses the same way I write a story or make dinner from whatever is left in the kitchen, beginning with a question or a problem or an interest, and working on from there. Each of these courses began with a sense of curiosity – a wondering – and each proceeded raggedly through unfamiliar texts and assignments to become what seemed real occasions for writing. Each was personal and arbitrary, and each reached beyond self to the world.

In fact, the idea of such a course went back to my early days at California State University-Northridge, when, working with poet Eloise Klein Healy, we designed a feminist theory- and literature-based creative writing class. The idea of the class was to use the sustained investigation of female difference – what Elaine Showalter then called 'gynocriticism' – as a lens not for reading but for writing. The idea for a topics-based creative writing seminar grew out of the original success of this class, but the difference I'm attempting to describe between that original class and these new more spontaneous classes was that the class I taught, first with Eloise and then on my own, was the product of intensive scholarly rigor and careful planning. As such, authority within it was constructed in familiar ways around the professor and her knowledge base. These new classes relied more exclusively on the spirit of intertextual play, and, like stories that grow entirely out of a single sentence, they grew spontaneously out of an idea.

The nonfiction writer, Sharman Apt Russell, whose work I greatly admired, has written books on a wide range of topics, from homesteading in the Southwest, to archaeology, butterflies, and hunger. When *The Anatomy of a Rose* came out some years ago, I was struck by both its depth and breadth. I'd known Sharman by then for quite some time, and I'd never known her to know anything about flowers. And I remember saying to her, 'So, you took a walk in the desert one day when the cactus was in bloom and you decided to write about flowers.' Sharman smiled and allowed that, yes, that was pretty much how it had happened. Sharman has what has always seemed to me to be an insatiable curiosity about the world, and that, as much as anything, seems to drive her process. And that, too, is part of the logic of the courses I'm describing.

Several things happen in such a course: (1) the professor is, *de facto*, dislodged as the center of authority, the person to whom students turn for the answer, the one who's in charge of what happens; (2) students themselves are not just given permission to become active agents in their own learning, they are required to do so, and – more – the class, the other learners, depends on each other doing so; (3) a kind of modeling occurs for what is popularly called 'lifelong learning,' where students participate in problem- or curiosity-based inquiry and writing; and (4) writing itself is linked, in important ways, to other writing and the world, and its practice becomes more explicitly intertextual, the way writers work.

Not surprisingly, this practice of teaching into the void originated in an accident of memory and timing, as once I proposed to teach a class on the nonfiction novel. But by the time my turn came around for that graduate seminar, I'd forgotten my original intent and ended up teaching, instead, a reading-based writing class on genres that problematize the distinction we make between what we know to be true and what we're convinced we make up. I taught novels (among them, Tim O'Brien's *In the Lake of the Woods* and Norman Mailer's *Executioner's Song*), nonfiction (Jon Krakaur's *Into the Wild* and Sheila Nickerson's *Disappearances, A Map*), memoir (William Kittredge's *Hole in the Sky* and Mark Doty's *Heaven's Coast*), and it was some time into the class before we discovered that one thing almost every book shared in common was a disappearance – whether of person or place, whether through mystery or death. And then we came to understand that disappearance might be said to constitute the single definitive point beyond which we can tell fact from fiction. Another defining focus of the class I did not plan beforehand turned out to be our current obsession with things that are 'true' – not a riddle we ever solved, but one we learned better how to worry. Students wrote, in the class, according to their own preoccupations, responding as writers with their own writing. And it was that – their own writerly investment in the texts – that framed the weekly seminar reports and kept the class continually surprising and new.

Since then, I have taught a course that attempted to examine the works of writers who write about writing and how their writing about writing is reflected in their writing. In this course, we read paired books – Grace Paley's *Just as I Thought* with her *Collected Stories*; Italo Calvino's *Six Memos for the Next Millenium* with *If On a Winter's Night a Traveler*, Annie Dillard's *Living by Fiction* with *The Living*, William Gass' *Fiction and the Figures of Life* with *In the Heart of the Heart of the Country*, Milan Kundera's *The Art of the Novel* with *The Book of Laughter and Forgetting*. Although I had read some but not all of the texts I assigned, I had never held the writers' aesthetics up against their fiction before and sometimes, as it turned out, that mirroring was highly provocative, and sometimes it remained opaque. For the students, who wrote both aesthetics papers and work that might be said to reflect those aesthetics, the process of framing writerly intertextual questions proved challenging and productive.

My next such course was a course in lifewriting, inspired by certain conversations with Wendy Bishop on the subject, in which we spent much of our time trying to distinguish between such genres as memoir, autobiography, personal essay, and autobiographical fiction. It wasn't knowing – not knowledge – that came from the class, but questioning.

'I don't know,' I found myself saying over and over. 'What do you think? Let's figure it out.'

'Aren't you sure of what you're saying?' I began by quoting Foucault's (1972: 17) 'Introduction' to *The Archaeology of Knowledge*. 'Are you going to change yet again, shift your position according to the questions that are put to you ...? ... Do not ask,' he writes, 'who I am and do not ask me to remain the same'.

By George, I want to say, I understand that logic. For teaching, like writing itself, will take us, when it is really teaching, beyond ourselves and into that which we do not – we cannot – know, at least not until the very moment that it comes into being.

As I wrote in that first syllabus:

> We ask these questions to give ourselves pleasure and to extend the labyrinth [...] for this class [...] has no known outcome. I am saying this from the outset in anticipation of our mutual longing for certainty. The operative mode of the classroom will predictably be uneasiness. That is the only way we can proceed.

And of course, throughout that term, we were uneasy, we were vexed, we were anxious and frustrated, but yet, we also produced uncommon levels of discussion, writing, and excitement.

'I didn't know any more than you did,' I later remarked to one of those students.

'Maybe so,' she said, but as if she wasn't buying it, 'but you knew how to frame the questions.'

And maybe framing questions and the process of engaging them is the best that we, finally, can do. And maybe it's just a trick I use to keep myself interested, and interesting. For if, as Robert Frost (1995 edn) says, 'No surprise for the writer, no surprise for the reader,' the same is probably true of teaching too. Perhaps what finally sustains both writing and teaching, for me, is nothing more than the capacity to be surprised. As I think about all the ways received ideas about authority have worked to silence me throughout my life, my ambivalence about it is shockingly transparent. We spend years accumulating credentials. We stack our publications up next to our degrees. Then, one day, we find that all of it – all – is not enough, and probably never was.

Based on the success of these classes, and of a more recent international literature-based creative writing workshop, we have designed a new special-topics based workshop as part of our undergraduate major. This course will routinely make available to all of our students the opportunity to stumble upon something new. And while this course, which I have long desired, is exciting for me, I don't approach it without some anxiety.

In her college application essay, a young friend wrote affectingly about shaving her head. An introverted girl, she acknowledged that for many years she had hidden behind her long shroud of dark hair and that when she emerged she felt naked, vulnerable, and strangely exposed to the world. But she also discovered in herself an 'an emerging capacity not only to connect with other people, but also with [her] intellectual and artistic curiosity. In this unfamiliar spirit of openness, [she] began to embrace a new concept of education that enabled [her] to accept the world, which had once seemed so neatly constrained, as chaotic, unpredictable, and full of possibility.'

Conventional authority keeps things controlled and constrained. It's not messy, and it often feels powerful. But if, as this young woman also wrote, 'In that trash can lay my keratin cloak, and outside lies my life,' it's at least worth entertaining the possibility that, at least some of the time, one true obligation of teachers is to step from behind the shroud of the certitude of what we know and into whatever lies beyond. What we stand to gain may be a place of learning that may be chaotic or unpredictable, but also, as the bald girl well knew, rich and full of possibility. Only first, we have to let go.

Note

Gratitude is extended to the young friend who granted permission to quote her graduate school application essay is here.

References

Foucault, M. (1972) *The Archaeology of Knowledge, and The Discourse on Language* R. Swyer (trans.). New York: Pantheon.

Frost, R. (1995) The figure a poem makes. *Collected Poems, Prose, and Plays.* New York: Library of America.

Showalter, E. (1985) Feminist criticism in the wilderness. In E. Showalter (ed.) *The New Feminist Criticism: Essays on Women, Literature and Theory* (pp. 243– 70). New York: Pantheon.

Part 3

Course Design

Chapter 10

Contracts, Radical Revision, Portfolios, and the Risks of Writing

WENDY BISHOP

> When writing an essay, we 'should start without any fixed idea of where we are going to spend the night, or when we propose to come back; the journey is everything.' (Virginia Woolfe, quoted in Heilker, 1996: 91)

> Writing, revising, editing, workshopping, revising again – these all motivated me to rework my texts (or at least think about different ways to revise) as I showered, walked to class, brushed my teeth, and ate lunch. (Haley, student)

A response-workshop-with-portfolios structure transforms the writing workshop into what I call a writing-intensive zone, since it places students under production demands that mimic a practicing writer's schedule. While those in composition have imported workshop models, those in creative writing have generally done less work exploring and analyzing teaching practices and have been more accepting of a traditional, authoritative model of instruction posited on a novice-student and master-teacher dynamic.[1] Generally, creative writing instruction has not focused on how evaluation discourages *and* encourages student writers' entry into the revision process and concurrently supports them in learning to understand themselves as writers. By developing authority-conscious pedagogy, we can discover how useful some of these methods can be for improving our lives – teachers' and students' both – in creative writing courses.

The classroom I recreate here asks students to explore the essay form – though it can be adapted easily for other genres – through the development of portfolio writings. When portfolios are used in response workshops, students focus on their material – texts that are revised, edited, workshopped, *revised again*, and constantly thought about; writers immerse themselves reflectively and practically in a writing life, 'developing our work within a predictable structure of group response and idea exploration' (Brooke, 1991: 1). They are, as

Virginia Woolfe suggests, on a writer's journey. They are, as Haley testifies, constantly and actively creating.

Until end-of-term grading takes place, portfolios can create a version of what Peter Elbow (1993) calls an 'evaluation-free zone.' As they compile portfolio essays, students write informally and then more formally, undertake invention exercises and style revisions, and share their drafts in sessions that elicit response, not ranking or grading; these sessions include small and large peer-response groups and student-and-teacher conferences. Portfolios are potentially evaluation free because the teacher resists grading (but not necessarily responding) until the end of the course. Grade deferment allows writers and teachers to focus on revision; every text is open to further consideration until the class disbands.[2]

The writing-intensive zone in which I'm most interested is one that allows students to take risks: attempt new rhetorical techniques, explore challenging subjects, try hunches and wild guesses, push drafts into dislocation, or pull initially fragmented, tangential thinking into a more satisfying whole. Writing students need to do this because, unlike the commonly taught thesis/support essay, the nonfiction essay (personal essay, creative nonfiction, exploratory essay, *the* essay) is a speculative text.[3] Aldous Huxley claims, 'For, like the novel, the essay is a literary device for saying almost everything about almost anything' (Heilker, 1996: 48), but teachers of writing know that this commodious form still can, and must, be learned, explored, perfected. As with the novel, as with poetry, as with any genre, writers improve their craft through practice that entails controlled exploration, including opportunity for, education in, and rewards for revision.

I teach revision by offering a course schedule that *demands* revision, by offering revision instruction and opportunities; by requiring an experimental, radical revision assignment; by orchestrating community-response sessions that encourage revision; by nurturing a class attitude that revision is worthwhile; and by insisting on class publishing that illuminates the benefits of revision. Teachers of other genres or of multi-genre courses will see that the same techniques and organization can be adapted to those courses. Whatever the genre addressed, the goal remains transferring what one has learned as an expert writer by allowing students to gain control over their own, evolving texts.

To set up such a writing-intensive class, I ask students to draft a set number of essays across a term. Their nonfiction is shared in small-group sessions several times, and then each of the first papers is published in a class anthology, either printed or posted on-line. In a recent workshop, we held a full-class workshop on five essays per class anthology. That is, in this 20-student workshop course, four class anthologies are published across the term with five highlighted essays discussed each workshop. The essays that aren't highlighted – that is, responded to by the whole class – still receive a reading from two assigned peers. Therefore, each time a class anthology workshop is convened, five students receive 20 responses and all other students receive two, in-depth responses.

When students see each other working in drafts or examine the diversity in our anthologies, implicit and explicit style and revision lessons take place. One student has seen an earlier draft in a small-group response session, now pushed further for class publication, and he notes the improvement. Another student sees that a peer gets a positive response from the class community for a technique, and she tries that technique in her next piece. They learn by doing.

I encourage risk-taking and experimentation by deferring product grades to final portfolios (70% of the final class grade) and by offering significant participation credit (30% of the grade). That's not enough. I also use modified contract grading. Currently, it works this way: complete all assigned work in good faith to earn a B; exemplary work as evaluated by teacher and student in the products of the portfolio and through class participation earns an A; and less than good-faith efforts receive a C or lower. While this structure sounds simplistic, we discuss evaluation at some length in class. While some readers may be disturbed at the apparent grade inflation represented by this contract, I set the contract demands as high as the grade.[4] Since I aim to create a text-intensive class, students who participate tend to have produced work that I'd rank at the B level. I'm also grading, through participation credit, a student's development of a writing identity and an understanding of what writers do when they write. Working hard at becoming a better writer garners a B-range grade, and my students make their own decisions about how much effort they will invest in the course.

Finally, I ask that the fifth class essay (drafted during the final class weeks along with the fourth piece) be a radical revision – a reworking of essay 1, 2, or 3 that is so experimental *for the writer* that it may fail. This piece, like all portfolio essays, is accompanied by a process cover sheet (the narrative of writing the essay), but the radical-revision cover sheet can exceed the normal one-page limit since the story of experimentation – and sometimes disaster – can be very good writing (and reading) indeed.[5] Jason wrote in his process paper:

> I went into class thinking myself to be beyond the criticism of mere peers, to be a writer whose only valuable input would come from the likes of my teachers, superiors. I was wrong. Incredibly wrong. My classmates showed me as much without any hesitation [...].

Real feeling exists in Jason's narrative, as do real dangers: this student read his classmates as willing and ready to have him take up personally important topics and allowed them to find out about his past and experience his concerns in the present. The classroom we create must safely support such disclosure, a writerly disclosure, not a merely therapeutic one: the writer is going public with exploratory thinking, and readers of that thinking must be trained to help improve it. Even as I ask students to form a writing community, I have to ask: how real do I want that community to be? Will I be able to help each student negotiate the public and private identities that all writers negotiate, constantly? Can I help them explore the art of 'narrating a journey toward some understanding of a textual, personal, or political problem' (Atkins, 1990: 17)?

Added to these identity negotiations are practical negotiations of authority: will I feel comfortable with students' resistance to deferred grading? Can I create the appropriate degree of autonomy and risk while still orchestrating assignments and a class structure? Can I convince these writers that they learn more by experiencing the evaluation-free, writing-intensive zones than by my telling them what to do? Certainly, I'm taking risks in attempting these complex goals, and my risks – sometimes discussed with my students – are part of what helps this community work. As I orchestrate, sometimes I'm guessing, sometimes I'm taking chances: teaching is much like writing.

To teach genre, convention-making, and convention-breaking, students contract with me concerning the topics, styles, and potential audiences for four of five of their essays. I assign the first as the term starts – we can't be writing intensively without writing immediately – while I'm setting up response groups and full-class workshops. I ask for an extended writing exercise that investigates one's writing history (telling stories of past writing classes, learning to write, texts that succeeded and didn't, writing habits, and so on) and then ask each writer to explore any desired variation of one of the following topics: examine your voice, tell why you write, tell how you write, or explore professional writing in your field. The writing exercise generates ideas toward those topics; small groups discuss topic choices and share rough, professional-quality drafts (typed, readable, completely drafted, but not yet finished). During this period, when we're talking about writers – what they do, how they do it – we're also negotiating term writing contracts:

> Your contract should take the form of a memo from you to me telling me what writing projects you'll undertake this term. Your first paper is a variation of the assigned first paper choice of topics. You'll list that topic as well as options for papers 2, 3, 4 and a guess as to which paper (1, 2, 3) you'll choose for your radical revision (paper 5). You'll list two or three possible substitute papers: if you get stuck during drafting, switch to one of these pre-approved substitutes. You may re-negotiate your contract/papers at any time in the semester by conferencing with me.

Here, I am the authority – telling students not *what* to write but *to* write. I insist on my editor's choice – on negotiating, on playing agent, publisher, goad, nag, celebrant:

> For your contract, balance literary/imaginative nonfiction, including autobiography, with more transactional, work-a-day writing: reports, reviews, analyses. That is, include (a) primarily nonfiction (essayist) prose; (b) practical work; and (c) experimental work.
> Suggestions:
>
> (1) If you choose to include a maximum of one piece in another creative genre – drama, short story, a group of 2–4 poems – you should expect to increase the length of your writing process cover sheet for this paper to short essay length. I will be responding to the description of the process of learning about composing in this genre as much or more than to the pieces of drama, fiction, or poetry. *Including other genres is optional.*
> (2) My definition of experimental work is this: *experimental to you.* In your contract memo, discuss the way that undertaking a piece of writing will push you into new writing territory.
> (3) Indicate potential/possible audiences/publishers for these papers.

With this contract, each student creates his or her own, individualized writer's experience without my abdication of the teacher's influence.

Contracts function as revisable Tables-of-Contents, promises, predictions that this much good writing can proceed from this writer, and contracts demystify the act of compiling a portfolio. Instead of an eternally deferred, unknown collection of work for the teacher, the writer plans, predicts, alters, and controls the contents of the portfolio via the contract which is itself subject to revision. Students can work at their own paces within the confines of certain due dates for anthologies and workshops. The contract and portfolio establish a sequence of work just as a professional writer schedules work using desires and deadlines.

When this type of class is set up – contracts confirmed, response groups trained, full-class workshops functioning – what distinguishes it from any other writing workshop? I struggle with the students' desire that I teach them a particular style or, better yet, instantly transform them into great writers. I care, instead, that my students change in some of the many possible ways available, develop stronger writers' identities, broaden their style repertoires, and so on. I believe the risk-taking stance and radical-revision paper teach a great deal of what can be taught about technical elements of style: together we need time with texts, respect for those texts we write, and those others write. Certainly, we need any lingua franca that helps us to articulate what we're learning – *lead, conclusion, cumulative sentence, informal register, academic discourse* – but as much (and often more), we need drafting and invested writing.

Many writing students bring along their strong (often school-induced) beliefs about individual voice (usually they're looking for a singular one) and literary experimentation (Joycean, sometimes Woolfian). Those more journalistically inclined may believe voice is achieved merely by existing, rather than through writing one's existence. Others assume that they will attain a strong style through osmosis, primarily through close reading of master writers or, more romantically, that a strong and distinct style is accessible to a talented few.

The radical-revision assignment focuses our style discussions. We list on the board 50 ways to radically revise; we borrow from Winston Weathers' (1990) definitions of Grammars A and B; from Lillian Bridwell-Bowles' (1992) feminist exploration of diverse discourses – personal/emotional writing, breaking boundaries of textual space, language play, and so on; from group brainstorming that suggests we change point of view or time of day, interweave texts, use other media, create bumper stickers, or compose collaboratively.[6]

After reading about Grammar B, John wrote an experimental meditation on spaces that provide him with unusual sanctuaries (part of a city storm drain, an abandoned silo, a rural bridge, and an opening in the base of a huge cypress tree). Briefly, Grammar A is traditional, school grammar which relies on order, unity, consistency. Grammar B is a flexible and experimental style that often ignores the conventions of Grammar A as it is generally taught; instead, Grammar B, as used by expert, professional writers, emphasizes sentence experimentation, textual collage, synchronicity, and poetic tropes and techniques.[7] Influenced by Weathers' discussion, John incorporated rough line drawings in his essay and used crots (space-separated prose segments) and fragments effectively. The day we responded to John's draft, our workshop was transformed: arguments arose over the verities of English grammar, but most of us praised the piece (a revision won a department award).

Steve's radical revision of his initial 'How I Write' essay turned into a song entitled 'Keep Me Moving Along': Steve's original draft was pretentious, and many classmates urged him to write a more honest draft and, for his final class performance, to sing the song with an acoustic guitar. That day, he managed to convince the entire class to sing along, and he provided a tape and lyric sheet in his portfolio.

Radical revisions create classroom carnival, turning the text upside down, freeing its author from worries about the text's potential for failure. Radical revisions are ungraded, part of the portfolio and class participation. When writers are turned loose in an evaluation-free learning zone, they see that writing can be pleasurable. Nonfiction draws many of us for the same reasons it drew early practitioners like Montaigne (1957: 611): 'If my mind could gain a firm footing, I would not make essays, I would make decisions; but it is always in apprenticeship and on trial'. The pleasure of the play of mind across and into ideas is a pleasure we need to afford our writing students in all genres if they are to become more expert thinkers and writers.

Collecting work in a portfolio lets the writer compound the natural benefits of creative writing. If, as Scott Russell Sanders explains, the 'essay is a weighing out, an inquiry into the value, meaning, and true nature of experience; it is a private experiment carried out in public' (Heilker, 1957: 89), then the portfolio of essays allows for a more thoughtful analysis of a variety of private experiments made public.

Experimentation = risk. Therefore the temporarily evaluation-free zones of the portfolio and contract grading. Therefore writing-intensive workshops. Because, who ever heard of just a little bit of risk? And my audience of writers – rightly – is not ever completely convinced that I *really* mean for them to take risks. How could they be, since, as writing teacher Lad Tobin reminds me, I never entirely give up my authority? Eventually, I have to transfer responsibility for writing back to writers.

This transfer can happen during radical revisions because the radical revision is both an assignment and a teaching/learning location.

I'm an authoritative orchestrator, using portfolios, risk-taking, and radical revision to shape the classroom activities and using myself as writer-model, responding best, I expect, to those who take to my lessons, become writers like me, multi-generic, multi-drafting (even as I acknowledge this is not the only possible writer's experience). 'As soon as I find myself giving up on a student or, on the other hand, feeling tremendous personal pride in a student's work, I need to question my own motives. I need to discover in what ways my biases and assumptions – both conscious and unconscious – are shaping my teaching' (Tobin, 1993: 38–9). Tobin's words remind me to study my own classroom even as I participate in it, and, always, to reflect on it as I plan a new version.

Thinking of Tobin's warning, I read this student carefully:

> I like how we get to choose our own topics in this class. It makes the writing more enjoyable and definitely makes reading everyone else's more enjoyable. [...] I like having other people's input and think that this workshop is very helpful, but I still feel like it is only school writing – and having twenty other teacher's comments instead of only one. (Anonymous in-class freewrite)

Have I created a class of 20 writers or 20 teachers? And what does that mean? I know what I'd like to think:

> I feel that my writing is definitely a part of me and that is why I am often very self-conscious about it. I'm not always pleased with my writing and I wish I could be better at it. I don't think I'm that BAD of a writer, I just know I can, or wish I could be, better at it. It is the same way with me as a person – there is always something more I can do to help others in order to make me a better person – sometimes I just need a swift kick to get me going. (Anonymous in-class freewrite)

If my teacher's role is to give the swift kick, I have every sense that this orchestrated, writing-intensive, portfolio-and-response workshop does so because of its design.

It's demanding of me and of students:

> I need deadlines. This class provided me with more than an adequate number of them (I have a gift for understatement). I write my best from about 10 until 2 in the morning (I edit the following afternoon).

I think this is a result of habit, but it is nonetheless true. Without deadlines, I have trouble forcing myself to work at those hours. I am concerned that after this class I will do less work since I am deprived of those deadlines. (Jason)

At the end of the term, in self-evaluation letters like Jason's, writers reflect on this class. Although a self-evaluation letter could allow the student to manipulate the teacher, it becomes the capstone to a long journey, a narrative *and* persuasive essay, perhaps, in that the writer is persuading me (but also him- or herself) about what took place along the way.

I'm looking for insights, honesty, and care. And I've read enough courses' worth of these letters to discount teacher-pleasingness. Most often, I encounter prose in which the writer discovers meaning, and I, reading later, after the class has ended, have the rare privilege of discovering too: pleasing and disconcerting things, large leaps of learning and sometimes relatively little change at all.

During your class, I realized that I am not just a writing student, but a writer. In fact, I will always be both. I used to think there was a difference. I earned an A mainly because I became so immersed in what I was writing, the class became secondary to the work. My essays were good kids out on their own, your class the proud parent, always there to provide stability and guidance. I already know what I want to write next (I think?) and will use the methods I learned right here. Although 'there is no limit to my ignorance,' at least I am no longer confused about why I write, how I write, how I will continue to write, and how to find the people willing to print and/or buy it! (John)

John's insights, of course, please me, but I'm also disconcerted. Proud parent? And here I thought I was the writer with writers, the orchestrator. I have to admit that I'm seen through; I'm an authority, oxymoronically pushing student autonomy through the demands of portfolios.

My students teach me to attend to what I already know: I have to negotiate complex, conflicting classroom roles, and they do the same when they enter small and large response groups, conference with me, and write for us all.

No kiss-ass letters wanted. None given. I learned most not from you, but from those around me. I learned humility, respect for diversity, and the art of communication. But that's what you intended, isn't it?

Not to teach us, but for us to teach one another. I was challenged by others. I tried to keep up. I tried to surpass. I tried to meet the challenge. I tried! (Mike)

Mike didn't follow any of my suggestions for writing a final course self-evaluation (turning in only one paragraph instead of the one or two pages of analysis I requested), yet I graded him up from the B he suggested to B+, based on his final portfolio drafts and his radical revision. Mike's letter would sound like manipulation unless you knew him, and knowing him has to be factored in. He often challenged me in class and in conference, and he was excruciatingly polite in person but impolite in his body language, attendance, and responses to other student writers. His comments, particularly at first (and somewhat to the last), were relatively harsh and often patronizing. Yet, he awarded himself only a B, a striking humility for the Mike who wanted *my* teacher's answers and trusted best, at first, my imagined long arm of the law.

During the course, Mike wanted me to define good writing. In class and during several serious one-to-one conferences, he asked me to provide a universal definition, something I knew was impossible to do. He let me know that by not doing so, I was, in his opinion, failing at my work. He wanted, perhaps needed, models and directives. I cleared some room in our workshop schedule and planned for a class freewrite on the topic, followed by a class discussion. Mike missed that class when we discussed good and bad writing, by which time almost everyone acknowledged that we didn't agree as readers, that we could work both into and against conventions.

Unperturbed by some teasing about missing the big class, Mike started intensively working on his radical revision – a video to accompany read-aloud sections of his earlier essay on working at an AIDS hotline center. He played the video and read on the last day of class. Silence. Then applause. He scheduled no final conference. He left the note I share here. And a portfolio of writing. I'm absolutely sure that this class, particularly the way his peers worked with him and around him, touched Mike. I think about his resistances as well as my pep talks to myself throughout the term and about learning to trust him to find his way – both resistance and trust seemed to pay off.

How many writing courses did I teach that term? One, organized around risk-taking and radical revision and made possible by the power of contract and portfolio grading and of portfolios for showcasing each writer's developing identity and texts. Twenty, for the number of writers involved and how they responded. I read the final portfolios, and I enjoyed myself. I anguished over a B– or B+ and felt good over raising a self-estimated A– to an A. Grading – on a five-point scale, on a check/check+/check– scale, on a pass/fail scale – never goes away: even contracts are completed or not completed, adequately or inadequately.

When I started to draft this essay, I didn't know how to do justice to the complexity of writers' voices and experiences that filled draft after draft of the conceptual space of *portfolio*. I started to perform for my imagined peer readers and I drafted a stiff, stolid, how-to beginning. Then I realized: I'd be embarrassed to take such prose to my own writing workshop. I recall:

> I say to myself, 'Can this be done?' Well the only way to know is to write it and see. (John)

> The hero of the essay is the author in the act of thinking things out, feeling and finding a way; it is the mind in the marvels and miseries of its makings, in the work of the imagination, the search for form [...]. (William H. Gass, quoted in Heilker, 1996: 92)

So I reminded myself that I was in my writing-intensive, evaluation-free zone, and I got to work on a riskier version, a re-creation of a classroom that teachers and the writers they teach can use.

Notes

I thank the students quoted here – Haley, Jason, Mike, John – for their enthusiasm, their hard work, the lessons they taught me, the writings they left me with me, and their permission to use their names and work.

1. See Bishop and Ostrom (1994); Haake *et al.* (1989).
2. See Belanoff and Dickson (1991); Yancey (1992).
3. See Heilker (1996).
4. In their 1993 research, Connors and Lunsford examined how teachers graded sample papers (A 9%, B 39%, C 37%. D 12%. F 3%) and found these figures comparable to grades given by teachers *circa* 1915–1930 (p. 220). The results of contract grading are not that different than the results of grading individual papers. As with any evaluation method, teachers using portfolios must articulate their developing sense of grading scales and where they situate themselves within department, institution, and/or national averages.
5. See Bishop (1991) Going up the creek without a canoe, (1995) Teaching 'Grammar for writers' means teaching writing as writers, and (1997) *Teaching Lives* for additional discussions fo class structures.
6. See Korn (1997).
7. See Bishop (1997) *Elements* and Weathers (1990).

References

Atkins, G.D. (1990) The return of/to the essay. *ADE Bulletin* 96, 11–18.

Belanoff, P. and Dickson, M. (eds) (1991) *Portfolios: Process and Product*. Portsmouth, NH: Heinemann-Boynton/Cook.

Bishop, W. (ed.) (1997) *Elements of Alternate Style: Essays on Writing and Revision*. Heinemann-Boynton/Cook.

Bishop, W. (1991) Going up the creek without a canoe: Using writing portfolios to train new teachers of college writing. In P. Belanoff and M. Dickinson (eds) *Portfolio Grading: Process and Product* (pp. 215–27). Portsmouth, NH: Heinemann-Boynton/Cook.

Bishop, W. (1995) Teaching 'Grammar for Writers' means teaching writing as writers. In S. Hunter and R. Wallace (eds) *The Place of Grammar in Writing Instruction: Past, Present, Future* (pp. 176–87). Portsmouth, NH: Heinemann-Boynton/Cook.

Bishop, W. (1997) *Teaching Lives: Essays and Stories*. Logan, UT: Utah State University Press.

Bishop, W. and H. Ostrom (eds) (1994) *Colors of a Different Horse: Rethinking Creative Writing, Theory and Pedagogy*. National Council of Teachers of English.

Bridwell-Bowles, L. (1992) Discourse and diversity: Experimental writing within the academy. *College Composition and Communication* 43 (3), 349–68.

Brooke, R. (1991) *Writing and Sense of Self: Identity Negotiation in Writing Workshops*. Urbana, IL: National Council of Teachers of English.

Connors, R.J. and Lunsford, A.A. (1993) Teachers' rhetorical comments on student papers. *College Composition and Communication* 44 (2), 200–23.

Elbow, P. (1993) Ranking, evaluating, and liking: Sorting out three forms of judgment. *College English* 55 (2), 187–206.

Haake, K., Alcosser, S. and Bishop, W. (1989) Teaching creative writing: A feminist critique. *AWP Chronicle* 22, Oct./Nov., 1–6.

Heilker, P. (1996) *The Essay: Theory and Pedagogy for an Active Form*. Urbana, IL: National Council of Teachers of English.

Korn, K.H. (1997) Distorting the mirror: Radical revision and writers' shifting perspectives. In W. Bishop (ed.) *Elements of Alternate Style: Essays on Writing and Revision*. Portsmouth, NH: Heinemann-Boynton/Cook.

Montaigne, M.E. (1957) *The Complete Works of Montaigne* D.M. Frame (trans.). Stanford: Stanford University Press.

Tobin, L. (1993) *Writing Relationships: What Really Happens in the Composition Class*. Portsmouth, NH: Heinemann-Boynton/Cook.

Weathers, W. (1990) Grammars of style: New options in composition. In R.L. Graves (ed.) *Rhetoric and Composition: A Sourcebook for Teachers and Writers* (pp. 200–14) (Third edn.). Portsmouth, NH: Heinemann-Boynton/Cook.

Yancey, K. (ed.) (1992) *Portfolios in Writing Classrooms: An Introduction*. Urbana, IL: National Council of Teachers of English.

Chapter 11

An 'A' for Effort: How Grading Policies Shape Courses

SUZANNE GREENBERG

When I first began teaching creative writing, I aligned my authority with the gods of reason. If students entered my classes thinking that their work would be evaluated based on that hard-to-define *talent*, my job was to rid them quickly of their preconceptions. There seemed to me few real creative writing prodigies, after all. Besides, as a graduate student, I already regularly had watched writers turn from ugly ducklings to swans after a summer vacation. So, my students wanted to know, if I was resolutely not grading on *talent* – and their first writing and the discussions that followed led me to believe that talent was what they hoped to be graded on – what was my grading based on? Logic, I told them. Reason. They looked at me with blank faces. I showed them the grid.

In those first semesters, I based my grades on carefully formulated percentages: 10% Exercises, 10% Small Group Participation (discussion of exercises), 5% Logbooks (a type of journal), 15% Written Reviews of Assigned Reading, 20% Short Story, 20% Revision of Short Story, 10% Summary Comments on Students' Stories, 10% General Class Participation. Similar breakdowns could be generated for a course in another genre.

When students asked me for clarification, I fine-tuned my criteria and created handouts to support this fine-tuning. For example, when students asked me how their stories would be graded, I created a single-spaced handout, 'Guidelines for Short Story' (not to be confused with my 'Guidelines for Revision of Short Story' or separate sheets that could be generated for poems, essays, or plays). I divided these guidelines into two sections, 'Mechanics' and 'Content.' To help justify why I might choose a particular grade, I offered stern advice, such as the following: 'If you break any mechanics rules (not indenting each time someone speaks, etc.), have a very good reason for doing this.' Under the content criteria, I went on to dictate that 'All stories should include at least two human characters, setting, dialogue, conflict and a consistent point-of-view,' certain I was now addressing the basics and finally sounding like a real English teacher, well on my way to justifying any grade I might give.

As a response to students who asked me how they would be graded on the small-group participation, I created a handout entitled 'Small Group Guidelines.' In it, I established my criteria, which included the following tedious but, I hoped, official-sounding instruction: 'On days you will be meeting in small groups, you are expected to bring in a *typed* copy of the assigned exercise for each member of your group as well as a copy for me. Members will all exchange work and then establish an order in which to read aloud and discuss exercises.' Students wanted to know, was 10% simply given for *completing* all exercises, or did they have to complete them a certain way? I instituted the check-minus, check, check-plus system and explained that to receive the complete 10% students would need a majority of check pluses. How did they earn check pluses anyway? A majority? Did this mean, for example, that 51% check pluses and 49 checks and check minuses give students the edge?

And so my semesters tediously chugged along. New questions, new fine-tuning, new handouts. Perversely, the more details I gave about how exactly I planned to grade, the more often my authority was challenged, and the more time my students and I spent discussing grading instead of writing. In other words, I had achieved exactly the opposite of what I had intended to achieve: instead of creating a classroom where students felt free to focus on their writing because evaluation was clear, I had created a classroom of grade-focused monsters.

Finally, it occurred to me, after resorting to finer and finer calculations, that there was something very wrong with my system. So, I threw it out and started again. If my previous grading system had obviously failed so dramatically, why not try a complete reversal of it; that is, offer my students no explanation at all for how I intended to calculate the final grade? But this was the late nineties, and what I privately began to think of as god-like grading – simply bestowing grades at the end of the course – wouldn't fly at my university.

Assessment was a prominent buzzword and the butt of faculty's wry jokes. As I went through my own reconsideration of how to assess my students' creative work, our English department was undergoing an external review, followed by an internal review of the external review. While much was made about the pedagogical usefulness of such assessments, many of us felt that they became exercises in bureaucratic futility. I vowed to make sure that whatever new methods I put into place to assess my creative writing students didn't feel equally riddled with redundancy.

Still, I couldn't simply stick my students with their first and last grade at the end of the course without revealing to them anything about my method. Not only did this feel mean-spirited, I'd certainly end up in grade appeals hearings without much of a defense. I decided to hide behind the polite guise of portfolio grading. While they'd receive written comments from me throughout the term, instead of being graded all along, students would present a packet of work to me at the absolute end of the course with an essay explaining what they submitted and how they saw their work evolving, and then they would receive a grade from me in the mail along with their other grades. If they wanted their portfolios back with comments – and many more, it turned out, did than didn't – they could pick them up early the next term or include a self-addressed stamped envelope to receive them sooner.

An entire body of pedagogy has been written on portfolio grading, and I began reading it to justify my own position. I found positive recommendations for portfolio grading in the 1995 CCCC Committee on Assessment report and in articles in the journal *Assessing Writing*. In *Portfolios Across the Curriculum and Beyond* and in the second edition of *Portfolio and Performance Assessment*, I found more support for the process approach that portfolios offered as well as practical advice I could apply when actually using portfolios in my courses.

Interestingly enough, much of the research on portfolio grading had been done in the field of composition, not creative writing. This shouldn't have been surprising, for those working in the field of rhetoric and composition have long been analyzing what works and what doesn't when it comes to grading student work. After all, guiding curriculum for the large number of usually mandatory first-year composition classes most often falls under the authority of rhetoric and composition specialists. If many of these experts were sending legions of graduate assistants into their first composition classes with a recommendation to use portfolio grading, this was yet more justification for trying it in creative writing classes.

But perhaps even more convincing was an essay I came across by Peter Elbow, perhaps best known for *Writing Without Teachers*, a book that approaches *all* writing as a creative act. The essay indirectly backed my contention that the more I detailed how my students would be graded, the more my students tended to focus on the percentages I had established instead of their writing. In this essay, Changing grading while working with grades, Elbow (1998: 174) writes, 'the more levels [of grading] we use, the more untrustworthy and unfair the results'. He argues for what he terms 'minimal grading,' that is, three or four levels instead of the current A, A-, B+, etc., system (p. 175) since 'the more levels we use, the more chances students have to resent or even dispute those fine-grained distinctions we struggled so hard to make in the first place' (p. 174).

While he didn't cite the *exact* problem I was having, I felt an uncomfortable recognition. Wasn't asking for clarification on exactly how to earn a check plus instead of a check awfully similar to focusing on the hazy difference between an A– and a B+? True, his students were writing essays and mine were writing fiction, but this made his point even more painfully clear to me. I had been turning my elective creative writing classes into classes in which students struggled with grades instead of language. With the support of Elbow, I finally felt vindicated in tossing away my elaborate handouts and jumping into what felt like the refreshing waters of portfolio evaluation.

The truth was, though, I did not have absolutely pure intentions. While I *did* want my students to focus on their work, not minute fractions of their grades, and to take responsibility for their own progress and development, in truth, I also wanted to put off grading their creative work for as long as possible. In other words, when it came to grading, I was a coward.

During the first semester in which I instituted my new grading policies, I reviewed the syllabus tentatively with my students on the first day of class. I read the section titled 'Final Grades' aloud: 'Assuming you don't have more than three absences, your final grade will be based on the completeness and quality of your written work and class participation. A Portfolio collected at the end of the semester (handout to follow) will give you an opportunity to highlight your best work.' While I read, I waited for the challenges to begin. But they didn't. We put away the syllabus and got to work.

Not that portfolio grading is perfect. I still count exercises and absences, and I still have to come up with final grades, which I dislike doing. But now, at least, grading is not my students' main focus, and it is mine only for a week or so as I read through each heart-felt, carefully constructed portfolio at the end of each course.

True to the promise on my syllabus, I created a handout on how portfolios are to be constructed. This handout has two sections: 'Required Elements of Portfolios' and 'Optional Elements of Portfolios.'

While my actual handout is far more detailed than the following synopsis might suggest (it includes an explanation of what I mean by a thorough revision, for example), my handout establishes three portfolio requirements, which can be adapted for other genres or multi-genre courses:

(1) A 250-500 word *typed* essay that discusses both their development as writers over the course and how they chose the work to include in their portfolio.
(2) All original short stories with my comments and at least one of those stories thoroughly revised.
(3) *Some* of the exercises completed in class.

Optional components of the portfolio include:

(1) Reviews of readings attended.
(2) Revisions of additional stories workshopped during this semester.
(3) Written comments on stories from other students.

When I grade these portfolios, I grade primarily as a process reader. I look for development, including thoughtful essays explaining how students had come to make given changes to their stories. While I don't go as far as Christopher C. Weaver (1998) in his essay, 'Grading in a process-based writing classroom' – he privileges student cover letters *over* the actual work (p. 145) – I do want to see thoughtful commentary in their cover letters, not pandering. And if one of their stories was already close to being polished when they turned it in for workshop, I want to see that they've tackled the less perfect story instead.

Having worked with portfolio grading for several years, I finally handed out a questionnaire to my classes recently to find out whether or not they would rather have received grades throughout the semester. A few were clearly frustrated at not knowing where their grades stood. As one student writes: 'It's good to know how you're doing. Plus you'd have a chance to "redeem" your grade at the end. Kick it in overdrive.'

Some were conflicted, as the following student's comment exemplifies: 'I would have rather had some guidelines at the beginning but it is hard to call. Writing is kind of like an art. How can you put a grade on expression? Yet, being a college course, some parameters must be set for a grading criteria.' Another suggested a mid-term grade would have helped. While I appreciated the frustration of the student who wanted to know where she stood in the middle of the semester, similar in some ways to the one who needed to know if he should 'kick it in overdrive,' I reminded myself – and each class since more regularly – that students are always free to stop in during my office hours to discuss how they are doing. One response – 'How can you put a grade on expression?' – raised a question with which I continue to grapple.

The majority – yes, 51% or more – however, clearly didn't mind not receiving a grade until the end of the course. As one student put it, 'If I were graded all along, I would have felt as though I had to watch everything I was doing to get a good grade. Instead of being creative, I would have probably worked to impress.' Another responded this way: 'I like not having the pressure of feeling like you had to write really good stories in the beginning.' Yet another wrote, 'I think to receive grades would trivialize the work.'

This final response illustrates my – and many others' – real problem with grading creative writing at all. Grading *can* trivialize the work. Yet, most of us teach in communities where grades are the common currency. If creative writing is to be recognized as a worthy academic subject – and many of us are still battling department assumptions that what we teach is simply fun or, at best, a kind of sideways means for improving students' overall writing skills – we cannot opt out of the responsibility for grading.

In addition, we can't, finally, grade solely on process. The final product must figure into the course grade, or we can be left in the untenable situation of awarding a mediocre writer with an A simply because he worked diligently all term long. How different is this than giving a math student an A because he worked through all the steps in a difficult problem before coming up with the wrong answer?

So talent does ultimately figure into final grades in courses I teach. Or, at least, what I, as a reader, perceive as glimpses of talent, writing that for whatever reason makes me feel enthusiastic about what I do for a living.

Try as I might have to disregard talent in favor of hard work, sometimes I feel as if I've come full circle. In an article written for the *New York Times Book Review*, fiction writer and literary editor Walter Kirn (2001) discusses his concern about the trend in book reviewing of giving every book 'a gentleman's C.' To avoid rumors of covert intentions, he wonders if the book reviewer is 'splitting the difference between his likes and dislikes, his enthusiasms and aversions, and turning out copy so bland and uninteresting that no one will want to read it in the first place, but all will declare it fair-minded and unbiased?' (p. 8). Is this what I've worried about, I wonder, as a creative writing instructor? That I seem fair-minded and unbiased?

The final grades that I now give reflect necessarily not only a student's efforts and progress but also my own private enthusiasms. In his essay, 'How a writer reads,' Stephen Minot (1989) argues in favor of transmitting one's enthusiasms to one's students. 'Good teachers of creative writing don't just teach the techniques; they infect the students with certain enthusiasms simply by being in a closed room with them long enough for the virus to catch' (p. 93). As readers and writers who care about writing enough to be invested in it as our chosen profession, how can our private enthusiasms – one student writer's particular way of characterizing a neighbor, another's precise turn of phrase in the second paragraph of an otherwise flawed story – not affect how we determine grades? Aren't we doing our students a disservice when we pretend to put our readerly and writerly expertise aside in favor of so-called objectivity? As artists ourselves, we have an obligation to let students in on, and honor, our own biases and connections to written texts.

Yet, as is the case with most creative writing professors I know, after all the hair pulling and teeth gnashing, I often end up recording a majority of Bs. My Cs, Ds, and Fs are generally reserved for the students who, to varying levels, don't make much of an effort, show up irregularly, or invest little in discussion and less in revision. My students take the classes I teach as electives. Most of them work hard, and, so, they earn their grades.

Still, there is more to my majority of Bs. When we give Cs to creative writing students who come to all our classes, participate in discussions, complete all their work, and revise according to their peers' and our suggestions – students who, in general, work hard all term long – we are not telling them that their work is average, even if this is what we intend to say. Instead, we are telling them that they have, in some way, failed. We are not grading in the vacuum of the university. We live in a culture where grades occur well beyond the university. Mainstream magazines have recently taken to grading television shows, movies and even books, and no one is flocking to C-rated movies, reassured they are perfectly within the average range of acceptability. In California, restaurants receive, from the health department, the same letter grades my students do. And just as my creative writing students know there is nothing truly satisfactory about a C, no one I know eats in a C-rated restaurant, even though reassured that it is, on average, clean. Even my children's dentist gives out report cards. Children and parents alike wait eagerly, knowing full well the difference between a B– and a C+ can be a follow-up visit to treat a nasty cavity. My majority of Bs partially reflects this reality.

Perhaps, though, my biggest concern with giving the so-called average, hard-working creative writing student a C is that we may be turning that student away from writing – and taking more creative writing courses – even as we're missing something crucial, a glimpse of latent talent. Recently, in discussing applications for our next class of graduate creative writing students, a colleague made a case for a student I had rated as average by simply reading aloud a sentence so profoundly beautiful that I was compelled to go back and reread the entire application. My colleague's enthusiasm was, if not contagious, convincing, and this student was eventually voted into our program. It's too easy, perhaps, to cut off a student's options.

In his introduction to *Writing on the Edge*, guest editor Elbow (1999, 2000) writes that, in judging which stories to include and which to reject in this special issue of true stories, he felt initially as if he were 'having to grade people's lives' (p. 4). He's argued, too, in *Everyone Can Write*, that grades only indirectly motivate writing students (2000: 403) and that while 'high-stakes assignments' are valuable, 'the more [grading] levels we use, the more untrustworthy and unfair the results[,...] the more chances students have to resent or even dispute those fine-grained distinctions we struggled so hard to make[,...] the more we establish a competitive atmosphere[,...and] the more work for us' (p. 407). No wonder my early attempts to delineate evaluation in finer and finer detail backfired. As creative writing instructors, try as we might to be fair – and even, perhaps, objective – evaluation, on some level, is what we do. Whether the work is actual fiction or simply barely fictionalized life experience in stories, poems, plays, or essays, if it's any good, students often feel unreasonably close to the work they've labored hard to create. To recognize the relationships among the evaluator, the evaluated texts, and the authors of those texts is to bring authority-conscious pedagogy to bear in order to understand how grading policies and practices shape a creative writing course.

When I grade now, I reward both hard work and talent, even if these qualities may not both reside in the same student in equal amounts. By keeping track of completed exercises and attendance even as I require final portfolios, I'm able to reward the student who stays on track, comes to class, and participates. By paying attention to which students are incorporating into their final drafts those concepts we have been discussing – concepts that range from using dialogue correctly to moving from summary to scene – I'm able to reward hard work. By allowing my private enthusiasms to matter, I'm also able to reward glimpses of talent.

While I still often have to squint to determine the difference between the fine hues of two adjacent grade demarcations, now when I dread a term's end, it's more likely because I'm going to miss a particularly vibrant group of students than because I'm afraid of awarding these same students their final grades.

References

Cole, D.J., Ryan, C.W. and Kick, F. (1985) *Portfolios Across the Curriculum and Beyond.* Thousand Oaks: Corwin.

Elbow, P. (1998) Introduction. Changing grading while working with grades. In F. Zak and C.C. Weaver (eds) *The Theory and Practice of Grading Writing: Problems and Possibilities* (pp. 171–84). Albany: State University of New York Press.

Elbow, P. (2000) *Everyone Can Write: Essays Toward a Hopeful Theory of Writing and Teaching Writing.* New York: Oxford University Press.

Elbow, P. (1999, 2000) Introduction. *Writing on the Edge: On Writing and Teaching Writing* 10 (2), 11 (1), 4–11.

Far, R.C. and Tone, B. (1998) *Portfolio and Performance Assessment: Helping Students Evaluate Their Progress As Readers and Writers.* Fort Worth: Harcourt Brace.

Kirn, W. (2001) Remember when books mattered? *New York Times Book Review* 4, 8–9.

Minot, S. (1989) How a writer reads. In J.M. Moxley (ed.) *Creative Writing in America* (pp. 89–95). Illinois: NCTE.

Weaver, C.C. (1998) Grading in a process-based writing classroom. In F. Zak and C.C. Weaver (eds) *The Theory and Practice of Grading Writing: Problems and Possibilities.* (pp. 141–50). Albany: State University of New York Press.

Chapter 12

Gender and Authorship: How Assumptions Shape Perceptions and Pedagogies

SUSAN HUBBARD

Our culture is rife with gender stereotypes and with experiences that tend to privilege one gender over another, so it should be hardly surprising when gender-specific assumptions are voiced by creative writing students, colleagues, scholars, and friends. Yet, some part of me always *is* surprised. Acknowledging and discussing gender stereotypes seem to me important tasks for the teacher and practitioner of creative writing. Ignoring or dismissing stereotypes serves only to strengthen them and to mislead students about their roles and possibilities as poets, prose writers, or dramatists.

In terms of oral and nonverbal communications, abundant literature indicates that men and women communicate differently. Even before Deborah Tannen's work found a popular audience, sociolinguistic studies[1] asserted that women, unlike men, tend to speak hesitantly, posing questions and qualifying their assertions; that women are less likely than men to speak in mixed groups and are more likely to be interrupted; and that women's talk is more likely to be about everyday, personal, and practical concerns. Scholars also have asserted that men and women *write* as differently as they talk and communicate nonverbally. But in creative writing, few scholars, writers, or empirical studies support such differences. After reviewing available research and conducting my own, I have come to think that studies documenting differences between male and female writers often are biased by the researchers' expectations (i.e. by gender stereotypes).

My research began and continues in the classroom, sparked by incidents such as this one: in an intermediate fiction workshop, I asked for a volunteer to open the discussion of a classmate's story. The first student to speak, a young man in his junior year, said, 'This is a woman's story, not the kind of thing that interests me.' Another student, a young woman, chimed in, 'Yes, this is definitely a woman's story. It's all touchy-feely, full of relationships.'

130

I've been encountering comments such as these since I began teaching creative writing in 1981, and they've never ceased to intrigue me. For starters, I myself don't consider so-called women's writing and men's writing distinct genres, except in a historical sense or in the sense that publishers of literature anthologies have chosen texts to define those categories. When I first began teaching, my response to comments such as those above was to bypass them and refocus the discussion. 'Let's talk about the story itself,' I'd say. But a majority of students, I've found, believe that men and women write in distinctly different ways, and these beliefs emerge in many writing projects and workshop responses.

I continued to think about these comments and the authoritative way in which they were expressed. In workshops, authority can be seen to belong to the student author whose work we're discussing, and to the workshop leader, who shapes the discussion and ultimately grades the work. A good workshop is like a good collaborative novel in that participants agree on some basic aspects of craft and share common aesthetic goals, but respect individual variations in plot and style. A student critic who lacks such respect can harm or even destroy the workshop dynamic.

These questions about such students' assumptions, over time, led me (and Dr. Gail Stygall) to compile an annotated bibliography of essays and books about gender and writing, which later was issued by the University of Wisconsin's Wisconsin Bibliographies in Women's Studies series. The questions, too, led me to use that bibliography to begin my own research, which I've shared in paper presentations and publications. They also led me to design a new workshop, Gender and Fiction, to foreground gender issues in a creative writing class. And they continue to lead me to continually review and revise the ways in which I teach.

In February 1997, the Association of Writers and Writing Programs' *The Writer's Chronicle* published my essay entitled 'Sexing the writer: Gender stereotypes in the writing workshop,' which centered on a survey I conducted of 60 undergraduates in creative writing classes at the University of Central Florida. I administered the survey during the first week of classes and asked respondents to identify themselves only as male or female. In 1998, I repeated that survey with an additional 52 students, asking them, 'Do you think that men and women write stories differently?' Of the total (112) students surveyed, 97 answered the question affirmatively. In the original group, 49 responded affirmatively, eight negatively; three weren't certain. In the second group of 52 students, 48 responded affirmatively and two negatively; two weren't certain. Here are some sample responses:

Women tend to write more on love and fantasies. Men tend to write more on escape from the unknown.

Men focus on the more concrete, tangible details. Women seem to be more interested in the emotional perspective.

Men's and women's minds work differently. This makes it happen that subjects will be treated differently.

I believe a woman can have the ability to be more passionate and in depth than a man. In most cases it seems that a woman is more observant to detail.

Stereotypically speaking, women are more sensitive and will write more 'touchy, feely' material. Men will write about self, self vs. others, self vs. nature, etc.

Most definitely! In almost everything we do in life men and women have different viewpoints. I think usually women see things from more of a deep viewpoint. Men seem to be more general. I think men think more than they appear to, they just don't express it as well as women.

When men approach writing they seek the facts, search for the pure plot and the bottom-line results. There's usually a bang at the end. Women on the other hand write with pure emotions, adding hypothetical motives and exploring many possible results and reactions. Sometimes they write in a circle.

Most of the comments pertained to choice of subject and/or structure and style of material. I found no significant gender-based patterns in the responses; that is, as many women as men believed the author's gender affected or determined the writing.

Each time, as the semesters went on, I noted that my students' own fiction didn't fit the stereotypes. Men wrote about relationships, but so did women. Women wrote about adventure, fantasy, and crime, as did some men. Violence and sex were popular topics, no matter what gender the writer. Some men wrote flowery prose. Some women wrote short sentences and plot-driven stories. Students' plots were structured every way imaginable. I couldn't deduce any pattern. Where, then, do the stereotypes come from, if not from the students' own work? My subsequent reading of literary, gender, queer, feminist, and composition theory has yielded preliminary answers and led to many more questions.

First, does gender affect content? According to Rust Hills, an *Esquire* editor who wrote *Writing in General and the Short Story in Particular,* 'man's fiction' traditionally has meant 'adventure, fantasying, apparently-hard-boiled-but-at-the-bottom-sentimental stories of sports or crime or outdoor life,' while what he terms 'ladies' fiction' is 'soupy, romantic' (1980: 1). Hills' categories reflect most directly magazine audiences for short fiction in the 19th and early 20th centuries but, apparently, are credible to many of today's students as well.

Composition teacher Robert J. Connors, in his article 'Teaching and learning as a man,' describes a 'male genre of writing' this way: 'It is a commonplace that young men in our classes *want* to write adventure or achievement narratives, quest stories of different sorts, or arguments that allow them to remain emotionally distant or to vent strongly-held opinions' (1996: 150). Connors asserts that young men's topic choices reflect their training from an early age to focus on tasks and to put aside personal feelings. He cites a passage from an essay written by a young man, describing three young men who shoot a horse for fun, and comments upon it: 'What is the teacher to say about the casual male brutality here, brutality of a kind unimaginable from a female student?' (p. 152).

Is it unimaginable? Not to me, nor, I suspect, to many others. Recent stories I've received from women students deal graphically with heroin addiction, murder, child abuse, and rape, some told from the point of view of the victim, others from the point of view of the dealer or perpetrator. And I suspect that many women, like many men, are taught at early ages to focus on tasks and put aside personal feelings. One assumes Connors premises his assertions on experiences that he feels are indicative of general trends and truths, but others' experiences may well contradict them.

In *Gender and the Journal*, Cinthia Gannett (1992: 97–8), too, describes 'women's writing' as focusing on

> daily life, family events, relationships; the functions are generally those of personal or social (not necessarily public) utility. Women have tended to write texts close to life, to use those texts in immediate and practical ways in their lives, and to use them, paradoxically, to challenge the dichotomy of public sphere and private, the mutings their discourse and ideas were subject to.

While its assertions may be true historically, this passage may strengthen the stereotype that women naturally veer from the factuality and brutality of a world more readily explored by men.

Critics and scholars have often perpetuated those stereotypes. As Dale Spender (1989: 21) aptly notes in her book *The Writing or the Sex,*

From Jane Austen to Barbara Cartland – there is the implication that all women's writing is romance, in much the same way as all women's talk is gossip. And a content analysis of the writing cannot possibly support such a classification scheme. Look at the domestic melodrama of Thomas Hardy, at the romances of D.H. Lawrence. Clearly when men write romance it's called something different. It is the sex and not the writing that is responsible for such a judgment.

Some critics have taken the position that only women writers are able to write effectively from a female point of view about certain topics, such as childbirth or rape. This position limits the contemporary storyteller unnecessarily. Surely, the developed imagination transcends gender, and creative writing coursework to develop writers' imaginations.

The attitude that women write better than men do about specific topics, and that men should not appropriate women's experience, grew from the realization that, until recently, the literature that dealt with these events was written almost exclusively by men. As Elaine Showalter (1985: 319) observes, we 'encounter the myths of female sexuality as seen by Hardy and Lawrence, and the wonders of childbirth as seen by Sterne and Hemingway'. Women writers and scholars in the 20th century began to correct the imbalance. Essays, anthologies, and courses focusing on women's writing examined the ways in which women's writing responds to the cultural, economic, and historical forces that excluded it from the canon. Today, any imaginative writer can write about any subject, without being silenced because of gender, ethnic background, class, or sexual experience.

Another question emerges. Does a writer's gender affect structure and style? At the onset of the 20th century, Sir Arthur Quiller-Couch's critical essays made clear distinctions between masculine and feminine writing styles: when a male writer would write directly and realistically, a woman would unavoidably do otherwise, because she possessed a feminine gift of rendering a scene vivid for us by describing it, not as it is, but as it excites her own intelligence or feelings. Quiller-Couch's stereotypes reflect those of classical rhetoricians, most notably Marcus Fabius Quintilianus (Quintilian, 1856), who, in the first century, advocated the masculine virtues of good writing: 'But let the embellishment of our style...be manly, noble, and chaste; let it not reflect effeminate delicacy, or a complexion counterfeited by paint, but let it glow with genuine health and vigor' (8.3.6).

Many composition theorists have long distinguished between male and female rhetoric. Males, they claim, tend to state conclusions first, then present the reasons that support them; women prefer an additive style, deferring conclusions until they are evident. Virginia Woolf's *A Room of One's Own* is often cited as the definitive example of female rhetoric because it 'is indirect rather than confrontational, seemingly digressive rather than linear, allows the reader to draw her own conclusions, uses first-person voice and second-person address, and depends a great deal on narrative and implicit analogy' (Rubin & Greene, 1992: 13). Tillie Olsen's story 'I Stand Here Ironing' comes to mind as embodying the same characteristics. But the description applies equally to the work of many contemporary male writers, among them John Irving, E.L. Doctorow, and John Barth.

Mary Hiatt in 1977 published a study of 100 books, fiction and nonfiction, 50 written by men and 50 by women. Contrary to stereotype, Hiatt found that men wrote longer sentences and used more exclamation points than women. Rubin and Greene, on the other hand, found that women students used more exclamation points than men. In my classes I find, to my dismay, almost everyone uses exclamation points – at the beginning of the semester, before they learn other ways to make their writing dramatic.

One of the most illuminating comparisons I've found of male and female styles is in Mary DeShazer's (1986) essay 'Creation and relation: Teaching essays by T.S. Eliot and Adrienne Rich.' DeShazer contrasts Eliot's assertion (in 'Tradition and the individual talent') that good writing must be impersonal, objective, and detached, with Rich's argument (in '"When We Dead Awaken": Writing as Re-Vision') that good writing is subjective, engaged, attached (p. 115). And in their respective essays, Eliot and Rich practice what they preach; he asserts his points with authority, using verbs such as *is, demands*, and *requires*, while her phrasing is much more tentative: *seems, suggests, relates*. But, style aside, Eliot's and Rich's arguments echo a classic division: the dualism of reason and emotion.

That dualism is the focus of *Manly Writing: Gender, Rhetoric and the Rise of Composition*. Its author, Miriam Brody (1993: 3), looks at the historical use of gendered metaphors in the rise of scientific writing and distinguishes between manly writing as 'plain, forceful, and true' and effeminate writing as 'ornate, unconvincing, and sometimes deceitful'. This distinction remains alive and well in many composition classrooms, where most of our creative writing students learn their basic writing skills and where many creative writing graduate students develop their pedagogy.

Elisabeth Daumer and Sandra Runzo (1986), in their essay

'Transforming the composition classroom,' ask, 'How are we to reconcile the pervasive message in feminist theory that language oppresses women with the fact that it is exactly this language that we are supposed to teach?' They assert that when students are taught 'the qualities of "good writing" as they are advocated in textbooks and rhetoric books–directness, assertiveness and persuasiveness, precision and vigor[,]' they are in effect being taught to write like men (p. 52). Their solution to this dilemma is to incorporate more texts by women in composition classes.

Brody (1993: 218), however, concludes by positing a progressive writing model: 'In this in-between place that we imagine, a place neither male or female, writers move freely between solitude and community, between single and shared authorship, and between assertion and qualification, conviction and doubt'. Brody's model gave me a vision of the kind of workshop I wanted to teach – indeed, the kind of writing community I wanted to inhabit. But before the model can be realized, its resident writers need to come to terms with the gender stereotypes they consciously and unconsciously hold.

I found provocative insights in Carol Tavris's (1993) book, *The Mismeasure of Women*, which I've used as a supplemental text in workshops. It ably delineates the similarities and differences between men and women and asserts that the most significant differences lie not in gender (or its related physical traits), but in power, resources, and life experiences. Tavris discusses the importance of resisting cultural feminism, which she defines as 'the appealing theories that women have a natural ability to be connected, attached, loving, and peaceful, that they speak in a different voice, have different ways of knowing, or different moral values' (p. 332). Even though the proponents of cultural feminism may have the best intentions – to redress social, cultural, and economic inequities – they tend to reinforce those inequities by promoting the idea that women by nature are suited to certain roles and professions that men are not. Both in the academic workplace and in fiction, poetry, and drama, cultural feminism, taken merely at face value, engenders stereotypes.

What are we to say, then, to those students (and colleagues) who are confident that men and women are essentially different in the ways they think, act, and write? First, we can take time to discuss gender stereotypes when they are voiced – in the classroom, in the committee room, and in the living room. Instead of ignoring stereotypical comments or treating them as irrelevancies, we can question them consciously and make time for dialogue in response. Second, we can encourage students (and friends) to read and write about the life experiences that reinforce their stereotypes. I've found that one of the most effective and overlooked ways to challenge the *status quo* is simply to take the time to describe it in full, precise detail.

Third, we can consider creating classes (and situations) that foreground gender issues. My Gender and Fiction workshop is an attempt to make gender an overt concern for the student writer. In its syllabus, I write:

> We'll consider how a writer's gender has been thought to affect the content, structure, and style of fiction; how gender may influence public perception of one's work; and how certain popular gender stereotypes manifest themselves in fiction workshops. We'll read and discuss a variety of theoretical approaches to these topics, as well as relevant fiction, in order to assess their implications for our own work.

Instead of bypassing comments as I used to do, I establish a new way to refocus the discussion of the story itself. My initial reading list for the course is wide-ranging; for instance, the assigned texts (aside from students' stories) include the following:

A Room of One's Own by Virginia Woolf
Shooting an Elephant by George Orwell
By Any Other Name by Santha Rama Rau
The Chrysanthemums by John Steinbeck
Gender Role Behaviors and Attitudes by Holly Devore
Discourse and Diversity: Experimental Writing within the Academy by Lillian Bridwell-Bowles
Excerpts from *Gender Trouble: Feminism and the Subversion of Identity* by Judith Butler
Excerpts from *Gender Outlaw: On Men, Women, and the Rest of Us* by K. Bornstein

These readings offer students a context in which to formulate and rethink their own ideas about gender and writing. My initial expectation was that a course focusing on gender and fiction would help students understand more explicitly the influence gender has in the world of writing and would encourage them to create characters and plots that acknowledge, confront, and/or correct, rather than unconsciously reinforce, such stereotypes. By and large, the course also helped students write better stories.

My fear – that the course would attract few students and probably those who least needed it – proved unfounded. Each time that it is offered, the course has a long waiting list comprising roughly equal numbers of men and women students with all levels of abilities and all manner of attitudes. This happy phenomenon is probably due less to the course material than to the generally overwhelming demand for creative writing courses.

I devote the first two classes to a two-page questionnaire that asks students to assess the influence of gender on their writing experiences. Their responses help me choose texts – to avoid stories and essays taught too often in other classes and to select others that seemed to meet their needs – and give me some useful material for class discussion. For instance, students are asked to write about a personal experience in which they were treated unfairly because of their gender. One young man wrote of being turned down for a babysitting job; a young woman wrote of being taken off a sailing team just before an important race. I share some of their paragraphs without identifying the sex of the author; students immediately begin to speculate, however, which leads to a discussion about why we associate certain sexes with certain kinds of experience.

The course requires students to complete two short stories (workshopped in class), to write a critical paper on the assigned readings (fiction, essays, articles), and to conduct research on an approved topic and present findings to the class. Through their reading and writing, students explore and confront a range of gender stereotypes, from those found in children's books and girls' juvenile fiction to those found in magazines and popular novels. In addition, what I insist upon is that opinions are substantiated with textual citations and relevant experiences and are voiced in a mutually respectful manner.

The course initially met with some resistance from students, and, during the first offering, two dropped out early on. One said the course upset her because it contradicted the traditional beliefs of her family; another simply said the 'gender stuff' got in the way of his writing. But the first student later asked me to direct her honors thesis, a collection of short stories about a woman's confrontations with Southern culture; I agreed and began to understand the reasons for her earlier discomfort. I've tried to make sure since then that my teaching style allows students comfortable space in which to disagree with me, each other, and the assigned texts – that my pedagogy is authority conscious.

The course has received very positive student evaluations, though some students complained about workload. A typical response was this one: 'Before this class, I never realized how much we tend to think of men and women as polar opposites. Now I see things I didn't before. My writing has improved, and so has my attitude. But we read about a hundred books this semester, and my eyes are tired.' Next time I offer the course, I'll shorten the reading list.

I consider even well-intentioned gender stereotyping of writing an oversimplification. The definitions and patterns I've discussed ignore other important factors – namely, class, race, ethnicity, and sexual identity. And they may lead us, as teachers of writing, to a facile reductionism – to identify in new student work the patterns that have been firmly established in the past and to ignore aspects that don't fit the patterns. If we are to create classrooms that embody the characteristics of Brody's progressive model, that encourage students to speak in all voices, then we need to help students recognize – and to be sure to recognize ourselves – all of the factors that shape their poems and stories. Acknowledging gender's place in the workshop is an important first step toward that end and represents a contribution to authority-conscious pedagogy that serves teachers and students alike, as well as our writing.

Notes

1. See Bernard (1972); Lakoff (1975); McConnell-Ginet et al., (1980); Thorne et al. (1983).

References

Bernard, J. (1972) The Sex Game: Communication Between the Sexes. New York: Atheneum.

Brody, M. (1993) Manly Writing: Gender, Rhetoric and the Rise of Composition. Carbondale: Southern Illinois University Press.

Connors, R.J. (1996) Teaching and learning as a man. College English 58 (2), 137–157.

Daumer, E. and Runzo, S. (1986) Transforming the composition classroom. In C.L. Caywood and G. Overing (eds) Teaching Writing: Pedagogy, Gender and Equity, (pp. 45–62). New York: State University of New York Press.

DeShazer, M. (1986) Creation and relation: Teaching essays by T.S. Eliot and Adrienne Rich. In C.L. Caywood and G. Overing (eds) Teaching Writing: Pedagogy, Gender and Equity (pp. 113–22). New York: State University of New York Press.

Gannett, C. (1992) Gender and the Journal: Diaries and Academic Discourse. Albany, NY: State University of New York Press.

Hiatt, M. (1977) *The Way Women Write*. New York: Teachers College Press.
Hills, R. (1980) *Writing in General and the Short Story in Particular*. New York: Bantam, 1980.
Hubbard, S. (1997) Sexing the writer: Gender stereotypes in the writing workshop. *The Writer's Chronicle* 29(4).
Lakoff, R. (1975) *Language and Women's Place*. New York: Harper & Row.
McConnell-Ginet, S., Borker, R. and Furman, N. (1980) *Women and Language in Literature and Society*. New York: Praeger.
Quintilian (1856) *Institutes of Oratory* J.S. Watson (trans. and ed.). London: Henry G. Bohn.
Rubin, D. and Greene, K. (1992) Gender-typical style in written language. *Research in the Teaching of English* 26 (1), 7–40.
Showalter, E. (1985) *New Feminist Criticism*. New York: Pantheon.
Spender, D. (1989) *The Writing or the Sex?* New York: Pergamon.
Tavris, C. (1993) *Mismeasure of Woman*. New York: Touchstone.
Thorne, B., Kramarae, C. and Henley, N. (eds) (1983) *Language, Gender, and Society*. Rowley, MA: Newbury House.

Chapter 13
Writing the Community: Service Learning in Creative Writing

ARGIE MANOLIS

One of the only literate members of the Greek community in Akron, Ohio, my grandfather recorded the community's stories in poetry. He died before I was born, but I wanted to be like him: to be at the center of things, taking down what happened. I knew that words had power and writers had authority. As a first-generation college student whose father is functionally illiterate and whose mother never had the opportunity to attend college, I also understood that my privilege as an educated person required hard work and a commitment to my community.

As an MFA candidate, I learned that becoming a writer with a capital W meant mastering the craft of a particular genre. In workshop, we focused on craft, rarely discussing what work our poems or stories might do in the world. When asked why we did not grapple with larger questions – what was our responsibility to our communities, or what might our communities think of our work – some professors responded that questions about community and audience were so personal that the writer had to work them out on her own. Others said that to ask such questions would lead to a fear of writing at all. Both answers were legitimate, but neither satisfied me. If I had these questions, didn't other writers have them also? Shouldn't we explore them collectively?

When I began to teach creative writing as a graduate student, I discovered how complicated it was to discuss audience and purpose in class. I talked to my students about the four authorities that govern any creative writing classroom: the teacher's authority, the authority of the authors we read, peer readers' authority, and the writer's authority to make drafting and revision choices. I suggested that writers should also consider the community's authority and its role in shaping their writing. My students were willing to buy, with some discussion and practice, the idea that peer critique was important, but when I suggested that community is not the same as peer readers, they balked.

When I suggested that sometimes *community* means a group of people more diverse than one's peers, and at other times, it means a specific group of people, or more than one group whose priorities conflict, they became confused.

After this faulty attempt at incorporating the idea of community into my classroom, I decided to seek out answers to my questions about community through my own graduate work instead of through my teaching. I participated in an internship meant to bridge the gap between writers and their communities. Each week, two peers and I went to a nursing home and worked with elderly people who lived in a locked unit for sufferers of Alzheimer's Disease or a related dementia (ADRD). We took props that might encourage the residents to remember and talk about their lives, such as shells from a beach vacation, fabrics and thread, or cooking ingredients. We wrote down what the residents said and created found poems from their words.

I was eager to do community work, but I found this work difficult and wrought with ethical complications. The residents' stories were particularly conducive to poetry because they came in flashes, small images or stories; they spoke in leaps not unlike the lyrical leaps poets take on the page. However, I couldn't justify using the residents to write poems they may not have been capable of writing if they did not have dementia. At the time, I understood little about dementia, but I knew it had difficult implications for those diagnosed and for their loved ones. I had no idea what use the poems or the project might have for the residents or their families.

Around this time, I discovered Kenneth Koch's (1997) book *I Never Told Anybody: Teaching Poetry Writing to Old People*. Koch worked with elderly people who were capable, at least, of understanding that they were writing poetry, though he describes a group of residents whose cognitive and physical abilities varied (p. 5). Like our sessions, Koch's centered around themes (p. 11) and involved a group of residents and facilitators (p. 5). The residents spoke the poems to Koch, another poet, and nursing home staff, who took down the words, read them back, and worked with the residents to revise them until they were satisfied (pp. 6–7).

By the time I discovered Koch's book, I knew his model would not be useful for people who suffered from ADRD. Most of the residents with whom we worked were incapable of fully understanding that we were taking down their words and making them into poems, nor would they have been capable of revising their work. Many enjoyed hearing their words read back, but only a few could remember having spoken them in the first place. Still, I was encouraged to know that our project had a context and that Koch, like us, aimed to break down the barriers between ordinary speech and poetry, which means, of course, breaking down the barrier between the poet as a revered expert and the poet as an ordinary person who takes the time to see the world in a particular way.

Koch's work, however, did not ease my ethical concerns; while his students had the opportunity to create poems they could fully appreciate, the residents from whom we recorded accidental poetry did not. Also, his use of the term *students* bothered me, at least partly, because of my inexperience as a teacher at the time. Even now, I have trouble with the idea of teaching elderly people how to write poetry; I am much more comfortable viewing such a project as a collaborative effort, one aimed at building bridges between differing experiences and types of knowledge.

Service Learning and Community Authority

Not until I began my first job as a teacher of writing did I realize how my discomfort with the conventional creative writing workshop's focus on craft and with the nursing home project came from the same source: a disengagement with the audience or readers of the work and, with it, a confusion about the purpose of the work and my responsibility as a writer. In my first summer in the small, rural town in Minnesota that I now call home, I reconnected to the purpose storytelling and poetry had held for me as a child, before I learned about character development or line breaks or metaphor. I began talking to elderly residents, mostly retired farmers, who congregated for breakfast at a diner in town. I did so with a desire to immerse myself in a new culture and with a wary outsider-ness – a necessary combination for a writer. I became fascinated with their stories, largely unknown in the wider culture. I wanted my students, too, to experience such conversations as part of their education as writers.

Soon, I would begin teaching at a small, public liberal arts college with a diverse student population, including students from nearly every county in Minnesota, 12 other states, and seven other nations. I was told students came to school here for reasons ranging from its reputation in the state, its relatively low cost compared to private liberal arts colleges, its commitment to diversity, and the opportunity to work closely with professors in small classes and on independent research. If given the opportunity to talk with the elderly people in their community, I thought, students from metropolitan areas might better appreciate their temporary home, and students from nearby rural communities might recognize the value in the stories of their own people. I hoped, too, that a community-based project would have a wide appeal for students who hoped to become published writers as well as students who wished simply to fulfill the art performance general education requirement.

For the last three years, as a requirement in my introduction to creative writing course, my students have planned and implemented weekly activities for residents of a nearby nursing home, most of whom suffer from ADRD. They record the conversations and write found poems from those conversations, which they read back to the residents and give to the residents' families. To integrate this community-based project into the course, I use the pedagogy of service learning.

Service learning – the use of community-based, participatory learning projects outside the classroom to complement and enhance students' academic experiences – has eased my discomfort about the ethical issues related to community-based writing and given me a practical model for course design that seeks to create writers who are engaged with and feel responsible to their communities. Service learning encourages students to meet identified community needs and course goals simultaneously. Students work in the community and connect the concepts and skills required of them as students to that work through reflection. In addition to the primary course objectives, service learning also meets several secondary objectives, including enhanced personal and interpersonal development, strong critical thinking, and an understanding of civic engagement that often leads to overcoming negative stereotypes and committing to social action (Eyler & Giles, 1999: 3–12).

This particular service-learning project addresses needs identified in a community assessment that happened before I arrived. Two needs that arose from that assessment were more intergenerational activities and more opportunities to grow as a diverse community. Our student body is 16% minority and mostly of traditional college age. Whatever their background, students rarely interact with the large, white, elderly population. In addition, as in many college communities, a clear town–gown division plays out regularly in the town and university newspapers and in conversations on and off campus. I wanted this project to potentially work toward alleviating all of these issues.

The project is also designed to meet the needs of the nursing home itself. I met with the activities director, who explained that programs for people with dementia focused mostly on large-group activities; the residents rarely had the one-on-one attention or small-group interaction therapeutic for this population. The activities director also wanted to get families more involved in the residents' lives. Later, I showed her a draft of my syllabus, and we agreed to work together. The project is now in its sixth year.

Goals, Needs, and the Creative Mindset

A series of concrete, known needs and goals runs counter to the creative writing tradition. We resist rules, resist authority, and, at times, even resist working with others. We may even resist the idea that creative writing can be taught or that students without natural talent should be in our classrooms. How can we, then, consider our classrooms as spaces in which students can do work meaningful not only to themselves as writers and learners but also to the surrounding community? How can we encourage beginning students to share their work with people outside the classroom when we also tell them that publication is earned only after years of practice, feedback, and revision?

I began the project with these concerns but have found, however, that collaboration and providing a final product for the community are necessary parts of organizing a successful project that is not exploitative. My community partner – whose work was essential – secured permissions from family members, chose residents who would benefit from the project, drew up a schedule, visited class frequently to train students, and planned a community celebration. The residents and their families are moved by the books of poems the students create for each family each semester.

Our collaboration, instead of forcing students to meet a series of prescribed needs or to see the community as a daunting authority, encourages students to ask the kinds of questions I want them to ask about purpose, responsibility, and audience. Instead of imposing my own ideas about community authority onto my students, I now encourage them to think critically about difficult questions. When should we respect the residents and their families by leaving out poems that might be difficult to read, or might not preserve resident or family dignity? When do we choose to write the poems anyway because they reveal the ugly truth of a terrible disease? Should we write a poem that we suspect is not actually true, but reveals a poetic truth? Students learn that, rather than allowing the questions to stifle the writing of that draft, they can discuss these questions safely with other writers after the first draft is complete.

This pedagogical approach also encourages students at all levels and with all kinds of talents to participate. For instance, the shy English major with a talent for writing and an ear for poetry in everyday speech who hopes to someday become a published writer can find poems while listening to the tapes and create thoughtful line breaks and titles for the work, even if she has trouble talking with the residents. As the course progresses, she learns valuable skills that help her think about the diverse communities through which literature can be inspired as well as her responsibilities to these communities. The psychology major whose work reflects little natural talent has the opportunity to grow as a writer and to hone the reflective skills she'll need in her work with the elderly, or another population, later.

How the Project Works

Because I remember how lost I felt when thrown into the nursing home for the first time as a graduate student and because good service-learning practice involves pre-service training and reflection, students spend the first five weeks of the semester preparing for the project. They read about aging, ADRD, intergenerational communication, oral history, local culture and history, and found poetry. They learn how to plan therapeutic activities for people with dementia that stimulate the use of senses and language, encourage reminiscence, and validate their memories and lives (Holden & Woods, 1998; Zgola, 1990). They also discuss current regional, national, and international controversies related to aging and disease. In these discussions, they consider the complexity of these controversies and their responsibilities as citizens and writers to grapple with them. They look at various models of community involvement and social action and consider how such models might inform their work. In short, these students get a crash course in various ways a liberal arts education can relate to any subject – in this case, to work with the elderly and to the writing of found poetry.

To prepare for writing found poetry, students read found poems by published authors, talk about how found poetry differs from original poetry, and consider the types of found poetry defined by Tom Hansen (1980) in his article 'Letting language do: Some speculations on finding found poems.' Will they write 'subversive found poems,' which remake the meaning of a text by changing its context (pp. 273–7), or will they write 'found poems of lyrical intensity,' concerned mostly with sound (pp. 272–3)? Or, are they creating a new kind of found poetry altogether? Students discuss what it means to be a writer of witness and consider what the poems might say about aging, dementia, contemporary rural life, and our responsibilities to the elderly and their families.

After this preparation, small groups of students plan activities for and meet with small groups of residents once a week for about an hour. The groups remain the same, so students get to know the residents well, even if some residents do not recognize or remember them from week to week. Students correspond with family members of the residents to learn about each resident's life history and to explain what they are doing. Based on residents' interests, students choose a theme for each meeting, bring props related to that theme, and plan introductory questions. They reflect on each session in writing. In the reflections, they narrate what happened; reflect on how their ideas about aging, disease, and community work are changing; and analyze what went well and what did not. These essays are a place where students grapple with difficult situations and questions on their own through reflection and articulation. I am the only one who reads them.

The students write found poems from tapes of the conversations, which they read back to the residents each week. At the end of the semester, students create a book of found poems – and final reflections – that is given to the residents and their families and caretakers. Families are invited to a reading and celebration; many family members attend, talk with the students, and express their appreciation for the project.

After the third year of the project, in addition to this celebration for families, students planned a community reading. After securing permission from the families, they also created a book of poems for the community; prior to this event, the poems were shared only with residents and their families and caretakers. The students invited local clergy, city government officials, business owners, and family members of the residents to read from the more than 500 poems collected in the first three years. The reading, held at a coffee shop owned by two local churches, was well attended by both people affiliated with the university and those who were not. As my students and I looked out at the audience, we realized the work we had done had bridged not only gaps between elderly people and young people, but also divisions between town and gown.

What About Creative Writing?

With all the community needs in mind, it's important that course goals do not get lost. To ensure this, I exert teacherly authority to lead discussions that connect the skills necessary for writing found poetry to the skills necessary for writing original work. In the process of finding poems on the tapes, students practice poetic conventions such as line breaks and titles and discover how these conventions inform the way a poem is read. They learn that writers must pay attention to discover poetry and narrative in daily life. The fact that they are working with language that is not their own helps them to understand diction and voice in new, useful ways. Students also learn to sustain and complete a long-term project. Finally, the critical thinking students apply to planning for, executing, and reflecting on the sessions transfers well to the kind of critical thinking necessary for successful workshopping.

Throughout the course, students also read published poems and short stories, read about craft, and work on their own poetry and fiction. They write several informal exercises as well as four formal assignments, including three poems and one short story, which they revise by the end of the course. Because of time constraints, however, only two of the four formal assignments are workshopped by the full class, although students receive written comments from their peers and teacher on all four assignments. This pedagogical choice means that students do not practice talking about their peers' work as much as they might in a more traditional class.

I still struggle with the decision to include fewer workshops in the course. I hope, however, that what students learn through the project makes up for less frequent workshopping. Students apply critical thinking and interpersonal skills when they work together to plan and conduct activities for the residents. They have the opportunity to enhance interpersonal skills, consider their civic responsibilities, and overcome negative stereotypes by interacting with residents and their families while they read and write about personal and cultural issues. And, students who take the course as part of their liberal arts education and not merely because they hope someday to publish gain both a sense of the hard work required to create polished writing and also the skills necessary to apply ideas from several disciplines to meet community needs.

Complicating Notions of Authority

My pedagogy, however, is unusual because I complicate the already complex notions of authority in the creative writing classroom. Students must come to terms with the multiple authorities that shape their work, including those beyond the four authorities usually present in creative writing classrooms – those of teacher, writers whose work is studied, peers, and student author. The elderly people with whom they work, their family members and caretakers, the staff at the nursing home, and all prospective readers of the found poems also become authorities whom they must respect, question, and resist, depending on the situation.

The practice of writing found poetry also complicates students' authority over their own writing. Writing found poetry is an exercise in humility – even more so, perhaps, than having one's poem or story workshopped. Students are co-authors, along with the residents. In a larger sense, too, their authorship goes beyond the speaker and poet to include their peers who participated in the conversation, the planning they conducted prior to the session, and the residents' complex and fragmented memories. This lesson may serve them well when they stumble upon the subject of their next original poem – or the subject of whatever research they do for their next course or work they will ultimately do in the world.

The instructor's authority also grows more complex in the service-learning classroom. The content of class discussions varies depending on what happens on site; students, then, become central not only to how skills and knowledge are acquired, but to which skills are practiced and which knowledge is acquired. Part of my role is to help students engage in problem solving around the multiple layers of authority they encounter. As David D. Cooper (1998: 51) notes in his article 'Reading, writing, and reflection,' teachers in the service-learning classroom should 'push [...] students to think critically and to engage issues in a more critically reflective way'. Sometimes, doing so involves asking hard questions and proposing uncomfortable points of view (p. 51). For instance, when a student wrote that staff seemed uncooperative and uninterested in the project, we looked at literature about nursing home culture as a class. I challenged students to consider why some staff were not invested in the project and to create plans of action for how we could change the situation.

The direction of conversations with students outside the classroom is also profoundly shaped by what happens on site and also complicates

my role. When students experience a difficult event, such as an angry outburst, we problem-solve together. When a resident who seemed uninterested in the project thanks a student for her poems, we celebrate together. I've talked to students who worried about the racism, sexism, and heterosexism they might face on sight about the ways residents have responded to me because of my gender and sexual orientation. I've also had the opportunity to work with several students on research, writing projects, and conference presentations related to the project, as well as the community poetry reading discussed earlier, thus changing my role from instructor to collaborator.

I still wonder whether spending more time on craft would ultimately have a larger impact on students' writing. Even at colleges and universities at which service learning is central to the institution's mission, many questions remain about how to reward faculty who spend time they might otherwise use for their own work on incorporating service learning into their courses (Ward, 1998: 155). But I am as likely to celebrate these questions as to worry over them. Overall, this pedagogy leads to more questions than answers. At the end of the course, we discuss what the books of poems had to say about aging, dementia, and life in rural Minnesota in the last century. Could the poems help readers understand aging and dementia? Would readers be more likely to act as advocates for the elderly? To get to know the elderly in their communities and listen to their stories? To understand the political forces that lead to the challenges rural Americans face? We are never sure how to answer these questions. But perhaps this is the lesson; no matter how much we think about the role community plays in our writing, we can't be sure of how our work will be read or how our readers will respond.

My three greatest passions – writing, service that leads to advocacy and social change, and meaningful personal relationships – are one passion and one journey. I pay attention to and honor the questions and contradictions. And ultimately, the authority in my classroom teaches my students to do the same.

References

Cooper, D. (1998) Reading, writing, and reflection. In R.A. Rhoads and J.P.F. Howard (eds) *Academic Service Learning: A Pedagogy of Action and Reflection* (pp. 47–56). San Francisco: Jossey-Bass.

Eyler, J. and Giles, D.E. (1999) *Where's the Learning in Service-Learning?* San Francisco: Jossey-Bass.

Hansen, T. (1980) Letting language do: Some speculations on finding found poems. *College English*. 42 (3), 271–82.

Holden, U.P. and Woods, R.T. (1998) *Positive Approaches to Dementia Care* (3rd edn). London: Pearson Professional Limited.

Koch, K. (1997) *I Never Told Anybody: Teaching Poetry Writing to Old People*. New York: Teachers and Writers Collaborative.

Ward, K. (1998) Addressing academic culture: Service-learning, organizations, and faculty work. In R.A. Rhoads and J.P.F. Howard (eds) *Academic Service Learning: A Pedagogy of Action and Reflection* (pp. 73–80). San Francisco: Jossey-Bass.

Zgola, J.M. (1990) Therapeutic activity. In N.L. Mace (ed.) *Dementia Care: Patient, Family, and Community*. Baltimore: John Hopkins University Press.

Part 4
In the Classroom

Chapter 14
Where Do You Want Me To Sit?: Defining Authority through Metaphor

CATHY DAY

> *We are the metaphors we learn and live by.*
> Ira Shor

It is the first day of a new semester. Students file into my creative writing course, adjust themselves in their chosen seats, and look up. Some are thrilled and expectant, others wary and indifferent. The occasional few are a tad hostile. Some don't bother to show up at all. All we're going to do is review the syllabus and my attendance policy, right? Wrong. On this so-called 'blow off' first day, we will talk about authority, albeit in a roundabout way.

Perhaps we are in a seminar room, sitting together around a conference table. Or we are sitting at desks in a circle. But in our minds, we sit at a metaphorical table. John desires the proverbial roundtable where everyone has an equal say. Jane sees a family dinner table where children are nourished and parents pass on wisdom. Joe sees a dinner table where children are ignored and parents pass the potatoes. Jonelle pictures herself at a chessboard facing an opponent; she strategizes her next move. James stands before a judge's bench, waiting for sentencing. Jackie is a dyed-in-the-wool company woman – she stands before the mahogany boss's desk, awaiting instructions. Even when we don't speak of this metaphorical table, it is always there.

I taught creative writing for years before I realized that it sometimes took a whole semester for us to communicate a basic but crucial bit of information to each other: where we expected to sit and needed each other to sit – symbolically – in the classroom. Students might want the same style of teaching their last instructor used: hands on or hands off, top down or bottom up. Each semester, I never know what to expect – and neither do they.

In creative writing classes, I teach students to use metaphor in their poems and stories but also use a metaphor exercise to gauge authority issues. On the first day of class (after introducing myself but before reviewing the syllabus and policies), I hand out a list of metaphors for the workshop. The metaphors are presented without my interpretation. The choice a student makes is not as important as his or her explanation and interpretation of that choice. After collecting the surveys, I tally the results, read aloud from the responses, and ask students to comment. This first-day exercise reveals the many different metaphors we've brought with us into the workshop and allows us to make the necessary adjustments. The list of metaphors I use is as follows.

The workshop is a/an:

- well
- guided tour
- athletic team
- dialogue
- workplace
- place of worship
- artist's studio
- chess match
- movie theater
- choose your own metaphor

I encourage anyone interested in this exercise to survey student responses anonymously because anonymity encourages valid and honest results. In my case, however, I knew that I wanted to write about this exercise, so I informed my classes about my intention to quote their responses while maintaining their anonymity.

The Workshop is a Well

In *Democracy and Education*, John Dewey (1916) asked, 'Why is it, in spite of the fact that teaching by pouring in, learning by passive absorption, are universally condemned, that they are still entrenched in practice?' (p. 38). The answer? Because it is easier – easier for the overworked teacher to stand tiredly at the well, easier for the student to assume the form of bucket. Semester after semester, the buckets keep coming, like *Fantasia*'s parade of pails and mops, an endless, sloshing stream. I am the well; hear me pour. The well's lulling monotony is tempting, but I do my best to resist becoming a bucket filler. However, many students (especially undergraduates) believe this is the way education should be – because they have rarely seen it work any other way. To them, my job is to fill them up with knowledge, and success is measured by how much they retain, how much water makes it home without sloshing out.

Some students interpret this metaphor more positively. 'Each week we (students) come and give of ourselves, like a well. You (teacher) take what we've given and show us how to make it even better. We don't all have the same quality of water.' This student sees the water emanating from herself; I am merely the Brita pitcher, filtering out impurities to help them achieve crystal clean prose and poetry.

The Workshop is a Guided Tour

In this scenario, I am a tour guide describing points of interest – to the left, the sonnet and sestina, and to the right, a Coover, Carver, and Kingsolver – so that the tourist/student can appreciate and learn more about creative writing. Success is measured by whether the tourist has come to appreciate this place and will perhaps visit again. Like the metaphor of the well, influence rests with the active guide/teacher while students sit back and enjoy the ride.

When I created this metaphor, I saw it as wholly unconstructive. Students in entry-level creative writing classes regularly choose it, though, and their interpretations have forced me to reevaluate my negative spin. Few beginning students are taking my class in order to be writers, and there's not a thing wrong with that. In college, I took a dance class. Partly, I was avoiding having to take a science course, but also, I was simply curious to see if I had it in me (I did not, but I tried very, very hard). One of my students wrote: 'We are new to this place and need to learn about it before making a decision about how this place will or will not affect our lives and what we write.'

I lived for a time near Gettysburg, Pennsylvania. Tens of thousands of men died here in 1863; hordes of turkey buzzards return each July looking (it is said) for that long-ago feast. In Gettysburg, it was easy to imagine tourists representing the different kinds of students I encounter. Students only interested in fulfilling a requirement or getting their feet wet are like the first-time tourists who took American History in high school. This type of tourist usually prefers to survey the past from inside a bus or car, listening to a recorded voice on a cassette purchased at the Civil War Wax Museum. Students who have tried their hand at writing before are like the more serious tourists. They are the novice history buffs who book time with National Park guides, professional historians who seem to know every rock of Devil's Den. A few disdain the title of *tourist* and certainly do not want a guide; these are the re-enactors, the hard cores, who come in wool uniforms bearing haversacks and muskets.

Like the tourists, some of my students come to fulfill a life-long dream, others because they just happened to be passing by. Whatever the reason, they keep coming. Like those park rangers, I smile and begin again the story I love so much to tell.

The Workshop is an Athletic Team

I am from Indiana, so the metaphorical implications of basketball have always been a part of my teaching lexicon. I often begin introductory courses by saying, 'Some of you are here because you just want to shoot around. Some of you want to learn some cool tricks. Some of you think you'll look snazzy in the uniform. Some of you expect to drill and practice – and that's the kind of player I'm looking for.' When young writers become experimental from the get go, I advise them, 'You can't slam dunk if you can't get the ball to the basket.' When students complain that my assignments are cramping their style, I talk about the movie *Hoosiers*. The coach (played by Gene Hackman) drills his players in fundamentals, refusing to let them shoot the ball, a skill they already possess in abundance. In the end, players and fans forget about this unpopular form of training when they win the state tournament, David-and-Goliath style.

Coaches know that there is one thing they can't give a player: talent. At a 1973 conference on the teaching of creative writing, Margaret Walker said,

I always feel the teacher really has only one real function, and that is to inspire his students to think. He can serve as a guide, he can encourage, but he can only teach the craft, how to manipulate the words effectively and powerfully, and when we have done that, the writers' natural genius and talent, proclivities and predilections, take over. (United States 77)

At every job interview, I was asked, 'Can creative writing be taught?' To me, it's like asking a basketball coach 'Can basketball be taught?' Of course it can, because we teach craft, not creativity. Or at least, that is what I do.

Because of my personal experience in sports, I see coaches as benevolent taskmasters – offering encouragement and, when necessary, telling players to get their act together. But I know that not everyone conceives the coach as positively as I do; Mary Swander's essay in this collection elucidates many of the difficulties associated with this metaphor. Students may see *coach* as synonymous with *tyrant*, imagining Bobby Knight screaming at players or throwing a chair across the court. Or they might think that _coach_ is synonymous with _hero_ and imagine Knute Rockne being carried off the field in the arms of his players. I certainly do not want students to see me in either light, so in order for the coach/player metaphor to operate effectively in the classroom, we must agree on what kind of coach/player relationship we are really talking about. Here is mine: There is no 'I' in 'team' or in 'workshop.' This corny expression is particularly appropriate to the workshop, a collaborative classroom that suffers when its stars begin to shine too brightly. A team stands a better chance of winning when ego is submerged for the greater good.

The Workshop is a Dialogue

Wallace Stegner (1988: 11) said, 'The best teaching that goes on in a college writing class is done by members of the class upon one another. But it is not automatic, and the teacher is not unimportant. His job is to manage the environment, which may be as hard a job as for God to manage the climate'. It is indeed difficult to conduct workshop as a dialogue, but it is what I shoot for: an extended conversation among peers with each participant contributing equally to the debate. It is the roundtable in its most ideal form, but I must admit that I have never seen it work in academia, only in informal writing groups attended by writers who were my peers.

The creative writing workshop is, by its very nature, a democratic environment, much more so than a class in the sciences, and perhaps even more so than other humanities courses. But ultimately, there is no getting around the fact that I have the final say-so; I have more experience, and I must assign grades. Despite these obstacles that might prevent true dialogue from taking place, Ira Shor (1996) says a utopian dynamic is possible in the classroom. In _When Students Have Power_, he argues for democratic sharing of classroom authority, which includes contract grading and collaborative learning. In an another work, _Empowering Education_, Shor (1992) emphasizes dialogue, something no self-respecting workshop can do without. 'Dialogue transforms the teacher's unilateral authority by putting limits on his or her dominating voice and calling on students to co-develop a joint learning process' (p. 90). I encourage students to listen to _all_ the voices in the room, not just mine.

I have found that a workshop of unmotivated, unsure students appreciates being told I want them to rise to the occasion. Given the opportunity to claim authority, many will. Then again, there are workshops – populated by overly confident students resistant to criticism, who take and take but do not give back – in which the last thing I want is to grant them more authority. In this case, I communicate the metaphor differently, pointing out that a dialogue is not necessarily a debate or an argument one wins, but a collective attempt to better each participant.

The Workshop is a Workplace

The best possible interpretation of this metaphor occurs when students see themselves as employees working for me, their employer. Some see the relationship positively: they want to know what is expected of them and to be promoted. They know (or at least, they expect) that writing takes work. I appreciate these kinds of students (I see a lot of myself in them), but where I might see a student with a good work ethic and a conscientious manner, I realize that others might very well see slavish obedience. Some might interpret the metaphor as altogether negative; perhaps, in their minds, the workplace kills the soul, work is drudgery, and authority figures are autocrats. My father has worked a job he hates for 34 years. To him, work is a necessary evil, a means to pay bills, put kids through college, and collect retirement. My dad would never choose the word *work* to connote something positive.

Students often extend the metaphor and see the college itself as a corporation in which the president is the CEO and the different departments are divisions of that corporation. The college, as one student said in her response, 'wants to be successful and maintain strength and cooperation within the company. If it fails, money will be lost, in application numbers and donations. No one will invest in a failing company, just as no one will invest in a failing college.' This kind of student sees me as a low-level department manager, not 'the boss.'

Or worse yet, students see their educational experience as a product, something they purchase. This consumer mentality produces students who consider themselves the employer, paying me to teach them to write. If they fail to learn, it is my fault, not theirs. In his 1997 *Harper's* essay, Mark Edmundson describes today's college campuses as 'northern outposts for Club Med' (p. 48) and 'retirement spread[s] for the young' (p. 40). New dorms, new gyms, new Stairmasters appear because 'if marketing surveys say that the kids require sports centers, then, trustees willing, they shall have them' (p. 40). When I taught in Mankato, Minnesota, two students campaigned for student government positions with the following plank in their platform: 'Our philosophy of the student being the consumer is really something that has been missing on this campus. Remember, without you, this campus is not possible. The administration and faculty need to recognize that the students on this campus are their customers' (_The Reporter_ p. 11). Ironically, I owe my previous job at the college of New Jersey to the customer-driven culture Edmundson decries; that teaching position was created in response to student demands for more creative writing classes.

The Workshop is a Place of Worship

Teacher and _preacher_ rhyme, after all. I am the preacher, giving sermons and reading from the Good Book. One of my students wrote:

I thought this class would work dictatorially. Creative writing to me was a religious service in which the teacher lectures on things the students, fallible and imperfect, will never become. Students are the humble but eager congregation. Outside class, our lives are lived with the sermon in mind. Try as we might to live up to the legacy set forth in the sermons, we never quite get it right.

I shared this student's pessimism about the value of this metaphor for the workshop – it was too solemn, and too much weight rested in the teacher/preacher's hands. But some students have convinced me otherwise. Another student said, 'I like to sit and listen and be inspired. Then I go home and do what the teacher says – write.'

Religious leaders work on the soul, from the inside out. Creative writing teachers who work in the same fashion flirt with disaster. In the introduction to his book _Narrative Design_, Madison Smartt Bell (1997: 10) says,

The strategy is to assume tremendous authority, elicit enormous trust, and then abuse both, deliberately and to the maximum. Psychological shock tactics. Similar methods are used by hypnotists when they're in a hurry, and by cult leaders everywhere. The purpose is to reach areas of the target personality that are otherwise inaccessible. For the religious, it's the soul; for the Freudian, it might be the id. The cult leader wants to get into this place to awaken his disciple to the glory of God. Your bloody-minded writing teacher, meanwhile, wants to get into this place to awaken his disciple to the glory of art.

There is a fine line between a patron saint and a demagogue. Like Bell, Stegner (1988: 44) warns that young writers should be trained, not invented. 'There are, of course, plenty of writing teachers who create cliques and coteries. I find them reprehensible – the wrong kind, bent on producing clones of themselves or their cult figures'.

Nobody sets out to be a teacher/cult leader, but it happens quite frequently, I think. Consider Robin Williams' character in the movie *Dead Poets Society*. Who would not want to be a teacher like Mr. Keating? Who really can? And should we want to? I must confess to a love/hate relationship with this much-beloved film and its troubling message. As Robert B. Heilman (1991: 417) wrote in *The American Scholar*, '[The film] says he was fired for fighting injustice. What he should have been fired for was making himself, instead of the works of literature, the object of adulation'. Yet, I remember vividly watching the movie for the first time, especially the final scene in which the defiant boys stand on their desks in tribute to their 'Captain.' When I have a good teaching moment, I liken it to that very scene. I try to keep in mind that, in the film, we never see Mr. Keating actually teaching anything from the beleaguered textbook, *Understanding Poetry*, only ripping out its farcical introduction.

The Workshop is an Artist's Studio

At first glance, this metaphor might seem very appropriate: novices staring at the blank canvas, brushes in hand. 'Soooooo,' I ask students who choose this metaphor, 'where do I come in?' Some look at me blankly or say they want to be alone. 'That's fine,' I say. 'But then you really shouldn't take a workshop.'

As Richard Hugo (1979: 3) says in *The Triggering Town*, 'Every moment, I am, without wanting or trying to, telling you to write like me. But I hope you learn to write like you. In a sense, I hope I don't teach you how to write but how to teach yourself how to write'. Some students come to me in a way Hugo would appreciate – they just want me to show them how to find the artist within: 'The art is already inside me but I don't know how to express it. You show me how to do that by saying things I already know but have never expressed.' Some only want me to enter the studio to declare whether the painting is a flop or a masterpiece – a task I refuse to perform. Some want me to stand behind them, offering sage advice, or perhaps taking it a step further: lacing my fingers with theirs around the brush so that it is difficult to tell who really painted the picture. This often happens with literal-minded, grade-conscious students, but I know it happens with better writing students, too. How many of my own first stories were written to please and pay homage to the writing teachers I admired?

A most unfortunate interpretation of this metaphor is this: I am the artist painting my vision upon students, blank canvases who blame my lack of artistic talent rather than their own inability to soak up the paint. Occasionally, I do get course evaluations that read (something to the effect of): *I think Cathy is a good writer, but why isn't it rubbing off on me?*

The Workshop is a Chess Match

'When you first play chess, you are taught by someone who has superior knowledge. You learn everything that the person teaching chess knows, but you'll never become better than the teacher unless you develop your own style, unless you work on your game on your own.' I like this student's interpretation better than my own, which is much more negative (perhaps because I have never been good at chess).

I saw the metaphor as adversarial, speaking to my least favorite kind of student: those who see me as an opponent and spend the semester trying to outwit me. In *When Students Have Power*, Shor (1996: 32) claims that this attitude is a direct response to the students' perception that they have little to no authority in the workshop:

> In the face of undemocratic practices, students do assert themselves, informally and subversively, by telling the teacher what they like and don't like, by disrupting class, by resistant nonparticipation, by faking interest, by breaking the rules[...]by cleverly 'playing the angles' to 'beat the system'.

Shor's answer is to vest the students with authority, a solution made possible – he freely admits – by his self-described 'tall white male body.'

> I was simply tall enough, confident in my white male physicality and my professorship[...]to draw on the authority of my gender, my color, and the activist times to take some risks. Different bodies, skin colors, and genders carry unequal authority into the room. (p. 24)

Redistributing authority in the creative writing classroom is difficult for any teacher to manage but becomes much more problematic for those who are not white, not male, not tall, not tenured.

Another student assured me that it would be good pedagogy for me to take a seat with him at the chess board, since the match is merely a 'mental challenge that yields the best out of everybody.' But I am not convinced. If I play this game, I will play to win. What happens when, after being forced to go head-to-head, I defeat my students? Or (oh, the horror!) what happens if they defeat me? Perhaps, I should remember Stegner's (1988: 60) advice:

> I have had students who could neither give nor take criticism without getting fiery red in the face and rough in the voice – so sensitive to personal slight that they could neither take it themselves nor dish it out, without a heavy component of hostility […]. If criticism affects you that way, you are very unlikely to 'make it' as a writer, because there is no way to learn, except through criticism – your own or someone else's.

Just as I became a better writer through criticism, I have to accept the fact that becoming a better teacher works exactly the same way, and I will not get better unless I am challenged.

The Workshop is a Movie Theater

Very few creative writing students choose this metaphor, thank goodness (though many literature students do). Here is a good example:

> Going to class is like seeing a movie for the first time. You never know how the ending will turn out. The type of mood the teacher (the movie) is in resembles the type of movie. If she is in a good mood, it's like an action-thriller, which you are happy to sit through. On the other hand, if the teacher brings in a bad attitude and takes it out on the kids, it is like a movie in which you just want to get up and leave.

I am heartened that most creative writing students do not see me as film flickering on a screen, nor themselves as movie patrons who have paid good money to be entertained. However, I must admit it pleases me to get a 'thumbs up' at the end of the semester and when good word-of-mouth brings new students.

It is impossible to discuss today's fiction workshops without taking into account the ways Hollywood affects the stories students write, the ways students analyze each other's work, and how they determine a story's success and/or failures. Our students are, as Edmundson

(1997: 42) says, 'the progeny of 100 cable channels and omni-present Blockbuster outlets'. By the time they arrive in my class, students have consumed and absorbed thousands, maybe millions, of stories via television and movies. In contrast, most have a hard time remembering the last unassigned book they've read. What good is my authority when I can only talk about a student's collage-crafted story in terms of Quentin Tarantino films? I would rather have the class compare the story to Susan Minot's 'Lust' or the William Gass classic, 'In the Heart of the Heart of the Country.' Perhaps, if I am lucky, my students have seen the movie adaptation of 'The Babysitter.' How unfortunate that their knowledge of this amazing story by Robert Coover is clouded by the image of a pouting Alicia Silverstone.

The Workshop is: Choose Your Own Metaphor

This choice garners a range of responses, and perhaps they are the most telling, because the students themselves create the metaphors. Here is a sampling of student-created metaphors:

- The workshop is like a record company where the teacher is the producer trying to aid the artists with their music. Along the way, the producer must discover the talent and guide the artist to stardom. [Stardom is defined as 'a good grade,' not a spot on the best-seller list].
- The workshop is a salad. You start out with some plain old lettuce, but then you spice things up when you add in foods from all the other food groups and from different countries, and then you top it off with some tasty dressing. My brain is just a plain old bowl of lettuce. Other students add variety to my salad and your professional critiques are the dressing that tops it all off.
- We are a dam, holding back a reservoir of art and creative thinking, while you are the operator struggling to turn a rusty valve to open us up to the outpouring of creativity that we seldom use in our everyday lives.
- The workshop is a movie. I am the new actor, and you are the director, telling me everything I do the wrong way. Since I have never acted before, I fear doing my best, since you might shoot me down.
- You are a midwife. The babies are our poems and stories. We are women giving birth. The midwife offers advice and facilitation that assists with the painful labor of extracting something from within the student.

- The workshop is a prison. The warden is present to keep all of the prisoners in line. She will make me follow strict rules. My previous lifestyle will have to change in order for me to conform; otherwise, I will be punished. I now have a choice to make. I can fight the system and attempt to maintain my former life, or I can conform and undergo a successful rehabilitation, thereby becoming a new and revised individual.

From the variety of these responses, one can certainly see that the creative writing workshop can be an amorphous, vague, exciting, and/or frustrating world for students.

By administering this survey the first day, I learn how much authority my students are willing or prepared to assume and am able to convey who I am as a workshop leader. The survey illustrates how metaphor operates, not just in the classroom but also in their everyday thinking about the world. Most importantly, the exercise allows my students to communicate with me in a way that might not happen otherwise, and it allows me to impart how I would like them to situate themselves – not their bodies, but rather their intellects, their attitudes. Before we make poems or stories, together we must construct the table around which we will gather to talk about them.

References

Bell, M.S. (1997) *Narrative Design: A Writer's Guide to Structure.* New York: W.W. Norton.

Dewey, J. (1916) *Democracy and Education.* New York: Free Press.

Edmundson, M. (1997) On the uses of a liberal education as lite entertainment for bored college students. *Harper's* September, 39–49.

Heilman, R.B. (1991) The great-teacher myth. *The American Scholar* 60 (3), 417–423.

Hugo, R. (1979) *The Triggering Town: Lectures and Essays on Poetry and Writing.* New York: W.W. Norton.

McBride, E. and Danielson, T. (1998) Advertisement. *The Minnesota State University Reporter* 7 May, 11.

Shor, I. (1992) *Empowering Education: Critical Teaching for Social Change.* Chicago: University of Chicago Press.

Shor, I. (1996) *When Students Have Power: Negotiating Authority in a Critical Pedagogy.* Chicago: University of Chicago Press.

Stegner, W. (1988) *On the Teaching of Creative Writing* E. Connery Lathem (ed.). Hanover: University Press of New England.

United States (1973) Library of Congress. Conference on Teaching Creative Writing. *Teaching Creative Writing.* Washington: GPO.

Chapter 15

Duck, Duck, Turkey[1]: Using Encouragement To Structure Workshop Assignments

MARY SWANDER

A couple of years ago, a tall, shy male student came into my office and said, 'I really appreciate the way you conduct the class. It's so opposite from the abusive basketball-coach method that I've experienced before.'

I instantly recognized what this man was trying to say. Twenty years before, I had used the abusive basketball-coach method to teach writing workshops. It had been modeled to me, and I adopted it, even though I had also suffered under the method. We all know how it goes. The teacher tells the students to go home, write, and come back with a finished piece. Then, in front of the whole class, the teacher rips the piece to shreds. In my very first undergraduate workshop, I knew I was experiencing a strange system.

'Write a short story for next week,' the instructor told us.

But isn't she going to show us *how* to write a short story? There must be parts, components to a short story, different styles and structures. Is she even going to explain the choices we could make? We had no text to illuminate these concepts. We were to learn through trial by fire, through negativity, through humiliation, through hearing what we and others had done wrong. In any other skill-building class, from foreign language to driver's education, students were asked to practice the basic steps of the craft, carefully mastering one chunk of knowledge before adding another. Why was the teaching of creative writing so different?

Because originally creative writing was not designed to be taught. When Paul Engle became the director of the Iowa Writers Workshop in 1945, he was a perceptive reader of literature and a charismatic entrepreneur. He poured his efforts into fund-raising, scouring the country for the best young writers in the United States and finding them financial support. Engle recognized that the United States, unlike Europe, had no sidewalk cafes where young writers might congregate and be mentored by those more experienced in their craft. The many voices in Robert Dana's (1989) *A Community of Writers* extol Engle for his enthusiasm and his drive that eventually brought the institution to national then international prominence.

As Stephen Wilbers (1980) documents in his book *The Iowa Writers' Workshop,* Paul Engle developed the workshop as a place where young, polished writers could come for a year or two and have their work critiqued. Engle assumed his graduate students already knew how to write. What they needed, he reasoned in this post-WWII era, was a kind of bootcamp where they would be toughened up to the brutality of the enemy: the attacking critics. He thought that his students should be given harsher criticism – for their own good – than any they would receive in the outside world. Then later, they would be able to take it. Like a man. In his introduction on the writer and place in *Midland: An Anthology of Poetry and Prose,* Engle (1961: xxi) states that 'tough and detailed criticism of a young writer can help him become his own shrewd critic so that, when he publishes, the critics will not have to be tough on him'. Engle's militaristic attitude prevailed. Many of the workshop students of that period were on the G.I. bill, returning vets who were familiar with this philosophy. And the workshop was mostly male. In our culture – especially in the 1950's – we saw the same buck-up attitude in the rest of academe, in the corporate world, and, yes, on the basketball court.

In the writing world, a teaching method that was initially used with sophisticated graduate students simply trickled down to all levels of instruction. By the mid-1960s, the Iowa Writers Workshop had gained prominence. Writers with advanced degrees began fanning out all over the country finding jobs at other universities and setting up writing programs that mimicked Iowa's in tone and structure. Young teachers tend to model their mentors, so the Iowa basketball-coach pedagogy spread throughout the English Department halls of high schools, colleges and universities. But there existed an important difference. When creative writing became 'democratized,' classes in poetry, fiction, and playwriting were offered to students with little developed literary skill. Yet most instructors of creative writing clung to a pedagogy intended for those young writers that Paul Engle had brought to Iowa City in the early days of his directorship: Flannery O'Connor, Constance Urdang, William Stafford, Mark Strand, and Charles Wright.

It wasn't until I began teaching poets-in-the-schools that I changed my attitude. I couldn't ask second graders to go write a finished poem and come back for a critique. So, I had to give the students building blocks in direct, understandable ways. I developed exercises and series of hands-on demonstrations of ideas and concepts. We wrote together collaboratively as a class, and I had students write in pairs to develop confidence and generate rough-draft material. After much success with these methods, I carried this building-block approach back to the university setting.

But suddenly, my authority in my new pedagogy was challenged, in part because I was a young woman. As linguist Deborah Tannen (1990: 239–241) points out, male and female ways of talking differ widely, with men taking a more agonistic view of interactions and women seeking to strengthen connections among people. I was diverting from the established male model by instigating a model based on care and connection. My authority was shot. And who challenged my authority the most? Women students. In the tangled web of interiorized inferiority, women expected a woman in authority to act more like a man than a man. Ironically, I found most male students welcomed the kinder, gentler approach.

Thirty years after Engle endorsed the abusive basketball-coach model of teaching creative writing, it has ceased to be just a gender issue. I have a male colleague who also used the skill-building model and positive reinforcement. Last year, he told me that a female student came into his office toward mid-term time and told him that their fiction writing class has so far been a complete failure.

'Why?' my colleague asked.

'Because you haven't made anyone cry yet. In my undergraduate classes, the professors always made students cry.'

Fortunately, the military model has been fading in the creative writing classroom. What we may be looking at here is a classic conflict between the attitudes of the so-called War generation and the Baby Boomers. Every creative writing instructor, however, must struggle with the inheritance of the basketball-coach method – that shrewd-criticism, buck-up, for-your-own-good approach – and how s/he establishes authority. And students must be made aware of what they're working with or against.

One of my favorite workshop stories illustrates the point: a woman in a graduate program somewhere in the Midwest was completely abused by her famous professor. He tore into her short story, grinding it into the ground, completely denigrating any talent she might have. The professor's tirade went on for most of an hour until the student fainted.

Her fellow students carried her off to the emergency room where she was put into a little booth. Next to her, on the other side of the curtain, a farmer lay on a gurney, full of wounds from a marauding turkey.

'Doctor,' the farmer said. 'You wouldn't have believed it. That turkey just went for the jugular!'

'I could believe it,' the woman student piped up. 'The same thing happened to me.'

Contemporary thinkers from psychologist John Bradshaw to feminist Gloria Steinem have written about the negative effects of shame and blame on the self-esteem of children. In *For Your Own Good: Hidden Cruelty in Childrearing and the Roots of Violence*, psychotherapist Alice Miller (1990) writes of what she calls 'poisonous pedagogy,' or the process of breaking a child's spirit – a practice much in vogue in Europe, especially Germany – in the early decades of the 20th century. This childrearing concept spread to the United States and, through the efforts of well-meaning German nannies, took hold in the upper-class families whose offspring became powerful leaders (pp. 59–60). 'Poisonous pedagogy' allowed adults easy control over children and was supposedly practiced out of love to save children from future suffering due to lack of discipline, for the child's 'own good.' Miller documents, however, that many of the children in this system grew to adulthood to verbally and physically abuse their children and seek to establish power over others in society. Miller also argues that this child-rearing technique produced citizens who were ready to obey the 'always right' political leaders.

So how do we cast off this outdated childrearing and educational method, move out of the emergency room and into a more constructive classroom? How do we implement a building-block model of teaching creative writing and still maintain our authority?

First, authority shouldn't be established through intimidation. Students don't learn through fear. Most students recoil from taking risks when they are reprimanded for flaws and imperfections. Most students either turn away in anger and reject everything the drill-sergeant teacher is saying or even stop writing. In the creative writing classroom, we long for students who easily assimilate feedback and are open to diving back into their projects, working at revisions with openness and energy. When I was a student at the Iowa Writers Workshop in the early 1970s, there was an astonishing number of us who for the first time experienced writer's block. In his essay, 'Mentors, fomenters, and tormentors,' W.D. Snodgrass (1999) reports that many of the writers in his era suffered from the same malady.

Writer's block shouldn't be the goal nor the norm. Instead, when a teacher approaches a class with a positive attitude, students usually respond in kind. I'm not suggesting condescending hand-holding that encourages dependence. Instead, after 25 years of teaching creative writing, I've learned to explain my workshop methods at the very beginning of each semester. During one of the first classes, I tell the students very directly that I teach differently from other professors. I tell the class that I want to oversee workshop student writing with an eye toward what is right with the piece before we dissect its faults. I explain that I'm all for looking at the weakness of a piece, but that examination is always with the goal of improvement.

I give examples from my own youthful workshop days. I remember once being in a class of very talented poets. One week one of my fellow students (who years later won the Pulitzer Prize) had come to the group with a beautifully wrought and moving poem. She read the poem aloud. Complete silence followed.

Finally, one member of the class said, 'I don't think you need that line break after the word *sofa* in the fifth line of the second stanza.'

The rest of the class agreed, then we spent most of the remainder of the time discussing the poem's line breaks, the addition of a comma here, the deletion of a word there. After 10 or 15 minutes, we moved on to the next page.

No one had said a word about the poem's ambition, the depth of its feeling, the range of its diction, the originality of its metaphors. Perhaps, we had all silently agreed on the poem's star qualities. But it's vital to articulate the good as well as the bad in workshops, lest the student leave the classroom thinking only, 'Well, I guess I wrote a poem with lousy line breaks.'

I also assign each student an advocate, one member of the class who will speak first in the discussion, who will look at the work with a larger perspective, seeking to delineate the scope and vision of the writing before concentrating on smaller issues. I'm especially mindful of the word choice *advocate* as someone who will try to get inside the work to such a degree that s/he will be able to speak for the writer's purpose, if not intent. Notice I don't assign critics. Rather, I encourage students to work with their advocates in pairs outside the classroom, showing each other their drafts before bringing their work to the larger group of peers.

Next, and very importantly, I introduce skill-building exercises, matching the quantity and degree of difficulty of the assignments with the level and sophistication of the class. I attempt to chunk down the elements of a genre to its basic components and let the students master one technique before progressing to the next. In his essay 'The lesson of creative writing's history,' D.G. Myers (1994) argues that the study of creative writing injects academe with a fresh and vigorous approach to literature. Literary scholars, modeling their work on the scientific method, tend to view literature from a distance. Myers believes that creative writers return a sense of imagination, intuition, and openness to the classroom. But creative writers could also benefit from the scientific method. I've found it helpful to analyze the structures of a literary work in components or units. Isolating these units within exercises helps keep the class concrete and focused.

In my undergraduate beginning playwriting class, for example, I begin with an exercise that asks students to define their theatrical sets. I want the class to begin to grasp the differences between a set that would work for the stage and one that would be successful for a screenplay (and even a setting that would be more useful for fiction):

ASSIGNMENT #1: SETTING
Think of any interesting location, then narrow your scope to a specific spot within that place. For instance, you might think of a farmstead. Think: farmstead, farmstead just outside a small town near Des Moines, kitchen in that same farmstead.

Then make a list as long as you can of all the specific sensory details you imagine in that place. What comes to mind in terms of sights, sounds, smells, tastes, textures?

From your list, write a short, pithy description of your setting.
Example:
A sunny farmhouse kitchen. There's an old stove, refrigerator, sink, and cabinets across one wall with potholders, dishtowels, and rubber bands hanging from the cupboard handles. Above the sink is a single window with well-worn cotton tie-back curtains. A large wooden table with chairs commands the focal point in the center of the room. On the table are piles of bills and receipts, ledger books, an old-fashioned adding machine. In a corner, a hall tree holds jean jackets, cover-alls, seed caps. At its base are several pairs of muddy rubber boots. There's a door to the outside and one to the upstairs bedroom.

Once we look at the exercise, I launch into a discussion of some dramatic concepts. How do we produce plays? How do theatre sets differ from movie sets? What kind of space is available? What kind of budget? Do you want to make your set realistic, non-realistic, or bare? How will the set effect the mood and tone of your script? Will your play become a comedy or tragedy? What kinds of dramatic action might take place in this set? What kind of business and smaller opportunities for movement on the stage? All plays need conflict – does your set suggest any conflicts? Presenting students with a variety of questions – whether it be in a poetry, fiction, or creative nonfiction writing course – allows them to better understand the choices they face in the writing process and helps define writing as a process.

The students digest these ideas and concepts, then go home to try and make them their own, returning the next class with a completed exercise. Here's a verbatim student exercise from my last playwriting class:

ASSIGNMENT #1: SETTING
The stage is darkened except for an area at center stage. There a shade light bulb illuminates while suspended over an antiquated and worn electric chair. Seated upright in the electric chair is a stuffed and tattered teddy bear. On the teddy bear's head is the electric chair's leather crown of electrodes. On the left armrest of the electric chair rests a Bible. Draped across the Bible and dangling off the armrest is a Cross-of-Jesus.

At first glance, this piece of writing is unpolished and contains some confusing and awkward sentences. In the military mode, the instructor might harp on the second sentence, reading it out loud and emphasizing its incoherence, questioning the use of the verb *illuminates*. 'Illuminates what?' I can hear the basketball coach shout.

I have come to believe that much of the shame-and-blame method of teaching merely covers up the instructor's inability to guide the student from point A to point B. The instructor usually knows intuitively that something is askew in the piece of writing but can't bring the proper linguistic tools to bear to address the situation. For example, instead of yelling at the student for the use of the word *illuminates*, the instructor might explain sentence combining, syntax, and the use of effective fragments. As a class exercise, the instructor might lead the group in an attempt to rewrite the first two sentences of the paragraph. The result might read something like this:

A bare, dark set. Center stage, a single light bulb dangles down over an antiquated and worn electric chair.

Once the student is able to grasp the magic of strong, straightforward, and clear units of syntax, he might then be asked to revise the rest of the paragraph on his own, returning to class a couple of days later with a smooth revision.

But let's go on. We must now look at the content of the paragraph as well as its style. What is happening in this set description? What dramatic questions does it raise? What potential for dramatic action and dramatic conflict does it create? The set description is filled with ambiguity, with curious juxtapositions, and with symbols. An electric chair with a teddy bear? Electrodes attached to the teddy bear's head? A Bible near the chair? With the Cross-of-Jesus? The class could explore the sentimentality behind the image of the teddy bear versus the harshness of the electric chair. The students might discuss the brutality of the image of the teddy bear wired into the electrodes. Or they might want to examine the resonances of the image of the Bible, its potential comfort or its potential hypocrisy. The instructor might ask about what kinds of characters would fit into this setting. What expectations does the set instill in the audience in the opening moments of the play?

For the following class period, I asked students to create characters to inhabit their sets:

ASSIGNMENT #2: CHARACTERS IN SETTING
Write two short paragraphs of description – one of a character who fits within your setting, and another of a character who does not. Your second character may have once fit into that setting, but no longer does, or s/he may be completely foreign to the spot. Your descriptions should include the gender, age, dress, and perhaps the attitude of your characters. Give your characters distinguishing names that match their personalities.

Next, get your characters talking. Pay attention to their vocal rhythms, their diction, or choice of words. Let them perform some simple, specific action with a part of the setting that reveals something about both the characters and the reasons why they are in that particular environment at that particular time.

Here's the above student delivering this sequential exercise:

ASSIGNMENT #2: CHARACTERS IN SETTING
Reverend Charles Goode, character number one, is an Afro-American minister. He appears to be in his middle fifties. He is dressed in the typical garments of a minister/priest, i.e., black suit, black shoes and white collar. Rev. Good's permanently furrowed brow reflects the inner turmoil that besieges him. The turmoil of a man whose commitment to God is in constant struggle with his deeply hidden carnal desires.

Character number two, Asa Guerra, who appears in spirit, is an eleven-year-old African-American male. Abandoned by his father at the age of three and raised along with eight other siblings by his mother he is clad in torn Levi's worn with an equally torn Nike T-shirt. On his feet are severely torn-up and laceless hi-top sneakers. Looking much older than his eleven years, he possesses an attitude of a streetwise thug, slick and volatile. The only symbol of his youth is that of a tattered teddy bear he always keeps nearby. This teddy bear, a gift, is the only remaining memory of his father.

(AS THE SCENE OPENS WE SEE REVEREND GOODE KNEELING IN FRONT OF THE ELECTRIC CHAIR. HE FACES THE AUDIENCE AS HE PRAYS.)

REV. GOODE
Dear Lord, I ask you to forgive me. Forgive me for giving up and allowing this young child to perish without the benefit of your salvation
(AS REV. GOODE CONTINUES TO PRAY, A YOUNG BOY, ASA, ENTERS STAGE LEFT. ASA WALKS UP TO THE ELECTRIC CHAIR AND RETRIEVES THE TEDDY BEAR.)

ASA
(TO THE TEDDY BEAR.) There you are. I thought I mighta lost you. (ASA SUDDENLY NOTICES REVEREND GOODE AND IS MORE UPSET THAN SURPRISED TO SEE HIM.) Reverend Goode!

REV. GOODE
(SHOCKED, THE MINISTER STOPS PRAYING AND LOOKS UP AND OUT INTO THE AUDIENCE. THEN HE BOWS HIS HEAD AND BEGINS TO PRAY AGAIN, VIGOROUSLY.) Oh Lord, why are you letting this happen to me? Haven't I been a humble and obedient servant? Didn't I not...

ASA
(INTERRUPTING.) Reverend Goode! You should have done a better job

REV. GOODE
(AGAIN THE MINISTER LOOKS UP AND OUT INTO THE AUDIENCE. BUT THIS TIME INSTEAD OF RETURNING TO HIS PRAYER HE SLOWLY STANDS AND TURNS TO SEE ASA STANDING NEXT TO HIM. THE MINISTER GASPS.) Holy Jesus!

ASA

Wrong again, preacherman. It's me Asa and you should've done a better job!

REV. GOODE

A better job!

ASA

Yeah, a better job!

REV. GOODE

I did the best I could! What do you want from me? My mission from the Lord was to save your retched soul from the depths of hell.

ASA

Depths of hell! If you wan't going to save me you should've got in touch with Jim Brown like I told you to! He could've saved my ass from that electric chair. But you didn't listen. All you want to do is get on your knees and go through all that praying crap. Praying and telling me how Jesus died for my sins. Shit if Jesus was suppose to die for my sins, then why wasn't he in that electric chair instead of me!

REV. GOODE

You still don't understand! After all these weeks you still don't understand!

ASA

Understand what. Man you're weak. You and all your talk 'bout saving souls. Mama always said you 'jack-leg' preachers all alike. Instead of savin' souls, you're all too busy worrying about parkin' those Florsheins under somebody's dinner table.

REV. GOODE

(SHOUTING.) I did my best!

ASA

Your best sucked! (REV. GOODE DROPS HIS BIBLE, RIPS THE WHITE COLLAR FROM AROUND HIS NECK AND THROWS IT ON THE FLOOR. HE STANDS UP, REACHES FOR THE BOY, GRABS HIM BY THE NECK AND BEGINS CHOKING HIM. THE BOY OFFERS NO RESISTANCE AS HE CONTINUES TO TIGHTLY HOLD ONTO THE TEDDY BEAR.)
What are you trying to do preacherman – kill me? Don't you remember fool, I'm already dead!

Again, one could establish authority by focusing on the mechanical problems in the writing. Yes, the punctuation and spelling need to be addressed and corrected. Or, one could focus on the ending and berate the writer for placing a wildly dramatic moment at the beginning of the script. But again, let's push on. In class, we did a cold, minimalistic staged reading, the characters moving about on the stage to capture at least some of the theatricality of the script.

Then, we discussed the tension between the two contrasting characters. We discussed costuming and how the characters' clothes accentuate their differences. We discussed props and how the Bible and the teddy bear become emblematic for the characters. We talked about diction and dialect and how the characters' speech patterns reflect their personalities. And we discussed conflict – how the script was already filled with tension, drawing us in, peaking our interest.

Finally, we examined the conclusion of the scene and raised questions concerning the significance of the dramatic action. Why was Reverend Goode trying to strangle the boy? The tension of the scene intensifies at this point. The audience discovers that they aren't in a realistic play, but in a non-realistic drama. But is the attempted murder over the top at this opening point in the play? How would you follow this scene? How might the playwright map out the rising and falling action of his entire one-act?

For the next month, the playwright struggled with these questions, moving through the remainder of the sequence of exercises for the course, one assignment designed to build on another. I introduced skills and concepts that would come to fruition in the completion of a well-written play by assigning exercises in dialogue and confrontation, in the development of scenes, in dramatic action, in extension of character and catharsis. The students wrote in response, taking one step at a time, trying out each technique, taking risks and not worrying about failure. If one exercise didn't work, they had the chance to rewrite it. The in-class critiques were not thumbs-up/thumbs-down judgments, but rather a process of pulling out a few nails, planing and gluing together parts to make sturdy and well-built pieces of art.

By the end of the term, this student and most others were more confident in their playwriting skills. They turned their own critical eyes on themselves and worked to rewrite and reshape their plays. In this step-by-step, choice-driven, authority-conscious pedagogical approach, little need existed for me to point out their works' faults. The above student wrote a gripping one-act about the confrontation between a dead, eleven-year-old criminal in Mississippi and the preacher who had tried to save his soul but not his body from the electric chair. The playwright moved the attempted strangulation to the end of the play and built up the contrasting characterization of the boy and the preacher. The plot thickened. An additional character was added – a young girl who had been molested by the preacher. In the end, the script was complex and hard-hitting.

I divided the students into small rehearsal groups. The members of the groups provided suggestions for revisions and brainstormed ideas to help shape each others' scripts. A new kind of authority was established – an authority that came from within each student in relationship to him/herself. And a sense of cooperation was in the air. Gone was the one-upmanship of most workshops. Gone was the abusive basketball coach.

I use a similar assignment-based method in other workshops, whether in poetry, fiction, or nonfiction. Continually, over the first third of the term, we study techniques. In poetry courses, for instance, we study particular fixed forms as well as free verse; we study persona, meter and rhythm, and metaphor and other figures of speech. In fiction and nonfiction courses, we study point of view, framing, and so on.

As the military model has faded over the past two decades, we have only begun to collectively and adequately document what replaces it, even though we struggle individually in our classrooms to form its alternatives and the assignments that might support a new, authority-conscious approach. Precise instruction on sentence construction and syntax are essential. A discussion of overall structure, whether in drama, poetry, fiction or nonfiction, is vital. Skill building, sequenced assignments, and exercises are good starting points – at least on the undergraduate level. Group work in a cooperative atmosphere is an additional help. I'm sure others could suggest many more aspects.

We can also pull back and take a look at our own cultural context, the worldview that generates our philosophies of teaching. Recently, I encountered two representations of poisonous pedagogy in our popular culture. A National Public Radio exposé on the Republic of Ireland reported on the parochial school system and detailed how the nuns have been historically taught to shame and blame the students. The idea was to ridicule the students to motivate them to achieve. And if they didn't achieve after that kind of treatment, then 'they weren't worth bothering with anyway.'

The very next day, I opened the sports page of the newspaper to an editorial about Bobby Knight, the most famous abusive basketball coach in the country. Apparently, many at Texas Tech University were bothered that Knight had been given a lucrative position there after having been fired for abuse elsewhere. The writer defended Knight and said that basketball players were used to abuse and took it as a matter of course.

The big deal is that people are beginning to understand the devastating effects of shame and blame and to realize that we don't have to endure or cultivate it. Encouragement in a step-by-step process enhances motivation. Mutual respect and cooperation ultimately create more authority in the classroom than the authoritarian and condescending attitudes that have been modeled in the past. Authority-conscious pedagogy offers other, better, more productive ways of doing things. Ways that help students attain goals. Ways that preserve human dignity.

Notes

1. Duck, Duck, Turkey is an American children's game in which a group of children sits in a circle. One child runs around the outside of the circle, tapping each child on the head and designating each *duck*. When the child taps the head of someone in the circle and says *turkey*, the turkey-child must get up and run to catch the child who had done the tapping. The turkey then circles the children, tapping them on their heads with the labels *duck, duck, turkey*. The word *turkey* refers not only to the bird but also to a person who is a somewhat annoying jokester or to a failed event. The word *duck* can refer to both the fowl and the the action of dipping one's head to avoid contact.

References

Dana, R.A. (1999) *A Community of Writers: Paul Engle and the Iowa Writers' Workshop*. Iowa City: University of Iowa Press.

Engle, P. (1961) Introduction: The writer and the place. In P. Engle with H. Coulee and D. Justice (eds.) *Midland: An Anthology of Poetry and Prose*. New York: Random House.

Miller, A. (1990) *For Your Own Good: Cruelty in Childrearing and the Roots of Violence*. New York: Noonday Press.

Myers, D.G. (1994) The lesson of creative writing's history. *The Writer's Chronicle* 26 (1), 12–14.

Snodgrass, W.D. (1999) Mentors, fomenters, and tormentors. In R. Dana (ed.) *A Community of Writers: Paul Engle and the Iowa Writers' Workshop*. Iowa City: University of Iowa Press.

Tannen, D. (1990) *You Just Don't Understand: Women and Men in Conversation*. New York: Ballantine.

Wilbers, S. (1980) *The Iowa Writers' Workshop*. Iowa City: University of Iowa Press.

Chapter 16
How To Avoid Workshop Dilemmas: The Use of Myth To Teach Writerly Concepts

AMY SAGE WEBB

Current creative writing pedagogy draws its authority from a constructivist orientation comparable to that of science education and even classical composition/rhetoric. We teach students to recognize relevant features and structures of story so that they may identify, diagnose, and practice them. The creative writing professor does not sit in the center of a workshop circle and tell people how to write a good story; instead, we teach the students how to recognize patterns and phenomena of story. We direct students how to read as writers, which means we teach them how to recognize some basic elements of a genre – in fiction, for instance, character, dialogue, setting, narration, and general structures of plot. These elements constitute a framework of analysis. Students of writing must learn to appreciate the work of other authors and to apprentice to their techniques; we must learn how to read for *how a piece of writing works* rather than for what it means.

The authority-conscious creative writing pedagogy expects that the creative writing classroom invites shared commitment. This expectation is not an abdication of professorial responsibility. Instead, it marks a paradigm shift in the creative writing classroom to focus on process rather than product. In composition, product may be a research paper, while process connotes the attenuated research, critical thinking, drafting, and revising skills necessary to produce it. Likewise, in the creative writing classroom, product may be a good story. Process, then, is the method of meaningfully interrogating one's own and others' work so that, by recognizing patterns and making deliberate, informed choices for technique, one may produce a lifetime of stories. The students and professor share a writer's means of appreciating literature intellectually and philosophically, as well as a serious apprenticeship of practicing the techniques that create it.

Challenges

A workshop-based methodology, no matter how it is structured, is not without its challenges. Knowing the elements of plot, character, dialogue, setting, and narration – or line, rhythm, and imagery in poetry – does not equate to knowing how to use them or how to advise one's peers to use them to best effect in a given creative piece. Rarely will student critique move well from the specifics of the work on the page to the general writing concept that informs and shapes it, either in their reading or their own work. Students can learn to recognize the elements of dialogue and setting in a story, but what those elements should or could be doing there takes breadth of reading and supple intellect – a vision that involves context and possibility. Without that vision, workshop can devolve into the cul-de-sac that I call the autobiographical and emotional dilemma, in which the author tells – or desperately wants to tell – students that the story is written that way because it happened that way. The class then validates the experience by saying what they 'like' or 'don't like' about it, or whether they have had similar experiences and can identify with the subject of the story. No discussion of craft or suggestions for revision can arise from this dilemma.

Equally problematic is the dilemma of neutrality, which is the class's inability to find a first comment with which to begin. Students might know about plot, character, narration, and dialogue, but beyond their own personal likes and dislikes, they struggle to determine which element bears mention with regard to a particular story. Beyond that basic checklist of the fictional, poetic, or dramatic elements around which nearly every creative writing textbook is structured, students need to be taught how to find paths toward discussion of the larger philosophical issues that give rise to a story's, poem's, essay's, or play's purpose and meaning. The shared commitment to workshop depends upon the ability of all class members to diagnose the purposes and the heart of the piece. This goal must come first in a decentralized workshop model if the students are to know (rather than being told by the professor) which elements need work. Proliferation of writing programs around the country means that undergraduate writers will not necessarily have prior training or experience. To embark upon a fruitful discussion of the story – what it needs, how to develop its plot and characters, how it is structured and told – the class first must focus discussion down to its most basic elements: what does the character want, and what is at stake for the character? Regardless of genre, discussions must be focused on craft.

Undergraduates have usually been taught in high school to read stories and poems for themes and symbols, and learning to read as writers with, for instance, a character-level focus can be difficult at first. Most easily identifiable in an overwhelming majority of stories is the primary element of desire or wanting that drives a character, sets a chain of events in motion, and brings the character into conflict with others. For example, the class might see a character's motivation as being that he wants to get back together with his wife. To understand the nature of the character's desire, *why he wants this* requires that the student understand the value of the wife and what is at stake for the character in the relationship. Motivation at both levels, both the wanting and the *why* constitutes the heart of the story. This is the entry into productive reading, discussion and analysis, and ultimately practice of writing short fiction.

I present here, then, a way to refocus a fiction-writing workshop within an authority-conscious pedagogy so that character motivation is central throughout the course. This approach can be adapted for other genres in order to prevent or dissolve the two most problematic classroom dilemmas – the autobiographical or emotional dilemma and the dilemma of neutrality – that otherwise work against fruitful discussion, re-envisioning, and other workshop goals that employ aspects of authority.

A mythological rubric

One way to help students begin thinking about the larger implications of what a character wants, or what is at stake in a story is to employ mythological questions as a rubric for reading and discussion. Myth enlarges human endeavor, struggle, and concern to a thematic level, and many contemporary scholars have examined myth in ways that make it philosophically intriguing and intellectually approachable for students. Noted for his work with Joseph Campbell in determining how myths provide structure for story, lecturer Sam Keen granted an interview with journalist Bill Moyers in 1991. The tapes and video of that discussion provide a list of questions that comprise most of the motivating forces for characters in stories, from our oldest oral tales to our most contemporary stories.

1. Where am I going?

In its largest (mythological) sense, this question implies all questions of a person's purpose in life, progress, and development. It is easy to apply this question thematically to any number of anthologized short stories. Students in a writing workshop quickly ascertain that the question also encompasses that difficult concept of character motivation. Where a character is headed, whether the path is desirable to the reader or not, implies the kinds of desires and goals that the character may have, as well as the desires other characters in a story may have for the main character. In other words, the question provides insight into what is expected and at stake for the character.

This question of direction is essential to the students themselves. Most undergraduates have clear ideas of whom and where they want to be, but few of them have a firmly developed idea of how they will get there. It is helpful to discuss in class how uncertainty can be as useful as certainty in setting a plot in motion. A character may act in order to set herself on a desired path (Norma Jean in Bobbie Ann Mason's (1982) 'Shiloh,' for example). Another character may fail to act, or may act inappropriately because he does not see his direction clearly (Leroy in 'Shiloh').

2. Who are my people?

Implied in the second question are all questions of belonging and searches for self-definition. This question moves from the initial 'where am I going' to 'who will go with me?' Students are keenly aware of the ways in which the second question affects the first. In other words, students know the ways in which one's friends and mentors can affect what kind of person one becomes. The same is true in fiction. Complications in plot usually arise from the conflicting desires of other characters. Thus, students see in the stories they read how a character's action might bring that character into conflict with other characters. Desire sets us in a direction, and once moving, we will eventually meet opposition, whether internal or external. This level of discussion is more useful for learning how to write fiction than the literary themes students have typically learned in high school (i.e. man against man, man against nature, man against himself). It is a new means of reading that lends itself to writing.

This mythological question also brings the class to the difficult concept of the value of other characters, for it raises the question of how a character defines herself. The first question about direction implies deeds. The second question about companions implies personality. When we ask who will go with us, we imply by negation the other question: who will *not* go with us? Who are *not* my people? Who will I have to leave behind? Students recognize how the type of person a character wants to be can determine the ways in which the character may act, make decisions, and interact.

In Fitzgerald's novel (1924) *The Great Gatsby* (1980), Jay Gatsby wants to be the type of person Daisy Buchanan can openly love. The narrator of John Updike's (1969) often-anthologized story 'A & P' features a character struggling with what kind of person he wants to be when his job forces him to confront two contradictory visions of himself. A similar struggle is evident in Ethan Canin's (1988) 'Star Foods' and Ron Carlson's (1997) 'Oxygen.' None of these characters can act or become unless he chooses between two models of behavior, and in each story the choice implies leaving someone behind.

The lesson of this second mythological question for the beginning writer is that characters in stories are not simply determined by what they want. They are also determined by whom they want, meaning the secondary characters in the story's landscape. The lesson the writer takes is that sometimes the best work the author can do in characterization is in detailing the others who surround her and how she reacts to them.

3. *Where did I come from?*

In its largest mythological sense, Keen's third question asks, where did everything come from? Many early stories are etiological, explaining natural phenomena. Myths in every culture arise to answer questions of origin and history, as well as questions of ontology and epistemology. Contemporary fiction does this too. Students have long had it suggested to them that literature addresses the human condition. How this might happen in their own stories, however, is often a matter of some confusion.

It might be argued that early forms of story (myth, parable, oral tale, folk tale) represent ontological and etiological inquiry (the nature of being and phenomena), whereas fiction after Modernism more accurately represents ontogenical and epistemological inquiry: questions about the development of the individual within the species and about the nature and limits of knowledge. For the writer, fiction is the confluence of the particular and universal. As writers we must read to recognize the individual and her limitations (issues of characterization and plot), but also the universal elements of humanity that the character and her failings exemplify (the 'mythos' that renders the story recognizable to the reader and provides meaning to the story).

In order to begin thinking about one's stories as larger than oneself, one must begin thinking about origins. How did I come to be who I am? Why do I think as I do? Expectations, history, and current conditions inform how one lives one's life, but it frequently happens that students oversimplify their characters and stories in order to fulfill some preconceived notion of how life and people are *supposed* to be. Beginning writers tend to exploit differences melodramatically. Being able to write of an encounter with a societally marginalized character such as an alcoholic or a homeless person requires that we go beyond the simple societal strictures and undertake some examination of how people are alike. This mythological question reminds students to look instead for similarities. Asking where one comes from is a process of attributing every character with beliefs and history while at the same time interrogating one's own.

Aristotle asserted that if we appreciate art and find beauty in it, we ought to find it likewise in its live counterpart – other human beings. And yet, we are a culture shaped by television and popular psychology more than by books. As such we learn how to classify behavior into categories and to judge by applying the jargon of popular therapy: alcoholic, co-dependent, bipolar. With this terminology, we can too easily dismiss the most relevant and interesting elements of the stories we read and write with the simple phrase, 'He has *issues*.'

We are trained by contemporary culture to respond from what Richard Schusterman (1997) characterizes as an 'aesthetics of absence,' meaning to what is not there, rather than from what we might call an aesthetics of 'presence,' what *is*. This equates to a learned cultural myopia, a failure of vision. The mythological question 'where did I come from' directs students to read more deeply into the world of the text that informs the characters as a means of understanding them. Where *did* the character come from? Where does the character *perceive* that she comes from? A writer who simply classifies and judges her characters will write parables, not stories. But a writer who can find recognizable, universal human elements in the history of any character she reads will probably be able to make recommendations to others about how to develop their stories and be able to see paths for developing her own.

4. Why is there evil?

This question implies the human response to pain, loss, and suffering. Perhaps the most traditional short story is the coming-of-age story, in which the character encounters the fact that the world is fractured or flawed. The price of knowledge is always pain. (Prometheus's punishment as well as Eve's tell us this). Thus, this mythological question also implies the human response to knowledge or growing up.

A common mistake of beginning writers is to focus too much on the facts of pain or injustice rather than on the character's response. We tell students to write what they know and what is important to them. Yet how wise is this advice when chief among subjects of importance to young writers are perceived slights and injustices, failed relationships, and hard lessons that still smart? The beginning writer's workshop is traditionally filled with stories of the things about which students feel strongly: villainous roommates, unworthy romantic choices, and cold-hearted authority figures. These are the known features of the world they inhabit. Each workshop usually has its assortment of villains from the news that are not what we know but what we have been taught to fear: kidnappers, rapists, and serial killers. These are the unknown, the unexplained, the threatening. Whether derived from the landscape of their lives or their fears, peers in workshop have a difficult time helping each other to develop stories about wrongdoing or suffering because beginning writers focus on the thing itself rather than its result.

No one and no idea is beyond our understanding if we meet the material with skill and on its own terms. Helpful here is for students to write about the evil deed from the point of view of the perpetrator. Evil is an abstract concept. It is a function of point of view. Few characters function out of pure malevolence; almost always, there is a complex psychological system of rationalization in place. Asking this mythological question – why is there evil? – requires that the writer actually determine how and why the character is wronged. Why does the character feel this way? What was at stake? The story can begin to focus on the character's response to the wrong-doing in the story only when the author understands that the character's suffering is directly proportional to whatever was at stake to begin with.

Learning to see character point of view and motivation as arbiters of good and evil in a story can teach students to envision likely structures for story. Something akin to Hegel's dialectics of inversion are implied in every story in which the world's failings, fracture, or evil have bearing on the main character. To create a category necessarily creates its opposite. If there is one whom I love, then implied by negation is that there is another category: those whom I do not love. Yet another negation is possible here as well, for if we can direct one type of emotion outward, then the possibility exists for directing another. Love implies the possibility of hate. In learning to write plots, it is helpful to learn to recognize that the story's direction is usually to move from one established concept to its inversion, and then to another inversion. Love begets hate. Hate begets self-hate.

For example: proportional to the love of Romeo and Juliet for one another is the hate of the Montagues and Capulets for each other. Proportional to the hate Romeo feels for the forces that drive him from Juliet is the hate he feels for himself when he believes his actions in the feud have resulted in her suicide. Likewise, when she wakes to find Romeo dead, Juliet's self-hate at her deception with the sleeping draught leads her to take her own life. This pattern of inversions proliferates especially in stories that take romantic relationships as their focus, but can be recognized in most stories. Learning to see what a character believes is evil teaches us to see what the character values in others and himself. The focus of discussion is redirected from the act itself to the implied values of the character who experiences it. When students begin to recognize this mythological question and the inversions it implies, they can begin to advise each other as to likely plot structures for their own work.

5. Who is in charge?

Asking this question is closely related to the question about the reasons for evil, for implied in this question is the human need to define both responsibility and justice. Students tend to place the character most like themselves at the center of the events in the story, thereby rendering the consciousness most similar to their own as the arbiter or reality. From this point of view, other characters can seem villainously 'flat,' to use E.M. Forster's (1954) term. In order to begin peopling one's stories with more realistic characters, one must ask who is in charge in the story, from the character's perceptions. Do the characters agree who is in charge? Does the power struggle in the story create other problems for the characters? Is the power struggle a result of design or definition? For example, in Faulkner's (1958) 'A Rose for Emily,' does Emily Grierson's family reputation give her power over the town, or does it give the town power over her? The story suggests that, in an almost biblical sense, naming a thing can give us power over it. And yet, by the same dialectical inversions suggested earlier, it is also true that what we name a thing can give it that power over us. If Emily asserts the Grierson name as a means of power, it becomes so: she does not have to pay taxes. But if Emily asserts that the Grierson name must connote a special social privilege to the town, she is then obligated to uphold that social status even when it imprisons her and denies her the possibility of love.

As with the question of why there is suffering, this question forces students to look beyond simple definitions of power in a story and to concentrate on the real issue, which is how characters react to power, whether perceived or actual. As with the question of evil or wrong-doing in a story, the writer's difficulty here can be a failure to look beyond the thing itself to see the implications of it in the story. The important factor in most stories is not the power dynamic of a social concept such as class or race; it is how the *characters* perceive this and how they react to it. How is their action dictated by the power they allow to operate in their lives? How do characters find themselves relegated to inaction as a result of their perceptions of who is in control? Students who can recognize this difference can provide better criticism to each other in workshop of their own stories. They can recommend how alterations in characters' perceptions of power can open up the story's plot. A boss in a story has an implied authority over a worker, and yet the best potential for the story might lie in re-examining the nature of that authority – does the worker perceive it as the boss does? 'Work' stories such as Updike's (1969) 'A & P' and Canin's (1988) 'Star Foods' achieve their interesting explorations of character and their different plots because each worker/narrator is re-examining and even re-naming his relationship to the employer.

6. What is the map of human life?
    This question implies the scope of one's development, especially in comparison to others. It also implies history applied to the self. As a means of evaluating human endeavor, stories throughout human history have attempted to define what is expected and therefore appropriate at different stages of life. Students benefit both as readers and as writers when they recognize their own expectations and the degree to which their stories and characters are predicated upon those expectations. For instance, is passion the province of the young? Are the old wise? Are children innocent? More important still is how the character in the story perceives the path of human life and her own place in it. Character motivation, that difficult *why* in the story, often derives directly from this question. We tend to want at different stages of life what we are taught it is appropriate to want. Real and imagined conflict often derives from comparison of the self to others at the same stage of development. These are the internal workings of character that lend depth and verisimilitude to a story. At the same time, characters' expectations imply larger, thematic issues about the culture from which the story arises.
    The tragedy of Romeo and Juliet is not simply that they cannot be together; it is that their desire runs contrary to the expectations of the

world around them. Contemporary love stories tend to exhibit the opposite view: the tragedy of the story is that the world around the lovers intrudes upon their desire for each other. The times in which we live have influenced our ideas of what it is appropriate to pursue and to expect at different ages. A good reader of fiction can begin to recognize that plot and characterization depend largely upon our views of what is appropriate for the characters in the world and time they inhabit. For example, the complications of Humbert Humbert's love for Lolita in Nabokov's (1955) novel arise from social assumptions about what is appropriate sexual behavior at different ages. One need not condone the relationship in the novel, but it is helpful to discuss the attraction of the older man to the adolescent girl with some understanding that the concept of childhood we now consider innate has really only come to the world rather recently. Likewise, before we dismiss a middle-aged character as a failure for having given up on business in order to go back to school at this point in his life, it is helpful to discuss whether the order of the character's pursuits and accomplishments is more important than the pursuits themselves. Students operate from a keen awareness of what they are supposed to be and do at different stages of their lives. Even the university classification of 'non-traditional' for any student starting college after age 22 or for students with children is suggestive of this map of contemporary human life. Recognizing it can be a means of finding a way in to the stories we read, and also to the stories we wish to write.

Learning Outcomes

This set of mythological questions, when used as a rubric for discussion of stories students read and for workshop of the stories they write, hones their abilities to think as writers about literature. Myth enables students to begin from the general concept as a means of working toward the particular evidence in the stories they read. Myth asks students to first identify the central issue or question by looking at the story from several different philosophical angles. This provides entry into discussion and a means of identifying more readily the issues of craft that are most important for the writer to consider in a revision. The discussion of those issues allows students to break the work down into smaller component elements of fiction: characterization, dialogue, narration, plot.

The mythological questions direct students to reason the other direction as well, beginning with the particular evidence in the story and learning to recognize the general concept behind it. Comparison and synthesis skills are honed and practiced, linking reading literature to writing creative fiction. To discuss via mythological questions, students must associate the particular evidence in one story with the particular evidence in another or their own experience in order to create a general concept that is larger than the components but which encompasses both of them. The story is the convergence of the particular (character) with the universal (human).

These six mythological questions provide every writing student with conceptual points for entering into discussion of any story. This solves the workshop dilemma of neutrality because no one is without means to begin talking about the work of a peer. Discussion can work from the general idea to the particular story and from the universal to the individual. So, the workshop also need never dead-end in the autobiographical and emotional dilemma either, as there is always a means of working toward or away from the individual experience.

Composition classes derive their pedagogical authority from models of argument, teaching students to recognize and to practice these in the argumentative research paper. Science and mathematics classes rely upon theories, laws, principles, and basic component skills. When structured around a rubric such as these mythological questions, the authority of creative writing pedagogy derives from similar principles. Clarifying and simplifying as they do the central character and thematic goals of the work, the mythological questions teach students to first read as writers and then to discuss their own work as reader-writers. Conceptual rubrics can be developed for other genres as well and adapted to a variety of particular creative writing exercises, assignments, texts, and discussions to address some of the debilitating dilemmas of workshops. The use of a conceptual rubric in the creative writing workshop moves students from reading to writing, from silence to discussion, from theory to practice, and from apprenticeship to ownership.

References

Canin, E. (1988) Star Foods. *Emperor of the Air: Stories*. New York: Harper & Row.

Carlson, R. (1997) Oxygen. *The Hotel Eden: Stories*. New York: W.W. Norton.

Faulkner, W. (1958) A Rose for Emily. *Collected Stories of William Faulkner*. New York: Random House.

Fitzgerald, F.S. (1980) *The Great Gatsby*. New York: Collier.

Forster, E.M. (1954) *Aspects of the Novel*. New York: Harcourt.

Mason, B.A. (1982) Shiloh. *Shiloh and Other Stories*. New York: Harper Collins.

Nabokov, V. (1955) *Lolita*. New York: Vintage International.

Updike, J. (1969) A & P. *Pigeon Feathers and Other Stories*. New York: Knopf.
Schusterman, R. (1997) The urban aesthetics of absence: Pragmatist reflections in Berlin. *The New Literary History* 28, 739–55.
Your *Mythic Journey* (1991) with Bill Moyers (filmography of Sam Keen). Director and Producer, Betsy McCarthy. Public Affairs Television.

Chapter 17

Writing in the Shadows: Topics, Models, and Audiences that Focus on Language

SANDY FEINSTEIN

While many students assume that reading and writing about Chaucer's poetry – or Shakespeare's plays or even Thackeray's novels – require the learning of an unfamiliar language that includes conventions of the time and cultural assumptions about those conventions, they do not enter a creative writing classroom with the same insecurities about language or aesthetics. Students' sense of personal investment is very different when it comes to writing poetry – so, too, fiction, nonfiction, or drama – than reading it; therefore, the demands of teaching Chaucer's poetry are considerably different from the demands of teaching students how to write their own poetry.

For the most part, students are unaware of what they don't know about their own language and how what they don't know matters in writing. Most do not realize they may lack a language by which to make their feelings sound genuine and mean something to someone other than their friends. In short, students need to discover ways of saying what they feel, or what they want to say, without repeating the same four letter words, the most recurring being *love*. Yet students often don't recognize this need. So, guiding them can take some delicate negotiations.

Method

Instead of steering students away from what some teachers see as a trite topic that encourages students to write in clichés, I offer pedagogic exercises and reading assignments that provide a variety of ways to use language to speak of love – a particularly popular topic with students. These exercises and reading assignments also have another intention: to destabilize the construct of authority as it has been understood historically, as one of the by-products of a canon, and to keep the idea of authority in the classroom in flux. While I draw from experience teaching poetry, this approach to destabilizing and keeping in flux authority by using a popular topic and unfamiliar models to examine audience and language can be adapted for assignments in creative writing courses focusing on other genres, including prose or playwriting.

When I first studied creative writing 30 years ago, my professor was a well-known male poet. Each weekly workshop session was pretty much the same: we discussed one another's poems. I don't recall being bored, but I know I was uncomfortable, not through any fault of the class, but because anticipating exposure is discomfiting. What I actually learned about poetry, though, came primarily from literature classes. Even in those classes in which we read female as well as male writers – classes on the novel, period courses in the 19th and 20th centuries – the model for conventional forms was always male: the sonnet belonged to Petrarch, Wyatt, Surrey and Shakespeare, then Milton, and the Romantic poets; the epigram to Martial and Alexander Pope; dramatic monologue to Robert Browning and Alfred, Lord Tennyson; imagism to William Carlos Williams and Ezra Pound; epic to Homer, Virgil, Milton; romance to Chaucer, Spenser, Sidney; villanelle to Dylan Thomas and Theodore Roethke, and on and on.[1] It didn't matter that women were or were not represented; the ideal form was typically identified with male writers. That was the canon.

In *Learning to Write Fiction from the Masters*, Conrad Barnaby (1996) begins with a truism about learning to write in any genre: 'Everyone will agree that the only way to learn to write is by reading and writing' (Preface). His purpose, he explains, is to 'expose would-be writers to passages from authors of acknowledged mastery' (Preface). Then, he offers examples of male and female writing primarily from the 19th and 20th centuries, though he adds, as a kind of postscript, 'Naturally, it would be splendid if one could read *all* the great books, starting with the *Canterbury Tales*.' Then, he lists additional early 'great books,' among which is not a single work by a female author (p. 251). Similarly, in more rigorously theorized discussions of writing, the focus on early non-canonical female writers is nominal. Renate Wood (1996) includes the better known Sappho (1991) in her triumvirate with two less well known male classical poets, Anacreon and Archilochus. Allen Grossman (1996), arguing that 'study of the founding stories, or paradigms, is fundamental to learning about writing with the intention to write' (p. 121), focuses on mythic constructs of Orpheus and Philomela, male and female characters, who, nevertheless, both originate in male authored stories.

The argument for the necessity of reading, of specific kinds and ways of reading, has done worse than privilege male over female models and contemporary over early models, it has privileged one kind of reader and reading over another, as D.G. Myers (1994) does in his contentious contrast of how literary scholars and creative writers read literature. Reading for writing is ownership, open to every kind of writer and maker of meaning. The teaching of how to read a text is a creative act that, ideally, results in creative acts, call them what one will: poetry, fiction, creative nonfiction, essay, scholarship. It's all creative writing, Myers's parochialism notwithstanding.

New reasons to read are always welcome. Paul Dawson (2003) offers an overview of the historical justifications for reading to write while suggesting that 'how a work is *composed* by the student is not as important as how it can be *read* in terms of the critical approach of Creative Writing' (p. 2). His point is well taken:

> the problem requires shifting the pedagogical focus of the workshop from narrowly formalist conceptions of craft to the social context of literature, but without diminishing the importance of craft as an intellectual skill, and without detracting from the purpose of improving students' writing. This means paying attention to the content of a literary work, as this is what connects it to the outside world, but without isolating content from form. (2003: 12)

Dawson seeks to accomplish this task by demonstrating 'how content is realized in the formal construction of a text, and this means shifting from a formalist poetics to a sociological poetics' (p. 12). The shift to a sociological poetics may be, unfortunately, yet another reason reading to write tends to privilege one's own time and society: it's easier to understand the relationship of audience to text, of content to form, to recognize allusions, politics, language and line choices and the play among it all. But the reader of literature of any time rewrites what s/he reads, inevitably, ineluctably, habitually. And it is the rewriting or re-creation, through appropriation and reinvention, that informs the relationship between the reading and writing I assign.

While students may recognize the omnipresence of love in poetry from Chaucer to the present day, they do not necessarily see the ways poets have made it new by making it their own, which is especially important for writers to understand. As varied and new as they may be, few writers have baldly and blandly confessed prosaically or pathetically and emotively complained declaratively.[2] In the models I use from early literature, the overtly confessional cannot be found, and the poetic conventions have little connection to the realism or naturalism that characterizes more contemporary literature. Put another way, lack of artifice is not a concept. Perhaps because I also teach early literature – Chaucer, Arthurian, gothic, and literature courses informed by history of science – I tend to use models that are atypical for creative writing classes. I have never seen any of my sample poems in any creative writing texts, not even in the otherwise eclectic *In the Palm of Your Hand*, a text I have used to supplement my approach. The expectation might be, then, that I use Chaucer for more than an expository frame in this discussion of creative writing pedagogy. In fact, though, I primarily use as models the poetry of writers whose authority has not been canonized, who do not, therefore, loom over students with a threat to their youthful presumption to dabble in the domain of the great.

Reading and Writing

I prefer to teach the poetry of those who are not as frequently read as their peers, some who were famous in their own time and place, others who wrote in the shadows of their more famous coevals. If not all felt the anxiety of influence in their own time, nevertheless their authority in our time is less established, reliable, assumed. It is the poetry of such overshadowed writers that students learn to read. Moreover, while the common wisdom may hold that students should be exposed to as much poetry as possible, if only to make up for how little they have read, I take the opposite tack, for the same reason, namely, that because students are not accustomed to reading poetry they need to learn to look closely at individual poems. Although I assign poems with a specific purpose or plan in mind, I always hope that what students learn will be, in fact, something other than what I have opted for as one particular outcome. It's a good start, too, if students come to see what they themselves are trying to do as part of a long, continuing tradition.

In my experience, most students are insecure with languages that do not sound like their own, indeed, with virtually anything that is unfamiliar. Therefore, it should come as no surprise that they are uncomfortable with the formal techniques of poetry, though many seem wedded to rhyme in their own work. Too many want meaning to be obvious and immediate, as their own poetry often makes apparent. In short, few know how to read poetry: they skim, reading it once as if it were unwelcome mail; even the best students rarely pause over lines and words if faced with a stack of poetry to read. So, I do not attempt to fill in the gaps in students' knowledge with long reading assignments. Instead, we read a few poems very closely. One intention of the reading, then, is to engage them in the poetry, to make them feel part of a tradition rather than alienated from it. By beginning to look at poetry purposefully, as models from which to learn what it means to construct a poem, to put one together and take it apart, ideally young writers become more comfortable with reading at random and as writers.

To get students accustomed to the lines and language of poetry, I begin by assigning poems that comprise the smallest possible unit: epigrams and, smaller yet, fragments. Most are unfamiliar with these classical forms. Yet these diminutive poems focus students' attention on the shape of a line and the concentration of a single thought or feeling.

Although there are a number of formal definitions for epigrams, I like that of Anne Rosalind Jones (1994), whom I heard define the form as a 'short rhymed poem, all the lines short, subject free, no more than 10 lines each.' The typical models for the teaching of epigrams would probably be Martial and Pope, but I prefer using the women poets Anyte (*c.* 300, Arkadian) and Pernette du Guillet (1520?, Lyon, France), the latter translated by Jones. Anyte (1991) offers a seemingly simple way to evoke common things through images: the grasshopper as 'nightingale of the field' and the cicada as 'oak-dwelling.'

After handing out an assortment of Anyte's and Pernette's epigrams, I have the students do a collaborative exercise. The objective is to define a familiar subject using concrete language in order to make the ordinary evocative. They are asked to form groups of three or four, choose one of the words in a list I provide, and then together come up with at least three different ways of describing that word. After writing a number of lines, they are asked to explain what they were trying to evoke in the description: what tone, image, sense, ideas. The exercise has, in the past, included the following common words: *evergreen*, *bunny*, *Mercedes*, *home*, *football*, *conch*. We talk about what they wrote and why. They also take the lesson of definition home with them when they are trying to find yet another way to talk about that difficult-to-describe-emotion we call *love*.

The epigram is a very comfortable form to teach, if for no other reason than it is short. It is also particularly well suited for discussions on how meter contributes to making meaning. Less formal than the epigram is the fragment. Contemporary literary journals such as *Thema* might be used to justify such an exercise, if one feels the need to demonstrate relevance to current expectations: *Thema* requires that 'the premise given must be an integral part of the plot [or poem], not necessarily the central theme but not merely incidental,' and their premises sound like fragments as in those announced for recent submission deadlines, 'The power of whim[,]' 'Paper tigers[,]' and 'Lost in translation.'

I choose to use classical fragments, especially those of Sappho,[3] a poet more usually recognized by name than by her poetry. Renate Wood (1996: 101), writing for other poets rather than for students, discusses Sappho as 'the first, with her "bittersweet Eros," to hint at ambiguity as a condition of the soul and at memory as something that can be jointly owned by separated lovers'. About the writing itself, she notes 'new attention to surfaces, and an abundance of epithets for the tactile emerges, ... a new acute awareness of becoming instead of being, which has an impact on the sense of time' (p. 102). Wood makes claims for the poet, rehabilitating her for her fellow poets, ascribing to her authority and position. Working with students, I emphasize the contrary, the questions Sappho (p. 1991) poses, the incompleteness that offers ahistorical rather than authorial ambiguities. Fragment 60, for example, asks a question that may well make the pens of college students race: 'Do I still desire virginity?' Or, for the vulnerable and hurt, fragment 40 offers an image to complement their own secret wishes: 'May winds and sorrows/Carry him away who condemns.' These poems express familiar feelings simply yet evocatively, such as 'I wish to say something to you, but shame prevents me' (p. 42). Sappho distills emotions in powerful images that belie the lines' categorization as only a fragment, as in 'Herdsmen crush under their feet/a hyacinth in the mountains; on the ground/purple blooms' (p. 49). Rather than complete the poems, or make the fragment part of a collaborative whole, students can imitate expressing their feelings in the restricted form of a clause, a question, an assertion, a statement, or a single image.

Formal Elements

Lady Mary Wroth (1983 edition) wrote not only in the inhibiting environment of a male literary culture but under the burden of memory as the daughter of a poetic father, Sir Robert Sidney, and as the niece of one of the most influential poets of the English Renaissance, Sir Philip Sidney. Wroth is specifically useful for teaching students various conventional forms, though her own poetry remained largely in obscurity until fairly recently.[4]

Wroth's sonnets provide opportunities to discuss organizing units such as stanzas, rhyme, and punctuation. They also show how narrative and dramatic situations can structure short, formal lyrics. The dream narrative is not only a literary convention, but also a popular theme in contemporary writing: then, as now, lovers and poets have been fascinated by sleep and the dreams that interrupt 'deaths Image.' Moreover, that the poem describes a dream may provide a rationale for the stylized nature of the images and, to the students, the seeming formality of the language. In addition, the poem offers a means by which to teach rhetorical strategies and techniques such as allusion, alliteration, metaphor, and metonymy. The form and language are, for most students, unfamiliar and, therefore, unnatural, even stilted, so I ask them to point to the words and syntax that create the impression of distracting artifice in order to discuss the effect, the tone, the voice, and how, if they experiment with words and syntax, they can create a persona, a voice, a variety of tones.

I assign selections from the sonnets to draw attention to rigidity of form and its functions, not because 'it is easier to write a sonnet, with its strict rules of rhyme and meter, than it is to write good free verse' (Moser, 1997: 4). One poem I have used to this purpose is the following sonnet from Wroth's *Pamphilia to Amphilanthus*:

When nights black mantle could most darknes prove,
   And sleepe deaths Image did my senceses hiere
   From Knowledg of my self, then thoughts did move
   Swifter then most swiftnes need require:

In sleepe, a Chariot drawne by wing'd desire
   I sawe: wher sate bright Venus Queene of love,
   And att her feete her sonne, still adding fire
   To burning hearts which she did hold above,

But one hart flaming more then all the rest
   The goddess held, and putt itt to my brest,
   Deare sonne, now shutt sayd she: thus must wee winn;

Hee her obay'd, and martir'd my poore hart,
   I, waking hop'd as dreames itt would depart
   Yett since: O mee: a lover I have binn.

The multiple effects of various techniques used specifically to describe love can shake students' assumptions about how feelings can be expressed; it is also one way to introduce the uses of figures and closed forms to represent passion. The juxtaposition of self-conscious artifice with a familiar emotional state is usually new to students; therefore, this kind of poetry may open their minds to other possibilities of what love feels like and to alternative ways to express intense, personal feeling.

Balancing Talking and Writing

In creative writing classes, there are, or should be, limits to talking. Students need to write more than they need – or even want – to talk about writing. Three straight hours of class time spent criticizing each other's poetry can cast a pall, discourage some students, even distress a few. At a certain point, talking can even be counter-productive. Young writers often benefit from an immediate application of what they have been told: to see what works and what doesn't, to get immediate feedback from the teacher or one another. Consequently, I break up the workshop's allotted time with reading, discussing, and writing.

Having read Wroth's sonnet as a model, I ask the students to do a 60-second freewrite in which they come up with alternative word combinations to describe *love*. Since we are not actually writing one-minute poems but generating words, students don't think that they are working out a poetry problem. It is a game, and they are too serious about their own poems to realize that playing such games have served poets before them.[5]

We use the sonnet as the model for different techniques with which they might experiment in order to find new ways to describe familiar emotions and thoughts. The closed-form poem is also helpful for teaching poetic conventions or rules that contemporary writers continue to follow: avoiding so-called weak words such as prepositions and conjunctions to end lines, avoiding over-punctuating, using active verbs, using concrete nouns, and avoiding and/or exploiting repetition. One can also discuss the use of embedded dialogue and indirect speech as well as what to some is a personal fixation, rhyme.

Dissemination, Delivery, Performance

In their time, Sappho, Anyte, Pernette, and Wroth depended on coterie exchange, oral performance, and private commissions. Anyte's poems include epitaphs that might have been commissioned for memorials. Therefore, I ask students to think about the limitations and potential of different forms of dissemination and recording of their poems. To this purpose, I require an assortment of projects that move students from the coterie experience of exchange to an increasing awareness of poetry as public as well as private.

The first project involves where to put their poems. They see words everywhere, but few seem to consider the implications of reading a billboard or a T-shirt, listening to a rap, carving words in a tree, or writing on the sidewalk. I want them to consider not only how they are surrounded by words, by poetic potentiality, but how some words work more effectively somewhere other than on a white sheet of regular-sized paper. So they are asked to write at least one poem on a surface other than paper. In a sense, this assignment brings poetry to people who would not necessarily read poetry. It also redefines the uses of surfaces: is it graffiti if it's a poem? If you wear a poem, whose product is it? Does a billboard still blight the landscape if it displays poetry rather than cigarettes? If it makes no sound, can it be a violation of personal space? Students think differently about the words they choose and about the feelings they want to express verbally when they consider a radical change of form and surface for alternative public displays.

I also reinforce these ideas on delivery and audience through another project concerned with public dissemination of individual and group portfolios. More specifically, students are asked to create a forum for interaction with their work: for example, by organizing a reading, constructing a home page, distributing a broadside, or desktop publishing a literary magazine. Again, the intention is to remind students that writing implies an awareness of, desire for, or assumption of an audience. Depending on what kind of dissemination they choose, they determine what sort of audience they desire for their work. Since they are one another's initial audience and since I want to avoid competitiveness and hurtful criticism, I begin with a collaborative exercise in which each student makes or rearranges a poetic line using my box of magnetic poetry; then, as a class, we affix our poem to a public surface, which, in the past, was usually a campus refrigerator.

Conclusion

Already in the 21st century, creative writing courses continue to increase in popularity, and the venues for poetry, fiction, nonfiction, and drama keep expanding: little magazines flourish, despite financial unprofitability; web sites seem to increase at a pace difficult to keep track of; contests multiply as reliably as lottery games. New forms and experiments feed off the new forms of dissemination. Still, if recent writing guides are any indication, the subjects have not changed very radically. Poetry, for instance, is still seen as representing the conflicts of the heart, as the handbook *In the Palm of Your Hand* demonstrates with its introduction and early chapters: when Kowit (1995: 7) begins his writing workshop chapter with the title 'Speak, Memory', what does he wish to evoke? Fewer students will recognize the allusion to Vladimer Nabokov's sophisticated autobiographical game of evasion than will recollect an image from their childhood or secrets of the soul that inhabit their minds and hearts. It may be for this reason so many more people write poems at some point in their lives than read poetry, for few are as interested in someone else's language of the self as in their own feelings and fantasies. The roles of authority in the creative writing classroom – whether these roles stem from the texts we read and then model or reject or from the texts we generate and the feelings that generate them – are and should be in flux. Finding one's heart in a poem, as a reader or writer, is like love: hard to say what it is or how it happens, yet it seems to be what many either yearn to have or desire to express.

Acknowledgement

I gratefully acknowledge the National Endowment of the Humanities Summer Institute 'Sappho and Lady Mary Wroth: Major Writers of Classical Antiquity and the English Renaissance,' directed by Judy Hallett and Jane Donawerth, at the University of Maryland, 1994.

Notes

1. These are the writers most easily found in anthologies, the fact of which canonizes them. I cite the Norton (1993) anthologies because they are among the most commonly assigned in survey courses taught in the United States.
2. This phrase is, of course, a play on Ezra Pound's present tense imperative to the modernists; 'Make it New' is also the title of one of his early books of poetry (1934).
3. See Sappho's fragments 60, 40, 42, and 49 respectively; in Rayor, pp. 79, 69, 70, and 74. The lines from Sappho quoted in the text are cited by fragment number.
4. Josephine A. Roberts's edition of *The Poems of Lady Mary Wroth* was largely responsible for recognizing the importance of this poet and making her poetry available.
5. I'm thinking here of Kenneth Koch as well as various language poets, including, for example, Charles Bernstein.

References

Anyte (1991) Epigram 14. *Sappho's Lyre: Archaic Lyric and Women Poets of Ancient Greece.* (pp. 224–31). D.J. Rayor (trans.). Berkeley: University of California Press.
Barnaby, C. (1996) *Learning to Write Fiction from the Masters.* New York: Plume.
Dawson, P. (2003) Towards a new poetics in creative writing pedagogy. *Text* 7 (1), 1–20. <http://www.gu.edu.au/school/art/text/april03/dawson.htm>.

Grossman, A. (1996) 'Orpheus/Philomela': Subjection and mastery in the founding stories of poetic production and in the logic of our practice. In G. Orr and E. Bryant Voigt (eds) *Poets Teaching Poets* (pp. 121–39). Ann Arbor: University of Michigan Press.

Jones, A.R. (1994) Lecture. NEH Institute on Women of Antiquity, *Women of the Renaissance*. University of Maryland, College Park, 13 June.

Jones, A.R. (trans.) (1987) *Women Writers of the Renaissance and Reformation* (pp. 224–31) Katherina Wilson (ed.). Athens: University of Georgia Press.

Kowit, S. (1995) *In the Palm of Your Hand*. Gardiner, ME: Tilbury House.

Moser, D. (1997) A new look for an old friend. *Smithsonian* August, 4.

Myers, D.G. (2003) The lesson of creative writing's history. *AWP Chronicle* 26 (1), 12–14. <http://www-english.tamu.edu/pers/fac/myers/lesson-of-its-history.html>.

The Norton Anthology of English Literature (vol. 2 of 2) (6th edn) M.H. Abrams *et al.* (eds). New York: W.W. Norton.

Sappho (1991) Fragments 40, 42, 49, 60, 65. *Sappho's Lyre: Archaic Lyric and Women Poets of Ancient Greece* Diane J. Rayor (trans.). Berkeley: University of California Press.

Thema (2001) Advertisement. *Poets and Writers* July/August, 66.

Wood, R. (1996) Poetry and the self: Reflections on the discovery of the self in early greek lyrics. In G. Orr and E. Bryant Voigt (eds) *Poets Teaching Poets* (pp. 97–120). Ann Arbor: University of Michigan Press.

Wroth, Lady M. (1983) Pamphilia to Amphilanthus. In J.A. Roberts (ed.) *The Poems of Lady Mary Wroth*. Baton Rouge: Louisiana State University Press.

Afterword

The Reason It Is; the Rhyme It Isn't

GRAEME HARPER and STEPHANIE VANDERSLICE

Because all signs indicate that creative writing teaching theory and practice is experiencing an upsurge in interest in English-speaking academia, *Power and Identity in the Creative Writing Classroom: The Authority Project*, offers an up-to-date blueprint of the very issues with which this burgeoning discipline is most concerned. One view of the collection's perspective on the American creative writing landscape by Stephanie Vanderslice, laid out here with Graeme Harper's analysis of how the book applies to current issues in British and other Anglophone creative writing scenes, will illuminate the differences as well as the commonalities globally and set the stage for sorely needed mutual understanding and cooperation. Indeed, such cooperation may provide the catalyst for a true renaissance of the field throughout the Anglophone world.

I. Creative Writing, Pedagogy, and Authority in the United Kingdom

I (GH) am, by nature and like many writers, skeptical of the word *authority*. It seems to me to be a word most often wielded to close off a passageway to something much brighter in our world, or something much darker, or something perhaps much, much more difficult to grasp. Dwelling in authority, we might well live unsoiled by the mud of that passageway, that way out of fixed modes of reason, the struggle to interpret more truthfully. Except, of course, that the air of what lies beyond is unable to be contained.

It seeps and you can be drawn to this seeping air of enlightenment and progression, which contrasts to the disinfected regimentation that here and there threatens our modern academe, a disinfection borne on the same principles of encasement and enclosure that creates a negative sense of the word *authority*.

For this reason, the authority of higher learning – and of this collection – is in growing understanding, not in trying to capture it.

205

Because it is not disinfected from human ignorance, ignominy, joy or sorrow, truth or error, it is not tied up in site-specifics, restricted to national boundaries, at the mercy of economics, or held entirely in the socio-political subject hierarchies of academe. You can't stand up and brandish your latest book until authority pops out. Nor does authority dwell in your dress sense or your title. Authority in higher learning is only possible if there is meeting of purpose, a coming together of like minds, a communication between points of intuition, and a moment in which to share all these.

Polemic can be protection. But, of course, the reason for many human exchanges is often learning. Like any animal keen on its survival, we seek to know more; and like any animal with empathy for its kind, we often seek to provide more. It is, to paraphrase Nancy Kuhl's 'Personal Problems: Authority and Therapeutic Writing,' a situation in which we are often both learner and teacher and, because of those roles, comfortably or uncomfortably, we are ultimately to act in a position of authority at one time or another.

Etymologically, of course, *authority* finds its way back to the word *author*. You can't easily chase the author out of creative writing discussion, nor out of literature, film and media, or theater classrooms, for that matter: human engagement, intuition, and ambition are bound up in authorship. In some cases, creative writing researchers, along with Anglophone literary and cultural critics, boldly misinterpreting the Barthesian argument, have argued passionately for reinsertion of the author into the critical-creative equation. It was never removed.

What strikes home, more so than this, though, when reading the essays in *Power and Identity in the Creative Writing Classroom: The Authority Project,* are the similarities and differences between the discussions in U.S. academe and the sense of where other discussions worldwide are currently heading. This has been very evident indeed in recent debates in the journal *New Writing: the International Journal for the Practice and Theory of Creative Writing.*[1] In the United Kingdom, in particular, and in Australia, New Zealand, and other Anglophone countries too, the relationship between what Anna Leahy has gathered here from U.S. colleagues and what is currently debated should receive close attention.

Take the book's first section, 'Understanding the Larger Influences,' for example. In Leahy's own essay, there's a concentration on what is called 'the workshop' in the United States. What a fine Victorian picture that conjures up here in Britain! Workshop: workhouse. When Charles Dickens was born in Portsmouth, his father, a naval clerk soon to be in deep debt, might well have consigned young Charles to 'the workshop' if not that Charles's ambition itself built for him his own private workshop – and a creative writing one at that!

So, the creative writing workshop: sure, such things exist in British university education, but not in the way they exist in the United States. They do not dwell in what might be called a workshop tradition, short as that American tradition may be. The teaching of creative writing is much closer in the United Kingdom to what is associated with the formal history of the study of English literature and its earlier gestation in such subjects as philology, rhetoric, and classics. Creative writing has emerged here from the tradition of university education in Europe and, therefore, has more carried along with it and has held much closer to the subjects that draw back down that tradition's timeline.

When D.G. Myers (1996: 168) concludes in *The Elephants Teach: Creative Writing Since 1880*, a book often quoted in the United States, that 'finally, creative writing had become a national staff of writers who teach writers who go on to teach, and to hope for tenure and promotion', he misses a key point: that any creative writer anywhere, Britain included, places self-understanding before institutional andragogy (a word referring to the distinct tenets of adult learning and used in Europe from the early 19th century). Myers, writing as a literature critic not as a creative writer, misinterprets the foundation on which creative writing higher learning is universally based and inserts instead a *post hoc* historicist literary criticism.

American War of Independence still smarting, perhaps, from a certain British perspective, it might be satisfying to read that 'Longfellow was the first American writer of any importance to choose an academic career to fill his stomach while his soul burned after literature' (Myers, 1996: 1). In Britain, we've had stomach-filling creative writers in universities right back to the birth of academe. As Harvard College was founded in 1636, it would appear that, according to Myers, one of the key institutions in the United States once had no creative writers of note working within it. But I think Myers, though he produced a useful literary critical study of its time, fails to completely understand the history and nature of creative writing on campus and the practices of higher learning associated with it, and does not engage fully with the differences and links between informal andragogy and formal pedagogy. What we now need are books built on a creative writer's sense of epistemology, not a literary critic's sense of historiography – and that is an aim to which *The Authority Project* certainly contributes.

Here in Britain, the workshop grew as an alternative to the critical literature seminar (or theatre, film, or media seminar). But because of a lack of separation bound up in the longer history of both formal study in academe and informal engagement with creative writing in universities, the American workshop model was met with a degree of skepticism. In addition, when Evie Yoder Miller talks in this book of 'the common goals and strategies of composition and creative writing classrooms,' we in Britain have some understanding but, as there is no such thing as an academic composition classroom, have some bemusement.

Because composition does not exist in British universities as in North American ones, neither does a three-way interface in English departments – composition, literary study, creative writing – added to by the involvement of others things like drama and film. Nor would I quite phrase it, from this British perspective, the way Miller does when she draws from composition terminology to say, 'I use texts in class that model an authority for students.' We'd probably simply talk about bringing in examples of good creative writing, and of bad creative writing too.

This brings us to the section of *The Authority Project* entitled 'The Teacher's Place, Voice, and Style' in which Mary Cantrell begins with the comment: 'What is wrong with those of us who teach creative writing? Unlike professors in any other discipline, we seem eager to relinquish our authority in the classroom.' In Britain, we don't relinquish it. Or, at least, we would not quite see it the same way. It is important to note that we do not have creative writing Master of Fine Arts programs in Britain; nor are these common in many of the other Anglophone countries that teach creative writing. In Britain, we have Master of Arts programs and doctoral programs in Creative Writing or Creative and Critical Writing, though such doctoral degrees have existed in Britain, and in Australia too for that matter, only since the early 1990s. Writers on campuses in the United Kingdom continue to be defined by their awards and publications and, increasingly, also by recognized formal academic qualifications in creative writing. But it would be wrong to think that the British approach to the subject, and the nature and style of the formal qualifications in creative writing, is necessarily the same as that adopted in the United States.

Picking up on the chapter by Audrey Petty, the postgraduate teaching market is certainly very strong in Britain, as it is in many circles worldwide. Part-time lecturing remains one of the key ways of staffing increasingly high-recruiting creative writing programs; what that means in terms of a writer's terms and conditions is, as yet, not entirely pleasing to the heart. As to 'teacherly identity,' a term mentioned by Rachel Hall in 'The Pregnant Muse: Assumptions, Authority, and Accessibility,' don't ask too many in creative writing in Britain, and beyond, what they believe their teacherly identity to be. Beyond North America and its MFA programs, the notion of the teacher-writer rings hollow, as it probably also did before the proliferation of graduate creative writing programs in the United States. Few writers I know on campus would want to be called 'teacher-writers.' Why anyone would want to take away our writerly identities by making us this hyphenated thing? Creative writers working on campus in Britain carry on a very long tradition of writing within the university, a tradition established even before the secularization of book culture some 700 years ago; they are no different than doctor-writers or publisher-writers or any other creative writer who is likewise sometimes involved in other pursuits. They are, in other words, creative writers.

Of course, as Katharine Haake points out, we don't know everything. Down the hall from my campus office, there's an internationally acclaimed chemist teaching graduate students, and he admits the same thing. He's not sweating it; nor should we. Higher learning is about discovery; discovery is organic: we all engage in it.

A soft spot for Wendy Bishop's work is a good thing; though her work has not traveled quite as far as some might imagine, it nevertheless carries authority and it's pleasing to see her essay in the section 'Course Design.' If, as she points out, the workshop is a 'writing-intensive zone,' then there's no doubt that the writing-intensive zone of many universities and colleges is beyond the classroom too. Never can we underestimate the power of the imagination to create without formal instruction and using the environment around it to generate the conditions for doing so. Creative writing on campus ensures that creative writing is valued; it does not ensure that it occurs at the highest level of learning. That, for the better, is a product of the individual and of culture.

And yet, an interesting point picks up on what Suzanne Greenberg says in her chapter in this volume. Once entering academe, both student and staff accept a policy of assessment. If you don't want assessment – to be subject to it, or to initiate it – then go write elsewhere. In Britain, we're currently engaged in a two-year national research project (ending January 2007)[2] to train people to better understand the nature of research in creative writing; this training project, which bases itself in the exploration of creative writing epistemology,[3] fits well with

the last 10 years of discussions around ideas of benchmarking or standardization. But assessment remains as difficult in creative writing as it is in any other subject involving aesthetic judgment.

No surprise that gender judgment, too, invades creative writing higher learning: where cultural context meets individual participation, gender becomes one of the grounds of difference, and one of the points of interest. Susan Hubbard usefully notes 'other important factors... namely, class, race, ethnicity, and sexual identity.' Indeed, if higher learning is to be best accomplished, it would be madness to leave such things as points of ignorance rather than nodes of understanding. Communication – of which creative writing is one part – certainly highlights personal and cultural difference as much as it confirms similarity. How we deal with this fact is indicative of our maturity as cognitively empowered creatures.

And so we gather to a rush of interest in this collection's last section: Argie Manolis working as a writing teacher in the community; Cathy Day considering metaphor and its uses in the structures and strictures of learning and teaching; Mary Swander focusing on encouragement (fine thing, too); Amy Sage Webb noting questions, mythological, and their uses; and, finally, Sandy Feinstein concentrating on models and topics. Thankfully Feinstein notes that she has not 'had to make students write.' Part of creative writing is determination and passion, just like with most things. If there are students who have to be made to write, they're doing the wrong course; it's far from our jobs as creative writers to be forcing square pegs into round holes.

If the authority of the institution or of the personal or public purse that usually pays for university and college education defines higher learning, then, thankfully, it is nevertheless not in *that* authority where learning dwells. *The Authority Project* shows that through the individual engagements of its chapter writers. Its debates are relevant, if different in parts, to those in Britain and beyond. Some readers won't agree with *all* the writers' interpretations, or with all their conclusions; but that's useful, too. It would be worrying if we did sit universally in agreement.

Of course, you can't buy true higher learning, or box it, or confirm its structure at a departmental meeting; it doesn't exist *because* of the classroom, and, no matter how many courses are constructed with it in mind, it does not live in a system of validation and approval that might well be held up to define a school of academic study. Higher learning is defined not by institutions, not by courses, not by structure or by function, but by human engagement, intuition, and ambition: it is creative fluidity, like the planet's life cycle, and our own. And it is this that gives validity to our work as creative writers on campus.

II. Creative Writing, Pedagogy, and Authority in the United States

Viewed through the expansive lens of teacherly authority in the creative writing classroom, *The Authority Project* sheds new light on many of the questions that have plagued creative writers in America since they entered the academy over a century ago and brings some newer issues deserving of attention to the forefront as well. As the field has grown rapidly over the last two decades and a wider variety of institutions of higher learning have included creative writing *per se* in their curricula, creative writers in the academy have increasingly become teachers, though not all would claim that title.

Chief among the sites of enduring struggle is the precarious position upon which creative writing has balanced, in one way or another, throughout its tenure in American academe. This is the dominant perception that, due to its inherent artistic roots, creative writing is, as Mary Cantrell writes in her essay, 'less academic, less rigorous . . .and [consequently] does not belong in an academic setting.' Fiercely divided loyalties between writing and teaching among academic creative writers and university and college administrators have not helped in reversing this so-called public relations problem, nor has a general, utter lack of interest in pedagogy – until recently – beyond that which could be effectively modeled or transmitted through osmosis. It is no surprise, then, that poet and novelist Jesse Lee Kercheval (1995: 119) describes her years studying with renowned writers at a prestigious graduate creative writing program as no more or less useful than 'sharing an elevator with someone famous for a little while'.

Undergirding these issues as arguably the most significant contributing factor to creative writing's Dangerfield-esque struggle for respect in the academy is the traditional liberal arts hierarchy that places artistic *production* well below the analysis of literature and relegates the *teaching* of that productive craft to an even lower status. While individual writers with hefty publication records may garner great respect in academe, creative writing as a field in American higher education shoulders a relentless burden of proof in its struggle to gain credence, a burden it has sometimes found difficult to bear.

Not far behind the struggle to stake a claim for creative writing's place in the landscape of American higher education itself is the age-old question as likely pop up in a department meeting as it is at a cocktail party where there are creative writing teachers present: 'But can creative writing *really* be taught?' Conspicuously, indeed logically, absent from discussions of how piano or oil painting techniques are transmitted, this question has begged to be put to rest since the first course in 'verse making' appeared on the University of Iowa course schedule more than a hundred years ago. To ask the question of whether creative writing can be taught is to imply, destructively, that we creative writers may not really be teachers and, therefore, may be fakes in our institutions of higher learning. In fact, several essays here make a solid go at closing this case once and for all, most notably Brent Royster's 'Inspiration, Creativity and Crisis: The Romantic Myth of the Writer Meets the Contemporary Classroom,' which lays some of the blame for the pervasiveness of this non-question on the tendency of writers themselves to romanticize their own inspiration and processes.

Another key creative writing issue in the United States, another issue *The Authority Project* meets head on, is the suggestion that the so-called groupthink of the unadulterated, amorphous workshop leads to the dry, passionless McPoem or McFiction, an assignation regularly leveled at the American literary establishment. Royster – and others here, though perhaps less overtly – suggests that any tendency towards common-denominator writing, though largely exaggerated in the press, may be attributed to the somewhat antiquated, product-centered workshop and offers a process-centered alternative that can encourage the development of authentic voice among beginning writers as it fosters 'continual writerly process and growth rather then expect and reward finished products.'

Also an enduring issue in the American creative writing scene updated in *The Authority Project* is the 'tension between writing as self-expression and writing as creative discipline,' as Nancy Kuhl puts it in her essay. Several other voices here offer varied perspectives on this tension, too, including Royster, Mary Cantrell, Anna Leahy, and others, indicating that when it comes to the complex issues of public and private writing, a healthy debate exists in the place of a party line. Likewise, Carl Vandermeulen takes on the difficulties of negotiating the relationships between teacher and students, as well as among students, in relation to the semi-public writing and the semi-private discussions of the workshop classroom. Tangential to these issues, moreover, the collection also addresses in numerous ways the problems of how best to cure beginning students of their tendency to ascribe effective writing as that which they can 'relate to' in its vagueness or interpret 'any way they want to,' a situation no creative writing teacher in the trenches can read about without a pang of recognition.

Evie Yoder Miller's 'Reinventing Writing Classrooms: The Combination of Creating and Composing,' moreover, considers a recurrent issue unique to American creative writing pedagogy: the commonalities between the creative writing and the composition classroom. In fact, leading creative writing/composition crossover figures such as Wendy Bishop, Hans Ostrum, Katharine Haake, Patrick Bizzaro, Mary Ann Cain, and many others, have long advocated that creative writing practitioners look to the innovative pedagogies of this American curricular phenomena – the general college writing course – for guidance in reflecting upon and articulating its own teaching practices. Perhaps, too, it is time that compositionists recognize what their field has gained and could gain from creative writing pedagogy. Miller makes an eloquent case for considering anew the enormous potentials these two fields possess for informing and strengthening one another.

Few discussions of creative writing in America today would be complete without attention to assessment, evaluation, and grading or marking. Until recently, most creative writing teachers rejected the notion of applying objective criteria to creative work as a futile exercise in fuzzy logic. Of late, however, in light of an increasingly assessment-driven mindset in education, several of the creative writing vanguard have increasingly – and appropriately – sought methods of introducing various kinds of evaluation into creative writing courses. *The Authority Project* is no exception. Wendy Bishop describes how, in borrowing from composition, she used portfolio and contract grading in her writing courses, while Mary Swander considers the historical origins of the 'abusive basketball-coach method' of teacher-response that unfortunately persists in some workshops today and Suzanne Greenberg examines the implications of letter grades in creative writing classrooms in the context of current U.S. grading norms.

Finally, *The Authority Project* necessarily confronts what has slowly been recognized in the last decade or so as the elephant in the corner of creative writing pedagogy: gender. Even today and even though my courses tend to attract a majority of females, when I ask my students to close their eyes and examine the romantic, mythical scene of a writer writing and then ask them to describe the writers they have imagined, they tell me they picture a white male. Conversely, many scholars note that as a field, creative writing has been feminized, if only due to its position in the literary hierarchy. As a result, gender in the creative writing class is a rich subject for the magnifying glass Susan Hubbard, Katharine Haake, and others hold up to it in these pages, suggesting an entirely new vantage point from which to understand its teaching.

Power and Identity in the Creative Writing Classroom: The Authority Project serves at once as an apt snapshot of creative writing in America in the early 21st century and, at the same time, as the next volume of what we hope will be an ongoing, increasingly rich interrogation of the theories and practices of teaching this elusive but eminently worthy subject. Moreover, it stakes a vital claim for creative writing's place on the American academic landscape and, as such, has earned a prominent position on my (SV) office bookshelf.

Notes

1. See Graeme Harper's (2005) 'The future of creative writing on campus'. In Graeme Harper and Richard Kerridge (eds) *New Writing: the International Journal for the Practice and Theory of Creative Writing* 1 (1). Clevedon: Multilingual Matters.
2. For details of the British national Arts and Humanities Research Board (AHRB) Research Training Program in Creative Writing (2005–2007, contact Graeme Harper (Graeme.harper@port.ac.uk).
3. For more on creative writing epistemology, see Graeme Harper's (2003) *Creative Writing at University: Key Pointers.* London: Drafts.

References

Kercheval, J.L. (1995) Interview. *Southwestern Review* Spring, 114–121.
Myers, D.G. (1996) *The Elephants Teach: Creative Writing Since 1880.* New Jersey: Prentice-Hall.

About the Authors

Wendy Bishop
Contracts, Radical Revision, Portfolios, and the Risks of Writing

Wendy Bishop taught writing at Florida State University for 18 years and lived in Tallahassee and Alligator Point, Florida. She is the author of *Thirteen Ways of Looking for a Poem: A Guide to Writing Poetry*; co-author of *Metro: Journeys in Writing Creatively*; and has creative nonfiction in *Crab Orchard Review* and *Alligator Juniper*, fiction in *Kalliope*, and poetry in *The Louisville Review* and *Cream City Review*. After a brief illness, she died in Tallahassee on November 21, 2003. Two weeks before she died, *On Writing: A Process Reader*, which she had finished in the hospital, arrived from the publisher. She has posthumously published *Acts of Revision: A Guide for Writers* and *Finding Our Way: A Writing Teacher's Sourcebook*, co-authored with Deborah Coxwell-Teague. Her husband, Dean, is working to put together a collection of selected poems that span a publishing career of 30 years. Dean, Wendy's children, Morgan and Tait, and her step-children, Jesse, Jeremy, Eowyn, Dean, and Jos miss her terribly.

Mary Cantrell
Teaching and Evaluation: Why Bother?

Mary Cantrell is a professor at Tulsa Community College and an adjunct professor at the University of Tulsa. She has presented research at the annual Associated Writing Programs' conferences. Cantrell has served on the staff of *Nimrod* since 1987 and participates annually in the *Nimrod* Awards conference. Her creative work has appeared in journals such as *Farmer's Market, Iowa Woman,* and *Mudfish*. She holds an M.A. from Iowa State University, where she held the Pearl Hogrefe Fellowship.

Cathy Day
Where Do You Want Me To Sit?: Defining Authority through Metaphor

Cathy Day teaches in the MFA program at the University of Pittsburgh. Her book *The Circus in Winter* was a finalist for the Story Prize, a 'Discover' pick at Barnes & Noble, and will be published in Germany and in Czechoslovakia. Her short stories and essays have appeared in *New Stories from the South 2000, Story, Gettysburg Review, Southern Review, River Styx, Antioch Review, Shenandoah,* and *American Fiction.* She holds an M.F.A. from the University of Alabama.

Sandy Feinstein
Writing in the Shadows: Topics, Models, and Audiences that Focus on Language

Sandy Feinstein is Honors Coordinator and Associate Professor of English at Penn State Berks. She has published articles and chapters on innovative teaching in a number of venues, from the journal *Studies in Medieval and Renaissance Teaching* to books devoted to pedagogy in higher education. Her scholarship on the Middle Ages and Early Modern Literature has appeared in *Chaucer Review, Arthuriana, Exemplaria,* and *Studies in English Literature (SEL),* among others. Her poems have most recently appeared in university press journals *pacific REVIEW* and *Nomad,* to name a few. She holds a Ph.D. from Indiana University.

Suzanne Greenberg
An 'A' for Effort: How Grading Policies Shape Courses

Suzanne Greenberg's short story collection, *Speed-Walk and Other Stories,* a finalist for the 2004 John Gardner Fiction Book Award, was the recipient of the 2003 Drue Heinz Literature Prize from the University of Pittsburgh Press. She is the co-author, with Michael C. Smith, of *Everyday Creative Writing: Panning for Gold in the Kitchen Sink.* Her fiction, poetry, and essays have been published in numerous magazines and journals, including *The Washington Post Magazine, Mississippi Review,* and *West Branch.* She teaches creative writing at California State University, Long Beach. She holds her M.F.A. from the University of Maryland.

Katharine Haake
Dismantling Authority: Teaching What We Do Not Know

Katharine Haake's most recent books are a novel, *That Water, Those Rocks*, and a collection of short stories, *The Height and Depth of Everything*. Her first book of stories was *No Reason on Earth* (1986). New work has appeared in *The Iowa Review, Witness, One Story*, and *The Santa Monica Review* and has been featured in the on line magazine, *Segue*. A recent recipient of an Individual Artist's Grant from the Cultural Affairs Department of the City of Los Angeles, she was also recognized as the 1998-99 Jerome Richfield Memorial Scholar at California State University, Northridge. Her other books are *What Our Speech Disrupts: Feminism and Creative Writing Studies* and, with Hans Ostrom and the late Wendy Bishop, the textbook *Metro: Journeys in Writing Creatively*. She currently chairs the Creative Writing program at California State University, Northridge, and lives in Los Angeles. She holds a Ph.D. from the University of Utah.

Rachel Hall
The Pregnant Muse: Assumptions, Authority, and Accessibility

Rachel Hall's work has appeared in a number of literary journals including *Black Warrior Review, The Gettysburg Review*, and *New Letters*, which awarded her their 2004 Fiction Prize and in the anthologies *Tanzania on Tuesday, Mamaphonic*, and *Fiction from the Crossroads*. She has received honors and awards from *Lilith, Nimrod, Glimmer Train*, the Bread Loaf Writers' Conference, and the Saltonstall Foundation for the Arts. She teaches creative writing and literature at the State University of New York-Geneseo where she holds the Chancellor's Award for Excellence in Teaching. Hall holds an M.F.A. from Indiana University.

Graeme Harper
Afterword: The Reason It Is; the Rhyme It Isn't

Graeme Harper (aka Brooke Biaz) is Chair of the UK Centre for Creative Writing Research Through Practice and Professor and Foundation Head of the School of Creative Arts, Film and Media at the University of Portsmouth. Honors include the National Book Council Award for New Fiction (Australia) and the Premier's Award for New Fiction. He has earned awards, grants, and fellowships from the Arts and Humanities Research Board; the National Endowment for Science, Technology and the Arts; the Arts Councils of England and Wales; the Eastern Frontier

Society (United States); and the British Academy, among others. Biaz's latest book of fiction is *Small Maps of the World* and latest short story is 'The Disappearing Father' in *The Dalhousie Review*. His new novel, *Filming Carol*, is forthcoming. Throughout 2004 Brooke was a BBC National Talent Awards featured fiction writer. He holds doctorates from the University of Technology, Sydney, and the University of East Anglia. He is Editor-in-Chief of *New Writing: The International Journal for the Practice and Theory of Creative Writing*, which, like the New Writing Viewpoints Series, is published by Multilingual Matters.

Susan Hubbard
Gender and Authorship: How Assumptions Shape Perceptions and Pedagogies

Susan Hubbard is the author of four books, two of which won national fiction prizes: *Walking on Ice, Blue Money, Lisa Maria's Guide for the Perplexed*, and *Lisa Maria Takes Off*. She co-edited *100% Pure Florida Fiction*, an anthology. Her short stories have been published in nationally and internationally circulated journals, including *Ploughshares*, *TriQuarterly*, and *The Mississippi Review*, and have been taught across America and in the United Kingdom. Her work has been translated into French, German, and Italian. Her scholarly research has been internationally presented, published, cited, and consulted. She is a past President of the Association of Writers and Writing Programs. She's taught at Syracuse University, Cornell University, and Pitzer College. Currently she is Associate Professor of English at the University of Central Florida and, in 2004, was named one of the '20 Coolest People in Orlando,' which makes her very, very nervous about the quality of life in Orlando.

Nancy Kuhl
Personal Therapeutic Writing vs. Literary Writing

Nancy Kuhl's chapbook, *In the Arbor*, is a winner of the Wick Poetry Chapbook Prize and was published by Kent State University Press. Her work has appeared in *Verse, Fence, Phoebe, The Connecticut Review, Puerto del Sol, Cream City Review*, and other magazines. Her manuscript, *The Wife of the Left Hand*, was a finalist for the National Poetry Series book contest and the AWP/Donald Hall Award for Poetry. She is co-editor of Phylum Press, an independent publisher of innovative poetry. She is the Assistant Curator of the Yale Collection of American Literature at the Beinecke Rare Book and Manuscript Library at Yale University. She is the author of two exhibition catalogs published by the library and distributed by the University Press of New England: *Intimate Circles: American Women in the Arts* and *Extravagant Crowd: Carl Van Vechten's Portraits of Women*. Kuhl holds an M.F.A. from Ohio State University and an M.L.S. from State University of New York at Buffalo.

Anna Leahy (Editor)
Who Cares – And How: The Value and Cost of Nurturing

Anna Leahy is an Assistant Professor at North Central College, where she earned the institution's scholarship award in recognition of her creative and critical writing. She recently served, with Stephanie Vanderslice, as the coordinator of the Association of Writers and Writing Programs Pedagogy Team. She has contributed to *The Journal of the Midwest Modern Language Association* and the journal *Pedagogy* and to the Association of Writers and Writing Programs, and the Modern Language Association conferences. Other work appears in *Encyclopedia of American Poetry*, *Facts on File Companion to the American Short Story*, and *American Studies International*. Her chapbook, *Hagioscope*, won the Sow's Ear Award, and her poems appear in *Connecticut Review*, *Quarterly West*, *Third Coast*, and others. She earned a fellowship at the Vermont Studio Center and holds a Ph.D. from Ohio University and an M.F.A. from the University of Maryland.

Argie Manolis
Writing the Community: Service Learning in Creative Writing

Argie J. Manolis teaches creative writing and composition at the University of Minnesota, Morris, where she is also the coordinator of the service-learning program. Her poems have been published in *So To Speak*, *Spoon River Poetry Review*, and *Mochila Review*, among others. She has been invited to present aspects of her work in service learning at several national conferences and has received institutional and statewide awards for her advising and service. Manolis holds an M.F.A. from Arizona State University.

Evie Yoder Miller
Reinventing Writing Classrooms: The Combination of Creating and Composing

Evie Yoder Miller teaches creative writing and composition at the University of Wisconsin-Whitewater. Prior to this, she taught at the high school and community college levels. She has presented research at the Association of Writers and Writing Programs conferences, and some of her short fiction, poetry, and essays have appeared in various small press publications. Her first novel *Eyes at the Window* was named a Borders Original Voices selection when it was published in 2003; a paperback edition followed in 2004. Miller holds a Ph.D. and M.A. in English with a concentration in Creative Writing-Fiction from Ohio University and an M.A. in Education from Union College.

Audrey Petty
Who's the Teacher?: From Student to Mentor

Audrey Petty was born and raised in Chicago and now holds a teaching position at the University of Illinois. Petty's stories were first featured in an issue of *Callaloo* devoted to emerging Black women artists. Her stories and poetry have since appeared in *StoryQuarterly*, *Nimrod International Journal*, *Crab Orchard Review*, and *Gumbo: An Anthology of African American Writing*. More work is forthcoming in *Saveur Magazine* and *The Massachusetts Review*. She is currently at work on a novel. Petty was awarded an Illinois Arts Council grant, a Tennessee Williams Scholarship at the Sewanee Writers' Conference, and a residency at Hedgebrook. Petty holds an M.F.A. from the University of Massachusetts.

Brent Royster
Inspiration, Creativity, and Crisis: The Romantic Myth of the Writer Meets the Contemporary Classroom

Brent Royster earned an M.F.A. in poetry from Bowling Green State University, where he is currently finishing a doctorate in rhetoric. His poems have been published in *Center: A Journal of the Literary Arts*, *Cimarron Review*, *Green Mountains Review*, *Iron Horse Literary Review*, *Mochila Review*, *The North American Review*, *Quarterly West*, *South Carolina Review*, and other notable journals. He teaches writing and literature at Ball State University in Muncie, Indiana. Royster has received an AWP Intro Journals Project Award for poetry.

Mary Swander
Duck, Duck, Turkey: Using Encouragement to Structure Workshop Assignments

Mary Swander is a Distinguished Professor at Iowa State University. She is the author of several books of nonfiction, including *The Desert Pilgrim: En Route to Mysticism and Miracles*, which was a Barnes &

Noble Discover selection, and *Out of This World.* Her poetry collections include *Heaven-and-Earth House* and *Driving the Body Back,* which as been reissued. Individual poems, short stories, and essays have appeared in *The Nation, The New Republic, The New Yorker,* and *Poetry,* among others. Swander has won numerous prestigious awards, including a Whiting Award, a National Endowment for the Arts grant, and the *Nation*-Discovery Award. She is also a regular commentator on the radio, has co-authored a musical, and adapted *Driving the Body Back* for the stage. She holds her M.F.A. from the University of Iowa.

Carl Vandermeulen
The Double Bind and Stumbling Blocks: A Case Study as an Argument for Authority-conscious Pedagogy

Carl Vandermeulen is a Professor at Northwestern College in Iowa. He currently advises the college newspaper and literary journal and supervises student teachers. He is the author of *Photography for Student Publications* and the editor-publisher for Middleburg Press. His publications include pedagogical articles, poetry, and creative prose in venues such as *Trends* and *Scholastic Editor.* He has made numerous professional, scholarly presentations at conferences of such organizations as the National Council of Teachers of English, the Cultural Studies Symposium, and Teaching and Technology and is extending the research he began for *The Authority Project.* He holds his Ph.D. from the University of Nebraska.

Stephanie Vanderslice
Afterword: The Reason It Is; the Rhyme It Isn't

Stephanie Vanderslice holds an M.F.A. in fiction writing from George Mason University and a Ph.D. in English from the University of Louisiana at Lafayette. She has published fiction and nonfiction in *Writing on the Edge, New Writing,* the *Louisiana Review,* the *American Literary Review,* and the *Deep South Writer's Conference Chapbook* among other journals and anthologies. Vanderslice writes frequently on creative writing pedagogy and is also co-editing, with Kelly Ritter of Southern Connecticut State University, *This is (Not) Just to Say: Lore and Creative Writing Pedagogy.* She is an Associate Professor of creative writing at the University of Central Arkansas, in Conway, Arkansas, where she lives with her husband and two sons.

Amy Sage Webb
How To Avoid Workshop Dilemmas: The Use of Myth to Teach Writerly Concepts

Amy Sage Webb is an Assistant Professor at Emporia State University, where she directed the Center for Innovation and received grants for writing and for public arts in Kansas. She has served as a Coordinator for the Association of Writers and Writing Programs' Pedagogy Forum. Webb contributed a chapter to the textbook *Mooring Against the Tide: Writing Poetry and Fiction* and is working on an advanced fiction-writing textbook. Her fiction and nonfiction have appeared in *Clackamas Literary Review, Eclipse, Red Rock Review,* and other periodicals. She holds an M.F.A. from Arizona State University.